KU-306-875

Nineteenth-Century Europe

HISTORY OF EUROPE

PUBLISHED

Early Medieval Europe 300–1000 (2nd edn)
Roger Collins

Sixteenth-Century Europe
Richard Mackenney

Seventeenth-Century Europe 1598–1700
Thomas Munck

Eighteenth-Century Europe (2nd edn)
Jeremy Black

Nineteenth-Century Europe
Michael Rapport

History of Europe
Series Standing Order
ISBN 0–333–71699–X hardcover
ISBN 0–333–69381–7 paperback
(*outside North America only*)

You can receive future titles in this series as they are published by placing a standing order. Please contact your bookseller or, in the case of difficulty, write to us at the address below with your name and address, the title of the series and the ISBN quoted above.

Customer Services Department, Macmillan Distribution Ltd
Houndmills, Basingstoke, Hampshire RG21 6XS, England

Nineteenth-Century Europe

Michael Rapport

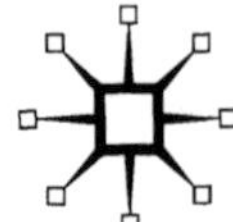

First published 2005 by
PALGRAVE MACMILLAN
Houndmills, Basingstoke, Hampshire RG21 6XS and
175 Fifth Avenue, New York, N.Y. 10010
Companies and representatives throughout the world

PALGRAVE MACMILLAN is the global academic imprint of the Palgrave Macmillan division of St. Martin's Press, LLC and of Palgrave Macmillan Ltd. Macmillan® is a registered trademark in the United States, United Kingdom and other countries. Palgrave is a registered trademark in the European Union and other countries.

ISBN-13: 978–0–333–65245–9 hardback
ISBN 10: 0–333–65245–2 hardback
ISBN-13: 978–0–333–65246–6 paperback
ISBN 10: 0–333–65246–0 paperback

This book is printed on paper suitable for recycling and made from fully managed and sustained forest sources.Logging, pulping and manufacturing processes are expected to conform to the environmental regulations of the country of origin.

A catalogue record for this book is available from the British Library.

Library of Congress Cataloging-in-Publication Data

Rapport, Michael.
Nineteenth-century Europe / Michael Rapport.
p. cm.—(History of Europe)
Includes bibliographical references and index.
ISBN 0-333-65245-2 (cloth) – ISBN 0-333-65246-0 (paper)
1. Europe—History—1789–1900. I. Title. II. History of Europe (St. Martin's Press)
D299.R26 2005
940.2'8—dc22

2005042963

Printed and bound in Great Britain by
CPI Antony Rowe, Chippenham and Eastbourne

Для Гелэна и великего Мирабо

And all is dross that is not Helena

Contents

List of Maps

Preface

All historians believe that their chosen period is of special significance, or at least of particular interest. I have yet to come across anyone who has pounced on a topic because they believe it is dull: obscure, perhaps, but not dull. I shall therefore avoid the temptation to laud the fascination of Europe's 'long nineteenth century' too much. None the less, the era *is* exciting – inspiring and alarming in equal measure. For a start, it is anchored at either end by the astonishing collapse of the French absolute monarchy in 1789 and the eruption of the First World War in 1914. It is marked by a dramatic economic and social transformation, which in turn engendered serious political anxieties and tensions. The political landscape also changed, both in the sense that new European powers emerged – Italy and Germany obviously, but also smaller independent states such as those of south-eastern Europe – and also in the sense that more people became involved in politics. It is this last development which forms the main, though not the only, theme of this book. Marc Bloch, the great French historian, wrote that 'unity of space is mere disorder. Only a central problem provides a work with unity.'[1] I found the telling in an orderly fashion of the story of the multitude of dramas which unfolded between 1789 and 1914 to be quite a test. In the end, the 'central problem' around which I have organised the others is the rise of mass politics. Its origins are discernible in the eighteenth century before the French Revolution, with the expansion in the educated public. The Revolution itself posited the 'people' as sovereign and sought to mobilise them in support of the new order, but at the time it failed to reach or to convince most Europeans. In this sense, 1848 was a pivotal moment because it was a Europe-wide event in which many countries witnessed popular participation in politics for the first time. Thereafter, few regimes, no matter how authoritarian or conservative, could ignore public opinion. The question as to how to integrate into the state those groups which had formerly been excluded became an important preoccupation. The emergence of mass politics came in the last decades of the nineteenth century and the first years of the twentieth century. Within the expanding civic arena, men and women, including workers and peasants, expressed their concerns more and more in political terms and through political and social organisations. The conflicting social pressures were such that this era witnessed the development not only of liberal and democratic movements, but also of those presaging the authoritarian and totalitarian regimes which haunted the twentieth century. I am acutely aware that the danger in pursuing this narrative is that it might become too narrowly focused, if not suffer from tunnel vision. I hope, however, that social, economic and cultural developments have not suffered too much at my hands. In my experience of teaching this period to undergraduates, I have learned that students often request a book which, first and foremost, gives them a chronological framework around which they can build their reading in depth. I hope that this present volume fulfils the former role and goes some way towards pointing students towards the latter, which is well served by a wealth of superior works. If this book piques some curiosity about the period, then it will at least have served a constructive purpose.

University of Stirling Mike Rapport

Acknowledgements

This book could not have been written without the immense support (both unwitting and wilful) of a staggering cast of characters. Jeremy Barker first switched me on to this period many years ago now; the good history teachers of our youth are the unsung heroes of later academic work. I shall never quite understand why Jeremy Black asked me to write this book – perhaps he detected in me the insane edge required for such an undertaking, but I owe him my thanks for this opportunity, for his early encouragement and for his later comments on a full draft. I am especially grateful to Terka Acton, Sonya Barker and Felicity Noble at Palgrave for their immense reserves of patience (far more than I deserve). I am extremely fortunate to be working in a department in which I can count so many colleagues as friends, and from whom I have learned so much about the nineteenth century. These include, in particular, Bob McKean (*moi velikii vozd'*, from whose knowledge of Russian history I continue to profit; I enjoy our conversations immensely); Jim Smyth (for – naturally – some of the grislier aspects of social history); Emma Macleod (whose meticulous knowledge of late-eighteenth and early-nineteenth century Britain will never cease to impress me); Jacqueline Jenkinson (for telling me about Mary Seacole); David Bebbington (for leads on British history) and our external examiner, Kathy Lerman (for her thoughts on Wilhelmine Germany). The department in general has been very supportive and I should like to thank all colleagues, but especially Michael Penman, Richard Oram, Robin Law, Annabelle Hopkins, Linda Bradley and Kitty Tollan, for easing the pressure in different ways. At a time when bureaucracy is coursing through academia like an incapacitating disease (*administrativitis horribilis* – a cure still eludes scientists), I owe a special debt of gratitude to Jim Smyth and George Peden who have, over the past year, performed a truly heroic task in shielding me from the worst of the paperwork. I have also greatly benefited from conversations about south-eastern Europe with Dejan Jovic. My students at every level have given me plenty of food for thought. Their interests, questions and ideas have, to a very large degree, determined the framework and selection of material for this book. The two anonymous readers of the first draft gave me excellent pointers – I am sorry that time and space have not allowed me to incorporate all their ideas. Naturally, the errors in this book are my own. Many depositories were plundered for this work, but staff at the University of Stirling Library in particular have been tremendous (if I wore a hat, I would doff it to Gordon Willis, Helen Beardsley and the Document Delivery Service in particular). Thanks also to the libraries of the Universities of Glasgow and Edinburgh and to the National Library of Scotland. At a more personal level, my parents have very kindly prodded me with questions such as 'Have you finished IT yet?' My wife and I lost a much-loved and noble companion during the final weeks of editing: our eminently easy-going cat (Mirabeau, Gingernut – like all cats, he had many names) kept me company as I wrote this book, sitting next to the computer, sometimes *on* the computer. He is much missed.

My greatest debt, as always, goes to Helen. She encouraged me through the cold sweats and crises of confidence, read over numerous chapters, and offered some very wise advice, some of which, to my cost, I have followed imperfectly. I have also benefited from her knowledge of urban history: the references to Glasgow, Edinburgh and Scotland in the text have been inspired by her own doctoral work. Helen's place in the dedication is a small token of my love and gratitude.

Abbreviations

AHR	*American Historical Review*
AHY	*Austrian History Yearbook*
CEH	*Central European History*
CJH	*Canadian Journal of History*
CSSH	*Comparative Studies in Society and History*
EHQ	*European History Quarterly*
EHR	*Economic History Review*
ESR	*European Studies Review*
FH	*French History*
FHS	*French Historical Studies*
HE	*History of Education*
HJ	*Historical Journal*
JCEA	*Journal of Central European Affairs*
JCH	*Journal of Contemporary History*
JGO	*Jahrbücher für Geschichte Osteuropas*
JICH	*Journal of Imperial and Commonwealth History*
JMH	*Journal of Modern History*
JSH	*Journal of Social History*
P&P	*Past and Present*
PBA	*Proceedings of the British Academy*
RHES	*Revue d'Histoire Économique et Sociale*
RHMC	*Revue d'Histoire Moderne et Contemporaine*
RR	*Revolutionary Russia*
SEER	*Slavonic and East European Review*
S-F	*Südost-Forschungen*
SH	*Social History*
SR	*Slavic Review*
TRHS	*Transactions of the Royal Historical Society*

Part I

Revolutionary Europe, 1789–1815

1 Europe in 1789

When Pope Pius VI visited Vienna in March 1782, he was greeted with adoring crowds of tens of thousands of people choking the streets around the imperial palace and even cramming boats cluttering the River Danube.[1] The Pope was undoubtedly more popular among Austrians than his Viennese host, the Habsburg Emperor Joseph II. The Austrian ruler was one of the great reforming monarchs of eighteenth-century Europe, but his efforts to change the diverse administrative, fiscal and social institutions of his sprawling central European empire came up against opposition at almost every level of society. To reform anywhere in Europe was to attack an array of customs, privileges and religious practices, upsetting a lot of people, including the privileged orders of the nobility and clergy, townsfolk sheltering behind both their city walls and their special rights, and the pious peasantry.

This conservative society was an overwhelmingly rural world. In eastern Europe (the classic division between east and west is the River Elbe), the countryside's population was heavily burdened with seigneurial obligations which, as in East Prussia, approached a form of servitude. Sometimes, particularly in Russia, Poland and parts of the Habsburg empire, peasants were actually serfs, meaning that they were bound to the land upon which they worked and legally subject to the authority of the landowner, who imposed a wide variety of controls. Yet though most western peasants were legally free, for those who were poor and landless, life could be as hard, if not actually harder in times of economic distress, as it was for serfs. Peasant ownership of land, while greater in the west than in the east, varied wildly from region to region. Where peasants did own land, only a minority owned enough to support their families, supplementing their incomes by sharecropping (whereby peasants, literally, received a share of the crop in return for their labour), craftwork or seasonal migration. Peasants in the west also owed seigneurial obligations and dues to landlords, had to pay taxes to the State and to the Church (the tithe), and were liable to military recruitment.

Across Europe this struggling peasant society was dominated by those who owned proportionately the most land: the nobility. Their control or influence over the people who worked on their estates gave them political and social predominance. Although not a closed caste in most parts of Europe, the power of the nobility was grounded in hereditary privilege, namely exemptions from taxation and frequently exclusive access to the higher posts in the state administration, the Church, the judiciary and the military. Yet not all nobles were rich; they ranged in wealth from the scented aristocratic popinjays of the marbled French court at Versailles to the struggling Hungarian 'sandalled' gentry (who, it was said, could not afford boots). Poorer European nobles frequently proved to be the most intractable in defending their privileges because this was all that differentiated them from the mass of the peasants.

In many parts of Europe, the importance of the nobility in provincial and village administration, justice, law and order, tax collection and military recruitment reflected the weakness of the central government. In certain states, aristocratic power was entrenched in formal political institutions: the Polish *sejm* (where a single noble had the right to veto any legislation: the *liberum veto*), the Hungarian diet or the British parliament could present formidable opposition to the government. In the Holy Roman Empire (Germany, roughly speaking), certain states had *Stände*, or Estates, which usually represented the main 'orders' in society, but were dominated by the two most privileged, the nobles and the clergy. In France, the Estates-General had not met since 1614. Where French provincial estates still met, they had some control over the distribution of the tax burden, but little power to oppose royal edicts. Instead, noble power was entrenched in the *parlements*, the thirteen sovereign courts, of which the one in Paris was the most important. These noble-dominated institutions had the right to register any royal edict before it became law within its jurisdiction. When a *parlement* refused to do so, it could issue a 'remonstrance', laying out the legal reasons behind its decision, which sometimes set the battlelines for a confrontation with the King.

The nobles shared influence with the clergy, whose power was partly economic, particularly in Catholic and Orthodox Europe where the Church was a great landowner (holding a tenth of the land in France and ensnaring a million serfs in Russia). The clergy exerted social and moral influence. Where standards of literacy were low, the peasantry learned of new laws from the pulpit. The Church might also levy its own tax, the tithe. The churches were the main, or frequently the only, source of welfare provision and of education. The harsh existence endured by much of the eighteenth-century population gave an importance to the spiritual comfort offered by priests, ministers, monks and nuns. There is evidence of a decline in religious belief, or at least of observance, in certain parts of Europe, such as in France, but non-attendance at church did not necessarily signify deep-rooted unbelief. Popular religious rituals, processions and belief in miracles were derided by some educated people as 'superstitions', but they offered both solace and an explanation for the natural world to many ordinary Europeans. There was, of course, a dark side to this piety, often translating into bigotry and persecution of other religious groups, particularly Jews. Religious devotion fostered a conservatism which reacted angrily against any challenge from overly ambitious reformers.

In urban Europe, particularly in the larger cities, inhabitants may have been less susceptible to the Church and noble influence. Towns were frequently sources of economic and cultural dynamism, particularly when they engaged in commerce, or were homes to academies, universities and the intellectual flowering of the Enlightenment. Yet towns also had institutions, privileges, corporations and guilds which were equally conservative forces. Townsfolk usually enjoyed exemption from labour obligations and conscription, while proportionately the tax burden was lighter than in the countryside, although food prices were often higher because of tolls or customs dues payable at the gates by merchants. Urban artisans gathered in guilds, which restricted entry into the trade or craft, tried to control standards and methods of production and created a corporate identity among their members through processions, initiation rites, help in times of sickness or death, and special religious services.

In the hierarchical society of late eighteenth-century Europe, one's status was defined by the amount of privilege one enjoyed, which was in turn determined by a range of factors. Among the most important was geography: those born in towns, or in certain provinces, would enjoy exemptions or rights which others did not and these privileges were defended by provincial estates, legal institutions and guilds and municipal corporations. Birth was another major criterion: nobles, alongside the higher clergy (who in any case usually came from the nobility), were the most privileged subjects of all, while serfs, born into hereditary bondage to the land, had none. It was also determined by occupation: service in the armed forces or membership of a guild, amongst other things, might have brought certain privileges; theoretically, function was the most important determinant of privilege and status. Society was viewed not in terms of social and economic 'class' but as being arranged into 'orders' or 'estates', divided between those who prayed (the clergy), those who served the state (the nobility) and those who worked (the Third Estate). Within each of these categories there were widely varying levels of wealth: the Third Estate encapsulated everyone from the wealthiest non-noble financier to the migrant labourer whose job was to light the street lamps every evening. The notion of a 'corporate' society, or a 'society of orders', was therefore a very different concept to more recent ideas of social and economic 'classes'.

Yet there were forces of change. In the long run, the most significant was population growth. From 118 million in 1700, it swelled to 205 million in 1800, exploding to 481 million by 1913. Poverty, unemployment, urban overcrowding and, in the countryside, land hunger caused by the pressures of population growth were anxiously noted by contemporaries and the 'social question' – how to deal with poverty – became one of the great issues of the nineteenth century. None the less, by 1789 there were the early, if faltering, signs of the sustained economic growth which marked the nineteenth century and which, in its later decades, would finally absorb much of the burgeoning population. In agriculture, crops new to Europe, such as maize and potatoes, were being introduced, as were new farming techniques. These practices would gradually spread from earlier pockets in Britain, the Low Countries and Catalonia to other parts of Europe over the course of the nineteenth century.[2]

Most contemporaries were more impressed by the growth of trade. The volume of trade increased dramatically, much of it driven by European overseas expansion and by slavery. Towns such as Amsterdam, Glasgow, Liverpool, Bordeaux, Marseille, Lisbon and Cadiz, which faced the non-European world, prospered, while older commercial centres, such as Venice, Seville and Toulouse, ill-placed to take advantage of the global expansion in trade, began to stagnate. At least navigable rivers and new roads meant that overseas produce was marketed inland.[3] The old regime economy was changing in manufacturing, as well. Merchants were beginning to break down manufacturing processes into simple stages, dividing the labour among unskilled workers – often peasants in the 'proto-industrial' or 'cottage' industries – for cheaper, large-scale production, rather than buying finished articles from skilled artisans. The factories associated with industrialisation, with heavy investment in new machinery and with large concentrations of workers, had begun to appear, especially in Britain, but also in certain isolated spots on the continent. One cannot yet speak of a proletariat with a working-class identity. It is also difficult to speak of a 'bourgeoisie' in the sense of a capitalist class whose self-confidence and wealth was drawn from commercial growth and from industrialisation. In the later eighteenth century, the term 'bourgeoisie' applies to a broad – and diverse – band of people. They did not perform manual labour, but nor were they nobles or clergy. Some were certainly capitalist in the sense that they engaged in commerce, manufacturing and finance, but more often than not the bourgeoisie grew out of state service in the government bureaucracy and the judiciary, as well as the professions. Like the nobility, the wealthier bourgeois were landowners.[4] The early origins of the European crisis did not lie in the rise of this middle class but in a political struggle between the rulers and the privileged orders.

European monarchs were pushing for administrative and fiscal efficiency and economic development for one central reason: endemic warfare. There were no fewer than sixteen major European conflicts between 1700 and 1790, and one historian estimates that more territory changed hands in this century than in either of the two preceding ones, which were hardly peaceful times.[5] A ruler's purpose was to promote the interests of the state, which meant expanding its power and territory.

Consequently, international politics were cut-throat. The price of weakness and defeat were amply illustrated in 1772, when Poland lost 211,000 sq km of its territory and 4 million inhabitants, as Prussia, Russia and Austria each gorged themselves on a share of the First Partition in 1772. The frequency, the expense and the high stakes involved in European conflicts drove states to increase revenue, to ease recruitment and to tap the resources of the population more effectively. These aims implied wide-ranging reforms in both state and society.

In pursuing these changes, rulers harnessed new ideas of government and society – including those stemming from the Enlightenment – and challenged traditional conceptions. The Enlightenment had so many often conflicting strands, arose in so many places and spanned such a wide period of time that it would be misleading to describe it as a coherent intellectual movement. Generally, the Enlightenment was the intellectual flowering of the eighteenth century which subjected social and political institutions to often withering criticism. The Enlightenment was bound together by a belief in the capacity for human reason to overcome fear and to allow people to explore their environment, shaping it and mastering it. Implicit in this was support for social and political reform and an attack on intolerance, bigotry, superstition and, sometimes, on religion itself. The Enlightenment certainly had radical implications, though the philosophers were not revolutionaries.

The epithet 'Enlightened Absolutists' has stuck to rulers and ministers who encouraged or at least tolerated some of these new ideas about government, law and society. While it would be wrong to discount humanitarian motives altogether (to cite one example, Grand Duke Leopold of Tuscany abolished torture and capital punishment in 1786), the main thrust of Enlightened Absolutism was to enhance the state's power and wealth. The efforts of European governments to release the productive capacities of society naturally entailed an assault on the privileges and influence of the nobility, the Church, provinces, municipal corporations and guilds. Investment in state education meant reducing clerical influence in schools and universities. Encouraging commerce and manufacturing frequently involved undermining the guilds and urban corporations. Freeing the peasantry from seigneurial dues and obligations was an assault on the privileges of their aristocratic landlords. The first blows to the traditional social order, therefore, came not from revolutionaries but from royal governments seeking to enhance the power of the state at the expense of the traditional, corporate society.

A government's challenge to vested interests could result in dangerous political conflict. Embittered Swedish nobles assassinated Gustav III at a masked ball in Stockholm in 1792. When the Habsburg Emperor Joseph II introduced his peasant reforms into Hungary in 1785, it not only brought tensions between the Magyar nobles and their peasants bubbling to the surface (in Transylvania, it spurred up to thirty thousand

Romanian serfs into revolt),[6] but also set the nobles and the Crown on a collision course. By 1789 the Magyar nobility were on the brink of revolt and, as he lay dying in February 1790, Joseph was forced to retract his decrees. In Poland, the Partition of 1772 sparked a programme of reform between 1775 and 1788 in law, education and the conditions of the peasantry. Yet the Polish nobles (*szlachta*) opposed the law code drafted by Andrzej Zamoyski when rumours multiplied that he was working towards reforms in serfdom. In France, the failure of the government's efforts to reform in the 1770s and the 1780s would, of course, prove to be a disaster not just for the monarchy but also, eventually, for its opponents among the privileged orders.

In the later decades of the century, the battle between reform and privilege took a radical turn. To fire up public support in the struggle, the privileged orders began to demand political reform, sometimes with representative government. Other people took these ideas very seriously, joined in the fray and turned this demand for wider access to political life not only against the government but also against the privileged themselves. By 1789, therefore, a three-way struggle was developing in European states between reforming, administrative monarchies, conservative or reactionary interests opposed to change, and radical movements. The emergence of a radical wing of opposition was made possible by the expansion in literacy. In the hundred years after 1690, literacy rates for men in France rose from 29 per cent to 47 per cent, while for women it rose from 14 per cent to 27 per cent. In Germany, literacy among the adult population increased from approximately 10 per cent to 25 per cent over the eighteenth century. Europeans witnessed an explosion in the press. In France 148 new titles appeared in the 1770s alone and there were no fewer than 151 titles in Germany in 1785. Although the number of subscribers to these journals was usually low, the number of people who actually had access to each copy – in clubs, coffee houses and pubs – was far greater. The notion that there existed a 'public opinion' independent of Church and State emerged.[7]

European radicalism was conditioned by a new sense that the public – the 'nation', the 'people', the 'citizens' – had rights which extended beyond the limits of the corporate, privileged society of the elites. Basing their demands on a radical interpretation of both recent Enlightenment ideas and adapting older, libertarian traditions, certain groups of people demanded wider access to public office and political representation. Such movements drew support and leadership from disenchanted bourgeois, but they also included liberal-minded nobles and sought increasingly to obtain widespread popular support. In many countries, they referred to themselves as 'patriots', meaning that they would put the needs of the nation above the exclusive privileges of the Church and the nobility. The excitement and debate generated among the public by the American Revolution (1775–83) added momentum to such movements. Though a minority of the population, they were usually articulate and geographically widespread, and they occasionally succeeded in securing popular support and actually toppling their governments.

A movement among Genevan burghers, excluded from high politics by the urban patriarchs, came to a head when they seized power, only to be put down by international intervention with French, Piedmontese and Swiss troops in 1782. Patriots in the Netherlands overthrew the Stadholder before being efficiently swept aside by a Prussian army in 1787. That year, Belgium rebelled against Joseph II's reforms, which attacked traditional legal, administrative and ecclesiastical institutions. The patriots divided between conservative Statists and radical Vonckists, however, and they were crushed by an Austrian counter-attack in 1790. These defeats for European patriots suggested that if enlightened reform had been blunted by the resilience of privilege, the old regime in Europe had at least weathered a storm of radical opposition. In fact, when combined with demands for political representation, nowhere would the failure of reform be more explosive than in France.π

2 The French Revolution, 1789–1804

One of the oldest explanations for the Revolution of 1789 in France has been that it was a social upheaval in which a bourgeoisie asserted itself against the old order dominated by the nobility. Feudalism was destroyed in 1789, clearing the way for the development of a new, capitalist order based on the wealth and influence of the bourgeoisie.[1] This view, usually dubbed 'Marxist' because of its emphasis on class conflict, has since been challenged by the 'revisionists',[2] who suggest that it is not possible to speak of the bourgeoisie and the aristocracy as two antagonistic classes with conflicting social and economic interests. Some French nobles engaged in commerce and industry; as a group the aristocracy were not universally opposed to social and economic change. On the other hand, wealthy non-nobles sought to join or imitate the nobility, rather than destroy the aristocratic order. At the wealthier reaches of the French nobility and the middle classes, a common elite of 'notables', it has been argued, was emerging by 1789. This was fed not only by the aristocracy's commercial and financial interests, but also by the prosperous bourgeoisie's determination to sink its money (once it had made it in business) into land and to 'live nobly' on its estates, rather than reinvest it in commerce or industry. The elite was therefore bound together by common social and economic interests, but also by a shared culture in the Enlightenment.[3] These land-owning notables emerged from the Revolution to control France, but, as other historians have emphasised, this did not preclude tensions within the elite, both before the French Revolution and in the nineteenth century.[4]

More recently, historians have interpreted the French Revolution as primarily a political transformation, with its roots in eighteenth-century political culture and ideas.[5] A new political culture – the ideology, rhetoric, symbols and practice of politics – was forged, whereby the shift of power from the monarchy to the 'people' was expressed in a variety of ways. With the eighteenth-century emergence of 'public opinion', there had been lively public debate on politics and, in the process, terms such as 'nation', 'liberty', 'citizen' and 'patriot' gained currency in the decades before the Revolution.[6] During the upheaval, the issue was how to put the ideals associated with them into practice.

In the background was a financial crisis, severely aggravated by the cost of the successful French intervention in the American War of Independence, which left the Crown quivering on the brink of bankruptcy. Attempts at fiscal reform were jammed by the political gridlock caused by aristocratic resistance in the *parlements*, which enlisted the support of public opinion because they successfully presented themselves as the defenders of public liberties against the despotic intentions of the Crown. Public suspicion of the monarchy was merely aggravated when the extent of the royal debt was uncovered in August 1786 by Louis XVI's Controller-General of Finances, Charles Alexandre de Calonne. His efforts to bypass the *parlements* with a show of consultation through a handpicked 'Assembly of Notables' in 1787 backfired when the Assembly insisted that only the Estates-General – the representative body of the whole kingdom – could consent to new taxation and to reform. The *parlements* took up the same cudgel and rejoined the battle. Crown and judiciary were locked in a bitter political struggle between August 1787 and May 1788.

The King won the first round of the fight when he had the leaders of the Paris *parlement* arrested on 5–6 May 1788 and the power of the sovereign courts razed. In cities across France, people took to the streets in violent protest. In Grenoble's 'day of tiles' (7 June), citizens clambered on the rooftops to defend the Dauphiné's *parlement* by hurling roof-slates down onto royal soldiers. In an effort to calm the opposition, Calonne's successor, Loménie de Brienne, gave way. In August he summoned the Estates-General for 1 May 1789 and then resigned. Louis XVI gave control of the empty royal purse to the Genevan, Jacques Necker, who had a reputation for financial genius and, crucially, enjoyed public confidence. Necker, though accepting the poisoned chalice, declared that he could undertake nothing without the consent of the Estates-General.

The aristocratic opposition had little time to savour its triumph because within weeks it lost public support, with momentous consequences. In September the Paris *parlement* declared that the Estates should assemble 'according to the forms observed in 1614'. This meant that each order – clergy, nobility and the commoners (the Third Estate) – would meet and vote separately. The implications were that the two privileged orders would always combine and drown out the views of the Third Estate. Radical, or 'patriot', opinion, which up to now had virulently backed the *parlements*, argued that, as the Third Estate represented the vast majority of the people, it ought to have twice the number of representatives. The three estates should meet together and vote by head, which would give the deputies to the Third Estate the decisive role in the proceedings. The hot air blown over café tables and the ink which spilled onto pamphlets in this debate sharpened some of the concepts which would lay the ideological foundations of the French Revolution. The most famous contribution was *What is the Third Estate?* (February 1789) penned by Emmanuel Sieyès. Influenced by the Enlightenment philosopher Jean-Jacques Rousseau, he baldly declared that the Third Estate represented the nation, which was a community of equal citizens sharing the same rights. The nobility and the clergy could be part of this nation, but only if they abandoned their privileges.

The elections to the Estates-General were held between February and June – the great length of time owing to the complexity of the proceedings. Yet it gave a wide section of the French population an opportunity for political participation unprecedented since 1614: all male taxpayers over the age of 25 could vote. *Cahiers de doléances* (lists of grievances) and requests for the attention of the estates were also drawn up. The scale of popular participation meant that no one was unaware that the estates of the realm were meeting in Versailles. Everyone (except perhaps the court itself) had high expectations of the results, even if most peasants simply wanted redress of local grievances.

When the estates met on 5 May, divisions immediately appeared among the first two orders. Two-thirds of the clerical delegates were not aristocratic bishops or abbots, but parish priests whose election marked a revolt of the lower clergy, recruited from the ranks of the peasantry, against their superiors. Amongst the nobles, progressives such as Lafayette, hero of the American War, represented a liberal minority facing the conservative provincial squires. The Third Estate presented a united phalanx and was dominated by well-to-do lawyers and office-holders – those accustomed to public speaking and state affairs. The defiance of the Third Estate was expressed when, bolstered by defections from the clergy, it declared itself the 'National Assembly' on 17 June. Three days later, meeting at the royal tennis court, the National Assembly swore not to disperse until it had drawn up a constitution for the kingdom. Concessions offered by Necker on 23 June pacified no one, and popular protests in Versailles and Paris persuaded large sections of the 'patriotic' nobility to join the National Assembly. Louis finally yielded on 27 June and ordered the remaining nobles to follow suit. Events at Versailles had excited much of the wider public, particularly in Paris, where the Palais-Royal with its cafés and shops was a centre for news and gossip. Yet figures at the court – probably, at first, without Louis's knowledge – had decided to put an end to all opposition by using force. Egged on by Queen Marie-Antoinette and by the King's younger, intransigent brother, the comte d'Artois, the minister of war had begun moving troops around Paris and Versailles.

It was now that the French people proper – not just 'public opinion' – entered into the politics of the Revolution and brought about the collapse of royal authority in the country at large. A feeble harvest in 1788 brought acute food shortages in 1789, and food riots spread across the country. In Paris, where 80,000 were unemployed in December 1788, artisans linked the economic crisis to the political situation and they adopted 'patriotic' slogans and ideas. The King's dismissal on 12 July of the popular Necker was seen as the signal for the troops amassed around Paris to march on to the city. With no means of defence, crowds of artisans and journeymen searched for weapons and gunpowder. Stocks of the latter had been transferred to the Bastille, the fortress-prison whose ramparts dominated the eastern, artisan districts of the city. On 14 July the Parisians stormed the fortress, shaking the King's resolve. He refused to send in his troops to crush the insurrection after his officers warned that they could not guarantee obedience from their men. With royal authority in tatters, the National Assembly – now calling itself the Constituent Assembly – began the task of giving France a constitution.

The absolute monarchy also collapsed under the weight of a peasant revolution. The peasantry had been under long-term pressure from their landlords, who in the decades leading up to 1789 sought to maximise their revenue by reviving seigneurial rights and dues which had fallen into disuse.[7] The simmering resentment which this caused was expressed violently even before 1789. In the summer of that year, peasant restiveness was spurred on by the 'Great Fear', in which peasants took up arms to defend themselves against ragged bands of beggars, their ranks swelled by the economic crisis, who sparked rumours of hordes of brigands in the pay of the privileged orders.[8] With the news from Paris in July, the countryside exploded in revolt as the peasants seized the opportunity to destroy seigneurialism. One of the first tasks of the National Assembly would be to restore order in the countryside.

On the night of 4 August, in a fit of near-hysterical altruism, the members of the Assembly rose, one by one, to renounce seigneurial rights and dues, including the church tithes. In the hangover of the following days, however, the 'abolition of feudalism' was then carefully hedged in by strict definitions. The definitive decree on 11 August abolished outright those charges and obligations which had been related to personal servitude, while others were redefined as property rights, for which the peasantry had to pay compensation to their landlords. The decrees of 4–11 August were aimed at calming the countryside, but the peasants in many regions, once having risen against the exactions of their landlords, were hardly likely to bow under this compromise, and resistance continued into 1790.

However, 4 August did more than just abolish seigneurialism. It amounted to a rejection of privilege of all kinds – personal, corporate and local. It therefore left an open field upon which a new administrative, fiscal and political system could be planted. Departments, each roughly equal in size, wealth and population and administered by an elected council, would replace the provinces. The first local elections were held in the summer of 1790. The Declaration of the Rights of Man and the Citizen (26 August 1789) proclaimed equality before the law, freedom from arbitrary imprisonment, fiscal equality (taxation would be shared amongst citizens according to their ability to pay), and freedom of thought, opinion and religion. It also proclaimed that the nation was the source of all sovereignty. Most revolutionaries, however, believed that in practice only those with a certain amount of property or commerce should dominate political life.

The suffrage was therefore given only to 'active citizens' – men who paid the equivalent of three days' worth of labour in annual taxation, accounting for about 15 per cent of the population. The King, meanwhile, was given only a suspensive veto over legislation, a loss of authority to which Louis himself was never reconciled. In the streets, the question of the royal veto and the limited franchise outraged the radicals of the now-flourishing Parisian newspaper press, including the *Ami du peuple*, produced by the fiery doctor-turned-journalist Jean-Paul Marat.

The most divisive issue of all, however, was the reform of the Church. The Assembly intended to pay off the state debt by selling off its lands. In November 1789 all church property was declared to be 'national property' (*biens nationaux*) which would be auctioned off to repay the state's creditors. Meanwhile, they and government officials would be paid in paper bills (*assignats*), which could be used in the land auctions, but which in practice began to circulate as paper money (they became legal tender in April 1790). Deprived of its income, the Church had to be reshaped. The solution was the Civil Constitution of the Clergy of July 1790. Priests were henceforth to be elected by the local 'active citizens' and were to be paid salaries by the state. The conservative press and the first *émigrés* – people who had fled abroad to escape the Revolution – seized the opportunity to co-ordinate ultra-Catholic opposition within France. Under pressure from both counter-revolutionaries and radicals, the National Assembly took a fateful decision on 27 November 1790. It laid down an oath of loyalty to the Civil Constitution, to be sworn by all priests. About half of the French clergy (non-jurors or 'refractories') refused: the French Church was split down the middle and non-juror priests would emerge as the moral leaders of the counter-revolution in many parts of provincial France.

Across the frontiers, the *émigrés* provided another focus for opposition, although their real significance probably lay in the fact that their very existence aggravated the creeping sense amongst the revolutionaries that there was dangerous opposition to the new order. Louis XVI himself wavered between hostility, reluctance and acquiescence in the reform of France. He and his family, it is true, had been roughly treated at the hands of the Parisians. On 5–6 October 1789 a famished crowd of 6000 women, angered by both the scarcity of bread and the King's reluctance to give his approval to the early reforms of the Revolution, marched to Versailles. They forced the royal family to move to the Tuileries Palace in Paris (with the National Assembly trailing behind a few days later). In the night of 20–21 June 1791 the beleaguered royal family made a desperate bid to flee the country, but they were stopped at Varennes, not far from the frontier, and ignominiously drawn back to Paris.

For the left, which sought to push the Revolution into a more democratic direction, the flight to Varennes was a sign that the constitutional monarchy had failed. Republicanism was now openly voiced in the press and in political clubs, such as the Jacobins which had a national network of some 200 societies, rocketing to 900 in the wake of Varennes. The Cordeliers, though merely a Parisian club, drew on a more popular membership, was more radical and forged links with like-minded societies throughout the city. This club organised a petition calling for a referendum on the King's fate. On 17 July 1791 the National Guard shot dead 50 of the demonstrators who gathered on the Champ-de-Mars to sign it. The repression which followed forced the nascent republican movement underground. The Jacobins split between the minority, led by Maximilien Robespierre who had wanted to sign the petition, and the majority (who now formed a separate Feuillant society) who remained loyal to the constitutional monarchy.

In the months after the summer crisis, the National Assembly ratified its political work in the Constitution of 1791. The new Legislative Assembly first gathered on 1 October as the seeds of a renewed political crisis were germinating. Radicals had believed that the flight to Varennes was the prelude to an invasion by the Austrians, whose Emperor, Leopold II, was brother to Marie-Antoinette. Matters were not helped by the Declaration of Pillnitz in August, in which Leopold and Frederick William II of Prussia declared their intention to restore the rights of the French monarchy – but only if other monarchs joined them. While there was little prospect of that, it reinforced the impression that Austria and Prussia were planning to support an invasion led by the *émigrés*, whose numbers had swollen substantially in the wake of the Varennes crisis.

In the Legislative, the centre was held by the Feuillants, who wanted to make the Constitution of 1791 work and who sought stability and peace to give it the best chance of survival. Their opponents sought precisely the opposite: war. The left-wing 'Brissotins' (Jacobins led by Jacques-Pierre Brissot), hoped that war against the German princes who harboured the *émigrés* would force the King to chose sides for or against the Revolution. The Brissotins could exploit the crisis in order to gain ministerial posts, capturing the Crown for the left. To the right, the Fayettists assumed that their idol Lafayette would be appointed to lead the French armies, would return in triumph and would crush the left and strengthen the monarchy. Louis XVI himself wanted war because he believed that the forces of Austria (which would be France's main adversary in a conflict with the Holy Roman Empire) would sweep aside the ramshackle French army and restore the absolute monarchy. In the cut-and-thrust of the increasingly bitter debate, Louis was forced to sacrifice his monarchist ministers in March 1792 and appoint, much against his will, a Brissotin government with the support of a large and clamorous section of the Legislative Assembly. With the balance now tipped in favour of war, it was declared on Austria on 20 April 1792. Prussia, which had signed a defensive alliance with Austria in February, entered the fray in May.

The war – as Louis had secretly hoped – began disastrously. The Austrians and the Prussians brushed aside the French army and marched on Paris, where the revolutionaries cried treason. Marie-Antoinette, it was said, was at the heart of an 'Austrian Committee'. Suspicions hardened when the King dismissed his Brissotin ministers on 10 June. Ten days later, the Paris crowds, spurred by empty stomachs, reacted by invading the Tuileries. The allied commander, the Duke of Brunswick, issued an ill-advised manifesto whereby he warned that Paris would suffer 'exemplary and forever memorable vengeance' if the King or his family were harmed. This 'Brunswick Manifesto' was counter-productive. The Legislative had already proclaimed a state of emergency, *la patrie en danger*. Patriotic provincial contingents of the citizens' militia, the National Guard, now swarmed through Paris on their way to the war and the Parisian radicals could count on their support. On 10 August, as the Prussians edged closer to Paris, these units provided the backbone of an insurrection organised by the Parisian districts ('sections'). The insurgents stormed the Tuileries, massacring the Swiss Guards and forcing the King and his family to take refuge in the Legislative Assembly.

The Legislative Assembly imprisoned the royal family and called elections, based on near-universal male suffrage, for a Convention which was to draft a new, republican constitution. The crisis itself did not abate. Thousands of priests, aristocrats, Swiss Guards and other 'suspects' were imprisoned. As the allies continued their slow but relentless march on the capital, the militants feared that these prisoners would be a fifth column, bursting from their confinement and massacring Parisians as they slept. In the September Massacres, instigated at the wild urgings of Marat, a mob broke into the jails. The gutters ran with blood as nearly one and a half thousand prisoners, mostly petty criminals and prostitutes, were slaughtered. The military danger did at last pass: on 20 September the dysentery-ridden Prussians were turned back by a French artillery barrage and bayonet charge at Valmy. The following day, the Convention first met and, on 22 September, it proclaimed a Republic. In December, the Convention tried Louis XVI for treason. The final decision on his fate – whether or not he should be put to death – was passed by only one vote. Louis XVI (or 'Louis the Last', as some republicans hopefully dubbed him) was guillotined on 21 January 1793.

The King's execution split the republicans. The more moderate among them, the Brissotins, who came to be called the Girondins (because much of the leadership came from the Gironde), had been swept into power by the revolution of 10 August, but they opposed the

King's death. Their left-wing opponents, dubbed the 'Mountain' because they sat on the higher benches in the Convention, now dominated the Jacobins, as their erstwhile friends among the Girondins had been expelled from the club. The Girondin–Jacobin struggle for power would become a fight to the death, against the background of the most desperate crisis faced by the young Republic.

Its birth was greeted with a flush of military success: the Prussians retreated after Valmy and the Austrians were defeated at Jemappes on 6 November. Yet victory brought its own problems. The French poured into Germany, occupying much of the left bank of the Rhine, and swarmed into Belgium. This last move brought the Republic into a headlong collision with Britain, alarmed by the surge of French military power along the continental seaboard, and with the Netherlands, as the French began to press on their southern frontier. France declared war on both countries on 1 February 1793. By the summer, the French were fighting not only Austria, Prussia, Britain and the Netherlands, but also the Italian state of Piedmont-Sardinia (whose provinces of Savoy and Nice had been occupied by the French in September), Spain (March 1793), Portugal and the Kingdom of Naples (July). In Russia, Catherine II was making bellicose noises, although in reality she had her eyes fixed closer to home. Meanwhile, French volunteers, considering the war won, began to drift homewards. The army's strength was being depleted just as the Republic had multiplied its enemies. The Prussians and the Austrians counter-attacked, with the Austrians inflicting a heavy defeat on the French at Neerwinden (18 March). France was soon invaded on every frontier.

In desperate need of troops, the Convention decreed the conscription of 300,000 men in February. When imposed in the west of France in March, regions such as the Vendée, Brittany and Normandy exploded in revolt. These spontaneous outbursts of violent peasant protest soon developed into a full-scale Catholic–Royalist rebellion with the leadership of local nobles and priests. In the Vendée, the open war was not contained until December, whereupon it developed into guerrilla warfare. While confronted with popular counter-revolution in the west, the Convention was faced with an economic crisis, which put it under pressure from a closer quarter – the popular militants of Paris.

The Parisian popular movement, which had provided the political (if not the military) mainspring of the insurrection of 10 August, was still gathering strength. Called *sans-culottes* because they disdained 'aristocratic' breeches, and mobilised by the Paris sections and the popular political clubs, the militants were driven by anger at economic scarcity and high prices. They were socially a heterogeneous group – not a working class, but rather a 'coalition' of master-craftsmen and the journeymen who worked and lived with them.[9] They also had leadership in the form of the radical *Enragés* (literally, the 'wild ones'[10]), who demanded the death penalty for hoarders, fixed prices (a 'Maximum'), and the utmost prosecution of the war (*guerre à l'outrance*), and who believed that the *sans-culottes* represented a purer form of democracy than the Convention. The journalist Jacques-René Hébert echoed all this in the *Père Duchesne*.

The logic of the Jacobin position in the Convention (where they were a minority) suggested that an alliance with the popular movement would allow them to defeat the Girondins. They also proposed most of the practical, if authoritarian, measures to deal with the political and social crisis. In March and April, the Convention built the basic machinery of the Terror. This included a Revolutionary Tribunal to try those accused of treason and a Committee of Public Safety, elected by the Convention to deal with the war effort. To this was added a Committee of General Security charged with policing. Together, the two committees would emerge as a strong, executive government during the Terror. Deputies were also sent to the provinces as 'representatives on mission' to mobilise the population for the war effort and to crush counter-revolution. The Convention also recognised local surveillance committees, which the Parisian sections had established spontaneously in August. At the same time, the Jacobins began to voice support for some *sans-culotte* demands. The Maximum, which fixed prices on bread and grain, was voted through on 3 May. Consequently, in the insurrection of 31 May–2 June, the *sans-culottes* and the Parisian National Guards purged the leading Girondins from the Convention and the government, bringing the Jacobins to power. They hurriedly drafted a new constitution, based on universal and direct male suffrage. The 'Constitution of 1793' would become a *sans-culotte* rallying cry, but it would never be implemented. Instead, the Republic would descend into the Terror. The immediate consequence of the coup was to fan the flames of civil war. Local conflicts between Jacobins and moderates, exacerbated by the economic crisis, had already erupted in Marseille and Lyon. Now, important cities such as Bordeaux, Caen and Toulon joined in an anti-Jacobin, 'Federalist' revolt.

Faced with the daunting task of coping with the military, social and political crisis, the Jacobin solution was the Terror. This was effectively extraordinary, emergency government – a state of siege. Historians seeking to explain the Terror lurch between two flags.[11] Rallying around one there are those, including the 'Marxists', Georges Lefebvre, Albert Soboul and George Rudé, who stress the circumstances which forced the revolutionaries to take drastic measures to defend the Republic. Marshalled around another are those, such as François Furet and Lynn Hunt, who argue that the Terror was produced by the Revolution itself, that it was the logical product of revolutionary ideology and rhetoric which, by claiming to speak for 'the nation', implied that all opposition was against it and was, therefore, illegitimate and counter-revolutionary.[12] With this mentality, the violence was virtually inevitable and indeed was inherent in the Revolution. As Simon Schama bluntly puts it, the Terror was 'merely 1789 with a higher body count'.[13]

Yet the Terror was a monster with more than one face. It aimed at providing effective emergency government to respond to the crisis, but there were also measures which the Convention had to pass – not always willingly – as the price of pacifying the *sans-culottes*. The Terror, in other words, was not just the creature of revolutionary ideology, but was also shaped in response to intense pressures 'from below'. There is much to be said for seeing 'the Terror' as being cast by conflicting 'terrors',[14] for it was a violent struggle within the Revolution between different interests and visions of the new order. It is true that the Convention came to accept the measures demanded by the popular militants because it considered them regrettable but essential for social stability and the war effort. In fact, the *levée en masse*, though a *sans-culotte* idea, brought the Convention to its feet. This 'mass levy' decreed universal conscription and the mobilisation of all civilian society for the prosecution of war. There is, moreover, no doubt that ideology helped to shape some of the machinery of the Terror. The Law of Suspects of 17 September 1793, for example, defined those liable to arrest in the broadest terms, including those whose words could be construed as counter-revolutionary. Yet it is no coincidence that the most radical measures were implemented after 4–5 September, when a mass demonstration by the *sans-culottes* led by Hébert pushed the Convention into declaring Terror the 'order of the day'. Until then, the revolutionaries had been dragging their feet over popular measures passed in the spring and summer, including the Maximum, a forced loan on the rich, the death penalty for hoarders and the creation of 'revolutionary armies'. These were marauding columns of Parisian militants who would terrorise the provinces and requisition grain for the city. Now, faced with the very real threat of insurrection, these measures were finally put into practice. On 29 September the General Maximum extended the price controls to a plethora of items. It also imposed a cap on wages, but in practice, for as long as Hébert's henchmen controlled the Paris municipal government (the Commune), it resisted that part of the Maximum. The grislier acts – including the executions of Marie-Antoinette and the Girondins in October – were aimed at placating *sans-culotte* desires for tough measures.

The most notorious atrocities outside Paris were committed by the Convention's own members – the representatives on mission. Yet the term often given to this phase – the 'anarchic' Terror – suggests that the Convention itself had little direct control over it. The 'Federalist' revolts were suppressed one by one. Marseille was recaptured in August, Lyon and Bordeaux in October, though Toulon, which in August had opened its port to the British rather than face the vengeance of the Convention, held out until 20 December. The representatives on mission wreaked horrific punishment on these rebellious cities. In Lyon, Joseph Fouché and Jean Collot d'Herbois found the guillotine too slow, so in the *mitraillades* cannon-fired grapeshot, blasting their victims into mass graves. Nowhere, however, was the repression more bloody than in the western areas affected by the royalist uprisings. The open war in the Vendée ended with successive republican victories over the royalists in December – and they were accompanied by the slaughter of thousands of rebels. In the most important city in the region, Nantes, the representative on mission, Jean-Baptiste Carrier, was responsible for the *noyades* (mass drownings) of his victims in the river Loire. Eventually, the most brutal of the representatives were reined in by the government, who recalled them to Paris to account for their actions.

The Terror, clearly, did not emerge all of a piece right from the start, but it evolved in response to conflicting pressures between the war, counter-revolution, civil strife and the economic crisis, and the popular militancy which that engendered. Many of these problems were of the revolutionaries' own making and they certainly viewed their predicament through the opaque lenses of their ideology, which helped to shape their often appalling responses. Yet the crisis was real enough. Without it, it seems unlikely that the punitive mentality which was certainly present in 1789 would have been given such wide, institutional expression. The haphazard way in which the Terror developed also meant that there was no single ideology or set of aims at play. Rather, the institutions of the Terror were shaped by conflicting demands and pressures, both external to the Terror (the war, the economic crisis, the civil war) and within it (the popular movement, the representatives on mission, the Convention and the committees).

Indeed, by the end of 1793 some voices were demanding a retreat from the Terror. The tide of the war was slowly beginning to turn, with the British and Austrians suffering (albeit indecisive) defeats in September and October respectively. By the end of the year, 'Federalism' had been defeated and the open war in the Vendée contained, though the guerilla war would grind on in its atrocious fashion for years to come. In November, therefore, Georges-Jacques Danton called for fewer executions, clemency and an attack on the extremists. He was eloquently supported by his friend Camille Desmoulins, in his journal the *Vieux Cordelier*. An influential member of the Committee of Public Safety, Maximilien Robespierre, watched this campaign for 'indulgence' with interest. The 'anarchic' Terror, he believed, was creating more enemies than it was actually destroying. Above all, most of the French population was deeply offended by an atheistic assault on religious belief ('dechristianisation') launched by some of the representatives on mission in the provinces. In Paris, the militants and the Hébertist Commune took up dechristianisation with gusto. Although it had been given some encouragement by the official adoption of the new revolutionary calendar and a decree deporting refractory priests in October, Robespierre and his closest colleagues on the Committee of Public Safety were alarmed by violent peasant reactions provoked by the anti-religious zealots. The 'anarchic' Terror had to be reined in.

On 4 December (14 Frimaire in the new republican calendar), the Convention passed a law asserting central control over the Terror. The Committees of Public Safety and General Security now directly controlled all authorities, from the representatives on mission to the local surveillance committees. The revolutionary armies were merged into a single organisation and kept on a tight government leash. All this encouraged the 'Indulgents', especially when some of Hébert's extremist allies were arrested. Through the winter, the Jacobins and the popular movement turned in on themselves as they struggled over the direction of the Terror. The Hébertists wanted to intensify the Terror; Danton and the Indulgents sought to mitigate or even end it, and the Robespierrists in the government wanted to shear the Terror of its excesses, while using it to deal with the crisis. The Robespierrists triumphed in March, when the Hébertists were arrested, tried, and guillotined, and in April, when Danton and his associates followed them. That the *sans-culottes* did not stir to defend their Hébertist champions suggested that they were becoming a spent militant force. The revolutionary army was abolished altogether and the Commune was purged and packed with Robespierrists, who in July would impose the unpopular Maximum on wages, with fatal consequences for themselves.

It is perhaps only with the Robespierrist triumph over the 'factions', that the Terror can be regarded as being driven as much by ideology as by circumstance. It became a means by which, in particular, Robespierre and his acolyte, Louis de Saint-Just (the pallid 'Angel of Death') could impose their own, spartan vision of a Republic of Virtue on the Convention. The Terror became, more than ever, a means of suppressing dissent.[15] The Law of 22 Prairial (10 June) decreed that defendants arraigned before the Revolutionary Tribunal would have no defence counsel and sentence was to be passed within 24 hours. This law instigated the 'Great Terror', a seven-week period during which most of the entire Terror's victims in Paris perished under the guillotine. Between March 1793 and late July 1794, 2639 people were decapitated in the city, 1515 of them during the 'Great Terror'. Yet under the surface Robespierrist pontifications bred resentment in the Convention and Robespierre himself was suspected of aspiring to a dictatorship. Moreover, representatives on mission who had been recalled to explain themselves were unsure what the government had in store for them. In the streets, the *sans-culottes* now only sullenly accepted the rule of the committees. There was a growing sense that the Terror had achieved its purpose. The French defeated the Austrians at the Battle of Fleurus on 26 June and streamed into Belgium. In Paris, the government's grumbling, fearful opponents in the Convention finally combined their parliamentary forces. On 9–10 Thermidor (27–8 July), Robespierre and his associates were overthrown and executed. The *sans-culottes*, fuming at the Maximum on wages, scarcely shuddered. Purged of the leading Jacobins, the surviving members of the Convention – who became known as the Thermidorians – began the process of dismantling the Terror. In December 1794 they were bolstered by the return of the 71 surviving Girondins, orientating the Convention towards moderate republicanism.

The last five years of the Revolution up to the advent of Napoleon Bonaparte was dominated by two major problems. Firstly, the republicans had to steer the Revolution between the two extremes of counter-revolution and Jacobinism. Secondly, they had to bring the war to a victorious conclusion. For as long as the war persisted, so opposition would flourish. Neither the Thermidorian Convention, nor the Directory which succeeded it, found workable solutions, which helps to explain the creation of the Napoleonic dictatorship.

It was not, however, for want of trying. The Thermidorians closed down the Jacobin club in November 1794 and, in the provinces, they connived at the onslaught of royalist mobs wreaking carnage on the Jacobins in the 'White Terror'. Yet the real threat from the left came not from the Jacobins but from one last great outburst of popular insurgency in Paris, in a revolt bred of despair. The Thermidorians repealed the Maximum on 24 December 1794, a decision which proved to be disastrous. Within days, Europe was in the icy grip of the harshest winter since 1709. Food supplies dwindled desperately and, freed from controls, the prices rocketed. The Convention was invaded by crowds in April and May 1795 (Germinal and Prairial Year III), with men and women demanding 'bread and the Constitution of 1793'. When the Prairial uprising was suppressed, it was the final defeat of the *sans-culottes*. On the right, the threat of counter-revolution was contained in July when a royalist force which had landed at Quiberon in Brittany was defeated. A royalist insurrection in Paris in October (Vendémiaire) was crushed with the help of the 'whiff of grapeshot' fired by artillery under Napoleon Bonaparte.

By August the Thermidorians had produced a new republican Constitution (that of Year III, or 1795), which established the Directory. All male taxpayers were given the vote in a system of indirect suffrage to two legislative councils, which in turn elected a five-member executive Directory. The essential aim of this Constitution was to avoid the popular 'anarchy' of direct democracy on the one hand and royalist counter-revolution on the other. The Directory drew its support from those who had done well out of the Revolution: government officials, army officers, manufacturers and landowners who had bought church property. Of all these people, the most important were the thirty-thousand-odd wealthiest *notables*, who with indirect suffrage were the people with the real ability to affect the balance of power in Paris. The Directory therefore rested on narrow foundations; there were vast sections of the population, particularly among the peasantry and the urban masses, who saw nothing in the Directory to satisfy their needs and who were open to royalist or Jacobin blandishments. There was also a widespread breakdown in law and order, expressed in an upsurge of brigandage (spurred by a further economic crisis in 1796), by another outburst of 'White Terror' in south-eastern France in 1797 and by deserters sheltered by war-weary peasants. With its slender popular base, the government was always obliged to secure the support of either monarchists or Jacobins. In what was called *la politique de bascule*, the government therefore jostled from left to right. In the coup of Fructidor (September 1797), the army was used to purge the legislature – and the Directory itself – of those politicians suspected of monarchist sympathies. In May (Floréal) 1798, it was the turn of the Jacobins to be 'Florealised' when it looked likely that they would make large electoral gains. They had their revenge in June (Prairial) 1799, when a 50-strong Jacobin rump exploited a renewed military crisis (France appeared to be on the brink of a Russian and British invasion) to carry moderate support for emergency measures reminiscent of the Year II (1793–4). They also forced three directors to resign, electing three left-leaning candidates in their place. Yet they were dominated by the cerebral Emmanuel Sieyès, who would engineer the downfall of the Directory in the coup of Brumaire (November 1799).

The main beneficiary of the Brumaire coup was, however, Napoleon Bonaparte. His rise to power was the fatal symptom of one of many illnesses with which revolutionary politics was riddled: the war. The military crisis of the summer of 1799 encouraged a royalist uprising around Toulouse, while the Jacobins confidently asserted themselves in the Prairial 'coup'. In October an uneasy truce with the royalists in the Vendée broke down. All this alarmed moderate republicans, and, though all these threats, including that of invasion, had receded by November, the near-catastrophe finally proved to even the Directory's own supporters that the regime needed strengthening. Sieyès was among those who wanted to revise the constitution by increasing the power of the executive. In Bonaparte he saw a successful and popular general who could do what was necessary. Yet in the coup of 9–10 November 1799, Bonaparte himself gobbled up the lion's share of the political prizes. When his soldiers closed down the legislature, a rump of deputies were formed into two commissions which, as requested, did not just 'revise' the existing constitution, but tore it up altogether. Power was invested in a three-man Consulate, in which pre-eminence was taken by Bonaparte, as First Consul, for the other two had merely consultative voices. The cogs for a dictatorial machine then slotted relentlessly into place.

The Consulate (1799–1804) was an authoritarian regime which

explicitly sought to preserve some of the less radical gains of the Revolution. Immediately after Brumaire, some twenty Jacobin legislators were exiled, but the First Consul also made it very clear that the restoration of the monarchy was out of the question. Politically, the Consulate was organised by the Constitution of the Year VIII (1800). It worked as a plebiscitary dictatorship: universal male suffrage was restored, but its impact was limited by an elaborate system of indirect voting, broken down into no fewer than four progressive – and increasingly exclusive – stages. At each stage, the First Consul nominated local officials such as mayors, departmental administrators and prefects. Prefects, created in 1800, were to be the agents of the central government in the departments, with wide powers of administration, policing and appointment, carrying out the will of the First Consul. When the Constituent Assembly created the departments in 1789, the intention had been to decentralise authority by making local government elected by 'active' citizens. The Constitution of 1800 reversed the flow of power, even though the circuitry remained the same: by their very uniformity, the departments proved to be just as effective as a means of central control as they were of local initiative. The legislature consisted of a Tribunate, a Legislative Body and a Senate, which was hand-picked by Bonaparte. Legislation was initiated by the Consulate itself, but the real weapons in Napoleon's dictatorial arsenal were the 'constitutional amendments', called *senatus consulta*. Drafted by Napoleon and rubber-stamped by the senators, without any debate in the other chambers, they were the means by which Bonaparte effectively ruled by decree, silencing opposition in the legislature.

Yet, like all dictators, he could only enforce his will on France with a certain amount of acquiescence from below. He obtained this compliance with his achievements in his early years in power. Bonaparte developed and made use of the legacy inherited from the French Revolution. In fact, these first five years of his rule were the most constructive of his entire regime up to 1815. It was no accident that Bonaparte consolidated his power at a period when France was at peace – or almost so. The war-weary French people probably wanted peace at almost any price, while the old republican elites wanted peace with victory. The First Consul gave them this. In 1800 he defeated the Austrians at Marengo and made terms with Austria at Lunéville in 1801. That same year, the resignation of one of the French Republic's most implacable opponents, the British Prime Minister William Pitt, cleared the path for negotiations with the British, who signed the Treaty of Amiens with France in March 1802. This lull was all too brief and Franco-British hostilities rekindled in May 1803, but on the continent the Napoleonic Wars did not really begin in earnest until 1805. Consequently, the years from 1801 to 1804 were tense but relatively peaceful. It was no mere coincidence that the two referendums by which he was successively voted Consul for Life (1802) and then hereditary Emperor (May 1804) came at this time.

Peace was one of the First Consul's strongest cards, but it was not quite the trump to win the game altogether. The ace was the Concordat which, signed in July 1801 and published at Easter 1802, healed the rift between the Revolution and the Church. The Pope accepted the sale of church lands, while in return Catholicism was recognised in France as 'the religion of the great majority of citizens'. The state would pay all French bishops and 3500 parish priests. While there was to be a clerical oath, it would not be to any constitution, but would be a simple promise to obey the laws. This went a great way to healing the decade-old schism in French society. It calmed all but the most intransigent Catholic royalists, helping to pacify the rebellious western French provinces. Other reforms consolidated the revolutionary, secular state, albeit with a decisive authoritarian twist. The Education Law of 1802 created the *lycées*, secondary schools intended to train the sons of the *notables* as administrators, engineers and military officers. Primary schools for the peasant masses were intended as a means of enforcing the use of the metric system and of eliminating local dialects, or *patois*, in favour of French by teaching basic literacy. From 1808 the whole education system – including institutions of higher education such as the *Polytechnique*, the elite engineering school founded in 1794 – would be forged together as the 'University', directed by a Grand Master. It was a centralised structure under the direct control of the government. Napoleon also codified the fifteen-thousand-odd decrees passed since 1789 in the Civil Code, promulgated on 21 March 1804. The 'Napoleonic Code' recognised equality before the law, the abolition of privilege, the principle of careers open to talent and property rights. But it also reversed some of the more advanced revolutionary legislation. For example, while the Revolution gave illegitimate children full rights of inheritance, the Civil Code gave them only to those whose parents had eventually married. The Revolution's liberal divorce legislation of 1792 was revised: the petitioners required the prior consent of their parents before a divorce could go ahead. These terms were aimed at restoring patriarchal authority within the family.

Collectively, these reforms were successful in binding the revolutionary elites to the Napoleonic regime. Throughout his rule, however, Napoleon went further: he rigorously pursued a policy of *amalgame*, or amalgamation, whereby he made it clear that he did not care about a person's political past – Jacobin, royalist, moderate – provided that he was now loyal to him. Those who served him well were rewarded with lucrative positions in the government and with honours and titles. A decoration, the Legion of Honour, was created in 1802. Later, under the Empire, a hereditary imperial nobility was formed in 1808, but it was to be an open elite. Promotion into it – and demotion out of it – was based on state service. Later, too, rewards of estates in the Napoleonic Empire's far-flung conquests kept the elites sweet, but for now the pinnacle of achievement was appointment as a senator, bringing with it influence and an extraordinarily fat salary.

Yet the regime was a dictatorship and, while there were plenty of carrots, there were also some heavy sticks. Opposition to Napoleon was most virulent first when the Consulate was taking its initial faltering steps and secondly after the terrible defeat inflicted on the Empire in Russia in 1812. In the early years of his dictatorship, the main danger came from intransigent royalists and republicans. Napoleon blatantly exploited two royalist conspiracies in 1800 and 1804 to squeeze the life from the Jacobins and the royalists in turn. Even the feeble parliamentary opposition was muzzled. Bonaparte feared that the veteran republicans in the legislature would try to disrupt the safe passage of the Concordat and, less than three weeks before it was due to be presented, both the Tribunate and the Legislative Body were purged of their more troublesome members. The Tribunate itself would later be abolished as a 'useless institution'. Leading liberal opponents of the regime, such as Madame Germaine de Staël (Necker's daughter) and Benjamin Constant (later an important liberal ideologue during the Bourbon Restoration) were exiled. The press was strictly controlled: in January 1800, 60 Parisian newspapers were shut down, leaving only 13 still publishing. By 1810 even they were reduced to four, all of which were subject to prosecution if they criticised the regime.

Napoleon extended the repression into the provinces. He ruthlessly pursued royalist guerrillas, particularly in the Vendée, where he set up military commissions to try and summarily execute rebels. Similar measures were also used, however, against the wave of brigandage which had afflicted the Directory. Otherwise, a close eye was kept on political opposition through a well-oiled police system under the former Terrorist, Joseph Fouché (who, it was believed, even kept a file on Napoleon himself). The police were empowered to arrest dissidents and to hold them without trial – 2500 of them in 1814. The movement of workers was controlled with the introduction in 1803 of the *livret*, a passport which contained an individual's employment record and personal details. No one could be given a job without a *livret*, which therefore became a means by which employers and officials alike could ensure quiescence. By these methods, as well as by securing possibly the widest support of any French regime since 1790, Napoleon had secured his position in France by 1804. He would now turn outwards, building on the military conquests of the Republic, and exploiting the resources and institutions at his disposal, to embark on the greatest-ever surge of French power in Europe. It would also prove to be the last.

The French Revolution was not primarily a social transformation. The 'abolition of feudalism' trumpeted by the revolutionaries on 4–11 August 1789 was not the dramatic step suggested by the stirring language of the decrees. Apart from the argument, put forward by Alfred

Cobban, that nothing resembling feudalism really existed in France by 1789, the August decrees did not destroy all the dues paid by the peasants to their landlords. Certainly, those related to personal servitude, such as serfdom, forced labour and the seigneur's hunting rights, disappeared, but the rest (and financially the most onerous) were redefined as property rights and could only be redeemed by the peasants with cash payments. Peasant land-ownership was enhanced by the sale of church lands, although by how much varied from region to region. In the Nord, peasant ownership increased from 30 per cent of all land to 42 per cent between 1789 and 1802 (and a third of the purchasers were previously landless peasants). In areas such as the Beaujolais and the Paris basin, however, peasant gains were tiny. Although 10 per cent of all land changed hands, middle-class and noble landowners benefited the most and remained the predominant proprietors in France. By being forced to share the highest office in the military and government and even local influence with non-noble landowners, the nobility undoubtedly lost a good deal of prestige and authority. Yet by 1815 they still owned at least 20 per cent of all land in France. While this is a substantial decline from the estimated 25–33 per cent in 1789, it enabled them to enjoy considerable authority: 41 per cent of Napoleon's prefects were recruited from the old nobility and they remained influential deep into the nineteenth century. In 1846 a quarter of all members of parliament were scions of the old regime nobility.[16]

The Revolution, therefore, did not destroy noble wealth and power, although it did reduce it. Nor did it bring a triumphant, capitalist bourgeoisie to power. Many of the obstacles to economic development were certainly swept away – internal customs barriers were abolished in August 1789, as were guilds in March 1791. In June 1791, the Le Chapelier Law banned workers' associations, which undoubtedly benefited employers, but even so the French economy evolved slowly, retaining traditional, pre-industrial and small-scale modes of production well into the nineteenth century. The wealthiest bourgeois, even if they had originally made their money in commerce and industry, preferred to invest it in more secure and traditional places, such as land and government bonds. As before 1789, therefore, the land-owning bourgeois had economic interests similar to those of the nobility and had the same aspirations to share in their cultural and social life, though there were tensions within this common elite of *notables*.

The main impact of the Revolution was political: it was one of the great founding deeds of modern politics, both democratic and totalitarian. The liberating principles proclaimed in the Declaration of the Rights of Man and the Citizen in 1789 have subsequently been repeated, if not quite verbatim – most notably in the United Nations Declaration of Human Rights in 1948.[17] Nor were the ideals empty rhetoric: the revolutionaries gave equal rights to Jews in September 1791. On 4 February

1794 the slaves in the colonies were emancipated, although this was a desperate response to their insurrection in Saint-Domingue, led by Toussaint L'Ouverture. When Napoleon restored slavery in the French colonies, Saint-Domingue rose up and in 1804 won its independence as Haiti, to this day the longest-lived republic in the western hemisphere after the United States. In France, the Revolution provided adult *men* with the first taste of electoral politics. Perhaps the widest experience of democracy was in the elections to the Estates-General in 1789, with the greatest participation in any election during the Revolution. William Doyle argues that 'the elections of 1789 were the most democratic spectacle ever seen in the history of Europe, and nothing comparable occurred again until far into the next century'.[18] Thereafter, the turnout for elections and referendums in the French Revolution dwindled as popular hostility and apathy took hold during the successive crises of the 1790s. Yet even during the referendum on the Constitution of 1793, the 1.8 million men in the local, primary assemblies who voted in favour, represented a decent turnout (30 per cent) given that France was embroiled in civil war. Certainly, the 'modernity' of the experience of voting should not be exaggerated. In many primary assemblies, candidates were elected in the age-old way that peasant communities made decisions – by acclamation. The revolutionary experience of electoral politics was not, therefore, a fully-formed, recognisably 'modern' system, but Malcolm Crook's description of the Revolution as France's 'apprenticeship in democracy' is certainly apt.[19]

In the wider civic sphere, the Revolution introduced politics and ideas of citizenship to a wide audience in a number of ways. The press flourished with the collapse of censorship. At its peak, Hébert's extreme *Père Duchesne* claimed a circulation of 200,000, although that was primarily because in 1793 his allies dominated the War Ministry, which ensured that it was distributed to soldiers at the front. Perhaps more important were journals such as *La Feuille villageoise*, which was aimed specifically at peasants. Although average runs ranged between 8000 and 16,000 copies, they reached a much wider audience, as each copy was passed from one reader to another or read aloud for the benefit of illiterates. Consequently, one estimate suggests that it reached a quarter of a million people. Political organisations also brought political debate to a large number of people: in 1794 there were some six thousand Jacobin clubs dotted about France, mostly in small towns, but in south-eastern France they were found in many villages, too.[20] While this enormous number may have more to do with the pressure for political conformity at the height of the Terror than with real political commitment, the existence of 1250 at the end of 1791 was a sincere response to the crisis in the constitutional monarchy. The mobilisation of the urban working population was certainly dramatic. An estimated quarter of a million Parisians took up arms in the crisis of July 1789. Later, the

Parisian popular movement may have mobilised only a minority of the population (attendance at section meetings ran at 10 per cent in 1793),[21] but this was impressive enough, given that at this time most people had to devote so much time and energy to survive grinding poverty.

There were limits to this democracy. The poorest males were denied the suffrage under the Constitution of 1791 and even in the elections for the Convention in 1792, domestic servants were not allowed to vote. The most important exclusion, however, was women. Nevertheless, their disenfranchisement did not prevent them from participating in politics – and having a direct impact on the Revolution – in other ways. Women's involvement was driven primarily by economic issues, but this was politicised: the problem of subsistence, as David Andress has written, was the issue which women used to 'reinsert themselves' into politics.[22] The march by 7000 women on Versailles on 5–6 October 1789 is the most famous episode, but women also participated in the protest on the Champ-de-Mars on 17 July 1791 and in the Germinal and Prairial uprisings of 1795. The radical women's political club, the *Citoyennes Républicaines Révolutionnaires*, was founded in May 1793 by Pauline Léon and Claire Lacombe, who were associated with the *Enragés*. The society's programme was a radical cocktail of political and economic demands, including the right of women to bear arms in defence of the Republic, but also for the Maximum and policing the grain trade. The government's forcible closure of the society on 30 October 1793 was driven partly by prevailing gender attitudes at the time. The spokesman for the Committee of General Security, Jean-Baptiste Amar, informed the Convention that women were 'not very capable of [the] lofty meditations and of serious cogitations' required for politics.[23] None the less, between 1789 and 1793, before the ban on women's clubs, France had no fewer than 52 women's or mixed-gender political societies (one of them royalist, in Avranches). Women did not win political rights during the Revolution, but they did win some civil rights. In September 1792 the Legislative Assembly legalised divorce, and research by Roderick Phillips has shown that women were more likely than men to be the petitioners (71 per cent in Rouen, for example).[24] In September 1793 and January 1794 the Convention decreed that inheritances had to be shared equally among both male and female heirs.

Yet the Revolution also had its darker side. The bloodletting cast a long shadow over the nineteenth and twentieth centuries. In the early nineteenth century, republicanism and democracy were associated with the extremes of the *sans-culottes* and the Terror. A deep schism was left in French society. On the one hand, there were those who supported the Revolution because they believed in the ideals of 'liberty, equality, fraternity', because they had gained materially from it through careers or purchases of land or because it represented military victory and glory.

On the other hand, there were those who loathed it, including the clergy, much of the nobility and the peasantry. The Catholic clergy resented the Revolution's triumphant secularism and its destruction of the Church's wealth. For the nobility, even if it did not, in the long run, suffer much loss of its property and influence, the nightmarish memories of persecution in the 1790s did not disappear. The peasantry, as we have seen, did not benefit as much as it wanted from the Revolution. For them, after 1789 the new order represented little more than conscription, taxation and an assault on their traditional way of life, with the attack on the Church and the sale of church lands drawing bourgeois landlords, with their urban values, into their communities. Indeed, in large parts of rural France – the Vendée (where perhaps 400,000 people were killed), Brittany, Normandy and the areas of the south affected by the 'White Terror' in 1794–5, 1797 and 1815 – the peasants did not mobilise in support of the Revolution, but in opposition to it. These regions would remain resistant to republicanism for decades to come. The bitter divisions left long political and deep social scars which made consensus an elusive prize for most of the nineteenth century.

3 The European Impact, 1789–1815

In 1789, European responses to the French Revolution were generally positive, at least among the intellectuals and politicians. Across the Rhine, some of the great writers of the German Enlightenment – not least Johann Wolfgang Goethe – kept an aloof distance from the celebrations. Yet the vast majority, among them Friedrich Schiller, greeted the news of the fall of absolutism in France enthusiastically. In Italy, reformists such as Pietro Verri (in Milan) and Dalmazzo Vasco (in Piedmont) were inspired to try vainly to press political reform on their rulers. In Britain, supporters of parliamentary reform welcomed the French Revolution as an imitation of their own 'Glorious' Revolution of 1688–9. Some people, of course, spoiled the party. In Italy, Vittorio Alfieri started to write his anti-French tract, *Misogallo*, in 1790. That same year, the Irish politician and intellectual, Edmund Burke, rounded on the British parliamentary reform movement and the French Revolution itself with *Reflections*, a long, florid, but blistering attack. His book sparked a passionate debate which attracted some radical big guns: Mary Wollstonecraft's response, *Vindication of the Rights of Man*, was one of the first, followed by Thomas Paine's *Rights of Man* (published in two parts in 1791–2). The most violent initial reaction to events in France was from Catherine II in Russia. In 1790 she had a nobleman, Alexander Radishchev, condemned to death (commuted to exile in Siberia) for publishing his *Journey from Saint Petersburg to Moscow*, in which he castigated serfdom and warned of an uncontrollable insurrection if matters did not improve.

Few European politicians, however, were at first as alarmed by the Revolution as the Tsarina. In fact, most positively welcomed it, as domestic turmoil left France weak and distracted from European ambitions. The elderly Austrian foreign minister, Count Wenzel Kaunitz, welcomed the Constitution of 1791: '[it] renders France far less dangerous than she was under the old régime. If it is a bad one, she will be the only sufferer.'[1] As late as February 1792, William Pitt told the British parliament that 'unquestionably there never was a time in the history of this country, when, from the situation of Europe, we might more reasonably expect fifteen years of peace than at the present moment'.[2] Even the sabre-rattling of the Prussians and the Austrians at the Declaration of Pillnitz in August 1791 was designed for show, rather than a serious effort to galvanise a European crusade against the Revolution. Their objectives in taking up the French gauntlet in 1792 were not to destroy the Revolution, but to exploit French weakness for territorial acquisitions. Yet the French Revolutionary Wars unexpectedly unleashed the awe-inspiring power of the French state over much of Europe. The war, not revolutionary ideals, endangered the Old Regime the most. It was also the most direct way in which the vast majority of Europeans felt the impact of the French Revolution.

The French Revolutionary and Napoleonic Wars, 1792–1815

The French Revolutionary Wars were fought from 1792 to 1802. There was a 14-month pause and then the conflagration reignited in the Napoleonic Wars, first smouldering slowly in 1803 before bursting into flames in 1805. Conflict continued unabated until 1815, except for a brief period of peace between Napoleon's abdication in April 1814 and his return to Paris in March 1815. All stages of the great European struggle were bound together by one overwhelming factor: they were waged to curtail attempts by France to establish hegemony over Europe. In this respect, therefore, the 'French Wars' were not an ideological reaction by the Old Regime against the principles of the French Revolution, but rather a continuity of the 'balance of power' politics of the eighteenth century. It was precisely because France's adversaries followed old habits that the wars lasted for so long. It was not just that the French were formidable adversaries but also that the states which allied against them had their own priorities in addition to defeating France, namely territorial gains and strategic advantages over their nominal allies. This was an understandable but fatal product of eighteenth-century 'balance of power' politics, where alliances were temporary arrangements which only lasted for as long as all powers could gain from them. Yet the hard knocks sustained by the European powers, as one anti-French coalition after another fell apart, eventually forced them to work together – but it took more than two decades of almost continuous conflict to achieve that unity.

The French themselves, for all their liberating rhetoric at the start of the war in 1792, rapidly embarked on conquests once they started winning. Initially, the Brissotin warmongers had promised a war of peoples against their tyrants – 'War on Castles! Peace on Cottages!' – but these cosmopolitan principles evaporated once the possibilities of expansion opened up in the autumn of 1792. On 19 November the Edict of Fraternity promised French help to the oppressed peoples of Europe, but their land and property also provided much-needed money and supplies for the enormous French armies which now invaded the Rhineland and Belgium. On 15 December a further decree abolished seigneurialism in the conquered territories, but it added the sobering details about who was to pay for the costs of the French occupation: the liberated people themselves. The revolutionaries in Paris wanted to exploit the stunning extent of their first victories by consolidating them into permanent strategic advantage. On 31 January 1793, Danton declared: 'The limits of France are marked out by nature. We shall reach them at their four points: the Ocean, the Rhine, the Alps, the Pyrenees.' The objective of 'natural frontiers' meant annexations. Pushing the French border up to the crest of the Alps meant absorbing Nice and Savoy from Piedmont. The real problem was the Rhine, for that meant annexing all of Belgium, a southern slice of Dutch territory and the left bank of the Rhine in Germany. Meanwhile, neither Prussia nor Austria, nor the states of the Holy Roman Empire which had lost out from the French annexations, would freely accept such a looming French presence in Germany. The British, meanwhile, could not accept French expansion along the continental coast with direct access to the North Sea and they entered the war, along with the Netherlands, on 1 February. For as long as France refused to relinquish its claims to the Rhine frontier and for as long as the other European powers refused to yield over this, so the war would continue until one side or the other was ground into submission.

It is important not to overstate the belligerents' purely power-political motives. Governments may have been primarily moved by such considerations, but in some states, such as Britain, public opinion counted for something in politics. The French Edict of Fraternity could not be ignored, as it sounded like a bugle call for international revolution, and in Britain, where a small but vibrant radical movement demanding parliamentary reform was gathering momentum, the government was alarmed. Meanwhile, the outrage across Europe caused by the execution of Louis XVI in January 1793 certainly swept some politicians along: in Britain, public opinion regarded the conflict with France as a war against a nation of regicides, while the anti-French backlash in Spain may have prodded the government towards war.[3] At the very least, the public response meant that the British and Spanish governments knew that their decision for war would enjoy widespread popular support.

France survived the onslaught of the First Coalition in 1793–4, but only by terrorising its own population. As Robespierre and his acolytes fell in July 1794, the Revolution was on the offensive once again, sweeping the Austrians from Belgium and entering Germany and the Netherlands. In the frozen winter of 1794–5, the French swept through the Netherlands, forcing the Dutch not only to sign a punitive peace, but also to establish a republican regime (the first of many 'sister republics') which would ally with France. This strengthened the French grip on Belgium, which was annexed in October 1795, a process eased by Prussia's withdrawal from the war at the Treaty of Basle in April 1795.

Poland had been partitioned for a third time earlier that year and Prussia's territorial appetite was, for now, satiated. Its troops committed in the west were now required to help digest the slice of territory in the east. Even Austria, though still in the fight, was willing to abandon Belgium (the Austrian Netherlands) because it hoped that in subsequent peace negotiations it would receive Bavaria as compensation. The First Coalition was falling apart. With northern Spain overrun, the Spanish monarchy not only negotiated a peace treaty at Basle in July 1795 but was also forced into an unlikely alliance with the French Republic in October.

French armies floundered in Germany in 1796, but General Napoleon Bonaparte invaded Italy in April in order to threaten Austria from the south. Piedmont, reeling from the impact, sued for peace. Napoleon crossed the Alps and entered peace negotiations with the Austrians at Leoben in April 1797. At the subsequent Treaty of Campo Formio in October, they were forced to accept the French annexation of the left bank of the Rhine. The Emperor then had to summon the diet of the Holy Roman Empire to begin the arduous process of working out the compensation for those German princes who would lose territory in the bargain. Austria's surrender of the integrity of the Holy Roman Empire left it all but moribund. At the end of the year, Joseph Görres wrote a caustic obituary: 'the Holy Roman Empire . . . fully conscious and consoled with all the sacraments, died peacefully and piously as the result of a total paralysis and attendant apoplexy'.[4] With Campo Formio, the War of the First Coalition was over. Britain was the only European power left fighting.

The Rhine was now the French frontier, while in northern Italy Bonaparte had bartered Venice in return for Austrian recognition of his personal creation, the Cisalpine Republic. Yet the dramatic surge of French power meant that few European states were willing to accept it for long. Bonaparte's invasion of Egypt in May 1798, aimed partially at threatening the British position in India by reaching the Red Sea, brought Turkey into the war. The Tsar, Paul I, was enraged by the French seizure of Malta en route, as he had both strategic and religious interests there: he had established a Russian Grand Priory of the Order of Malta, which had ruled the island prior to the French invasion. In the Second Coalition, therefore, Britain (as always) and Austria (as always) joined Russia, Turkey, Portugal and Naples in the struggle against France. A further burst of French power led to the creation of more sister republics, satellite states intended to provide their French masters with troops and resources as needed: the Roman Republic in February 1798, the Helvetic (Swiss) Republic in March and the Parthenopean (Neapolitan) in January 1799.

Yet this phase of French expansion was short-lived. The British fleet trapped Bonaparte's army in Egypt in 1798, and, in 1799, Austro-Russian forces swept the French out of Italy. Differences in aims, however, split the allies and helped prevent an invasion of France itself. While Russia and Britain wanted to force the French back to their old frontiers, the Austrians demanded territorial compensation for Belgium and the left bank of the Rhine. This split the Austro-Russian forces, leaving the latter alone to face a French army in Switzerland, where they were defeated at the Battle of Zurich in September. By the time Bonaparte came to power in November, therefore, the crisis for France was past. A fuming Tsar Paul pulled out of the war in 1800 when the British, having taken Malta from the French, held on to it. In 1800 General Moreau led a French thrust against the Austrians in Germany, while Bonaparte led the attack on them in Italy, defeating them at Marengo in June. The Neapolitans were forced to sue for peace in March 1801, while Portugal, invaded by France's Spanish allies, caved in during May. The Austrians left the war with the Treaty of Lunéville in February 1801. The French conquests of the 1790s were confirmed, the Habsburg grand dukes were expelled from Tuscany, which became the Kingdom of Etruria ruled by a Spanish Bourbon. The First Consul was trying to restore Spanish influence in Italy as a means of offsetting that of Austria, which held on to Venetia. Yet it showed how far Napoleon was willing to jettison republicanism for the sake of power politics. In return, France received the vast Spanish territory of Louisiana in North America. Britain, now isolated, opened negotiations leading to the Treaty of Amiens in March 1802. With neither side conceding much, this was a mere lull. The French Revolutionary Wars were now over, but the Napoleonic Wars were about to begin.

The Napoleonic Wars were fuelled first and foremost by Napoleon's own dynastic ambition and seemingly unquenchable thirst for French (for which read 'his') power. He ignored the provisions of Amiens by failing to withdraw from the territories conquered beyond the Alpine and Rhine frontiers. Instead, Napoleon became 'President' of the Cisalpine Republic, annexed Piedmont directly onto France, and invaded and became 'Mediator' of Switzerland. He began to organise overseas expeditions which appeared to threaten British imperial interests. Finally, Napoleon virtually dictated the *Reichsdeputationshauptschluss* in 1803, the law proclaimed by Francis II in Vienna and by which German rulers were compensated for the loss of the Rhineland. This amounted to a dramatic reshuffling of territory. In the process of 'mediatisation', where the larger German powers absorbed the smaller principalities, membership of the Holy Roman Empire was reduced from 365 states to 40. Austria, Prussia and the major *Mittelstaaten* (medium-sized or 'middle' states) – Bavaria, Württemberg and Baden – were the main beneficiaries. They had been strong enough to prove their viability to Napoleon, who was the real force behind the *Hauptschluss*. The First Consul's purpose was to strengthen the middle states eager to resist the encroachments of Prussia and Austria. Mediatisation also undercut the power of the knights of the Holy Roman Empire, since much of their land had been in the ecclesiastical states. The destruction of the latter entailed 'secularisation' – the closure of religious houses, the sale of church land – which appealed to both the French republicans and the enlightened German intellectuals. Moreover, the need to absorb hundreds of thousands of new subjects would oblige the middle states to embark on political reform.[5]

Yet there was no respite for Germany from the French hurricane. In the opening phases of the Napoleonic Wars in May 1803, the French swept into Hanover (because Britain's George III was Elector). This eventually persuaded Tsar Alexander I, who was then angered by the French abduction of the duc d'Enghien (a leading *émigré*) from the neutral territory of Baden, to seal a formal alliance with the British in April 1805.[6] Austria, though its treasury was empty after years of warfare, was pushed into the Third Coalition when in March 1805 Napoleon incorrigibly converted his 'Republic of Italy' into a kingdom, with his stepson, Eugène de Beauharnais, as viceroy in Milan, and annexed the Ligurian (Genoese) Republic. Prussia, however, remained aloof: the benefits of co-operation with France had been made all too obvious in the *Hauptschluss* of 1803.

The first major scalps went to both sides simultaneously. The French and Spanish fleets were mauled at Trafalgar by the British under Horatio Nelson (who was killed in the battle) on 21 October 1805. The day before, the French *grande armée* had entrapped an Austrian force at Ulm in Bavaria and was now bearing down on Vienna, which fell in November. Napoleon shattered an Austro-Russian army at Austerlitz on 2 December 1805, which was followed by a crushing peace treaty imposed on the humbled Austrians at Pressburg. This example dissuaded Prussia from joining the Third Coalition. By January the British and the Russians had been swept out of Italy and the French reconquered Naples, forcing the Bourbon royal family to take refuge, along with the British, in Sicily. From 1808 Naples would be ruled by Napoleon's Marshal, Joachim Murat. In 1806 the Dutch ('Batavian') Republic was converted into the Kingdom of Holland, under Napoleon's brother, Louis. Napoleon's dynastic aims and the harsh punishment which he meted out to his defeated enemies were not a formula for lasting peace.

Prussia was finally persuaded to join a Fourth Coalition with Britain and Russia when Napoleon announced the organisation of the Confederation of the Rhine (*Rheinbund*) in 1806. This sucked most of the middle states of western and central Germany out of the Holy Roman Empire. Napoleon's *Rheinbund*, which grew to include 39 German states by 1808, had effectively destroyed the 1000-year Holy Roman Empire and formed a loose confederation of states allied to France, acting as a buffer against Austria and Prussia. It also thrust

French influence deep into the heart of Germany. When Prussia took up arms, with British encouragement, its great army – to the great shock of almost everyone – was torn to pieces at Auerstedt and Jena in October 1806 and Berlin was occupied.

After Jena, Napoleon marched into Poland to meet the Russian challenge, helped by a Polish insurrection against Russian rule. In November 1806 a 30,000-strong Polish force raised by Polish patriots in French service entered Warsaw. In February 1807 the French and Russian armies mauled each other into a standstill at Eylau (Iława), before the French defeated the Russians at Friedland in June. Defeated but still unbroken, Russia got off lightly at the Treaty of Tilsit that same month, but the terms inflicted on Prussia were harsh. The kingdom lost swathes of territory, and had to pay an indemnity and bear the costs of a French military occupation. A restored rump of a Polish state, the Grand Duchy of Warsaw, was carved out from the Prussian partition and was to be ruled by Napoleon's ally, Frederick Augustus, King of Saxony. Prussia was forced to recognise not only the *Rheinbund*, but also the imposition of French rulers on the Kingdom of Westphalia (Jérôme Bonaparte) and the Grand Duchy of Berg (Napoleon as regent for his young nephew, Louis). Prussia's army was to be limited to 40,000 men. In July 1807, at a meeting on a raft floating on the River Nieman at Tilsit, Tsar Alexander I and Napoleon effectively carved up continental Europe into spheres of influence. Russia received a large chunk of Prussian Poland and was secretly to be allowed to grab Finland off the Swedes. In 1808–9 Russia duly invaded and annexed it. In return, France received Russian recognition of the French conquests so far and a promise that Russia would join the Continental System.

The Continental System was a European blockade of British commerce declared by Napoleon in Berlin in November 1806. It would prove to be the undoing of French power in Europe. Britain and France tried to strangle each other through economic warfare, but the British had two great advantages: a good fleet and money of their own. The French taxed and conscripted from their conquests and their allies, but provoked resentment. The British creamed off funds from their considerable commercial and imperial activities, and were able to subsidise their war-weary continental allies throughout the conflict, constantly persuading and cajoling the European powers to field yet another army against the French Emperor. Meanwhile, their navy allowed them to defy Napoleon's attempt to block British trade from Europe. In August 1806 the British stopped the Danes from joining the blockade – and thus bottling up the Baltic Sea – by invading Denmark and bombarding Copenhagen. This did not prevent the blockade from biting into the British economy, but life was breathed into the allied cause by Napoleon's efforts to force the Continental System on Portugal. In November 1807 a Franco-Spanish force swept across the Portuguese frontier and took Lisbon the day after the Regent, Prince John, had fled for Brazil, allowing Napoleon's Marshal Jean Junot to take charge. Yet French troops had not simply passed through Spain on the way to Portugal: they actually occupied certain northern Spanish fortresses as well. This foreign occupation and Spain's share in the humiliation at Trafalgar in 1805 were blamed on Manuel de Godoy, King Charles IV's chief minister. Godoy and Charles were unpopular because they had pursued a programme of reform aimed at reducing the power of the nobility and the influence of the Church. Meanwhile, Charles's son and heir, Ferdinand, was an avowed conservative and, with the foreign policy humiliations, his star began to rise. In March 1808 his supporters toppled Charles IV and Godoy in an insurrection at Aranjuez and proclaimed their leader King Ferdinand VII. Both sides appealed to Napoleon for support, which was rather like asking a wolf to escort a flock of sheep. The French Emperor obligingly offered to mediate, and summoned the fractious royal family to Bayonne where he imprisoned them in April, placing his brother Joseph on the Spanish throne.

Popular support in Spain backed Ferdinand, who became known as the 'Desired King'. A network of his supporters tried to overthrow French rule in Madrid on 2 May 1808. If the insurrection failed in the capital (up to five hundred Spaniards were killed), it spread to the rest of the country, where the fiercely independent provinces set up governments of their own – juntas – in order to mobilise local resistance to the French. By June 1808, the long, bloody, Spanish war of independence had begun. It was joined, too, by insurrections in Portugal, where local juntas recognised the authority of a central committee in Oporto, which proclaimed loyalty to the exiled Prince Regent. In August a British–Portuguese force under Sir Arthur Wellesley (the future Duke of Wellington) defeated Junot, who negotiated the withdrawal of his troops from Portugal. Britain now had a foothold in continental Europe and, supported by the Spanish insurrection against the French, Wellesley could embark on the Peninsular campaigns, the 'Spanish ulcer' which would sap Napoleon's strength.

In central Europe, a brief but spectacular challenge by a resurgent Austria ended when the French, helped by a counter-attack by their Polish allies, defeated the forces of Archduke Charles at Wagram, outside Vienna, in a closely-fought battle in July 1809. At the Treaty of Schönbrunn in October, the Austrians lost their Illyrian provinces, which would be ruled directly from Paris. Austria's Polish territories were shared between the Grand Duchy of Warsaw and Russia. The Habsburgs had to pay a heavy indemnity and reduce their army to 150,000 men. In 1810 they also had to suffer the indignity of seeing the Habsburg Archduchess, Marie Louise, getting married to the Corsican usurper, who was trying to give his dynasty some respectability. The Austrian defeat marked the end of the Fifth Coalition raised against

France. Its remnants proved more resilient in Iberia, where the French under André Masséna counter-attacked in 1810, but were repulsed at the Torres Vedras fortifications around Lisbon and chased back into Spain in 1811. In July 1812 Wellington defeated the French at Salamanca and entered Madrid.

While the French were being harried in Spain, Napoleon's relations with Russia deteriorated. Russia's entry into the Continental System had been economically disastrous for the nobility who had benefited from grain exports to Britain. Napoleon's threat to restore the Kingdom of Poland, the French annexation of the Netherlands and north-eastern Germany, including the Duchy of Oldenburg which was ruled by the Tsar's brother-in-law, angered Alexander. The Tsar began to impose heavy tariffs on goods from Napoleon's domains and considered making the first military move against the French. In the end, it was Napoleon who blinked first. Having amassed an enormous army, he invaded Russia in June 1812. After the appalling slaughter at Borodino in September, the Russians abandoned Moscow. The exhausted French staggered into the city, which was promptly burned to the ground, possibly by accident but perhaps too by Russian patriots. In October the notorious retreat began, with Napoleon's forces harried by Cossacks and the biting Russian winter. By the time his forces crossed the River Berezina, they numbered a mere 20,000 out of the original 375,000.

The terrible defeat in Russia was a turning-point. It severely reduced Napoleon's forces in eastern Europe, while they were being bled white in Spain. It also gave other powers – not least Prussia, where a far-reaching reform programme was in full throttle – the chance to strike back. The Prussians raised an army of 270,000 men, and, with the Russians invading Poland, they joined the war against Napoleon in March 1813. By June, a Sixth Coalition was forged of Britain, Spain, Portugal, Russia, Prussia and Sweden. It was funded by the heaviest British subsidies yet. Austria, cowed by the painful experiences of 1805 and 1809, and worried by the dangers of Russian expansionism, warily refused to commit itself. Napoleon fought a rigorous campaign in Germany and it was only when the French Emperor rejected the offers of Clemens von Metternich, the Austrian foreign minister, for mediation that the Habsburg emperor was persuaded to march against France. In October the allied forces combined at Leipzig, defeating the French and inflicting heavy casualties in a three-day 'Battle of the Nations'. With this coalition victory, French power in Germany collapsed as one state after another defected to the allies. Sweden meanwhile knocked out one of Napoleon's few remaining friends, Denmark, by a lightning invasion in December 1813–January 1814. In Spain, Wellington defeated the French at Vittoria in June 1813, and by early 1814 he had invaded southern France. Further north, Napoleon had been forced to abandon the Low Countries and the allies were crossing the French frontier. By

March they were approaching Paris. On 2 April the Napoleonic Senate declared their master and creator deposed and proclaimed the restoration of the Bourbon monarchy in the portly shape of Louis XVIII. Two days later Napoleon abdicated. He left for exile on the Italian island of Elba at the end of the month. His escape in February 1815 and his return to Paris in March, opening the final 'Hundred Days' of his empire, was dramatic. The allies declared him an outlaw and the French army broke itself on the reef of combined British, Dutch and Prussian forces at Waterloo on 18 June 1815.

The French Revolutionary and Napoleonic Wars were less a conflict about ideological differences than about the balance of power – the efforts of the European states to reduce the persistent attempts by one of their number to secure hegemony over them all. Yet the continuity with eighteenth-century power politics should not be overstated. In fact, the reason the war dragged on for so long (claiming 7 million dead) was because the balance of power politics had failed. The explosion of French power could be contained only with unprecedented effort and great human cost. The reason for this was the administrative and military strength unleashed by the French Revolution.

Ideology did have a role. Neither side was willing to recognise the legitimate existence of the other and this gave the war a violent intensity which surpassed that of earlier eighteenth-century conflicts. Two examples will suffice to illustrate this. First, for a brief period – in the same poisonous atmosphere of the Terror which generated the bloodthirsty law of 22 Prairial – the law of 7 Prairial Year 2 (26 May 1794) declared that the French forces would not take any British or Hanoverian prisoners. This rule was extended to Spanish troops fighting the French *after* the Terror, on 11 August that same year, but it was repealed on 30 December. Norman Hampson has uncovered one incident in which the law was, literally, executed,[7] but it seems that it was very rarely carried out in the field. Yet it shows that the French revolutionaries were seeing the war in Manichean terms, as a struggle of good against the dark forces of despotism. Secondly, on the coalition side, the allies employed methods against revolutionary France which they would probably never have deployed against what they regarded as a 'legitimate' government. The British forged the *assignat* in order to hasten the Republic's economic collapse and they encouraged the murderous civil war in the west of France. If ideology did not *cause* the war, it *nurtured* it and conditioned the way in which it was fought. Extreme ideological differences helped to dehumanise the enemy, intensified the conflict and made it harder to negotiate without appearing to compromise on the principles upon which, at least publicly, governments were claiming to stand.

Otherwise, while there were some technological innovations, weaponry had changed little. French Revolutionary and Napoleonic tactics, however, stunned the opposition. New tactical ideas came from the military theorists of the old royal army, such as Jean-Baptiste de Gribeauval, Jean du Teil, Jacques Guibert and Pierre de Bourcet. Gribeauval and du Teil developed tactics which involved more flexible use of artillery so that it could be moved about on the battlefield, blasting the precise points in the enemy's line in co-ordination with the infantry attacks. How the infantry was formed was Guibert's innovation: it abandoned marching in lines (which maximised a unit's firepower) in favour of attacking in columns, which allowed for rapid deployment and momentum in the assault. In fact, as columns were especially vulnerable to the raking fire from enemies in line formation, the French would form in a mixed order of line and column. Thanks to de Bourcet's thinking, the French army moved across the countryside in a different way. Eighteenth-century armies conducted their campaigns by marching along supply routes and living off established supply depots. The French army, however, was broken down into smaller divisions which marched independently along separate routes, living off the land. The French army could move faster, get behind the enemy and were harder to pin down by a larger force. The trick, which Napoleon would perfect, was to ensure that, once the enemy was found, these divisions all converged on the same point at the same time. If the French found the enemy first, skirmishers would be sent out to harass the opposition and probe for weak spots. Such troops, operating as they did in small detachments, had considerable scope for initiative, which was why the coalition armies, with their emphasis on rigid, inflexible discipline, looked at them askance.

Other explanations for French success, however, have lain not so much in their tactics but in patriotic fervour and the success of the revolutionaries in mobilising the entire French society for the war effort. This has been lent some support by John A. Lynn's study of the Army of the North. He draws on official reports and private correspondence to underline the point that patriotism did provide a motivation for the French army. Public festivals, praise in the press and promises of a bright, republican future had the effect of bolstering morale, of letting the troops know that their sacrifices on the battlefield were appreciated by the public behind the front line. The actual provision of state support given to widows and to wounded veterans no doubt also helped.[8] In official propaganda, the soldiers of the Republic were the *défenseurs de la patrie*, which is a long way from Wellington's later epithet on his own troops, 'the scum of the earth'. The difference was reflected in discipline: the French Revolution abolished flogging in the army (though not in the navy) in 1790, while British soldiers had to wait until 1881 to be spared the lash. Yet not all historians have accepted that patriotism was a motivation. It is certainly true that early appeals for volunteers were met with enthusiasm, but after the initial victories in late 1792 the soldiers drifted home. Conscription, from the time it was first imposed in 1793, was met with violent opposition and desertion, which ran at 8 per cent in 1796. The political motivation of many recruits may be doubted. It is true that when the Hébertists controlled the French war ministry in 1793–4 they distributed copies of the extremist *Père Duchesne* at the front. Yet, as Tim Blanning suggests, the troops may have found more mundane uses for the paper.[9] Whether by coercion or by patriotism, the French were certainly able to mobilise a significant proportion of their own population – and then that of their conquests. The *levée en masse* of August 1793 was, in effect, the first call for what would be called 'total war' in the twentieth century. Regular conscription, with annual call-ups for specific 'classes' (age groups) was not decreed until the Jourdan law of August 1798. It was this system and not the *levée en masse* of 1793 which, once he had repressed the worst of the desertion, was at the root of Napoleon's success. None the less, the most important reason for French success was the extraordinary lengths to which they went in order to milk their conquests dry of human and material resources.

Occupation, Collaboration and Resistance: 1792–1814

In the first years of the war, the exploitation of territories occupied by the French was party due to the fact that their own economy was threadbare, so their campaigns had to be fuelled from new territories. In June 1795, for example, the whole left bank of the Rhine was ordered to disgorge 22 million *livres*, although this was reduced in July to 10 million because, quite simply, the population, already reduced to penury, could not pay. Picking the conquests bare soon became a standard way in which the revolutionaries waged war. In 1796–9 Italy bore a heavy burden of pillaging: when Bonaparte marched into Milan in May 1796 he announced a 'very small contribution' of 20 millions *livres*. Moreover, its churches and cities were stripped of works of art and state treasuries emptied of gold (some 45 million *livres*' worth was carted off to Paris in 1796 alone).[10] Wherever the French armies invaded, the mass requisitioning of food supplies to feed the soldiers proved disastrous for the local population, particularly in the already harsh economic conditions of the late 1790s. This foraging came on top of 'official' seizures at the behest of the government in Paris: commissioners seized money, food and items on a long shopping list, including machinery, works of art, livestock and horses. Under Napoleon, Europe was subjected to a more sophisticated form of economic exploitation. The Continental System was established by the Berlin Decree in November 1806. Every European port under French rule was to deny entry to British imports. There was a dual purpose to the blockade: to weaken the British economy and to boost French manufacturing and agriculture by creating a European market closed to British competition. European merchants and governments found ways of circumventing the blockade, while British sea power made the system hard to enforce in practice. It also committed Napoleon to foisting it on recalcitrant European countries, which explains the French attack on Portugal in 1807 and the invasion of Russia in 1812, both of which had disastrous consequences for the French Empire.

The French also drafted men from the local population into the armed forces. Under the Republic, the annexation of Belgium (1795), the Rhineland (1798) and Piedmont (1799) allowed the French to impose conscription directly on these territories. Elsewhere, they established 'sister republics', whose main function was to act as buffer states against France's enemies, and, above all, to raise armies of their own to fight on France's side, so that, as the Director La Revellière-Lépeaux put it, the entire territory from the Netherlands to northern Italy would be 'an uninterrupted continuity of territory . . . a nursery of excellent soldiers and a formidable position'.[11] Napoleon merely expanded this system of exploitation, even if the 'republics' became 'kingdoms' to emphasise his dynastic aims. The 700,000-strong army which invaded Russia in 1812 was not composed entirely of Frenchmen: there were 90,000 Poles and Lithuanians, as well as Germans, Swiss, Italians, Spanish and Portuguese. On average, the French Empire proper provided a third of all Napoleonic forces – and, owing to annexations, not all of these were French – while satellite and allied states provided the rest of the cannon fodder. It was only after the defeats in 1812–13, as Napoleon's empire began to collapse, that France itself began to bear the brunt of taxation and conscription.

Napoleonic Europe had three different spheres (see Map 3.1). There was, first, the French Empire, which included France and the annexations ruled directly from Paris, including Belgium, the Rhineland and Piedmont and, at its height, Genoa (1805), Parma and Tuscany (both 1808), the western parts of the Papal States and the 'Illyrian Provinces' (1809), the Netherlands (1810) and Hamburg, Bremen, Lübeck and the Grand Duchy of Oldenburg (1810–11). Secondly, the French satellites were states or regions which retained a separate political identity, but which were governed directly by Napoleon or his French acolytes. These included the Kingdom of Italy (formed in 1805), the Kingdom of Naples (1806), the Kingdom of Holland (until 1810), the Kingdom of Westphalia and the Grand Duchy of Berg. Finally, there were the allied states, with their own dynastic rulers and nominally independent but which, for various reasons, supported Napoleon. These included the Kingdoms of Bavaria, Württemberg, Saxony, the Grand Duchy of Baden and the Grand Duchy of Warsaw. In these ways, France enjoyed a brief and final fling of European hegemony.

Exploitative as French dominance was, there was another side to the

Map 3.1 Napoleonic Europe, 1812

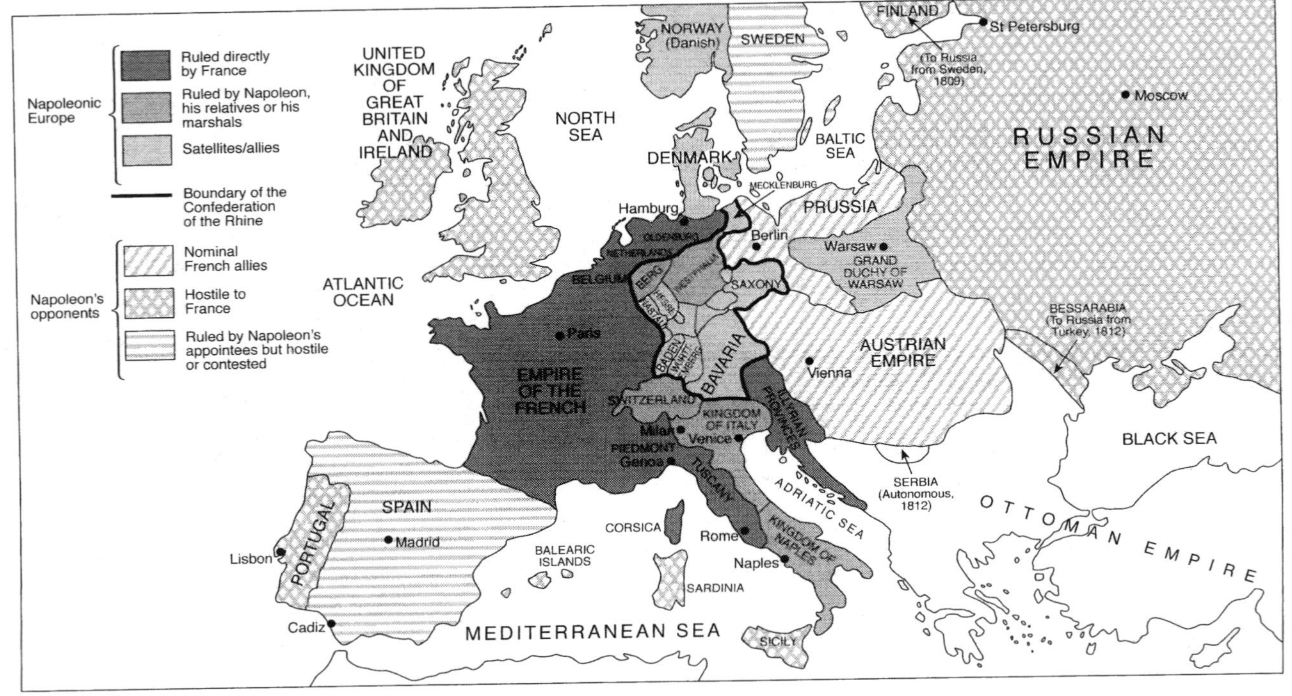

balance sheet. Some revolutionary reforms were introduced in most conquests, but the constantly turning tide of the war in the 1790s meant that the Republic's efforts barely took root. Even so, in annexed Belgium – despite a popular insurrection against the French in 1798 – the system of departments, law courts, policing and education were sown on the hostile soil and, with time, germinated. Once the Napoleonic era opened, countries such as Belgium settled under long-term French occupation and so the more constructive facets of French rule began to bear fruit and gained some acceptance, at least among the elites. In Piedmont, nobles, officials and even ordinary citizens grew to appreciate the smooth and impartial workings of French administration and law, as opposed to the rather capricious system of the Savoyard monarchy. Moreover, people appreciated the great and usually successful efforts of the *gendarmerie* in combating brigandage, which was endemic in the mountainous areas of the kingdom. In the Kingdom of Italy, Eugène de Beauharnais introduced streetlighting and vaccination and secularised government in the areas formerly ruled by the Pope.

The Concordat was to have brought religious freedom for all. In most countries of Europe, religious minorities – and especially Jews – had been tolerated, but that meant just that: they were allowed to live and work without official harassment, while being subjected to a wide range of restrictions. Anti-Semitic legislation was often popular amongst pious, Christian Europeans, so Napoleonic officials had to struggle against these prejudices. Generally, the more direct the French control, the more complete was Jewish emancipation, particularly in western Germany. In Italy, however, when in 1808 the French authorities tried to outlaw the passages in the traditional Easter sermon which blamed the Jews for killing Christ, riots exploded in Pisa. In the Grand Duchy of Warsaw, anti-Semitism amongst the *szlachta* and the peasantry forced Napoleon to acquiesce in the suspension of Jewish emancipation for ten years, on the grounds that Jews were not yet properly assimilated into Polish society. The point made by Michael Broers is a valid one: 'when the Napoleonic regime was at its most enlightened, it met its fiercest internal, popular resistance'.[12]

The Napoleonic Code introduced, in theory, civil equality, which meant the abolition of labour dues and obligations for the peasantry, the opening of careers to merit rather than to noble birth, and equality before the law. Historians, however, differ on their views as to how effectively these principles were applied. Martyn Lyons emphasises the positive work of the Napoleonic Empire. In the satellite states, subjected to strong French influence, the 'Napoleonic Revolution' went far: serfdom was abolished where it existed (in Berg, and, in theory if not in practice, in the Grand Duchy of Warsaw), while personal labour obligations were also swept away (Berg, Westphalia). Allied kingdoms such as Bavaria followed suit on serfdom. Nobles' rights to administer justice on their manors were removed in the Kingdom of Naples. Aristocratic privileges were abolished everywhere except Poland. In Germany this meant that non-nobles who could afford it were allowed to buy land (entails) which, under the old law, belonged exclusively to the nobles and could not be sold. Napoleon did not necessarily aim to encourage peasant land ownership, but he did seek to promote civil equality and individualism.[13]

Geoffrey Ellis, however, is less optimistic that the Napoleonic impact was so liberating. Napoleon sought to create a new elite to govern French-dominated Europe, an *amalgame* of old nobility and new, bourgeois servants of the Napoleonic state. This was, above all, a *French* imperial elite, rewarded for its loyalty with estates, called 'grand-fiefs', and lands which could be inherited but which could only be sold with his permission. These rich prizes were carved out from land seized from the former rulers in Italy, Germany and Poland. The value of these donations depended upon the income which they yielded, so in these cases the abolition of seigneurialism was conveniently ignored. Allied states, of course, were in a better position than the satellites to resist the full egalitarian implications of the Napoleonic Code, and the elites did so. The Polish nobility at first opposed the introduction of the Napoleonic Code into the Grand Duchy of Warsaw in 1808, but were then keen to exploit those aspects of the laws which gave them control over their peasants. Although the Duchy's constitution of 1807 abolished serfdom, it persisted in practice. In Naples, Murat set about trying to abolish feudalism, rationalise administration, introduce the Napoleonic Code and reduce the state debt inherited from the Bourbon monarchy by selling off church lands. Efforts to restore the common lands enclosed by landowners and to divide them up amongst the peasants foundered on the resistance of the local elites by 1811. Similarly, as elsewhere in Catholic Europe, in Naples there was great hostility towards the provisions for divorce in the Napoleonic Code, so that only one petition had been received by 1814.[14] Although the nobles lost their old privileges almost everywhere, they remained wealthy and powerful by virtue of their landed wealth. When confiscated ecclesiastical and princely lands were sold off, the old nobility itself seized the opportunity to expand its estates. Ellis implies that, far from undermining Old Regime society, Napoleon actually strengthened certain aspects of the old European order.[15] Napoleon was driven less by a desire for revolution, than by his own dynastic ambition. In order to rule effectively, he needed the co-operation of the elites, which meant quietly shelving anything which alienated them. In any case, the support of the elites always remained conditional on Napoleon being able to win victories; only that would guarantee their careers and their plump livelihoods. Once defeat set in after 1812 they were more willing to listen to the blandishments of the conservative or liberal opposition.

The other great obstacle to the 'Napoleonic Revolution' lay in the demands of the war: Napoleon needed troops, money and supplies. Some of his most lasting reforms were aimed not at spreading the benefits of the Revolution but primarily at tapping the resources of the conquered territories more effectively. The introduction of the French system of administration and effective policing in the form of the *gendarmerie*, while certainly appreciated by some Europeans, were intended to provide the stability and the efficiency required for the thorough exploitation of the conquests. French revolutionary institutions were therefore introduced, but all too often their benefits were drowned out or compromised by the crushing wave of demands for money and conscripts.

These policies stoked resentment. Local people simmered with anger at the seizures of coin and crops and the attacks on the Church, but it was usually the imposition of conscription which, as in France itself, caused that anger to boil over into insurrection. Examples of this include Belgium in 1798, where a peasant revolt against conscription had to be put down with force, and a simultaneous wave of violent protest in the Rhineland. In 1809 the Tyrol rose up against conscription imposed by France's Bavarian allies. It was given backbone by the militia led by Andreas Hofer and coincided with the Austrian counter-offensive that year. Even after the Austrians were defeated at Wagram, the Tyroleans fought on until Hofer was captured, dragged in chains to Mantua, and shot. These revolts had strong religious dimensions: Belgian rebels were often led by priests and believed that wearing holy relics and symbols would protect them against the hail of French bullets. Other rebellions against French rule had strong religious motives: in southern Italy, the counter-revolutionary insurrection of February–March 1799 was led by Cardinal Fabrizio Ruffo, who proclaimed a holy war against the Godless republicans. Although he landed from Sicily in Calabria with only four followers, he rallied the peasants to form the Most Christian Armada of the Holy Faith, the *Santafede*. His actions sparked a series of spontaneous uprisings across the south, until, in June, he took Naples itself. There was also a social dimension to this revolt, for while the Neapolitan Jacobins and their French supporters had failed to abolish seigneurialism, Ruffo promised to do.[16] Further north, in Tuscany, Italians rioted, shouting 'Viva Maria!' and set upon the detachments of French troops and their Italian 'Jacobin' sympathisers. The same pattern repeated itself when French authority collapsed in Italy in 1813.

The most dramatic of all the cases took place in Spain, where the guerrilla war, though organised in the name of King Ferdinand VII, was not directed by him, but by the regional juntas. The guerrillas were extraordinarily successful in disrupting the Napoleonic regime and may have caused as many as 180,000 French casualties. By being spread out around the country, they tied down thousands of French troops who might otherwise have been deployed against Wellington. Militarily, the guerrillas provided a screen behind which the British could organise their forces in Portugal, preparing for each successive campaign in Spain until the final, successful one in 1813. The guerrillas also prevented the French from establishing regular, efficient administration and policing, by attacking officials, robbing postal couriers and plundering tax receipts. They also made any would-be collaborators think twice before helping the French: those few *afrancesados* who did remained a tiny minority.

Prussia experienced the upsurge of popular opposition to France in a different way. Prussian ministers realised that the only way to defeat Napoleon would be to harness the same energy and talent which he had inherited from the French Revolution. Prussia had some able ministers willing to carry through these progressive changes: Karl vom Stein and Karl von Hardenberg. After the bruising defeat at Jena in 1806, it was clear that not only the Prussian army but society itself would have to be rejuvenated. The lot of the peasantry was, on paper at least, improved with the 'October Edict' of 1807, which made peasant purchase of land easier, granted equality before the law and encouraged peasants to develop their farming by giving them greater freedom to sell their own crops. The October Edict also proclaimed that from 1810 there would be no more serfdom. There was even talk of creating a *Volksarmee*, a people's army modelled on the French citizen-army of the Revolution. In reality, such radical provisions were hard to implement against the resistance of the aristocratic Junkers – and this was a struggle which would be carried over into the post-Napoleonic era. Prussian peasants were expected to pay compensation to their landlords for the loss of income which these new freedoms entailed. Even so, Stein's short-lived ministry (he was in power from 1806 to 1808) brought down bitter opposition from the Junkers – and from the French, who feared the energised Prussia which might emerge from these reforms. Napoleon strong-armed King Frederick William III into dismissing him. After a series of weak ministries, Stein's ally, Karl von Hardenberg, assumed the mantle of reform when he became Prussia's first ever Chancellor in June 1810. He embarked on a programme aimed at religious toleration, freedom of expression, opening careers to merit, and granting civil rights to Jews. After the French defeat in Russia, conscription was decreed and reserve *Landwehr* units created, so that, by the time of the Battle of Leipzig in 1813, Prussia could field 280,000 men. Hardenberg did not want a political democracy – quite the contrary. He sought to give as much freedom as possible to the individual, but with absolute power to the government when it dealt with political matters. Yet, in the process of their reforms, Stein and Hardenberg became, despite themselves, the leaders of a 'German War of Liberation' which unleashed popular, patriotic energies. None the less, if the main German states of Austria and Prussia had survived the French Revolution and the Napoleonic Empire intact, it was not without having to adopt some of the reforms of the Revolution. Even Francis II's cautious, conservative Austria implemented some changes. In June 1808 an Austrian *Landwehr* was created, the penal code was overhauled and in 1811–12 a General Civil Code was issued.

In Russia, where noble wealth was heavily based on serfdom, emancipation carried with it the threat of aristocratic resistance. Nobles showed that they were quite capable of getting rid of Tsars whom they did not like. Paul was killed in 1801 because of his oppressive regulation of the lives of the nobility, but also, allegedly, because he began to change things for the serfs: in 1797 he imposed a ban on more than three days of labour obligations a week. Under Alexander I there was a fleeting moment in which Russia might have taken a path towards constitutional monarchy. Soon after his accession in 1801, Alexander appointed an 'Unofficial Committee' of his liberal-minded friends, including Mikhail Speransky and the Polish liberal, Prince Adam Czartoryski. Yet Alexander never fulfilled his early promise as a law-giver. Even when he had granted constitutions to Finland in 1809 and to Poland in 1815, his approach to government suggested that he was reluctant to cede his autocratic power. The reasons for this were inextricably bound up with the two great problems of Russian society – the influence of the nobility and serfdom. In an empire where there were 20 million serfs and where there was only a tiny urban middle class, the nobility would dominate the legislature. Such a parliament would make any progress in abolishing serfdom or improving the conditions of the serfs difficult, if not impossible. If the Tsar wished to avoid creating a reactionary bastion of privilege at the heart of Russian government, he would first have to address the problem of serfdom. The great liberal reformer, Mikhail Speransky, ran into this problem when he drafted constitutional plans for the 'Unofficial Committee' in 1802–3 and concluded that there could be no political progress without the emancipation of the peasantry and the education of public opinion. The Tsar was thus caught in a vicious circle: he could not abolish serfdom without clashing with the nobility, but he could not grant a constitution without abolishing serfdom. Alexander banned the introduction of serfdom into newly-conquered areas – Poland, Bessarabia and Finland – and he would abolish it in the Baltic provinces (roughly, present-day Estonia, Latvia and Lithuania) between 1816 and 1819, but he did nothing to abolish it in Russia itself. Yet despite the yoke of serfdom, the people rallied to the Tsar when Napoleon invaded in 1812; the Russians called their struggle the 'Patriotic War'.

Contemporaries were impressed by the strength of this sort of popular conservatism across Europe. It was a powerful weapon in the struggle against the French Revolution and its principles. It was certainly an important factor – perhaps it was *the* factor – in explaining why the French had such little success in exporting their revolution. They certainly had their sympathisers in other European countries – radicals, 'patriots' or 'Jacobins' in the 1790s who later under the Napoleonic Empire became Bonaparte's most loyal administrators. In general, the European Jacobins of the 1790s and Napoleon's collaborators sprang either from the radical movements which existed prior to 1789 or they were enlightened reformers disillusioned with the failures of their own rulers or their slow pace of reform. In Belgium, the French could rely on former supporters of the radical patriot, Vonck, or even on former servants of Joseph II's Austrian regime, frustrated by the conservative, Catholic resistance of Belgian society to secularisation and administrative reform. Yet everywhere they were in a minority, even if they were geographically widespread (as in the British Isles and Italy) or represented a cross-section of urban society (as they did in Mainz in the Rhineland). They were perhaps most numerous in the Netherlands (where the Patriot movement had put down roots in the 1780s) and in Italy.

Yet, in general, European Jacobins (who usually called themselves 'patriots') offered little in the way of a viable social programme to garner widespread support. They generally upheld property rights and, except for the abolition of seigneurialism, offered the peasantry and urban masses little other than democracy to ease the problems of poverty. There were important exceptions, such as the radical wing of the Italian Jacobins who wished to impose limits on property ownership and offer free and universal education, progressive taxation, a distribution of church land amongst the poor, and a welfare state.[17] European Jacobins were usually based in the cities; their influence rarely penetrated the countryside. In the Kingdom of Naples, where rural, often bourgeois, landowners opposed the local seigneur by adopting republican principles, they were treated warily by a suspicious peasantry.

Determined repression by old regime governments put off those moderate sympathisers of the French Revolution who were reluctant to use revolutionary means. Yet the main factor in the defeat of European radicals was that, as a minority, they were overwhelmed by the force of popular resistance. Too weak to rise up themselves, they were often dependent upon French military support to gain power – as in the Netherlands in 1795 and in Italy during 1796–9. Yet that also meant that their French masters could dictate policy, and in the later 1790s the Directory did not shy away from purging the more radical Jacobins, whom it distrusted. Once the French support collapsed, as it did in Italy in 1799, the hapless Jacobin regimes, associated with demands for taxes, conscription and provisions and with the attack on the Church, were easily toppled by popular insurrections and invading allied armies. Even in Ireland, where an ostensibly revolutionary uprising took place in 1798, the republican movement, the United Irishmen, could barely impose itself on what appears to have been essentially a Catholic peasant insurrection, driven by sectarian hatred and deep-rooted grievances against Protestant landlords. In Poland, the uprising of March 1794 against Russian occupation, led by Tadeusz Kościuszko, certainly drew some inspiration from the French: there were revolutionary tribunals to try traitors and a *levée en masse*. In May, to harness popular enthusiasm, serfdom was abolished, though certain labour dues remained. Yet Kościuszko could not go too far for fear of alienating the Polish nobility, and there was little hope of securing the support of the Ukrainian and Belarussian peasants, who loathed their Polish landlords. The uprising was eventually crushed when the Russian General Suvorov took Warsaw on 8 November 1794. It must be acknowledged that European radicalism failed in the 1790s, but in some places it left important legacies. In Italy, the Jacobins had debated the idea of national unity, putting it on the agenda for the first time. The United Irishmen represented a democratic, non-sectarian form of nationalism which would inspire subsequent generations of liberal nationalists. Under French rule, former 'patriots' would provide Napoleon with some of his most committed administrators, but sometimes their disillusionment led them into the liberal opposition to Napoleon. The more radical forms of Jacobinism would also inspire the first European socialists.

An issue debated by historians has been whether or not the popular resistance to the French, and the reforms of governments such as those of Prussia, brought forth the rise of modern nationalism. Historians such as Tim Blanning and Michael Broers have pointed out that this was not the case.[18] Blanning has shown that Rhenish resistance to the French was based far more on traditional loyalties to the Church and to their sovereign rather than to any abstract idea of German nationality. German intellectuals, such as Johann Gottlieb Fichte, and organisers of the German nationalist movement, such as Ernst Arndt and Friedrich Jahn, certainly thought about a truly national – that is, pan-German – crusade against Napoleon. Governments – and almost certainly most of their subjects, including the Prussians – did not think in terms of uniting Germany. In Spain, the term 'War of Independence' implies a nationalist struggle, yet the guerrillas operated on a regional basis. They were commanded by the provincial juntas, who were very reluctant to co-operate with each other. Moreover, it is sometimes said that this was a struggle motivated by loyalty to the imprisoned King Ferdinand VII and to the Catholic Church. In fact, the guerrillas frequently pillaged the Church, while their leaders often proved indifferent to the fate of the Spanish monarchy. The uprising is probably best seen as a *reaction* to French rule. Spanish people fought not for the Spanish nation nor even for the Church and King but because they sought to protect their local communities from the exploitation of foreign military occupation.[19]

Yet something positive did emerge from the wreckage of the terrible conflict and Spain was one of its most important cradles: liberalism, a term bequeathed to the modern age by the Spanish resistance to

Napoleon. The provincial juntas were, at least, co-operative enough to convene the Spanish parliament, the Cortes, which opened in Cadiz in September 1810. Elected on a very broad suffrage, the Cortes returned a large number of deputies committed to reform. They included those who had served the enlightened absolutists, Charles III and IV, as officials, members of the juntas and reforming clergy from the Catholic Church. These people, whose views were radicalised by the war, became known as liberals. Their conservative opponents were called *serviles*, because they were said to prefer slavery to freedom. Under liberal influence, the Spanish parliament issued laws which proclaimed the freedom of the press, abolished the Inquisition and proclaimed that the Spanish nation was sovereign, although the state would be a constitutional monarchy. These principles were enshrined in the liberal Constitution of 1812, which provided for near-universal male suffrage and which, like the French Constitution of 1791, limited royal power to a suspensive veto. The Spanish Constitution of 1812 became a key document for radical and liberal aspirations in Europe after 1815.

In Italy the Napoleonic episode stimulated political debate among the intellectuals, army officers, liberal clergymen, government officials and lawyers who had direct dealings with the Napoleonic system. Even where they opposed French rule, they supported reform and frequently looked to the Spanish Constitution of 1812 as a model. These Italian liberals formed underground societies, the most famous of which were the Carbonari, which aimed at revolution, first to get rid of the French and then to establish constitutional government in Italy. Some did in fact envisage Italian unity, though others were content to argue for constitutions within the existing states. Once the Napoleonic regime was gone, these liberals switched targets when it was clear that the restored Italian rulers had no intention of initiating political reforms. Similarly, some of the Russian army officers who marched across Germany in 1813–14 were impressed by the Prussian reform movement. Once they returned to the stifling atmosphere of post-war Russia, these officers would form the kernel of the liberal opposition to the autocracy. In Germany, students who joined the struggle against the French in 1813 returned to offer their leadership to younger colleagues in the *Burschenschaft* movement. After 1815, patriotic Poles would positively adopt their Napoleonic inheritance as it recalled their struggle alongside their French allies against Russian despotism. Both liberating and repressive, the revolutionary and Napoleonic episode had shaped the battlelines for the political conflicts of the next generation. No matter how much those who had lost wealth, power and prestige might have wanted it to do so, in 1815 European society would not be able to return to the way things had been in 1789.

Part II

Conservative Europe, 1815–1850

4 The Conservative Order

For the victorious powers, war and revolution, in the light of recent experience, marched together, one darkly shadowing the other. Few states or peoples were left untouched or unchanged by the almost unbearable strains of the conflicts of 1792–1815. War had brought with it the danger of revolution or, at the very least, the necessity of reform. Conversely, revolution seemed to carry the threat of war, since the French revolutionary and Napoleonic regimes had appeared to recognise no international law, but were driven only by their own uncontrollable impulse to spread their ideas and institutions. For the politicians in 1815, therefore, the twin task was both to prevent the outbreak of another major European war and to suppress revolution in Europe. Both revolutionaries and their conservative opponents were immersed in the culture of 'Romanticism', which rejected the cool rationalism of the Enlightenment in favour of human feeling. Liberals and radicals could celebrate the heroism of individuals struggling against repression, while conservatives would stress the piety and loyalty stirred by the people's innate attachment to their religion and their ruler.

For almost four decades, European governments proved to be better at preserving the general European peace than in preventing domestic revolution. The reasons lay partly in the way in which states handled the Napoleonic legacy. While the Kings of Spain, Piedmont and Naples expressed an uncompromising will to eliminate all traces of the Napoleonic era, few governments actually did so, finding instead that the strengthening of state efficiency under French tutelage suited their interests. While naturally extirpating the superficial traces of Napoleonic rule, governments often retained the changes themselves, or their essence. For this reason, recent historians have emphasised that the label usually applied to the period between 1815 and 1848 – the 'Restoration' – is not an apt description.[1] In their pursuit of stability, governments frequently compromised with the legacy inherited from the revolutionary and Napoleonic era. Few governments were avowedly reactionary, instead pursuing moderate change – often against powerful reactionary voices – in order to consolidate their grip on their subjects. Yet this did not stop them from being repressive towards liberals and radicals. Post-1815 politics took the shape of a three-way contest between conservative reform, reactionary resistance and revolution. This shaped the political ideologies and practices which would leave indelible traces on Europe.

The initial concern was how to contain France. The first Treaty of Paris, before the Hundred Days, had been considered by some of the allies, especially Prussia, as too lenient, for France was to keep her frontiers of 1 November 1792. Napoleon's brief return stretched the patience of the allies. Even so, the terms of the second Treaty of Paris, signed on 20 November 1815, while more punitive, were still aimed at containment rather than the abject humiliation of the vanquished. Britain, in particular, understood that the latter would merely make domestic stability in France much harder to sustain. France was reduced to her frontiers of 1790, except that she was to hold on to the annexed papal enclaves of Avignon and the Comtat Venaissin. The works of art looted during the Revolutionary and Napoleonic Wars were to be returned, and France was to pay an indemnity of 700 million francs. An allied army of 150,000 men was to occupy northern France at French expense for three to five years. It turned out that, with the help of a loan from British and Dutch bankers and a public subscription to government bonds, France paid off its indemnities quickly, so, at the Congress of Aix-la-Chapelle in 1818, the allies agreed to end the occupation.

The European rulers and diplomats who assembled at Vienna in November 1814 to discuss the general European peace settlement also had to consider ways in which every land-grabbing European power might be restrained. Britain and Russia emerged from the Napoleonic Wars as the two dominant European powers. While Britain was more concerned with its overseas empire and commerce, the question of how to contain the crushing might of the Russian Empire was an awe-inspiring problem. The German problem was how to create an arrangement which allowed neither Austria nor Prussia to swallow up the middle states, while also keeping Germany strong enough to resist French and Russian threats. Arrangements had to be made for Italy, which had been so vulnerable to French invasion, and Poland, which had been carved up in 1795 and then restored by Napoleon as the Grand Duchy of Warsaw.

The Vienna 'Final Act' was signed on 9 June 1815, nine days before Waterloo (see Map 4.1). France was hemmed in to the north by a united kingdom of Belgium and the Netherlands and the Prussian annexation of the Rhineland, which supported the Grand Duchy of Baden along France's eastern frontier. In the south, Piedmont was bolstered by a powerful Austrian presence in Italy. Germany was arranged into a Confederation (*Bund*) of 39 states, including Prussia and Austria, with a federal diet, which was an assembly of diplomats sent by all German governments to discuss common concerns. The *Bund*'s purpose was to contain Austro-Prussian rivalry by guaranteeing the existence of the smaller states. Poland, put to death as an independent state, was reduced to the free city of Krakow; the rest was partitioned again by Prussia, Austria and Russia, although Tsar Alexander I endowed his share, the 'Congress Kingdom', with a constitution. The Italian problem was

Map 4.1 Europe, 1815–1878

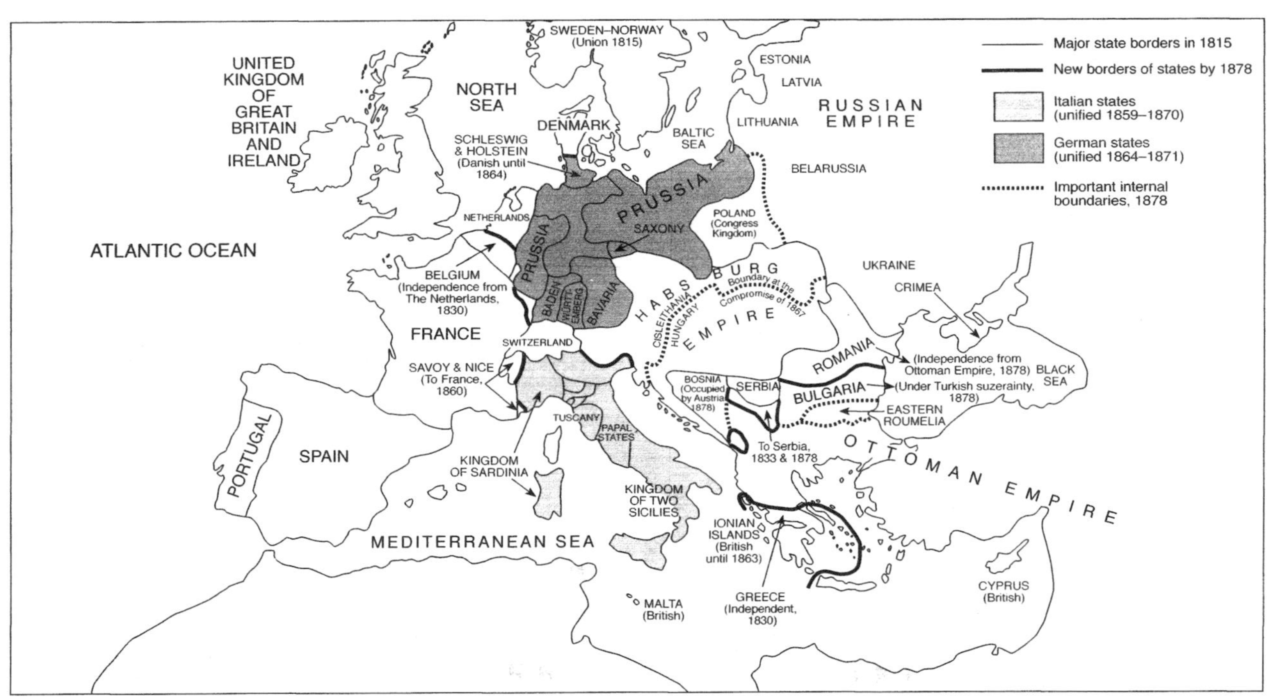

resolved by putting the peninsula under the heel of Austria, which acquired Lombardy and Venetia. Moreover, Habsburg princes ruled four other states (Tuscany, Parma, Modena and tiny Massa and Carrara) and, in June 1815, Ferdinand of Naples signed an alliance with Austria guaranteeing his throne. Napoleon's King of Naples, Marshal Murat, was deposed after the Hundred Days and shot when, in October 1815, he boldly tried to recapture his throne. Elsewhere, Norway, though offering some diplomatic resistance, was incorporated into a union with Sweden and the slave trade was outlawed.

Reaction or Reform?

The primary purpose of the settlement was to build a stable international framework in Europe. In this it was certainly successful: there was to be no conflict between the great European powers until the Crimean War of 1854–6 and there was no general European war until 1914. Its determination to ignore the aspirations of European peoples cannot be judged too harshly, because dreams of national unity or liberation were not widespread in 1815, except perhaps in Poland. Yet when nationalists in Poland, Italy, Germany and Belgium began to flex their muscles over the next generation, the European order began to look like a stifling system, obstructing national aspirations in the name of conservatism.[2] It also seemed to be hostile to liberal aspirations for representative government, although Britain, France, the Netherlands, Norway and Poland were among those states with representative institutions in 1815. In a flourish of German constitutionalism between 1814 and 1820, the southern states of Hesse-Darmstadt, Baden, Bavaria, Nassau and Württemberg drafted constitutions as a means of integrating their new subjects acquired in the 'mediatisation' of 1803. Yet this did not, as conservatives feared, release a liberal cascade in central Europe. The act establishing the German *Bund* stipulated that all member-states should have representative institutions, but this was interpreted in a conservative way. In Austria, the provincial diets had little capability to challenge royal power. In its provinces outside the German Confederation, the Habsburg monarchy ruled without representative institutions as much as possible. King Frederick William III of Prussia had promised a constitution to his subjects on several occasions, most recently in 1815, and his minister, Hardenberg, saw a parliament as the best way of defending his reforms against reactionary Junkers. Yet agitation in Germany and an outburst of revolutions in southern Europe in 1820 persuaded the King to turn his back on the idea.

How far the international system was intended to suppress liberal ideas and nationalism was, in fact, a source of division among the great powers. In November 1815, Britain, Prussia, Austria and Russia renewed their coalition in a 20-year Quadruple Alliance, which would guarantee the Peace of Paris. French aggression would be an immediate cause of war and the overthrow of the restored Bourbon monarchy occasion for consultation. Article Six of the alliance provided for regular meetings of these powers for discussion of measures 'the most salutary for the repose and prosperity of Nations, and for the maintenance of the peace of Europe'.[3] This clause laid the foundation for the 'Congress system', which was based on the idea, emerging from the bitter experience of the Napoleonic Wars, that European powers acting together 'in concert' would be an effective way of ensuring general peace. Whether or not this gave the powers the right to suppress revolutionary movements in other states became a matter of debate.

The British rejected the notion that they had the right to meddle in the internal affairs of other states, but the other powers disagreed and joined together in the Holy Alliance. Inspired by Tsar Alexander and signed by Russia, Prussia and Austria in September 1815, it stressed that the monarchs would be guided by 'the precepts of that Holy Religion, namely Justice, Christian Charity, and Peace'. They agreed that 'they [would], on all occasions and in all places, lend each other aid and assistance', leading their armies 'to protect Religion, Peace, and Justice'.[4] Most European states eventually subscribed to the Holy Alliance, but not the British. From 1820 the congress system itself would break down over this disagreement as liberals and nationalists tested the strength of the conservative order.

Prince Clemens von Metternich epitomised the post-war system. Austrian foreign minister from 1809 and Chancellor from 1821, Metternich recognized that the Habsburg empire was the most vulnerable of all European powers to the twin threat of revolution and war, precisely because it was a polyglot ragbag of territories. Though not the strongest of European states, Austria was the most influential power in a hulking region, which Metternich's rival, Count Franz Kolowrat-Liebsteinsky, called Metternich's 'forest of bayonets', spreading across central Europe. Under Metternich, Austria played a central role in crushing revolutionary movements in the 1820s and 1830s. Within the Austrian empire itself, the government maintained a secret police to keep watch over suspects, the press and theatres, and to listen in to what must usually have been idle chat in cafés. Censorship, including the interception and opening of mail, was conducted by the Secret Cipher Chancellery, which by 1817 was sifting through the 1000 letters which arrived daily in Vienna. Publishers could not print anything other than government tracts without prior approval.[5]

Metternich was not, however, an ultra-reactionary. He was not opposed to reform if that strengthened the state against its revolutionary enemies. In 1815–16, he lent both advice and diplomatic support to the Pope's reformist minister of state, Cardinal Ercole Consalvi, when he was besieged by his reactionary *zelanti* enemies in 1815–16. In 1821 he promised King Ferdinand of Naples that Austrian troops would crush the revolution there, but added the condition that Ferdinand embark on reforms to provide efficient government. Metternich was rather more successful in dispensing such advice to other rulers than in applying it to Austria itself. He did make plans for economic and administrative reform, as he sought to promote both economic development and government efficiency, but they came to little. The severest limit placed on reform in the Habsburg monarchy was its financial embarrassment, aggravated by Metternich's counter-revolutionary campaigns. Between 1815 and 1848 the army swallowed up 40 per cent of the budget, while interest on the state debt gobbled up another 30 per cent. These financial troubles were a potentially fatal source of weakness. Lack of money needed to help the stricken population in the economic crisis of the 1840s contributed to Metternich's downfall in March 1848.

Yet day-to-day Habsburg rule was usually efficient and free from corruption. Lombardy and Venetia enjoyed lighter taxation than under French rule, while in Galicia the Ruthenian (Ukrainian) peasants came to regard Habsburg officials as their protectors against their Polish landlords. The secret police, while certainly employed against revolutionaries, were also used, ironically, to gather information to ensure that the government had an understanding of local needs.[6] Moreover, in contrast to Joseph II's attempts to 'Germanise' the empire in the later eighteenth century, Metternich tolerated the nascent cultural and linguistic movements which arose among the elites of the non-German peoples of the empire, like the Czechs and Magyars. Few could predict that they would later feed into nationalist movements; for the time being the government saw such activities as a means of diverting local elites from politics.

Financial constraints ensured that Emperor Francis's attempt to rule as an absolute monarch in Hungary failed. In 1812, he had angrily dissolved the Hungarian diet, swearing never to convoke another. Yet imperial decrees could only be enforced with the co-operation of the nobility, whose power was deeply entrenched in the Hungarian counties, each with its own assembly ('congregation') and court, which became focal points for the resistance of the Magyar gentry. In 1821 the Austrian intervention against revolutions in Naples and Piedmont compelled the Emperor to demand new taxes and recruits from Hungary. Throughout the year the counties refused to co-operate, compelling Francis to summon the Hungarian diet for 1825. While a defeat for royal absolutism, this was not a liberal triumph. The diet was primarily a parliament of the nobility, who sought to entrench their political position, privileges and control over their peasants and to defend the use of Magyar over German. They therefore opposed not only royal absolutism, but also reforming Hungarian aristocrats who worked with the Emperor's Hungarian Chancellery in the hope that royal power could be harnessed to develop Hungarian society. Out of this contest sprang Hungarian liberalism.

In Germany, Frederick William III of Prussia may have rejected constitutionalism, but he never contemplated reversing Stein and Hardenberg's reforms. Administrative reform gave some unity to the expanded Prussian kingdom by creating a system of provinces, each with a government commissioner, an *Oberpräsident*, although the monarchy was not powerful enough to overcome Junker resistance to centralisation in East Prussia. In January 1820, in a move which would be of great future significance, Hardenberg successfully enacted the State Debt Law, declaring that any new debts assumed by the government had to be approved by the estates of the whole kingdom. Of more immediate importance was the Provincial Estates Law of July 1823, which granted the individual provinces representation on estates which were none the less arranged so that they were dominated by the nobility and could not challenge the royal government. This ensured that demands from non-noble delegates for a wider political role became a feature of Prussian political life over the next two decades

In France, Louis XVIII, brother of the guillotined Louis XVI, came to the throne with a charter in June 1814 which represented a compromise with France's revolutionary legacy. Louis recognised that the political, legal and fiscal structures created by the Revolution had succeeded, where his Bourbon predecessors had failed, in creating a centralised, uniform system of government. He had no desire to restore the provincial and corporate privileges, *parlements* and estates which had proved so aggravating to earlier French kings. Louis also sought to preserve his throne by healing the bitter political schism which was the legacy of the French Revolution. The charter therefore retained some of the revolutionaries' achievements. Freedom of religious worship was guaranteed, but Catholicism was to be the state religion. France was to have representative government, though with a suffrage restricted to the 110,000 wealthiest men. The principle of careers open to merit and the sale of *biens nationaux* were recognized. Moreover, the charter promised an official 'forgetting' of 'opinions held, or votes cast, prior to the Restoration'. Napoleonic personnel would hold on to their posts. This equilibrium was upset by the Hundred Days. Many Napoleonic officials and army officers who had retained their posts in 1814 slipped back over to the side of the Emperor. After Waterloo, French ultra-royalists demanded retribution and, in the south, they acted on this urge. Led by the King's younger brother, the comte d'Artois and his nephews, the ducs d'Angoulême and de Berry, the royalist organisation, the *Chevaliers de la Foi*, acted to harness popular, Catholic royalism. From June to August 1815, they unleashed the 'White Terror' against those associated with the Revolution, such as buyers of *biens nationaux*, former Jacobins and Bonapartists. Bands of royalist peasants and artisans killed around 200 people, while 3000 were imprisoned without trial and thousands more were put to flight. Moreover, the elections to the Chamber of Deputies were held in this feverish atmosphere and the ultra-royalists won a majority of seats. This *chambre 'introuvable'* ('rare' chamber, as Louis ironically dubbed it) confronted the King's own government with demands for repressive measures against those who had betrayed him. In the entire White Terror, between a quarter and a third of all French officials lost their posts – people who would be open to the blandishments of republican or liberal critics of the Bourbon restoration. The White Terror had poisoned the politics of the Bourbon monarchy right from the start.

Louis XVIII managed to swing the regime back on to its conciliatory course when he dissolved parliament in April 1816 and ordered fresh elections, which returned a less reactionary chamber. The next four years saw a period of moderate government – from 1818 under Elie Decazes. None the less, conciliation could not survive for long in the mutual animosity between 'ultras' and liberals. A reactionary backlash was sparked, first, by the election to parliament of a veteran republican, the *abbé* Henri Grégoire in 1819. The second traumatic blow to moderation came in February 1820 when the duc de Berry, third in the line to the throne, was stabbed to death by a lone Bonapartist assassin. To the ultras, both events were the natural result of liberalism.[7] Moderates were also alarmed: the King dismissed Decazes and a Law of General Security, allowing the arrest of anyone suspected of subversion, was passed. Censorship was reimposed and a 'double vote law' gave the wealthiest 25 per cent of tax-payers a second vote in special electoral colleges. The brakes on reaction were lifted altogether when Louis died in 1824 and was succeeded by his brother, Charles X, who was an ultra-royalist. Charles retained the ultra ministry of comte Joseph de Villèle, whose policies set the government on a collision course with the liberal opposition. In 1825 Villèle proposed to indemnify former *émigrés* who had lost property during the Revolution; the King was empowered to grant legal recognition to women's religious orders; and a law on sacrilege (unenforced in practice) punished profanity with a maximum penalty of severing a hand before beheading. In 1826 the government tried (in vain) to restore primogeniture and the following year it presented (again in vain) a new censorship law which it stupidly described as 'a law of justice and love'. When Charles reviewed a jeering National Guard in April 1827, he dismissed the entire corps. It was an ominous sign that the Bourbon monarchy had not succeeded in reconciling itself to France's revolutionary legacy.

The conservative order in Britain weathered a period of smouldering post-war discontent and radical agitation until the economic recovery of the early 1820s. Yet the virulence of popular protest and the existence of real revolutionary conspiracies up to 1820 led some among the political elites to regard some adaptation of the old regime as a necessary response. Moreover, the state was faced with the task of integrating its reluctant Catholic Irish subjects, bound into the United Kingdom by the union of 1800. Yet concessions to political and religious reform met with opposition from ultra-Tory reactionaries, whose conception of society was based on hierarchy and the supremacy of the Protestant Church. The pressure for change was greatest in Ireland, where demands for Catholic emancipation, which meant the removal of civil disabilities, were orchestrated by Daniel O'Connell, a scion of Catholic Irish gentry and a nationalist opposed to the union. He skilfully exploited rural discontent to forge the Catholic Association (first established in 1823) into a wide, popular movement for emancipation. Irish Catholics, who could vote for Protestant candidates, increasingly defied their landlords in the way they voted. The groundswell persuaded the Tory government under the Duke of Wellington to bolster its position by rallying all Protestants to its side. The Test and Corporation Acts, barring Protestant dissenters from public office, were abolished in February 1828. Yet this concession merely encouraged liberal (Whig) reformers to keep up the pressure. Tories such as Wellington and Robert Peel embraced the change as inevitable, particularly when sectarian violence in Ireland simmered on the brink of civil war. The ultra-Tories rallied to the defence of the 'Protestant Constitution' and led a popular anti-Catholic campaign which collected almost a thousand petitions against Catholic emancipation, which became law regardless in April 1829.[8]

In Spain and Italy, reactionary rulers at first tried to efface all traces of the revolutionary experience. Ferdinand VII's reactionary teeth sank into both the Napoleonic regime and Spain's liberal Cortes. On his return from exile in France in April 1814, he received the support of the *serviles* in parliament and his victory was assured on 4 May when royalist army officers under General Francisco Elío backed Ferdinand and 'pronounced' against the liberal constitution of 1812. With the support of the military, Ferdinand dissolved the Cortes and proscribed the liberals. Ferdinand then banished the *afrancesados* for their collaboration with the French. The Jesuits and the Inquisition returned and seigneurial rights were restored. Yet even Ferdinand seems to have wavered between his own reactionary impulses and the need to strengthen the state through reform. While resurrecting the old provincial privileges (*fueros*) in November 1815, he also appointed a commission to review them. Seigneurial justice, entails and nationalised church lands were not restored to their original owners.[9]

The shock of a liberal revolution between 1820 and 1823 persuaded Ferdinand to set the Spanish monarchy on a more resolutely reformist course. The Inquisition, abolished by the revolutionaries, remained so. The army was purged not only of liberals but also of *serviles*. The finance minister appointed in 1824, Luis López Ballesteros, sought to fight off bankruptcy with fiscal and economic reforms and he overlooked a liberal or even an *afrancesado* past when he appointed administrative and financial experts. The *serviles*, however, felt that their loyalty had been snubbed. They switched their allegiance away from Ferdinand to his brother, Don Carlos, whose ultra-royalism and religiosity were much more to their taste, and they were increasingly dubbed 'Carlists'. Ominously, they formed secret societies and their paramilitary wing, the 100,000-strong Royal Volunteers, remained under arms after the defeat of the liberals in 1823, despite Ferdinand's efforts to disband them. Fearing an ultra-royalist coup, Ferdinand recalled a large number of liberal army officers and, in 1827, the Carlists rose in southern Catalonia. This 'Revolt of the Aggrieved' was easily crushed, but it was an early warning of the storm which would be unleashed on Spain on Ferdinand's death in 1833.

In the northern Italian kingdom of Piedmont in May 1814, King Victor Emanuel I and his minister, Count Carlo Cerruti, unleashed a bloodless reaction, the *Palmaverde*. All those who had served the French state were dismissed and all French laws and institutions (including Turin's botanical gardens) were abolished. In the Papal States, the *zelanti* (zealots) among Pope Pius VII's cardinals went so far as to abolish vaccination and street lighting because they had been introduced by the French. In Naples, the restored King Ferdinand IV appointed Prince Antonio Canosa as minister of police in January 1816. A five-month reign of repression was unleashed against Murat's supporters. Yet, even in these states, the Napoleonic order had planted roots and the reaction provoked otherwise loyal but reformist opinion. In Rome in July 1816, the Pope had to appoint Cardinal Ercole Consalvi as secretary of state to calm tempers down. Before being toppled by a *zelanti* resurgence in 1823, Consalvi amnestied those who had worked with the French, recognised the sale of church property and restored some of the reforms introduced under Napoleon. In Naples, Austrian pressure forced Canosa's dismissal and his rival, Luigi de' Medici, tried to steer the state along a reformist course. In Piedmont, even Victor Emanuel found something good in the French legacy: the *gendarmerie* was recast as the *carabinieri* in July 1814, and between 1818 and 1820 a reformist minister, Prospero Balbo, worked hard to repair some of the damage committed in the *Palmaverde*.

The one state which became progressively more reactionary after 1815 was Russia. Alexander's drift towards reaction was partially driven by his mystical religious convictions, encouraged by the bigoted Orthodox monk, Photius. From 1817 the universities were purged of 'the repugnant spirit of deism'. In 1824 the Tsar appointed as education minister Admiral Alexander Shishkov, whose attitude was that too much schooling was bad for people. The authoritarianism of the Tsarist regime was epitomised by Alexander's friend and head of Chancery, Count

Alexei Arakcheev, who was appointed in 1816 to form 'military colonies', intended to solve the problem of demobilisation after the war. Peasants who had been conscripted into the army could not be returned to serfdom, so the Tsar would set aside land to settle these soldiers alongside peasants, all of whom would own their land outright. The gradual merging of these two groups would create a class of land-owning, peasant-soldiers who in peacetime would devote themselves to farming, but in war would serve the Tsar in battle. Yet the peasants resented being uprooted from their homes and balked at the military discipline to which they were subjected. Arakcheev put down a peasant rebellion at Chuguev in the Ukraine in 1819, but the Tsar wanted to persevere: 'even if I have to cover the road from Saint Petersburg to Novgorod with corpses'. By 1825, 750,000 men, women and children had been settled in these colonies. Although a further insurrection occurred in 1831, the project was not entirely abandoned until 1857.

The Liberal Challenge

The mild reforms enacted by governments before 1830 did not convince everyone of the desirability of the conservative order. In the generation after 1815, these sceptics included people who had been directly involved in the Napoleonic experiment (and had been punished for it) or who had joined the liberal opposition to it and were disappointed by the shape of the post-war order. Most liberals sought to compromise between the more radical, democratic implications of the French Revolution and the stabilising weight of the monarchy. Consequently, in countries with constitutions, liberals aimed to increase the power of the legislature as against that of the monarchy, or to secure a limited extension of the franchise. In countries without representative government, liberals sought to establish it and, while generally committed to the rule of law, the more radical among them were not shy of using subversive or revolutionary means when confronted with an oppressive regime. Moderate liberals admired the Charter of 1814, or the British parliamentary model, but radicals were stirred by the more democratic Spanish Constitution of 1812. The radicals' emphasis on democracy – based on the idea that sovereignty resided in the nation – also made them nationalists in some parts of Europe. They demanded either freedom from foreign rule (as in Poland and Italy) or national unity (as in Germany and again in Italy). In this period, nationalists were also liberals; for them, national freedom marched alongside individual liberties. Their emphasis on personal freedoms led liberals to commit themselves to the free market. Individuals should be given the liberty to improve their lives through education and hard work. While liberals were concerned with the 'social question' of poverty, they generally rejected solutions which involved state intervention or the redistribution of wealth. Instead, they believed that governments should remove restrictions to economic development, allowing the free market and individual initiative to eliminate poverty.

Excluded from power, liberals laid great emphasis on freedom of speech and organisation as the basis of civil society, which they idealised as the arena for rational debate and free association, independent of the state. While frequently subjected to censorship and repression, civil society was not entirely stifled before 1848. As such, it was the place where liberals could express their alienation from the conservative state. Civil society was socially exclusive, because illiteracy was generally high: in 1850, it ranged from 95 per cent in Russia, through 75–80 per cent in Spain and Italy, 40–45 per cent in the Habsburg monarchy and France, and 20 per cent in Prussia and Scotland to an impressively small 10 per cent in Sweden. At the same time, the cost of books and newspapers – and of their distribution – was still prohibitive for most people. By its very nature, therefore, civil society was primarily the preserve of nobles and the middle classes, but with a small but growing number of articulate, literate workers and the occasional peasant knocking on the door from the outside. Despite its social exclusivity, however, it was not devoid of dynamism, for the public sphere was growing between 1815 and 1848.

In France, the press saw an impressive growth after the stifling years of Napoleonic rule. The circulation of the top ten most popular Parisian daily newspapers rose from about 50,000 in 1824 to 120,000 by 1840, while the total number of periodicals increased from a meagre 45 in 1812 to a more respectable 197 by 1829.[10] In Germany, the number of books published in Prussia more than doubled between 1821 and 1840 – despite the repression enforced by the Karlsbad decrees. The number of reading rooms and libraries expanded, and, as literacy rates were relatively high in Germany, political messages could reach peasant homes through cheap broadsheets. German choral societies and professional and gymnastic associations provided fronts for political organisation. As Wilhelm Riehl commented, 'Public life stormed and raged in the theatre and concert hall because there was nowhere else it was allowed to storm and rage.'[11] In Poland, a minority conspired against the rule of the three partitioning powers, but others turned to the literary world to express their political views. The poetry, literature and history which dripped from the pens of Adam Mickiewicz, Juliusz Słowacki, Zygmunt Krasiński and Joachim Lelewel explored themes such as submission, servitude, vengeance, liberty and democracy.[12] In Italy, 120 new journals appeared between 1815 and 1847, published by local academies, clubs and annual 'scientific congresses'. These congresses gathered aristocratic and bourgeois people from across the Italian states and so helped to forge a national consciousness amongst the elites. In Russia, where censorship was more stringent than anywhere in Europe, historians have none the less discerned an increase in the reading public, among university students, the intelligentsia of St Petersburg and Moscow and a provincial readership.[13] The Tsarist regime paid a back-handed compliment to this when Peter Chaadaev published his *First Philosophic Letter* in the journal *Teleskop* in 1836. He depicted Russia as an uncivilised pariah amongst nations. Rather than allow any public engagement with Chaadaev, the Tsar declared him insane and exiled the publisher of the journal.[14] There were women journalists and writers who engaged in public debate, but most had to adopt male pseudonyms. In France, the cigar-smoking Amandine-Aurore Dupin was better known as George Sand. Flora Tristan suffered the consequences of using her feminist pen too freely when her estranged husband shot her in the shoulder.[15] Aristocratic women could oil the public sphere through their hospitality and their own erudition in salons, where politics and literature were discussed. In Russia, Zinaida Volkonskaia, wife of one of the Decembrists, organised salons where the aristocratic liberals discussed their ideas before their ill-fated uprising in 1825.[16]

Conservatives greatly exaggerated the subversive potential of liberalism and nationalism. Metternich claimed that there was a vast international conspiracy afoot, co-ordinated from Paris by a central committee. Such anxieties bore little relation to reality, but they conditioned the government's repressive response when evidence of revolutionary activity did appear. Until the mid-1820s, the fountainhead of liberalism was not France, as Metternich feared, but Spain. Under the rule of the Cortes, many educated Spaniards had enjoyed the experience of a free, civil society, with newspapers, societies and open political debate. This was now smothered in the reaction which followed Ferdinand VII's restoration. Liberal opposition within the Spanish army would play a central role in Spanish politics and would be the key to the coups d'état, or *pronunciamientos*, against Ferdinand in the post-war period – there was an attempt in 1817 – but finally, in 1820, the spark of a military coup set Spain alight. Since 1810, Spain's colonies in South America had been fighting for independence and the King's abrasive efforts to raise taxation and enforce conscription in Spain were resented.

On 1 January 1820, liberal officers in Cádiz, among them Major Rafael del Riego, declared for the Constitution of 1812, with the support of their soldiers who had no wish to die in the Americas. After faltering, the coup gathered pace as uprisings in other cities toppled the royal government. In March Ferdinand yielded, restoring the Constitution. The new liberal government abolished seigneurial rights, entails, the Inquisition and censorship, suppressed the Jesuits and other monastic orders and nationalised their lands. Yet the liberal ministry was composed mostly of moderates, fearful of social revolution and willing to restrict the franchise. The liberals split between these *moderados* and the radical *exaltados*, including Riego, who felt that 'their' revolution had been betrayed. The *moderado* government responded by banning political clubs and reimposing censorship. In 1821 the persistence of rural poverty and the reimposition of conscription (to continue the fight in South America, because the liberals were as attached to the colonies as the royalists) drew the already apathetic peasantry further away from the liberal regime and made them more open to *servile* influence. Peasants fled their villages to join bands of brigands and royalist guerrillas in the mountains: there were 122 local revolts against the liberals in 1820–3. The *exaltados*, frustrated by the weakness of *moderados* against the royalists, formed a secret network of societies, the *comuneros*, across 50 Spanish cities.[17] They organised insurrections from the autumn of 1821 and they won the 1822 elections. Yet though Ferdinand was obliged to appoint an *exaltado* ministry, its very radicalism played into his hands. *Exaltado* attacks on the clergy spurred on the *serviles*, who had formed counter-revolutionary juntas in three different provinces, culminating in the establishment of an alternative royalist government in the Catalan hills. While the crisis weakened the liberal regime from within, the wrecking ball which demolished it was French intervention. Villèle's ultra-royalist government had been straining on the leash to bolster its popularity with a successful French military adventure. In April 1823, 100,000 French troops ('the sons of Saint Louis') invaded Spain against minimal resistance from the bedraggled liberal forces, who made a last stand in Cádiz, where they surrendered on 30 September. Ferdinand exacted his vengeance on the liberals, whose leaders, including Riego, were executed or had their property confiscated. The Church, army, bureaucracy and legal system were purged. Yet the official reaction was mercifully brief. The worst of the violence was committed by peasants, whom the *serviles* had organised as 'Royal Volunteers'. When Ferdinand had calmed down, he himself introduced his own, mild reform programme. He still stamped hard on dissent, however, and the French commander in Spain, the duc d'Angoulême, prophetically wrote, 'this country will tear itself to pieces for years to come'.

The Spanish *triennium* inspired liberals elsewhere in Europe. In neighbouring Portugal, a liberal revolt broke out at Porto in August 1820, toppling General Beresford, the effective regent in the absence of João VI, who had been living in Brazil since the royal family fled into exile in 1807. When João proved to be reluctant to return, two successive coups in November by army officers, the first by moderates, the second by radicals, established the Spanish Constitution of 1812 as the basis for the reform of Portugal. The liberal regime was toppled when, encouraged by the French intervention in Spain, a counter-revolutionary mutiny broke out in the army. King João returned to Portugal when a liberal insurrection broke out in Brazil in 1821, but, impressed by

French and British models, sought to rule as a constitutional monarch. Disillusioned reactionaries turned to his younger son, Don Miguel, whom they attempted to enthrone in a coup in 1824. With João's death in 1826, his eldest son, Don Pedro, who was regent in Brazil, was summoned to succeed his father. Don Pedro, however, was enjoying his liberal experiment in South America, granting Brazil a constitutional charter in 1823. Reluctant to leave, his solution was to grant Portugal a similar constitution and to abdicate in favour of his seven-year-old daughter, Maria da Glória, who was to be married to Don Miguel, her uncle. It was an attempt to heal the liberal–reactionary schism but, though Miguel swore to uphold the 1826 Charter, he revoked it in 1828 and had himself crowned King. The collapse of a liberal revolt in Porto led to 14,000 arrests and the confiscation of property from no fewer than 80,000 families. Some of those who fled into exile would join up with Don Pedro to arrange the downfall of the usurper.[18]

The Spanish example also stirred liberals in Italy. The largest revolutionary organisation there, the Carbonari, had an estimated 60,000 members in the south alone. At a minimum, the Carbonari sought to overthrow Austrian dominance and to establish representative government. The first eruption occurred in the Kingdom of Naples. In July 1820 a small but carefully-planned revolt encouraged a popular uprising in the impoverished countryside, but their victory was sealed when one of Murat's former officers, Guglielmo Pepe, led three regiments of King Ferdinand's army over to their side. As the revolutionary forces advanced on Naples, the King conceded the Spanish constitution of 1812 and appointed his son Francis as regent. Francis appointed a moderate liberal government, including Pepe. The Carbonari network ensured that, when parliament met on 1 October, radicals would be strongly represented, though facing a majority of moderate and conservative landowners. The division between radicals and moderates weakened the Neapolitan liberals, while their potential support in Sicily drained away in a civil war. The Sicilian revolution of July 1820 witnessed a split between reactionaries, who saw Neapolitan rule and liberalism as the enemy, and the Carbonari, who wanted to share in the constitutional government won in Naples. When the Austrians crushed the Neapolitan revolution in March 1821, Sicily was in no state to help. The Austrian attack was launched after the Troppau Protocol, adopted by Austria, Prussia and Russia in November 1820, gave great-power approval for the intervention, though France and Britain remained aloof. A further conference at Laibach in January 1821 was attended by Ferdinand, who secured a promise of Austrian help. Yet just as the reaction triumphed in southern Italy, another revolution erupted in the north.

In Piedmont, liberal army officers cast Victor Emanuel's Savoyard dynasty in the role of liberating northern Italy from Austrian rule and conquering Lombardy in the process. They invested their hopes in

Charles Albert, second in line to the throne, whose family had accepted the Napoleonic regime. In March 1821 a group of army officers took over the fortress of Alessandria, raised the Italian tricolour, and proclaimed the Spanish Constitution of 1812 and the independence of the 'Italian Federation', with Victor Emanuel as King of Italy. Victor Emanuel, however, balked at ruling as constitutional monarch, and a further military uprising in Turin forced him to abdicate and appoint Charles Albert as regent. Charles Albert proclaimed 'the Constitution of Spain', but the first in line to the throne, Victor Emanuel's brother Charles Felix, declared his opposition to any change in the system of government. Charles Albert himself showed his true colours when he fled to Novara, held by troops loyal to the old regime. Charles Felix then appealed to Austria, Prussia and Russia, whose rulers were still at the Laibach conference, for help against the liberal regime in Turin. Charles Felix's forces, backed by Austrian troops, swept aside all resistance and marched into Turin on 10 April.[19]

The reaction was harsh and accompanied by a resurgence of clericalism. In Piedmont, hundreds of liberals fled as 97 death sentences were handed down. The Neapolitan reaction was marked by the brief return to power of Canosa, who used the reactionary secret society, the Calderari, to persecute those who had joined the revolution. Several Carbonari were publicly executed. Even though Canosa, after pressure from Austria, was dismissed, long prison terms and executions continued under the reformer, Medici. The army and the government were expunged of anyone involved in the constitutional regime of 1820–1, leaving a new generation of embittered officials and officers seething against the absolute monarchy. In Lombardy, though unaffected by the revolution, the Austrians put over ninety leading Carbonari on trial, condemning forty of them to lengthy spells in the Spielberg, a fortress which gained notoriety in the 'black legend' of Austrian rule in Italy.

The Italian Carbonari inspired French revolutionary organisations opposed to the Bourbon restoration, particularly the Charbonnerie, a wide network of revolutionary groups organised into cells. Members included former Napoleonic army officers and officials and a younger generation of students and journalists. This radical opposition was a loose alliance of both republicans and Bonapartists, for whom the limited concessions to the revolutionary inheritance did not go far enough. They worked with certain liberals, particularly those who supported the rival Orléans dynasty, but they did not agree with them over what would replace the Bourbon monarchy. The Charbonnerie was probably too loosely organised to pose a serious threat to the regime, but it was responsible for failed conspiracies, most notably in Belfort, Marseille and Saumur in December 1821, and La Rochelle and Thouars in 1822. The most effective liberal opposition, however, would prove to be the moderate, parliamentary kind – the *doctrinaires* – who claimed to abhor both absolute monarchy and revolution. They did not seek to overthrow the Bourbon monarchy, but rather to hold the King to the Charter. They had some gifted ideologues, including Benjamin Constant, François Guizot and Pierre Royer-Collard.

For conservatives, even Britain did not seem to be safe from the possibility of revolutionary tumult, though most organisations were actually committed to legal means. Whig (moderate liberal) Hampden clubs, whose membership was originally restricted to the wealthy, were opened up to workers and labourers to demand for the extension of the franchise. In 1817 alone, a weary House of Commons was bombarded with more than seven hundred petitions for reform.[20] The campaign had little chance of success because the Whigs were a minority in parliament. Some of the protests which accompanied political agitation were accompanied by violence, which alarmed the elites. One of three mass meetings at Spa Fields in 1816 degenerated into violence. An attack on the Prince Regent's coach in 1817 led Parliament to suspend habeas corpus. In 1819 the British liberal Sydney Smith was warning: 'there will be a war of the rich against the poor'.[21] The sense of impending civil conflict in Britain was intensified by the 'Peterloo' massacre in 1819 when Manchester workers were slaughtered by cavalry as they attended a political meeting. An anxious parliament passed the 'Six Acts', which empowered local magistrates to ban public demonstrations, close down private meetings, search for firearms amd seize seditious writings, and imposed a tax on newspapers and changed legal procedure to strengthen the prosecution. Such measures seemed to be justified when, in February 1820, the police uncovered the Cato Street conspiracy, in which a small group of radicals plotted to assassinate the entire government. More dramatically still, in Scotland in early April, Lanarkshire and Glasgow weavers marched in support of a 'revolutionary government'. This 'Radical War' was nipped in the bud when government cavalry scattered the marchers.

Opposition in Germany flowed from the nationalist organisations which had fought Napoleon. These included the gymnastic *Turnerschaft*, founded in Berlin in 1811 by Friedrich Jahn, and the *Burschenschaften*, radical, patriotic student societies, first established at the University of Halle in 1814. The *Burschenschaften* wanted both German unity and a constitution. They held a festival at Wartburg Castle in Eisenach in October 1817, but the movement split between radicals who envisaged a democratic Germany and moderates who wanted unity while retaining Germany's existing political institutions.[22] Almost as alarming to the authorities was the submission of a petition, drafted in 1818 by the nationalist democrat Joseph Görres, to the Prussian government. It carried over three thousand signatures from the Rhineland, underlining strength of feeling for political reform. The authorities were thoroughly alarmed. In December 1817 even Hardenberg wrote to Metternich, fearfully claiming that 'Jacobinism, which is almost everywhere raising its head' needed to be combated by a common German law to muzzle the 'unbridled license of our gazetteers and journalists' who were being protected by the smaller German states.[23]

The authorities did not have to wait long to tighten the screws on the radical opposition. The assassination of the reactionary playwright, August von Kotzebue, in March 1819 persuaded the German Confederation to enact general measures of repression. Kotzebue was stabbed to death by Karl Sand who, though acting on his own initiative, was an unbalanced member of the radical core of the Jena *Burschenschaft*. Delegates from the *Bund* responded in August with the Karlsbad decrees, which ordered the dismissal of any professors who abused 'their legitimate influence over the minds of youth' and the enforcement of laws against secret associations. The decrees also imposed restrictions on the press and established a central commission at Mainz to investigate 'secret revolutionary activities and demagogic associations' in Germany.[24] *Burschenschaft* members were imprisoned or exiled. The reaction also throttled constitutional tendencies within Germany. Metternich successfully pressed the *Bund* to defend the principle of monarchical government in its Final Act of June 1820. Frederick William sidelined Hardenberg, whose ideas for a Prussian constitution were now in shreds.

Metternich, however, faced opposition within his own 'forest of bayonets' – in Hungary, where a liberal consciousness emerged during the acrimonious sessions of the Hungarian diet of 1825–7. Emperor Francis's representatives threatened the fractious but conservative Magyar nobles with the abolition of serfdom if they did not co-operate. Yet a group of liberal nobles, characterised by Count István Széchenyi, stood astride the chasm between the autocratic court and the conservative opposition. As a patriot, Széchenyi wanted to promote the Magyar language, and, as a liberal, he envisaged the social and economic development of Hungary within the protective shell of the Habsburg monarchy. The dilemma of such a political position was that, on the one hand, the Emperor had the power to force the pace of reform, but at the risk of eroding Hungary's constitutional rights; on the other hand, greater autonomy would mean handing more power to the conservative nobility who would never permit the reform of Hungarian society, not least the abolition of serfdom. There was another problem: the patriotic defence of the Magyar language might alienate Hungary's national minorities – Slovaks, Romanians, Serbs, Croats – who would fear for their own rights. Hungarian liberalism was a delicate balancing act over social, political and ethnic issues.[25]

In Russia, liberalism was first carried by aristocratic army officers who had breathed the fresh oxygen of freer societies in the West during the last years of the Napoleonic Wars. Frustrated at what John Gooding has aptly called Alexander's 'barren liberalism',[26] they began to organise subversive societies with the aim of overthrowing the Tsarist autocracy and establishing constitutional government. They drew support from intellectuals, frustrated reforming bureaucrats and fellow army officers. In 1816 the 'Union of Salvation' was formed in St Petersburg. Like Western liberals, however, the Russians soon split between moderates and radicals. The former claimed to eschew revolution in favour of education, the abolition of serfdom and political reform. The radical conscience of the movement, the army officer Pavel Pestel, proposed the abolition of serfdom with some redistribution of land and the establishment of a democratic republic. The division between a moderate 'Northern Society' and Pestel's radical 'Southern Society' became formal in 1821. The liberals' opportunity came when Tsar Alexander I died suddenly. On 14 December 1825 the conspirators struck as Tsar Nicholas I was ascending the throne. They mustered 3000 troops on Senate Square in St Petersburg, but failed to capitalise on the initial surprise. Raked by grapeshot, the rebels scattered. In the south, the Chernigovsky regiment rose up, but was put down in a skirmish near Trilesy on 3 January 1826. In the repression, five Decembrists (as the insurgents would later be known) were hanged, including Pestel, and 116 were exiled to Siberia.[27]

The consequences of this first Russian revolution were far-reaching. The insurrection taught Nicholas that his brother's grip on the Empire had been feeble. He created His Majesty's Own Chancellery, the Third Section of which was in charge of state security. Its 16 men belied its real power: the 60 gendarme units, originally established in 1815, were its main source of information, as they reported on political activity, corruption and public opinion. The Third Section also received as many as five thousand denunciations a year and it employed a host of informants, gaining a fearsome reputation for invasiveness. Nicholas's relationship with his people, which was later starkly defined in 1833 by his minister of education, Sergei Uvarov, as 'the joint spirit of Orthodoxy, autocracy, and nationality' (later described as the doctrine of 'Official Nationality'), was not to be slighted in any way by the babbling intelligentsia. Rigorous censorship was therefore imposed by the press statute of May 1826. Postmasters were ordered to open mail and copy the contents of any suspicious letters, passing them on to the Third Section. This stifling atmosphere alienated the intelligentsia: denied any legal outlet for constructive criticism, whenever they spoke independently it could only be *against* the regime, and often at great personal risk. This 'parting of ways' would ensure that the Decembrist revolt would mark only the beginning of the Russian revolutionary movement.[28]

Cracks in the Edifice

The conservatives saw off the revolutionary challenges of the early 1820s, but in the process they broke the facade of international, counter-revolutionary solidarity. In November 1820 the Holy Alliance powers – Austria, Russia and Prussia – proclaimed the principle of counter-revolutionary intervention at a conference at Troppau (in Austrian Silesia), held to discuss the crises in Spain and Naples. The Troppau Protocol declared that the powers had an 'indisputable right in contemplating common measures of safety against States in which the Government has been overthrown by Rebellion'.[29] Yet France and Britain objected, the latter protesting that the Protocol claimed for the reactionary powers 'the exclusive privilege of meddling in the internal affairs of independent States'.[30]

Yet, at the Laibach (Llubljana) conference in Slovenia in January 1821, the Holy Alliance powers pressed on with their programme of intervention, authorising Austria's assault on Naples. In October 1822 a congress at Verona permitted the French (now seeking a prestige-enhancing adventure for domestic political purposes) to attack the liberal regime in Spain. For the time being, however, the split between Britain and the other great powers was healed by their co-operation over a dramatic event in the Ottoman Empire – the Greek struggle for independence.

Greece was part of the Ottoman Empire, which was a multinational state organised in the *millet* system, whereby people were identified according to their religious affiliation. This gave the Sultan's predominantly Orthodox Christian subjects some autonomy, although they were always legally subordinate to Muslims. The Sultan's government in Constantinople, the Porte, had only a loose grip on its subject peoples and worse, it could not control the local authorities who abused their power. Attempts at reform by Sultan Selim III between 1789 and 1807 had been emasculated by opposition from the powerful Muslim landlords, the *ayans*, and by reactionaries in Constantinople who objected to the intrusion of Western influences on the Islamic state. A revolution in Serbia in 1804, which eventually gave the principality autonomy, originated as a Serb reaction in the name of the Sultan against the excesses of the local rulers, including the *ayans*, and the elite imperial guard, the Janissaries. Selim's cousin, Mahmud II, who ruled from 1808 until 1838, continued the attempt to curb the powers of the Janissaries and the *ayans*.

These developments were watched with keen interest by the great European powers. Britain, France and Austria feared that Russia would exploit Turkish weakness in order to seize territory in south-eastern Europe and, above all, make a bid for the straits linking the Black Sea to the Mediterranean. Serbian autonomy in 1812 was evidence of further

Ottoman decay in Europe. This was followed more alarmingly by the Greek War of Independence, which occurred, firstly, because power in Greece had slipped away from the Sultan's officials to the *ayans* and bandit warlords, the *Kapitánioi* (whose followers were called *Klephts* or *Armatoloi*). Secondly, Greek merchants had come into contact with the ideas of the Enlightenment and of the French Revolution. In 1814 a group of them in Odessa founded a 'Friendly Society', the *Philiki Etairia*, which steadily grew across the Greek community in the Ottoman Empire. The spark flashed during the attempt (beginning in 1819) by the Ottoman government to subdue the Albanian *ayan* who dominated the region, Ali Pasha. The advancing Ottoman army ensnared Ali in his city of Janina, but began to pillage from Greek peasants. By the spring of 1821, therefore, thousands of Greek *Klephts* and *Armatoloi* had joined Ali Pasha to resist the Turks.

The war against Ali Pasha and another against Persia stretched the Turkish military, which provided the *Philiki Etairia* with its chance. The society ambitiously saw itself as the vanguard of a movement for the liberation of all Christians in south-eastern Europe, with Russian support. The insurrection therefore began in the Romanian principalities because the local ruling elites, the *Phanariots*, were Greek and because the Turks, by an agreement in 1802, were not allowed to move troops into Moldavia or Wallachia without Russian permission. In March 1821 a Greek in Russian service, Alexander Ypsilantis, crossed from (Russian-controlled) Bessarabia into Moldavia, proclaiming that an army of 70,000 Russians would soon arrive to support the uprising against the Turks. Yet the Romanian peasantry rose not against the Turks but against their Romanian landlords and the Greek officials. The Tsar, who was then at the Laibach conference and in no mood to encourage revolution anywhere, refused to support the revolt and gave the Turks the permission they needed to march into the principalities. The rebellion collapsed.

Yet the struggle was quickly rekindled in the Peloponnese. It was started by the *Etairia* in April 1821 and, with the Turkish forces engaged against Ali Pasha and the Persians and in Romania, the revolution gathered pace. When Ali was assassinated in February 1822, the Greek *Kapitánioi* were ready to fill the political vacuum and the *Armatoloi* lent their considerable weight to the *Etairia*'s insurrection by waging a guerrilla war against the Turks. By the summer of 1822 the insurgents controlled the Peloponnese and nearby islands, which became a base for supplies and naval operations. Helped by their considerable seamanship, the Greeks managed to hold on until 1825, but they dissipated their strength in a civil war. Besides fighting the Turks, the new Greek government, elected by a national assembly in Epidaurus in December 1822, was also trying to assert its authority over the fiercely independent *Kapitánoi*. The Greeks paid the price for their divisions when, having been fought to a stalemate, the Sultan called on Mehmet Ali, Pasha of Egypt, for military assistance, promising him Crete and the governorship of the Peloponnese for his son, Ibrahim. Egyptian troops landed in Greece in February 1825 and the Greek positions, including the Acropolis in Athens, were retaken one by one.

The Greek cause, however, was saved by great-power intervention. Russian and British commerce in the Black Sea was being disrupted by the war and the Tsar saw himself as the protector of the Orthodox peoples of the Balkans. Britain, France and Austria feared that Russia might exploit the revolt in order to establish an independent Greek state under its control. The great powers, therefore, had interests in controlling the crisis. Meanwhile, public opinion in all European countries, including Russia, was strongly pro-Greek. The 'Philhellenism' of educated Europeans was based on their classical education, which led them to see the Greeks as romantic descendants of the Ancient Greeks, struggling heroically for their freedom. By the Treaty of London in July 1827, France joined Britain and Russia in agreeing to mediate between the Greeks and the Sultan. In order to prevent the Turks and Egyptians from pressing home their military advantage, the allies sent a fleet under Admiral Edward Codrington to blockade the coast. Codrington found the Muslim fleet anchored at Navarino, where he learned that, despite a truce signed by Ibrahim, Turkish and Egyptian troops were still operating on land. In a four-hour carnage on 20 October, the combined French, British and Russian squadrons destroyed the Turkish–Egyptian fleet. The Battle of Navarino ensured Greek independence, which was recognised by the great powers at the Treaty of London in February 1830. A year later, they chose Otto (Othon in Greek), son of King Ludwig of Bavaria, to be King of the new constitutional state.

Meanwhile the independence of an expanded Serbia had been secured by a war between Russia and Turkey. In March 1826 Tsar Nicholas pressed the Sultan to honour both the Treaty of Bucharest (1812), which guaranteed Serbian autonomy, and the 1802 agreement by withdrawing his forces from the Romanian principalities. The Turks, their hands tied in Greece, could barely refuse. In October 1826 they signed the Convention of Akkerman, agreeing to Nicholas's demands, but Navarino poisoned Russo-Turkish relations. Mahmud renounced the Convention and war broke out in April 1828. After a hard-fought conflict, Mahmud sued for peace in August 1829. At the Treaty of Adrianople, he recognised Serbian autonomy, with Miloš Obrenović as hereditary prince. In November 1833 the Russians also forced the Sultan to grant Serbia six districts to the south.

The collapse of Ottoman power in Serbia and Greece seemed to demonstrate the perils posed by international conflict to any conservative state which failed both to strengthen itself and to keep revolutionary impulses in check. Yet no great power wanted to see the Ottoman

Empire collapse altogether. At the Treaty of Adrianople, Russia certainly annexed territory in the Caucasus and on the Danube delta, but Tsar Nicholas restrained his greater ambitions because he feared the consequences of a full-scale Ottoman collapse and the potentially revolutionary effects of a long war. Yet the intervention in 1827 set an ominous precedent for south-eastern Europe: that of great-power interference in the complex politics of Ottoman decline. The Greek War of Independence was a harbinger of future great-power entanglements in the region. In another bad omen for the future, the northern Greek frontier set along the Arta-Volos line by the great powers in 1830 left three-quarters of the Greek population under Turkish rule. This fuelled nationalist irredentism, which, among all the emerging states of south-eastern Europe in the nineteenth century, would prove to be both an affliction for the countries directly involved and a temptation for the great powers who sought to exploit it. Eric Hobsbawm exaggerates when he writes that the 'permanence of the 1815 settlement . . . lay in ruins', since the great powers actually co-operated in finding a resolution to the crisis. Yet, in the long run, he is right: Turkish disintegration would turn south-east Europe 'into a battlefield of the powers'.[31] The conflict which did spell the end of the Vienna settlement – the Crimean War of 1854–6 – would be rooted in the problem of Ottoman decline.

5 Social Crises and Responses, 1815–1848

The period between 1815 and the 1848 Revolutions was bordered by two severe social crises – the desperate years between 1816 and 1818, and the tragedy of the 'Hungry Forties' of 1845–8 – and punctuated by others in between. All regimes faced opposition which arose as a direct protest against poverty or as an attempt to exploit popular discontent. This opposition underwent important changes in the decades before 1848. Socialism, which offered alternative visions for the organisation of work and society, spread among artisans and workers who feared the cold breath of destitution. Workers became more adept at political organisation and so found new forms of expression and of protest. Yet socialism, class-consciousness, trade unions and popular political organisations remained the activities of a minority and remained geographically restricted. Europe still remained a predominantly agrarian society, and the inhabitants of the countryside still resorted to traditional forms of social protest. This was also true of most urban artisans and workers.

Population Growth and Economic Change

The underlying cause of the social unease was a burgeoning population as yet unaccompanied by the rapid economic development which later provided sufficient employment and improvements in the quality of life for most people. Contemporaries anxiously watched the accelerating pace of population growth. In 1798 the British clergyman, Thomas Malthus, published *An Essay on the Principles of Population*, which argued that the swelling numbers of people would outrun the means of subsistence. Unless the increase was restrained by 'preventive checks' (meaning sexual restraint and a delay in marriage), then 'positive checks' – those 'terrible correctives to the redundance of mankind', famine, disease and war – would do the job instead.

The rise in population probably did not occur because 'fertility rates' were increasing, or, put another way, because people were having more babies. Where the birth-rate increased or remained high, as in southern Italy, it was in a response to high rates of infant mortality. The underlying cause of the population rise appears to have been a general decline in mortality: more people were staying alive for longer. This was probably the result of a range of factors. Changes in agricultural production, including the introduction of new crops such as the potato, may have made the food supply more consistent and varied. The virtual disappearance of bubonic plague from Europe (caused by a decline in the black rat population) in the eighteenth century and then inoculation programmes against diseases such as smallpox may also have contributed. Europe's smallest people – children under the age of five – benefited most from the decline in mortality, and people who survived infancy could expect to live a lot longer than the average lifespan. The survival of more children into adulthood increased the number of young, fertile people of marriageable age who would go on to have children of their own.

In the second half of the century, agricultural change and industrialisation, better transport and, eventually, the growth in real wages in later decades ensured a more reliable supply of affordable food and a more varied diet. Such economic development ensured that the crisis predicted by Malthus did not occur. Industrialisation, therefore, eventually allowed European society to support the growing population. Better standards of living created a check of their own: parents started to limit the size of their families to protect their living standards. Knowledge of contraception became more widespread in the late nineteenth century. In Britain, prosecutors obligingly publicised birth control when they tried to ban a handbook on contraception in 1877.[1]

Yet all this was in the future. In the decades before the rapid economic growth after mid-century, the burgeoning population threatened the countryside with overpopulation and the towns with unemployment. Ireland was faced with a desperate, Malthusian crisis. The population had grown from 7.2 million in 1821 to around 8.3 million by 1845 when catastrophe struck. The rural labourer, who received a cabin and a potato patch in return for work on a tenant-farmer's land, and the cottager, who had a dwarf-holding, suffered most during the famine which bit in 1845–7. Between 800,000 and 1.5 million people died. The trend of escaping rural poverty by emigration, already present (about a million Irish people left between 1815 and 1845), accelerated. In 1851 the Irish population had dropped to 6.5 million owing to a combination of death and flight. The fall continued, so that by 1911 there were just under 4.4 million people in Ireland.

Emigration was a solution for other Europeans: about 60 million left in the nineteenth century alone. Most set sail after 1850, and especially in the great wave which began around 1885, but it did occur in the first half of the century, particularly in times of abject poverty – 1816–18, 1828–32 and 1845–8. In 1818 an official in the Prussian province of Westphalia reported:

> The craze to emigrate to America has become an epidemic in the two counties of Wittgenstein and is arousing our special concern . . . In

> neighbouring Hesse-Darmstadt the same wandering spirit is said to have erupted. . . . The local authorities . . . see the main cause . . . in poverty and the recent severe difficulties in gaining a livelihood.[2]

In all, some 1.5 million Europeans left between 1800 and 1845. Yet when compared with the later rush, emigration was not rapid enough to ease the problems of poverty. Nor was economic growth rapid enough to absorb the surplus population. The economies of most countries did not 'take off' (when the expansion of new industries becomes sustained) until after 1850.[3] The only countries to experience such sustained growth before 1848 were Britain, Belgium and certain regions of France and Germany.

Britain was the unquestioned leader by 1850, but even its ability to support its rapidly expanding population in the late eighteenth and early nineteenth centuries was achieved only with great effort. Agricultural production rose, primarily as a result of agricultural innovations, the expansion of the area under cultivation and the enclosure of common land (which none the less deprived much of the rural population of important grazing and foraging rights). Food production increased, but so too did prices and rents, owing to growing demand. English cottagers, hemmed in by these pressures and by the loss of the commons, were reduced to low-paid farm-workers. In the Scottish Highlands from the 1770s, landlords sought to boost their incomes by clearing crofters from their estates and replacing them with sheep, whose wool was more profitable than rents. The pace of the Clearances gathered after the Napoleonic Wars, and migration from the Highlands was accelerated by the potato blight of 1846, when some 150,000 people faced terrible privation. By 1800 Britain was a net importer of all grains, but the landowners who produced British crops were protected by the Corn Laws of 1815, a tariff system imposed on imports of foreign grain. For all these reasons, British agriculture only just held its own against the press of population growth.

Other parts of rural Europe also struggled under the pressure. The French countryside reached its maximum population density, peaking in 1846, which, with a property-owning peasantry, entailed a subdivision of holdings and an increasing number of sharecroppers all looking for land to farm. Overpopulation allowed landowners to push down the wages of agricultural labourers, sometimes to subsistence levels. The peasantry became more vulnerable to poor harvests as the population density increased. Some of the pressure was eased by new crops such as maize and potatoes and by the growth of rural industry, such as woollens (in the Champagne) and lace (in Normandy). The potato helped to sustain the poorest inhabitants, but the blight of this crop between 1845 and 1851 inflicted terrible misery. A mark of the poverty of rural France was the movement of people in search of work. Though seasonal migration was a centuries-old tradition, the numbers involved were remarkable: half a million people a year left their department. Many of these were gone for years, a migration which affected one in five rural families. Peasants did try to control population growth through the use of contraception (although the most common form, condemned by the Church, was coitus interruptus, which became known as the 'French sin' to other Europeans) and, in fact, French population growth was slower than elsewhere in Europe. Yet the growth was sufficient to put land and food supply under intense pressure. The situation was not all bleak; there were signs of vitality, particularly from the 1840s. Certain regions began to specialise in crops such as wine, sugar beets and livestock for the market rather than for subsistence. In the long term, this specialisation and the development of a rail network, both of which began in earnest in the 1840s, would reap fruit in later decades, mitigating the effects of harvest failures. From around 1860, regional variations in prices of grain narrowed and subsistence crises became a thing of the past. Fear of famine, which had done so much to prompt rural violence, receded.[4]

Across the frontier, the German countryside was faced with a similar problem of overcrowding.[5] Yet the general trend of German agriculture in this period was to expand more than adequately to meet this new demand, despite the subdivision of peasant holdings, which doubled the number of farms from 1 million in 1816 to 2 million by 1858. The boost in agricultural production was achieved by expanding the extent of the land being farmed: 14 million hectares were cultivated in 1800, and by 1850 this had expanded to 25 million, 7 million of which came from ploughing up common land. New crops, particularly the potato, were introduced to wider areas and livestock increased, which also increased the amount of fertilizer available. Cash crops – particularly sugar beets – made their first great leap in production in 1837–40. Yet these undoubted strides could not hide short-term fluctuations in prices and in production, which caused great distress. In times of poor harvests, as in 1816–17 and again in 1845–7, the problem of rural poverty intensified. Yet, in a terrible irony, land-owning peasants also suffered from an overabundance of grain in the 1820s, particularly in the exporting regions of Germany, such as East Prussia. After the crisis of 1817, two factors conspired to bring about a collapse in cereal prices: the good harvests of the early 1820s and the impact of the British Corn Laws, which reduced sales of Prussian grain in one of its most important markets. While severe for the great noble landowners, it was disastrous for those Prussian peasants who had been emancipated from seigneurial bonds by the decrees of 1807 and 1811. They were unable to make their redemption payments and some impoverished souls were desperate enough to resort to becoming bondsmen (*Insten*) on noble estates. This was a form of serfdom in all but name: the peasants would become tenants, performing labour services as they did before the Emancipation of 1807. The German economist Friedrich List described the harsh existence of the freer peasants of the west and the south who scratched out a living by farming their tiny plots, subsisting mostly on potatoes.[6] One estimate has almost half the German population living in poverty.[7]

In the Habsburg monarchy, agricultural productivity increased at a rate of 1 per cent between 1789 and 1841. Some of this expansion was due to swamp drainage and the clearing of forests. The potato, once resented by Austrian peasants as food for pigs, gained gradual acceptance, although its use in making spirits no doubt increased its appeal. Yet peasants still remained oppressed by seigneurial dues and obligations; generally, the further north (into the Czech lands) and east (into Hungary and the Ukrainian province of Galicia) one went, the more onerous the labour obligations became. In Italy, the sharecropping (*mezzadria*) system common in the north and the centre fell under heavy criticism from agrarian reformers, for whom *mezzadria* was a dead weight on the economy as it prevented innovation and the fusing of landholdings into large-scale, commercial farms. Yet the system persisted into the twentieth century, not least because it gave the landlords a large measure of social control over their tenants.[8] In the south, nobles successfully resisted the effects of the reforms of the Napoleonic era which, on paper at least, abolished seigneuralism in the Kingdom of Naples. Sicilian nobles, who did not experience French occupation, managed to cling on to their privileges even longer. Rather than innovate, landowners tried to earn a living by squeezing as much as they could from their tenants, while increasing food production by expanding the land under cultivation. This scarcely scratched the surface of the problem of rural poverty in the south, and pressure was not eased until after 1880, with the onset of mass emigration.

In Russia, serfdom persisted until 1861. Yet for all the justifiable moral reservations which contemporaries had over it, the way the system operated actually allowed it to absorb the population increase. Serfs gave their labour (*barshchina*) to their landlord in return for an allotment, the use of communal pastures and meadows, a home and a small garden. As each household had as many allotments as there were husband-and-wife teams (*tiagli*) to work them, the amount of land available to each extended family increased with the number of married couples within it. Though the system discouraged peasants and landlords alike from innovating (since the allotments were redistributed periodically), it has been argued that it allowed Russian agriculture to produce higher yields of grain than is usually supposed. Yet in times of crisis the suffering of the peasantry was terrible, as in the famine and cholera epidemic of 1848–9.[9] Moreover, serfs were subject to the discipline – often violently inflicted with the knout or whip – not only of the landlord's bailiff but also of the village elders, the patriarchs, who enforced the will of the peasant community on recalcitrants.

Agricultural life in both western and eastern Europe presents a bleak picture, if for different reasons. Generally, expansion in agricultural production kept the expanding population fed, but there were signs by the mid-1840s that the land in some parts of the west had reached its limits in supporting the growing numbers of people. Meanwhile, the spectacular and sustained economic growth driven by industrialisation lay in the future in most places. In Britain, the application of new technology was patchy until the sustained take-off after 1830. The preconditions were there: first, population growth offered an expanding labour market; secondly, technological innovations in textiles and steam power in the eighteenth century, though localised, would help drive further development; thirdly, the dominance of British sea power gave British manufacturers access to world-wide markets, not only for their products but also for the raw materials for which they were developing an insatiable demand; fourthly, Britain had an advanced banking and credit system – while manufacturers mostly depended upon their own accumulated profits for reinvestment, they were also able to turn to banks;[10] fifthly, where previously the costs of overland transport had been prohibitive, Britain now had an excellent road and canal system, which opened up coal and iron ore fields for exploitation.

The momentum, which gathered in the 1830s, came from the development of the railways. The first line was opened between Stockton and Darlington in 1825, but it was not until George Stephenson's steam engine first rolled along the new Manchester–Liverpool line in 1830 that the day of the steam-powered locomotive had arrived. Profits from British overseas trade and the cotton industry were sunk into the railways and, recovering from a crash in 1836–7, investment peaked in 1847. The subsidiary industries upon which the railways depended were faced with an unprecedented demand, encouraging technological innovation in the coal, iron and engineering industries in particular – but also in brick production, required for the construction of bridges, tunnels and dykes. By 1860 Britain not only produced 50 per cent of the world's cotton goods but also 50 per cent of its cast iron and nearly 60 per cent of its coal and steel. In 1850 it produced three times as much pig-iron and spun cotton as the next most advanced economies of Europe combined – Belgium, Germany and France – and had twice as much installed steam power. Moreover, industrialisation represented an important structural shift in the British economy. If in 1801 some 36 per cent of the population worked in agriculture, fishing and forestry, this had declined to 22 per cent 50 years later. The proportion employed in manufacturing, mining and construction increased from 30 per cent to 43 per cent. Accompanying this structural change in the economy was an important social transformation. By 1851 – and at the time this was not true of any other country – more than half of all British people lived in towns of over 2500 people (54 per cent in fact, an increase from 33 per cent in 1801), a significant proportion (25 per cent) in the ten cities of over 100,000 people.

Other European countries certainly did not witness the same spectacular growth, but certain regions did experience industrialisation, even if the penetration of technology was not yet so deep. As in Britain, German industrialisation began in certain textile regions, such as the Rhineland and Saxony, but the second wind came from the railways. Once the railway network began to thread its way across the land, home-grown rail, coal, iron and engineering industries developed. The speed with which these grew stemmed from an availability of capital – German manufacturers of all kinds were keen to use them to open up markets – and because both politicians and economists recognized the strategic value in developing a network. While the work was usually undertaken by private firms, as in Britain, the state financed the projects indirectly by seizing the land required and by guaranteeing payments to investors. The first German line was lain in 1835 between Nuremberg and Fürth. In Prussia the beginnings of a web centred on Berlin was discernible by the early 1840s. This development stimulated the German iron and coal industries, although the acceleration occurred after 1850. German industrialisation, in other words, was gathering pace in the 1840s, but craftworkers still constituted 68.5 per cent of the manufacturing workforce in 1848, down from 75 per cent in 1800. Most of the mechanised and heavy industry was focused in certain areas – in the Ruhr, along the Rhine and in Saxony.

Elsewhere in Europe, modern forms of technology and organisation were still localised islands in a sea of traditional methods, but the exception to this was Belgium. In proportion to its size, it was the most industrialised country in Europe, because it sat on top of a vast seam of coal which swept in a huge subterranean arc from northern France, through Hainault and Liège and into Germany. Consequently, Belgian manufacturing was the only industry other than that in Britain to switch almost entirely from charcoal to coal-fired furnaces and steam power. By 1850, the Liège-Hainault arc was producing the equivalent of 77 per cent of the pig-iron output of all the German states put together.

France, however, was closer to the European rule, combining patches of technological advance on a far bigger tapestry of traditional methods. The cotton factories in Alsace, where hand-spinning had disappeared by 1825, and the great iron furnaces of Le Creusot and Saint-Étienne were impressive establishments. Northern France secured a great advantage when its coalfields were be exploited extensively from the 1840s, giving a cheap and plentiful supply of power for machinery. Until then, however, much of the production of cotton cloth took place in cottages, as manufacturers exploited the cheap labour of rural outworkers in the north and in Brittany and Normandy. In Lyon, the silk weavers (*canuts*) retained control of artisanal methods, using the Jacquard loom with great skill; no power looms appeared there until 1843. The first French railway tracks were laid in 1832 between Saint-Etienne and Lyon, primarily for coal, but, as in Britain, the potential for passengers was soon realised and the line carried 171,000 people in 1834. A political debate between those who favoured state control and those who supported private enterprise was resolved by the law of 1842, which gave the state control of planning the network (a web radiating out from Paris), along with the financial responsibility of supporting the construction. Private companies would then lease the lines, provide the rolling stock and run the rail services. As a consequence, the iron industry enjoyed boom years in 1835–8 and 1845–7, but French coal supplies were either inadequate or too expensive to meet the rise in demand, so the shortfall had to be made up with imports.

The textile industry in the Habsburg monarchy witnessed some technological developments, with the introduction of machinery, steam power and the factory system in the suburbs of Vienna, Bohemia (especially Prague and Reichenberg) and Moravia (Brno). By the 1840s the Austrian government saw the military importance of the railroads, while financiers such as Salomon Rothschild saw economic benefits and pressed for the introduction of a steam railroad system to the monarchy. A decree of 1841 envisaged the construction of lines linking Vienna to Prague, the Bavarian border and Milan – although Italy's first railway line was in fact constructed in the south, linking Naples with Portici as early as 1830. Spain had one industrial region – Catalonia, where by 1845 the cotton industry was almost entirely mechanised.

In Russia, it has been argued that serfdom hampered economic development because it was unproductive, failed to produce an internal market for manufactured goods and kept the labour force tied to the land.[11] More recent work, however, has challenged this view. While serfdom prevented great innovations in agriculture, industry could use serf labour. Where landowners had access to raw materials, they could establish factories on their estates, and use what was termed 'free' labour, serfs who paid the *obrok* – dues in money or goods – instead of the *barshchina*. They used their industrial earnings to pay their dues to their landlords. By 1825, 95 per cent of the labour force in the rural cotton industry was recruited in this way. By mid-century, three networks of such proto-industry had developed in Russia, mass-producing goods using traditional methods organised on a large scale, involving textiles, metalworking and tanning, and, in the village of Mstera, painted icons.[12]

Economic development, however, came at a cost. In the long run, industrialisation raised standards of living for most Europeans, but, in the medium-term, the change was not easy for workers. While wages (at least for adult men) were higher in factories than amongst most of the handicraft trades – and they certainly towered above the earnings of farm labourers – the precocious growth of manufacturing economies was fitful, with 'boom and bust' trade cycles. As productivity grew rapidly, it eventually outstripped demand, leading to a slump in trade – behind which lurked unemployment and misery. This occurred in the years around 1830 and immediately before 1848. Moreover, for those who worked in the new machine-driven factories, the rhythm of labour was different – and more demanding. Pre-industrial working life had been harsh. Poor families pieced together a meagre living with a mix of agricultural work, crafts and charity – an 'economy of makeshifts' – but the working day was frequently driven by how long daylight lasted. The week, particularly in Catholic countries, was punctuated by religious festivals and holidays. For journeymen and apprentices working in a skilled trade, working relations with employers were complex, going beyond the imposition of work discipline and the payment of wages. The relationship between master-craftsman and his journeymen and apprentices was peppered with abuse and violence, but the master did have certain duties – not least to train up apprentices and to give them a chance of becoming employers in their own right. In factories, however, the machine determined the pace of work – and machines rarely, if ever, stopped. Working days of 16 to 18 hours were timed by the clock, the tasks were monotonous and the conditions were unhealthy if not downright dangerous (very young children were used in textile mills because they could slide underneath the machines and tie together broken threads). The employment of women and children was of course nothing new, but the new industrial work was performed outside the home in insalubrious conditions. The dust, high temperatures and humidity in airless textile mills may account for high levels of tuberculosis and scrofula amongst workers. Workers unaccustomed or unwilling to adapt to the more demanding rhythms of the factory led employers to impose discipline by threatening dismissal or levying fines for lateness or poor work.

Legislation did take steps towards improving working conditions, but there were limits to how far politicians were willing to go to interfere in private enterprise. In Britain in 1833 and France in 1841, laws restricted the employment of children in factories. Further British laws in 1842, 1844, 1847, 1850 and 1853 gave further protection for women and children in mines and factories. Other workers did not benefit from protective legislation until 1867. There were some signs that employers themselves were beginning to grasp that long working hours, with little time for rest or leisure, could be counter-productive. In 1841 an Alsatian textile manufacturer named Gros cut down the working day by a mere half-hour and saw productivity rise by an impressive 4 per cent. Other entrepreneurs began to follow his example over the following decade. The Habsburg monarchy banned child labour in factories in 1842, although the law was hard to enforce.

Yet those who suffered most in this period were not the factory workers, but those who still laboured in the crafts. This was not necessarily because their jobs were endangered by the rise of machinery and the factory system, although many of them, understandably, blamed this for their predicament. In Britain, the hand-loom weavers were right to do so: the number of power looms rose dramatically, from 55,000 in 1829 to 100,000 in 1833, so by the 1840s some 250,000 hand-loom weavers, suffering from plunging wages, eked out a living. Their trade had virtually disappeared by 1850. In the Czech lands, the introduction of textile machinery pressed spinners and hand-loom weavers against the wall; between 1780 and 1840 their numbers halved in Bohemia. Elsewhere in Europe, however, hand-loom weavers increased in number as the population grew and as mechanisation in the textile industry was only just beginning. In France, their numbers expanded in areas such as Normandy, where textile manufacturers could 'put out' work to cottagers who were cheaper than the urban workforce. Craftworkers of all kinds, in fact, increased in number in Germany, where they rose from 1,230,000 in 1800 to 2 million by 1847. This expansion made life difficult, for several reasons: first, the increase in the supply of labour depressed wages; secondly, in the more skilled trades, it became less likely that the larger numbers of journeymen and apprentices would become master-craftsmen; finally, craftworkers frequently sold to a local market, which meant that their goods depended on demand from the rural population. In times of agricultural crisis, demand for their products would tail off.

Craftworkers were also experiencing important structural changes. If they resisted new technology, they were being subjected to a more 'capitalist' *organisation* of production. This change predated, often by several decades, the introduction of machines and large-scale factories. It involved operating with economies of scale by producing large amounts of goods using large numbers of cheap, unskilled workers. Merchant-tailors in the Parisian clothes trade, for example, while not having any new technology at their disposal, would undermine the artisans by employing large numbers of less skilled workers, often women, who commanded half the wages of journeymen. The entrepreneurs broke production down into specific tasks. Each out-worker or sweatshop performed the same, repetitive stage in producing ready-made clothing in standard sizes. These mass-produced goods were cheaper than the individually tailored suits and dresses produced by the artisans. So while the sales of the Parisian clothing industry doubled between 1825 and 1847, it was the large-scale entrepreneurs who wolfed down most of the profits. Those artisans who could not compete were forced to become wage-earners themselves or they engaged in subcontracting – *marchandage* – whereby they took on some of the work offered by the merchant-tailors. Either way, for journeymen and apprentices this meant a deskilling of their trade and lower wages.[13]

Poverty and Welfare

Aristocratic and middle-class Europeans of all political perspectives anxiously discussed what less fortunate people in town and country were directly experiencing – 'pauperism', or the grinding existence of life on the very margins of subsistence. Rural overcrowding, while perhaps not as immediately obvious as it was in urban slums, made life just as precarious as it was for the poor of Europe's cities. In Germany, rural farm-hands frequently lived in the most miserable of conditions – in one-room cottages, sometimes squeezed in with farm animals, in attics or even in stables. Yet contemporaries were more alarmed by overcrowding in the cities. The period from 1811 to 1850 witnessed Europe's most rapid urbanisation, even though by the latter date the vast majority of the European population still lived in the country. London grew from an already heaving metropolis of just over a million in 1801 to a swarming ants' nest of 2.68 million by 1851, Europe's largest city by far. Industrialisation is, of course, one explanation, but towns also expanded because they were sources of employment in the craft industries for casual, unskilled labour, and were traditional destinations for seasonal workers. Paris, whose population grew from 700,000 in 1815 to over a million by 1850, is a good example. Moscow grew from 250,000 to 365,000, a product less of industrialisation than of an expansion in the handicrafts, especially in textiles. Charity and social assistance were more likely to be offered in the larger population centres. Naples, whose population grew from 350,000 to 449,000, had a burgeoning population of poor, the *lazzaroni*, who were kept quiescent by charity doled out by an anxious royal government.

Construction in housing, however, did not keep pace with the growth of the urban population. There were civic improvements, many of which were undoubtedly of wide benefit – gas lighting was introduced in German cities from the 1820s, and Berlin got its first pavements in that same decade. Cemeteries were moved away from city-centre churches into municipal burial grounds removed from densely-populated areas. Public buildings – city chambers, law-courts, schools, government offices – were constructed as an expression of civic pride, but little was done in this period for the housing stock of the poorest citizens. Before the development of public transport (the cost of travelling across Paris in the horse-drawn tram was prohibitive for most workers), workers' accommodation was close to their workshops or factories. This in itself might have been tolerable in small-scale, artisanal districts, but it was the picture of living hell in industrial cities, where chimneys belched smoke and the noise of factory machinery resounded through the streets. Ulster-born William Cooke Taylor painted a grim portrait of Manchester in 1842: 'its narrow streets, its courts and cellars, have been abandoned to the poorest grade of all. There they live, hidden from the view of the higher ranks by piles of stores, mills, warehouses, and manufacturing establishments.'[14]

Slums emerged in the dilapidating city centres because there was little expansion in affordable housing. In the Ruhr, where mines and iron foundries opened where there were no substantial towns, miners lived in huts, making the region resemble a shanty town. In cities everywhere, high rents meant that workers sublet or shared accommodation with others, while the 'dangerous classes' of casual, unskilled labourers were crammed into apartments, attics or dark, dank cellars – sometimes several families to a room. A report on the population of Paris after the cholera epidemic of 1832 explained that the outbreak caused more deaths in the central districts 'because nowhere else is the space more confined, the population more crowded, the air more unhealthy, dwelling more perilous and the inhabitants more wretched'.[15]

Politicians were well aware of the problem, but they were not inclined to offer much in the form of state welfare. There was some genuine concern for the plight of the poor. In 1832 the municipal government in the northern French textile town of Lille received a report which described the housing of the poor in truly shocking terms:

> In their obscure cellars, in their rooms . . . the air is never renewed, it is infected; the walls are plastered with garbage . . . If a bed exists, it is a few dirty, greasy planks; it is damp and putrescent straw . . . The furniture is dislocated, worm-eaten, covered with filth. . . . The windows, always closed, are covered by paper and glass, but so black, so smoke-encrusted, that the light is unable to penetrate.[16]

In these conditions stalked a new and terrifying disease: cholera, which reached European Russia from Asia in August 1829 and spread westwards, with ghastly symptoms – prolific vomiting, diarrhoea, dehydration and, as a police report recorded on the first victim in Hamburg in 1831, 'the extremities ice-cold, hands and feet blue, and eyes sunken'. Overcrowded districts were particularly vulnerable because the bacteria spread through the water supply, which, with poor sanitation, was rapidly infected. The disease was lethal: a quarter of a million people died from the illness in Hungary in 1831 and when it reached Hamburg in 1832, 3349 people contracted the disease, almost half of whom (1,652) died.[17] Although cholera affected all of Europe and killed bourgeois, nobles, workers and peasants indiscriminately, it was seen in the nineteenth century as 'a poor people's' illness precisely because it was more likely to break out in the overcrowded, filthy housing in which they were forced to live. Cholera did cause social instability: in 1831, Hungarian peasants massacred Jews, priests and landlords, whom they accused of poisoning wells. In 1832, violent disturbances in Paris, where 20,000 people died from cholera, can be linked to the outbreak there. It was no coincidence that when Napoleon III's Prefect of the Seine, Baron Haussmann, started to rebuild Paris in the 1850s he demolished those districts worst afflicted by the cholera outbreaks. Cholera added to the widespread malaise about poverty, which was seen as a danger to social order, even to civilisation, rather than as a symptom of economic dislocation. In the 1840s, William Lindley, a German-speaking British subject, studied the conditions of the poor in Hamburg, later concluding that 'lack of well-being encourages the pathological lust for destruction which, given the opportunity, turns against the possessions of the better-off'.[18]

Poverty was also regarded as a sign of immorality, and the problems associated with it, such as dirt, degradation, prostitution and alcoholism, were seen as its causes rather than its symptoms. In 1835 a doctor named Louis Villermé was ordered by the Academy of Moral and Political Sciences to investigate the 'physical and moral conditions of the working-classes'. Though genuinely shocked by the conditions which he witnessed, particularly among the textile workers in Lille, his explanation for them was blunt: the poor spent too much on 'costly pleasures'. Poverty, therefore, was the product of moral degradation.

Methods of poor relief reflected these attitudes. In Britain, the Speenhamland system (named for the Berkshire village where it was first applied in 1795) offered assistance to poor labourers in relation to the size of their families and the price of bread. A barrage of criticism from ratepayers pounded this practice and in 1796 the utilitarian thinker, Jeremy Bentham, came up with the idea of a 'workhouse' in which stringent conditions would encourage people to seek work rather than rely on poor relief. The Poor Law Commission appointed in 1832 adopted this solution. It argued that while the able-bodied poor needed to be discouraged from idleness, those who could not support themselves – the aged, the infirm and the orphans – should get the help they needed. The new Poor Law was passed in 1834: parishes would be gathered into 'unions', each of which would construct a workhouse funded by the local 'poor rate' and outside of which no able-bodied pauper would receive assistance. At least south of the border everyone, even the able-bodied if they were willing to stand the monastic discipline of the workhouse, had the right to poor relief. In Calvinist Scotland, under the Poor Law of 1845, they had no such right. The Irish Poor Law of 1838 followed the English pattern[19] and the notion of 'self-help' rather than dependence on charity prevailed everywhere in the British Isles.

In France, the Revolution had criticised the old regime system of poor relief as woefully inadequate. Yet plans for a state welfare system were scuppered by the financial pressures of the war. None the less, *bureaux de bienfaisance* had been established by the law of 30 November 1797 which made assistance the responsibility of local communities. The *bureaux* could provide food, clothing and money to paupers and they received limited state aid, but the bulk of the money came from local *notables*. After 1815 the *notables*, whether Catholic or liberal, saw themselves as guardians of a moral code of which charity was an important part, but which also implied a contract whereby they offered social assistance in return for political acquiescence. This usually unspoken assumption was made explicit in Piedmont, the most prosperous part of Italy, where Count Camillo di Cavour advocated 'legal charity' controlled by the elites who would thus reinforce their own social position against the danger of revolution from below.

The French state inherited a tradition from the old regime of providing public works for the unemployed. Despite its commitment to free-market principles, the July Monarchy established temporary workshops – *ateliers de secours* – during the economic crisis, which continued unabated in the wake of the 1830 Revolution. They were, however, a pragmatic response to the problem of public order in the early days of the new regime. Private charity, therefore, remained essential, as it did in the Netherlands, where poor relief was operated jointly by the 'Society of Charity', established in 1818, and the state. In such circumstances, worker militancy was bitterly resented as ingratitude. Some French workers protected themselves by organising mutual aid societies, which boasted a membership of a quarter of a million by 1852. They offered medical care, help in times of illness and a decent burial at death, in return for a monthly subscription of 1–2 francs (at a time when a skilled worker in Paris could, on average, earn 750 francs a year). Unfortunately, few of these mutual aid societies ever had the funds to pay their members unemployment benefit.[20]

In Germany, programmes for poor relief were introduced by bureaucrats whose main concern was for social order. Prussian officialdom did, it is true, have a strong ethos of serving public welfare, but their main concern stemmed from the effects of the reforms of the Revolutionary and Napoleonic era. The Prussian general law code of 1794 had established the principle that the state would look after the poor, and provincial workhouses (*Arbeitshäuser*) were established to perform the role of workhouses, prisons and hospitals in each province. Yet their means were inadequate and in practice poor relief remained the duty first of one's family, then of one's home community (*Heimatgemeinde*), which might also have meant the lord's manor. Landlords, guilds and municipal corporations looked after their own paupers, but only if they had lived, worked and paid taxes in the local community for some time. Poor relief in Prussia was, therefore, very localised and paupers would only go to the workhouse as a last resort. By freeing the Prussian serfs and by allowing freedom of movement (in 1816), Stein's and Hardenberg's reforms created the conditions, it seemed, for the rampant growth of a mobile and dangerous underclass. The former serf owners were freed of their moral obligations to look after paupers, while the division of common lands deprived villages of one of the means by which they supported them. In towns, population pressure, the decline of the guilds and the erosion of municipal privileges – which hitherto had included the right to deny outsiders residence and therefore poor relief – explains the rise in numbers of paupers in the urban environment.

The Prussian Poor Law of 1842 decreed that anyone who wished to receive poor relief had to have lived in the community for three years, which would be proven by the registration of all newcomers (*Meldenpflicht*). This system was full of pitfalls: plenty of paupers *had* to move frequently in search of work, which meant that they were never liable to poor relief. Landlords often agreed not to let out accommodation to people whom they suspected might be potential paupers. Some villages avoided registering newcomers altogether, preferring to pay the token fine for breaking the law rather than make the more costly payments to the poor. Consequently, *Meldenpflicht* was made stricter for 'considerations of police surveillance'. From becoming a means of social assistance, poor relief rapidly became an authoritarian means of keeping a watchful eye on all Prussian subjects.[21]

Socialism and Protest

Radical intellectuals would look at the problem of poverty through critical lenses. Initially, socialism (the term was first coined in France by Pierre Leroux in 1832) implied a system of thought which made the 'social question', rather than political reform, its priority. The three decades after 1815 were especially rich in socialist thought, precisely because they were *not* dominated by Marx. He had just begun to give coherent expression to his ideas when the 1848 Revolutions erupted. The most influential early socialists emerged in France. They drew inspiration from Enlightenment ideas and the French Revolution, including *sans-culotte* demands for price controls, for better wages and sometimes for an 'agrarian law' whereby farm land would be redistributed among the poor. The 'Bible' of the early socialists was Filippo Buonarroti's account, published in 1828, of Gracchus Babeuf's conspiracy, which in 1796 sought to topple the Directory and introduce an egalitarian republic in which land would be shared equally amongst each household.

The influence of 'Babouvism' threw up an influential theorist, Pierre-Joseph Proudhon, who is usually seen as an anarchist thinker who exerted a weighty influence on socialism. In *What is Property?* (1840) he famously replied to his own question that 'property is theft', but he did not reject property ownership altogether. He was critical of Communists such as Marx, declaring, in a less quoted aphorism, that 'Communism is oppression and slavery.'[22] Followers of Proudhon believed in a society of small producers which would take account of social justice, particularly through mutual associations. There would be no central state, only self-governing communes. These ideas naturally appealed to small-scale artisans who were trying to defend traditional methods of manufacturing against the introduction of the factory system or competition from unskilled labour. Proudhon also had a profound influence on the Russian socialist Alexander Herzen and the anarchist Mikhail Bakhunin, both of whom he knew.

'Utopian' socialists, best represented by Etienne Cabet and Charles Fourier, envisaged communities organised so as to guarantee social justice. To cushion the impact of economic change, Fourier argued in 1829, society should be organised into democratic, self-sufficient, agricultural communities called *phalanges*, where people would own their land but share the profits and live in communal buildings (*phalanstères*). Workshops would produce the goods needed by the *phalange* but people would perform a variety of tasks, changing frequently between them to make the work skilful, pleasurable and suited to the particular passions and aptitudes of each individual. Cabet's book, *Voyage en Icarie* (1840), described a land called Icaria where there was no private property: all the land was owned by the state, which was democratic, with a representative assembly. Ominously, however, individual liberty was regarded as 'a mistake, a sin, a grave evil',[23] because the needs of the community had to take precedence.

In the long run, the 'Utopian' socialists were outstripped by 'scientific' socialists. Their influence was great, primarily because they did not reject technology and economic change but saw them as stages along the path of progress. Thinkers such as Henri de Saint-Simon and the German Karl Marx offered explanations for economic and social development, while also offering a long-term vision for the future. To a large extent, this explains why Marx in particular would prove to be so important to socialist ideology after 1848. With his associate, Friedrich Engels, he argued in the *Communist Manifesto* (1848) that economic development would throw up two competing classes, a capitalist bourgeoisie and an industrial proletariat. Their struggle would culminate in a revolution in which the proletariat would triumph, eventually inaugurating a Communist society. In contrast, the aristocratic Saint-Simon (1760–1825) argued that the bourgeoisie and the proletariat would cooperate, because together they formed a single productive class, the *industriels*, as against the parasitic wealthy and idle, the *classe oisive*. Government should be dominated not by any particular social group but by 'technocrats', people who understood technology, production, finance and science. These people would ensure that the benefits of industrial development would be enjoyed by all.[24]

The extent to which these advanced ideas had an impact on workers and peasants in the first half of the century is an open question. Popular forms of protest were occasionally injected with political content, and not just in urban areas. Most rural protest remained rooted in the traditions of the past, reflecting the concerns of an economy which was still subject to harvest failures, dangerous oscillations in prices, population pressure and efforts by landowners to maximise their own revenue. There were food riots across Europe in the crisis years of 1816–19, 1828–32, 1838–42 and 1844–8. Their political motivation was sparse. In 1816 an eloquent rioter in East Anglia in England movingly declared: 'Here I am between Earth and Sky, so help me God. I would sooner lose my life than go home as I am. Bread I want and bread I will have.'[25] In south-west Wales between 1838 and 1844, tenant farmers, mostly men disguised as women (the uprising was dubbed the 'Rebecca Riots', although there were real women among them), protested, amongst other things, against the Poor Law, attacking the Carmarthen workhouse. They had their French counterparts in the Ariège in southern France between 1828 and 1832. There, peasant protesters dressed up as women (*demoiselles*) and chased out foresters and charcoal-burners. Such cross-dressing drew on rural traditions of carnival or charivari, a means by which the peasant community defined itself against the intrusion of the outside world, be that in the shape of new (possibly bourgeois) landlords, the developing national economy, or the demands of the state. Other traditional forms of rural protest included grain seizures, tax strikes and the burning of barns and ricks. 'Luddism' – the smashing of machinery (as in a wave of rural violence in the English Midlands in 1843–4, when threshing machines were destroyed) – represented an attempt by tenants and farm labourers to protect customary patterns of work and their livelihoods.

There were some early signs of peasant politicisation in these protests. The *demoiselles* of the Ariège were fighting the Forest Code of 1827, which overwhelmingly supported the landlords in their struggle to eliminate the peasants' customary rights of gleaning and grazing in woodland. In 1830 the *demoiselles* injected their protests with political rhetoric. They cried out 'Liberty!' because the *notables* themselves had proclaimed the July Revolution to be a triumph for freedom.[26] Yet these early signs of peasant politicisation were still rare. The food riots which swept across central Europe in 1847 seemed to have been driven primarily by economic despair. In eastern Prussia, protests took the form of 'hunger marches' in which hundreds of landless peasant labourers went tramping through the countryside *en masse* in search of food to be had by begging, looting and riot.[27] Republican leaflets were certainly found in areas of rural revolt in south-western Germany in March 1848, but these were more likely to have been produced by middle-class democrats seeking to harness popular discontent than to have come from an angry, peasant pen.[28]

If in western Europe evidence of peasant politicisation was ambiguous, in the east it was non-existent. In February 1846 the Ukrainian peasants of Galicia responded to an attempt by Polish nationalists to foment an insurrection against Austrian rule by rising up – but *against* the Polish revolutionaries. Over one week, 1200 Poles were killed, including officials, landowners and their families, many of whose bodies were mutilated, and 400 estates were plundered. In some cases they were quietly encouraged by the Austrian authorities, but the peasants needed little prodding: they took advantage of the momentary collapse of law and order to attack the people whom they regarded as their immediate oppressors – their landlords, not the Emperor. Peasants believed that they were committing mass murder in the name of the Emperor, who, it was said, had suspended the Ten Commandments in order to permit the slaughter.[29] In Russia, reported incidents of peasant protest increased over the decades before serf emancipation in 1861, but there were also forms of 'everyday resistance' which helped to ease the burden of serfdom. Peasants hid a part of their harvest from the greedy eyes of bailiffs collecting rents or dues and to avoid state taxes. Where they had to labour on the lord's land, they might drag their feet, working at a maddeningly slow pace. They also engaged in poaching and stealing wood (sometimes, in an ironic cycle of exploitation, as a means of paying the *obrok*).[30]

Western-European workers were more likely to be politicised than peasants, especially in communities such as the Parisian artisan districts, where traditions merging politics with social protest were already well-established. Even so, the extent of working-class politicisation should not be exaggerated: even where there were traditions of political expression, artisans and workers did not always have the organisation by which to further political or even economic ends. Workers' organisations – guilds, trade unions or 'combinations' – were outlawed in many parts of Europe. In France they had been banned in 1791, but artisans still participated in legal or semi-legal organisations, such as the *compagnonnages* (national networks of journeymen and apprentices). The *compagnonnages* supported apprentices as they went on their traditional 'tour de France', learning their trade as they moved from town to town. These organisations also tried to represent the journeymen in their disputes with master-artisans and merchants over rates of pay. Mutual or 'friendly' societies were also established, to which workers paid monthly dues in return for insurance benefits in times of sickness, retirement and death. These were subject to the scrutiny of the authorities but they were tolerated because they were regarded as important safety nets for their members and therefore contributed to social stability. In the Habsburg monarchy, the Prague cotton printers who went on strike in June 1844 (the violence was such that the army had to be brought in) were organised through their mutual aid societies, but this contrasted with other Czech workers who had no such organisational base. In Germany, most states banned labour organisations, and though guilds survived in some places, they were helpless in the growing use of outworkers by entrepreneurs. Even where workers' combinations were not forbidden (they were not made illegal in Prussia until 1845 and in Hanover until 1847), workers were not allowed to strike. In Britain, the Master and Servant Act of 1823 threatened miners with imprisonment for breach of contract (which included striking). Unions had been banned in 1799, but there was some relaxation of the law in 1824, which allowed workers to form unions and to gather funds, though not to strike. An amendment the following year prosecuted anyone who tried to strike or coerce people to join a union. It was not long before the law bared its teeth. In 1833 a group of farm labourers in Tolpuddle in Dorset formed a 'friendly society', only to be transported to Australia for taking forbidden oaths.

Beleaguered European artisans therefore turned to direct action against machinery and factory organisation. Luddism and burning down factories could occur wherever craftworkers felt threatened by mechanisation. Britain saw a serious outbreak of such activity amongst the textile workers in Yorkshire and the Midlands in 1811–16. There were outbreaks of French Luddism in the southern woollen industry in 1816–19; among Parisian artisans in 1829–33; among weavers in the south-east and the Champagne in 1840 and 1847–8, and during the 1848 Revolutions, with the burning of textile factories in cities across the country.[31] Craftworkers might also organise 'interdictions' through the *compagnonnages* and mutual aid societies, urging their colleagues not to accept employment on premises which adopted machinery. A wave of machine-breaking and attacks on factories occurred in Germany and around Vienna during the outbreak of the 1848 Revolutions.

Yet such forms of protest could only yield short-term results; artisans also turned to political action. Almost everywhere, it was the artisans and craftworkers – not the factory 'proletariat' – who were most receptive to radical and early socialist ideas. These appealed not only to their articulate sense of self-worth but also to their belief that the factory system and machinery were the primary causes of their suffering. Meanwhile, factory workers were usually unskilled, poorly-educated migrants from rural areas, and women and children. By and large, British radicals found most consistent support amongst the skilled but beleaguered craftsmen in such trades as shoemaking and tailoring. In 1838 a London cabinet-maker named William Lovett and the master-tailor Francis Place drew up the 'People's Charter', whose six points included universal male suffrage, secret ballot and annual elections. At the height of the 'Chartist' agitation, between 1838 and 1842, huge public meetings gathered wide working-class support in cities such as London, Birmingham, Glasgow, Leeds and Manchester. Two petitions presented to Parliament in 1839 and 1842 gathered, respectively, 1.3 and 3.3 million signatures. In 1842 the political agitation was accompanied by the 'Plug Plot', in which workers removed the plugs from boilers to extinguish the fires powering the machinery. Yet Chartism only attracted mass support in times of economic slump; its leadership gave out ambiguous support to strike action and was confused over the use of revolutionary violence. It petered out in 1848.

More successful was a middle-class campaign to repeal the Corn Laws. Led by radical liberal proponents of free trade such as John Bright and Richard Cobden, the Anti-Corn Law League, founded in 1838, launched an assault on protectionism, which was blamed for high food prices. Besides the practical goal of encouraging social stability through cheaper bread, the campaign was a means of undermining the conservative order: because landowners benefited most from the tariffs on grain imports, the liberals could denounce the Corn Laws as a rampart of aristocratic privilege. When Chartist activity subsided from 1842, the campaign received more popular support. The Corn Laws were finally repealed in 1846, but this was less as a result of the extra-parliamentary pressure than of changes within the Conservative party. It split between those who sought to defend the landed interest through tariff protection and those who were convinced of the benefits of free trade, including the Prime Minister, Robert Peel, who led the parliamentary charge against the laws.

German apprentices and journeymen who migrated to cities such as London, Paris or Brussels in search of work were exposed to socialist ideas, and some of these artisans joined Marx's and Engels's Communist League, for which *The Communist Manifesto* was written. Most working-class associations were, however, either educational or were mutual aid societies. The former, the *Bildungsvereine*, mushroomed in the 1840s as the authorities grew more alarmed at the extent of social problems. They were usually sponsored by liberal businessmen and officials, who sought to promote workers' welfare by subjecting them to edifying lectures and readings. Members included not only artisans (few of the poorest workers joined these societies), but also professionals and employers, who expected to run them; as one businessman in the Rhineland put it, 'The proletarians should have our trust . . . but not a say in how things are run.'[32]

Inevitably, discussion of workers' welfare turned to the 'social question' and to politics. In 1847 the Berlin Handicraftmen's Association boasted some three thousand members and was supported by employers, but the radical Stefan Born claimed that it had quietly developed into 'a training ground for up and coming revolutionaries'.[33] In practice, however, radical ideas – republican or socialist – would not be widely disseminated amongst workers in Germany until the 1848 Revolution and after. Most worker protests before then were apolitical and economically driven. The most dramatic of these movements before 1848 was the Silesian weavers' uprising of 1844. Driven to despair by a crisis in the linen industry, they besieged the homes of the merchants and demanded compensation for their suffering from the merchants in the form of money or food. These demands were accompanied by 'cat's music' (noisy, cacophonous, 'rough' music), a traditional expression of social protest. The weavers do not appear to have been motivated by any wider sense of class identity, nor did their demands aim at any radical reorganisation of society. In many parts of the Habsburg monarchy, workers were divided by language: the workers in the third largest Czech industrial centre, Liberec (Reichenberg), were German, while Czech workers themselves tended to be first-generation migrants from the countryside, where they retained roots and an attachment to the land. Established workers in the factories frequently resented those in the cottage industries who undercut wages. In May–June 1843 they were the target of striking Brno factory workers. Viennese workers were described by Friedrich Engels as 'disarmed, disorganized, hardly emerging from the intellectual bondage of the old regime', without knowledge but with a 'mere instinct of their social position'.[34]

In France, however, working-class protest reached something of a watershed after the 1830 Revolution. The role of skilled workers in the Parisian insurrection that July – and the praise which they received from middle-class liberals for their bravery and patriotism – encouraged them to press their demands. These included a ban on factories and machinery and a demand for higher wages and a shorter working day. The response of the authorities was blunt: the Prefect of Police warned the workers that further demonstrations would be treated as breaches of public order. Workers' sense of betrayal by the new regime heavily influenced the precocious growth of the French labour movement. The Lyon silk-weavers (*canuts*), who were the best-organised of all French workers, added grist to the mill. Their insurrection of 1834 came as the government put their strike leaders on trial and just after parliament had passed a law banning large workers' organisations and political clubs. What began as an economic dispute arising from distress in the silk industry therefore became politicised. It was not socialists, but republicans in the form of the *Société des droits de l'homme* who made some progress towards politicising the strike. Yet in order to get artisan support, middle-class radicals had to back their demands for the 'right of association'. A nascent sense of working-class consciousness fused with older attitudes based on the *compagnonnages* and mutual aid societies. In the early 1830s the emphasis on organisation rapidly developed into the notion that 'association' meant not only individual trade unions but also working-class unity. As the *Echo de la fabrique*, the newspaper of the Lyon weavers, expressed it colourfully: 'if all the fraternities would . . . join hands to sustain each other', they would 'bring into being the bonds of the confraternity of proletarians'.[35] This sense of working-class solidarity and the relationship of the workers' movement with middle-class republicans would be severely tested in 1848.

6 Europe Overseas

It has been suggested – tentatively – that one of the most important consequences of the absence of a *general* European war between 1815 and 1914 was that it allowed European powers to divert their resources overseas, to subjugate non-European peoples under their imperial sway.[1] Yet the greatest orgy of European global expansion occurred in the later nineteenth century, when international relations were strained and when one might have expected the powers to focus desperately on European affairs. Meanwhile, the age when there was no war at all between the great European powers, 1815–54, witnessed nothing so dramatic as the 'scramble for Africa' which opened in the 1880s. In fact, in the first half of the nineteenth century the state which experienced the most dramatic territorial enlargement was Russia, which by 1850 was approaching the Manchurian frontier. Otherwise, while France and Britain certainly expanded their empires, the new conquests were undertaken in a very piecemeal fashion and sometimes even reluctantly. Moreover, two other imperial powers – Spain and Portugal – seemed to be in terminal decline.

In 1789 the European powers with great overseas empires were the western maritime states – Britain, France, the United Provinces, Spain and Portugal. Although it had lost the American colonies in 1783, Britain still held sway over Canada, a number of Caribbean islands (including Jamaica), large parts of India, a few other scattered possessions in Asia, New South Wales in Australia, and small parts of Africa, such as Sierra Leone. In North America, French influence, expelled from Canada by the British in 1763, still balanced on a toehold on the cod-fishing islands of Saint-Pierre and Miquelon off Newfoundland, but France's most important North-American possessions were in the Caribbean, namely the islands of Martinique, Guadeloupe and Saint-Domingue. On the South-American coast, France claimed the steaming, malaria-ridden Guiana, which proved almost impossible to colonise and became a penal colony (the 'dry guillotine' of the French Revolution). In Africa, it held an important trading post in Senegal, in the Indian Ocean the islands of La Réunion (then called the Île Bourbon), Mauritius and the Seychelles, as well as a few trading posts (*comptoirs*) in India. The Dutch empire included the Cape Colony, Ceylon (modern-day Sri Lanka) and Indonesia. Portuguese settlements clung on tenaciously in Mozambique, as did trading posts and fortresses along the Angolan coast (which fed the demand in Brazil for African slaves), and the islands of Goa (off the west coast of India), Macau (off China) and Timor in the south Pacific. The most valuable Portuguese colony was Brazil. The Spanish overseas empire was territorially the most impressive, sweeping through the rest of South America and much of Central America, including Mexico. Spain also planted Caribbean colonies, including Santo Domingo (sharing the same island with Saint-Domingue), Puerto Rico and Cuba; Louisiana in North America (acquired from the French in 1763); the Philippines and other Pacific islands (including the Marianas and the Carolines) and *presidios* (trading posts) in Africa.

Yet the French, Dutch, Spanish and Portuguese empires were decaying in the later eighteenth century and this was hastened by the French Revolutionary and Napoleonic Wars. France was deprived of the jewel in its imperial crown with the slave revolt in Saint-Domingue, led by Toussaint L'Ouverture, which began in August 1791. It led to the abolition of slavery in the French colonies on 4 February 1794, and, when Napoleon Bonaparte tried to restore it in 1802, a successful war of independence from which the republic of Haiti emerged in 1804. The French had also reacquired Louisiana off the Spanish in 1801, but for strategic reasons the First Consul opted to sell the vast territory to the United States two years later, a decision which, along with the loss of Saint-Domingue, represented the French abandonment of imperial ambitions in the Americas. Napoleon was more interested in bolstering French fortunes in Asia, but these plans came to nothing. Challenging the British grip on India was one of a number of reasons for his invasion of Egypt in 1798, where the French clung on until 1801, ravaged by plague and harried by British and Turkish forces. At the end of the Napoleonic Wars, the allies stripped France of all her overseas colonies. While Martinique, Guadeloupe, Guiana, Saint-Pierre and Miquelon, La Réunion, Gorée, Senegal and the trading posts in India (including Pondichéry) were restored to France, the first French overseas empire was a stripped carcass compared with its mid-eighteenth-century prime. The Dutch empire also appeared to be withering, losing the Cape Colony and Ceylon to the British, who emerged from the Napoleonic Wars as the great global power. They also managed to enhance their position in India in a series of wars against Indian rulers. The Muslim 'Tiger of Mysore', Tipu Sultan, was killed in 1799 when his citadel of Seringapatam was stormed by the British. A war against the Hindu Marathas, which finished in 1805 (and was waged by the East India Company without British government sanction), left the British on the cusp of imperial domination of the subcontinent.

The most dramatic consequence of the Napoleonic Wars, however, was the collapse of Portuguese and Spanish power in South America. At Trafalgar in 1805 the British had shattered Spanish sea power, and the Peninsular War of 1808–14 absorbed all Spanish energies. The war in

Europe consequently gave South American patriots the space in which to organise struggles for independence. The South-American wars first arose from resistance against French efforts to secure the loyalty of the Spanish colonies for Joseph Bonaparte, whom the French Emperor had placed on the Spanish throne. Fighting began in 1809–10 in Rio de la Plata (Argentina) and in Venezuela (which declared independence in 1811 and where the revolt was led by Simón Bolívar). In Buenos Aires, the colonists set up a junta in 1810 to rule Rio de la Plata, while another junta seized power in Caracas in Venezuela. These provisional governments declared that they were ruling in the name of King Ferdinand, but in practice it showed the colonists that they could govern themselves. The Constitution of 1812 had claimed to speak for Spaniards on both sides of the Atlantic, yet the Cortes, worried that it would be swamped by colonial deputies, limited South-American rights to parliamentary representation. Consequently, the South-American juntas rejected Spanish authority. Colombia joined the fray by declaring independence in 1813, followed by Uruguay (1814), Chile and Argentina (formally in 1816), Mexico (1820), Peru and Panama (1821) and Bolivia (1825). The war was bloody, brutal and prolonged, but by 1824, exhausted by the conflict, drained by domestic instability and diplomatically isolated, Spain had given up the fight. It took until 1836 for the Spanish government to swallow its pride and recognise Mexico, and it was another three decades after that before it offered the same courtesy to the other South-American states. The Portuguese, meanwhile, relinquished Brazil. After the French invasion of Portugal in 1807, the royal family fled to Rio de Janeiro. The immediate constitutional result was that in 1815 Brazil was granted the status of a kingdom so that it would have a purely dynastic link with the mother country. This did not prevent an independence movement from taking shape, and in 1817 an insurrection was crushed, only for a rebellion to explode once more in 1821. The exiled Portuguese King and Regent of Brazil, Don Pedro, was, unlike Ferdinand of Spain, willing to make constitutional concessions to the Brazilian liberals in order to maintain his own position. The liberal regime which had seized power in Portugal in Pedro's name in 1821, however, had no desire to relinquish control over the valuable colonial trade and sought to reimpose direct rule from Lisbon. Don Pedro, caught between Brazilian and Portuguese liberals, reacted by declaring Brazilian independence himself, rather than face overthrow at the hands of either. With British approval, Brazilian representatives proclaimed Don Pedro constitutional emperor of their new state.

By the end of the first quarter of the nineteenth century, it appeared as if European overseas imperialism was waning rather than waxing, with only the British overseas empire actually experiencing any growth. In fact, while some European powers certainly acquired new overseas territories, no European power in the four middle decades of the nineteenth century pursued an aggressively consistent policy of overseas expansion. The Spanish, Dutch and Portuguese wanted to cling on to what they still had and simply did not have the power to make new conquests, though Spanish and Portuguese governments occasionally tried to bolster their prestige with the odd imperial venture. After 1815 most French ministers had little interest in empire, not least because overseas expansion might bring down British hostility. The Bourbon regime justified the invasion of Algeria with reference to a diplomatic dispute which began in 1827 when the *dey* of Algiers insulted the French consul (he did, in fact, whack the Frenchman with his fly swatter), during an argument over unpaid French debts. Relations deteriorated from there, but the expedition against Algiers in June 1830 was really a desperate attempt to breathe some prestige into Charles X's monarchy, which was tottering on its last political legs. The succeeding July Monarchy had little interest in an empire because it had no desire to antagonise Britain. Yet once the French were established on the coastal rind of Algeria, it was hard to let go. The expedition had proved to be popular with public opinion, which celebrated a show of strength as if it were some consolation for the defeat in 1815. It would have taken a very courageous – and secure – regime to withdraw from North Africa. In maintaining the occupation, however, the July Monarchy entrusted the Algerian colonies to the army, which inadvertently set a pattern which would shape subsequent French expansion. Geographically far removed from the direct authority of the government, military officers acted on their own initiative. Without official authorisation, these commanders often expanded French commitments, either for strategic reasons or to satisfy their personal ambition. The governor-general of Algeria from 1835–41, Marshal Bertrand Clauzel, was ordered to restrict colonisation to the immediate areas surrounding the coastal ports. He ignored this directive and instead used the army to seize several inland towns. He drained marshes south of Algiers and established fortified farms which would be occupied by Europeans, whose numbers reached 37,000 by 1841. In the war against Abd el-Khader, who waged a Muslim holy war (*jihad*) against the French, Clauzel's successor, Marshal Thomas-Robert Bugeaud, pursued a scorched-earth policy to break Algerian resistance. El-Khader fought on until 1847, but by the time he surrendered, Bugeaud had extended French control over wider areas of the country. So, although the July Monarchy was, officially, uninterested in acquiring new territory in Algeria, the actions of its military commanders presented the French government with just that. To pre-empt Bugeaud, who dreamed of establishing a military colony of ex-soldiers-turned-farmers, the government enabled civilian colonists – French, Spanish, Italian, Maltese – to take over and farm land in Algeria, where 100,000 Europeans had settled by 1845.

Reluctant as the July Monarchy was to establish large colonies, it was interested in economic growth, and this did not preclude some overseas acquisitions. In 1842 François Guizot declared to parliament:

> What is appropriate for France, what is indispensable, is to possess sure and strong maritime stations at points on the globe which are destined to become great centres of commerce, to serve as a support for our commerce, where the fleet can obtain provisions and find a safe harbour.[2]

This policy of setting up stations (*points d'appui*) to support French commerce and naval operations justified the French occupation of Gabon in 1839; the Indian Ocean islands of Nossy-Bé and Mayotte in 1840–1; the Marquesas and Tahiti in the Pacific in 1842, and Grand Bassam and Assinie on the Ivory Coast in 1842–3. Even so, these acquisitions were handed to France as *faits accomplis* by marauding French officers, rather than as part of a predesigned policy. Guizot's policy of *points d'appui* therefore gave a rationale for conquests which had already taken place on individual initiative. The main concern of both Louis-Philippe and Guizot was to stay on good relations with the other European powers. They opposed the colonisation of Madagascar and any occupation of the coast of Indochina.

Napoleon III actually sought to cut back the pace of European colonisation in Algeria. He told the British ambassador in 1858 that he regretted that France had colonies: 'it is so difficult to maintain them in a prosperous state . . . they are a burden to the Mother Country'.[3] He tried to protect Muslim rights (particularly their property) against the rapacity of the French military, but elsewhere in Africa the now-familiar pattern re-emerged, with the Paris government being led by the impulses of its officers on the ground. This was most dramatic in West Africa. While Napoleon III was more concerned with re-establishing France as a great *European* power, the French governor in Senegal from 1854 to 1865, Louis Faidherbe, had visions of a great French empire carved out of Africa, linking up with Algeria. A mere captain, who was told at his appointment that this was not a new 'warlike era', used his meagre 1.5-million-franc budget to extend the French military presence (with the help of Senegalese troops), building forts and founding Dakar in 1857.

The French conquest of Indochina started, it is true, as a search for a viable naval base in south-east Asia. By the 1850s, however, after several setbacks, this had come to nothing, although France won a concession from the Chinese in Shanghai in 1850. Instead, overenthusiastic missionaries drew the French government into the region. French Catholics had won papal recognition as the leading missionaries when they were given control of six vicariates in China and Indochina. In 1848 the Annamese emperor, Tu Duc, banned all missionaries from Vietnam, and two French priests were executed in the early 1850s. The French badly mishandled the diplomatic negotiations to resolve the crisis and a sustained Catholic campaign persuaded Napoleon III to act in 1857. French forces arrived in 1858, and by 1862 had forced the cession of Saigon and three provinces of Cochinchina. While this certainly gave the French the port they had long craved in south-east Asia, most of Napoleon III's ministers were not enamoured with the idea of bearing the costs of a new colony. In 1864 they almost gave it up in return for an indemnity from Tu Duc. In 1867, however, the French commander in Saigon, Admiral La Grandière, seized the remaining three provinces of Cochinchina (the southern part of Vietnam, which also included Annam and Tonkin). This was against explicit orders from Paris 'to avoid anything which might upset the court of Hué [the ancient capital of Vietnam]'.[4] France was also drawn into Cambodia in the 1860s when a civil war between rival claimants to the throne brought the danger of British intervention. La Grandière, again against direct orders not to intervene (which, to be fair, he only received a week after he had made his move), reacted by establishing a protectorate over Cambodia. French imperialism therefore made dramatic gains in the half-century after 1815, but what Napoleon III told parliament in 1863 could apply to this entire phase of French expansion: 'our overseas expeditions do not represent the execution of any preconceived plan; they have been driven by force of circumstance'.[5]

Like France, Britain made important territorial acquisitions in the half-century after the Napoleonic Wars, but, like the French government, it often did so haphazardly. The experience of losing the 13 American colonies left some Britons sceptical about the benefits of an empire which was expensive to defend and which returned few benefits which could not, in fact, be reaped from free trade. Certainly, mid-nineteenth-century radical liberals such as John Bright and Richard Cobden objected to imperialism on these grounds.[6] While vocal and influential on the left of liberal opinion, however, these radicals were on the fringes of power, not at the heart of government. Official opinion, while reluctant to incur state expenditure and energy in an active effort to make new territorial acquisitions, was willing to use force and, if necessary, assume direct political control if deemed vital for British economic and strategic interests. As Palmerston put it with characteristic bluntness in 1860: 'trade ought not to be enforced by cannon balls, but on the other hand trade cannot flourish without security, and that security may often be unattainable without the exhibition of physical force'.[7] Meanwhile, most free-traders did not share Cobden's moral scruples and believed that commerce inevitably meant an exercise of influence in what was an unequal economic relationship. In 1846 one free-trader commented that, by Britain's very dominance of world markets, 'foreign nations would become valuable Colonies to us, without imposing on us the responsibility of governing them'.[8] Mid-century British imperialists preferred to extend and protect British interests in the world without the expenses of formal empire, but that did not mean that Britain was anti-imperialist. Instead, its influence over non-European peoples grew in subtler but no less effective ways to give it an 'informal' empire, extending British power more widely than its actual colonial possessions would suggest.

The British insistence on free trade was not, of course, driven by the rhapsodising ideals of a Cobden ('drawing men together, thrusting aside the antagonism of race, and creed, and language, and uniting us in the bonds of eternal peace'[9]), but for more pragmatic reasons. In 1848 Marx (and later Lenin) would explain it in terms of capitalism: industrialisation required a constantly expanding market, which sent the bourgeoisie scurrying across the globe, prising open and then defending commercial opportunities. That Britain's 'informal empire' based on free trade was a consequence of industrial development is a reasonable assumption, though perhaps not in the way Marx suggested. It is certainly true that Britain sold manufactured goods in return for raw materials and food (in the mid-1850s, 85 per cent of the volume of British exports was in manufactured products, while 61 per cent of imports was in raw materials). The cotton mills required a mass market, which could be met overseas. Overseas investment offered lucrative returns on the profits accumulated from industry and commerce. There was, therefore, a link between Britain's economic growth and British imperialism. Yet there was also an important domestic dimension to the conversion of the state to free trade – represented most dramatically by the abolition of the Corn Laws in 1846 and of the Navigation Acts in 1849. Britain was increasingly dependent upon grain imports to feed its people, just as the social dislocation caused by industrialisation threatened to rip apart the existing fabric of the social and political order. The government's anxieties over domestic problems led it to insist on free trade and to protect commercial routes and markets if necessary.[10]

It did not, however, want to get involved in costly colonial disputes if they could be avoided. The most that mid-century British governments wanted to do was to ensure that all trade – British or otherwise – was subject to the same rules, with no special privileges: a 'fair field and no favour'.[11] British treaties with Argentina in 1825, with the Ottoman Empire in 1838 and with Persia in 1841 aimed at securing open markets for all commerce, but this was because Britain could afford to do this: its commercial and industrial dominance left its competitors standing anyway.[12] Its relationship with overseas trading partners would not be equal; the Foreign Secretary, Canning, celebrated South-American independence with a startlingly frank expression of what historians have since called the 'imperialism of free trade': 'Spanish America is free, and if we do not mismanage our affairs badly, she is English.'[13]

British hegemony had at least one positive effect: it meant enforcing the ban on the slave trade, decreed in the Congress of Vienna's Final

Act, and, eventually, efforts to abolish slavery itself. The British slave trade had been abolished in 1807, though slaves in the empire were not emancipated until 1833. In 1815 Britain provided a naval force – the West African squadron – which would not only enforce the international law against the commerce in human beings, but would also coerce African rulers into accepting trade agreements. This was the 'imperialism of free trade' working together with anti-slavery. Yet others stepped in when the British moved out: Americans, French, Spanish and Portuguese could not resist the high profits which accrued from the transatlantic slave trade. The restored Bourbon rulers in France promised that slavery would be abolished in the French colonies, but it merely made the trade in slaves illegal in 1818. As no criminal penalties were applied, between 1815 and 1831 the plantation owners in the remaining French Caribbean colonies still managed to enslave a further 125,000 Africans who had been forced across the Atlantic. Slavery was not definitively outlawed in the French empire until 1848. Portugal officially abolished its slave trade in 1836 as it could not withstand British pressure to do so: the loss of a large part of its fleet to Brazil meant that it could not protect its own slavers. Yet that also meant that it could not enforce its own ban. Slave ships continued to sail from Mozambique and Angola, which drove the British government in 1839 to order the Royal Navy to stop and search Portuguese vessels, inflaming Portuguese opinion. In the 1830s and 1840s the slave trade in the Atlantic and Indian Oceans *grew*, as slavers continued to slip past the Royal Navy. While it declined thereafter, the commerce proved to be horrendously persistent. Even when slavery was abolished – in the Portuguese empire in 1875 and in Brazil in 1884 – the traffic continued. Lisbon was either unable or unwilling to enforce the abolition and by 1908 there were still some forty thousand enslaved 'labourers' on the islands of São Tomé and Príncipe, and probably about twenty thousand slaves in Angola in the early 1910s. The Portuguese Republic, established in 1910, eventually stamped out slavery.

British economic entanglements with the rest of the world almost inevitably brought political involvement in local affairs – and then formal political control – for several reasons. Clashes with local authorities over trading conditions might lead to military action. Misunderstandings born of cultural differences created friction between the British and local people, leading to conflict and then, once more, to formal British intervention. A desire to ensure the security of trading posts, routes and existing colonies led officials to act, sometimes without government approval, to extend the area under British control. The most famous instance of the British enforcement of free trade was in the Sino-British wars between 1839 and 1860. The East India Company had, since the eighteenth century, traded with China for its tea, for which the British public had by now acquired its insatiable taste. Yet while there was little Chinese desire for British cotton, there was an alarming surge in demand for opium, which was grown in India and then exported to China, chiefly through licensees of the East India Company. These licensees dealt with the 'hong' merchants, the only Chinese people allowed to trade with foreigners, in Canton, the only Chinese port open to foreign commerce. Yet popular demand for opium meant that an illegal trade in the drug spread and Chinese efforts to restrict British traders to Canton and to destroy cargoes of opium led to the first Opium War of 1839–42. This ended with the Treaty of Nanking, whereby five ports were opened to Britain, which also received Hong Kong. A second conflict, the Arrow War of 1856–8, was caused when the Chinese executed a French missionary and seized a British-flagged vessel, the *Arrow*. Franco-British forces occupied Canton in 1857, which led to the Treaty of Tientsin the following year, in which six further ports were opened to Europeans. A further clash led to a Franco-British occupation of Beijing in 1860, after which the British received Kowloon and partitioned the island of Chusan with the French. The wars in China were a classic case of 'creeping colonialism', in which the British, initially pursuing the principle of free trade (it did not seem to matter that the commerce was in a highly addictive drug), finished by expanding their formal empire. Similarly, the British invasions of Burma and annexations of territory there in 1824–6 and 1852 aimed at opening markets.

Cultural clashes might also lead to firmer British control. Since 1784, British-dominated India had been ruled by the East India Company and the British cabinet together, through a joint Board of Control, but this meant that the British government did not enjoy complete, direct authority over Indian affairs. This changed after 1857, when Indian soldiers rebelled in the great 'Mutiny'. The root cause of the uprising was an overzealous effort by British officials and missionaries to 'regenerate' Indian society in the 1830s and 1840s, a process which had begun under the governor-general, William Bentinck (1828–35), egged on by British radical reformers and evangelical Christians. In 1829 he formally banned ('for the good of mankind') the Hindu practices of *sati* (the self-sacrifice of Hindu widows by throwing themselves on to the funeral pyres of their husbands) and *thugi* (ritual killing in the name of the goddess Kali). While some Indians regarded the British measures as decent in principle, it also marked a departure from company policy, which had previously tried to avoid provocative meddling with local customs. An act of 1833 ended the East India Company's monopoly of trade in India, allowing the subcontinent to feel the full weight of British immigration and enterprise, which challenged Indian customs. The British annexation in 1856 of Oudh (which had been protected by treaty) brought Indian anger closer to boiling-point – not least because many of the Indian *sepoys* in the company's Bengal Army were from Oudh. Together, these developments seemed to point to a wider policy of

Christianising and Europeanising India. The pot bubbled over in 1857, when Indian soldiers were introduced to the new Enfield rifle, whose cartridges were encased in animal fat. Hindus, for whom cow fat was anathema, and Muslims, who were banned from tasting pork, were appalled. The resulting mutiny, which developed into a full-scale British–Indian conflict, lasted for 14 months and involved horrendous atrocities by both sides. The most important consequence – apart from a legacy of hatred and suspicion – was the India Act of 1858. This transferred all authority over India from the East India Company to the British crown. Missionaries were urged to be more sensitive to Indian customs, but the result of more than two decades of reforming zeal had been the assertion of direct government rule from London.

The protection of existing possessions, trading posts and commercial routes also accounts for British territorial expansion in this period. The British anticipated a future Russian invasion of India from the north because Russian influence had expanded in Persia from the late 1820s. They tried to install the exiled Shah Shuja as a puppet ruler of Afghanistan in order to pre-empt any Russian drive towards India's north-western frontier. A 16,000-strong army was sent into Afghanistan in 1838, but the expedition was a catastrophe: harried by guerrillas and local uprisings, the British tried to pull out in the winter of 1841–2; only one survivor reached the safety of the British garrison at Jallalabad. Yet the upshot of the war was that it drove the British to consolidate their hold on India itself, annexing first Sind (in 1843) and then the Punjab (in 1849) on the grounds that British commercial and strategic interests demanded it. The British East India Company also intervened and assumed control of Singapore (1819) and Malacca (1822) in Malaya when local power struggles endangered the flow of trade. In 1846 the island of Labuan off Borneo was seized to make shipping routes safer, while New Zealand (1840) and Natal (1848) were annexed to prevent tensions between European settlers, merchants and the local inhabitants from getting out of control. In West Africa, a similar, haphazard extension of British control took place in response to local circumstances. The hinterlands of older colonies such as Sierra Leone, on the Gold Coast, and the settlement in Lagos (formally annexed in 1851) were gradually encroached upon as British authorities tried to ensure the security of the colonies and of British trade in the interior. The British, therefore, did not resist the temptation (or, as imperialists no doubt saw it, the need) to annex new territories to their sprawling empire. Yet it was an uneven, haphazard growth, following a policy which preferred, in the classic formula suggested by John Gallagher and Ronald Robinson, 'trade with informal control if possible; trade with rule where necessary'.[14] Yet there were continuities between the haphazard European territorial expansion of the first half of the century and the great carve-up of the non-European world in later decades.

7 Europe between Revolutions, 1830–1848

The repressive response to the revolutionary violence of the early 1820s widened the schism between state and civil society in Europe. In the late 1820s liberal and radical grumbling was suddenly given new force by an economic crisis. Poor harvests – which ran for as long as five years between 1827 and 1832 – made food supplies scarce and prices high. There was also a depression in manufacturing, with a financial crash in Britain – the world's banker – in 1826, reducing credit and increasing bankruptcies. The link between the economic crisis and the political revolutions of the 1830s was not necessarily direct. The liberals were as alarmed by the potential for social upheaval as their conservative opponents and the crisis convinced them of the need for social stability.[1] Yet if they were reluctant to stir up popular opposition to the conservative order, it was often the economic protests of the peasantry and the artisans which gave them the decisive, revolutionary push.

The Revolutions of the 1830s

The political struggle between conservatives and liberals surged onwards in the later 1820s. In France, the liberal opposition had almost been whitewashed out by 1824, when it had only a tiny rump of 19 in the Chamber of Deputies. Yet the ill-advised, provocative policies pursued by the ultras under Charles X spurred a public reaction in which, in the later 1820s, the liberal opposition began to enjoy a revival. In 1827 François Guizot founded *Aide-toi le ciel t'aidera* (heaven helps those who help themselves), an organisation which supported liberal candidates and which helped liberal supporters who had been fraudulently denied the right to vote to get back on to the electoral rolls.[2] Liberals won 50 out of 75 by-elections in 1828 and 1829 and now dominated the Chamber. Charles X steeled himself for a confrontation by appointing his old ultra-royalist friend, Prince Jules de Polignac, to lead a government against the parliamentary majority in August 1829.

Polignac had no hope of obtaining a parliamentary majority, so the King tried to override it by dismissing parliament and calling fresh elections which, in June and July 1830, were even worse for the government. On 25 July the slide to revolution began when Charles X responded by issuing the 'Four Ordinances', or emergency decrees, which dissolved parliament again, ordered new elections, cut the electorate from 100,000 to 25,000 and established strict censorship. When these were published the following day, printshop workers, already groaning under the economic crisis, demonstrated in the streets. Liberals finally took leadership of the gathering riot, which turned into a revolt against the regime on 28 July. In two days of fighting around barricades, the crowds – mostly skilled artisans – stormed the Tuileries Palace and the government collapsed. Charles X abdicated and fled into exile. The liberals who took political leadership of the 1830 Revolution wanted neither a republic, which they associated with the Terror, nor Napoleon II, the emperor's son living in captivity in Vienna, for whom the artisans had shouted. They wanted stability and believed that the Charter of 1814, moderately reformed, would offer it. So they pushed aside popular demands and, on 9 August, Louis-Philippe, the duc d'Orléans, scion of the junior, rival line of the Bourbon dynasty, was chosen as 'King of the French'.

The French revolution of 1830 was the spark which nearly set ablaze the entire conservative edifice in Europe. One of the first places to be affected was Belgium. Its union with the Netherlands in 1815 had shown early promise. After the post-war economic crisis, foreign visitors were struck by Belgium's prosperity and few Belgians questioned the union at first. None the less, fiscal, religious and linguistic issues lurked ominously below the surface calm. Belgians believed that they inherited more than their fair share of the Dutch state debt and manufacturers resented the policy of low tariffs. Conservative Belgian Catholics remained fearful of Dutch Protestant influence, particularly in education and especially when the Dutch King William, following the advice of both Belgian liberals and Dutch Protestants, closed down Belgian Catholic schools in 1825. The linguistic issue was particularly prickly for the French-speaking Belgian middle classes, who had to learn Dutch if they wanted to access positions in the state and the liberal professions. In 1829, Catholics and liberals buried their differences and co-operated in a petitioning campaign for freedom of the press and freedom of education, which by February 1830 had gathered over three hundred and fifty thousand signatures (or marks from illiterate peasants). Though the King allowed Catholic schools to function once again in May 1830, he dismissed the petitions and enforced new press restrictions. The agitation coincided with the economic slump, which particularly hurt industrialising Belgium with high unemployment, factory closures, slumps in wages and high food prices.

Popular anger was sharpened when a tax on the milling of grain was levied to pay for King William's birthday celebrations. Food riots were given political direction on 25–6 August when a largely middle-class protest outside the Théâtre de la Monnaie in Brussels was joined by workers, and order collapsed in the city. Other Belgian towns joined the revolution and the liberals established a provisional government, the Commission of Security. The Dutch counter-attack with 6000 troops on 23 September was beaten back after four days of street fighting. Concessions made by the Estates-General were now too little to placate the Belgians, who formally declared independence on 4 October. Elections were announced for a National Congress and within a month Antwerp, though not the citadel, had fallen.

The great powers divided over a Dutch appeal to enforce the Vienna settlement by crushing the Belgian revolution. Tsar Nicholas I offered a quarter of a million troops for the purpose, but by the end of the year he was confronted with a revolutionary uprising in Poland. The great powers therefore brokered a cease-fire between the Belgians and the Dutch at a conference in London in November and recognised Belgian independence in December. They then approved the Belgian constitution and chose Leopold of Saxe-Coburg as King. The Dutch accepted the settlement early in 1831, but the Belgians defied the great powers because the territorial arrangement denied them the left bank of the Scheldt estuary, Luxembourg and Maastricht. An attempt by the London Conference to compromise at the expense of the Netherlands enraged Dutch public opinion and, in August 1831, the Dutch invaded Belgium, which was saved only by French and British intervention. In 1839 the powers, this time including the Dutch, recognised Belgian neutrality, a treaty which would have great import for the future.

The July Revolution in France also aroused great excitement in Switzerland, where liberals in the 'Regeneration' movement had begun to challenge the dominance of the cantons by the aristocratic patricians. While appealing to Swiss traditions of popular sovereignty, the liberals, influenced by the writings of Benjamin Constant, argued that direct democracy was dangerous; the people should be represented in assemblies. News of the revolution in France gave energy to the reform movement in the press, political clubs and public meetings. Faced with a groundswell of popular demonstrations, the cantonal governments yielded to the liberal demands. Each canton drafted a new constitution: most restricted the suffrage to men of property or education, who would elect a Grand Council to represent the people. Yet all Swiss citizens were guaranteed the basic freedoms of conscience, assembly and opinion. The failure of the liberals to resolve the economic crisis, however, stirred radical, democratic opposition, which turned violent in Neuchâtel, Basle and Schwyz. Conservatives smirked as the crisis ensnared the liberals and the country split between cantons dominated by the former and those won by the latter.

In Portugal, the revolution in France galvanised the liberal supporters of Don Pedro, who had been forced to flee to Brazil by his younger brother, the absolutist Don Miguel. Early in 1832, having relinquished the Brazilian throne to his son, Pedro landed in the Azores, where he restored the Portuguese Charter of 1826. The British also helped him raise a small force which landed at Porto in the summer of 1832. They determinedly resisted a 13-month siege by Miguel's forces, and support for the usurper began to evaporate. A further invasion by Pedro's supporters in the Algarve led Miguel to abandon Lisbon. In April 1834, Pedro signed an alliance with France, Britain and Spain which secured British money and naval assistance. 'Miguelism' was destroyed and Portugal became a constitutional monarchy.

France, Belgium, Switzerland, Portugal and, as we shall see, some German states witnessed the only successful revolutions in Europe in the 1830s. Elsewhere, the conservative order held, its bloodiest repression occurring in Poland. The Polish insurrection of 1830–1 was caused, above all, by the intransigence of Tsar Nicholas I, who succeeded in creating a yawning chasm between the Crown and the patriotic Polish nobility. Nicholas considered the constitutional liberties of the Congress Kingdom to be a dangerous example for the rest of the Russian empire. In 1828 the leaders of the Polish Patriotic Society were tried but acquitted of treason. Nicholas quashed the verdict and had the prisoners exiled to Siberia anyway. Rumbling discontent among younger army officers finally broke out in revolt in November 1830 when the Tsar mobilised the Polish army against the revolutions in France and Belgium. The insurrection was initially shunned by the liberal leadership, which still wanted to work within the Russian empire and to find a peaceful resolution. While a provisional government was formed in December, the liberal strategy was to negotiate constitutional concessions in return for ending the rebellion. Nicholas, aghast, refused outright to deal with people whom he saw as rebels. In defiance, the Polish parliament, the *Sejm*, deposed Nicholas as King of Poland.

Nicholas reacted in February 1831 by sending in a 120,000-strong army. While militarily Polish resistance was stubborn, politically their revolution fell apart. As the Russians advanced, so power in Warsaw fell successively to more and more radical wings of the Polish patriotic movement. The main issue was the conditions of the peasantry, particularly serfdom. The radicals wanted to harness popular enthusiasm for the revolt by freeing the serfs and emancipating the Jews. This split the revolution between conservative landowners and clergy on the one hand, and peasants and radicals on the other. Meanwhile, the Russians closed in on Warsaw, which fell at midnight on 7–8 September after a bitter struggle. The rebellion ended a 15-year period during which the Poles had enjoyed more political freedoms than at any time between 1795 and 1918. Besides the repression which followed (including the confiscation of nobles' land, penal servitude and Siberian exile for 80,000 Poles), the Poles lost the vestiges of statehood offered by the Congress Kingdom. The Polish army, the *Sejm* and the universities were abolished, while the 'Organic Statute' of February 1832 declared that Poland would be ruled by decree from St Petersburg.

In Italy, opposition had been aggravated by the reaction after the revolutions of the early 1820s. In Naples, most of the original Carbonari had fled, but the ranks of the subversive society were opened up to more popular elements, including peasants and artisans. Inspired by the French revolution of July 1830 and hopeful of receiving French aid, the Italian liberals rose up against their rulers in central Italy in February 1831 in Modena, Parma and the northern part of the Papal States, the Legations. They swept aside the authorities in these states, but they split between moderates and radicals, who disagreed over whether there should be a monarchy or a democratic republic. More importantly, the revolutionaries in the different cities refused to co-operate with each other; there was little sense of Italian nationalism at work, except among some of the radicals. The revolutionaries, therefore, failed to co-ordinate military resistance against the Austrians, who marched southwards in March, sweeping the revolutionaries aside. Yet the situation was still fragile in the Papal States, for as soon as the troops withdrew in July, the Pope was confronted by new disturbances. His secretary of state, Cardinal Bernetti, was forced to appeal for Austrian help once again in January 1832. This merely drew the Papal States deeper into Austria's orbit. Austrian troops held on to Bologna until 1838 and they would later occupy Ferrara. To add insult to injury, the great powers allowed the French to occupy Ancona until the Austrians withdrew from Bologna.

In Germany, the news of the 1830 Revolution in France set off a flurry of excitement. Revolutions in the small German states of Brunswick, Hesse-Cassel, Saxony and Hanover forced the rulers to grant basic rights to their subjects, along with constitutions. The radical *Burschenschaften*, which had been kept alive in the 1820s by the wives of the exiled or imprisoned leaders, were given a new lease of life. They organised new festivals, culminating at Hambach in the Palatinate in May 1832, where between twenty and thirty thousand people gathered in the largest mass meeting in Germany before 1848. Speakers were strident in their appeals for a democratic and united Germany. Women attended, but the invitation made it clear that they were meant only to 'adorn and enliven the gathering with [their] presence!'[3] The authorities were particularly worried by the evidence that the nationalist movement had broadened its appeal, since about a quarter of the participants were artisans and craftworkers. The governments of Baden and Bavaria mobilised army units nearby. The festival was followed by smaller imitations across Germany, but the liberals remained aloof from the radical nationalists. One liberal newspaper snarled that 'none of the popular representatives could be heard above the furious clamour of the demagogues'.[4] Liberals such as Ludolf Camphausen and David Hansemann preferred a parliamentary monarchy on the British or

Belgian models, with a restricted franchise, preferably achieved by reform rather than by revolution.

With the opposition divided, German governments struck back. The diet of the *Bund* passed the 'Six Articles', which restricted reporting on parliamentary debates, established a federal commission to keep watch on the proceedings of German parliaments, and empowered governments to reject parliamentary acts if they were 'incompatible with federal law'. The *Bund* also reiterated the Karlsbad decrees with the 'Ten Acts', which banned all political societies, meetings, speeches and insignia, increased surveillance of the universities, strengthened censorship and obliged all German states to exchange intelligence on subversive activities. By 1842, Prussia alone had imposed 39 death sentences and no fewer than 165 long prison sentences on members of the *Burschenschaften*. These measures may, in the short term, have silenced nationalist and liberal opposition, but it convinced many of the latter, hitherto attached to reform within the existing German states, that constitutional government could only be achieved within the framework of a united Germany, free of the restrictive *Bund*.

Metternich was the figure behind the reaction in both Germany and Italy, but the Habsburg monarchy itself was barely touched by the 1830 revolutions. There was some excitement in Prague and Vienna, but little which could seriously endanger the regime. Yet Metternich took no chances. He wanted (as he put it) to 'restore order' in France by sending in an Austrian army to crush the July revolution. The Austrian treasury was empty, however, and Emperor Francis and members of the royal family, including Archduke Charles who commented that ideas could not be conquered by bayonets, persuaded him that this was not possible. In 1833, Metternich met Tsar Nicholas I of Russia and Frederick William III of Prussia at Münchengrätz to reaffirm their mutual co-operation against revolution in Europe. At home, Metternich brushed off the suggestion that the best way to avoid revolution was by making concessions. Yet though Metternich sent Austrian troops to crush the Italian revolutions, this came at the price of having to consult the Hungarian diet, which gave a platform to the Magyar opposition.

In Britain, the repeal of the Test and Corporation Acts and Catholic emancipation in 1828–9 weakened the conservative grip of power, because the two measures split the Tories between reformists and ultras. The Whigs reinvigorated their commitment to parliamentary reform. When King George IV died in June 1830, general elections were held (as was customary). No one won an outright majority but, after decades in the wilderness, the Whigs came to power in November. By that time, revolutionary events in Europe had electrified the political atmosphere with the anticipation of reform. In the social distress of these years, popular radicalism revived, demanding universal male suffrage in enormous rallies in 1830 and 1831. The groundswell made Earl Grey's Whig government take notice. An acrimonious parliamentary battle over a reform bill led Grey in 1831 to ask King William IV to call fresh elections, which returned a strong pro-reform majority in the House of Commons. Yet the resistance of the House of Lords whipped up popular anger across the country. In Bristol, where the authorities lost control of the city, the bishop's palace was burned down (as most bishops in the Lords had voted against reform). When moderate, middle-class reformers began to take up arms, ostensibly to defend public order against such disturbances, a feeling grew that any further delay would lead to revolution. Yet still the Lords resisted and Grey resigned in May 1832. The Tories, however, were too divided to form an alternative ministry, opposition to the reform bill subsided and Grey, back in power, steered it through the Lords in June. The Whigs did not intend the 1832 Reform Act to be the first step towards democratisation; Grey explicitly ruled that out, although one in five adult males now had the vote in England (one in eight in Scotland) and this included workers in some cities. Nor did it represent the rise of the middle classes, although urban property-owners were enfranchised and urban areas benefited from a redistribution of seats. The landowners retained their influence in the county seats and still dominated parliament, whose composition of aristocracy and gentry remained almost unaffected.

Spain experienced a violent upheaval in the 1830s, but in a unique way: the struggle was not a liberal revolution against the conservative state, but rather a reactionary assault on a monarchy which was letting the liberals in by the back door. Ferdinand VII's reforms in the 1820s had alienated the Carlists. Yet when in 1830 the ailing King married the young María Cristina of Naples, who gave birth to a daughter, Isabella, the Carlists sought to ensure that Ferdinand's ultra-royalist brother Carlos, not Isabella, would succeed to the throne when the King died. María Cristina was no liberal, but she understood that her husband's erstwhile enemies would be her best allies against the Carlists when Ferdinand died. To prepare the ground, liberals were amnestied, the Royal Volunteers disbanded, and the army and administration purged of Carlists. After Ferdinand's death in September 1833, María Cristina became regent and she appointed a ministry of former *moderados*, who promulgated the Statute of 1834, which restored constitutional rule by providing a two-chamber Cortes, elected by a restricted, indirect suffrage, and left the Crown with significant powers, including an absolute veto.

On Ferdinand's death, guerrilla bands in the Carlist strongholds of Navarre, Catalonia and the Basque country rose up 'for the elimination of the liberal *canaille*'.[5] Led by local priests and gentry determined to defend Catholicism and provincial privileges against reform, their support was drawn mainly from the peasants of the mountain regions, who were deeply religious, conservative and hostile to urban ways. For this reason, Carlism had limited appeal; even the aristocracy, whose power was preserved in the new upper chamber anyway, were coming to see moderate liberalism as a creed better suited to an evolving society. The urban workers, middle classes, state officials and army officers remained loyal to María Cristina. Moreover, the liberals had diplomatic backing. The 1834 Quadruple Alliance with Portugal, France and Britain secured British naval and (critically) financial support, as well as supplies and forces of volunteers, including the French Foreign Legion. Carlism, therefore, had only a slim chance of victory; that it survived for so long as a military danger rested on the inaccessibility of its hill-top strongholds, its leadership and its organisation. It had an excellent guerrilla leader in T. Zamalacárregui, who trained an army of up to thirty thousand men before he was killed in 1835. The Carlists virtually formed a separate state in northern Spain, with its own bureaucracy, a university and an officer training academy. Yet they rarely broke out of their northern strongholds – Carlism's high-water mark was a determined march which came within sight of Madrid in 1837. Yet Carlism held no prosperous farming region and no significant towns, and so to recruit and feed its army it had to conscript and requisition from a narrow base of half a million peasants, who responded with desertion. The Carlist War ended in 1840 after the radical liberal general, Baldomero Espartero, drove northwards in 1839, scorching the earth as he went.

The liberal victory established Spanish constitutional government, which would survive – though punctured with authoritarian and republican phases – until 1923. Liberals of all stripes had drawn together during the crisis, and the Constitution of 1837 extended the suffrage, enabling peasant smallholders to vote, though it fell far short of the Constitution of 1812. The defeat of Carlism did not kill off the ultra-royalist threat, as there were insurrectionary outbursts in subsequent decades. Equally ominously for Spanish politics, liberalism survived the onslaught because the army had remained loyal. Its commanders would demand a share in the political spoils.

The revolutions of the 1830s split Europe between liberal states with constitutions, among them Britain, France, Belgium, Portugal and Spain, and conservative states in Italy, the Habsburg empire, Russia and most of Germany. Yet while this represented a significant breach in the conservative order of 1815, it did not bring about the revolutionary cataclysm which some conservatives had feared. Metternich, on hearing of the July Revolution in Paris, wept, 'My entire life's work is destroyed.' But he need not have worried. The revolutionaries of the 1830s were liberals, committed to constitutional government and perhaps some social reform, but also as anxious as conservatives about the danger of social unrest. In those rare instances when their revolutions were successful, the liberals were determined to consolidate their power.

They therefore had no desire to provoke the conservative powers by trying to export their revolution. The main losers of the 1830s were not the European aristocracy, who retained much of their political power and social influence, but the urban workers and the peasantry, even where the liberals triumphed. While they had provided much of the force behind the revolutions, they did not share in the spoils and they were not enfranchised. Indeed, the liberals, once they had gained power, proceeded to apply their economic doctrines, which had serious implications for the poor. In the aftermath, new political movements would develop to test the limits of both conservatism and liberalism.

The Emergence of the Middle Class?

In 1848 *The Communist Manifesto*, penned by the great German socialist thinkers, Karl Marx and Friedrich Engels, identified class conflict as the motor of political and social change. The contemporary age, they argued, was the 'epoch of the bourgeoisie', in which 'society as a whole [was] more and more splitting up into two great hostile camps, into two great classes directly facing each other: Bourgeoisie and Proletariat'.[6] Marx and Engels were almost certainly right to identify the emergence of a developing middle class, but their identification of a 'bourgeoisie' with industrial capitalism was too narrowly focused. Bourgeois capitalists did exist, but they were still a small portion of the European middle classes. These were neither a homogeneous nor a close-knit group with a consistent unity of interest. They were divided horizontally, in terms of wealth and status, ranging from the wealthiest non-aristocratic landowners and financiers, through the entrepreneurs, merchants and professionals to the lower middle class of master-craftsmen, minor officials and shopkeepers.

The first category was an expanding group: in Prussia, non-noble landowners, while they did not storm the citadels of the great latifundia, none the less extended their hold on some of the other estates, taking advantage of the indebtedness of both the Junkers and the peasant-farmers. By 1850, some 43 per cent of all manors – former aristocratic estates – were in the hands of non-nobles. This upper crust of the middle classes rapidly became 'feudalised'; they aped aristocratic lifestyles and tried to gain access to noble society. The nobles frequently resisted this influx of wealthy commoners – in Prussia they tried to bar them from local government institutions, and did so with some success. In Russia, the Tsarist state maintained the society of orders – or *sosloviia* – in which only the members of Russia's two great merchant guilds shared some of the privileges of the nobles, but they were not allowed to own serfs or buy land until the 1860s. Meanwhile, the nobility resisted the progress of commoners up the Table of Ranks, established by Peter the Great, which defined status according to the state service performed by the individual. In 1845 Tsar Nicholas I yielded to noble demands that commoners had to reach rank nine (rather than fourteen) before attaining personal ennoblement and rank five (instead of eight) before receiving hereditary nobility. Yet between 1836 and 1843 some 4700 commoners had been ennobled by reaching the eighth rank.

In France, the 15,000 *grands notables* – defined as those who paid over 1000 francs in direct taxation and who qualified to stand for parliament – dominated French political life. They consisted of both the *grande bourgeoisie* and the nobles, and 75 per cent were landowners. The 1830 Revolution in France was not so much a bourgeois revolution as the triumph of the more liberal wing of the *grands notables* over the royalists. Few people in the middle-class ranks below were enfranchised in the mild reform which followed. In Britain, access to the nobility for the wealthier middle classes was well-established. Untitled land-owning families had originated from professional, mercantile and manufacturing activity. Succeeding generations might engage in local politics or public service, including election to Parliament, which eventually led to ennoblement. As knighthoods were not hereditary, there was plenty of movement backwards and forwards across the formal frontiers which separated the noble from the non-noble elites. Intermarriage amongst them was also common; as early as the 1720s, in only 25 per cent of all aristocratic marriages were both partners from noble families. That figure remained stable until the 1880s when there was another downward shift to 20 per cent.[7]

For some observers, not least the Italian liberal Cavour who admired the British and French examples, an open elite was to be welcomed. It merged middle-class and aristocratic interests, ensuring social unity against the danger of social disorder and political revolution. In Italy, in fact, a land-owning upper-middle class had emerged and it shared many aristocratic attitudes. In the south, merchants and professionals exploited aristocratic impecuniousness to buy up land, and they did so primarily for status. Middle-class landowners (*galantuomini*) did well from the abolition of seigneurial rights and dues by the French regime in 1806–15, which put the old aristocracy under pressure while doing little to alleviate peasant poverty. They were also well-placed to make gains from the divisions of the commons and the sale of church land. Such 'new men' did nothing to change the way the latifundia were run, but rather they sought to squeeze a living from the rents paid by peasants. In the north, aristocrats – not middle-class entrepreneurs – frequently proved to be economically more dynamic. In Lombardy, the mercantile community was conservative, seeking to monopolise the luxury trades. The land-owning nobility looked more 'capitalist', exploring new agricultural techniques, raising cash crops and building silk-mills on their land.

While the bourgeois upper crust experienced frequent crossovers and, in some cases, a direct fusion with the nobility, there were also divisions within the middle classes. These included both horizontal layers of wealth and vertical fissures, in terms of *how* different groups earned their money and differed in their cultural and political values. Beneath the upper-middle class (or the *grands notables* in France) there was a wider section of people whose social position depended more directly on salaries and earnings from their work rather than on inherited wealth – professionals (lawyers, doctors, teachers), officials, businessmen and well-to-do landowners. At a local level, and particularly in rural areas, these people might enjoy a good deal of prestige because they were the most educated or wealthiest people in the village, enjoying frequent contacts with the world outside. In some parts of France, such people might include well-to-do peasants. In rural East Prussia, the middle class might consist of a few educated officials in the village, and perhaps some shopkeepers and artisans, while in the Rhineland, a more recognisably 'bourgeois' group of entrepreneurs and manufacturers had emerged. In a city such as Hamburg, which experienced very little growth in this period, the middle class was a more conservative, mercantile elite. Italian rural middle-class landowners or small-town professionals emerged as the mediators between the great landowners and the peasantry. Yet Italy, particularly in the south, was also littered with under-employed professionals who resented their exclusion from the government posts upon which so many of them depended for employment. Such individuals, like the Sicilian Francesco Crispi, turned to criticising the regime itself. A similar picture emerged elsewhere as classically educated young men in France and Germany found that there were simply not enough jobs to go around. The French satirist Albéric Second wrote that the world must be overpopulated because 'there were twenty times more lawyers than suits to be lost, more painters than portraits to be taken, more soldiers than victories to gain, and more doctors than patients to kill'.[8] This was the way the middle classes experienced the rapid population growth in the first half of the nineteenth century. Master-craftsmen and shopkeepers helped to form a lower-middle class whose position was often precarious – artisans struggling against more recognisably 'capitalist' forms of production and, above all, depending, like the shopkeepers, upon precarious local demand. The children of such small businessmen might seek employment in more secure jobs such as schoolteaching and state service as minor officials.[9]

Cultural and educational differences, though they did not necessarily rule out convergence in other areas of life, such as marriage, also divided the middle classes. The most extreme case was Russia, where law and custom reinforced the divisions. The liberal professions and the intelligentsia had no desire to be associated – at least in legal terms – with the grotty world of business and commerce, whose members were labelled as a separate 'trade and industry class' in the Russian *sosloviia*. In France, the classical education offered by the great secondary schools (*lycées*) meant that they were not suitable for young people who wanted to go into business or manufacturing, where many entrepreneurs still believed in the virtues of learning on the job. It was therefore unlikely that all members of the French middle class shared the same educational background. For those young people who were not able to go to a *lycée*, alternatives existed in the form of municipal *collèges* and vocational technical schools.[10] In Britain, the 'public' (i.e. private) schools often creamed off the sons (and, after the 1850s, girls) of the upper-middle class, while the expense excluded the children of less prosperous families, who were more likely to be educated in grammar schools. In Prussia, the sons of the land-owning elites, of professionals and officials tended to enrol in the prestigious *Gymnasien* for a classical secondary education which would lead into a university education and then a career in law or state service. Other schools were provided for the sons of well-to-do farmers, manufacturers and businessmen. These were the *Realschulen*, whose curriculum was intended to prepare these people for further education in trade schools and technical colleges.

While there was no coherent bourgeoisie, this is not to say that no one perceived a common identity or interest across these groups. All middle-class groups valued order and property above the dangers of social instability and revolution. Even when middle-class people participated or accepted revolutionary change – as in 1830 and again in 1848 – they also sought to restore order as quickly as possible and to prevent the revolutions from swinging into a more radical, social upheaval. The middle classes therefore broadly defined themselves against other groups – sometimes the aristocracy, sometimes the workers and peasants, but always against the 'dangerous classes', the underclass of paupers and migrants who seemed to endanger social order. To define the middle classes, however, as a broad layer lying between the conservative aristocracy and the poorer sections of society none the less includes a wide range of strata. German liberals, in fact, spoke of the *Mittelstand*, by which they did not just mean the middle class, but all productive sections of society, from the wealthiest financier to the independent craftsman. For liberals, the *Mittelstand* was the 'real nation', membership of which was determined, above all, by 'independence', which at its broadest meant anyone who was not a servant, a child or a woman, but which might also have excluded apprentices and journeymen. While the liberal conception of the *Mittelstand* therefore had limits, they went far beyond the confines of any single socio-economic group.[11]

What this all means is that the 'middle class' existed among contemporaries as a political concept. It was also a very real and influential *cultural* framework. Distinctively middle-class values did emerge in the first half of the century. These transcended many social strata and reached the better-off, skilled workers who either sought to emulate the middle-class way of life or who already shared the same values as middle-class citizens. Such values included 'respectability', which meant sobriety (in terms of both one's alcohol consumption and one's dress), dignity in one's behaviour and language, and cleanliness and tidiness. It also meant religious observance. 'Respectability' was to be expected of rich and poor alike, and observers of pauperism in the first half of the nineteenth century fretted, amongst other things, over the demoralising effect of alcohol and other forms of 'vice'. Even more problematic was the virtue of 'independence', which meant an ability to fend for oneself without having to lean on charity, poor relief or even members of one's family. In Britain, this notion would be expressed in *Self-Help*, the best-selling book penned by Samuel Smiles in 1859. Wealth, Guizot argued, was the fruit of ability and diligence, while poverty was the consequence of idleness and even stupidity. In Germany, 'respectability' was encapsulated in the Biedermeier style, which was a post-1848 term applied retrospectively – and scathingly – to a bourgeois retreat into the calm, private peace of domestic bliss. For women, respectability and independence had special implications, not least their exclusion from political rights. In Germany in 1827 the *Krug'sche Lexikon* suggested that women be denied full rights as citizens 'because of their natural occupation, which binds them to the house and makes them dependent on the male'.[12] The idea that woman's 'natural' role was as mother and wife in the home was part of a wider notion that there were 'separate spheres' for men and women. The former were made for public life and for work, the latter were virtuous, sensitive 'angels of the hearth', the domestic goddesses who graced the home and reared their children with good values.

Liberalism and Radicalism: The Resurgence

To contemporaries, of all the liberal regimes which came to power in the 1830 revolutions, Louis-Philippe's July monarchy in France appeared best to fit the label 'bourgeois'. Karl Marx memorably described the regime as 'nothing other than a joint stock company for the exploitation of French national wealth'. Yet those who seized political power were, socially, scarcely different from those who had lost it. After 1830 the Chamber of Deputies was still dominated by the *notables*, among whom were entrenched the old aristocracy. The purge of the structures of government after the revolution simply replaced those who had served the Bourbons with those who were more likely to have worked for Napoleon. The July insurrection was, therefore, a narrowly political revolution. The only major change to the Charter was that the suffrage was marginally extended; in Robert Tombs's crushing description, 'the electorate rose from 90,000 extremely rich elderly men to 170,000 very rich middle-aged men'.[13]

If this seems unheroic, then that is precisely what the July Monarchy aimed to be. It wanted to provide stable, parliamentary rule for the economic development of France. It sought to wrest control of education away from the Church and establish a system of state schooling. It was, in other words, a moderate liberal order. The regime sought to steer a middle way between what it saw as the 'anarchy' of democracy and the 'tyranny' of royal despotism. As that also entailed avoiding war in Europe, no other nineteenth-century French regime tried so hard to live in peace with its neighbours, although even it had its bad moments. The July Monarchy also witnessed a period of sustained economic growth – some of the fastest in French history – even though the regime itself was wary of the social dislocation caused by too rapid a pace of development. The late 1830s saw a dramatic road-building programme, but more important was the 1842 railway law, a result of which was the construction of 900 miles of railway track, which in turn stimulated a boom in the related industries of iron and steel, engineering and coal mining. In 1833, moreover, François Guizot's education law obliged every commune to have a primary school, an important (if, owing to poor resources, faltering) step towards universal education.

Yet these undoubted achievements did not impress the regime's opponents. Among them, naturally, were ultra-royalists, who came to be called Legitimists because they supported the 'legitimate' Bourbon dynasty. In the summer of 1832, Legitimists under the duchesse de Berry, (widow of the duke murdered in 1820) tried to raise the Vendée in revolt. Only a few hundred royalists took up arms and the Duchess was arrested. None the less, while the Legitimists would never reconquer power nationally, the wealth and social influence of the old nobility ensured that they remained a weighty political presence.

A more persistent threat to the regime came from the left. With the triumph of the liberal opposition in 1830, the extreme left – republicans and Bonapartists – were left out in the cold. Republicans drew strength from nationalism, offended by the cautious foreign policy of the July Monarchy. They claimed that the government should be trying to reassert French prestige in Europe and eradicate the shame of the 1815 peace settlement. When the French government failed to help the Polish revolutionaries in their struggle for independence from Russia in 1831, Paris was contorted by four days of rioting. Republican organisations, such as the *Société des droits de l'homme*, organised protests, encouraged workers' strikes and supported uprisings in Lyon and Paris in 1834 (the background to Victor Hugo's novel, *Les Misérables*). The government responded with prosecutions of republican newspapers and restrictions on the rights to form trade unions and political associations. In

1835, republicans retaliated with an assassination attempt on Louis-Philippe. In the terrible carnage of the bomb blast, 14 people were killed, while the King escaped with minor bruising. In the public revulsion which followed, the government secured the passage of the 'September Laws', which made it easier to secure a conviction in political trials and imposed severe restrictions on the press. Not everyone in the regime accepted these measures – the King himself was reluctant to abandon his liberal principles – but republican violence and the September laws embittered the divisions in French political life.[14]

Yet the republican opposition was itself divided. After 1835, moderates sought reform through legal methods, while radicals still tried to destroy the regime by revolution. Among the latter, important figures, such as Auguste Blanqui, were drawn towards socialism. This gave radical republicanism some appeal amongst the artisans of Paris; after an insurrection in 1839, they made up 87 per cent of those arrested. Yet radical organisations remained small, their newspapers were published clandestinely, they were infiltrated by informers, had no funds and, unlike the Charbonnerie in the 1820s, had no support in the army. A mass uprising would only occur in times of desperate economic crisis – and the republicans would have to wait until the later 1840s for that.[15]

For most republicans, the failure of revolution in the 1830s bolstered the position of the moderates who wanted peaceful reform. Yet under the dominance of the ministry of François Guizot between 1840 and 1848, the July Monarchy set its face against reform. The Chamber of Deputies was dominated by a solid phalanx of Guizot's supporters, so republicans organised an extra-parliamentary campaign to put pressure on the government. Political societies were banned, so the republicans held banquets and drafted petitions in order to rally public support. Predictably, the movement was divided between moderates around the newspaper *Le National* and radicals whose mouthpiece was *La Réforme*. Moreover, in 1846 Guizot comfortably won the elections with an increased majority; there seemed to be little need to pay much heed to the gaggle of reformers outside. 'Enrichissez-vous', he once advised them (get rich, in order to qualify for the vote). Yet Guizot's parliamentary majority disguised the strong sense of frustration which large parts of society felt at their disenfranchisement. By 1848 there were ten newspaper subscribers for each of the 18,000 electors in Paris, which is fitting testimony to the exclusion of most of civil society from national politics.

Spain and Portugal witnessed the establishment of moderate, liberal regimes similar to the July Monarchy in France. After the liberal victory over the Carlists in 1840, the Spanish *moderado* government sought to undercut the power of the more radical *progresistas* by placing restrictions on the suffrage and reducing the autonomy of elected local government. This assault on the Constitution of 1837 led to *progresista* riots. Both sides appealed to General Espartero, fresh from his victorious campaign against the ultra-royalists. Espartero assured the government of his loyalty, but he also refused to accept the constitutional changes. When the regent, María Cristina, refused to withdraw the proposals, however, the radicals once more took to the streets, and forced her to appoint Espartero as prime minister. She then abdicated in October 1840, leaving Espartero in control as regent. The general broadened the suffrage, allowing the *progresistas* to dominate the Cortes, but he offered little else, falling under the influence of a clique of army officers. Early *moderado* attempts at a counter-coup failed, but Espartero began to haemorrhage support, starting with economic troubles in Catalonia, where the general resisted demands from manufacturers for protective tariffs. In November 1842 he bombarded a revolt in Barcelona into submission. Yet he was toppled in June–July 1843 after his suppression of press freedom produced an alliance of disillusioned ('pure') *progresistas* and *moderados*.

The victors found a leader in Ramón María Narváez, a liberal army officer who would become prime minister in May 1844. Opposition, both on the extreme left and the extreme right, was crushed. A three-month workers' uprising (the *Jamancia*) in Barcelona was violently suppressed at the end of 1843. In 1846–9, Narváez crushed a Carlist insurrection in Catalonia (the 'Second Carlist War'). Though ruthless, Narváez was committed to a constitutional government, but one in which a wealthy oligarchy remained in control. In 1845, therefore, he allowed the *moderados* to reform the political system with a new constitution. Royal power was boosted so that the monarch could suspend the legislature at will. Members of the upper house, the Senate, were appointed for life rather than elected. Trial by jury was suspended for press offences. In 1846 the suffrage was restricted to a fraction of the wealthiest citizens. Power was, in effect, given to a landed elite of the nobility and wealthy bourgeois, akin to the French *notables*. Narváez's authoritarianism aimed to ensure the stability of this order, or, as he put it, to 'save the constitution'. Like the July Monarchy in France, however, the regime sought to create a stable framework for economic and social development. A uniform tax system and criminal code were created and later an agreement was reached with the Church recognising the sale of ecclesiastical lands, while the foundations of a national system of education were also laid.

A similar social elite was empowered in Portugal after Don Pedro's triumph in 1834. In September 1836, however, radicals, akin to the Spanish *progresistas*, rose up in Lisbon and forced the restoration of the more democratic constitution of 1822. French and British diplomatic pressure forced the 'Septembrist' regime to compromise in the Constitution of 1838. This was opposed by conservative 'Chartists' who, determined to consolidate the grip of the elites on national politics, favoured the original Charter of 1826. They came to power in 1839 on the resignation of the Septembrist government, which had put down a Miguelist revolt in eastern Portugal but which was riven by internal divisions as it tried to placate the Church. The Chartist government, like Narváez's Moderate regime in Spain, sought to lay the foundations for a modern, centralised state, but in the economic crisis of 1846–7 it was beset by attacks from reactionary Miguelists and Septembrists, both of whom exploited peasant unrest. The appointment as prime minister in October 1846 of General Saldanha, Portugal's answer to Narváez, sparked a Septembrist revolt in Porto. It engulfed northern Portugal in civil war until June 1847, when British and French military help enabled Saldanha to stamp out the uprising.

As constitutional states grappled with their opponents, the absolutist states struggled with domestic problems of their own. In Russia, Tsar Nicholas made half-hearted attempts to grapple with the problem of serfdom. His attitude was summed up in 1842 when he declared serfdom 'an evil which is palpable and obvious to everyone, however to touch it now would be even more harmful'.[16] He feared that radical reform would unleash a wave of peasant disorder caused by excited expectations, or stir conservative nobles into revolt. He therefore established a series of 'secret committees' to discuss the problem and they came up with some limited reforms, but nothing approaching outright abolition. The burden of serfdom continued to weigh heavily on Russian consciences.

Meanwhile, the repression after the Decembrist revolt marginalised the liberal intelligentsia. 'Enlightenment', recalled one contemporary, 'became a crime in the eyes of the government.'[17] Yet Nicholas's reign saw important developments in Russian political thought. 'Westernisers' believed that Russia's problems stemmed from its failure to develop along lines similar to other European states, including the evolution of legal institutions and parliaments. 'Slavophiles', on the other hand, idealised the distinctiveness of the Russian people. Ivan Kireevski argued that Russian society had been distorted by the reforms of Peter the Great in the early eighteenth century, and by Western influences ever since. The great virtue of the Russian people was its sense of community and piety as against the individualism and rationalism of Western liberalism. Russian virtues were embodied in the peasant commune. Slavophilism naturally lent weight to conservative arguments, but its relationship with the Tsarist regime was ambiguous. Slavophiles wanted to return to a golden age before absolutism (another Western import), when the Tsar ruled with his people, represented in the estates, the *zemskii sabor*. This would heal the rift between the state and the people. Slavophiles also hated serfdom and they demanded a free press, but the emphasis on Russian qualities lent itself to a chauvinistic form of nationalism.[18] Yet Slavophilism was adaptable to other, more radical ideas. Alexander Herzen, who, on inheriting his father's wealth, left Russia for exile in 1847, saw the Russian commune, with its co-operative spirit amongst peasants, as the basis of a Russian form of socialism. Mikhail Bakhunin regarded it as the egalitarian and democratic foundation of an anarchistic society. These ideas would influence succeeding generations of Russian revolutionaries.

Financial troubles had prevented the Habsburg monarchy from pulling that perpetual thorn – Hungarian opposition – from its side. In October 1830 the aristocratic diet provided Metternich with 50,000 troops to crush revolution in Italy, but liberal tendencies were beginning to emerge among those who were more thoughtful about Hungary's problems. It was around this time that the term 'public opinion' won common currency in Hungary. It buzzed with excitement over a book published in 1830 by Count István Széchenyi, entitled *Hitel* (*Credit*). It argued that Hungary's problems lay primarily in the privileges of the nobility. Peasant labour services (the *robot*), he argued, were less productive than free labour, while the persistence of entails meant that the property could not be used as security for loans which could be sunk into agricultural improvements. Sensational as Széchenyi's ideas were for the time, they were not the most radical. During the diet of 1832–6, a lawyer and deputy named Lajos Kossuth began to write 'parliamentary reports' which were circulated (in manuscript) among reading circles and clubs (*kaszinós*) across the kingdom. When he founded a newspaper, *Pesti Hírlap* (*Pest News*) in 1841 (which eventually attracted 5000 subscribers), he argued that anyone who had something to say about politics or society should be permitted to have a voice. During the 1840s the moderate Széchenyi and the radical Kossuth waged a stormy press debate, foreshadowing Magyar divisions during the 1848 Revolution.

The liberalisation of Magyar politics did not go unopposed. Four radical Hungarian lawyers were arrested by the government in 1836, Kossuth was imprisoned in 1837–40 and the liberal Baron Miklós Wesselényi was sentenced to three years' imprisonment in 1839. Hungarian conservatives also mobilised against the liberals. Among the most vocal were the poor ('sandalled') nobility, who had the most to lose from the loss of their privileges. Encouraged by Metternich, they waged a violent campaign of intimidation in the elections to the 1843 diet, but while they succeeded in chasing some liberal candidates away from the county meetings, the diet of 1843–4 had a reformist majority. In 1846 Metternich sponsored the creation of Hungary's first political party, the Conservatives, which, unlike hotheads such as Kossuth, promised to respect the rights of the national minorities (which drew even Széchenyi into the party). From Vienna's point of view, this was part of a wider scheme to raise the possibility of Slav separatism in order to bring the rebellious Magyars to heel. Meanwhile, Metternich appointed special administrators to rule the troublesome counties directly. The atmosphere of the later 1840s was therefore tense but also expectant as Hungarian electors went to the polls in 1847. While the liberals did not have it all their own way, a diet was returned which discussed peasant emancipation and the abolition of the nobles' tax privileges.

Magyar nationalism gave impetus to a 'national revival' in Croatia. Croats were stirred by the threat that Magyar would become the only official language in Hungary. Yet the Croats understood that they constituted a tiny part of the kingdom and could easily be ignored, so some nationalists, led by Ljudevit Gaj, formulated a wider form of nationalism, Illyrianism, which sought to unite all South Slavs, while also forging a common language. Neither goal was an easy task, but Gaj was encouraged by Metternich, who allowed him to publish his journal, *Danica* (*Morning Star*), in 1835. In the literary flourish of the 1830s and 1840s, Gaj made the remarkable achievement of persuading Croatian writers to abandon the dialect of the Zagreb region (kajkavian) in favour of the štokavian dialect, which was used by Slavs further south, including Bosnians and Serbs. This was in fact the culmination of a long acculturation since the eighteenth century but, for Gaj, cultural unity would lead to political co-operation. The plan, however, ran into Serb opposition and Slovene indifference. The Slovenes were ruled directly from Vienna, so had no fear of Magyar nationalism. The Serbs were Orthodox (while the Croats were Catholic) and had their own independent state to look to. In the Serbian principality itself, the overthrow of the Obrenović dynasty in 1842 and the enthronement of Alexander Karadjordje was the work of liberals who envisaged an expanded Serbia defined by its Orthodoxy and its štokavian dialect and defiant of both Austria and Russia. When Metternich understood the dangerous implications of South Slav nationalism, he withdrew his support for Gaj's newspaper in 1843.

The Habsburgs also faced troublesome opponents amongst its German-speaking subjects. From the 1830s Austrian liberals were increasingly irritated by government and Church interference within civil society, and were frustrated by the worry that Metternich's conservative policies, by stirring nationalist opposition, were actually endangering the unity of the Habsburg monarchy. While censorship and police harassment were never as stringent as the liberals claimed, they were still exasperating. Clerical influence in education – the Jesuits were allowed to teach from 1836 – was taken as a sign that the monarchy was trying to bolster its power with the moral authority of Catholicism. The political police were neither numerous nor efficient, but their very existence – and the fact that they were not above using intimidation against people suspected of harbouring 'dangerous' ideas – made them despised. At the same time, the censorship could not cope with the sheer volume of material and it was easily evaded. Austrian writers had their works published abroad, particularly in the German press, which could then spill back into the Empire. Metternich was the main target of their attacks. Their ideas circulated in cafés and private salons, as well as in cultural and professional 'circles', such as the Juridical–Political Reading Club (which would provide much of the liberal leadership in 1848), the Concordia Circle (a literary and artistic society) and the Lower Austria Manufacturers' Association. The opposition found a political voice in the Estates of Lower Austria, which met in Vienna and whose demands for economic and political reform became shriller towards 1848.

In Germany and Italy, radical and liberal opposition to the existing order gathered momentum in the 1840s. The nationalist flourish of the early 1830s was forced underground when the repressive political system held firm. The German states did achieve a customs union, the *Zollverein*, but this was not intended as a prelude to unification. The idea for a single German market was floated at the end of the Napoleonic Wars by businessmen frustrated by Germany's myriad customs barriers which slowed down trade and made it more costly. The Prussian reformers took notice, but they saw the *Zollverein* very much in terms of Prussian rather than German interests. A customs union would stimulate the Prussian economy by opening up German markets to competition. It would also link the centre of the Prussian kingdom with its western part, blocked off by the territory of other German states. Prussia, which took the first step in 1818 by unifying its own internal customs system across its vast swathe of northern German territory, became a single market for more than ten million people. The southern states were worried by competition from the north, while Metternich recoiled from a single market as the first step towards political unification and as a dangerous extension of Prussian power. Prussia raised high external tariffs against the smaller states to force them into line. Encouraged by Metternich, Bavaria and Württemberg resisted, forming their own customs union in 1828, but the liberalised regimes which came to power in the 1830 revolutions in Saxony and Electoral Hesse brought their states into the *Zollverein*. The economic critical mass built up as more governments saw fiscal and economic benefits in joining the union. In 1831 Bavaria and Württemberg themselves opened negotiations for entry. On 1 January 1834 all customs barriers within the *Zollverein* were lifted. Important states such as Hanover still refused to join, but the most important exclusion was Austria. Although the union would prove to be a tool by which Prussia could lever the smaller German states into following its policies, for as long as Prussia itself remained opposed to political unification, the *Zollverein* would remain an economic agreement.

In any case, the proponents of political change were as divided after 1830 as they were beforehand. Republicans, who sought a unitary, democratic Germany, were a small though active minority, many of whom spent long spells in exile. In Switzerland, a group under the influence of the Italian nationalist Mazzini formed 'Young Germany', which sought to spread its democratic and nationalist ideals amongst German workers. In 1835, however, it could only boast some two hundred members in 14 different clubs, though its influence amongst craftworkers may have been wider. Some German radicals absorbed socialist ideas and in 1847 the Communist League emerged under the leadership of Karl Marx. Liberals, meanwhile, still sought constitutional monarchy with a limited suffrage. The repression of the 1830s led them to discuss politics behind the respectable fronts of professional associations, choral societies and reading clubs.

In the early 1840s both liberals and radicals benefited from a swell of popular nationalism during a war scare. French support for Mehmet Ali of Egypt's attack against the Turkish Sultan in 1839 led the other great powers to intervene. France began military preparations to support its demands for compensation through a revision of the Vienna settlement. Germans, puffed up with nationalist sentiment, anxiously awaited a French surge across the Rhine, while Prussia won hearts and minds by mobilising no fewer than 200,000 men to face the crisis. In contrast, the feeble response of both the *Bund* and impecunious Austria undermined confidence in the latter's claims to German leadership, while exposing the former as woefully inadequate. Patriotism was kept on the boil in 1840 when King Christian VIII of Denmark started a policy of imposing central control over his predominantly German duchy of Holstein. German nationalists were infuriated and by 1847 the revived gymnastic clubs boasted 250 branches with 85,000 members, while choral societies had recruited 100,000 members and held national festivals annually in 1845–7.

The international crises also revived liberal parliamentary fortunes: they underscored the need for German states to strengthen their defences, but the money required allowed liberals to wring out political concessions. In Baden, they pressed for a citizens' militia and legal reforms. Grand Duke Leopold's reactionary minister, Friedrich von Blittersdorf, was ousted by a vote of no confidence in 1843. Bavarian liberals resisted the conservative, Catholic policies of Chief Minister Karl von Abel, who resigned in 1847 in disgust at King Ludwig's affair with the dancer, Lola Montez. In Württemberg, liberals under Friedrich Römer performed well in the 1844 elections and grasped the right to review spending on foreign policy. The cost of Prussia's mobilisation during the Rhine crisis showed that the kingdom would not be able to sustain a major conflict for long, while Frederick William's desire to develop Prussia's railways also demanded money. Yet Hardenberg's State Debt Law of 1820 committed the King (since 1840, Frederick William IV) not to raise loans without consulting the estates of the realm. Liberals seized the opportunity to press for constitutional government. In 1844 Frederick William summoned a 'United Diet', consisting of representatives from the Prussian provincial assemblies, for 1847.[19]

If nationalism and liberalism were flourishing in Germany, they were still struggling to put down roots in Italy. In the Papal States, the government successfully opposed the liberals by appealing to the latent loyalty of the masses, recruiting 75,000 peasants into paramilitary units (Centurions) by 1833. Italian liberalism and nationalism flailed in a sea of popular indifference or hostility, not least because few of their proponents addressed the social concerns of the urban poor and the peasantry. Yet the balance was not tipped entirely against them. The experience of the early 1830s showed that the absolutist governments were dependent upon Austrian military support to keep domestic opposition at bay. Vienna therefore enjoyed unwelcome and unpopular influence in their domestic affairs (Metternich, in fact, forced the Pope to disarm the Centurions in 1836 on the grounds that they were a danger to social stability). Meanwhile, the repression added to the legacy of bitterness and the sense of alienation shared by segments of the social elites towards their rulers. That their regimes rested on the support of the loyal, pious masses merely reinforced their resistance to change.

The opposition drew lessons from the experience of the early 1830s. The tactics of the Carbonari had been inadequate to the challenges of revolution and the star of the great Italian nationalist, Giuseppe Mazzini, began to rise. He placed more emphasis on open propaganda than on revolutionary conspiracy. A great uprising of the Italian people would bring a unitary, Italian republic, which flew in the face of the regionalist sentiments expressed most famously by his contemporary, Vincenzo Gioberti, who wanted a loose Italian federation led by the Pope. Both Mazzini and Gioberti were popular. Mazzini's revolutionary organisation, 'Young Italy' (founded in 1831), could reasonably have laid claim to 60,000 members by 1833. He was opposed to socialism, but his emphasis on democracy appealed to the articulate artisans of the cities. Gioberti's 1843 book, *Of the Moral and Civil Primacy of the Italians*, had sold no fewer than 80,000 copies by 1848; as the title suggests, Gioberti was not shy in shouting Italian superiority from the rooftops. Mazzini, in contrast, saw all nations as unique but equal, like the different strings of a harp. The real appeal of Gioberti's 'Neo-Guelph' vision lay in his attempt to harness Catholicism to the national cause, while Mazzini was secular in his outlook.

These ideas could not be put into practice without power, especially to challenge the Austrians. The only candidate for military leadership of the national movement was Piedmont, as it was the strongest of the independent Italian states. Piedmont, however, was transmitting mixed messages. King Charles Albert was hostile to the idea of unification and would develop expansionist designs for the benefit of his own dynasty. He was, however, an economic reformer: tariffs on grain imports were reduced in 1834, and this was followed by a series of measures liberalising trade. While workers' guilds were abolished in 1844, they were permitted to establish mutual societies. Charles Albert codified the laws and appointed the Marchesa Giulia di Barolo to reform women's prisons. Piedmont, therefore, had some progressive credentials, making it a tempting candidate for Italian nationalists seeking the military might for their designs. Yet in 1846 they anointed another champion – the new Pope, Pius IX (Pio Nono). He had read Gioberti and he showed some early liberal promise, giving an amnesty to political prisoners, appointing a liberal secretary of state and nominating commissions to prepare various reforms. In 1847 he relaxed censorship. These developments generated a good deal of excitement in Tuscany and Piedmont, where rulers made similar concessions, and the agitation for reform spread to the Austrian-controlled regions of Lombardy and Venetia, as well as to Naples and Sicily, where revolts were suppressed.

While liberals scored political successes in Germany and were being galvanised in Italy, Metternich sought to shore up the ramparts of the European conservative order, and the Habsburg monarchy in particular, by annexing the free city of Krakow in 1846. The city had been a nerve centre for Polish patriots during their disastrous attempt to foment an uprising against Austrian rule in Galicia. Yet the Austrian seizure of Krakow was Metternich's only success in stemming the gathering tide of opposition. The first breach in the conservative defences came in Switzerland in 1847 when radicals gathered at festivals and shooting contests, spreading ideas for a unitary, democratic nation-state. In the Aargau in 1844 the radical government closed down the monasteries and sold off their property. Catholic Lucerne responded by allowing the Jesuits to take over its seminary. Both provocative actions sparked a wider confrontation across the Confederation. Anti-Jesuit feeling galvanised radicals in other cantons, and units of their volunteers, the *Freischäler*, marched from Aargau on Lucerne in March 1845. A number of Catholic cantons reacted by forming the *Sonderbund*, an alliance aimed at defending themselves against such attacks, but also at preventing a reform of the Confederation. When the Swiss diet met, the radical cantons had a slim majority and demanded the dissolution of the *Sonderbund*. In November 1847, after an attempt at compromise failed, civil war erupted in which the radicals swept the conservatives aside. In September 1848, a new federal constitution was approved which compromised between radical desires for a centralised state and conservative wishes to preserve the autonomy of the cantons. The victory of the Swiss radicals was a defeat for Metternich. While he sent money and arms to help the conservative cantons, he could do little else: Britain and (at the last minute) France refused to support intervention.

The liberal, reforming fever beginning to grip Italy also alarmed Metternich. He reinforced the Austrian garrison (permitted by the

Vienna settlement) in the papal city of Ferrara. Pius's loud protests (echoed, tellingly, by Charles Albert of Piedmont) reinforced the Pope's liberal credentials and his popularity amongst Italians. By the end of 1847 an Austrian attempt to turn back the rising tide of Italian opposition by force seemed increasingly likely. Early in 1848, in Lombardy, resentment over taxation and conscription was expressed by a boycott of tobacco (since the tax on it was a source of revenue for the Austrian government). Tensions between the Austrian garrison and the non-smokers erupted into violence which, though contained by the authorities, simmered resentfully. In Sicily, however, an uprising erupted in Palermo in January 1848, when the combined forces of the urban poor, peasants, liberal nationalists and conservatives hostile to Neapolitan rule drove the royal forces from the island. The revolt spread to Naples, where King Ferdinand was forced to promise a constitution. This was the first of the European revolutions of 1848.

8 The European Revolution, 1848–1850

The Collapse of the Conservative Order

The revolutions of 1848 were revolutions of hope and despair. The political excitement and agitation across Europe after the mid-1840s aroused expectations of radical change, but these were dashed by the bleak landscape of the worst economic crisis of the nineteenth century. It started in 1845 with both an agricultural disaster, which forced food prices up, and a cyclical crisis remarkable for the violence of the economic slump. In agriculture, harvests in 1846–7 were again poor, and the potatoes, the great back-up crop, were afflicted with blight, turning them into an inedible mush. Ireland was the worst hit – these were the years of the terrible famine – but the crisis was severe elsewhere in Europe. In manufacturing and commerce there was an abrupt fall in production, which sent unemployment spiralling catastrophically upwards.[1] The crisis therefore exposed the shortcomings and weakness of the conservative order. Governments, faced with the rising challenge of liberals and radicals who were testing their capacity to resist, collapsed with awe-inspiring ease in 1848. Europe was engulfed in a wave of revolutions on a scale not seen again until 1989.

The kick which brought the edifice tumbling down was the fall of the July Monarchy in France. Despite the economic crisis, no one expected a republic to arise from the rubble. Rather, in 1847–8, republicans were peacefully pressing the government for suffrage reform with a campaign of public banquets. The government's clumsy efforts to ban a radical banquet in Paris on 22 February led to demonstrations, an escalation of violence and, on 23 February, the dismissal of Guizot, followed swiftly by the abdication of Louis-Philippe himself. Leading republican politicians and journalists formed a provisional government which, on 25 February, proclaimed the Second Republic.

The news of the events in Paris spread rapidly to other European capitals, where conservative regimes collapsed under the weight of insurrections. Austria's Italian satellites began to slip away as Grand Duke Leopold of Tuscany and even the Pope were forced to grant constitutions. Most significantly of all, in Piedmont, Charles Albert issued the *Statuto* – a constitution – on 4 March. German governments were persuaded, cajoled or bluntly forced to concede rights such as press freedom and trial by jury, to allow the creation of citizen militias and to promise constitutions. Apart from the hapless Louis-Philippe, however, the only monarch to lose his throne was King Ludwig I of Bavaria, who abdicated in favour of his son rather than end his love affair with his unpopular mistress, Lola Montez. In Berlin, demonstrations developed into full-scale street fighting on 18 March. Four days and 250 deaths later, Frederick William IV promised a constitution. Across Germany, voices were raised demanding a national assembly which would draw up a constitution for a unified state. In Heidelberg, 51 leading German liberals met on 5 March to organise a 'pre-parliament' for all Germany, which met in Frankfurt on 31 March. Violent protests left Vienna under the control of a citizens' militia and a students' 'Academic Legion'. Most sensationally of all, on 13 March the Emperor dismissed Metternich. Two days later the Habsburg court promised a constitution. The revolutions now erupted in Budapest, Prague, Milan and Venice. The Hungarian parliament began to enact parts of Lajos Kossuth's programme, including the abolition of serfdom. The revolutions in Venice and Milan, where uprisings toppled Austrian rule, were accompanied by a Piedmontese invasion of Lombardy as Charles Albert sought to rally nationalist opinion behind his bid to expand his kingdom.

With the empire now under foreign attack, the Habsburg monarchy had to make concessions to its domestic opponents. The 'April Laws' gave the Hungarians an annual parliament, elected on an extended franchise which included the urban middle classes and the land-owning peasantry. Hungary was to be a separate constitutional monarchy with only a dynastic link to Vienna. The Czechs were granted linguistic equality with the Germans in Bohemia and the Bohemian diet was summoned. This fell short of the single parliament for all the Czech lands (which also included Silesia and Moravia) demanded by Prague liberals, who formed a National Committee which became, in effect, a provisional government. In northern Italy, the Austrian forces, under Marshal Joseph Radetzky, pulled back to the northern 'quadrilateral' of fortresses, leaving the Italian liberals in control of Milan and Venice (where Daniele Manin was proclaimed President of the Venetian republic).

Elsewhere in Europe, governments survived either by yielding or by resorting to repression. In Denmark, liberal demonstrations in March compelled Frederick VII to concede a fully constitutional regime, while in Sweden 30 protesters demanding an extension of the suffrage were killed by troops in Stockholm. In Norway, the socialist Marcus Thrane organised a Chartist-style movement for social reform and universal male suffrage, but the parliament was unsympathetic and the authorities arrested 117 people. In the Netherlands, William II was confronted by demonstrations in The Hague and Amsterdam. He split the opposition by bringing moderate liberals from the States-General into the government on 13 March. A commission reformed the constitution, which strengthened parliamentary powers. Radical opposition in Belgium was emasculated by King Leopold's rapid concession of a wider suffrage. Britain avoided revolution – narrowly, it seemed at the time – when a monster demonstration organised by the Chartists in London on 10 April was met by a determined government response: 100,000 volunteer 'special constables' were recruited to bolster the police. In Spain, Narváez's iron rule defended the Constitution of 1845 against both the extreme left and the Carlists. In April 1848, Tsar Nicholas I of Russia established a censorship committee to oversee all publications. The circle of revolutionary intellectuals around Mikhail Petrashevsky was arrested in May and, in the seven years between 1848 and Nicholas's death in 1855, intellectuals and academics were virtually silenced.

Where the revolutions of February and March succeeded, the various people who had contributed to the liberal victory naturally expected some say (or all the say) in the creation of the new regime. Liberals wanted to contain the revolutions within political limits, securing constitutions with or without universal male suffrage. Radicals wanted to go further, with greater democratisation and fundamental social reform. The latter drew strength from the underlying social crisis, which allowed them to gather the support of workers and sometimes peasants. At the same time, all these groups now had greater freedom and confidence to press their demands. There was a flowering of political activity in the form of clubs, the press and mass demonstrations. Yet the conflicting political and social aspirations amongst the revolutionaries made the task of conservatives in destroying the liberal regimes easier. Politics in the liberalised regimes rapidly polarised and the revolutionaries turned against each other. In some parts of Europe where nationalist aspirations were proclaimed, the alienation of other ethnic and linguistic groups fatally damaged the liberal order.

Social Conflicts: Workers and Peasants

For the new governments, worker unrest was the most immediate and obvious danger. The potential for violent social conflict within the cities loomed, as radical artisans sought to press home their protests against the factory system and the use of unskilled labour, while workers in general demanded state action to tackle poverty and unemployment. Liberals responded that the political freedoms now secured gave workers the capacity, in the long run, to ease their poverty. Thus breaches within the precarious revolutionary alliance between workers and middle-class liberals appeared at the very start. The new regimes did offer some assistance as stopgaps. The liberalised government in Vienna tried to relieve poverty by lowering taxes on food and setting up public works projects. In Prague, food prices were reduced, relief funds collected and the unemployed set to work on public projects. In Venice, the new government provided work in the tobacco factories and the naval arsenal, but after a series of disturbances in May, Manin appointed a committee of public vigilance which kept watch on the urban poor of porters, boatmen and street hawkers.[2] Public works were set up in Berlin to ease the immediate misery of unemployment. The French provisional government sought to soothe tensions by establishing National Workshops to 'guarantee work for all citizens' and appointing the 'Luxembourg Commission', which was presided over by the two socialist members of the government, Louis Blanc and Alexandre Martin ('Albert'). The commission was to discuss labour questions and to listen to workers' delegates. It drafted some reforms, including a reduction in the working day.

Yet working-class radicals were determined not to see a repeat of the 1830 revolution, from which they drew no benefits. In Paris, socialist ideas came frothing to the surface, as workers organised themselves into 'popular societies'.[3] In their clubs, newspapers and demonstrations, workers discussed the idea of pushing the revolution towards a 'social republic', which would take action over poverty and working conditions. Two well-disciplined workers' demonstrations were staged on 16 March and 16 April, the first led by the revolutionary socialist, Auguste Blanqui. The results of the elections, held with universal male suffrage on 23 April, reflected the social anxiety and resentment which this militancy stirred amongst most of the French population. To prevent bankruptcy, the provisional government had increased direct taxation by 45 per cent – the '45 centimes' – which was hated not only by the wealthy, but also by the peasantry, who were led to believe that this extra money allowed Parisian workers to idle in the National Workshops. The elections returned a majority of 'moderates' (usually monarchists), dismaying workers and radicals who now feared for the future of social reform, and for the Republic itself. Workers were killed in violent protests in Rouen. In Paris on 15 May a demonstration organised by the radical clubs invaded the Constituent Assembly, which finally prompted the reaction from the conservative majority.

The Luxembourg Commission was closed down and on 20 June the Constituent Assembly voted to disband the National Workshops, which now employed an alarming 115,000 previously unemployed workers. Mass protests began on 22 June and developed into an armed insurrection – the 'June Days' – in which workers fought not just to keep open the workshops, but also for the 'social republic'. Fierce fighting in barricaded streets lasted until 26 June when at least fifteen thousand workers lay dead and some twelve thousand more were arrested. The main consequence of the June Days was to heighten social antagonisms. The peasants supported the government. National Guard units from wealthier Parisian districts fought against the workers. Liberal republicans saw in the June Days a struggle between 'order, liberty, civilisation' and 'barbarians, desperados emerging from their lairs for massacre and looting', as the moderate republican newspaper, *Le National*, put it.[4] Social fear set the Second French Republic on the path of reaction.

German workers created associations to press their demands; strikes, particularly in northern German cities, broke out in April over wages. Stefan Born, an apprentice printer, established a Central Workers' Committee in Berlin, to which a large number of labour associations affiliated. It appealed for solidarity among workers, but it rejected the notion that workers should struggle against the bourgeoisie; social reform would come through legal means in a new parliamentary democracy. In August 1848 a congress of workers met in Berlin, with 40 delegates from 31 associations, including the first German trade unions. It hammered out a wide-ranging reform programme, including a welfare system, free state education and a progressive income tax. Moderate as the incipient labour movement was, no fewer than 70,000 people left Berlin out of fear of social revolution. When the first regular troops returned to the city at the end of August, they were greeted ecstatically by people anxious for law and order.

The extreme left sought to exploit German workers' grievances, but labour and political radicalism did not always march in step. The Cologne Workers' Association, with 8000 members by the summer, sought to steer the workers away from political action. Its main goal was to put moral pressure on the bourgeoisie for a peaceful transition to a socialist society. Its membership consisted primarily of journeymen and labourers, attracted to its approach because, as Jonathan Sperber suggests, they were 'schooled to passivity, to living from charity, by decades of un- and underemployment'.[5] When its leadership was arrested in early July, however, Marx and his associates took it over, transforming it into a political organisation with close ties to the democratic movement. In the process (and also because the organisation started to levy dues), its membership fell from thousands to hundreds.

Viennese workers noisily voiced their economic demands through public meetings and collective bargaining with their employers. Less politicised than their French or German counterparts, Austrian workers placed their faith in the political leadership of radical students, but radical journalists began to make an impact with their appeals for proletarian unity, their attacks on employers and their demands for the government to do more for the poor. In April, some workers started to refuse to pay rents, prompting the government to support the creation of a Security Committee, backed by the new National Guard 'to safeguard public security, peace, and order, and to guard the personal and property rights of all inhabitants'.[6] Mindful of the June Days in Paris, the government was reluctant to shut down the public works altogether, so instead reduced the workers' pay. Between 21 and 23 August, spontaneous street demonstrations, with women in the lead, turned violent and between six and eighteen workers were killed. As after the Parisian June Days, anxious people saw the uprising in terms of social conflict. The conservative *Wiener Zeitung* declared that 'at this moment there came into being a proletariat that formerly did not exist'.[7]

The poverty of urban workers would prove to be one of the most important factors in the ultimate collapse of the revolutionary regimes. In 1848–9 there was little sign of economic recovery to take the sting out of worker militancy, while the measures promoted by liberal regimes were unequal to the depth of the social crisis. Although the most dramatic working-class insurrections were spontaneous, radicals consistently sought to exploit the grievances and channel them towards political goals. At the same time, conservatives pointed to the fearsome power of working-class demonstrations to claim that workers were intent on destroying social order, even civilisation itself. Most liberals and middle-class people were alarmed enough to seek to roll back some of the political freedoms which had made worker militancy possible.

The year 1848 also saw the collapse of the old regime in the countryside. Peasants protested against their burdens: in the east, against serfdom and seigneurial rights; in the west, over access to forest and common lands and against taxation, low wages, indebtedness and their remaining seigneurial obligations. French peasants, protesting against the Forest Code, chased away state foresters and invaded private woodland. Such actions were also widespread in western Germany and northern Italy. In the Rhineland, peasants seized land and burned manor houses and tax registers. For western-European peasants, the 1848 Revolutions were to prove a grave disappointment. In France, they were immediately faced with the '45 centimes' tax and they feared the rumoured 'communism' of urban workers. Disappointed in the new Republic, they protested by turning back to their traditional patrons, the rural *notables*, in the April elections.

Western German peasants seized the chance to throw off their remaining seigneurial burdens and to protest against taxes and redemption payments. While abhorring the violation of property, German liberal governments accepted the attacks on seigneurialism itself and sought to restore calm by formally abolishing the remaining rights and dues. In Baden, urban democrats tried to harness peasant aspirations to hold on to land which they had seized, and some of the rural population was active in a republican uprising in April 1848. Elsewhere in Germany, the peasants settled down once the concessions were made, giving monarchs the advantage of rural peace when the opportunity came to strike back against the liberal regimes. In East Prussia, indebted peasants were still economically dependent on the aristocratic landowners and suffered acutely in the social crisis. They rioted throughout the spring, but through it all they kept a deep-rooted faith in their King; in the elections some even wrote 'Frederick William IV' on their ballot papers.[8] In such circumstances, it was easy for the conservatives to recruit the peasantry into the cause of the 'King and Fatherland'.

The impact of the revolutions on the central-European peasantry was even more dramatic than in the west, because their burdens were weightier. In the Habsburg empire, peasant violence, particularly in Bohemia, forced the authorities to abolish the *robot* (labour services) on 28 March 1848. On 11 April, the government in Vienna issued a manifesto promising to free all peasants from all dues and obligations on 1 January 1849, albeit with redemption payments. In practice, landlords in Cisleithania (the Austrian, as opposed to Hungarian, parts of the empire) lost very little in the emancipation. They were now free of direct responsibility for the peasants, who were weighed down with redemption payments over two decades. Though this compensation was a third less than the amount originally envisaged, it was enough to allow the landlords to introduce technology into their estates, giving them a competitive advantage over the peasant smallholdings. Meanwhile, the reforms allowed the Emperor to pose as the emancipator of the peasants, who now sought to defend their gains, their religion and their beloved monarch by siding with the forces of order.

In Hungary, the nobles responded to peasant unrest with emancipation. The abolition of serfdom, tithes and seigneurial rights and dues on 18 March was enshrined in the 'April Laws'. Urbarial farmers (those who held land which could be neither freely sold nor inherited) were now granted full ownership. Yet the gentry retained absolute ownership of their own domain land, meaning that they could legitimately evict their tenants and former serfs, who became landless labourers. Peasants still owed labour services to the county authorities and were barred from owning vineyards. Nobles, meanwhile, still enjoyed exclusive rights (regalia) to sell wine, hold fairs, keep birds, hunt and fish. The peasants, therefore, tested the limits of the reforms by further unrest. The conflicts were aggravated where the landlords were Magyar and the peasants were Romanian (as in Transylvania) or Serbs (as in the south). The social and ethnic violence was such that, on 21 June, the minister of the interior declared the entire kingdom under a state of siege, dispatched troops into the countryside and had the peasant ringleaders arrested. Later, the peasantry would refuse to rally en masse to the liberal Hungarian regime when it faced its gravest crisis.

In Italy, Neapolitan peasants occupied estate lands, alarming moderate liberals and all property-owners, who supported the deployment of National Guard units to restore order. With the peasants now being repressed by the liberal regime, King Ferdinand saw his chance and, in a coup on 15 May, purged the parliament of radicals, making the moderates, terrified of social revolution, dependent upon him – and his soldiers – for the maintenance of order. In northern Italy, the revolutionaries made little headway in winning over the peasants. In Lombardy, the economic crisis, conscription, a forced loan and requisitioning by the Piedmontese army alienated the rural population. By July they opposed a war which they believed to be for the benefit of their landlords. Some peasants even began to cheer the Austrian commander – 'Viva Radetzky!' Moderates like Stefano Jacini began to think that an Austrian restoration would be preferable to the 'evils of anarchy' which would be unleashed by a peasant insurrection. In neighbouring Venetia, the situation was initially more promising. Manin abolished the hated head tax and reduced the imposition on salt, but he then had to choose between keeping peasant support with further reforms and conciliating the rural and mercantile elites, whose financial backing was essential. Manin chose the latter, while the Austrians shrewdly promised not to reimpose the head tax. The peasants now had little to lose if the Austrians won.

The European peasants started out as a revolutionary force in 1848, spurred by their deep social and economic grievances. Yet their targets were invariably local: they struck at their immediate oppressors, their landlords and local representatives of the state, such as tax collectors and forestry officials. After the initial outbreak, they usually fell under the conservative spell when the reforms offered by the liberal regimes dried up. When the counter-revolution came, peasants either stood aside or rallied enthusiastically to the conservatives.

The Centre Collapses: Political Polarisation

Liberals wanted the 1848 Revolutions to be primarily a political transformation, ending with the creation of constitutional states. Social change, they argued, would evolve from the free ownership of property, the play of market forces and the personal freedom of the peasantry. This middle ground was challenged by both the extreme left and the conservatives. In the crises of 1848–9, the latter won more influence as most people were progressively drawn away from the liberal centre to support the forces of law and order against the radicals. The liberals themselves, forced to choose between their own libertarian principles and the restoration of order, generally opted for the latter. The resulting political polarisation ultimately finished in a victory for the conservatives because, in the end, they had greater forces and support at their disposal.

In France, the repression of the June Days led workers to desert the liberal Republic, while the moderate republicans turned towards authoritarian methods to face down the crisis. General Eugène Cavaignac, commander of the troops who put down the June uprising, had been appointed temporary head of government. In July, a decree reduced the popular clubs to impotence. In August, a law imposed restrictions on the press, forcing the closure of several newspapers. Paris was officially under a state of siege from June until October 1848. The rightward drift of the liberal republicans left an opening through which a man with a familiar name stepped into power: Louis Napoleon Bonaparte.

Louis Napoleon was the nephew of Napoleon Bonaparte. He had made two blundering attempts to seize power from the July Monarchy in 1836 and 1840. Sentenced to life imprisonment, he escaped in 1846, reappeared in Paris in 1848 and was elected to the Constituent Assembly. For Parisian workers, the name Bonaparte was associated with the glories of the Napoleonic Empire and with their aspirations for social reform. The peasantry remembered Napoleon as the 'people's Emperor', making his nephew a promising alternative to the *notables*. For 'moderates', the Napoleonic tradition meant strong, authoritarian government: even monarchists were willing to back Louis Napoleon, provided he crushed the left and cleared the way for a restoration of the monarchy. In December 1848 he won the presidency in a landslide election and the conservatives prepared to make their counter-offensive.

In Germany, radicals and liberals agreed that the nation should be united through the election of a national parliament at Frankfurt, which would draw up a constitution. Yet they concurred on little else. The *Vorparlament* (pre-parliament), which was to prepare for the elections to the National Assembly, rejected the republican programme of the Badenese radicals, Friedrich Hecker and Gustav von Struve. They reacted by returning to Baden where, on 12 April, they proclaimed a republic and mustered a 6000-strong force, including peasants, before being routed by the combined government forces of Baden, Hesse-Darmstadt, Nassau and Württemberg. Meanwhile, the *Vorparlament* decreed that the suffrage would be determined by the separate states, permitting most of the liberal governments in Germany to restrict the vote to property-owners or taxpayers. Most of the delegates elected to the National Assembly, which first met in May, were therefore constitutional monarchists. In June they voted to appoint Archduke John, a Habsburg, as the interim executive of the German empire.

The German radicals were not yet beaten. The democrats in the Frankfurt parliament were a large and vocal minority. Most of these, like Robert Blum, would have accepted a monarchy as the price for unification, while working for universal male suffrage and social reform. Yet a smaller group of revolutionaries, including Arnold Ruge, were set against compromise. They appealed to workers and the poor on the streets of cities like Frankfurt, Berlin and Cologne, urging them into a second revolution for an egalitarian, social democracy. In June, one of Ruge's colleagues, Julius Fröbel, led a Democratic Congress in Frankfurt, to which 89 associations from 66 cities sent delegates. A central committee was established in Berlin to co-ordinate propaganda and agitation against both conservatives and liberals alike. Their success in attracting working-class support was mixed. Those on the extreme fringes, such as the Communist League of Marx and Engels, drew in intellectuals and skilled workers, but its newspaper, the *Neue Rheinische Zeitung*, presupposed an educated readership and criticised the guilds, which many workers wanted to revive. In September, however, a mixture of social distress and radical agitation led to a violent confrontation in Frankfurt between the liberal authorities and the radicals, who mobilised the highly-politicised workers in the city.

The spark was a war against Denmark over Schleswig-Holstein. The duchies were ruled by the Danes and were legally inseparable, but Holstein was part of the German Confederation and had a mostly German population. German liberals and radicals took it for granted that Holstein would remain part of a united Germany, but the question was whether or not Schleswig could also be detached from Denmark. On 21 March 1848, King Christian VIII of Denmark raised the stakes by announcing the formal annexation of Schleswig as an integral part of his kingdom. An insurrection of Germans in both duchies was met with force by a Danish army, and the rebels asked Prussia for help. To German public acclaim, the Prussians duly marched into Schleswig, but diplomatic pressure from Britain and Russia forced them to withdraw in May and to sign an armistice at Malmö in August. The German provisional government in Schleswig was disbanded. When the Frankfurt parliament, after some prevarication, ratified the armistice in September, a public meeting of 12,000 people called by the radicals proclaimed the armistice as treasonous and called for a second revolution. Alarmed, the liberal administration in Frankfurt called on troops from Austria, Prussia and Hesse-Darmstadt to protect the parliament. 2000 soldiers prevented the crowd from storming the building, with 60 deaths on all sides, including two conservative deputies. The tremors were felt across Germany, but it was in Baden that a further revolutionary outbreak took place in response. On 21 September the incorrigible Struve, just out of prison, marched across the frontier from Switzerland with a handful of friends, including the young Wilhelm Liebknecht. They proclaimed a German republic but were again crushed after four days.

The September crisis poisoned relations between the liberals and radicals, and strengthened the conservatives. Conservatives and liberals alike now feared a second revolution, and the German administration under Archduke John encouraged liberal governments in the various states to provide troops to crush the radical threat. In the autumn, Prussia, Hanover, Saxony, Weimar and Bavaria – all with liberal ministries – sent contingents to help restore order in Saxe-Altenburg and Saxe-Meiningen. Conservatives were talking ominously about the 'bullet solution'.[9]

Political divisions among the revolutionaries were opening opportunities for reaction in the one country whose support for German unity was essential: Prussia. The elections to the Prussian diet took place in May, returning a mixture of nobles, middle-class liberals and democrats, peasants and some artisans. It soon became clear that the liberal prime minister, Ludolf Camphausen, could neither command a majority in parliament nor control the Berlin democrats, who seemed to be running amok. In May, the King left Berlin for the safety of Potsdam, where conservatives rallied around him. Army officers and landowners established 'King and Fatherland' associations to marshal the peasantry behind the monarchy. In June, political temperatures in Berlin rose after a railway workers' insurrection, led by democrats. Camphausen chose to resign rather than call in the army, but the conservatives sensed that the tide was turning in their favour. The King forced the resignation of yet another liberal cabinet in August and prepared for a coup against parliament. In September he appointed the reactionary General Wrangel to command the army around Berlin. In October the citizens' militia killed 11 striking canal workers and the last liberal Prussian cabinet resigned, its efforts to steer the regime between revolution and reaction in tatters. On 5 November, Wrangel's troops swept through Berlin, disarming the militia, dissolving parliament, declaring martial law and closing down political clubs and newspapers. Belatedly, Prussian democrats now rallied to the cause of the parliament, trying to support a tax strike called by liberals. It had little impact, as the people who paid the most tax were precisely those who wanted a return to order.

None the less, the victorious conservatives avoided a complete reaction. On 6 December, Prussia received a constitution from the King, who was buying time to bring the crisis under control. Some ministers were toying with the idea of a German empire dominated by Prussia, which would have to be a constitutional state if it were to secure widespread support. The final version of May 1849 split the voters into three classes of taxpayers, so that the wealthiest 5 per cent of Prussian males were represented by a third of the seats. The King confirmed the emancipation of the peasants from their remaining obligations and the abolition of the fiscal and judicial privileges of the nobility. He pleased artisans by restoring the guilds in 70 trades. Yet the conservative victory in Prussia endangered the liberal regimes elsewhere in Germany. As the Frankfurt parliament made loud protests against the royal coup in Prussia, the moderate left-wing delegates formed the 'Central March Association', aimed at uniting all shades of opinion in defence of the liberal revolution. Half a million members in 950 clubs were affiliated to it, but the German National Assembly was now unable to impose its will on the two great powers, Prussia and Austria, for, in the latter, the forces of reaction had triumphed in October.

Austrian radicals broke from the liberals when the Emperor issued his promised constitution in April. They were disappointed because the suffrage was restricted, the Emperor had an absolute veto and much of the upper house was to be appointed by the sovereign. Austro-German nationalists fretted that the new Austrian parliament might pre-empt Austrian inclusion in the united Germany. On 15 May a radical Central Committee organised a demonstration of 10,000 armed workers, supported by the students of the Academic Legion. The government yielded, declaring that there would be no upper house and no property qualifications (which was understood to mean universal male suffrage). Yet the radicals could not celebrate for long. Feeling endangered by the crowds, the royal family slipped out of Vienna, making for Innsbruck, from where Ferdinand issued a 'Manifesto' to his people on 20 May, denouncing the 'anarchical faction'.[10] The echoes of Louis XVI's flight to Varennes in 1791 were not lost on the radicals, who crowed that the days of the monarchy were numbered. Yet the horrors of a republic, which to everyone but the radicals meant 'anarchy' and 'communism', alarmed most of the Viennese. The liberal government moved to disband the Academic Legion and close the university, which sparked student protests on 26 May. The ministry again caved in, confirming the concessions of 15 May and allowing the establishment of a joint liberal–radical Security Committee responsible for law and order in the capital. This was, however, the last great victory of the left; the radicals were now beginning to swim against a tide of public hostility.

Pro-government deputies standing for 'law and order' and a return to the April constitution dominated the chamber after the June elections. The radicals were then swept aside as they helplessly watched the workers' August insurrection being crushed. The liberals on the Security Committee asserted themselves and managed to carry its own abolition. In September, a network of constitutional clubs, aimed at defending the liberal settlement of March–April against 'republicans' and 'anarchy', spread across Austria, attracting up to thirty-thousand members and including both liberals and conservatives making common cause against the left. The radicals belatedly rallied to the defence of the liberal order in October, when the court and the army launched their counter-attack against the 1848 revolution. The reaction, however, was made possible by events in other parts of the Austrian empire.

The Springtime of Peoples

The liberals and radicals of 1848, with few exceptions, were also nationalists, although their precise aims varied and conflicted. The revolutions in Italy were dominated by the question of national unity, which divided the republicans from the moderates. There was, moreover, the stubborn persistence of localism – loyalty to one's dynastic ruler, one's province or city (*campanilismo*), rather than to the more abstract idea of 'Italy'. Pope Pius IX seemed to be fulfilling his early promise when he gave his army vague orders to support Charles Albert's campaign against the Austrians. Yet any real unity of purpose was fragile. A need to temper domestic, republican opposition by taking the initiative against Austria and his own desire to annex Lombardy to Piedmont drove Charles Albert's decision for war. The Italian revolutionaries, meanwhile, split over whether to risk supporting a drive for national unity under the ambiguous Charles Albert, or to work towards reforming their own, separate states before dealing with unification. Most republicans opted for the former, agreeing to an uneasy political truce with the liberals, who were more enthusiastic about Piedmontese leadership. In any case, Charles Albert forced the issue by warning the liberal government in Milan that he would withdraw from the war unless it agreed to hold a plebiscite over a Piedmontese annexation of Lombardy. Meanwhile, Austrian forces had regrouped and, in May, counter-attacked through Venetia. Faced with the stark alternative of being abandoned to the Austrians, in the summer the Lombards and Venetians held referendums which overwhelmingly supported the annexation of their respective provinces by Piedmont. Nominally, at least, all of northern Italy was a kingdom united under Charles Albert.

Like Piedmont, other states pursued their own interests rather than national unity. Grand Duke Leopold of Tuscany squabbled with Charles Albert over territory belonging to Modena and Parma. King Ferdinand II of Naples was especially worried by the expansionism of Charles Albert, whom he regarded as a rival for pre-eminence in Italy. Neapolitan liberals had cajoled him into sending troops northwards to join the struggle against Austria, but now, strengthened by his coup on 15 May, he ordered his forces back to prepare for the reconquest of Sicily. The Pope's enthusiasm had already burned out when on the brink of war with Austria, a Catholic power. Anxious also over republican stirrings in Rome, he had withdrawn from the war at the end of April.

The full commitment of Papal and Neapolitan forces might just have tipped the balance against the Austrians. As it was, in the broiling heat at Custozza on 25 July, Radetzky's forces routed the Piedmontese. The Austrians re-entered Milan and, on 9 August, Charles Albert agreed to an armistice, whereby he abandoned Lombardy. The failure of independence and unification under monarchist leadership sparked a republican backlash. The 'second wave' of revolution, which would sweep the rest of Europe in 1849, actually began in Italy in the summer of 1848.

Radetzky's victory was applauded by German nationalists in both Austria and Germany. They had also cheered as Prussian troops were, in May, sent in to crush a Polish uprising in Poznania, which they saw as part of Germany. Narrow-minded nationalism was not, of course, confined to the Germans; it was the curse of almost all European liberals and republicans to regard their own national interests, such as territorial boundaries and the rights of ethnic minorities, only from their own national perspective. Ethnic groups struggling for self-rule or unification were reluctant to concede much to other nationalities, let alone collaborate. National hatreds were most damaging to the liberal cause in the Habsburg empire, where the imperial government had little difficulty in playing off the different nationalities against each other. In April 1848, conservatives exploited ethnic hostilities in Galicia between Poles and Ruthenians, who, particularly in the east, were respectively landlord and serf. The governor, Count Franz Stadion, secured Ruthenian support by issuing an emancipation proclamation, undermining Polish demands for autonomy. He also crushed the Polish National Committee in Krakow (which was shelled by Austrian artillery). The next to fall were the Czechs. In April, the movement for German unification spurred the Czechs to seek to offset German nationalism by calling for a Pan-Slav congress to be held in Prague in June. The idea provoked a withering storm of anger from Germans and Magyars. The latter feared that it would encourage separatism amongst the Slavs (which in fact it explicitly disavowed), while the former insisted that Bohemia was part of Germany. Trouble began when the liberal Czech historian František Palacky infuriated German nationalists by rejecting an invitation to attend the Frankfurt parliament on the grounds that Bohemia was not German.[11] In Prague, the German-speaking population had organised a 'League of Germans' to counter the Czech demands for the unity of the three provinces (Bohemia, Moravia and Silesia) and linguistic equality with German. A bitter war of words ensued.

The June uprising in Prague, which put a premature end to the Slav Congress, further aggravated these relations. The insurrection occurred because the commander of imperial forces in Bohemia, the authoritarian Windischgrätz, was heavy-handed in his efforts to restore order. The first weeks of May saw worker unrest, a demonstration in defence of press freedom and a prison riot. Army patrols now tramped through the streets, while cannons were wheeled ominously on to vantage points over the city. The tension snapped on 12 June when some twenty-five thousand people clashed with troops, built barricades and began a six-day uprising, the bloodiest in the Czech revolution. On 17 June, Windischgrätz (whose wife had been killed by a stray bullet) bombarded the city, killing up to two hundred people, mostly manual workers. The vast majority of the insurgents were Czech, and though some German radicals joined the insurrection, most joined with conservatives in celebrating Windischgrätz's 'triumph'.[12] The Frankfurt parliament had even considered asking Prussia, Bavaria and Saxony to provide troops to support Windischgrätz. In Prague, the uprising marked the beginning of the reaction: a state of siege was declared, those suspected of revolutionary activity were arrested and the Czech National Committee was closed down. Yet Windischgrätz was shrewd enough to realise that the government in Vienna needed the support of moderate Czechs against Austro-German radicals. He lifted the state of siege on 20 July, two days before the all-Austrian parliament met in Vienna. The Czech delegates, deeply wary of what they saw as liberal Austrian tendencies towards centralisation and, worse, radical desires to drag the Czechs into a united Germany, duly supported the government. Meanwhile, the Habsburg court had been manoeuvring against the Hungarians. In doing so, it found allies among the Slavs and Romanians, alarmed and antagonised by Magyar nationalism.

For Hungarian liberals, 'Hungary' meant the lands of the Crown of Saint Stephen, which included vast areas not populated by Magyars. The best way to ensure unity, they believed, was to grant all inhabitants rights as individuals, while discouraging – and indeed repressing – separatist tendencies. Non-Magyars, Kossuth believed, would have no need of special national rights when as individuals they were being made citizens of a wider, Hungarian polity. He also argued that the unity of the kingdom made it necessary for the official language to be Magyar.[13] Demands by the subject nationalities for special treatment were seen as 'reactionary' and divisive. In northern Hungary, the small Slovak national movement made moderate demands and supported the Emperor when the Magyars brushed them aside. More dangerous were the Romanians, the Serbs and the Croats. In 1848, Romanian nationalists within Hungary wanted, at a minimum, a separate status for their two Churches (Uniate and Orthodox), as well as legal recognition of their nationality. The March 1848 revolution had, however, alarmed the Hungarian and Saxon magnates whose privileges were under threat. Their opposition to the abolition of serfdom stoked up the hatred of the Romanian peasantry against the Magyars. On 15–17 May, 40,000 people, mostly peasants, converged on Blaj to support a 'National Petition' which demanded the abolition of serfdom, civil rights and Romanian representation in the Transylvanian diet, as well as a separate Romanian parliament, militia and educational system.[14] Successively the Transylvanian diet (dominated by Magyars), the Emperor (under Magyar pressure) and the Hungarian parliament rebuffed the Blaj demands. This left the Romanians with two choices: union with the Danubian principalities or autonomy from Hungary within the Habsburg empire. The former option looked more attractive in June when Romanian liberals in the principalities, disgruntled with the restrictive Russian-imposed constitution, the 'Organic Regulations' of 1832, toppled the ruling prince in Wallachia and established a provisional government in Bucharest. Tsar Nicholas I pressurised the nominal sovereign, the Ottoman Sultan Abdülmecid, into joining him in destroying the Romanian revolution in September. The Transylvanian Romanians turned to the second solution, which entailed a struggle against Hungary on behalf of the Habsburgs. Imperial troops supported the peasants and the Romanian border regiments when they rose up in October and drove the Hungarian forces out of Transylvania. This war, the bloodiest and the longest conflict during the revolutions, would last until August 1849. In savage interethnic strife, 40,000 people would die and 230 villages would be destroyed. This revolt had broken out as the Hungarians were facing another invasion – from the southern Slavs, again backed by the Habsburg monarchy.

The Croats of the empire's 'Military Border' had their own grievances: when not at war they farmed, but in large communes called *zadruga* which could barely cope with the population increase of the nineteenth century. Yet the Croats of the Military Border were fundamentally loyal to the Austrian Crown because their freedom from manorial obligations gave them a status above other peasants in 'Civil' Croatia (formally part of Hungary), who remained serfs. In March a liberal Croatian National Congress met in Zagreb and, brushing aside the objections of the Croat gentry, abolished serfdom and demanded full autonomy with a Croatian parliament under the Habsburg Emperor. While Vienna was alarmed by these demands, the imperial court also recognised that the loyalty of the Military Border was a powerful weapon against the Magyars. The Emperor duly appointed the conservative, anti-Magyar Baron Josip Jelačić as Croatian Ban, or Viceroy, and, in April, to the command of the Military Border. Conflict was also brewing further east between Magyars and Serbs. In May, with the backing of the independent Serbian principality, 8000 Hungarian Serbs met at Sremski Karlovci (Karlóca in Hungarian) and proclaimed an autonomous province, Voivodina. Like Croatia, Voivodina recognised the ultimate sovereignty of the Habsburg Emperor, but not the authority of the Hungarian government. Its governing committee incited Serbian peasants against Magyar landlords and the crisis developed into open war between Hungary and the Voivodina Serbs. The latter, supported by their own troops from the border regiments, held their own against the Hungarians, fighting off an attack on Sremski Karlovci in June. Jelačić sought to harness this Serb nationalism as well as Croatian patriotism against Hungary: on his arrival in Zagreb on 5 June, when he was sworn in as Ban, he declared the unity of Orthodox Serbs with Catholic Croats a 'single-blooded nation of two faiths'. He exploited the Hungarian attack on Voivodina to wrest wide-ranging powers from the Croatian national assembly, the *Sabor*, which he then closed down in July, though not before it had abolished serfdom in Civil Croatia. With the blessing of the Austrian court (and with supplies provided by the Austrian war ministry) Jelačić then prepared to turn against the Hungarians. The advance units of the Croatian army crossed the River Drava into Hungary in September, but were defeated at the village of Pákozd, only 30 miles from Budapest (see Map 8.1). Jelačić asked the Hungarians for

Map 8.1 The survival of the Habsburg Empire, 1848–1914

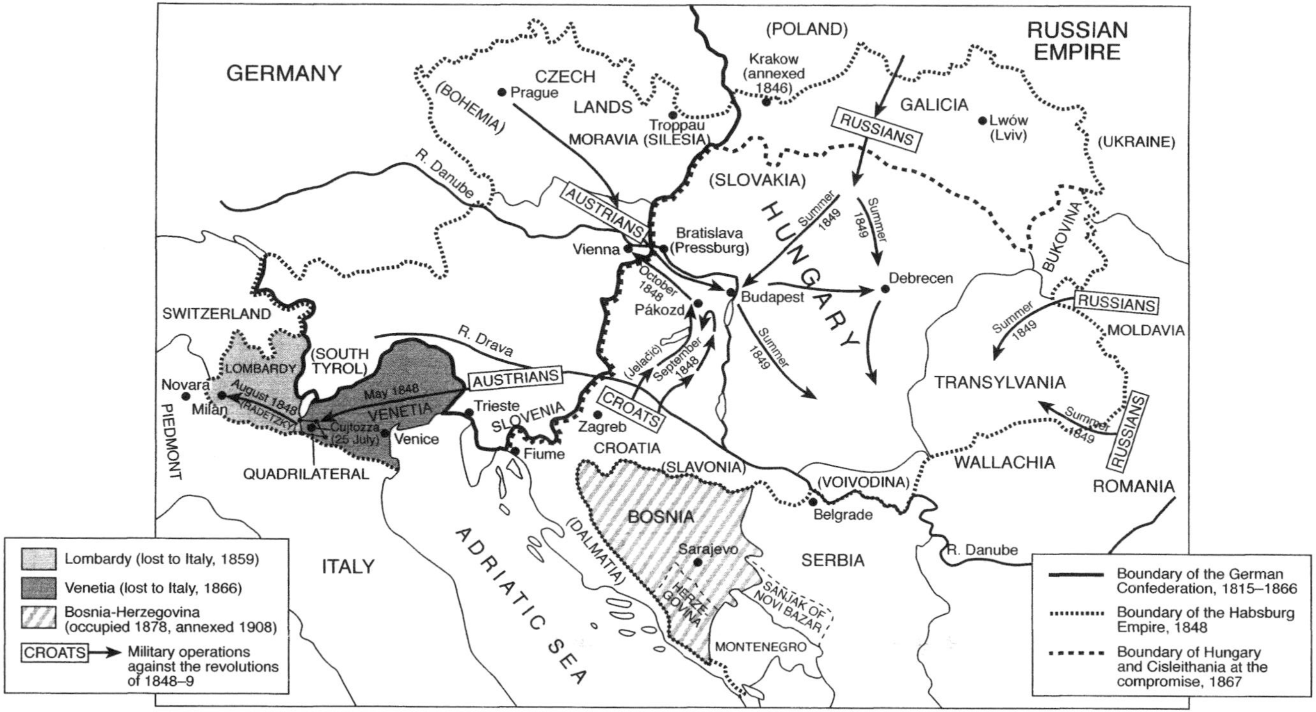

- Lombardy (lost to Italy, 1859)
- Venetia (lost to Italy, 1866)
- Bosnia-Herzegovina (occupied 1878, annexed 1908)
- CROATS → Military operations against the revolutions of 1848–9

- Boundary of the German Confederation, 1815–1866
- Boundary of the Habsburg Empire, 1848
- Boundary of Hungary and Cisleithania at the compromise, 1867

a three-day truce, which he used to withdraw, not back to Croatia but towards Vienna to support Windischgrätz in containing the revolution there. Before he arrived, a radical uprising had erupted in the Austrian capital.

The immediate spark for the Viennese insurrection was the outbreak of open war between the Habsburg monarchy and Hungary. A final effort by the court to negotiate with the Magyars failed when its commissioner, Count Ferenc Lamberg, a Hungarian conservative, was killed by a mob on his arrival in Budapest on 28 September. The Viennese court was finally and unambiguously set on crushing the Hungarian revolution by force, issuing a declaration of war on Hungary on 3 October. The Austrian radicals opposed the war; the Magyars, with their defiance of the monarchy and their fight against Jelačić, seemed to represent the strongest political shield against the forces of reaction. Through the press and the political clubs, the democrats mobilised students and workers, including women, who tried to prevent troops from leaving to fight the Magyars. On 6 October these efforts sparked fierce street fighting and, with conservatives fleeing the city, political initiative fell to the left, both in Parliament and among the students and the radical clubs, which were directed by a Central Committee.

Parliament established a Permanent Committee to organise Vienna's defence against the combined forces of the garrison encamped outside the city, Jelačić, who arrived on 10 October, and Windischgrätz, who had marched from Prague. On 22 October, Ferdinand ordered the Austrian parliament to leave Vienna and move to Kroměříž (Kremsier) in Moravia by 15 November. On 28 October, Windischgrätz's artillery opened fire on Vienna and his troops began to storm the city. Only a Hungarian victory could save the Austrian revolution, but two days later Jelačić's forces beat the Hungarians back at Schwechat – a mere two miles from Vienna. On 1 November when Windischgrätz and Jelačić formally entered the city, 2000 Viennese had been killed in the fighting.

The defeats inflicted on the liberal order in 1848 gave the opportunity for radicals to seize the initiative. It was only when this second wind had died down that the revolutions truly came to an end. In Germany and France, radicals took the fight from the capital cities, where they had been comprehensively beaten, into the provinces and the countryside. It was, however, in Italy and in Hungary that the second wave first began to swell, in response to military defeat.

The Second Wave of Revolution and the Victory of the Reaction, 1848–51

Charles Albert's defeat at Custozza discredited the monarchist path to Italian independence. Piedmont was thrown into crisis by the defeat and, in December, Charles Albert bowed to popular pressure to appoint none other than Vincenzo Gioberti as prime minister. Gioberti urged Charles Albert to reassert his leadership over the movement for Italian unity, which entailed restarting the war. And it was for the next round of that conflict that the King now prepared. In Tuscany, the government's lukewarm support for the war sparked a republican uprising in August, after which Grand Duke Leopold was forced to appoint the radicals Domenico Guerrazzi and Giuseppe Montanelli as ministers. A massive public demonstration in January 1849 forced the government to concede universal male suffrage and the Grand Duke fled in February. In Rome, the Pope's moderate prime minister, Peregrino Rossi, was stabbed to death on his way to Parliament on 15 November. The next day a crowd, incited by the political clubs, forced Pius IX to flee to Gaeta, leaving the capital in the hands of an interim government, which held elections based on universal male suffrage in January 1849. On 9 February the new assembly proclaimed the Roman Republic, which radicals such as Mazzini and Giuseppe Garibaldi saw as the first step towards a united, democratic Italy. Yet the two most powerful kingdoms, Piedmont and Naples, would never countenance such a vision. Naples had been in the throes of reaction since the royal coup of 15 May 1848 and Ferdinand II's troops were busy subduing the Sicilian separatist movement, which collapsed when Palermo was taken in February 1849.

Charles Albert's decision to resume the struggle against Austria in March 1849 was disastrous. The ill-prepared Piedmontese were routed by the Austrians at Novara. Facing an Austrian invasion and a republican uprising in Genoa, the King chose to pre-empt a disaster for his dynasty by abdicating in favour of his son, Victor Emmanuel II, and signing an armistice with Austria. The terms were generous, not least because Radetzky had no desire to fan the flames of Italian republicanism. With the most powerful Italian state defeated, the rest of Italy could put up only a feeble resistance, and Austrian troops overran Tuscany. Under Garibaldi, Rome held out until 2 July, not against the Austrians but against the French. President Louis Napoleon Bonaparte, courting the support of French conservative Catholics, gave orders for the Roman Republic to be crushed. On his return, Pius IX restored absolute rule. Only Venice remained. The city, though shelled by artillery across the lagoon, starving and cholera-ridden, held out until 27 August when imperial troops entered the city. Ironically, the first soldiers to arrive in the city were Hungarian.

In Hungary, the Croatian invasion in September 1848 gave strength to the radical opposition, but the crisis produced neither a radical revolution, nor a scurrying of moderate liberals towards conservatism. Rather, the left-wing liberals, led by Lajos Kossuth, stole the thunder of the extremists by carrying out their policies. They were able to do this because, for all their bluster, the radicals had little influence over the peasantry, while the urban working class was small. So initiative fell to the tougher liberals, who established a National Defence Committee. On 3 October, with the Austrian declaration of war, this committee became Hungary's emergency government, with Kossuth as President. The original liberals, albeit bereft of their moderate wing, remained in control and it was achieved by a parliamentary vote. It was, as Istvan Deak suggests, a 'lawful revolution'.[15]

The committee mobilised the country's resources in an early form of total war. The liberals expanded the citizen army (*honvéd*), used Hungary's gold reserves to purchase arms and grain from abroad and built up their war industries. After the defeat outside Vienna on 30 October, Hungary was thus able to survive both the Austrian counter-attack – which succeeded in taking Budapest itself in January 1849 – and a Romanian invasion supported by imperial troops. In echoes of the Terror of the French Revolution, the crisis gave renewed vigour to the radicals, who, while failing to secure universal male suffrage and the abolition of serfdom in the diet (now at Debrecen), established revolutionary courts. These handed down 122 death sentences to (mostly non-Magyar) 'traitors'. On 19 April, Hungary declared independence from Austria. In May, the Hungarians retook Budapest, and Kossuth was elected governor (or virtual dictator) of Hungary, which now faced a new threat – from Russia.

Tsar Nicholas I had always been inclined to use his army to crush the liberal regimes, but he had specific reasons for helping the young Habsburg Emperor, Francis Joseph, to destroy the Hungarian revolution. He suspected the Hungarians of trying to foment the revolt in the Romanian principalities; he feared that an independent Hungary would weaken Austria, allowing Prussia to dominate Germany; and he worried that the Hungarians would inspire his Polish subjects. Hungarian resistance, the caution of the Russian advance and illness from scurvy and cholera delayed Hungary's final collapse, which came in August. Kossuth resigned and fled into exile. The tiny rump of the National Assembly met at Arad and dissolved itself. The last Hungarian resistance, in the fortress of Komárom, was snuffed out on 2 October. While the Russians (and Nicholas himself) admired the courage of their Hungarian adversaries and pressed for a full amnesty for them all, the Austrian government granted this only to the rank and file. Five hundred people were sentenced to death, with 120 of these judgments being carried out, but this does not include the summary executions of guerrillas. Fifteen hundred people were imprisoned for up to twenty years, although many were amnestied in the 1850s. The Hungarian constitution was declared null and void by the very act of rebellion. Pro-Austrian officials took over local government. Austrian law was introduced, and the Hungarians also lost their police, the *Pandurs*, who were replaced by an Austrian *gendarmerie*. The uniformity stretched to fiscal and economic policy: up to 1851, Vienna gradually introduced the Austrian tax and customs system to Hungary, though the abolition of the tariffs between Hungary and Austria removed a long-standing Hungarian grievance.

For the rest of the Habsburg monarchy, the persistence of the Hungarian revolution had serious consequences. After the defeat of the Austrian revolution in October 1848, Prince Felix zu Schwarzenberg was appointed to form a new government. Schwarzenberg was not opposed to reform, but he believed in the traditional Habsburg way of achieving it: from above. He wanted to restore Habsburg authority, centralise the monarchy and, to some extent, Germanise it. The cabinet which he appointed therefore included some who had been associated with the liberal measures of 1848, namely Franz Stadion and Alexander Bach, a one-time democrat. On 2 December 1848 this government pressed the feeble-minded Ferdinand to abdicate, replacing him with his nephew, the 18-year-old Francis Joseph, who had not been compromised by the concessions made in March. The Constituent Assembly was reconvened on 22 November as a rump in Kroměříž, because the Emperor needed Czech and Austro-German support in the war against Hungary. Yet the government ignored the constitution produced by the Kroměříž parliament and imposed three acts of its own on 4 March 1849: a bill of rights, a law compensating landlords for the abolition of serfdom and a constitution. This last document was Stadion's work. It gave more power, including legislative initiative, to the Emperor, who appointed the government and made all decisions regarding imperial matters. Some of the achievements of 1848, including civil rights and the abolition of serfdom and seigneurial obligations, were retained. The legal equality of all nationalities was proclaimed, but the Hungarian, Bohemian, Transylvanian and Croatian diets were abolished. Administrative uniformity and centralisation would erase the nationality question; the empire was no longer to be a multinational but an anational state. In practice, the Emperor did not even convene the parliament promised in Stadion's constitution. Only the upper house, the *Reichsrat*, would meet and it would be appointed by the Emperor as an advisory body. On 31 December 1851 the 'Sylvester Patent' restored royal absolutism.

The counter-revolution in the Habsburg empire struck a heavy blow against plans for German unification. The *großdeutsch* (greater German) solution, which would have included Austria in the united Germany, was closed down when Schwarzenberg declared the Habsburg empire to be a unitary state, thus detaching German-speaking Austria from Germany. Yet there were German liberals who preferred a 'smaller German' (*kleindeutsch*) answer because it would be dominated by Prussia, with its enlightened bureaucracy and its leadership of the *Zollverein*. That Prussia retained a constitution after 1849, while Austria returned to absolutism, merely reinforced its more progressive credentials.

The Frankfurt parliament produced the German constitution in March 1849. That same day, Frederick William IV was elected as hereditary Kaiser (Emperor) of the German People. Yet though 29 German states accepted the constitution, they were not the most powerful and Prussia itself rejected it. In April, Frederick William castigated it as 'the dog-collar with which people want to chain me to the 1848 revolution'; he would not accept a 'crown from the gutter'. He closed down the lower chamber of the Prussian parliament and promised military help to any government opposed to the Frankfurt constitution. The other larger German powers – Austria, Bavaria, Hanover and Saxony – joined Prussia and recalled their deputies from Frankfurt. At the end of May the remnants of the parliament, now mostly of the left, withdrew to Stuttgart in Württemberg, where it was forcibly closed on 18 June.

This coup de grâce was a direct result of the second wave of revolution in Germany. When Frederick William rejected the constitution, the radicals mobilised, with the Central March Association playing a leading role. In Cologne, three separate radical congresses (including a socialist one organised by Marx) and two liberal conventions were held in May. There were outbreaks of revolutionary violence in the Rhineland involving up to fifteen thousand people, including peasants. An uprising in Saxony followed King Frederick Augustus II's closure of Parliament. Prussian troops brought in to restore royal authority killed 250 insurgents in four days of fighting in Dresden. Maximilian II of Bavaria was faced with an insurrection in the Bavarian Palatinate, from where revolutionaries tried to link up with republicans in Rhine-Hessen and Baden, which – not for the first time – was proclaimed a republic. The Prussian army overran the radical forces, though 6,000 republicans held out in Rastatt until late July. One in every ten was shot and 80,000 Badenese emigrated to North America in the aftermath.

The revolutions were over in Germany, but the issue as to how the various states would be ordered was still unresolved. Prussian conservatives sought to exclude Austria from Germany, which would then be dominated by Prussia. Only ultra-conservatives were now hostile to the notion of unification in any form. In May 1849, Prussia, Saxony and Hanover, soon joined by other German states, forged the Erfurt Union to press ahead with a plan for a federal Germany. Yet when Bavaria and Württemberg refused to join (neither wanting Protestant, Prussian dominance) and instead entered into an alliance with Austria, Hanover and Saxony withdrew in early 1850. War nearly erupted when Vienna wanted to heed two appeals to the restored *Bund*, one from Denmark (regarding Holstein) and the other from Hesse, for help in suppressing stubborn revolutionaries who were still resisting. Prussia opposed Austrian intervention, as it would strengthen the *Bund* and weaken the

Erfurt Union. Both sides mobilised their armies, the Austrians backed by the Bavarians. When the Austrians invaded Hesse on 1 November, only the intervention of Tsar Nicholas and Frederick William's fears over the potentially revolutionary consequences of an all-out war made Prussia yield. On 29 November, at an agreement at Olmütz (Olomouc), the Prussians were forced to disband the Erfurt Union. German unity – whether from below in 1848–9 or from above in 1850 – had failed.

In France, the consolidation of authoritarian rule did not occur without resistance from the radical left, which was making an impact in rural departments. This was because the radicals were working hard to mobilise peasant voters. In the parliamentary elections of May 1849, their candidates emphasised social reform, proclaiming themselves supporters of the 'democratic and social Republic', so they were called *démoc-socs*, or, simpler still, 'socialists'. The *démoc-socs* promised tax reductions and access to cheap credit, all of which would appeal to the hard-pressed peasant smallholders smarting from the on-going economic crisis. In some areas, 'red' candidates supported peasant resistance to the collection of the '45 centimes' tax. The *démoc-socs* took 170–80 seats (out of 750) and hoped to build on these foundations by winning the elections of 1852 when both the three-year term of the new Legislative Assembly and Bonaparte's presidency expired.

As the ambitions of the left grew, so did the fears of the conservatives, for whom an authoritarian solution began to look increasingly attractive. In June 1849, *démoc-soc* protests against the French intervention in Rome were dispersed by the army in Paris, Lyon and the rural south. Repressive legislation against political clubs, public meetings and the press followed arrests of left-wing deputies. Yet in the by-elections held on 10 March 1850 to fill the 21 seats left vacant, the *démoc-socs* held on to 11. The right asserted its strength in the National Assembly by voting a law on education (the Falloux law) on 15 March 1850, which expanded the role of the Catholic Church in the state education system and permitted the establishment of private Catholic schools. In April, the by-election victory of an outspoken opponent of the Falloux law, Eugène Sue, prompted the Assembly to disenfranchise 30 per cent of the electorate across France in May.

Yet conservatives were still alarmed by the buoyant mood of the *démoc-socs* as they worked among the grassroots as 'their year' of 1852 approached. Louis Napoleon Bonaparte appeared to be the only right-wing candidate who could gather enough votes to deny the *démoc-socs* victory in the presidential elections of 1852, yet, according to the constitution, he could not stand for a second consecutive term. Bonaparte campaigned tirelessly to amend the constitution, making no fewer than fourteen provincial tours in 1849–51, shamelessly telling audiences what they wanted to hear. To republicans he offered his support for the constitution of 1848 (an implicit condemnation of the restriction of the suffrage), while to conservatives he hinted that he might support a restoration of the monarchy. He used his presidential patronage to place his own supporters as prefects in the departments, as commanders in the army and as officials in the government ministries. At the end of July 1851, however, the amendment was defeated in parliament by an unholy alliance of republicans and Orleanists (who saw in the Bonapartes a competing dynasty). Louis Napoleon therefore resorted to a coup d'état. In the early hours of 2 December, police arrested leading opposition leaders, while troops occupied the National Assembly. Republican efforts to organise popular resistance were stymied in part by Bonaparte's proclamation restoring universal male suffrage and, in Paris, resistance was feeble. In the provinces, however, the coup was opposed by a great insurrection. Nearly seventy thousand people took up arms, principally in the rural districts of south-eastern and central France where *démoc-soc* propaganda had made its deepest impact. The uprising was too far removed from the centres of power to pose a serious threat and, once the authorities brought up troops, it was easily crushed.[16] The repression was efficient and sweeping: almost 27,000 people were arrested, of whom 10,000 were sentenced to deportation. Although Bonaparte himself commuted many of these penalties, the unexpected violence unleashed by his coup indelibly marked his new regime.

Achievements and Lost Opportunities

The 1848 revolutions were not a complete failure. Few of the constitutions introduced in 1848 survived the collapse of the liberal regimes, but some formerly absolutist monarchies retained some form of parliamentary government. The fact that Piedmont and Prussia were both henceforth constitutional monarchies would be of great significance to the futures of Italy and Germany. In France, universal male suffrage was reintroduced in 1848 and this time, bar the brief interlude in 1850–1, it was there to stay. Of equal importance in the long term was the abolition of serfdom and seigneurialism in central Europe; while certainly applied in such a way that it benefited the landlords, it was never reversed. The revolutions also gave millions of people their first direct involvement in politics: male workers and peasants voted for the first time in Germany and the Habsburg monarchy, where peasant deputies – most notably the Ukrainians from Galicia – were returned to the imperial parliament in Vienna. How far the peasants actually understood the political process and how far the experience advanced peasant politicisation is admittedly open to question. In September 1848, the Czech liberal press was reporting that peasants did not understand the meaning of such terms as 'democrat', 'reactionary', 'despotism' and 'hierarchy', though one can surely forgive them for finding the slippery notion of 'sovereignty' hard to grasp.[17] The political mobilisation of large sections of the European population was achieved not just through the formal means of elections and parliaments but also through the civil liberties which allowed political clubs (whether conservative, liberal or radical) and workers' organisations briefly to flourish. In Paris and Berlin, workers made use of the freedom to associate, organising guilds, mutual societies and, sometimes, nascent trade unions. In Germany, 1848 is taken as the traditional birth-date of the German labour movement.

The 1848 revolutions did little to emancipate half of the European population: women. They were excluded from the franchise everywhere and the deep-rooted prejudice – among many women as well as most men – against women's political participation ensured that few voices would be raised in support of their rights. One exception was a Hessian democrat (who still could not be accused of exploding sexual stereotypes) who declared that depriving women of the right to vote would be as unfair as denying them the pleasures of 'cooking, sewing, knitting, darning, dancing and playing'![18] More typical of left-wing attitudes was the leader of the Mainz Democratic Association, Ludwig Bamberger, who, while objecting to women's 'perfumed slavery', none the less asked: 'Who wants to eradicate differences which are present in nature?'[19] Some women challenged the limits of citizenship. In France, Jeanne Déroin announced her candidacy for the *démoc-socs* in Paris in the May 1849 elections, but was not supported by the rest of the radical movement. None the less, 1848 did witness women's political participation in more informal, but no less influential ways. In Paris, several political societies admitted men and women as equals, although most allowed women to attend but not to speak. In Germany, thousands of women collected money for a German navy (a popular national cause), while women's clubs were established in Berlin, Mannheim, Mainz and elsewhere. In Mainz, the Humania Association was founded in May 1849 by Kathinka Zitz-Halein to support 'needy patriots' with money, clothing, bandages and nursing in the radical uprising of that summer. In this way, women would show themselves worthy of citizenship; 'we must cease being just women', wrote Zitz-Halein, 'and become entirely citizens and patriots'.[20] Similar organisations supported the May insurrections in Saxony, Nassau, Frankfurt and Heidelberg. In Prague, middle-class women established the Club of Slavic Women, aimed primarily at promoting women's education. They also held two public meetings in August 1848 to protest against Windischgrätz and his treatment of the city. The second meeting resulted in a delegation being sent to Vienna, which secured the release of some political prisoners and permission to establish a Czech school for girls which finally opened in 1860.

1848 weighed heavily on the second half of the nineteenth century, both through its visions of reform and its rekindling of the fear of revolution. Many of the ideas expressed in 1848 were eventually implemented, albeit in different guises. This was not because the post-revolutionary regimes suddenly accepted liberal and democratic ideas. Rather, it was because the problems which bubbled violently to the surface in 1848 did not disappear. Constitutionalism, nationalism and the social question were all issues which the conservative victors could not ignore for long; not least because the accelerating pace of economic and social change after mid-century made these problems more urgent. Even in Russia, where the Tsarist regime's triumph over the revolution appeared to be so complete, the repression proved to be, in David Saunders's apt description, a 'Pyrrhic victory'.[21] After 1848, most governments understood that they had to show more flexibility towards new ideas, institutions and developments and that repression alone would only alienate civil society from the state and generate radical opposition. Much of the emphasis after the reaction of the 1850s, therefore, was on integrating different sections of society – first the middle-classes, then the workers and the peasantry – into the political order. This demanded a more flexible form of conservatism, which in the process absorbed some of the lessons of the mid-century crisis. Meanwhile, the defeats of the revolutions taught liberals, nationalists and radicals to change their tactics and ideas as they pursued their aims. In many respects, therefore, European politics in the second half of the century were concerned with the shadows and legacies of 1848.

Part III

A New Era? 1850–1879

9 A New Era?

The conservative order reasserted itself in the 1850s, but it was not an age of all-out reaction. The shock of 1848 gave a new flexibility to conservative thinking. Political stability and the defence of the existing social order meant adapting to economic and social change, which accelerated after 1850, even harnessing the forces which had erupted in 1848. This 'new realism'[1] was driven not just by a fear of revolution but also by the new instability in international affairs. The decades after 1848 witnessed a breakdown in the old certainties of the Vienna system, whereby a tacit assumption that war and revolution were interconnected led the great European powers to act with restraint. The Crimean War of 1853–6 did not altogether destroy this 'concert of Europe', but the conflict was the first of no fewer than four wars between great European powers up to 1878, a year which also witnessed the conclusion of a major war between Russia and the Ottoman Empire. These struggles helped to reshape Europe, with the emergence of Italy and Germany in the centre and of Romania in the east. Moreover, the wars forced dramatic change on the two great absolutist powers, Russia and Austria. Even they could not be blind to the need for reform if they were to weather the renewed instability in the international climate.

The New Conservatism

In western Europe, the pragmatic conservatism of the post-1848 era was embodied in Louis Napoleon's France. The Bonapartist regime combined authoritarianism with more than a nod to popular sovereignty, economic development and social reform. Within weeks of his coup in December 1851, a plebiscite gave Louis Napoleon overwhelming popular approval and a year later, after a further referendum, he was proclaimed Napoleon III.[2] For many voters Bonapartism represented the revolutionary legacy – and rejection of the Orleanist elites – without the anarchy of the Second Republic. The constitution of January 1852 had given Bonaparte sweeping powers, including the exclusive right to initiate legislation. Elections held every six years were based on universal male suffrage, but the government designated 'official candidates', lending them considerable support while harassing opponents. Louis Napoleon also used his powers against the republican opposition, reducing the ranks of the National Guard, strictly licensing cafés and censoring the press.

The authoritarian regime actively sought the support of the population, disseminating almanachs, songs and Napoleonic prints, subsidising newspapers and publishing decrees in an effort to instil loyalty. Napoleon III's populism aimed at giving the impression that he stood above the traditional elites, but he could not rule France without their help. Even the Emperor's ministers were not committed Bonapartists, but were frequently Orleanists whose influence and experience were too great to ignore. Napoleon III himself asked: 'How do you expect the Empire to run smoothly? The Empress [Eugénie, whom he married in 1853] is a Legitimist, Morny is an Orleanist, my cousin Jérôme-Napoleon is a Republican, I am a socialist; only Persigny is a Bonapartist and he is mad.'[3] In Parliament, Orleanist *notables* – landowners, businessmen, officials – predominated and rallied to the Empire less out of conviction than out of fear of social anarchy and political turmoil. Once the danger receded with the return of economic prosperity in the 1850s, Parliament would try to assert itself. The regime was also forced to compromise with local conservative interests, which most prefects found more practical to conciliate rather than challenge. Moreover, while most Catholics welcomed the coup in 1851, Napoleon III could never take their backing for granted and the Church was still a strong source of support for Legitimists, particularly in western France. In 1859, when Napoleon III brought France into the war of Italian unification, destroying the Pope's political power in Italy, he lost the support of significant sections of Catholic opinion.

The Second Empire was not, despite Napoleon III's impulses, a truly autocratic regime. It was certainly authoritarian and repressive. When workers in Lyon went on strike in 1855, the authorities made 132 arrests. Three hundred members of republican secret societies were arrested between 1853 and 1859, so opponents of the regime found it safer to organise behind legitimate fronts, such as mutual aid societies. From 1854, however, the regime began to loosen its grip on political opposition. Political clubs were still illegal and press restrictions remained, but republican journals made their first cautious appearance and in the 1857 elections republican candidates attracted half a million votes and won five Parisian seats. Yet this flowering of political freedom was fragile. A gruesome but unsuccessful bomb attack led by the Italian republican Felice Orsini on Napoleon III in January 1858 brought a new wave of repression. Under the Law of General Security, 500 people marked for their involvement in the June 1848 insurrection, or in the subsequent *démoc-soc* agitation, were rounded up, with most being deported to Algeria. This was not simply a response to Orsini's attack, but was part of a deeper, authoritarian impulse within the regime, as Orleanist journals were also closed down.

Yet Napoleon III also sought to disseminate the view that the regime was the friend of the worker and the peasant – and this was not entirely cynical. He appointed the former Saint-Simonian, Michel Chevalier, to the state council to advise on economic matters. Napoleon III pursued a vigorous policy of state intervention in the economy to promote rapid economic growth. This would not entail nationalisation: Louis Napoleon's coup in 1851 was justified on the very grounds of forestalling such socialist ideas. Instead, it meant that the state had to play an active role in boosting the economy which, Napoleon III hoped, would improve the conditions of the poor. In the long run, however, these policies neither eased social tensions nor integrated the workers within the Second Empire.

In Spain, Queen Isabella II had escaped the revolutionary torrent of 1848, but the underlying dangers of social instability pushed the bedrock of the *moderado* regime – property-owners, officials, manufacturers and merchants – further towards the right. The Queen secured the resignation of her *moderado* prime minister, Narváez, in January 1851 when he refused to sign a Concordat with the Church on the grounds that it undermined state supremacy over ecclesiastical affairs. His replacement, Bravo Murillo, was a neo-absolutist, who signed the Concordat, but who also sought to restrict the already narrow suffrage and reduce the Cortes to an advisory body. This went too far for the *moderado* notables, who were reluctant to relinquish their hard-won power. Their main weapon lay within the army, among liberal officers who saw their role as the defence of the Constitution of 1845.

The trial of strength occurred in the summer of 1854, when a *pronunciamiento* by the *moderado* General Leopoldo O'Donnell was eventually supported not only by the more radical *progresistas*, but also, to O'Donnell's discomfort, by workers' insurrections in cities such as Valencia, Barcelona and Madrid. When the government toppled on 17 July, power fell to the *progresistas* whose steely politicians and army commanders used the threat of social revolution to force the Queen to come to terms. Espartero returned to power and he promptly suppressed the more radical democratic clubs and newspapers. There followed a two-year liberal *bienio*, in which a mainly *progresista* government and single-chamber Cortes laid the infrastructure for the economic expansion which continued up to the late 1860s. Yet though the *progresistas* were monarchists, they angered the Queen with attacks on church property while failing to alleviate peasant poverty and to abolish conscription and the hated taxes on consumption.

Isabella easily rid herself of the *progresista* government, which had little popular support. In July 1856 she dismissed Espartero and appointed O'Donnell against the parliamentary majority. O'Donnell's soldiers routed the *progresista* militia with professional efficiency and resistance collapsed.[4] O'Donnell, however, was no creature of the court; his Liberal Union was a coalition of *moderados* and right-wing *progresistas* committed to the Constitution of 1845. When he defied the

Church by pressing on with the sale of church lands, the Queen angrily dismissed him in October, but she could not manage the political elites without him. O'Donnell's subsequent 'long ministry', which lasted from June 1858 until March 1863, was careful both to conciliate liberal opposition and to curry popular support. Membership of the Cortes was carefully manipulated and the press restricted. In a pattern of political management which would recur later, real political life in the country lay not in the Cortes, but in *caciquismo*, whereby local notables exchanged votes for government patronage. Disenchanted *progresistas* abandoned the Liberal Union, joining the chorus of criticism from the left. Some democrats, among them Francisco Pi y Margall, had begun to speak in terms of 'socialism', by which they meant a state role in improving working conditions, arbitrating in labour disputes, providing credit for peasants and allowing them to benefit from the sales of church land and entails. Torn between the hostility of the court and the opposition of the left, O'Donnell haemorrhaged supporters and, in February 1863, he resigned. The fall of O'Donnell opened a period of instability which would last for more than a decade.[5]

In Britain, as in most other parts of Europe, stability was encouraged by the economic boom which started around 1850. When they looked across the sea to continental Europe, most British subjects breathed a sigh of relief that they had avoided the twin traps of authoritarianism and republicanism. The state remained firmly in the hands of the landed gentry. While the franchise had been extended to well-to-do middle-class householders in 1832, those who were actually elected remained the same; in that respect, there was no difference between the liberal Whigs and the conservatives. The Whig Lord Palmerston told his parliamentary colleagues in 1852, 'we are here an assembly of gentlemen and we who are gentlemen on this side of the House should remember that we are dealing with gentlemen on the other side'.[6] Both Whig and Tory cabinets were composed of noble landowners, yet their conservatism was pragmatic. The occasion for Palmerston's magnanimous recognition that even the Tories were 'gentlemen' was the announcement by the conservative prime minister, the Earl of Derby, that his (short-lived) government did not intend to restore the Corn Laws, despite his own colleagues suffering from the fall in agricultural prices in the early 1850s.

One part of the British Isles which did not share in the post-1848 relief was Ireland, where the years after 1850 were a period of psychological, social and political adjustment to the catastrophe of the great famine. Social tensions intensified, particularly between the landlords and the relatively prosperous tenant farmers. Although during the famine the latter tended to be much harder on the starving, the image of the bad landlord was a compelling one. The landlords themselves did little to dispel this impression, as after 1848 they continued to maximise their income from the land by demanding increased rents, which led to violent confrontations. These social divisions were given political expression after the Franchise Act of 1850, which quadrupled the rural electorate, enfranchising the tenant farmers, who would become the backbone of resistance to the landlords. Landlords continued to exert what they chose to see as their 'fair and legitimate influence' over their tenants, by promises of rent reductions, or threats of increases and, ultimately, eviction. Against landlordism, a slogan first heard in the 1830s – 'Tenant Right' – became a political platform for tenants who demanded free sale (of their lease to another tenant), fair rent and fixity of tenure. In 1850 the Irish Tenant League was formed to press for these reforms and it allied with the 'Irish Brigade' (MPs promoting Irish interests in the British parliament) to form the Independent Irish Party in 1852. The IIP lost credibility when two of its prominent members accepted office in Lord Aberdeen's government (1852–5). Yet not for the first time and not for the last, the central issues which would challenge the landed interest in Ireland were being given organised political expression.

Piedmont was the only Italian state to emerge with a constitution from the 1848 revolutions. The suffrage was restricted to those who owned property and who passed a literacy test (some 8 per cent of the adult male population). King Victor Emanuel was left with control of the armed forces, foreign policy and full executive powers to apply and make laws, provided Parliament did not overturn them. Yet his absolutist impulses were restrained by a tendency, represented by moderate reformers such as Cesare Balbo, which considered a moderate constitution as the best bulwark against republicanism. Above all, a liberal state would strengthen the King's aspiration to provide moral and political leadership for the rest of Italy. Their advice prevailed and the King was well served by his moderate liberal prime ministers, Massimo d'Azeglio (1849–52) and Camillo di Cavour (1852–61).

The policies of these ministers made Piedmont look like the France of Guizot and Louis-Philippe. They wanted to curb the influence of the Church, to stimulate economic development and to put their own ministerial authority vis-à-vis the King on a legal, parliamentary base. Though Cavour was not above bending or even breaking the constitutional rules, paying secret service money to the press, closing down opposition newspapers and using government officials to influence elections, he never wanted to destroy parliament altogether. For him it was the best defence against both democratic radicalism and royal absolutism. Cavour's reforms and his success in rooting the monarchy in parliamentary soil made Piedmont appear to be the most modern, liberal state in Italy. Yet Cavour, later seen as the architect of Italian unity, showed little interest in the 'Italian question' during the early 1850s. The King, for one, was downright hostile to the idea of unification; he blamed the disasters of

1848–9 not only on his abdicated father but also on those patriots who had chased 'the phantom of Italian independence'.[7] None the less, Victor Emanuel did like the idea of Piedmontese pre-eminence in Italy. This seed would eventually germinate into an active anti-Austrian policy from the mid-1850s.

In neo-absolutist Austria, Francis Joseph did not even rule with a prime minister; Schwarzenberg, who did suddenly in April 1852, was not replaced. Under the uniform system devised by Alexander Bach, in theory no nationality would enjoy special privileges but in practice German would be the common language of the empire, which gave the Austrians an immediate advantage in government and administration. The empire was to rest on the pillars of emperor, army and Church. The Concordat of 2 August 1855 caused more offence among liberals than the Sylvester Patent. It rolled back some of Joseph II's secularising reforms, which had survived even Metternich's alliance of 'throne and altar'. Catholicism was to be 'maintained for ever' in the empire, with its property sacrosanct and with the state relinquishing some of its responsibilities over marriage, law and education. The Emperor promised not to alter any laws on religion without first consulting the Pope. At least neo-absolutism did not restore the old powers of the nobility; after all, the monarchy was determined to share its authority with no one. Manorial justice was gone for good and the new royal judiciary, while authoritarian, proved to be fairer and more efficient. Yet the absolute monarchy could not eliminate the sense of grievance which stemmed from the repression, particularly of nationalist aspirations, in the aftermath of 1848. Little distinction was made between those ethnic groups who had remained loyal in 1848 and those who had rebelled, prompting a Croat to sigh to a Hungarian, 'We received as a reward what you were given as a punishment.'[8] The Italians of Lombardy and Venetia, of course, remained restive. An uprising of Mazzinians in Milan in 1853 was put down, while Lajos Kossuth still tried to keep the Hungarian nationalist flame alive from his exile in Constantinople. Martial law was not lifted in Hungary until 1854.

In Germany, conservatives were in little doubt that they would have to confront a revolutionary challenge again, as they witnessed the rapid economic growth after 1850. A strong current in conservatism therefore grudgingly accepted constitutions, economic development, nationalism and the expansion of the state, provided that they reinforced the position of the traditional political elites. The Prussian foreign minister, Otto von Manteuffel, wrote in 1849, 'the old times are gone and cannot return. To return to the decaying conditions of the past is like scooping water with a sieve', while the historian Leopold von Ranke warned one of Frederick William IV's advisers, 'the storms of today must be met with the institutions of today'.[9] This did not mean, of course, wilfully embracing every new idea. The *Bund*, restored in May 1851, re-enacted the oppressive legislation of 1819 and 1830–4. Even in traditionally constitutional states such as Baden and Württemberg, rulers long weary of parliamentary politics exploited the weakness of the liberal opposition to appoint ministers willing to apply a firm hand against the legislature. The new constitutions granted in 1848 were revoked in these states, as well as in Hanover and Saxony. In 1853 and 1856, two Prussian municipal laws strengthened government powers over urban affairs. The police in Berlin were put under military orders and were to report on every aspect of social and political life. The border police and the rural gendarmerie were increased and undercover agents monitored all signs of unrest. Prussia may now have been a constitutional state, yet strong authoritarian tendencies remained.

However, the extent of the reaction should not be overdrawn. Most German states, including Prussia, retained parliamentary institutions. The revolutions' abolition of the last relics of seigneurialism was enforced. The Prussian minister-president, Count Friedrich von Brandenburg, understood that popular anger had to be answered if there was to be no further violence in the countryside. In March 1850 some six hundred and forty thousand peasants were unburdened of their seigneurial obligations – three times the number of serfs freed by Stein and Hardenberg at the end of the Napoleonic Wars. In a more conservative move – but one none the less designed to secure the support of the artisans – Brandenburg also restored the guilds, which had been one of the key demands of craftworkers in 1848.

While Austria and Prussia, in their different ways, strived to keep revolutionary forces at bay in the 1850s, the reordering of Germany was one issue which would not go away. Prussia had shown that it was striving to strengthen its position within the Confederation. The continuity implicit in the restoration of the *Bund* was an illusion. In December 1853, Otto von Bismarck, Prussia's minister at the Frankfurt diet, wrote ominously that Prussia and Austria were 'breathing each other's breath' and that, in the long run, the latter must give way, or be forced to do so.[10] Prussia probed Austria for weaknesses, seeking ways of reducing its influence. Austria had to stomach a Prussian move to forge a tax union with northern German states (the *Steuerverein*) in autumn 1851. Prussia parried Austrian efforts to give the *Bund* wider powers and, in 1853, to join the *Zollverein*; Vienna had to be happy with a separate trade agreement with Prussia. Prussian policy was not, however, consistently hostile. For conservatives, including the King, the priority had to be the maintenance of the Junker-dominated social order, which meant that Prussia could not go embarking on a potentially destabilising collision course with the other German 'superpower', no matter what Bismarck might say. Consequently, the temperature of Austro-Prussian relations fluctuated between simmering hostility and cool conservative co-operation. Frederick William IV himself used the death of

Schwarzenberg in April 1852 to send Bismarck (of all people! – it seems that he was chosen because of his strong anti-liberal reputation) to Vienna to seek a new spirit of collaboration with Austria, evoking memories of the Holy Alliance of 1815. This would prove to be futile, for a conflict was stirring in the Black Sea, a war which would rupture the conservative 'Vienna system'.

The Crimean War, 1853–1856

Although most of the combat took place on the conflict's eponymous Black Sea peninsula, the origins and course of the Crimean War ranged widely. Its primary causes lay in the 'Eastern question', the political tensions arising from the gradual decline of the Ottoman Empire. Before 1848 there was a consensus – albeit one infected with mutual suspicion – to shore up the Sultan's power and, whether Turkey liked it or not, to deal with crises through international co-operation. By 1853 this grudging spirit of collaboration had broken down, particularly between Britain and Russia. Fear of Russian expansion, popularised in the press, had stoked Russophobia among British public opinion for a generation before the outbreak of the Crimean War. The Russian southwards advance towards the straits, into the Caucasus (see Map 9.1) and towards Persia and Afghanistan in the 1830s and 1840s was matched by British expansion into India; two great empires were about to collide across a broad Eurasian frontier which once separated them. Control of the straits leading from the Black Sea into the Aegean was an important source of these tensions. Russia had scored a diplomatic and strategic victory when it provided Turkey with military support in 1833 against the Egyptian invasion led by Mehmet Ali. The treaty of Unkiar Iskelessi that year forged a defensive alliance between the Tsar and the Sultan, giving Russia access through the straits in the event of war. This was unacceptable to the two major maritime powers, Britain and France. Tsar Nicholas I at least understood this and in June 1841 he signed the Straits Convention with the other European powers, in which the Sultan agreed to allow no foreign warships through the straits while the Ottoman Empire was at peace. Yet Mehmet Ali submitted to the Sultan in 1841, so the danger of another attack on Turkey – and therefore Russia's chances of increasing its influence by dealing directly with the Porte – had diminished. When the Tsar visited London in 1844, he strongly hinted that Britain and Russia might now partition the Ottoman Empire.[11] The danger of a Russian surge towards the straits and the threat to India appeared to be alarmingly real to British politicians and the public alike. These anxieties were reinforced by the expansion of British economic interests within the Ottoman Empire, particularly in textiles, grain and plans for a railway towards India. As Britain was now

Map 9.1 The Russian Empire in Europe, 1772–1914

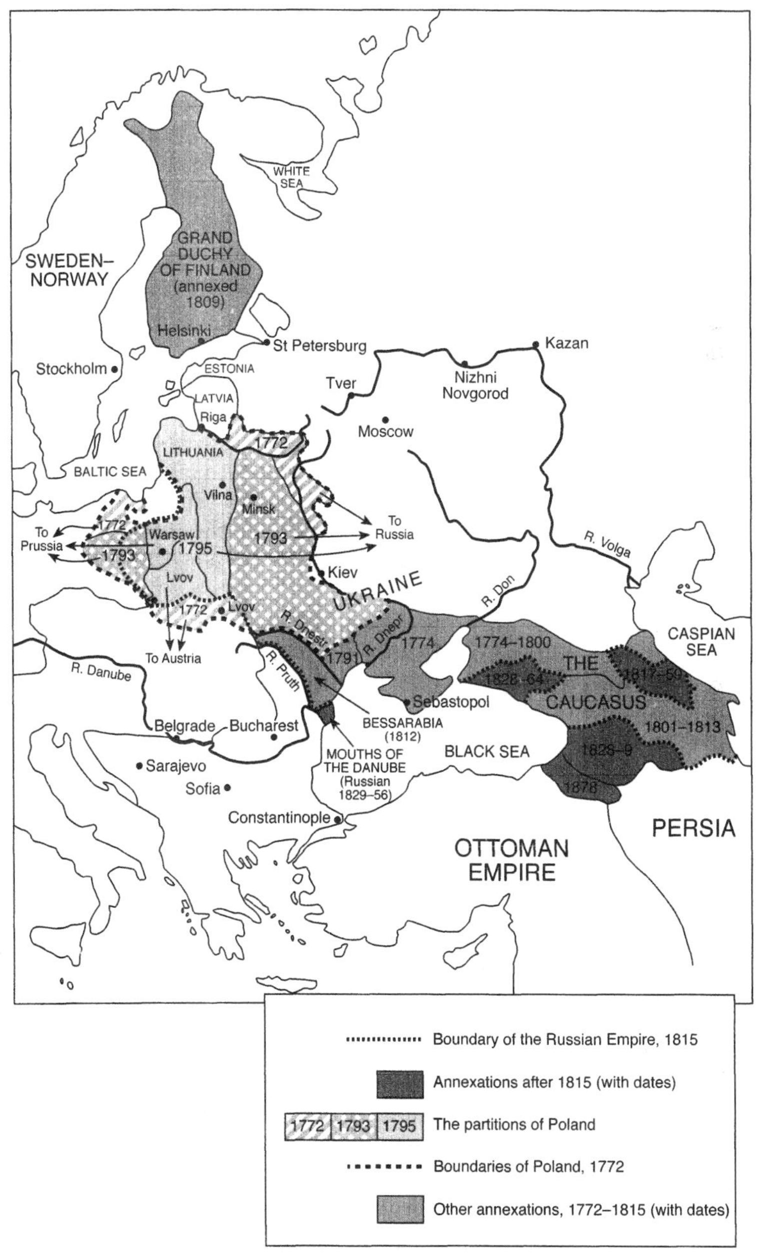

Russia's main commercial competitor in the Black Sea region, control of the straits became an economic as well as a strategic problem. Mutual suspicion and hostility between Russia and Britain would break out into conflict over a series of misunderstandings.

Meanwhile, the Vienna system no longer exerted the same restraint as it had before 1848. The conservative triumph over the revolutions had, ironically, intensified attitudes seeping through the sinews of international politics like a slow-acting poison. The Tsar, fresh from his success at destroying revolution in Hungary, assumed that he could depend upon Austrian support, or at the very least its benevolent neutrality, in any major international dispute. It was a fatal miscalculation; Schwarzenberg had already predicted that one day Austria would astonish the world with her ingratitude towards Russia. In France, Napoleon III's name alone raised expectations among French nationalists that his regime would be committed to revision of the 1815 peace settlement in Europe. His own justification for French expansionism rotated around *la politique des nationalités*, the notion that Europe should be ordered by national self-determination. His preferred tool was negotiation, but he was willing to go to war if it satisfied domestic political needs for 'glory'. His attempts to seduce French conservative support at home led him to support Catholic possession of the keys to the Holy Places, the Christian sites under Ottoman rule in Palestine, to which the Orthodox clergy also claimed privileged access.

On the surface, the Holy Places dispute looks like a trivial squabble, but it had wide political reverberations. In December 1852 when the Sultan succumbed to Napoleon III's pressure and gave Catholic monks the keys, he ran headlong into the rights claimed by the Orthodox clergy. The slight antagonised the Tsar who, by the Treaty of Kuchuk-Kainardji of 1774, claimed to be the protector of the Sultan's Orthodox subjects and whipped up religious fervour among the Russian population. This issue was the match which ignited the dangerous fumes gathering around the wider Eastern question. Nicholas suspected Napoleon III of deeper political motives, telling the British ambassador to St Petersburg that French policy implied breaking the Ottoman Empire up into 'little republics, asylums for the Kossuths, Mazzinis and other revolutionists'.[12] To pre-empt French intervention in Turkish affairs, Nicholas again proposed the partition of the Ottoman Empire between Russia, Britain and Austria. The British responded coolly, promising only not to seal any agreement over the Eastern question without consulting Russia. Meanwhile, Nicholas's blunt proposition stirred British anxieties that the Russians were in fact preparing the ground for an assault on Turkey. Ultimately, therefore, the Crimean War stemmed from different views and suspicions arising from the decline of the Ottoman Empire.

The fatal misunderstanding occurred over the Menshikov mission to Constantinople. Prince Alexander Menshikov was sent to negotiate with the Sultan over the Holy Places dispute. It followed an Austrian diplomatic mission led by Count Christian von Leiningen to prevent a Turkish invasion of its rebellious principality of Montenegro. Austria feared that a full-scale war would stir up Slav nationalism within the Habsburg monarchy and also allow the Turks to strengthen their military presence close to the Military Border. Bolstered by Russian support, Leiningen's ultimatum in February 1853 browbeat the Turks into withdrawing their forces from Montenegro. The Russians now proceeded with every confidence that they too could cajole Constantinople into yielding over the Holy Places and that, in doing so, the Austrians would repay Russia for its earlier backing by supporting its demands. Overall, the aim of the Menshikov mission appears to have been the maintenance of the Ottoman Empire as it stood, while restoring Russian influence in Constantinople. While the British government advised the Sultan to make concessions, the underlying fear of Russian expansionism stoked popular Russophobia. With misguided confidence, the Tsar believed that the British government would brush off public opinion and honour its commitment to co-operate with Russia over the Ottoman Empire. When the Sultan conceded some but not all of Russia's demands, Menshikov left Constantinople in disgust, issuing an ultimatum to the Sultan, who, now confident of British and French support, ignored it. The two Western powers assembled their fleets in Besika Bay in June 1853, the Russians invaded the Romanian principalities on 2 July and the Porte, bolstered by popular fervour demanding a *jihad*, declared war on 4 October 1853. The war might have remained a Russo-Turkish conflict but for the devastating Russian naval victory at Sinope on 30 November when all but one of the Turkish ships were sunk. In Britain, this 'massacre' was denounced by the press and the groundswell of public opinion swept aside the remaining resistance to war in the cabinet. After the Franco-British fleet sailed into the Black Sea with orders to force the Russians back to port, Britain and France each declared war on 27 and 28 March.

The Crimean War was global in its range, not least because the two hegemonic powers which had emerged in 1815 – Britain and Russia – were on opposite sides, with the former seeing the struggle in terms of containing the ambitions of the latter. Consequently, there was a naval war in the Baltic; fighting involving Russians, Turks and an Islamic insurrection in the Caucasus; minor engagements in the White Sea and expeditions along the Pacific coastal outposts of the Russian empire. The worst of the fighting was, however, on the Crimean peninsula, where the allied campaign aimed at capturing Sebastopol, Russia's formidable Black Sea naval base. Combat raged until September 1855, when the south side of Sebastopol fell to the allies. Although the young Tsar Alexander II wanted to fight on, the diplomatic ring began to tighten and he agreed to enter peace negotiations in January 1856. The

Crimean War was a harbinger of the horrors of modern, industrialised warfare: the use of ironclad ships, sea mines and the devastatingly accurate and penetrating Minié rifle, against which the older Russian smoothbore muskets were no match. The siege of Sebastopol witnessed almost a year of trench warfare, with all the misery later associated with the First World War.

'What a slaughterhouse!' exclaimed an appalled General Pierre Bosquet after the Battle of Inkerman in November 1854.[13] It was an apt description of the entire conflict, which killed 638,000 people – 474,000 Russians, 95,000 French, 45,000 Turks, 22,000 British and 2000 Piedmontese, who entered the war on the allied side. The vast majority – three-quarters in the case of the French, who had the best medical provision – died not from combat but from disease, mostly cholera and typhoid. On the British side, the single-minded determination of Florence Nightingale and 40 nurses succeeded in overcoming military prejudice and red tape to improve vastly the conditions in British military hospitals, while the much-loved Jamaican Mary Seacole tended British wounded on the front line.[14] Russian suffering was the sharpest: as there were no railways south of Moscow, their forces were supplied by animal power, which struggled in the winter. One regiment took five months to reach the Crimea from Nizhni Novgorod. The obvious logistical and technological gulf between the Russians and their opponents was to be one of the great spurs to reform in the flanks of the lumbering Tsarist order.

At the Treaty of Paris, signed on 30 March, Russia ceded part of Bessarabia and abandoned its protectorate over Moldavia and Wallachia. The Black Sea was neutralised, meaning that no power could sail warships or maintain bases there, effectively bottling up Russia's maritime route to the Mediterranean. The Sultan pre-empted any discussion of Russian protection over his Orthodox subjects by proclaiming the equality of all religions and ethnic groups, a radical break with the Ottoman tradition which held Muslims as the superior caste. The war had serious repercussions on European international relations. Diplomacy never ceased during the war, first because both sides tried to seduce Prussia and Austria into their camp and secondly because the European powers worked collectively to find a diplomatic solution to the conflict. The survival of concert diplomacy may, in fact, have prevented the Crimean War from becoming a general European slaughter. The Austrian government, fearful of the impact which the Tsar's proposals for south-eastern Europe would have on Slav nationalism, angered by the Russian occupation of the Romanian principalities, and struggling financially, had neither the will nor the means to support Russia. On the contrary, Austrian forces were mustered along the Russian and Transylvanian frontiers, forcing a Russian withdrawal from the principalities in August 1854. It was a stunning diplomatic victory for Austria, but it came at the price of exasperating Russia and putting Vienna's finances even further into the red. Yet Austria did not win any friends in the West either. While concluding an alliance with France and Britain on 2 December 1854, Austria withdrew into neutrality as the immediate Russian threat in south-eastern Europe receded. Austria's discomfort was Prussia's gain. King Frederick William IV declared his neutrality in February 1854 but, despite some rude anti-Russian noises emanating from Crown Prince William and his liberal circle, this was less troublesome to Russia than Austria's irritating tightrope act. Prussia had no vital interests at stake and so had no need to emulate Austria's threatening, armed neutrality. Piedmont, another of Austria's enemies, sought to capitalise on the war, entering it against Russia in January 1855 in the hope of wringing some rewards at the peace settlement. The allies, however, were trying to drum Austria into the conflict and had to guarantee the existing order in Italy. Though Napoleon III's foreign minister, Count Alexander Walewski, dropped the bombshell of the Italian question on to the diplomatic table in Paris, Piedmont made no material gains.

Yet the Crimean War had cracked open the 'Vienna System' in an important way: for 35 years after 1815 the only 'revisionist' power was France. Then, after Olmütz, Prussia began to bide its time, waiting for the opportunity to shake up the old arrangements within Germany. Continental Europe's greatest power had now been forced back from the Danube and driven off the Black Sea; Russia, the guarantor of conservatism in Europe since 1815, was also now a 'revisionist' power. The new Tsar, Alexander II, later chastised himself for making peace on such damaging terms: 'I signed the Treaty of Paris and it was cowardice!'[15] For two decades, Alexander's foreign policy aimed at testing the will of the other powers to enforce the treaty. Most of Russia's energies, meanwhile, were channelled into domestic reform. The conservative 'Holy Alliance' of Russia, Austria and Prussia had fractured and the broad consensus over the Vienna settlement had evaporated. The main beneficiaries were France, Piedmont and Prussia: their ire would be directed against Austria, while Britain and Russia stood aside. Austria was the real loser of the Crimean War.

10 Unifications and State-Building

The Unification of Italy

The first sign of the Austrians' precarious position came from Italy. Cavour, one of the mongers of the War of Italian Unification in 1859, aimed at expelling them from the peninsula and annexing the Austrian provinces of Lombardy and Venetia to form a northern Italian kingdom under his King, Victor Emanuel. Neither Cavour nor Napoleon III, his partner in the undertaking, wanted a united Italy, which would be harder to control and might fall prey to the radical, democratic nationalists. Yet Cavour was also more convinced that he could use Italian nationalists to fire up anti-Austrian feeling in Italy and to rally support for Piedmontese policy without unleashing the red spectre of 1848. Cavour's change of heart was partly thanks to the Italian National Society, established in July 1857, which included both liberals and the more pragmatic republicans, such as Garibaldi and Manin, who left the more doctrinaire democrats such as Mazzini out in the cold. It accepted Piedmontese leadership as the only viable way to liberate Italy from Austrian domination, while postponing the argument over the shape of the new Italy until later; for the time being it safely bottled up the mischievous genies of republicanism and socialism. Its strength lay in its recruitment of local elites, whose personal, official and business contacts allowed the society to spread its message. This policy was not without its dangers for the nationalists: an Italy forged with Piedmontese steel might remain permanently under the hammer of the Savoyard monarchy and assume a conservative shape. Moreover, the Piedmontese military alone could not beat the Austrians; the Italians would need French help, so conspicuously absent in 1848. Yet it was doubtful whether Napoleon III would resist the temptation to use the nationalist cause simply to grind the new Italian state permanently under his Bonapartist boot.

Cavour, however, had his own reasons to risk seeking French help. In the 1857 elections, his parliamentary support was whittled down to a paper-thin majority, with a surge to the clerical, conservative right. On 30 July 1858 the Austrian ambassador to Paris noted that Cavour 'needs some hard fact which he can exploit in an Italian sense' to save his political skin.[1] Cavour had, in fact, obtained this 'hard fact' ten days previously at a secret meeting with Napoleon III at the spa town of Plombières in the Vosges. They agreed that Italy would be split into four different states: Piedmont would dominate a kingdom of Upper Italy, most of the Papal States and Tuscany would form a central Italian kingdom, and the Pope would hold on to Rome and its surroundings, while the Kingdom of Naples would remain untouched. All four would join an Italian confederation on the German model, but under the presidency of the Pope. The aim was not, therefore, Italian unity, but a loose federation which in practice would be dominated by Piedmont. Napoleon III did not want a unitary state which could challenge France.

Instead, he was driven by a potent mixture of other motives at Plombières. His desire to make his dynasty respectable was fed by the marriage of Victor Emanuel's daughter, Clotilde, to the Emperor's cousin, Prince Jérôme Napoleon. Cavour calculated that, should the French emperor then fight a successful war in Italy, 'the Napoleonic dynasty [would] be consolidated for one or two generations'.[2] It would also steal the thunder of the republican opposition which was re-emerging in France. The attempt on his life in 1858 by the Italian patriot Orsini, who enjoyed noisy support from French republicans, convinced him that he urgently needed to make the Italian cause his own. Napoleon III also seized the opportunity to reverse one of the humiliations of 1815 by securing a promise of Nice and Savoy from Cavour, in return for the 200,000 French troops who would join Piedmont against Austria.

Having secured French support, Cavour's parliamentary majority widened and Piedmont's claim to lead the national movement was almost unassailable. Cavour now provoked Austria into making the first aggressive move. He subsidised the National Society, noisily recruited Italian patriots and mobilised the Piedmontese army, until, on 27 April 1859, an Austrian army invaded. It was a disastrous reaction for the Habsburgs: French and Piedmontese forces drove the Austrians back into Lombardy, defeating them successively at Magenta (4 June) and Solferino and San Martino (both 24 June). These were bloody battles; the Swiss doctor Jean Henri Dunant, who helped to treat the wounded at Solferino, was so appalled that he helped to establish the Red Cross at the Geneva Convention in 1864. Francis Joseph received news that there was real danger of an insurrection in Hungary, while Austrian liberals were stirring opposition in Vienna as well. He sought a quick peace with Napoleon III.

The French Emperor was obliging: his forces lacked the arsenal to take on the Austrians, who had withdrawn to the quadrilateral of fortresses; he was anxious about Prussian intentions on the Rhine; and, most alarming of all, Cavour's ambitions now went beyond what was agreed at Plombières. After Magenta, he encouraged members of the National Society to stir up revolt in northern Italy, with some success. In June, liberals seized power in the duchies of Parma and Modena and in the city of Bologna in the papal province of Romagna, calling for their annexation by Piedmont. So far, this was in accordance with Plombières, but Cavour was also in touch with Italian patriots in Perugia and the Papal Marches, while a revolution in Florence had toppled Grand-Duke Leopold of Tuscany on 27 April. The mercurial Cavour now appeared to be working towards a Piedmontese annexation of these provinces, which were originally intended to be part of the central Italian kingdom. Napoleon III therefore tried to derail Cavour's plans by unilaterally sealing an armistice with Francis Joseph at Villafranca on 11 July. The Austrian emperor agreed to cede Lombardy, except for the quadrilateral, to Piedmont. There would be no other territorial changes: Venetia would stay under Austrian rule; the Papal States would remain intact under the Pope; the rulers of Modena, Parma and Tuscany would be restored; Napoleon III even dropped his claims to Savoy and Nice. Cavour's ambitious plans for the complete expulsion of Austria and for an Upper Italian Kingdom were demolished at one diplomatic blow and he angrily resigned when Victor Emanuel accepted these terms.

Yet the situation in Italy rapidly slipped from Napoleon III's grasp. The provisional governments in central Italy, ignoring the Villafranca armistice, elected assemblies which persisted in demanding their annexation by Piedmont, introducing Piedmontese law and administration, and welcoming the commissioners sent by Cavour. Napoleon III pressurised Victor Emanuel to turn a deaf ear to the clamour, but the British government regarded an expanded Piedmont as a bulwark against a resurgent France. Palmerston pressed Victor Emanuel to recall Cavour, who regained office on 21 January 1860. He immediately set about making arrangements to annex central Italy, including Tuscany. Plebiscites, skilfully organised with the help of the National Society in March, voted overwhelmingly in support of Piedmontese annexation. To sweeten a bitter Napoleon III, Cavour presented Nice and Savoy to France.

Now Mazzini stepped into the maelstrom, alive to the dangers of French domination and Piedmontese dynastic ambitions. An Italy united by a popular insurrection would foil both.[3] Mazzini saw his opportunity in the south, where the conditions of the peasantry made the situation combustible. An insurrection on 4 April 1860 in Palermo provided the spark which fired up the Sicilian peasantry and, though the authorities contained their revolt by the end of the month, it gave the Mazzinians the opportunity to strike.[4]

They were led by Giuseppe Garibaldi, who was disgusted with Cavour's old-school diplomacy and with the surrender of Nice, his home town, to France. He now aimed to force the issue of Italian unification by invading the south. He gathered a force of '1000 Red Shirts', who were actually closer to 1100 people: students taking drastic action to avoid exams, veterans of 1848 and young middle-class and aristocratic idealists, including a woman, Countess Martini Salasco, an officer amongst Garibaldi's scouts. In May they set sail from Genoa, landed at Marsala in Sicily, defeated a small Neapolitan force at Calatafimi and entered Palermo on 2 June (see Map 10.1). Garibaldi's success lay not only in his martial prowess but also in his political acumen. When Garibaldi's promise of tax and agrarian reforms fell short and when he imposed conscription, the peasant revolt turned against him and, while persisting in sincere efforts to improve rural conditions, Garibaldi and his Sicilian comrade, Francesco Crispi, were also ruthless in crushing the unrest. Sicilian landowners therefore found security in Garibaldi's new order, which, it soon became clear, meant unification with Piedmont.

Across the straits in the Kingdom of Naples, King Francis II (who had succeeded Ferdinand II in 1859) tried to prevent a revolution by granting a constitution on 25 June. Neapolitan liberals, hostile to absolutism and to Garibaldi's republicanism in almost equal measure, saw through this ruse and looked to Piedmont as the surest guarantor of a constitution and social order. The peasantry, meanwhile, having heard of Garibaldi's promises to their Sicilian counterparts, were stirring in anticipation of his arrival. In a vain attempt to impose himself on the situation, Cavour sent agents to Naples to provoke a liberal insurrection to establish a pro-Piedmontese government. Garibaldi landed in Calabria on 18 August and the peasants greeted him as a liberator as he marched on Naples, which he entered on 7 September, Francis having fled the previous day.

Cavour was frantic; he could not be sure that Garibaldi would easily relinquish his conquests in the south, from where, with Mazzini's encouragement, he could march on Rome. With Napoleon III's assent, he pre-emptively sent Piedmontese troops into the Papal States on 18 September, sweeping the Pope's army aside, though Rome, as it had been since 1849, was still protected by French troops. The Piedmontese then prepared to confront Garibaldi's forces which, in fact, were in no state to fight on. The peasants of the south, like the Sicilians, were disappointed in the new order and an upsurge in brigandage was assuming the proportions of an open civil war. Neapolitan liberals and property-owners saw their best hope of salvation in the establishment of robust authority. Garibaldi himself concluded that strong government, with a regular army and efficient policing, was required. Piedmont provided the model.

Garibaldi therefore surrendered his southern conquests to Victor Emanuel, whom he hailed as 'King of Italy' at Teano on 25 October. The stark alternative was civil war. In October–November a plebiscite, with the exertion of 'influence' in an open ballot, produced an overwhelming result in favour of 'a single indivisible Italy with Victor Emanuel as constitutional king'. The new Italian parliament, which met in Turin after elections in 1861, proclaimed Victor Emanuel II King of Italy on 17 March. Garibaldi soon repented of his magnanimity and sought to regain the initiative by completing unification on radical

Map 10.1 Italy, 1815–1870

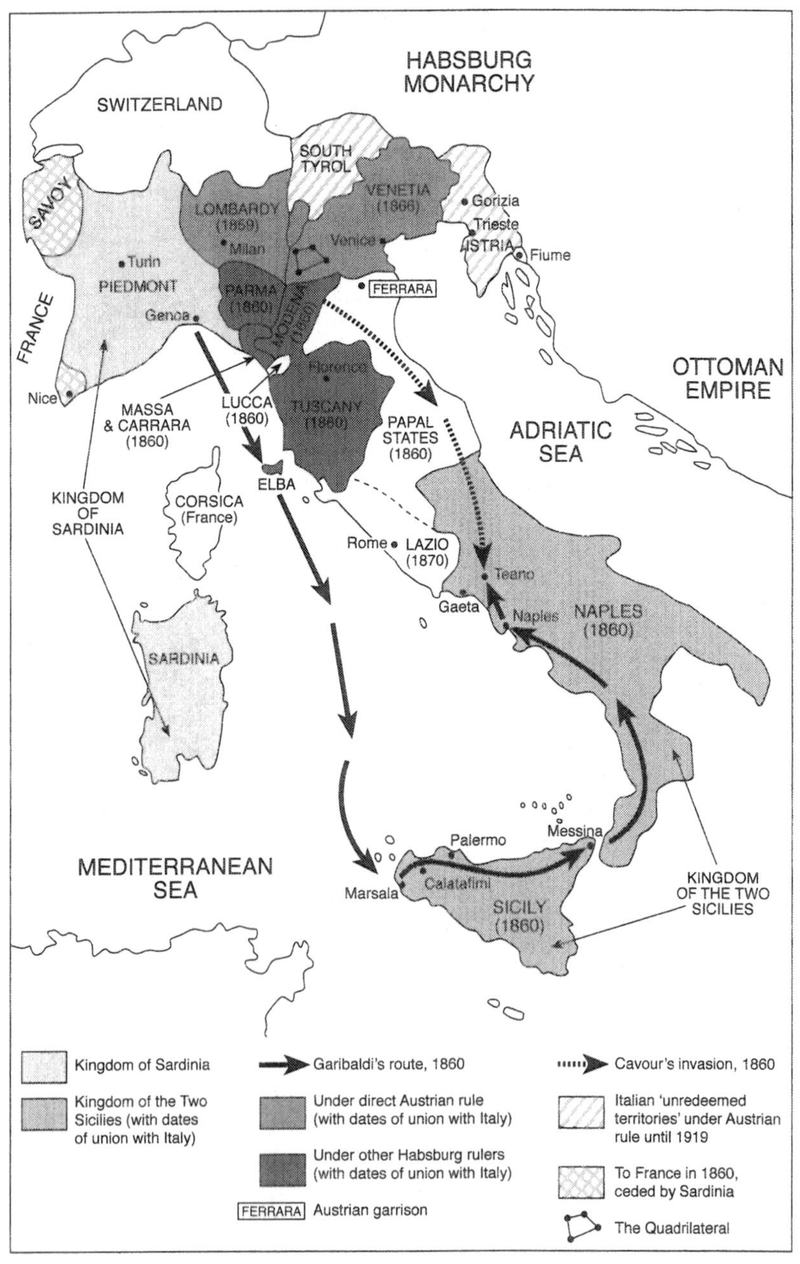

terms. In August 1862 he marched on Rome with a volunteer army but was defeated by government forces at Aspromonte. He tried again in October–November 1867, but this time was stopped by the French troops protecting the ancient capital. In the south, both Bourbon royalists and republicans tried to channel the endemic peasant revolt and brigandage towards political goals. In 1866 in the old Sicilian capital, Palermo, the two extremes collaborated in an insurrection which took five days to crush. On the mainland, certain regions of the former Neapolitan kingdom – Calabria, Basilicata, Puglia – became Italy's Vendée and the authorities responded with martial law, executions, hostage-taking and blockades of villages. Resistance was not extinguished until 1865. Venice was eventually added to the new kingdom on 3 October 1866, the fruit of Italy's alliance with Prussia in Bismarck's war against Austria. Rome fell after Napoleon III was captured by the Prussians at Sedan in September 1870 and the French withdrew their troops from the city. A prisoner of Italian circumstances in 1859–60, Napoleon III had unwittingly started the process of unification. A prisoner of the Prussians in 1870, he could no longer prevent its completion.

German Unification

The Italian drive for unity offered a source of inspiration for German liberals. The *Nationalverein*, (German National Society), founded in 1859, was modelled on the Italian equivalent, seeking to bind local liberal organisations into a nationwide *kleindeutsch* movement. It was given momentum when the darker side of nationalism stirred in 1860; the French annexation of Nice and Savoy in 1860 seemed to presage an attack on the Rhineland, which provoked a spontaneous outburst of popular German nationalism. This was accompanied by a revival of the fortunes of the liberals, who won parliamentary majorities in Baden and Württemberg and increased their seats in other *Mittelstaaten* such as Hanover, Hesse-Darmstadt and Nassau. From 1858 a 'New Era' opened in Prussia when Frederick William IV, whose mental health had been deteriorating, succumbed to a stroke and Crown Prince William took over as Regent. He dismissed his father's conservative ministers and appointed a liberal-leaning government which wanted to reverse the diplomatic defeat at Olmütz, primarily through a programme of 'moral conquests'. Reform and respect for the rule of law would 'earn Prussia the political respect and give it the position of power that it [was] not able to achieve by its material might alone'.[5]

The signs that a united Germany might just arise from civil society and take a liberal shape were promising in 1860. Besides the *Nationalverein*, which was relatively small at 25,000 members, the relaxation of laws against associations in most German states permitted a flowering of professional, choral, gymnastic and rifle societies which in 1861–2 formed national committees and, over the next three years, held national festivals proclaiming their support for unification. By 1865 the gymnastic societies boasted 167,000 members and the choral societies 60,000, while the riflemen's festival held in Frankfurt in 1862 drew 8000 participants.[6]

Even so, there were limits to this liberal nationalist upsurge. The industrial working-class and rural labourers were not entirely excluded, but liberal nationalism remained primarily a movement of the *Mittelstand.* In January 1863 the *Nationalverein* rejected an appeal for membership from a workers' deputation, arguing that they should concentrate on self-improvement and leave national issues to the middle class. Ultimately, liberal society was weakened by its failure to widen its social base, which meant that it could not rally popular support against the authoritarian counter-attack. Moreover, the movement was still divided between *großdeutsch* and *kleindeutsch* visions. South German Catholics, who in any case enjoyed their own social organisations, looked askance at a nationalist movement which threatened to exclude Austria. The *Reformverein*, established in October 1862 to further the *großdeutsch* dream, was itself split between liberals and pro-Habsburg conservatives.

The shape of the German Empire which emerged in 1871 was the product of struggle, both external, between Prussia and Austria, and internal, between liberals and conservatives. The 'New Era' turned out to be a false dawn, which darkened with a constitutional crisis in Prussia in the early 1860s. Despite his early promise as a liberal, Crown Prince William (crowned King on his father's death in January 1861) was committed to royal power. When the liberal majority in the *Landtag* blocked army reforms proposed by his ultra-conservative war minister, Count Albrecht von Roon (who, among other things, sought to reduce the importance of the citizens' militia, the *Landwehr*), court conservatives steeled William for a confrontation that might even finish with a coup against the constitution itself: without a 'change of system,' Roon wrote to his friend, Bismarck, 'we should be heading under full sail into the mire of parliamentary government'.[7] Yet despite twice dissolving Parliament, in December 1861 and March 1862, the King was confronted with increased liberal majorities after each subsequent election. The King reacted by appointing Bismarck, notorious for his contempt for liberal talking shops, as minister-president on 22 September 1862. In fact, Bismarck started by trying to persuade the liberals that Prussia could achieve great things if only they would yield to the King. Prussian leadership of Germany, he declared, flowed not from Prussia's liberalism but from its power, for the great issues of the day would be resolved 'by blood and iron'.[8]

The liberals took this memorable but unfortunate choice of words as the throwing down of a gauntlet. In the year from October 1862, Bismarck twice closed the *Landtag* down to overturn a liberal majority, 'disciplined' as many as a thousand liberal officials and muzzled the liberal press. By October 1863 he was muttering, 'the Prussian monarchy and our present constitution are irreconcilable things'.[9] The liberals had clung on tenaciously for over three years, buoyed by successive electoral victories, but they had weaknesses. They did not really command widespread popular support; only about a third of those eligible to vote bothered to do so in 1862–3, which was hardly an overwhelming endorsement. Liberals rejected universal male suffrage, which led Bismarck to consider a populist alliance with the workers and peasants. At a meeting with the socialist Ferdinand Lassalle, who disliked the middle-class liberals as much as Bismarck, Lassalle promised, 'Give me suffrage and I will give you a million votes.'[10] Only the King's hostility to such a radical solution prevented such an alliance. Bismarck's victory over the liberals would stem instead from his foreign policy.

The struggle between Austria and Prussia was waged on both political and economic fronts. The two central issues were the reform of the *Bund* and Austrian membership of the *Zollverein* (see Map 10.2). States politically hostile to Prussia, such as Hanover, Saxony, Württemberg and Bavaria, might have supported Austrian admission into the customs union or tried to direct it towards protectionism, but Prussian economic might was too powerful to ignore. Prussia's economic growth was dramatic in the two decades from the mid-1850s, becoming Germany's largest producer of coal and iron. While having obvious military benefits, the economic expansion also made Prussia a valuable trading partner. Whenever the *Zollverein* came up for renewal (as it did every 12 years), Prussia was, therefore, able to dissuade other states from supporting Austrian membership.

In the early 1860s, Austria and Prussia engaged in a final struggle over the *Zollverein*, which became enmeshed in a dispute over reform of the *Bund*. Prussian negotiations with Napoleon III over a commercial treaty in May 1860 sparked opposition from Germany's main protectionist states, Austria, Bavaria and Württemberg. In June, a meeting between William I and Francis Joseph at Teplitz, where they discussed co-operation in Germany and a customs agreement between Prussia and Austria, led Prussian and Austrian industrialists to make conflicting demands for, respectively, free trade and protection. In the ensuing dispute, Austria and Prussia resurrected conflicting plans for reform of the *Bund*.[11] In 1862 Prussia defiantly concluded a trade agreement with Belgium, ratified the French commercial treaty and announced that its renewal of the *Zollverein* treaties would be conditional on other members' acquiescence. In August 1863 Bismarck foiled an Austrian effort to reform the *Bund* by bullying William I into staying away from

Map 10.2 The German Confederation, 1815–1866

Boundary of the German Confederation (to 1866)

Boundary of the North German Confederation, 1867

Boundary of the German Reich, 1871

Prussia in 1815

Habsburg Empire in 1815

BAVARIA (1833–4) Other major German states (with dates of joining Zollverein) the discussions, which collapsed without Prussian participation. This would be the final attempt to resolve the 'German question' by a negotiated settlement.

Bismarck's behaviour – not least his support for Russia as it crushed a Polish insurrection in 1863 – damaged Prussia's image among German liberal nationalists. He was therefore not yet in a position to go on the offensive – diplomatic or otherwise – to drive Austria out of Germany altogether. Meanwhile, Austria's best hope of defending its position in Germany now seemed to lie in co-operation with Prussia, after the futility of confrontation. The occasion for this collaboration was a crisis with Denmark over Schleswig-Holstein, which had been brewing since 1855, when the Danes drafted a constitution which integrated the duchies fully into Denmark. The German population protested and nationalists across Germany joined the clamour. By 1863 the Danish government, under pressure from *Eiderdan* nationalists who claimed that Denmark proper extended as far as the River Eider, seemed willing to surrender Holstein to the German Confederation in return for the full integration of Schleswig into Denmark. This ran headlong into the claims of German nationalists, who insisted that the two duchies were inseparable, were distinct from Denmark and should be admitted together into the *Bund.* In September 1863 the Danes brushed off German protests and produced a unitary constitution for Denmark and Schleswig, while declaring that Holstein would have its own constitution. The crisis finally bubbled over in November when Frederick VII of Denmark died, leaving no male heir who could claim both the Danish throne and the duchies. Frederick von Augustenburg, who would have inherited the duchies had his father not relinquished them to Denmark at the Treaty of London in 1852, proclaimed himself Duke of Schleswig-Holstein. Germans of all political stripe, *grossdeutsch, kleindeutsch*, liberal or conservative, could rally to the Augustenburg cause, which would have brought the duchies into the German Confederation. While Austria hoped that their independence within the *Bund* would frustrate Prussian expansionism, Bismarck aimed ultimately to annex them, conflicting reasons which led both states to march together against Denmark. In late 1863, acting on the orders of the federal diet, troops from Austria, Prussia, Saxony and Hanover first occupied Holstein and then, in February 1864, invaded Schleswig and Jutland. After abortive peace negotiations in London in the spring, the war resumed until July when the Danes sued for peace.

Vienna's foreign minister, Rechberg, had hoped that collaboration with Bismarck would return Germany to the dual hegemony of Austria and Prussia. Yet Austria was again excluded from the *Zollverein* on its renewal in 1864, finishing Rechberg's ministry. Austria and Prussia repeatedly clashed over what to do with the duchies. In August 1865 a compromise was reached at Bad Gadstein, whereby Prussia would administer Schleswig, and Austria would run Holstein, where Prussia would be able to site bases. Liberal nationalists in parliaments across Germany bitterly denounced the agreement as a betrayal of the very principle of self-determination, but they were also beginning to divide. The display of Prussian arms against Denmark impressed northern liberals with the possibility of using Prussian power in the national cause, which meant compromising with Bismarck. 'German unity', wrote one, 'is more important to me than a few paragraphs of the Prussian constitution.'[12] For many liberals, national unity would come first, the arguments over political liberties would come later. Others, particularly in the south, were alarmed at the prospect of 'the absorption of Germany into Prussia'. The liberal opposition in Prussia itself was split over whether or not to compromise their liberal principles at home, in order to give Bismarck the means to pursue an energetic German policy. In any case, the minister-president still pursued the liberals with special malice. He dissolved the *Landtag* in June 1865 and everyday harassment bit deeply: liberal manufacturers did not get government contracts, liberal doctors were passed over for public health positions, and judges were given salary increases for political loyalty. Finally, Bismarck broke the liberal opposition by engineering a war to expel Austria from Germany.

In April 1866 he signed an alliance with Italy, which would last only for the duration of the conflict, at the end of which Italy would receive Venetia. Both sides mobilised their forces. The flash point was reached on 1 June when Austria asked the diet to decide over the future of Schleswig-Holstein. Prussia reacted by invading Holstein, whereupon Austria proposed that the *Bund* take military action against Prussia. Bismarck warned the other German states that support for Austria's motion would be regarded as a declaration of war. The majority, seeing the danger in Prussian expansionism, backed Austria by nine votes to six. Prussia declared the dissolution of the *Bund*, calling on all members to forge a new German state under Prussian leadership and, on 16 June, invaded Saxony, Hesse-Cassel and Hanover for resisting. The Austrians roundly defeated the Italians at Custozza and in the naval battle of Lissa, but the Prussians crushed the Austrians at Sadowa (a battle also known for the river fort, Königgrätz) on 3 July. On that date, the last shadows of the *großdeutsch* dream evaporated. At the Treaty of Prague on 23 August, Prussia swallowed up Schleswig-Holstein, Hanover, Hesse-Cassel, Frankfurt and Nassau, and in October Austria surrendered Venetia to Italy. The wars of German unification have been described as a Prussian 'conquest of Germany'.[13] This is a particularly apt description of the war of 1866. The destruction of four sovereign states, together comprising four and a half million people, with the dispossession of three rulers and the rapid 'Prussification' of the new 'provinces', stirred dismay among Prussia's new and reluctant subjects.[14] The surviving states north of the River Main were bound into a North

German Confederation. Its constitution (ratified in 1867) provided a two-chamber parliament arranged to ensure Prussian predominance, but with universal male suffrage for the lower house (*Reichstag*) to keep the liberals in check. It became the basis of the constitution of the German Empire in 1871. Bavaria, Baden, Hesse-Darmstadt and Württemberg in the south were all that remained of the 'Third German' counterweight to Prussian power, while Austria withdrew from German affairs and – to Russian anxiety – looked eastwards.

The war cracked open the fissures within the liberal opposition. Most nationalists initially opposed the conflict, as Germans were fighting Germans, yet the mood changed with the speed of the Prussian triumph. Prussia had shown that it had the power – the blood and iron, as Bismarck had promised – to achieve German unity. At the same time, in the elections to the Prussian *Landtag* (held on the same day as Sadowa), conservatives tormented their liberal opponents by shamelessly playing the patriotic card. According to one slogan, one was either 'for or against the soldiers'.[15] The final blow was Bismarck's indemnity bill, whereby he promised to restore constitutional government in return for Parliament's approval of all the expenditure made since 1862 without its consent. Faced with overwhelming public enthusiasm for the monarchy, most liberals accepted this compromise, which was passed on 3 September 1866. Seventy-five deputies opposed it, including the old Progressive Johann Jakoby, who warned against the liberal 'capitulation' to Bismarck: 'Unity without freedom is a unity of slaves.'[16] The liberal split became formal in June 1867 when supporters of the indemnity bill formed the National Liberal Party against their erstwhile allies among the Progressives.[17]

Yet Bismarck did not control the national movement. The National Liberals still aspired to a *kleindeutsch* state, which was not yet complete, while Bismarck recognised that a Prussian conquest of the remaining southern German states would antagonise France and doubted that Protestant Prussia could easily absorb the Catholic south. Pro-Prussian parties in southern German parliaments secured little support except in Baden. The new *Zollverein* treaties passed in the teeth of parliamentary opposition in all four southern German states, but it was especially fierce in Bavaria and Württemberg. None the less, Bismarck saw unification as necessary because otherwise these states might ally with Austria or France. However, he understood that complete unification would be possible only when France was weakened and when southern opposition was more muted. Yet, over the next two years, nationalist impatience with Bismarck's policy of waiting on developments seemed to be strengthening the liberal opposition, while southern German regionalism became more strident. In 1870, therefore, he provoked another war, this time against France.

French relations with Prussia had been deteriorating since the Austro-Prussian conflict. Bismarck leaked the story of clumsy efforts by

Napoleon III to seek compensation in the Rhineland. The southern German states were alarmed enough to seal military alliances with Prussia. Undaunted, in August 1866 Napoleon III privately proposed a French annexation of Luxembourg and Belgium, in return for French acceptance of German unification. Bismarck simply stored this particular stick of diplomatic dynamite for later use. The cause of war with France came from Spain, where a revolution had toppled Queen Isabella II in 1868 and the victorious liberals were looking for a new monarch. Early in 1870 they invited Prince Leopold of Hohenzollern-Sigmaringen, from the distant branch of the ruling Prussian dynasty. Bismarck knew that this would infuriate the French and he hoped that the ensuing international crisis would strengthen his hand against both the Prussian opposition and southern German hostility. In June, therefore, he prevailed on a reluctant Leopold to accept the Spanish throne. When a French ultimatum forced Leopold to stand down, the French foreign minister, Antoine de Gramont, managed to pluck defeat from the jaws of victory. He persuaded Napoleon III that a Prussian guarantee was required to the effect that no Hohenzollern would ever be put forward for the Spanish throne. When the French ambassador to Prussia accosted King William on 13 July at Bad Ems, he was politely assured that the affair was closed. The discussion was measured enough, but when the King telegraphed Bismarck to inform him of the meeting, the Prussian minister-president edited the telegram to wave it like 'a red rag upon the Gallic bull'.[18] This insidious manoeuvre had its provocative effect on French public opinion, which bounced the government into declaring war on 15 July.

France, like Austria in 1866, had no friends: the southern German states had allied to Prussia and were carried on a wave of patriotic German feeling in which conservative and democratic opposition to 'Prussianisation' was swept aside. As Karl von Dalwigk, Hesse-Darmstadt's foreign minister, resignedly declared, they were 'completely in the talons of the eagle'.[19] Vienna had no desire to become embroiled in another war in Germany, while Tsar Alexander II loathed Napoleon III because he gave moral support to Poland. British public opinion was enraged when Bismarck leaked Napoleon III's designs on Belgium and Luxembourg to *The Times* newspaper. The war was a French disaster. Early in August, Prussia and its German allies launched an attack through Alsace and Lorraine, trapping one French army around Metz and, on 1 September, another – including Napoleon III himself – at Sedan, where 500 Prussian artillery pieces blasted the French. To end the slaughter, the Emperor surrendered the following day. The news reached Paris that evening, and on 4 September the rump of republican deputies proclaimed a republic in France. The Wars of German Unification had sired not only a German state but also the Third French Republic, a regime whose birth was deeply painful. Paris was besieged by German troops, its civilians subjected to the full horrors of starvation, disease and bombardment (40,000 people died, mostly children and the elderly). The four-hundred-thousand-odd defenders of the French capital pinned their hopes on an army which Léon Gambetta (the inspired, beer-swilling republican who had escaped from Paris by balloon) had promised to raise in the provinces. The French army trapped at Metz surrendered on 29 October, however, and this released some two hundred thousand German troops who could march on the Loire to prevent Gambetta's forces from reaching the capital. On 28 January the government signed an armistice with the Germans.

By then, Bismarck's unified German state had taken shape. Once the conflict had begun, Bismarck worked on his most important war aim: winning over the southern German states. He was helped by a wave of nationalist sentiment; if the south was to be 'won' rather than 'conquered', there could be no sign of pressure from Prussia. During the negotiations which followed in the autumn of 1870, Bismarck was not, in fact, averse to using a mixture of threat and compromise. By the end of November all four southern states had signed treaties joining the German *Reich*. Concessions were made to particularism: the new Empire's *Bundesrat*, the upper house of parliament appointed by the individual state governments, received expanded powers. Bavaria retained the right to control residence within its borders; it kept its own railway, postal and telegraph systems and its army would be a self-contained unit within the German army. Bavaria and Württemberg would both enjoy permanent seats (along with Saxony) on the military and foreign affairs committees of the *Bundesrat*. Württemberg's rights were not as extensive as those enjoyed by Bavaria, but the King there had the right to appoint his army commanders, while in peacetime only local troops would be posted within the kingdom. Baden was allowed to raise its own taxation on beer and spirits. The great symbolic moment was finally reached in the Hall of Mirrors at Versailles on 18 January 1871, while the war was still raging around Paris. In the name of the assembled German princes, Grand Duke Frederick of Baden hailed 'his imperial and royal majesty Emperor William!' The King of Prussia was now 'German Kaiser'.

Making a Nation

'We have made Italy,' Massimo d'Azeglio said. 'Now we must make the Italians.'[20] It was equally important for Bismarck to 'make Germans'. Italy and Germany were not the creations originally envisaged by the prophets of the nation-state. Their creation was less the expression of the popular will than of the power of hegemonic states – Piedmont and Prussia – and the political elites. The unifications depended less on revolution 'from below' than on policies imposed 'from above'. The new states were therefore faced with a multitude of problems, such as their relationship with the Catholic Church, the persistence of regionalism, and the integration of workers and peasants alienated by social problems. Meanwhile, despite the conquest of Venetia in 1866 and Rome in 1870, Italian national aspirations were unsatisfied, with Trieste, the Trentino and the south Tyrol pressed firmly under Austria's thumb. To nationalists, these territories were unredeemed – *terre irredente* (hence irredentism). Bismarck's German Reich was confronted with the opposite problem: it had national minorities – Poles in the east, the French in Alsace-Lorraine and Danes in the north – who might be subject to irredentist claims coming from the other side of the border.

The struggles between the new states and the Catholic Church were part of a wider European cultural struggle between secularism and religion in the later nineteenth century, and the stakes were being raised during this period. Pope Pius IX condemned liberalism, socialism and secularism in the 1864 *Syllabus of Errors*. In July 1870 the Vatican Council added the doctrine of papal infallibility, meaning that the Pope spoke with divine authority on religious matters and so could not be contradicted. Against this ideological background, the fraught relations between the Church and the new Italian state were also bluntly political, as unification occurred at the Pope's expense: he first lost the Papal States and then, in 1870, Rome itself. It was difficult for devout Italian Catholics to be loyal both to the Church and to the new kingdom. In Germany, a third of the Reich's citizens were Catholic, many of whom had been hostile to the Prussian (for which many read Protestant) bid for unification.[21]

The Pope reacted to Italian unification with an interdict (*non expedit*) forbidding Italian Catholics to vote or to stand in elections, undermining the legitimacy of the liberal order. The Italian state responded in 1867 with the expropriation of church land, the closure of religious orders (in which some 4000 houses were suppressed), a ban on pilgrimages, the introduction of military service for priests, civil marriage and the extension of equal civil and political rights to non-Catholics. This anticlerical backlash merely stimulated an upsurge in Catholic piety. The mutual hostility made it easier for the Italian government to annex Rome in September 1870. Yet Church–State relations evolved into a 'fractious cohabitation'[22] rather than, as in Germany (or in France), an all-out war. The liberal 'right' recognised the Church's influence and compromised in 1871 with the 'Law of Guarantees', which recognised the Vatican as an independent state, provided the Pope with an annual compensation and guaranteed his freedom to communicate with Catholics worldwide. Pius gave this compromise short shrift and the *non expedit* was reiterated in 1874, 1881 and 1886. With a papal ban on political participation, however, no Catholic party emerged to defend specifically Catholic interests.

By contrast in Germany, Catholics reacted to unification by forging the Centre Party in 1870 to protect the Church and Catholic schools against secularisation, while opposing any extension of the power of the new Reich over the states. It also promoted social reform to attract workers back to the Church. These doctrines allowed the centre to align with both the left and the right as it saw fit. For Bismarck, Catholicism was bound up with the regionalism of the south, but also with the potential for separatism in Alsace-Lorraine and nationalism in the Prussian-ruled parts of Poland. Bismarck accused the Polish clergy of awakening Polish nationalism from the pulpit and in their primary schools. The opening of the *Kulturkampf* – the struggle between the German state and the Catholic Church – he later claimed, 'was decided for me preponderantly by its Polish side'.[23] He was also dependent on liberal support in the *Reichstag* and calculated that, as supporters of the secular state, they would be rallied by a resolute policy of anticlericalism. Identifying enemies of the new order (*Reichsfeinde*) was also a means of galvanising wider public support, since Catholics, though significant, were a minority, accounting for a third of the population. Socialists would be subjected to the same targeting, and for the same purpose, a few years later.

The first step was taken when the Catholic section of the Prussian education ministry was closed. In December 1871 the 'pulpit paragraph' of the German Criminal Code penalised priests who 'endangered public peace'. When Bismarck failed to persuade the Pope and the German bishops to withdraw their support from the Centre Party, he stepped up the campaign from the summer of 1872. Across the Reich over the next three years the Jesuits were banned, the Expatriation Law of 1874 enabled the expulsion of priests who breached the pulpit paragraph and civil marriage was introduced. Prussia was even stricter: the May Laws of 1873 obliged trainee priests to attend state universities; church appointments were to be vetted by the state, and the registration of births, deaths and marriages was put under state supervision. In 1875 Prussia outlawed all religious orders. While anticlerical liberals were enthused by this assault on what they regarded as a conservative institution, the *Kulturkampf* failed to destroy Catholicism as a political and social force. If anything, it rallied Catholics around the Church and the Centre. In 1874 the party's seats in the *Reichstag* were boosted from 63 to 91 and thereafter its number of deputies never dropped far below a hundred until 1912. Catholicism's resilience was due to its support and organisation in the grassroots, with its own press and associations. Bismarck's policies also stirred the hostility of conservative Protestants anxious about secularisation.

By the late 1870s the political situation had evolved. Both the captains of heavy industry and the Junkers – an alliance of 'iron and wheat' – put Bismarck under pressure to introduce tariffs in the depression after 1873. Bismarck was coming to regard protectionism as a means of bolstering the conservative, landed base of the Reich while also supporting the vital industries which gave Germany its military might. Tariffs, once imposed, were also a means of raising money without having to beg the *Reichstag* for new taxation. Protectionism, however, also meant breaking with the liberals, who supported both free trade and anticlericalism, while the Centre had strong support among Catholic farmers and landowners who backed tariffs. An important obstacle to Bismarck's change of direction was removed in 1878 when Pius IX died; he was succeeded by Leo XIII who wanted reconciliation. Bismarck's tariff bill in July 1879 was the break with his erstwhile allies, the National Liberals, who split between the more conservative, who supported protectionism, and those who remained faithful to the doctrine of free trade, who joined the Progressives. There was little any of these groups could do to stop Bismarck from purging their colleagues from the state administration. Bismarck then abandoned most of his anticlerical legislation, though the *Kulturkampf* did not entirely fizzle out until 1887.

In Italy, where the vast majority of the population was Catholic, religion was closely associated with regionalism or separatism. None the less, particularism could not be eradicated overnight. The new regime tried to impose administrative uniformity based on 69 'provinces', each with a prefect, and municipalities (*comuni*), whose mayors were appointed by the central government. The army, the civil service and the judiciary were also standardised across Italy, but in the early years they were dominated by the Piedmontese. The government would also sponsor public commemorations of the *Risorgimento*, expand education and encourage economic development, but it would take time to shape the likes of the Tuscans or the Sicilians into Italians. Cavour (who died in 1861) had hoped that the fruits of liberalism would persuade Italians of the benefits of citizenship in the new state, but the constitution was the same as the Piedmontese *Statuto* of 1848. Its limited franchise gave the vote to a mere 2 per cent of the population in 1860. Consequently, and despite a limited extension of the suffrage in 1882, power remained confined to the liberal elites, who were divided between a 'left' and a 'right'. In practice, these ideological differences were blurred by *trasformismo*, whereby governments 'transformed' opponents into supporters by favours and position. Governments came and went, but in practice little – even the personnel – actually changed at the centre. The political system therefore worked to ensure that there was stability in government, but at the cost of creating a schism between 'legal' Italy (the political establishment) and 'real' Italy (society at large).

Much of 'real' Italy remained blighted by poverty, leaving many people without a stake in the new order. The peasants were subjected to conscription and a uniform tax system, including the *macinato* (grist-tax) which inflated bread prices. It was the source of violent resentment and there were riots against it in 1869. The problem of poverty was especially acute in the south, where endemic brigandage exacerbated the situation in the 1860s. The limits of the liberal order were revealed by its limited success in tackling the 'southern question', the problem of reconciling the *Mezzogiorno* (south) with the new state.[24] The challenge was how to integrate the southern elites while at the same time alleviating the desperate social problems of the masses. The dilemma was exposed after March 1876 when the liberal 'Left', most of whose parliamentary deputies represented southern constituencies, ousted the government of the liberal 'Right', which had been in power since unification and whose strongholds were in the north. The new prime minister, Agostino Depretis, cautiously chose to conciliate the southern elites by, among other policies, supporting protectionism, which did little to tackle the fundamental problem of poverty. The urgent problems faced by the liberal order in Italy, its apparent inability to resolve them, and the practices associated with *trasformismo* all planted the germs of disillusionment. In 1882 the author of the statement that the Italians were congenitally prone to indiscipline and needed iron rule to guide them was no arch-conservative, but a former *Garibaldini*, Pasquale Turiello.[25] Still, the new parliamentary state survived to take root – slowly and fitfully – in Italian society.

German workers footed the bill for Bismarck's conciliation of conservative interests and, like the peasantry in Italy, were not easily integrated into the new order. The tariffs of 1879 raised the price of German grain by as much as 50 per cent over foreign wheat, which hit real wages. The workers, however, were finding a voice in socialism. In 1875 the German Social Democratic Party (*Sozialdemokratische Partei Deutschlands* – SPD) was founded at Gotha, with a programme which combined Lassalle's vision of state-supported workers' co-operatives with the Marxist aim of overthrowing the bourgeois–capitalist order, albeit by peaceful, legal means. With universal male suffrage, the SPD scored some early electoral successes: it received 10 per cent of the popular vote and 12 seats in the *Reichstag* in 1877. It boasted 38,000 members in 291 local branches. Bismarck, however, watched these developments – and the wider problem of the rapid growth of a working class – with alarm; the working-class internationalism of the socialists seemed as dangerous to the Reich as the Catholic Church. His chance came after two attempts on the Kaiser's life in May and June 1878. In the sincere public outrage, Bismarck enacted anti-socialist legislation, depicting the socialists as *Reichsfeinde*. When the liberals opposed his original bill, he dissolved the *Reichstag* and, in the ensuing electoral campaign, had no difficulty in declaring his opponents to be weak and unpatriotic. The liberals only avoided a total collapse by supporting the anti-socialist law, although they did impose amendments protecting the rights of SPD deputies and ensuring that the law itself had to be renewed after two and a half years. Otherwise, it banned all societies 'which aim[ed] at the overthrow of the existing political or social order through social democratic, socialistic, or communistic endeavours'. The socialists would survive the persecution, not least because, like the Catholics, they were well organised at grassroots level. None the less, the legislation endangered the political integration of German workers into the Reich.

The Nation-States of South-Eastern Europe

The Italian and German states are the best-known products of the collapse of the Vienna system in the 1850s, but the impact also reverberated in south-eastern Europe. The great-power intervention to rescue Turkey from the Russian onslaught during the Crimean War underscored the weakness of the Ottoman Empire, while the examples of Italian and German unification inspired Slav, Romanian and Greek nationalists alike. In Greece by 1861, King Othon, who had whittled down the powers of parliament to rule as a virtual autocrat, was faced with violent opposition from student demonstrations and military conspiracies, often in favour of the 'Great Idea', the union of all Greeks in one state. He sought to undercut this opposition by securing the Ionian Islands from the British and an anti-Turkish alliance with Serbia and Montenegro. His efforts came to nothing and in October 1862 the garrison in Athens deposed him and established a provisional government. France, Britain and Russia, the guarantors of Greek independence, imposed Prince William of Denmark upon the throne (as George I), but as a sweetener the British transferred the Ionian Islands to Greece in 1863. The Greek Constituent Assembly endowed Greece with a single-chamber legislature, universal male suffrage and a secret ballot – one of the first states in nineteenth-century Europe to adopt such reforms together. Nationalist thirst for Greek unity, however, remained unquenched. Sporadic Greek insurrections against Turkish rule on Crete finally culminated, in August 1866, in an uprising supplied by the Greek government with arms, provisions and even army officers. The Greeks also fomented insurrections in Macedonia, Thessaly and Epirus to divide Turkish efforts. They looked for allies, and found the Serb ruler, Prince Michael Obrenović, receptive; he dreamed of forging a regional alliance for an all-out war of liberation against Turkey.

Obrenović, pursuing the idea of South Slav unity, saw Serbia cast in the same role as Piedmont. In June 1862, Serbia and Turkey came to the brink of war when a Serbian mob attacked Belgrade's Turkish garrison (permitted under the terms of Serbia's autonomy). When the Turks bombarded the city, the great powers brokered a compromise whereby Turkish civilians would leave the principality but four Turkish garrisons would remain. In the next five years of uneasy peace, Obrenović stoked Slav nationalism, particularly among the Bulgarians and in Bosnia, but, with no plans for land reform, he failed to attract mass peasant support. Obrenović signed an alliance with Greece in the summer of 1867, but the costs of his expansionist plans provoked domestic opposition. Obrenović was assassinated by supporters of the rival Karadjordje dynasty in June 1868 and succeeded by his young cousin, Milan. The liberal opposition pressed their programme on to the regency which followed and, in 1869, Serbia became a constitutional state. Serbia's gain was Greece's loss: it had to fight Turkey alone. The insurrection on Crete was crushed by 1869 and the devastated island would remain a smouldering issue between Turkey and Greece.

While Serb and Greek nationalist aspirations were frustrated, the Romanians made a dramatic breakthrough. Unification was driven primarily by domestic politics, but it was also a by-product of the Crimean War. The Treaty of Paris in 1856 had ended the Russian protectorate in Moldavia and Wallachia, so the way was open to revise the Organic Statutes imposed by Tsar Nicholas I. Each principality would now elect an assembly to advise an international commission on a new constitution. However, before he duly summoned the two assemblies in 1857, the Sultan also seized the opportunity to appoint two princes to act as governors of the principalities. The assemblies, though elected by a very limited suffrage of some thirteen thousand voters, reacted by calling for the union of the two principalities under one prince. The great powers intervened with a conference in Paris which in August 1858 created the 'United Principalities of Moldavia and Wallachia', under Turkish suzerainty but subject to the supervision of the European powers. While the principalities were declared 'united', in fact they each had a prince elected for life, with their own separate legislatures based on a narrow suffrage.

In January 1859, however, the unionists in the two assemblies engineered *de facto* unification by both electing Alexandru Ioan Cuza as Prince of Wallachia and Moldavia. The powers, including Turkey, accepted Cuza's election and, in 1861, a single assembly for the two principalities, but ruled that the union would only last for his lifetime. Unionists pressed Cuza to make the unification permanent but the prince understood that he could not push his luck too far with the European powers. Cuza, who modelled himself on Napoleon III, sought to court the support of the wider population with benevolent reforms, while governing with an iron hand. He introduced the metric system and a law code, and nationalised the property of Greek Orthodox monasteries. He broke conservative *boyar* (gentry) opposition in the assemblies by extending the suffrage and he abolished personal servitude and dues for the peasantry. His land reform, while dramatic (2 million hectares were transferred to the peasantry), still left 70 per cent of all agricultural land in the hands of the *boyars* and the state. Nationalists were not averse to exploiting the 'land question' to further their cause, and nationalism was Cuza's nemesis. Conservatives who resented his reforms and liberals tired of his authoritarian ways gathered around the cause of unification, full independence and a constitution. In the night of 22 February 1866 a coup, led by the former '48er, Ion Brătianu, found Cuza in his bed and forced him to abdicate. According to the Paris Convention, the union should have been dissolved, but the provisional government acted quickly, searching for a prince who would be appointed as hereditary ruler. The Romanians eventually found the Prussian Prince Charles of Hohenzollern-Sigmaringen. There was some domestic opposition to the choice, particularly in Moldavia, where the Orthodox clergy worried about his Catholicism. Riots in Iaşi were put down by the army, and Charles was confirmed as King by a referendum.

Napoleon III called a great-power conference in Paris in March 1866 but, other than by going to war, there was no way of forcing the Romanians to back down. In any case, nationalists were forcing the pace of change: on 10 May the Romanian Constituent Assembly declared Romania 'one and indivisible' and proclaimed Charles as King Carol I. The Sultan and the Tsar both mobilised their forces along the frontiers, but the British wanted to avoid war, while the French supported Romanian unification. Meanwhile, Austria was facing a more serious danger – Prussia – and could ill-afford to become entangled in south-eastern Europe. With the outbreak of war in Germany, Tsar Alexander II was more willing to give way over Romania and, isolated, the Turks compromised. By an edict issued on 23 October, the Sultan recognised Carol as hereditary ruler of the 'United Principalities' (studiously avoiding the term 'Romania'), although he had to pay tribute to Constantinople. The flimsy 'Crimean system', based on the 1856 Treaty of Paris, had been torn apart; the way was once more open for Russia to press its interests in the Black Sea.

Ironically, nationalism in south-eastern Europe was given a boost by the *Tanzimat*, the efforts of successive Sultans to reform the Ottoman Empire. Among his many contributions, Abdülaziz secularised the *millets* (religious groups within the empire) so that authority passed from the clergy to lay representatives. He also guaranteed the rights of the individual and sought to strengthen imperial authority over the local power-brokers, all in the hope that the sting would be taken out of the nationalist scorpion. Yet among the Turks, liberal 'Young Ottomans' were frustrated because the reforms fell far short of a constitution, while conservative clerics and much of the Muslim populace resented the potential loss of their pre-eminence (though in fact they continued to dominate the structures of the state). In Ottoman Europe, the reforms inadvertently stoked nationalism; as *millet* leadership passed from the clergy to the lay Christian elites, so the overarching Orthodox identity fragmented among the different nationalities. This was expressed by different ethnic groups among the Sultan's Christian subjects each demanding recognition as a separate *millet*, with its own national church.

In 1871 Abdülaziz yielded to the demands of the Bulgarian Orthodox clergy, students, local officials and trade guilds for a separate Bulgarian *millet*, with its own Orthodox leader (*exarch*). This clashed with the Greek Orthodox hierarchy's traditional leadership of the entire Christian *millet*. They hit back by declaring the Bulgarians to be heretics. The issue was especially explosive in Macedonia, where the loyalties of the mixed Greek and Slav population could be claimed by either Church. Beneath the religious clash, therefore, lay a deeper, ethnic conflict among the Sultan's Christian subjects.

The Ottoman decline opened a Pandora's Box of conflicting national aspirations. Croatian and Serb nationalists embraced various forms of the 'Yugoslav' ideal, which envisaged the union of the southern Slavs – excluding the Bulgarians but including the Macedonians. Greek nationalists embraced the 'Great Idea', which aspired to the union of all peoples whom they deemed to be Hellenic, including the Macedonians. Bulgarian nationalists dreamt of a 'Greater Bulgaria', embracing Macedonia. Romanian irredentism held fast to the 'Dacian ideal', the historic claim to territory based on the ancient Roman province of Dacia, but which at least excluded Macedonia. As the nationalist aspirations of one group overlapped territorially with those of the others, they would foster ethnic conflict. Yet for as long as the Ottoman Empire remained the primary obstacle to the realisation of these separate goals, nationalists almost everywhere in south-eastern Europe could envisage co-operation against this common enemy.

They aimed, above all, at fomenting a great peasant revolt against the Sultan and exploited peasant anger over taxation, compulsory labour services on the Sultan's railway projects, and land tenure (since Muslims remained the dominant landowners). A particularly sore spot was Bosnia-Herzegovina, where, of a total population of some 1.3 million, there were 400,000 Muslims, of whom 10,000 formed a landlord elite, mostly absentees living in Sarajevo. The actual farmers were primarily Orthodox Christian sharecroppers who, on top of taxes, paid as much as half of their crop to their landlords. Between 1871 and 1875 sporadic peasant unrest became endemic. In Macedonia and Bulgaria, the Turkish state inadvertently piled an additional woe on to the peasants: the settlement in the 1860s of up to two hundred thousand Muslim refugees fleeing Russian expansion in the Caucasus. They did not integrate easily into local society and many turned to brigandage, adding to the peasants' fear and loathing.

In 1875 this volatile mix of grievances caught alight. A financial crash in 1873 had left the Turkish government in danger of bankruptcy and it sought to maximise its revenue by squeezing what it could from existing taxation. In Bosnia, the appearance of the tax collectors in January 1875 came after a disastrous harvest. The revolt started when peasants, unable to pay the officials, fled to neighbouring Montenegro, while troops and police ransacked their abandoned villages. The insurrection, a response to economic distress, spread as peasants clashed with Turkish soldiers. Nationalists tried to impose a political stamp on the revolt: committees across the frontier in the Slav provinces of the Habsburg empire, in Montenegro and in Serbia sent arms, provisions, money and volunteers to back the peasant rebels.

Meanwhile, a Bulgarian nationalist insurrection was crushed in April 1876. The peasantry were unwilling to risk joining the uprising and most of the elites were content with the concessions made by the Porte a few years earlier. The nationalists had to depend upon the initiative of local village notables such as priests, teachers, students and master-artisans. In destroying the revolt, the Sultan used Muslim irregulars, the *bashi-bozuks*, and the Caucasian refugees, as his regular forces were tied down in Bosnia. Both sides committed atrocities: Bulgarian insurgents slaughtered Muslims, and they in turn wreaked their revenge, rarely discriminating between rebellious and loyal peasants. The rising was over within weeks, but some thirty thousand people had been killed, although this death toll pales in comparison with that in Bosnia-Herzegovina, which claimed about a hundred and fifty thousand lives. It was, however, the 'Bulgarian atrocities' which grabbed world attention. European governments were swayed by outraged public opinion. That more Muslims than Christians might have been killed was ignored. In Britain, traditionally the defender of the Ottoman Empire, Gladstone managed to discredit the pro-Turkish policy of Disraeli, who was therefore in no position to intervene in the war which erupted between Turkey and Russia in 1877.

In the 1870s both Austria–Hungary and Russia were watching developments carefully. The Austrians, having been burned by nationalism in Italy and Germany, were alarmed by the Bosnian revolt, fearing that it might encourage South Slav separatism. There was also the danger that Russia might stoke up Slav nationalism. An influential Pan-Slav movement had emerged, arguing that Russia should compensate for its defeat in the Crimean War by taking up its true national mission: protecting all Slav peoples and forging an alliance or even a political union with them. At its most expansive, it envisaged that Constantinople would be 'reconquered' for the Orthodox faith and would become the new capital of the Slav empire, as Nikolai Danilevskii argued in his 1869 book, *Russia and Europe*. Pan-Slavism did not dictate official Russian policy in the Balkans; after all, it threatened to promote revolutionary nationalism.

None the less, it encouraged freelancing Russians and south-eastern Europeans to work together and, in the process, alarmed the Austrian government about Russian intentions. Russian volunteers joined the Serbian and Montenegrin forces which, in June 1876, invaded Bosnia to eject the Turks. Russian public opinion urged the Tsar to intervene and defend Serbia from the Turkish counter-attack. Meanwhile, the Austrian government threatened the Croatian *Sabor*, where the over-zealous National Party responded enthusiastically to the Bosnian revolt. Yet both Austria–Hungary and Russia stopped short of challenging each other. The Austro-Hungarians wanted permission to help the Turks crush the Bosnian insurrection, while Russia wanted to prevent the Turks from inflicting a crushing defeat on the Serbs. So while Vienna allowed Russia to issue an ultimatum to the Sultan to stop fighting the Serbs (October 1876), Russia let the Austro–Hungarians send in forces to put down the Bosnians. The temptation, however, was too great for the Russians not to exploit the crisis and reverse some of the losses of the Crimean War.

The opportunity came when Abdülaziz was toppled in a coup led by Midhat Pasha, a liberal who wanted far-reaching political change in the Ottoman Empire. The European powers had already been trying to impose a comprehensive reform programme on Constantinople, but the constitution which Midhat foisted on the new Sultan, Abdülhamid II, went much further (though it was short-lived; once war broke out, the Sultan seized the chance to dismiss Midhat and to restore absolutism). The Porte's rejection of the foreign reform programme in April 1877 was the pretext the Tsar needed to go to war. As its forces marched, Russia secretly promised to allow Austria–Hungary to annex Bosnia-Herzegovina and not to build a large Slav state from the wreckage of the Ottoman Empire.

For the Romanians the conflict presented an opportunity. In 1876 Ion Brătianu's National Liberal Party had wrested power from the conservatives on the back of its demand for full independence from Turkey. Romania now declared war on the Sultan. The Russians hoped that a swift victory would allow them to dictate terms to both the Porte and the Slav states, but the Russians needed Romanian help to break Turkish resistance at the siege of Plevna. As the Russians stumbled, Montenegro, Greece and then, in December, Serbia seized the chance to stake their nationalist claims by joining the fight against Turkey. When Plevna finally fell, the Russian forces moved forwards again, taking Adrianople in January 1878 and signing an armistice with the Turks at San Stefano on 3 March. Its terms were electrifying.

The armistice recognised Serbian, Montenegrin and Romanian independence, and, while Russia took back the areas of Bessarabia lost in 1856, all three states made territorial gains. The most dramatic development was the creation of the new 'Greater Bulgarian' state, in breach of

Map 10.3 South-eastern Europe, 1804–1914

Russia's promise to Austria–Hungary. Bulgaria would be autonomous within the Ottoman Empire, but it would be immense, encompassing all of Macedonia and stretching from the Danube to the Aegean, so enjoying access to both the Black Sea and the Mediterranean. The emergence of such a vast Russian satellite was a hair-raising result for the rest of the region and the great powers alike. For the Greeks, San Stefano was a disaster; it came just as they struck into Ottoman territory. The armistice allowed the Turks to shift their forces southwards to crush their invasion. The Russians, in fact, had accepted that any peace agreement was subject to the discussion of the European powers and probably saw San Stefano as a haggling position. The peace negotiations were held at the Congress of Berlin in 1878, the last great milestone of congress diplomacy before the First World War. The Treaty of Berlin (see Map 10.3) sliced off large helpings of territory from Russia's proposed Bulgarian mass, reducing it to a third of the original size, so that it now extended only as far south as the Balkan Range. An Assembly of Notables would elect a prince, who would be approved by the great powers and confirmed by the Sultan. South of the Balkan Mountains, a new province, Eastern Rumelia, was to be governed by an assembly and a governor chosen by a commission of the European powers and accepted by the Sultan. Bulgaria was thus partitioned, with both halves remaining under Turkish suzerainty. Macedonia reverted to direct Ottoman rule, and while Serbia and Montenegro became fully independent states, the territory which they had gained at San Stefano was drastically cut back. Yugoslav dreamers were given a rude awakening when Austria–Hungary was given the right to occupy Bosnia-Herzegovina, albeit provisionally and under Turkish suzerainty, and to garrison the Sanjak of Novi Bazar, which divided Serbia from Montenegro. Romania surrendered southern Bessarabia to Russia but received in return the territory of Dobrudja, an outrage to nationalists, as the lands lost to Russia were part of the historic province of Moldavia. None of the new states, therefore, accepted the peace settlement as permanent. In the years to come, the overlapping irredentist goals would be a source of tension and conflict, not only between these countries but also among the great powers. The Austro-Hungarian occupation of Bosnia, while aimed at dousing the flames of Slav nationalism, would draw the Habsburg monarchy deeper into the affairs of the region, which was also witnessing a resurgence of Russian power. South-eastern Europe now emerged fully as one of the great stress zones in international relations.

11 Containing the Tempest: Reform and Consolidation

With the breakdown of the Vienna system in the 1850s and the gathering pace of economic and social development, European governments of all political colourings undertook reform in order to preserve the existing order. In Russia and the Habsburg empire, the stimulus for the reform programme was a confluence of domestic and international crises. Yet even in countries where there was less urgency, reform was undertaken to strengthen the establishment. In Britain and France, institutional change resulted as governments and elites tried to consolidate themselves by integrating new social groups or political tendencies within the regime. In all cases, however, it proved difficult to contain the forces of opposition intent on a more radical overhaul of the system. In Russia, the shortcomings of the 'Great Reforms' of Tsar Alexander II stirred revolutionary opposition, while France and Spain in the early 1870s witnessed the creation of republics as the previous regimes – for different reasons – failed. Within a generation of 1848, the political face of Europe had changed. Except in the Russian Empire, where the autocracy remained intact, parliamentary institutions (with widely varying degrees of suffrage) had become the norm. None the less, in various ways (including electoral manipulation, patronage and dominance of the upper chamber) the elites – nobles, bourgeoisie or a blend of both – managed to retain political control.

Reforming the Conservative Order

Alexander II became Tsar in 1855, as the serious shortcomings of the Russian military machine had been brutally exposed in the Crimean War. At home there were alarming signs that the long-abused peasantry was protesting in ever more violent ways. Alexander II's more progressive advisers would launch the era of the 'Great Reforms', of which the most dramatic was the emancipation of the serfs in 1861. There is some controversy over the government's motives. The most obvious explanation is that the reforms were a response to military defeat and to the need for Russia to develop economically and socially if it were to remain a great power. There is also some evidence that the Tsar was worried by the danger of a peasant insurrection. The government's own reports recorded 216 peasant disturbances in 1835–44, rising to an alarming 348 in the following decade. In 1856 Alexander ruffled some noble feathers when he warned them that 'sooner or later it would be necessary to change serfdom and that it was better for this change to begin at the top than at the bottom'.[1] Yet for conservatives – and possibly the wavering Tsar himself – the danger of rebellion was a very good reason *not* to emancipate the peasantry; in the past the very whiff of freedom had spurred excited peasants into disobedience and revolt. More positive motives included changing attitudes among enlightened government officials and progressive landlords, who were coming to see serfdom as an obstruction to economic growth. A free agrarian labour force would be more productive, enabling landlords to profit from growing European demand for Russian grain. Mounting criticism and guilt about serfdom played a role in convincing nobles and officials of the evils of the institution; even Nicholas I had admitted that it was wrong. A swell in the support for reform had been developing within the Russian bureaucracy for decades. Restrained under Nicholas's iron rule, the enlightened bureaucrats came of age under Alexander II. Many of the reforming officials, such as Nikolai Miliutin and Sergei Soloviev, wanted nothing less than an overhaul in the relationship between state and society. They were not liberals; few, if any, supported a constitutional monarchy. However, like the enlightened reformers of the eighteenth century, they wanted to purge the entire state of *proizvol*, the arbitrary, corrupt and abusive exercise of power, seeking instead to establish *zakonnost*, the rule of law whereby government would act according to established laws. They did not want to give Russian subjects political rights, but the process of reform meant enlisting public support and, after peasant emancipation, redefining the relationship between the state and the people. This implied more 'openness', free discussion and transparency between government and its subjects; the Russian term was *glasnost*. Alexander, in fact, permitted public discussion of serfdom because in December 1855 he abolished his father's '1848 Committee', which eased censorship. The purpose was to co-opt public opinion behind reform, against the expected opposition of conservative nobles.

Yet, despite all this, the reforms would not have happened unless Alexander himself had been persuaded of the need for deep-rooted change. The young Tsar was, in fact, a reluctant reformer; he had no desire either to relinquish any power as an autocrat or to unravel Russia's hierarchical society. The zealous reformers certainly shaped the final outcome of the emancipation, but they did not start the process. Those who put the freedom of the serfs on to the statute book were conservative officials originally appointed by Nicholas, who were less likely to be influenced by progressive currents. The solution to this apparent conundrum is probably that the short-term shock of military defeat, given momentum by a developing crisis in the rural order, convinced conservative officials of the urgent need for change. Yet the precise terms and the wider implications of emancipation demanded serious attention, which was why the more progressive officials then won the initiative. Once convinced of the need for emancipation, therefore, the Tsar was forced to concede further reforms in order to deal with its consequences. He never intended the changes to be as far-reaching as they turned out to be.

One of the prickly issues to be grasped was under precisely what terms the serfs were to be freed and, during this brief period of *glasnost*, there was no shortage of suggestions. In 1858 Konstantin Kavelin published an article brashly demanding that the peasants gain freedom *with land*, in contrast to the government's own assumptions. The public's fevered anticipation of sweeping change alarmed the Tsar. In 1859 he banned all public discussion of the peasant question and later (in 1865) he would impose a new censorship law. Yet Kavelin's bombshell had fallen with pinpoint accuracy on to the essential question. Emancipating the serfs without land would ensure that the government retained noble support, but it would also create tens of millions of landless peasants (almost a third of the 74 million people in Russia were serfs in 1858). Progressive officials, such as Nikolai Miliutin, therefore proposed freeing the serfs with land while making them compensate the landowners for it. The big question was how. The heady public excitement over the issue was hard even for arch-conservatives to ignore and some of their number, including Iakov Rostovtsev, dramatically came around to Miliutin's way of thinking. Divisions amongst conservative officials allowed the reformers to prevail and, though it took over two years of careful drafting, the law was promulgated on 19 February 1861. The emancipation was heavily weighted in favour of the landlords, since they received government compensation for the land given to the peasantry, who in turn were saddled with repaying the government over 49 years. However, an institution which had characterised Russian society for over two centuries had gone for good.

As landlords no longer 'owned' serfs, the peasants were now subject only to the state. Yet the government in St Petersburg could not possibly deal with so many people in such a vast empire. The Tsar was forced, therefore, to accept some public involvement in local government. In 1859 the *volosti* (cantons) were created, with officials elected by the peasants. None the less, *volost* influence was offset by the establishment in 1863 of representative institutions at a higher level (the *zemstva*) elected in each district for three years by three different classes (landowners, urban property-owners and the *volosti*). These district assemblies would then choose the members of the provincial *zemstva*. In 1870 a similar representative element was introduced in the cities. The responsibilities of the *zemstva* – which had tax-raising powers – were vast, including economic development, public health, roads, prisons and education. The rural *zemstva* were, however, dominated by the nobility; they were intended to compensate the gentry for the loss of their influence over the peasants, whose daily lives were still managed by the village commune (*mir*). The peasants were also treated differently by the law, as separate *volost* courts would handle peasant cases.

Emancipation made an overhaul of the Russian army possible. In its old form, peasants were conscripted for 25 years, which more or less meant for life; the authorities could barely return fully-trained soldiers back to their villages as serfs. Now it seemed safer to allow peasants to serve in the army for shorter periods of time. From 1862, following the suggestions of Dmitri Miliutin, Nikolai's brother, the army recruited more people each year, but for a shorter term (seven years), after which they would be put on the reserve list and could be recalled in wartime. In fact, this increased the number of trained soldiers who could be mustered; by 1870 there were 553,000 reservists. In education, universities were given greater control over their own affairs in 1863. In a series of legal reforms, local justices of the peace would be elected by the district *zemstva*, judges were to be well-paid (and so less susceptible to bribery) and trials were to be open and held before a jury.

The limits of the great reforms were imposed by the awkward fact that the Tsar had to cling on to the nobility. He needed their co-operation in local government, in the law courts and in the army to protect the autocracy and to keep order in the empire. The result was that the reforms had serious limitations: the terms of emancipation and local government reform favoured the nobility. While he allowed his advisers to explore limited constitutional changes, Alexander had no intention of relinquishing his autocratic power. These restrictions and the persistence of censorship alienated liberals and angered radicals. While liberals hoped that a Tsar would at some point grant a constitution, the more determined opponents of the regime sought to rally dissatisfied peasants to the cause of revolution. In 1881 this opposition succeeded in mortally wounding the 'Tsar Liberator' in a bomb blast.

The danger to the Tsarist regime lay not in any revolution from below; the peasant masses proved stubbornly resistant to revolutionary blandishments. The immediate threat came from state officials, army officers and students frustrated by the limits of reform and by the lack of political freedom. The closure of the universities in 1861 and, above all, the arrest of the liberal nobles of Tver province in 1862 suggested that the regime would not tolerate even a 'loyal opposition'. The Tver nobles had meekly suggested that the success of the abolition of serfdom depended upon 'consultation with the people' and that the economic burden of emancipation should fall on all classes, not just the peasantry.[2] When mysterious fires burned in St Petersburg, the official investigation could not find any culprits, but the government seized the opportunity to close down two organs of the revolutionary movement, the *Contemporary* and *The Russian Word*. The editor of the former, Nicholas Chernyshevsky, was arrested and exiled to Siberia. The state's falsification of evidence against him infuriated wider liberal opinion. Moreover, in their surveillance of dissidents, the Third Department (political police) had hoped to incriminate loyal but progressive officials such as Prince Alexander Suvorov, governor-general of St Petersburg.

In such circumstances it was hard to sustain a middle ground; liberals who sought to press for political change within the law were allowed no space in which to do so. Initiative fell to those who were prepared to take violent action rather than 'waste their breath on discussions of . . . parliamentarianism and legal points and the devil only knows what', as Barazov, the radical in Ivan Turgenev's *Fathers and Sons*, puts it. Populists turned their back on Western liberal traditions and hoped instead to forge an egalitarian society based on Russian peasant life. In August 1862 the underground organisation 'Land and Freedom', inspired by ideas disseminated in Chernyshevsky's *Contemporary* and in Herzen's *Bell*, was established. It anticipated a peasant insurrection over the drawbacks of the emancipation edict. Its propaganda tried to appeal directly to the peasants, sometimes using embarrassingly 'folksy' language.[3] Some cooler heads realised that educating the peasantry would take years, or even generations, but the revolutionaries were excited because the government itself recorded 647 violent incidents in 42 provinces immediately after the emancipation edict. The most serious violence occurred in Kazan province, where a peasant named Anton Petrov informed a crowd in Bezdna that the genuine edict gave the peasants 'real' freedom, with land which they could occupy immediately. Should any landlord resist, he told them, 'bang him on the head. The Tsar will reward you.'[4] Soldiers dispersed the gathering, killing 41 and wounding 70. Although Petrov (who was summarily tried and shot) claimed to be speaking in the name of the Tsar, the Populists hoped to channel peasant anger towards the regime itself.

Another hope for the revolutionaries came from Poland, where a nationalist insurrection erupted in 1863. Alexander's reform programme led Polish patriots to speak hopefully of a 'thaw' in the Tsar's treatment of the Poles. Alexander certainly planned to make concessions; he needed stability as he proceeded with his reforms. Yet Alexander would not yield any of his autocratic powers by restoring the constitution of 1815 or even implementing the 1832 'Organic Statute'. He was also reluctant to encourage Polish nationalism since, from the Polish point of view, Poland had to include the Ukrainian and Belarussian lands held before the first partition in 1772, territories which Russian patriots dubbed Russia's 'western provinces'. The real tragedy of these irreconcilable claims was that many of the peasants who toiled in these lands were neither Polish nor Russian, but Belarussian and Ukrainian, oppressed by Polish and Russian landlords alike.

Otherwise, Poles were readmitted into the civil service from 1857. The Polish language was taught once again in Lithuanian schools. Jews were allowed to leave the 'Pale' of settlement and to enter the state bureaucracy. The Catholic Church was given a new lease of life when the long-empty archbishopric of Warsaw was filled. A medical academy was opened, and an agricultural society, an assembly of progressive landowners, was permitted to meet to discuss land reform and serfdom. It rapidly became a surrogate parliament under its moderate president, Andrzej Zamoyski. The medical academy and the art school became centres of revolutionary conspiracy in Warsaw, where radical and moderate students were called respectively 'Reds' and 'Whites' (the first use of these political terms).[5] During the insurrection, these labels were applied respectively to the radicals who worked immediately for revolution and land reform, and to the moderates, who defended the interests of the gentry, accepted clerical influence and – initially – wanted to secure concessions by persuasion. The point of no return came after violent clashes in 1861 when Polish demonstrations were violently repressed in February, April and October. The Tsar followed a policy of repression alternating with mild concessions, in a bid to split the Polish Whites from the rest of the opposition. Yet, by this stage, the gap between the Russian regime and Polish public opinion had widened so much that even the cautious Zamoyski refused to work with the new viceroy, Alexander's brother Constantine, who was appointed in May 1862. A National Central Committee, inspired by the Reds, was formed in Warsaw, and many of the Whites submitted to its authority in November, paying the secret 'national tax' aimed at funding the uprising.

The insurrection of January 1863 was sparked by the imposition of conscription. The National Central Committee proclaimed itself the provisional government as it unleashed a guerrilla war on the Russians, although there was no major rising in Warsaw. The insurrection gathered momentum as the peasants responded to the promises of the Reds, which was precisely why the Whites initially had no intention of joining the revolt. The Reds were weakened as the fighting took its toll, however, and the Whites steadily gained in influence, imposing themselves on the revolution by mid-April. Together, the Reds and the Whites forged an underground state, with its own system of taxation, communications and policing. The Russian general charged with investigating it managed to joke when he reported to Constantine: 'I have come to one conclusion, namely, that I don't belong to it . . . nor does Your Imperial Highness.'[6]

The insurrection, however, suffered from several weaknesses: militarily, the insurgents were mostly civilians – artisans, workers, students, intellectuals, peasants and gentry, whose training consisted mostly of bloody experience on the battlefield itself. While Red propaganda managed to stir the Lithuanian and Belarussian peasants, those of the Ukraine, embittered by social grievances against their Polish landlords, slaughtered young Polish democrats who tried to propagandise amongst them. Moreover, there was no intervention by the European powers. In February, Bismarck had promised Alexander Prussian military co-operation in suppressing the revolt. Alexander could therefore safely ignore British and Austrian offers of mediation and French proposals for an international congress.

The Russian army took over in Poland as the Tsar gave General Feodor Berg full powers, while in Lithuania the governor-general Mikhail Muraviev, a Decembrist-turned-reactionary, fully earned his epithet, the 'hangman of Vilna'. Under pressure, the Whites and the Reds turned on each other. The latter seized control of the insurrection in September, and instigated a reign of terror against Whites and Russians alike. As the revolution polarised, many Poles were trapped in a dilemma: support for the Reds meant reprisals from the Russians, but failure to back the insurrection meant being subjected to 'revolutionary justice' by the Reds. The final phase of the uprising was played out when the Russians responded to a bomb attack on Berg with terrorist measures of their own: heavy fines, executions and the sequestration of goods and property. The intense repression and the struggle against the Whites destroyed the Red government, and in October direction of the uprising fell to a dictator, Romuald Traugutt. He worked hard to rebuild the Polish forces by allowing them to lie low over the winter and then imposing a *levée en masse* in the spring of 1864. In December 1863 he also declared the emancipation of the peasantry with land. The Tsar, however, following the advice of Nikolai Miliutin, outbid the Polish revolutionaries by offering Lithuanian, Belarussian, Ukrainian and then Polish peasants outright ownership of their land, without redemption payments. While the reform may have secured some peasant quiescence, in the long run it did not create a Polish peasantry loyal to the Tsar. The revolt, which was finally suppressed in April 1864, had mobilised more peasants to the Polish cause than the insurrection of 1794. In the aftermath many Polish nobles were exiled and their estates confiscated. Polish civil servants were purged and Russian was declared the official language. The Catholic Church was forbidden to communicate with Rome. Bishops who refused to obey were dismissed and there were forcible conversions from the Uniate Church to Orthodoxy in Russia's 'western provinces'.

It was not just Poles who suffered. As the uprising spread into Belarus and the Ukraine, so these regions felt the heel of the Tsarist boot. Belarus lost its only institution of higher education, the Agricultural Institute, and Catholic teachers were sacked.[7] While supporting Polish independence, Ukrainian patriots did not necessarily advocate their own political separation from Russia. Nikolai

Kostomarov, an influential member of the Ukrainophile intelligentsia, argued that Russia and the Ukraine were historically equal partners. He hoped that greater freedom for the nationalities of the empire would accompany the Tsar's reforms. Kostomarov's vision was overly optimistic. After the Polish insurrection, the *hromady* (literally, 'communities'), societies promoting Ukrainian language and culture, were suppressed.[8] Most Ukrainian books were banned in 1863, while Peter Valuev, the minister of the interior, declared the language to be merely 'Russian contaminated by Polish influence'.[9]

The backlash spread to Russia itself. 'Land and Freedom' was broken up by the police in 1863. The next major socialist act was taken by an extremist group, the 'Organisation', forged by Nikolai Ishutin in 1864 and with a shady inner circle with the blood-curdling name of 'Hell', whose members believed that a single act of violence – the assassination of the Tsar – would spark a widespread peasant revolt. In April 1866 an attempt by Hell on the Tsar's life was foiled and, bolstered by the public outrage (dubbed 'patriotic syphilis' by one fuming radical), the regime unleashed three years of reaction. It scarcely merited Herzen's term for it – the 'White Terror'. Alexander II was now certainly convinced that reform and order were incompatible and he replaced his more liberal-minded ministers with conservatives. Yet he refused to undo the earlier reforms, though two journals were closed down and a handful of radicals arrested. Most of the 'Terror' came from the reaction of the mobs who beat up anyone who looked like a 'revolutionary'; blue-tinted glasses were meant to be a give-away sign. Meanwhile, a hard core of revolutionaries, adopting Ishutin's uncompromising style, pressed on, rejecting reform and liberalism, and working only for the revolution. These 'nihilists', such as Peter Tkachev, who envisaged mass terror, and Sergei Nechaev, the inspiration for Feodor Dostoevsky's novel, *Demons* (1873), and author of the notorious *Revolutionary's Catechism* in 1869,[10] accepted the need for appalling levels of violence in the pursuit of the revolution. They rejected the notion that the peasants had to be gradually educated before they awoke to their full revolutionary potential. Instead, a core of hardened revolutionaries would seize power and then impose the new order on a benighted population, by terror if necessary.

In November 1869 Nechaev had one of his followers brutally murdered for betrayal, and the details of his behaviour which emerged during his trial (he was sentenced to life imprisonment) further discredited the revolutionary movement. These events convinced the less extreme revolutionaries that violent acts alone would not work. The ideologue of Populism, Peter Lavrov, argued in his *Historical Letters* that while an elite party would lead the revolution, their role was to work for the people's benefit. In 1874 and 1875 some two or three thousand men and women, mostly students on summer break, went out 'to the people' in order to win over the workers and peasants to the cause of the revolution. This first serious attempt at forging a mass revolutionary movement in Russia was unsuccessful, as peasants rejected the advice of the students. Two young revolutionaries later recalled pursuing a hapless peasant driving a sled in October 1873: they 'kept running, shouting about taxes and revolution' until they could no longer keep up.[11] Conservative village elders handed over many such enthusiasts to the authorities. In all, some 770 people, of whom 158 were women, were arrested. The 'To the People' movement had failed, but, in contrast to the nihilists, the idealism of the 'pilgrims' touched public opinion when they were brought to trial. In August 1876 'Land and Freedom' was relaunched. While it adopted the tactics of the 'To the People' movement – members actually settled permanently in villages among the peasants – it also tried to exploit the grievances of the urban workers. In 1876, led by the young Georgii Plekhanov, it tried in vain to take over a demonstration by unemployed workers in St Petersburg. When, in 1878, Vera Zasulich tried to shoot Feodor Trepov, governor-general of Saint Petersburg, in revenge for the flogging of one of the protesters, she was acquitted by a jury. Other members of 'Land and Freedom' killed the head of the Third Department and a police official in Kiev. In 1879 the bloodshed split the Populists between those who placed greater emphasis on education and those who saw violence as an essential revolutionary tactic. The former joined Plekhanov in the 'Black Repartition', while the latter formed the 'People's Will'. As the Plekhanovites left the country for exile, the initiative fell to the terrorists, who made several assassination attempts on the Tsar.

Shaken by the attempts on his life, the Tsar appointed Mikhail Loris-Melikov as interior minister to restore order. Student agitators were hanged in a brief but harsh period of repression. After that, however, Loris-Melikov suggested some political reform, the proposals for which would be submitted to a consultative council of *zemstva* and town representatives. The aim was to detach the nobility from the revolutionary movement, but it is doubtful whether this would have calmed the political situation. The People's Will was new in that it drew most of its members from the middle class and the educated workers, with little noble involvement. The Tsar, however, accepted the proposals on 28 January 1881. Whether or not they would have been the first step towards a constitutional monarchy will never be known; on that same day Alexander was killed by the 'People's Will'.

The political reforms in the Habsburg monarchy were a direct response to military defeat. On 15 July 1859, three days after signing the armistice with Napoleon III at Villafranca, Francis Joseph issued the 'Laxenburg Manifesto', in which he announced the peace and promised to pursue the welfare of his subjects through reform. The manifesto aimed at quieting grumblings of opposition among Viennese liberals, financiers opposed to the costs of the war, tax-payers defying treasury officials and Magyar '48ers' like Kossuth who were trying to foment a new Hungarian revolt. Conservative nobles – particularly Hungarians and Bohemians – also resented the anational, neo-absolutist centralism of the Bach system.

The Emperor started by dismissing Bach. There followed two constitutional experiments, both aimed at preserving the authority of the monarchy. It was to the conservatives that Francis Joseph listened first. The Hungarian Count, Antony Szécsen, argued that to save the Habsburg empire, the Emperor had to seek the allegiance of the nobles by restoring the 'historic rights' of the non-Germans. The old diets and privileges would entrench noble power, minimising concessions to liberalism. The October Diploma of 1860 consequently expanded the membership of the *Reichsrat* to 100, chosen by the Emperor and by the restored *Landtage*, the provincial diets dominated by the nobles. The Hungarian chancellery and diet were restored, while the Croats got back their *Sabor* and *Ban* and received their own chancellery. These concessions pleased few people; for Austrian liberals the *Reichsrat* was not a real parliament, while the reforms offered little to the other nationalities. The October Diploma floundered in this atmosphere of widespread public hostility.

The second constitutional experiment therefore reversed the direction of reform and sought to restore uniformity and Habsburg centralism, but in the outward form of a constitutional monarchy. Anton von Schmerling, the new interior minister, had a patent issued on 4 February 1861, converting the *Reichsrat* into a two-chamber parliament, with an aristocratic upper house and a chamber of deputies elected by the *Landtage*. Both these diets and the lower chamber would be divided into four *curiae*, or classes (the large landowners, towns, rural communities and chambers of commerce), which ensured that both German and conservative interests would be well-represented. The *Reichsrat* assumed control of the state budget and could initiate legislation, but otherwise had very little power. Schmerling's 'sham constitutionalism'[12] (in the hard judgment of one historian) convinced few people and would last only a few years.

Even the support of Austro-German liberals for the government was qualified. Although centralism tended to benefit the German-speakers, who also liked to see Hungarians and Slavs put in their place, they also wanted greater constitutional concessions. Meanwhile, Hungarian liberals led by Ferenc Deák demanded nothing less than the 1848 Constitution in return for Hungarian support for the Habsburg monarchy. When the Magyars boycotted the *Reichsrat*, the Emperor retaliated by closing the Hungarian diet in August 1861. The Croatian nobility demanded the restitution of the full rights enjoyed by the *Sabor* in 1848, whereupon Schmerling dissolved the Croat assembly. The Czechs withdrew from the imperial parliament in June 1863, resentful of German dominance. The Poles and the Italians also refused to attend the *Reichsrat*.

The surge of Prussian power in Germany forced the Emperor to begin to compromise at home, and Schmerling was dismissed in 1865. Then, with their *großdeutsch* dreams impaled, along with Austrian power in Germany, on Prussian steel at Sadowa, Austrian liberals started to recognise a need to accommodate the non-German nationalities of the Empire. Moderate Hungarian liberals, such as Deák and Gyula Andrássy (both former '48ers'), were willing to accept some common policies and institutions with Austria, provided that Hungary enjoyed domestic autonomy. The other nationalities seized the opportunity to press their claims, but their moderate leaders had long recognised that ultimately their security depended upon being part of a larger imperial state. The Hungarians and Austro-Germans, however, had no intention of sharing power with the other nationalities. The new imperial foreign minister, Friedrich von Beust, grudgingly recognised that the most realistic course consisted of luring the Austro-German liberals away from Bismarck's emerging German state with the promise of constitutional reform, alongside a compromise with the Hungarians, the Emperor's most powerful domestic opponents. Together, the Germans and Magyars could rule the Slavs.[13] On that much the Hungarians agreed; Andrássy declared, 'the Slavs are not fit to govern; they must be ruled'.[14] Conservative and Slav opposition, which would have preferred a federalist solution, was brushed aside. The Austro-Hungarian compromise (*Ausgleich*) was ratified by the *Reichsrat* and the Hungarian diet in May and June 1867.

The *Ausgleich* created the 'dual monarchy' of Austria–Hungary. Hungary and Cisleithania (meaning the lands outside the kingdom of Hungary) would have their own governments, answerable, respectively, to the Hungarian diet and the Austrian *Reichsrat*. Hungary would enjoy autonomy in handling its domestic affairs, including the concerns of the other nationalities, except that Francis Joseph, as King of Hungary, would have a veto on public spending and appointing powers for certain posts. While the Hungarian parliament had the right to initiate legislation, the monarch had to give his assent to the bill *before* it was debated. The kingdom itself was expanded to include Transylvania, while the old Croatian–Slavonian military frontier was abolished and absorbed by Hungary. A customs union, renewable every ten years, would help bind the two parts of the monarchy together. The common coinage and postal system from the days of Bach survived. Command and control of the armed forces remained in imperial hands, but Hungary was allowed to maintain its own army as well as to vote for the contingent supplied to the imperial forces. Foreign and military policy and the related finances would be handled by common imperial ministries, which met, together with the Austrian and Hungarian prime ministers, in a cabinet in which the Emperor still took the final decisions. Yet the common ministries were responsible to parliamentary institutions. The delegations, which met alternately in Vienna and Pest, gathered 120 representatives – 60 each from the Austrian and Hungarian parliaments – with the power to determine every ten years the common defence and foreign policy budget. This would then be submitted separately to the Austrian *Reichsrat* and the Hungarian diet for approval.

Croatia was offered some concessions in its own 'Compromise' (*Nagodba*) with Hungary in 1868. The Hungarian minister-president would henceforth appoint the Ban, while the *Sabor* could communicate only with the Hungarian government – not directly to the Emperor. So while Croatia retained autonomy over its own affairs, it was treated as if it were an integral part of Hungary. The Croats also sent 40 deputies to the Hungarian diet and had 5 of the 60 Delegates. While Croatia paid 55 per cent of all its tax receipts into the common Hungarian expenses, there was no way of accounting for their actual use. Demands from Romanians, Serbs and Slovaks for equal treatment were brushed aside. They had to be content with the Nationalities Law of December 1868, which gave the same civil rights to all citizens in the kingdom and which guaranteed the use of the local language in law, the schools and administration up to county level. At higher levels – parliament, government and higher education – the official language was to be Magyar.

In Cisleithania, the internal arrangements were pronounced in the Basic State Laws of December 1867. The emperor retained a veto on all legislation and the power to appoint the minister-president, who was not responsible to the *Reichsrat*, while the Crown could rule by decree when parliament was not in session. There were no changes made to the *Reichsrat* itself, to the *Landtage* or to the system of suffrage, so the government, by exerting its influence on the diets, could determine whether it obtained a German, centrist majority or a Slav, federalist one. None the less, the constitutional arrangements were not completely barren of liberalism. The *Reichsrat* passed laws protecting the freedom of speech, press, worship and education. All offices were declared open to merit and the judiciary was to be protected from political interference by the government. The Liberals managed to restore civil marriage, extend state control over education and, in July 1870, end the Concordat in retaliation against the decree of Papal Infallibility. The *Reichsrat*'s law on nationalities recognised the equality of all such groups, including the right of each to preserve its own culture and language. None the less, non-Germans had to speak German if they wanted to progress into higher education and administration.

Unsurprisingly, the most vocal opposition to the Compromise came from the subject peoples. The Poles demanded autonomy, the Slovenes their own diet, the Italians of Trentino their own province and the Czechs the concessions of 1848 and the union of all their provinces. The Czech deputies boycotted the *Reichsrat* and visited Moscow to raise the banner of Pan-Slavism. The government imposed martial law in Prague. In 1871, however, the emergence of Bismarck's mighty German Empire led Francis Joseph to try to redress the balance against German nationalism with Slav loyalty. He recognised the unity of the Czech lands under the Bohemian Crown, which would be governed under 18 'Fundamental Articles', guaranteeing the Czechs autonomy, though not giving it parity with Hungary. This went too far for the Austro-Germans, particularly those who lived in Bohemia. German nationalists rioted on the streets of Vienna, while, in Hungary, Andrássy opposed the concessions as an attack on the dualist compromise, warning the Austrian minister-president, Count Karl Hohenwart, 'Are you prepared to carry through the recognition of Bohemian state rights with cannon? If not, do not begin this policy.'[15] Hohenwart tried to steer a middle course between Czech nationalism and Austro-Hungarian opposition in October 1871 by watering down the Fundamental Articles, which the Czechs rejected. Short of employing force against both sides, there was no way out of the impasse, but the Hungarians had thwarted reform of the *Ausgleich* in favour of the Slavs.

Within Hungary, the main issue would be how to maintain the Compromise simultaneously against the other nationalities, Austria and the Crown. The Transylvanian Romanians gathered at a mass meeting in March 1869 to protest against the *Ausgleich* and boycotted the Hungarian diet, while nationalists resurrected the 1848 dream of union with Romania. The greatest challenge, however, came from Croatia, where a National Party had opposed the *Nagodba*. They agitated constantly against the pro-Hungarian Bans, forcing the resignation of one in 1871 and then another in 1872. In response, Andrássy (who became imperial foreign minister in 1871) secured the disbandment of the Croatian border regiments, which he feared could be used against the Magyars. When the Croat soldiers mutinied in June 1871, martial law was imposed and, under these conditions, the conservative, clerical right won the 1872 elections to the *Sabor*. The following year, the Archbishop of Zagreb brokered a compromise, whereby some of the powers of the Ban were reduced but the Croats were allowed to keep a greater proportion of their revenue. Slav and Romanian hostility convinced the Hungarians by the mid-1870s that nothing less than a programme of 'Magyarisation' – the forced assimilation of the subject peoples – would succeed in quelling the nationalities question. The opportunity came when the left-wing liberal Kálmán Tisza pragmatically ditched his ultra-nationalist opposition to the *Ausgleich* in 1875 and merged with moderates led by Deák (one of the architects of the Compromise) to form the Liberal Party. Assurances from the Emperor not to arouse the Slavs and Romanians against the Hungarians calmed all but the most diehard of radical Magyar resistance. After landslide elections in June, Tisza became Hungarian minister-president and, reassured by Francis Joseph's promises, he could begin a vigorous Magyarisation programme.

Reform, Consolidation and Failure

Débâcles in foreign policy had been a prime mover behind the reform of two of the most conservative regimes in Europe. Diplomatic or military defeat also led constitutional regimes to adapt. In the Netherlands, King William III, an admirer of Napoleon III, had responded too enthusiastically to the Emperor's suggestion in 1867 that he sell the Grand Duchy of Luxemburg to France. In the parliamentary furore which followed, the liberal opposition succeeded in securing enough votes to reject the foreign policy budget. When new elections returned the liberals in 1868, the King, who had tried to keep the conservatives in power against the majority, accepted the resignation of his government. The legislature had asserted itself on the monarchy; henceforth, Dutch governments were held to account by parliament.[16] In Denmark, defeat in the Schleswig-Holstein war shamed the ruling liberals, so it was the conservatives, dominated by the landowners, who steered through parliamentary reform in 1866. This was made all the more urgent because Denmark had, in fact, two constitutions – that of 1849 and that of 1863, the second rushed through in a bid to absorb the two duchies. The new constitution was, unsurprisingly, shaped so that rural constituencies, property-owners and royal appointees dominated the *Rigsdag*. Across the straits in Sweden in 1859, King Charles XV had inherited 'Scandinavianism' from his father, Oscar I. This emphasised the common 'Nordic' heritage of the Danes, the Norwegians and the Swedes and underpinned the Swedish dynasty's ambitions to inherit the Danish throne, in the process uniting the three Scandinavian kingdoms. Yet these dreams evaporated in 1864 when the Swedish government and *Riksdag* countermanded Charles's promises of military help to Denmark. To shore up his position with popular support, the King supported the Swedish liberals in 1865 in replacing the traditional four estates (since 1617, the peasants, towns, nobles and clergy). A more recognisably modern two-chamber legislature was created, and first met in 1867.

Reform in these countries was driven to varying degrees by foreign policy setbacks. Yet Britain and France, the main victors of the Crimean War, also reformed. Regimes there were trying to consolidate themselves in the face of social change and domestic political pressure. The parliamentary reform of 1867 in Britain did not arise from any serious crisis. In the early 1860s William Gladstone emerged as the great hope of the radicals of the Liberal Party, who had never accepted that 1832 was the last word in parliamentary reform. The radical Reform League, established in 1864 in the enthusiasm generated by Garibaldi's visit to London, enjoyed both middle-class and trade-union leadership, and held mass meetings in support of universal male suffrage and the secret ballot. In the same year, a less radical, middle-class organisation, the National Reform Union, was created to advocate the secret ballot and votes for all ratepayers. In Scotland, demands for reform were bound up with the 'Scottish Rights' movement, which stemmed from a widespread feeling since the 1850s that Scottish affairs were not being dealt with adequately by the government in London. Few people, least of all the radicals themselves, anticipated that their mass meetings would have much impact; John Bright admitted in 1866 that the 'multitude' was not able 'to make a very effective demonstration of strength'.[17]

It was, however, precisely *because* of social stability that ultimately the arguments for reform were accepted among both Liberals and Conservatives. Among the former, a great obstacle was removed with the death in October 1865 of Palmerston, a staunch Whig opponent of further political change. He was succeeded as prime minister by John Russell, who argued that an extension of the suffrage was possible because of the growing political maturity ('improvement and intelligence') of a wider section of the population since 1832. These political considerations did not mean that there was no social fear. More cautious politicians feared that an extension of the franchise would lead inexorably to the pitfalls of 'democracy', of which the 'despotism' in France was a prime example. Speaking against Russell's reform bill in the spring of 1866, the Whig Robert Lowe fearfully argued that, with the vote, 'the working men of England, finding themselves in a full majority . . . will awake to a full sense of their power'.[18] When the bill failed, the Reform League and Reform Union stepped up their campaign with protests across the country. The fear engendered by a cholera epidemic that summer was compounded by riots in Hyde Park in July. Matthew Arnold later remembered his father ranting, 'flog the rank and file, and fling the ringleaders from the Tarpeian rock!'[19] Few people outside the Reform League, therefore, advocated universal male suffrage. The aim of extending the franchise to include some workers was primarily to detach the skilled, articulate workers from the rest of the working class, to integrate them within the political nation and so dissuade them from fostering their own, more radical working-class movement.

Russell resigned after the failure of his reform bill, and Queen Victoria asked the Conservative peer, Lord Derby, to form a minority government. His leader in the House of Commons, Benjamin Disraeli, was convinced that if the Tories remained a party of landed reaction, it would be doomed to perpetual opposition. A Tory-sponsored reform bill, by contrast, would secure popular support for the Conservatives. However, to obtain a majority in the House of Commons, he needed to detach the radical Liberals from their party. The 1867 Reform Act, therefore, came at the end of a Disraelian tightrope act as he lured the radical vote while not alienating the aristocrats in his own party. The act enfranchised more people than Disraeli had originally intended, theoretically doubling the electorate to include two in five men in England. In practice, a residence qualification of a year for urban householders barred the large numbers of workers who moved frequently. Moreover, an eighth of all seats were still controlled by landowners. A separate Scottish act in 1868 almost trebled the urban electorate and increased the number of rural voters on a less dramatic scale. John Stuart Mill's amendment to enfranchise women was rejected, but the fact that working-class men could vote while middle-class women could not appeared to be an anomaly, made all the more striking because in the 1870s women could be elected on to school boards and as poor law guardians. In 1867–8, women's suffrage committees were established in the larger cities, and 2 million signatures supporting women's enfranchisement had been collected by 1876.

For all its shortcomings, the Second Reform Act had profound effects on British politics. To reach the enlarged electorate, the political parties had to rely more on electoral organisation and on coherent political programmes than on personal contact, patronage and influence. The era of mass politics was emerging – particularly when the secret ballot was introduced in 1872, which at last enabled workers and rural voters to slip away from the political influence of employers and landlords. This did not, however, signal the rise of a socialist party. In 1874 the first working-class MPs were elected as Liberals, whose values were shared by the skilled workers. The desire to 'tame' the less 'respectable' workers who had acquired the franchise was one of the motives behind the 1870 Education Act establishing district school boards which were empowered to set up elementary schools.

The working class did not show the gratitude which Disraeli might have expected in the elections of 1868. The Liberals increased their majority and William Ewart Gladstone formed his first government. He declared that his mission was 'to pacify Ireland'. Problems there ran too deep to be resolved by any palliative such as franchise reform. The Tenant Right movement persisted in trying to challenge the dominance of Irish politics by Whigs and Tories, both of whom represented landlord interests. The problem was also exploited by the Irish Republican Brotherhood (IRB – the Fenians) founded in 1858. Inspired by Mazzini, its 50,000-strong membership included tenant-farmers and poorer, agricultural labourers, but was drawn primarily from the urban, lower middle class. Its central aim was to secure independence for Ireland through violence. In 1865 the government suppressed the Fenian press and arrested three Fenian leaders. When the insurrection did come in 1867, it was ill co-ordinated and easily suppressed by the police. In Britain, Fenian attempts to rescue prisoners in Manchester and London left a policeman dead and a dozen killed by a bomb. Yet the Irish population proved to be less revolutionary than the Fenians had hoped, and did not stir. Fenianism made more of an impact with its public campaigns, developing a romantic form of Irish nationalism, while the trials, imprisonments and amnesty campaigns which followed the 1867 uprising gave Fenians a public platform. As a secular movement, Fenianism also exasperated the Catholic Church, which tried to harness nationalism with a rival 'National Association', founded in 1864. These various expressions of Irish nationalism provoked the Presbyterian population. Once Gladstone had disestablished the (Episcopalian) Church of Ireland in 1869, a cause on which Presbyterians and Catholics agreed, the former felt more in common with their fellow-Protestant Episcopalians than with the Catholics and would be drawn increasingly towards unionist Toryism. In 1870, Gladstone's Land Act aimed to ease tensions in the countryside, but fell far short of the demands of the Tenant Right movement. After Gladstone lost the 1874 elections, Irish MPs began to demand a more radical solution, striking a middle course between Tory unionism and Irish republicanism – a separate Irish parliament within the British Empire, or 'Home Rule'.

Napoleon III began to 'liberalise' the Second Empire towards the end of 1860 as a means of consolidating his regime and his dynasty. He had no intention of creating a parliamentary regime, but aimed to concede only as much as would secure the loyalty of the potentially troublesome Orleanist notables.[20] The need was all the greater because Napoleon's free-trade treaty with Britain in 1860 was unpopular within certain industries where republicanism stirred, while his role in Italian unification had angered his erstwhile allies in the Catholic Church. From November, against the advice of most of his ministers, the Emperor allowed the legislature to debate matters of general policy, suggest amendments to bills and publish unedited records of its debates. From December 1861 Parliament was permitted to debate the budget clause by clause. By strengthening parliamentary prerogatives, Napoleon may have hoped to 'entrench' his dynasty in representative institutions which would offer continuity and stability. The reforms were not concessions forced under severe pressure, but they were still a sign that Napoleon III had not been able to make the elites bend to his will. The reforms allowed some moderate republicans to make their peace with the regime; Emile Ollivier declared in 1861 that the Empire was no longer incompatible with 'liberty'. Yet while the bulk of the voting population still rallied to the Empire, Legitimist, Orleanist and republican voices were raised more freely in the pulpit, in the press and in the election campaign of 1863. The government's candidates won by a landslide, but a quarter of the ballots were against the regime, despite its energetic efforts to promote official candidates and to intimidate the opposition press. The republican electoral committee in Paris was prosecuted as an illegal public assembly, yet eight of the nine deputies returned by the capital were still republicans.

These results tested the willingness of the regime to reform further. Napoleon III rejected calls from the Orleanist leader, Adolphe Thiers, for the 'necessary freedoms' (of the individual, the press and elections), for ministerial responsibility and the right of parliament to initiate legislation. Instead, he tried to bypass the Orleanists by forging a populist alliance with the peasants and workers. While grain and wine prices were high the peasantry prospered, and the regime could count on them for support, although protest in areas penetrated by the *démoc-socs* never entirely died out. Napoleon's approach to the workers, while driven by some genuine concern for their welfare, was primarily determined by the desire to take the sting out of worker militancy and to lure them away from republicanism and socialism. Consequently, his programme for dealing with the 'social question' in the 1860s was more radical than that offered by the moderate republicans. In 1862 he allowed a workers' commission, representing 200,000 workers in 50 trades, to elect 340 delegates to visit the International Exhibition in London. When they returned they demanded the right to form unions and to strike. In May 1864 a law recognised the 'right to strike', but without unions or picketing. In 1867, workers' associations were permitted to negotiate over such matters as wages, hours, insurance and apprenticeships. In 1864, French followers of Proudhon joined British skilled workers in forming the International Working Men's Association, which held its first congress in Geneva in 1866. Napoleon III spotted an opportunity to secure working-class support as alarmed Orleanists and moderate republicans condemned his populism as 'Caesarism'. In fact, most skilled workers equated socialism with republicanism, so the regime could not rely on their support; the Empire found that it had unwittingly unleashed a radical force in the French labour movement. The government took fright in 1868, closing down the French branch of the Socialist International. Police raided cafés (the regular meeting-place of workers) and clamped down on street protests. A strike wave around Lyon in 1869–70 left Bonapartists fuming about the workers' lack of 'gratitude'.

Napoleon III's efforts to conciliate first the *notables* and then the workers suggest that the Second Empire's liberalisation was the product of a muddled response to conflicting political pressures. In the later 1860s those pressures became heavier as Napoleon's earlier foreign policy triumphs soured. With the danger from Prussia becoming more apparent, reports on French public opinion warned, 'faith in the star and good luck of the Emperor have weakened'.[21] Napoleon III tried to patch over his worn-out prestige in January 1867 by offering further political reforms, but the opposition would not let him off the hook. Thiers berated the Emperor for allowing a new and dangerous German power to emerge and when Napoleon III replied that, in fact, Prussia did not pose a serious threat, this gave the opposition the excuse to derail government plans to introduce universal conscription. A further blow came in Mexico, where Napoleon had supported the Habsburg Archduke Maximilian's claims to the throne, against Juárez's liberal regime. Maximilian was shot in June 1867. Five months later, French troops were used to defend Rome against an expedition led by Garibaldi. Both events suggested that Napoleon III had lost his touch and was supporting conservative rather than liberal causes.

In the last years of the Empire, Napoleon III was confronted with an upsurge of opposition; political rallies drew crowds of thousands and electoral meetings frequently degenerated into rioting. Republican organisations sprang up, first under the guise of social clubs, masonic lodges and agricultural societies, and then, in the run-up to elections in May 1869, as electoral committees. With the benefit of hindsight, republicans recalled 1868–70 as a sustained 'war against the Empire'.[22] They were themselves divided. The more radical members of the younger generation, such as Jules Ferry and Léon Gambetta, demanded some social reform, while denouncing moderate veterans such as Louis Garnier-Pagès as bourgeois and conservative. In fact, mindful of the lessons of 1848, the radicals wanted to avoid socialism and had no desire to unleash a popular insurrection over which they would have no control. They therefore sought to mobilise working-class political action behind a broad republican front, diverting it from its social aims towards a consensus based on an appeal to political liberty, civil equality, separation of Church and State, and universal and secular education. Republicanism offered a cautious social programme involving the defence of property and small producers through tariffs, tax reform and cheap credit, but with a commitment to social order. Some socialists foresaw that, once in power, the republicans would shelve their social promises. Émile Aubry warned Lyon workers: 'Do not compromise your growing power by dupe's alliances with bourgeois radicalism.'[23] Yet the republican rhetoric of democracy was not mere dissimulation to neutralise working-class radicalism. The idea that all republicans, whether workers or employers, could share the same political values was sincere and helped to sustain the unity for long enough to allow the republican regime to consolidate itself in 1870.

In 1869 the Bonapartists still had a majority in the Legislative Body, but the opposition had won 40 per cent of the vote and, in September, Napoleon III conceded to parliament a role in initiating legislation, though he sidestepped the question of ministerial responsibility. At the end of the year, however, he appointed Ollivier to lead the government, precisely because he could secure a majority in the Legislative Body. This was the birth of the short-lived 'liberal Empire'. Ollivier repealed the General Security Law of 1858, sacked prefects who had interfered in elections, and planned administrative decentralisation and an arbitration body for industrial disputes. Yet striking workers and socialist leaders were arrested and plans to abolish the workers' passport, the *livret*, were cast aside.

Ollivier nearly succeeded in his explicit aim of 'saving the dynasty'. A new constitution in March 1870 strengthened the legislative power of parliament and in May it was submitted to a plebiscite, during which the government shamelessly exploited widespread anxiety over social unrest. A vote against the 'liberal Empire', voters were told, was a vote for social revolution: 'the return of the Terror, the ruin of the countryside'.[24] The referendum recorded a massive majority (67.5 per cent) in favour. What was perhaps the most popular regime since 1789 was destroyed not by domestic upheaval but by foreign invasion. Napoleon's surrender to the Prussians at Sedan on 2 September brought the republicans out on to the streets in Paris, where the rump of republican deputies proclaimed the Third Republic and created a Government of National Defence to continue the war against the Germans. In the provinces, republicans took over from Bonapartist officials as the *Bulletin* of the new government roared, 'THE REPUBLIC MEANS ORDER!'[25] This promise would shape the institutions and the politics of the new regime in France.

While dedicated republicans sought to unleash patriotic fervour in order to continue the war against the Prussians, most of the population wanted to restore peace and social stability as quickly as possible. Elections held in February 1871 therefore returned a monarchist majority against the republicans in the National Assembly, which met at Bordeaux because Paris was being besieged by the Prussians. Thiers was duly elected head of the executive and he set about making peace with Prussia. For Parisian radicals, however, peace meant an end to the revolutionary impetus which promised social reform. In March, a struggle between Parisian National Guards and government troops over the possession of cannons in Montmartre sparked the uprising. The capital, isolated, elected its own government, the Commune, which was more republican than socialist and more Proudhonist than Marxist. It had little time in which to implement its social reforms, as the government forces which had besieged the capital for five weeks broke through the Communard defences, retaking the capital street by street in bitter fighting. The ensuing repression in the 'bloody week' in May 1871 was disproportionately brutal: while the Communards killed hostages, including 24 priests, government troops summarily executed some twenty to twenty-five thousand people.

Besides creating martyrs for the European left, the crushing of the Commune showed that the French Republic was both conservative and ruthless in defending what most people regarded as social order. Moreover, Thiers's government did this while signing the Treaty of

Frankfurt with Germany on 10 May. No one celebrated the loss of Alsace-Lorraine, the German occupation or the war reparations of 5 billion francs, but Thiers's success in bringing peace and order boosted confidence in the new regime. It managed to raise the funds to pay off the Germans and end the occupation by March 1873.

In any case, there was no obvious, viable alternative to a moderate republic, which Thiers, though a monarchist, was coming to recognise. The social republic envisaged by the Communards scared the peasantry and other property-owners, but the return of the Bonapartes was an increasingly distant prospect as Napoleon III died in Britain in 1873 and his son was killed by the Zulus at Isandlwana in 1879. Meanwhile, the monarchists self-destructed. Once German forces had withdrawn from France, conservative Orleanists joined with the Legitimists in parliament in voting Thiers out of office. Yet the two rival wings of the monarchist movement could not seal their alliance. They nearly reached a compromise, whereby the Orleanists would tolerate the childless Bourbon, the duc de Chambord ('Henri V'), on the throne, while on his death the Orleans dynasty would succeed. Chambord, however, showed no willingness to wake up to the late nineteenth century. He believed in divine-right monarchy, royal absolutism and the Bourbon white flag rather than the tricolour, which was too much for the Orleanists to stomach. Despite the hefty combined monarchist majority, there was no restoration.

As a stopgap, the Legitimist Marshal Patrice MacMahon was given a seven-year term as president (which established an important political precedent), but the more liberal Orleanists now preferred to compromise with the republicans. In the early 1870s both sides saw their constitutional concessions as temporary and waited for the opportune moment to assert their own programme. Yet from this process a constitution painstakingly emerged, seeking to avoid both authoritarianism and direct democracy. The Orleanists therefore accepted a republic (in January 1875) with universal male suffrage. In return, the republicans swallowed a two-chamber legislature (a Chamber of Deputies and a Senate), which provided political checks and balances, and a presidency, elected by both houses, which would offer continuity and stability. The conservative bulwark would prove to be the Senate, chosen by electoral colleges representing the departments. As local councils, regardless of population size, each sent one delegate to the departmental electoral college, rural areas had political influence out of all proportion to their already substantial share of the population. The importance of the Senate was that it had the right to veto legislation enacted by the lower house and could therefore make or break the policies of governments whose authority rested in its majority in the Chamber of Deputies.

The compromise, however, worked for the republicans precisely because the new order taking shape promised to be conservative. The mood of the country proved to be politically republican, but conservative in spirit. Supporters of the Republic won the elections to the two new chambers in 1876. The days of the so-called 'Duke's Republic' under MacMahon were numbered. The President contemplated a coup d'état in May 1877, but the army maintained its usual distance from politics. Legitimist efforts to intimidate the electorate at new elections in October availed them little. The republicans again won a majority and in 1879 they secured the Senate. MacMahon resigned, a symbolic moment in the demise of the Legitimist nobility as a political force. For the first time ever, the majority of French voters supported a Republic.

The Third Republic would prove to be (to date) the longest-surviving French regime since 1789, collapsing only with the Nazi invasion in 1940. The First Spanish Republic, by contrast, would survive for less than two years, from February 1873 until the last days of 1874. Spain after the fall of O'Donnell in 1863 was a state quivering on the brink of revolution. The entire political oligarchy, from ultra-royalist Carlists to the *progresistas*, was afraid of social revolution. In 1863 the *progresistas* alone could secure a parliamentary majority and, though they were monarchists, Queen Isabella was wary of their radicalism and refused to appoint them to form a government. Grassroots progressives therefore boycotted politics – the *retraimiento* – and moved towards an alliance with more radical democrats, who were tinged with republicanism. The *progresista* leader, General Prim, launched three abortive *pronunciamientos* between 1865 and 1867 in order to force political change without resorting to a popular insurrection, which would bring with it the dangers of social upheaval. Isabella tried to rule through increasingly authoritarian ministries, including two under Narváez (in 1864–5 and 1867–8), but in the process she bled even the support of the *moderados*, who by September 1868 were willing to join Prim and the *progresistas* in a *pronunciamiento*. The aim of the coup was to save constitutional government by putting the crown on a new head. It succeeded because it had widespread support among liberal army officers. Royal authority crumbled as even loyal officials and commanders, seeing a stark choice between the military coup and social revolution, chose the former as the best hope of preserving order. Isabella boarded the royal train and sped across the border into France and exile.

On the face of it, the authors of the *pronunciamiento* were right to fear the potential of social upheaval, particularly in Barcelona, where Catalan workers adopted the radical ideology of the democrats. Spurred by the economic dislocation caused by the American Civil War, they had organised mutual societies and cultural associations. During the coup, power in some Spanish cities fell to radical juntas. The middle-class leadership of the democratic movement – journalists and hard-up professionals – was also beginning to make inroads among the peasants, particularly in Andalusia, where traditional dreams of the *reparto* (division of the great estates among the impoverished rural population) proved easily adaptable to radical political messages. The leaders of the military coup now had to pacify this threat from the left. The new government – with General Francisco Serrano as regent and Prim as prime minister – therefore granted basic civil rights, trial by jury and universal male suffrage in return for the democrats' recognition of the constitutional monarchy. This offer split the democratic movement. The intransigents formed the Republican Party, exploiting peasant resentment, which continued to smoulder because the new regime neither abolished conscription nor lowered taxes. In October 1868 the Cuban War of Independence broke out, and it would outlast the revolution in Spain by three years. With the burdens it placed on government and society, the war encouraged the Republicans to strike at the liberal regime in a series of revolts in 1868–9, but the army kept the liberals firmly in the saddle.

The Constitution of 1869 provided for a Lower Chamber and a Senate, both elected by universal male suffrage. It proclaimed Catholicism as the state religion, but it permitted all other forms of religious thought. Convents were closed down and the liberals reduced state salaries for clergymen and introduced civil marriage and secular education. The state's 'disinheritance' of Catholicism alienated conservatives, for whom defence of the Church would remain a great rallying cry. After the international furore over the choice of Leopold von Hohenzollern-Sigmaringen as King, the liberals eventually accepted Amadeus, the Duke of Aosta, who tried to heal the potentially fatal schism between *moderados* and *progresistas* by domesticating it within a formal, two-party system. He did so, however, by influencing the electorate through royal and ministerial patronage. To change a parliamentary majority, the King needed only to dissolve parliament, while appointing a new interior minister who could exert government influence and ensure electoral victory for his own party. This system of *turno pacifico*, whereby a government was effectively appointed *before* it won a parliamentary majority in the elections, allowed the opposing political parties to take turns in power, with the King as mediator. The system would dominate Spanish politics, after the brief hiatus of the First Republic, for the rest of the nineteenth century and it had its equivalent in Portugal, where it was called *rotativismo*.

Yet the divisions amongst the Spanish liberals were too deep for the *turno pacifico* to ensure stability. The *progresista* ministry, appointed in July 1871, fell in July 1872 when it split between moderates and radicals. The latter joined the Republicans. When the King tried to integrate them by bringing them into government in August, the *moderados* boycotted politics rather than serve with republicans, leaving leadership in the hands of the radicals. They seized the opportunity to purge the army of conservative and *moderado* officers, prompting the King to abdicate in February 1873. The radical parliament was left with no other option than to proclaim a republic. The constitutional monarchy had destroyed itself.

The Republic itself proved short-lived; it could barely guarantee order against its own extremists and failed to conciliate the army and the social elites. The Republican leadership sought to legitimise the new order by the election of a Constituent Cortes. The army disintegrated as liberal officers deserted, discipline collapsed and conscription was abolished. Impatient republican activists, meanwhile, adopted a radical social agenda and proselytised among both the urban workers and the peasantry. In the south, they put federalist (or 'cantonalist') ideas into practice by establishing independent microrepublics strongly influenced by the anarchism of Proudhon and Bakhunin. In Andalusia, this federalist revolt fed on peasant expectations of the *reparto*, but by August the government had managed to muster enough forces to crush the uprising in two weeks of fighting.

A Carlist revolt was a more serious danger. Since the collapse of Isabella's regime in 1868, the ultra-royalists had been probing for an opportunity to revolt, and it finally came in the summer of 1873 when the Republic was weak and facing revolution in the south. The Carlists seized the Basque provinces and much of rural Navarre, but the urban centres remained loyal to the Republic. As in the Carlist Wars, the bedrock of royalist support remained the pious peasantry and it was for this reason that it was unable to break out of its traditional mountain strongholds in the north. None the less, by 1874 a northern royalist state, with its own postal system, telegraph service and administration, had been set up, fielding a 20,000-strong army funded by taxation, customs and dues paid by the local railway companies. Once the Republican regime had restored discipline in the army by the end of 1873, it began to demolish the Carlist state, but the task was not complete when the monarchy was restored at the end of 1874.

In January 1874, the Cortes was invaded by soldiers led by General Manuel Pavía, who declared that, in times of 'perverted government' and social breakdown, the army represented the national will (the excuse would be used by Franco in 1936). Pavía brought Serrano back into power to lead a conservative government. The anarchic experience of Republican rule had alarmed enough people to give momentum to a restoration of the monarchy, but the desire was particularly strong amongst younger army officers who were fed up with the political shenanigans of their superiors. The brains behind the operation was Antonio Cánovas del Castillo, who understood that Isabella had alienated too many people to be a palatable choice of monarch, so her 16-year-old son, Alfonso, became the figurehead of the Restoration. On 29 December 1874 the Army of the Centre declared a *pronunciamiento* in favour of Alfonso XII. The following day the Republic's short, tortured life came to an end.

With the Constitution of 1876, Cánovas aimed to create a political system which excluded the extremes of left and right, but which would forge a wide consensus amongst the ruling elites (only 5 per cent of the population could now vote). That consensus would be that no particular party ought to have an exclusive, permanent grip on power and that it was better to relinquish it peacefully than reignite the revolutionary struggles of the past. The *turno pacifico* returned and its lynchpin was the notables and the local bosses of the governing political party – the *caciques*. They had the power to bring out the voters and they did so in return for the promise of patronage from the new government. The *caciques* managed to dominate local politics, even after the introduction of universal male suffrage in 1890, because low levels of literacy (28 per cent in 1879) left the population vulnerable to manipulation. *Caciquismo* was justified on the grounds that it maintained the 'legitimate' interests of the great propertied families and local notables in the face of universal suffrage.[26] Yet when Spain faced a dire crisis, as it would in the disastrous year of 1898, it was easy to blame the corruption of *caciquismo* for national failings.

12 The Sinews of Power and the Means of Existence[1]

Underlying many of the political and social problems faced by states after mid-century were the upheavals associated with economic development. The emerging phenomenon of mass politics was, of course, a product of cultural changes, such as the growth of education and literacy, but it was also made possible by economic and social change. The increasing speed and lowering cost of transport and communications prised open markets, distributed written and visual material more widely and broke the isolation of rural communities, which were progressively tied more tightly into national life. The wider economic effects of steam travel – on the railways, on the rivers and on the high seas – would also change standards of living for the better for most people. While this can be measured primarily in terms of real wages (the amount people were actually paid in figures weighed against the cost of living), it also has a qualitative dimension. The greater disposable income enjoyed by most people gave them a more varied diet and fed a demand for new forms of mass leisure. At the same time, more people could afford to join associations, mutual aid societies, trade unions and political parties. Yet the economic transformation also came at a social price, including wider social differentiation and changes in the workplace, which was rarely to the benefit of the workers and peasants.

Steam power was the primary motor driving the rapid economic growth (at various times in various places after 1850), coming between the earlier advances in textiles and the later emergence of 'new industries' such as chemicals, electricity and light engineering. Railways spread like a thin veil across the face of Europe: if in 1860 the landscape was criss-crossed by almost 52,000 km of track (mostly in western Europe), by 1900 this figure had risen to 283,500 km. The early starters, Britain, France and Germany, had been joined by other European countries. These latecomers had been hobbled by a number of problems. Their access to raw materials had been less favourable, they were slower to adopt new technology, their social structures (such as serfdom in Russia) were conservative, or their governments were reluctant to unleash the social forces associated with industrialisation. Ultimately, railways were too dynamic a force for states not to take an active interest. They integrated markets, people and the state, while the need to compete with other European countries in terms of industrial capacity also encouraged governments to take an active role in developing the railways. Their strategic value was lost on no one; the development of the network in countries such as France, Spain, Italy and Russia was strongly influenced by such considerations. France, after the initial investment under the July Monarchy, experienced two major railway booms under Napoleon III, in 1853–6 and 1860–4, with a combination of state and private investment. The government tided the railways over during slumps in private investment and guaranteed a 4 per cent return for investors. Where larger rail firms proved unwilling to build branch lines, the government encouraged smaller companies to do so, seeing in their development a means both of winning over public opinion and of opening up rural France to the wider economy. In Spain, the first 500 km of track were built on private initiative between 1848 and 1855, but thereafter the government invested heavily in the system. Railways were constructed to link Madrid with outlying parts of the country, in order to act rapidly against revolutionaries and to penetrate incorrigibly Carlist areas. The Italian government subsidised both the construction and the running of railways from the 1870s. One of the primary aims was to bind the new state together and to overcome the particularism of the south. The Habsburg monarchy privatised the rail system in 1854 because the international crisis during the Crimean War left the state with insufficient funds to develop the network on its own. This ushered in a boom period until 1873, during which time the essential network was laid out, and after the slump of the 1870s the state clawed back the initiative with laws in 1879–83, starting the most dramatic phase of construction which lasted until 1913. Some of the most energetic track-laying took place in Russia: the great Trans-Siberian railroad threaded its way through the Urals and penetrated the Siberian forests towards Vladivostok between 1891 and 1901. In the great spurt of the 1890s, an average of 2820 km of track was laid each year.

The immediate economic impact of the railroads was to stimulate demand for iron, steel, coal and locomotives, which spurred mining, metallurgy and heavy engineering. German coal production increased from 9.2 million tons a year in 1850 to 247.5 million tons in 1913. In the same period, the amount dug out from British mines rose from an already hefty 50.2 million tons to 275.4 million tons; French coal production expanded from 5.3 million to 39.9 million, and that in Russia grew from a negligible amount to 30.2 million tons. The figures for pig-iron in the same period were, in Germany, an increase from 245,000 tons to 14.8 million tons, in Britain 2.7 million to 9.8 million, in France 561,000 to 4.65 million, and in Russia 231,000 tons to 3.87 million. These figures show, firstly, that Germany had emerged as Britain's most important heavy industrial competitor, and indeed was overtaking the early-starter as Europe's pre-eminent heavy industrial power. Secondly, France lagged behind Britain and Germany in terms of heavy industrial capacity. Thirdly, Russia, starting from a long way behind the others, was catching up, at least with France. These different fortunes need to be explained.

By 1914, Germany was producing two-thirds of Europe's steel and half of its coal, generating 20 per cent more electricity than Britain, France and Italy together and outstripping its competitors in chemicals (with a global monopoly on synthetic chemicals) and engineering. The value of its exports, 10 per cent higher than the French in 1890, was 60 per cent greater in 1911. Germany's impressive economic performance can be explained by a confluence of factors: between 1850 and 1910 the German population grew much faster (from 34 million to almost 65 million) than the French (35.8 million to a mere 39.6 million). Germany therefore had a plentiful supply of labour which, particularly from 1890, was absorbed by German industry, which also sucked in immigrants, particularly from Poland (some quarters in Ruhr mining towns became Polish-speaking and remained so into the 1920s). Germany was also blessed by a geographical accident which came into play, particularly after 1880. With the introduction of the Gilchrist-Thomas process in steelmaking from 1879, low-grade (phosphoric) German ore could be used in furnaces. This gave the Ruhr the advantage of having both its coalfields and its sources of phosphoric iron ore close at hand. German steelmakers, who had previously needed to import Spanish and Swedish ore, found their costs dramatically reduced. Navigable rivers such as the Rhine were efficient transport routes and therefore ideal locations for their steelworks.

Germany's late industrialisation proved to be a positive advantage in modern industries such as chemicals. Unburdened by heavy investment in older technology, unlike its French and British counterparts, the German chemical industry in the 1870s could leap straight into the most recent processes. German industry also had a plentiful supply of capital for investment: Germany had four major investment banks by 1914, which provided money for large-scale industry, but German industry also developed substantial joint-stock companies in which banks invested. By 1912 the capital of these companies almost equalled that of the banks. Industrial concentration in cartels, often regarded as stifling competition, was seen by contemporaries as a co-operative way of reducing wasteful rivalry between firms. The German Steelworks Association (1904), for example, controlled production and facilitated large-scale investment, but cartels were not always efficient. They could lead either to overproduction (and price falls) or underproduction (which periodically forced German industry to rely on imports, as in 1906 when there was a shortage of coal). Finally, the German state played an important role, purchasing and then running thousands of miles of railway and subsidising freight for German firms. The navy-building programme from the 1890s stimulated engineering and shipbuilding. To state-sponsored technical education in agriculture was added a system of craft schools and technical colleges to serve industry. These *technische Hochschulen* were supplemented by training schools provided by private firms.

By comparison with Germany and Britain, France appeared to be economically 'backward', but it has also been argued that it was merely taking a different path towards economic development.[2] The growth in French GNP (Gross National Product – the value of all goods and services produced, both at home and abroad, by businesses owned by people in the country) between 1860 and 1910 was certainly poor compared with the European average. It grew at an annual rate of 1.41 per cent, compared with the average of 1.88 per cent, while Germany steamed ahead with 2.57 per cent. Yet Germany had a larger and faster-growing population (rising by 1.17 per cent a year compared to France's 0.16 per cent). This means that if one looks at the annual growth of GNP *per capita*, then French growth was only marginally behind that of Germany: 1.25 per cent a year, compared with Germany's 1.39 per cent a year (and a European average of 0.96 per cent). In other words, French workers, peasants and entrepreneurs were only fractionally less productive than their German counterparts. Yet the figures also show that Germany enjoyed an easy lead in the supply of labour. Besides the slower birth-rate, the persistence of peasant smallholding, buoyed under the Third Republic by protective tariffs, made farmers reluctant to leave the land to which they had an emotional as well as an economic attachment. This did not necessarily hold back manufacturing of consumer goods such as lace in Normandy, which could be produced by rural outworkers, but it did not provide heavy industry with a ready pool of labour.

This shortage also meant that French industrial workers could demand high wages, which pushed up production costs. There were, of course, ways in which French entrepreneurs could overcome this. They employed women, who commanded lower pay, they encouraged peasants to commute to the towns by train and they used immigrant labour. In 1851, 380,000 foreigners lived in France and there were 800,000 by 1876. A further half a million entered the country in the next five years, accounting for 3 per cent of the population. Most of these people were from European countries, but the first immigrants from North Africa, the Kabyles, also appeared. Before 1920 (when it took first place) France was, in proportion to its total population, second only to the United States as a country of net immigration. The immigrants frequently brought important skills – the Belgians in textiles and mining and the Italians in artisanal trades including hatmaking and tailoring.

In heavy industry, however, France did not enjoy the same advantages as Germany in terms of access to raw materials (and the loss of the rich provinces of Alsace and Lorraine did not help). France in the 1870s still imported a third of its coal, and at a price. French coalfields, moreover, were concentrated in the north, while the great iron and steel centres, such as Saint-Étienne and Le Creusot, were in the south, which inflated transport costs. Some manufacturers therefore sought alternative forms of energy and by 1914 France was a world leader in the use of water turbines and hydroelectric power, with the first great projects harnessing the water power cascading off the Alps. French investors were more cautious than their German and British counterparts. Entrepreneurs tended to rely on family and business contacts to raise money, while banks tended to be seen as sources of short-term loans in times of crises, rather than as institutions to be tapped for long-term investment. None the less, the French state primed financial institutions for large-scale investment: the Crédit Foncier was founded in 1852 to fund urban building projects.

Yet to contrast the French economy with that of Germany (or Britain) is not to compare like with like. The fact that French per capita GNP did not lag significantly behind Germany's is a reflection of the value of the luxury goods produced in France, such as coaches, cabinets, fashion, wines and spirits. The small-scale, traditional methods of production were better suited to these goods. The concentration of French industry on luxury industries could be seen as a rational response to the dominance of Britain and Germany in heavy industry. It was a way to compete with those rivals for a share in global markets. This is not to say that advanced production techniques did not exist in France; towards 1914, some manufacturers, such as Renault and Citroën, were experimenting with new forms of industrial organisation, mass-production and so-called 'scientific management' (Taylorism), which strictly regulated working patterns by the clock. It was, however, precisely these innovations which stirred opposition among French skilled workers anxious for their status, earnings and working conditions.

By 1914 the Italian economy could similarly claim that, while it lagged behind in terms of heavy industrial capacity, it excelled in certain sectors. Italy underwent its great period of industrial expansion between 1896 and 1914, with a shift from the traditional activities in textiles towards metallurgy, chemicals and engineering. Like France, Italy remained a predominantly agricultural country, but, to overcome the country's paucity of coal, a combination of state and private enterprise harnessed hydroelectric power, which was derived from the water flowing down Alpine valleys. Northern Italy was therefore well-served by electricity, 90 per cent of which was consumed by industry. Milan was the first city in Europe to be illuminated by electric street-lighting, while electric trams were clattering through the city by 1893. The other great area of Italian finesse was in automobiles. Turin was a railway engineering centre, so there was already technological and carriage-building expertise on site; Fiat (*Fabbrica Italiana Automobili Torino*) was founded there in 1899. If at first the car industry was aimed at wealthy aristocratic playboys, by the outbreak of the First World War Fiat was beginning to expand its production to cater for a wider market, producing 4500 cars a year by 1914, although most of those were exported.

Russia was meant to be a classic case of 'backwardness'. The terms of serf emancipation in 1861 did not immediately create a pool of industrial labour. Russian peasants were bound to the land both emotionally and by the redemption payments, due over 49 years at 6 per cent interest. In any case, the prospect of a burgeoning Russian working class terrified the Tsar, his officials and the nobles. As Russian industry developed, however, so too did its industrial workforce, growing from an average of 950,000 in the 1870s to an average of 1.65 million in the 1880s. The government may have worried about the implications for social stability, but it was also concerned to keep pace with its rivals. In 1890 the minister of finance, Count Sergei Witte, warned, 'in relation to the needs of our country and in comparison with foreign countries our industry is still very backward'.[3] This issue of 'backwardness' has obsessed economic historians looking at Russia, but for Witte it was a matter of life and death for the Tsarist regime. His stringent programme of economic development focused on railway construction to stimulate the coal, iron and steel industries. The crucial period was the 1890s, when Witte secured foreign loans (particularly from Paris), high import tariffs and higher taxation to raise the money needed for industrial development. Instead of leaving money in the pockets of its citizens, who could then spend money on consumer goods such as clothes and food, the state took it to build up the capital needed to import machinery and to construct railroads and armaments. It may therefore have been that the population paid the price of industrialisation through enforced low living standards. Yet this view might have been exaggerated; Paul Gregory's research on Russian national incomes has shown that Russian agriculture was not as unproductive as previously thought. He also shows that in the 1890s the burden of taxation did not appear to lower peasant consumption of grain, suggesting that standards of living in the countryside were not adversely affected by the Witte system.[4]

The first great spurt of the 1890s (averaging 8 per cent annually) could not, however, be sustained because of the strain it placed on the government budget and the difficulties faced by Witte in securing further foreign loans in 1899. The Russian domestic market was too small for the capital goods being produced and from 1901 there was a slow-down, aggravated by the revolutionary upheavals of 1905–7. Yet enough fixed capital – factories, machinery – had been installed in Russia to lay the basis for further growth. The renewed expansion from 1909 to 1914 (at an annual growth rate of 6 per cent) was still dependent upon the state, as private investors were attracted by government contracts, particularly in its armaments programme. Yet much of the money came from joint-stock banks and the issue of shares by industrial firms. The extent of industrialisation should not be exaggerated. Traditional modes of production persisted, especially in the consumer goods produced by the cottage industries. Cities such as Moscow and St Petersburg had a 'dual economy', with industrial plants sitting alongside artisanal workshops producing clothes, shoes and luxury goods. In St Petersburg, 48 per cent of all wage-earners in 1910 worked in the service industries, a third of those as domestic servants. Even within the same factories, methods were often a mixture of the old and the new.

European industrialisation would not have been possible without an expansion in food supplies. In many parts of Europe, workers were often still 'worker-peasants' in contact with the rural world. In 1918 half of the industrial workforce in Russia still had access to family land and 20 per cent worked on it. Large-scale industrialisation, however, involved the specialisation of ever-increasing numbers of workers in manufacturing. Consequently, either agricultural production had to expand to feed those who no longer produced their own food, or provisions had to be imported. Europe witnessed both processes.

Agricultural productivity was increased either by expanding the area under cultivation or by innovation to make the land more productive. Rises in food production frequently grew out of both expansion and innovation. In European Russia, the area under cereal crops grew by 10 per cent between 1850 and 1900, accounting for a quarter of the increase in cereal production, while higher grain yields accounted for the rest. The amount of land dedicated to cereal production increased more dramatically after 1900, particularly in wheat and barley, which were export crops, suggesting that the gentry and peasantry were responding to the demands of the European market. These aggregate figures, however, hide serious regional differences. In the central Black Earth provinces, population pressure forced peasants to plough up fields which had been used to graze livestock. This reduction in pasture affected the availability of draft animals and manure, which reduced the productivity of agriculture in this region. In the more sparsely-populated provinces of southern Russia, the northern Caucasus, along the Urals and in western Siberia, however, cultivation expanded on to virgin soil in the first flush of fertility. There were also efforts to innovate. In the Black Earth region the spread of potatoes was a sign that peasants were relying on them as a primary food staple, but in other areas they were used as part of a four-crop rotation, which reduced the need for fields to lie fallow. Specialised cash crops such as sugar beets, cotton and tobacco began to appear, particularly on the estates of nobles who were trying to maximise their income after the emancipation. In the two decades before the First World War, investment in livestock outside the central Black Earth and Lower Volga regions also increased by 1.8 per cent a year. At the same time, investment in farm machinery and transport grew at an impressive 9 per cent per annum, though that reflects the initial backwardness of Russian agriculture. Overall, Russian crop production grew by an average of 2 per cent a year between 1860 and 1913, particularly in the export crops of wheat and barley, with rye increasing the most slowly. With the population increasing at 1.8 per cent, it seems that food production in Russia was, despite some terrible privation as in 1891, keeping pace, but the progress was regional not general. The hard-pressed Black Earth region, in particular, was left lagging behind the periphery. In Peter Gatrell's pithy judgment, 'in the centre, progress was peripheral, but on the periphery there was progress'.[5]

Germany was Europe's most advanced industrial power by 1914, but it actually experienced a very balanced development between sectors, still employing some 35 per cent of its workforce in agriculture. Over the course of the nineteenth century, German agricultural productivity trebled and this was primarily the result of innovation; overall, German land devoted to agriculture actually fell by 1.9 million hectares between 1878 and 1914. The tariff protection first introduced in 1879 did not discourage the great Junker landlords from adopting new techniques, while the peasant farms which dominated western Germany also showed a marked willingness to introduce new technology and methods. This was partly a result of state encouragement. From the 1860s agricultural schools and colleges were expanded, which improved the technical awareness of farmers, making possible the acceptance of new, more productive strains of crops (including the sublimely-named winter wheat, 'Rimpau's early bastard'). Moreover, banks tailored loans and mortgages to small farmers to encourage innovation and the use of technology. Mechanical reapers on German farms increased from 35,000 in 1895 to 301,000 in 1907, while the use of threshers doubled.

France's rural landscape remained primarily a patchwork of peasant smallholdings. Their subdivision into ever-smaller parcels actually increased from mid-century, when farms of under ten hectares accounted for 68 per cent of all agrarian property. This proportion increased to 85 per cent in 1882, with only a slight decrease by 1908. Naturally, the small scale of French holdings made investment in farm machinery not only impractical but also unaffordable, since the profitability of these farms was small. In 1882 about three-quarters of all French farmers did not have surpluses which they could sell on the market, so it was the 25 per cent who did who could introduce new technology. As late as 1892 the most advanced tool of which some three and a half million French farms could boast was a plough; threshing machines and mechanical reapers were few and far between. Yet the French agrarian economy was far from stagnant; in 1852, 100 male agricultural workers provided enough food for 459 inhabitants, but 30 years later that figure had increased to 590. The increase in food production actually outstripped the population increase and was able to support the greater number of people who were no longer working in agriculture. This expansion was most dramatic in northern France, particularly in the Paris basin, where larger-scale farming was already well-established, but it was slower in the south, where the subdivision of landholdings was more pronounced.

Large-scale, market-driven enterprises existing alongside small-scale peasant-holdings implies a dual economy in French agriculture. It was probably the former which accounted for the growth in production, but the extent to which small-scale farmers steered shy of agricultural change should not be exaggerated. They were certainly cautious about introducing new crops and often waited until their value had been demonstrated elsewhere, but they did slowly change. In one case – wine production – specialisation proved to be disastrous for smallholders. The development of transport links from the 1870s opened up world markets, which encouraged southern peasants to specialise in growing grapes, while buying grain from other parts of France to meet their own needs. Yet a disease called phylloxera, which attacks vines, made its first appearance in France in 1864 and, over the following decade, spread northwards. The recovery of the wine industry was made possible by the use of pesticides and by replanting the vineyards, but all this required considerable investment, so while small producers floundered, large-scale wine production became more accentuated. In the long run, however, the wider availability of staples from the commercial farms of the north, or from imports, encouraged French farmers to specialise in cash crops – vines, vegetables, sugar-beets – and in livestock. Peasants became more accustomed to a cash economy and more aware of the opportunities afforded by the market.

Italian productivity increased thanks to a combination of expansion and innovation. This was encouraged by the artificially high prices generated by the tariff wall of 1878. New machinery and chemical fertilisers were urged by travelling agronomes around 1900 and by specialist agricultural schools. The innovations were paid for by credit from rural banks. Farmers had doubled their wheat production by 1913, but only in the north, which boasted most of the educational facilities. State grants encouraged the draining of marshes and the irrigation of arid land. By 1915, 352,000 hectares had been reclaimed in this way, but only 2,300 hectares of it was in the south. Southern landowners had neither the capital nor, frequently, the inclination to make these investments, not least because of the conservatism of the local peasantry, who eschewed new methods as expensive, risky and time-consuming. The general expansion in agricultural production did not come without social upheaval. The widespread system of sharecropping (*mezzadria*) declined as both peasant land-ownership and the number of landless agricultural labourers rose. By 1911, of an agricultural population of 10 million, there were 650,000 peasant proprietors, but also 5 million landless labourers, a rural 'proletariat' who sometimes violently resisted the decline of the *mezzadria* system and who were behind a series of agrarian strikes in the 1880s. Italian socialists made their first rural inroads in Emilia and lower Lombardy, the areas most affected by these transformations.[6]

Economic growth and the expansion of markets, trade and rapid communication began to forge an integrated European – indeed global – market. International economic organisations, such as the World Postal Union (1878), were founded to encourage co-operation over practical matters, and agreements on the standardisation of railways, on maritime law, on copyright, on the spread of disease (including agricultural plagues such as phylloxera): there were no fewer than 129 such agreements between 1881 and 1910. Economic interdependence elicited optimistic judgements from contemporaries; in a 1909 bestseller, Norman Angell suggested that war could only bring economic disaster to all belligerents, so prolonged conflict was in nobody's interests ('the capitalist', he wrote, 'has no country'). Optimists who looked forward to the forging of a global market were disappointed by the rise of the 'new mercantilism'. This was the construction by almost all European states of high protective tariff walls from the 1870s, partly in response to the 'Great Depression' which struck parts of the European economy from 1873 and which grumbled on until 1896. The long-term slump was caused by falling agricultural prices. Grain-producing regions in the Americas and in the Black Sea region took advantage of falling transport costs and undercut grain prices on the European markets. The profits of agrarian interests were hurt, but there were also winners, particularly workers whose real wages rose as they had to spend less to feed themselves and their families. In Britain, for example, as global wheat prices collapsed in the 1880s, the price of animal foodstuffs – butter, meat and eggs – declined, but more gradually because demand increased as workers were having to devote a smaller proportion of their earnings to staples such as bread. Economic historians are now sceptical, therefore, about the actual existence of such a Great Depression, at least in the more advanced industrial societies such as Britain.[7] In predominantly agrarian countries, however, the collapse in prices hurt a wider section of the population. In Russia, cereal prices began to fall in 1880 and dropped almost continuously – punctuated only by the harvest failures of 1883 and 1891 – until 1900, but the various regions were affected differently. As the price of wheat declined less drastically than that of rye, the wheat-producing areas of southern-European Russia, where cultivation could be expanded into fertile, virgin land and where estates took advantage of lower transportation costs, still remained buoyant. The depression in prices bit harder into the rye-producing peasant agriculture of the Black Earth, where calls were heard for protection, not against foreign competition but against the more prosperous farming of the periphery of the Empire. In France, by 1895 cereal prices had been reduced by more than a quarter of their level in the early 1870s. Although the price of wine increased until the 1880s, owing to the scarcity caused by the phylloxera epidemic, the recovery from the disease caused a glut by 1900 and a consequent fall in prices. As land-owning peasants provided the backbone of support for the Third Republic, the agricultural crisis was an acute political problem. Peasant producers were among those who campaigned for tariffs in the 1880s. Unemployment rose in Germany and Britain, although there are no accurate figures. In Britain between 1870 and 1901 unemployment averaged between 4 and 5 per cent, but these numbers are only for those trades for which records were kept, so it was almost certainly higher, particularly amongst the unskilled who relied on casual work. None the less, the figures do suggest that, in terms of unemployment, this depression scarcely measured up to that of the 1930s.

Its importance lay in the fact that it was the agricultural producers who suffered from the price falls, which had a decisive impact on government policy. For example in Germany, where the country was becoming dependent upon foreign grain imports, the Junkers saw their share of the market decline and prices fall by as much as 15 per cent by 1875. Meanwhile, Prussia's triumph in 1871 had encouraged a speculative boom, stimulated by political euphoria, the injection of cash from the French war indemnity and easy credit. Joint-stock companies were formed at a rapid tempo, with shares being traded at inflated rates. The bubble burst when, in April 1873, a financial crisis in the United States and the crash of the Vienna stock exchange had a knock-on effect in Germany, with many of the new companies going bankrupt. As the depression bit, prices and production fell and unemployment rose; railway and engineering firms laid off as much as half of their workforces, and the drop in railway and locomotive construction decreased the demand for iron and coal. Calls for protective tariffs were heard from heavy industry, but also from textiles which were suffering doubly from the depression and, since the commercial treaties of the 1860s, from French and British competition. Bismarck finally succumbed to the powerful protectionist lobby in 1879. Other European powers also adopted protectionist policies in this climate; France raised tariffs in 1885, culminating with the Méline tariff of 1892. Russia retaliated against German protectionism with its own tariff in 1885, while those of 1890 and 1891 were intended to raise capital for industrialisation. Italy abandoned free trade in 1887, embarking on a ruinous trade war with France, which ran for more than a decade. Austria–Hungary doubled its tariffs in 1878 and made further increases in the 1880s. In practice, these countries did moderate their protectionist policies in agreements with specific countries. By 1914, however, only the United Kingdom still embraced free trade, although tariffs became a major election issue in 1905.

Despite protectionist policies, however, the era of the Great Depression actually witnessed significant rises in real wages, a consequence both of the decline in prices and of the rise in money wages, particularly in the more industrialised countries, where workers' earnings were generally higher than those of agricultural labourers. In Britain, real wages rose by a third between 1850 and 1875, and then by 45 per cent until the turn of the century, while in Germany and France they increased by roughly a third between 1870 and 1900. Although urban rents rose, the real wages compensated for this and improved the standard of living for many people. Workers were left with more disposable income to spend on a wider range of foods and consumer goods, such as clothing, which also fell in price in the last decades of the nineteenth century. While the consumption of bread – the staff of life for most urban and rural workers – remained stable, the amount of meat, tea, coffee and sugar consumed rose significantly in both Germany and Britain. In 1873 the average German bought 59 lb of meat, but by 1912 that figure had risen to 105 lb. In France, the price of cotton clothing had fallen by 50 per cent between 1873 and 1896 and workers were better dressed than they had been in mid-century. The increasing variety in diet was made possible by the transport revolution, enabling the rapid transit of perishables, and by developments in food processing (margarine was invented in 1869), canning and refrigeration. The first refrigerator ship put to sea from Argentina in 1877, carrying a consignment of mutton, and the first New Zealand lamb arrived in Europe five years later.

The wider availability of a greater variety of goods stimulated a dramatic transformation in the way people shopped. France led the way in creating the first shopping chains and department stores. In 1852 Aristide Boucicaut opened the world's first department store, the *Bon Marché* (immortalised in Emile Zola's 1883 novel, *Au bonheur des dames*). The grocer Félix Potin set up a chain of shops selling food in Paris. In this 'retail revolution', department stores and retail chains emerged across Europe, including Russia. In such shops, prices of goods were fixed, so that, while previously they would have haggled with the retailer, shoppers ceased to be active participants. Instead, they were meant to be passive consumers, lured into buying products through displays, bargains and advertising.

The benefits from rising standards of living were unevenly distributed. Even as workers' real wages rose, their share in the total amount of wealth declined. Between 1870 and 1900, for example, the workers' share in the gross national product fell by 26 per cent in Britain and by 55 per cent in Germany, while the share going to the top 5 per cent of earners in Britain in 1880 stood at a staggering 48 per cent. The extent of that concentration of income was unique in Europe, but such patterns, if less pronounced, emerged elsewhere: in Prussia the share of income going to the top 5 per cent of earners rose from 21 per cent in 1851 to

30 per cent by 1913. In other words, those who benefited most from economic growth were the wealthy, particularly the entrepreneurs who ran big business because it was there that the profits were the greatest. Among the working class itself, skilled workers enjoyed a more marked improvement in living standards than the unskilled, who were more likely to find themselves unemployed and dependent upon insecure, casual work. In Britain by 1900, unskilled workers were reaping only half of the income awarded to their skilled counterparts.

The differences in the quality of life between rich and poor were especially visible in urban areas. In 1800, Europe had 22 cities with over a hundred thousand people; by 1895 it boasted 120 of this size, with 10 per cent of the European population living in them. Urbanisation, however, brought social problems. Until the development of cheap, efficient public transport, European workers tended to live close to the factories or workshops. Sometimes they even lived *in* their place of work, sleeping alongside the machines, or under the workbench. In Paris, for example, before the *Métro* opened, public transport consisted of a few hundred horse-drawn omnibuses, but to travel on them cost the equivalent of a tenth of an average worker's daily wage in mid-century. Before the development of the infrastructure, therefore, workers tended to live in the same, overcrowded, insalubrious neighbourhoods which were being polluted by the factories. In Glasgow around 1900, the rapidly expanding working-class districts were those closest to the industries.[8] In St Petersburg, the industrial suburbs were poorly served by trams, so workers were driven to live in housing as close as possible to their factories or workshops, in noisy, polluted conditions: 'the factory buildings, houses, streets, and bustling crowds of people were covered with a thick layer of soot', wrote the radical worker Semyon Kanatchikov in the 1890s.[9] With workers having to live in overpopulated urban districts, rents soared and accommodation was subdivided, partitioned and shared by large numbers of people.

The rebuilding of Paris under Napoleon III, which destroyed the worst of the slums, inadvertently intensified the division between the wealthier west and the poorer eastern districts, where those unable to afford the higher rents were pushed out to the squalid fringes. In London, slum clearance began in the 1870s, but in the short term this actually reduced the stock of housing and so exacerbated the problem of overcrowding. Much of the destruction of slums took place to clear the way for railways entering the city. Ironically, if in the long run such transportation allowed workers to commute from cheaper housing in the suburbs, in the short term the displaced population of the urban poor, who still could not afford the rail fares, simply crammed themselves into the nearest and cheapest accommodation by the tracks. In 1911 some three-quarters of a million Londoners were still living in overcrowded conditions. Moscow, whose population grew at a rapid 4 per cent a year between 1900 and 1914 (three-quarters of this growth due to immigration from the provinces), had an average of between eight and nine people living in each subdivision of housing – which made it twice as crowded as either Vienna or London. In St Petersburg in 1904, over fifty thousand people were renting corners of rooms, sleeping on wooden boards or on the floor. Six years later, 63,000 people were living crammed together in basements prone to flooding.

None the less, conditions did begin to improve in some places. London showed the way in 1863 when it opened the first underground passenger service, the four-mile Metropolitan Railway, which in the first year of its existence carried 12 million passengers. In 1900 the Paris Métro opened. The development of cheaper, more efficient systems of public transport allowed more workers to commute to work rather than having to depend upon their own legs. Distinctly residential areas removed from the centres of commerce and industry developed – at least in larger metropolises such as London, Paris and Vienna. Although at first only affordable amongst the middle class and the skilled workers and later derided for their lifelessness and monotony, the suburbs offered the space, privacy and clean air which so many urban workers and artisans craved.

If there were inequalities in wealth distribution and housing, there were also gender differences in living standards. Even within the same families, men enjoyed more of the benefits than women. In 1908 the German Union of Construction Workers explained:

> It is like this in working-class families. The man, the one who after all has to work, consumes the largest share of the available food. The children too have as much as possible. In most cases, the mother is left out – she has to be satisfied with one or two mouthfuls if there is not enough to go round, and lives on bread, coffee and potatoes. A working man's wife makes daily sacrifices for her family. She is happy if nobody shouts for more, even if she is still hungry herself.[10]

Of course, the assumption that women did not work was a false one, and when women did work they were paid less than men for similar tasks. Women were always an important part of the workforce in manufacturing and agriculture and they remained so. The 1866 census in France showed that 2 million women worked in agriculture, while 1 million were involved in all forms of manufacturing. It is not easy, however, to disentangle the two types of activity. Among the agricultural workers, for example, women often supplemented their family's income not only by vine-growing but also by lace-making or silk-weaving. In Prussia in 1861, over a quarter of all women in employment (or almost 566,000 out of just over 1.9 million) were hired as day-labourers in agriculture, compared to 90,000 who worked in factories. In Russia in 1900, 25 per cent of all waged women were working as field hands. Demand for women's labour in European industry was strong because they commanded lower wages than their male counterparts. Women workers were often given different jobs from the men, which was meant to justify the wage differentials, even when the women had skills. This is well illustrated by the Lyon silk industry. Women and girls traditionally had important roles in the preparation of the silk for weaving, which in turn was done by both men and women, although male weavers (*canuts*) tended to monopolise the work involving the more prestigious patterned and brocaded fabrics. In the mechanised weaving mills which sprang up outside the city, however, the weavers were mostly unskilled, poorly-paid young women living in monastic *internats*, which were effectively factories with dormitories. In 1906 the silk-workers' union declared 'the silk spinning mills have become female prison camps'; women lived and laboured under close supervision and for poorer pay than their male counterparts in the city.

Their lower wages meant that women's presence in Europe's manufacturing labour force was very strong. In Baden's cigar and tobacco industry in the 1860s, women outnumbered men by three to two, a ratio which increased when entrepreneurs put out the manufacture of cigars to domestic industry. Women working as tailor's assistants in Hamburg in 1870 outnumbered men who did so by about four to one. In the Italian silk industry in 1900, 70 per cent of the workforce were women. In 1910, 900,000 women worked in the factories of the Habsburg monarchy, where in the Czech lands they made up 30 per cent of the workforce in ironworks. Women represented 45 per cent of the entire labour force in the French textile industry, which employed 70,000 women in the factories of the north. Women tended to concentrate in certain types of industry, particularly textiles. In 1907 in the Ruhr, women made up just over a quarter of all textile workers in Barmen, while the iron and mining industries of Bochum offered little employment for them (although the town did boast two women miners). While women accounted for one in three Russian factory workers in 1914, the proportion was higher (58.6 per cent) in textiles.

Male workers had misgivings about female competition. French and German trade unions frequently excluded women from membership, demanding instead a 'family wage', which would give men enough for their household, removing the necessity for women to work. Working-class people had imbibed the ideal of the wife and mother as the angel of the hearth, and a higher proportion of unmarried than married women held paid employment. In France in 1896, 52 per cent of all single women earned wages, compared with 38 per cent of married women. This imbalance may be explained by choice, child-rearing or the ability of adult offspring to contribute to the household economy. Yet it may also be the result of prejudice; some businesses simply would not employ older women, who were more likely to be married.

A fundamental change was the decline of domestic service as a source of women's employment – at least in western Europe (in Russia it remained, after agriculture, the most important form of women's paid work until 1917). In France in 1866, women accounted for three-quarters of all domestics. In Westphalia and western Prussia, domestic service was by far the largest single employer of unmarried women, of whom 35 per cent worked as maids, servants, cooks and the like. These women tended to be rural in origin, kept frequent contact with their families in the countryside and saw the work as a means of contributing to their income. Initially, therefore, domestic service was an extension of the peasant family economy. These attitudes changed, however, and, increasingly, young women regarded domestic service as temporary until they had saved enough money to marry, or even to train for another type of job (domestics accounted for the majority of account-holders in savings banks). If domestic service meant a move to a metropolis such as Paris or Berlin, the daughter could break away from parental control in the choice and timing of marriage. None the less, the work itself was far from emancipating, demanding 16 to 18 hours a day, celibacy and adherence to the strict rules and values often laid down by their middle-class employers. From 1880, domestic service began to decline as a source of employment. The spread of education and literacy and rises in standards of living increased expectations, so that young women were less willing to submit to the stringent conditions of service. Other opportunities, offering more independence for young, unmarried women, were a greater draw.

From the later nineteenth century the service sector associated with a maturing industrial economy expanded dramatically, offering new sources of work for literate working-class women as clerks, typists and sales assistants, and then as teachers and nurses. In 1891, 45 per cent of French post-office workers were women. In 1907, in Bochum in the Ruhr, 12 per cent of all single women were working in department stores, 10 per cent in the clothing industry and a smaller proportion in the food trades. The Bochum Chamber of Commerce noted that year that 'the salesgirls [were] now recruited more from those classes which earlier regarded experience as a domestic servant as the most suitable preparation for their later careers as housewives'. The city fathers may not have been champions of women's liberation, but this does show that women's work was changing. In 1910, 20 to 25 per cent of the workers in the six Parisian department stores were women. In fact, the 'retail revolution' in France offers a contrast with the British experience, in that most of the women recruited to French department stores tended to come from the urban lower middle classes, while in Britain they were more likely to come from working-class families. In work such as retailing, the postal and telegraph services and teaching, a marriage bar often functioned, meaning that once women had married, they were no longer expected, or even allowed, to continue working. Certainly, British women in these areas of employment – as in domestic service – were not allowed to marry and then keep their jobs. Ironically, therefore, as the forms of employment performed by working-class and lower-middle-class women changed, large numbers of them could not take advantage of the opportunities.[11]

New forms of work, in fact, were beginning to open up to better-off middle-class women, though this should not be exaggerated. A woman of the wealthy bourgeoisie was not expected to undertake waged work, but to live within the domestic sphere, supervising servants and sometimes playing an important social role as hostess for gatherings of her husband's business associates. Yet most middle-class women were not wealthy enough to live like this. They may have employed some servants, but maintaining the home to conform to the image of cleanliness, respectability and prosperity usually required domestic toil on their own part. Shopping and cooking, jobs for servants in the wealthiest homes, were tasks assumed by middle-class women, as illustrated by the appearance of cookbooks; Italy's first was published in 1891 (Pellegrino Artusi, *The Science of the Kitchen and the Art of Eating Well*). The introduction of gas, running water and then electricity certainly made life easier. Yet despite the status attached to bourgeois 'idleness', financial constraints often forced middle-class women to assume paid work, even if it was hidden; in Germany, the wives and daughters of low-paid minor officials might sew and embroider, selling their products to shops to supplement the family income. Such families began to attach greater importance to the acquisition of a high level of education and professional training for their daughters. Women often trained as teachers; in Prussia by 1896 there were no fewer than 14,600 women teachers, most of them in the state elementary schools. Similarly, teaching was an early career path for Russian middle-class women; until the 1870s the only way into the profession was as a governess in a private home, but thereafter women who graduated from state grammar schools were allowed to teach at primary level. In 1911, 62 per cent of the teachers in state schools were women, while that proportion rose to 71 per cent in schools run by the *zemstva*. Many of these were not only middle-class, but also daughters of the landed aristocracy, impoverished by the long-term effects of serf emancipation. By the First World War, moreover, 1000 women a year were graduating from Russian medical schools. The expansion of women's opportunities in teaching and medicine in Russia may be explained by the desperate need which both the state and the *zemstva* had for these skills – and because women were paid less than their male counterparts. In France before 1880 the only waged work considered acceptable for a middle-class woman was as a schoolteacher, but opportunities did begin to open up: in 1906 there were 573 women doctors, while from 1900 the legal profession at last began to admit women. In Italy, Maria Montessori became the country's first modern woman to acquire a medical degree in 1899.

These developments, however, are best seen as early signs for the future; it was not until after the Second World War that women began to enter the professions in significant numbers. In the late nineteenth and early twentieth centuries, women, no matter how educated or qualified, came up against severe obstacles. Teresa Labriola may have been a professor of law at the University of Rome, but the Italian bar turned down her application for membership in 1913. Less than 1 per cent of French lawyers were women after the turn of the century. In Russia, graduates from women's law faculties, founded in 1906, could only work as legal consultants rather than practise at the bar. In Germany, male students often had no objection to women studying law and medicine, but they had more reservations about them practising as equals in the world beyond academia. They were happier seeing women employed as their assistants rather than as fully-fledged equals. In Russia, the impressive proportion of women teachers should be set against their lower salaries and the formal bar from 1871 on women rising above the lower ranks of the profession. The high proportion of women teachers may be explained by the lack of possibilities in other professions. Russian women doctors struggled hard to earn respect from their male colleagues, prompting one female medic to call them 'the enemy'.[12] In France, while 49 per cent of the medical workforce was female in 1906, only 3 per cent of doctors were women. The rest worked in more traditionally 'feminine' spheres, such as midwifery and nursing.

If not everyone benefited equally from the improvements in standards of living, it is true that, for the first time, the number of people living on the very margins of subsistence declined in most parts of Europe. In Britain in 1800, for example, some two-thirds of the population had incomes hovering precariously around subsistence level, whereas by 1900 that proportion had halved. This was still a significant minority, however, and the unequal distribution of wealth in one of the world's most prosperous and powerful states was not lost on critics of capitalist society. In France, 73 per cent of the families of rural labourers received charitable assistance. That the average Russian family was better off in 1913 than in 1861 does not mean that they were no longer poor. A gauge of this poverty lies in the levels of infant mortality, which between 1907 and 1911 on average stood at an astonishing 245 per 1000 live births. This was a small improvement compared with earlier years, but it showed that, in terms of income and living conditions, Russia generally lagged desperately behind other European countries: infant mortality stood at 174 per 1000 live births in Germany, 128 in France, 151 in Italy, and 76 in relatively robust Sweden.

One of the main options for impoverished families was flight.

Though skilled artisans in search of opportunity crossed the oceans in large numbers, it was no coincidence that, when the great wave of emigration rose around 1885, the Mediterranean and eastern Europe accounted for most of it. Eleven million Italians left between 1890 and 1914, mostly from the poorer south, rather than the richer, industrialised north. Four million subjects of the Austro-Hungarian monarchy departed between 1875 and 1913, joined by 2.5 million Russians between 1900 and 1914 – and that despite the settlement of some two million people, with the encouragement of the Tsarist government, into Siberia. The overseas migrants were being driven away by poverty at home, but were drawn by a rise in demand for unskilled labour in North and South America, Australia, New Zealand and North Africa. The development of cheaper transport across the oceans made the passage more affordable. More prosperous countries still lost migrants; 3.5 million Germans left between 1861 and 1914, three million of them before 1895, but thereafter German industry absorbed the vast majority of the surplus population.[13]

The persistence of low incomes and the very fact that large numbers of families were dependent upon poor relief show that poverty remained a source of strain for a significant proportion of European families. It is scarcely surprising, therefore, that economic growth did not eliminate the symptoms of poverty, such as crime and alcoholism. As some working men sought refuge from the daily grind in pubs, cafés and taverns, the women and children suffered from the dissipation of their earnings. In 1852 a Swedish doctor, Magnus Huss, coined the term 'alcoholism' as a medical condition arising from excessive drinking. Historians have noted the high intake of alcohol amongst workers whenever they were faced with the pressures of industrialisation. One historian calls 1832–52 the 'golden age of inebriation' in northern Europe, while another discerns a 'great collective binge' in France in the later nineteenth and early twentieth centuries.[14]

In France after the 1870s, the correlation between high bread prices and high crime rates began to disappear and thefts of property may have been driven increasingly less by an urgency to feed oneself and one's family than by a desire to satisfy other needs. Yet such criminal activity was no less a sign of *relative* deprivation in a society which was as a whole becoming more prosperous. Poverty, therefore, remained one of the primary sources of criminal activity. In Russia, some unskilled St Petersburg workers, fleeced when they paid for their squalid accommodation, supplemented their scanty earnings by petty crime. While no overall figures exist, reported cases of 'hooliganism', a catch-all term describing a range of offences from disturbing the peace to crimes of violence and theft, seem to have been on the rise between 1911 and 1914. Across Europe, however, the proportion of reported crimes involving violence tended to decline, while those against property –

particularly theft – increased, although these tendencies should not be exaggerated; much of the violent crime probably went unreported and unseen, particularly in cases of domestic and sexual abuse. Urbanisation and industrialisation increased the levels of theft, fraud and suicide, while the murder and the arson rate (the latter a classic form of rural protest) fell. Those committing theft tended to be those with the least economic security, namely unskilled, casual labourers, although this was not always the case. Those convicted of pilfering in the Hamburg docks in 1906–10 tended to be the more skilled lightermen rather than the unskilled wharfmen, which may have reflected the opportunities for stealing available to the former (who worked unsupervised on the barges), rather than any lack of desperate need among the latter.[15]

Some women substituted their earnings by resorting to prostitution; in St Petersburg, while a domestic earned 5 roubles a month, the lowest-paid prostitute could glean 40 roubles. In that city there were an estimated 50,000 prostitutes and 500 brothels. Most of the women were in their late teens and had regular jobs, frequently as sales assistants, or were former domestic servants. Domestics were vulnerable to sexual abuse by their employers and lost their jobs if they fell pregnant. Abandoned, they lacked the community support experienced by many women industrial workers, for whom abandonment was a less common experience. Russian sales assistants were frequently forced into prostitution because not only did their wages scarcely stretch far enough to meet their own needs, their employers also demanded that they dress well, which put them under immense financial pressure. Much European prostitution was 'casual' in that women fell into it as a temporary expedient. This perhaps accounts for the large numbers involved. In Germany in 1900, estimates of the number of prostitutes varied between 100,000 and 200,000, and by 1914 they came close to a third of a million. London had so many brothels in the late nineteenth century that it was dubbed – in a mocking parody of Britain's proud boast to be the 'workshop of the world' – the 'whoreshop of the world'.

In the decades before the First World War, the state tried to address the 'social question' of poverty through reforms which are sometimes taken to be foundation-stones of the twentieth-century welfare state. In the late nineteenth and early twentieth centuries, governments were confronted with the mounting challenge as to how to persuade workers and peasants, who were increasingly finding a political voice, to accept their place within the existing political and social order. This quest for social stability was certainly one motive for state intervention. The decades before the First World War witnessed a remarkable development in almost all European countries. The state began to engage more in social policy, stepping in to deal with such questions as working conditions, health and poor relief, where previously private initiative, charity, the churches and local communities had borne the brunt of the responsibility. State action in these areas was not new, of course, but Germany (in the 1880s) and Britain (after 1905) adopted a rapid series of measures which dramatically expanded the state's role as a provider of social and welfare services. With Germany as the leader, other states, particularly in Scandinavia and the Low Countries, followed, though rarely as comprehensively as the German model suggested. Variously, old-age pensions, unemployment insurance and sickness insurance (introduced even in Russia in 1912), basic health benefits, more stringent regulation of working hours and conditions (particularly for women and children) and compensation for industrial accidents were introduced in most European countries. In France and Italy the measures were taken at a more hesitant and therefore less noticeable pace, while in Spain the record was sparse. Yet the same tendencies for the state to intervene were discernible and similar motives underlay the initiatives. First, governments were trying to persuade large sections of the population that they had a stake in the existing political and social order and to seduce them away from its critics; Bismarck, for example, spoke of 'killing socialism with kindness'. Secondly, Europe after 1870 was becoming a dangerously competitive place. The realities of imperialism, international tensions and rapid economic growth played on concerns over the 'degeneration' of the 'race', as nationalists and 'social Darwinists' likened the rivalry between nations to the struggle for survival in nature. Thirdly, however, there was a better awareness about the nature of poverty. If the prevailing attitude was still that poverty was the result of moral failings, social studies were beginning to piece together a more complex image of its causes and effects. New awareness of the issues surrounding indigence allowed social reformers to match their zeal with hard evidence to support their arguments. The weight and the nature of each of these factors weighed differently from one country to the next and even behind one reform and another. The result of the legislative wave was not a welfare state of the kind which would emerge in European countries after 1945, although one may discern its origins in these early reforms. None the less, it did mark a break – in some countries a radical breach – with nineteenth-century assumptions about the role of the state in society.[16]

13 The Cultural Clash and the Growth of the Public

Science and Religion

For beleaguered liberals and radicals facing the conservative onslaught in the 1850s, cultural activity became a means of waging war on the conservative order by other means. Above all, this entailed challenging the religious authority which legitimised the established order. Liberalism and radical ideologies therefore became associated with secularism, anticlericalism and a 'rational' belief in science over religious faith. In many respects, the fraught relations of the united Italian kingdom after 1860 with the Catholic Church, the German *Kulturkampf* in the 1870s and the tendency of Spanish liberals and republicans to identify displays of popular religiosity with a benighted, 'dark' Spain stemmed from this broad, European cultural current. Though not new in the nineteenth century, the conflict between, on the one hand, secularism and a confidence in scientific progress, and, on the other, religious belief as propounded by the conservative order and the established Churches, was intensified. Conservatives in the later nineteenth century were alarmed by a crisis in the European conscience, made all the more threatening by the emergence of mass culture, which threatened to undermine the moral foundations of the conservative order. In fact, the cultural clash between religion and science need not have been as manichean as it sometimes appeared. Many of the scientists themselves were religious and tried hard to deny neither the existence of God nor the importance of religion as a source of moral, though not scientific, truth. Meanwhile, there were clerics who were willing to accommodate scientific theories and discoveries within their systems of belief. None the less, the debate was poisoned by the adoption of dogmatic positions by extremes on both sides and by the enlistment of science and religion in the wider political conflicts of the age.

For most Europeans the first half of the nineteenth century was an era of religious revival, but among theologians, philosophers, historians and scientists there was a malaise. In *Vormärz* Germany, the biblical historian, David Friedrich Strauss, launched a frontal assault on the notion that the Bible was the direct word of God. In *Life of Jesus* (1835), Strauss argued that the authors of the Gospels were immersed in a particular culture, at least a generation after the death of Christ and at a time when Messianic expectations were running high. For Strauss, this explained the tenor of the New Testament, from which it was hard to discover the precise nature of divine truth, since it was written by human hands. Strauss was accused of trying to present Christ as a mythical figure and, with Germany still in the backlash of reaction against the revolutions of the early 1830s, he lost his job at the University of Tübingen.

Strauss was no atheist, but in France there emerged a creed which sought to root society in human ethics and science rather than religion. This was positivism, based on the theories of the French philosopher Auguste Comte. Comte published his writings between 1820 and 1854, the most important of which were his lectures, the *Cours de philosophie positive* (1830–42). His ideas were highly influential in the later nineteenth century, particularly but not exclusively in France (in Britain, he found an enthusiastic reader in John Stuart Mill, among others). Comte tried to explain the problems of his day by examining the world-views which shaped society. He discerned in the development of the human intellect a 'Law of Three States'. In the first 'theological' state, human beings interpret natural forces through animist beliefs, gods or a single divinity. In the second, 'metaphysical' state, people explain the world through abstractions like 'nature', 'progress' and 'evolution'. In the third, 'scientific', or 'positive' state, humans do not explain the universe through 'absolute ideas', but try to discover the immediate causes of phenomena and the scientific laws which govern them, through the application of reason and observation.[1] For Comte, the nature of society was determined by the intellectual stage: in the 'positive' state a new society would emerge, dominated by scientific thinking, industry and commerce. Comte, whose emphasis on reason and science owed an intellectual debt to Saint-Simon, shared with Marx a view of inevitable change in society. Unlike Marx, however, the passage of human society would not come about through economic development, social conflict and revolution, but through changes in the way people thought. For Marxists, ideas merely justified pre-existing social interests. For positivists, the relationship was reversed: ideas themselves changed and shaped society. Comte therefore argued that the most important precondition for social reform was an intellectual freedom in which each of the sciences would adopt the positivist approach, identifying general scientific laws about human society, and shedding theological and metaphysical explanations. Thus in positivist thought science would be the ultimate basis for the reorganisation of society. Human ethics, unhindered by theology, would be its moral basis.

Positivism naturally appealed to French anticlerical liberals and republicans, but it took a long time to spread widely. Notions of progress among Comte's contemporaries were shaped by eighteenth-century philosophers such as Giovanni Vico and Johann G. Herder. Napoleon

III's anticlerical education minister of the 1860s, Victor Duruy, believed in free thought, science and progress, but he remained a deist in his religious beliefs and was not influenced by positivism.[2] Yet Comte's influence became stronger under the Third Republic, though it remained very much the preserve of reformist, radical, middle-class intellectuals. Léon Gambetta and Jules Ferry were not fully-paid-up members of the positivist 'church', but they drew on Comte's ideas to forge a secular, radical basis for the Third Republic. Workers, however, were attracted more to the seductions of socialism than to the reformism of the positivists. In Britain, positivism was propagated, above all, by Frederic Harrison and it found fertile ground amongst the socialist intelligentsia of the Fabian Society.[3] Positivism was, in fact, one of the more developed philosophies amongst reformers who adhered to more inchoate secular notions of human progress and who put faith in science or economics rather than religion. Italian republicans and socialists of the later nineteenth century, such as Filippo Turati, founder of the Italian Socialist Party in 1892, shared a vaguely positivist commitment to social reform and anticlericalism, but it was also strong in the universities. Italian positivism was a loose commitment to science and to notions of inevitable, but gradual, social change. A different form of secular thought arose in Spain, inspired by the German philosopher, Karl Krause. Krause's ideas appealed to anticlerical Spanish liberals of the 1860s because they offered an alternative to the slavish imitation of French thinking. The Krausists were not irreligious (Krause had argued that all knowledge was ultimately divine in origin) but their emphasis on the individual's struggle for self-improvement, education and free thought appeared to be an assault on the authority of the Catholic Church. Its main proponent, Julián Sanz del Río, regarded the University of Madrid as the morally regenerating heart of the Spanish nation. When, in the conservative reaction which preceded the 1868 Revolution, Krausist professors were expelled from their posts, the liberal revolutionaries and intellectuals revolted against what they regarded as an intolerant Catholic state.

Theologians and philosophers were already struggling to digest some of these awkward ideas when the most controversial scientific thesis of the century was published: Darwin's theory of evolution. Charles Darwin did not intend to attack religious belief itself when he published *Origin of Species by Means of Natural Selection* in 1859. Like many of his contemporaries, he certainly sought to remove divine providence and intervention as a means of explaining how the earth, or life on it, changed over time. The theories of late eighteenth-century geologists such as James Hutton and his rival Abraham Werner had already caused a stir by suggesting that the earth was much, much older than the 6000 years allowed by the biblical creationists. Scientists who challenged this traditional view argued that the Bible was a source of moral and religious truth, but was not a reliable scientific guide.[4] Few scientists denied the action of God behind the *initial* creation of the earth, but since their theories contradicted the precise content of the Bible, they appeared to challenge its veracity. It was precisely for this reason that even scientists with religious convictions sought to unburden the natural sciences of the metaphysical debate. Among these was the British geologist, Charles Lyell, for whom the arguments over biblical authority were hampering scientific inquiry with dogma.

So when Lyell's contemporary, Charles Darwin, began his work in the 1830s, it was within a scientific culture which was still fervently debating the relationship between God and nature. Darwin's focus was initially narrower: he aimed to contribute to a long-running debate about the way in which the earth, and life upon it, had developed over its long existence. Jean-Baptiste Lamarck and Geoffroy de Saint-Hilaire had suggested that species developed slowly, adapting to their environment in a continuous process of organic change. Lyell (who examined the lava flows on Mount Etna) and Georges Cuvier argued instead that the earth's geological layers – and with them the fossil evidence that certain species had disappeared – were explicable by catastrophes. Each layer represented a different period, and different environment, which, for Cuvier, were each in turn destroyed by a great flood.

Darwin stepped into this debate with *Origin of Species by Means of Natural Selection*, the fruits of his research during his voyage to the Galapagos Islands and to South America on HMS *Beagle* between 1831 and 1836. Darwin emerged with a new theory – that of 'natural selection or the preservation of favoured races in the struggle for life'. Where there was competition for the means of existence, a member of any species was more likely to survive and reproduce if it had some physical variation giving it a competitive edge. Across generations, therefore, the successful variation would be preserved at the expense of the original form and, with time, the accumulation of mutations would be enough for, in effect, a new species to emerge. Darwin therefore lent weight to the theories of organic transformation and he explained it in terms of competition for the means of life *within* species. Yet Darwin also explained the divergence of different species over the course of time. In any given territory, the greater the diversity of species, the less competition there would be *between different species* for the means of survival, as each would find its own niche in the environment. Creationist theories had suggested, along the lines of the Book of Genesis, that different species had emerged from divine will. Darwin's book suggested that they evolved through accident and time rather than any providential design.

Some of the more scientifically-minded British churchmen took Darwin's ideas in their stride. The year after the publication of *Origin of Species*, seven Episcopalians, six of whom were clerics, published

Essays and Reviews. Much of the discussion focused on German biblical critics such as Strauss, but their acceptance of some of their points,[5] combined with the salute to Darwin's work as a 'masterly volume', provoked an uproar. The Archbishop of Canterbury issued an encyclical against *Essays and Reviews* and legal action was taken against its authors, who were deprived of their clerical positions for a year. This sentence was later quashed by the Privy Council, but not before 10,906 clergymen had signed a protest against the essayists' views. It was not only clerical intransigence which put science at odds with religion. Darwin's ideas – and those of the German biblical critics – were too compelling to resist for those who wanted to attack the Church and religion in particular or the conservative order in general. Marx gleefully wrote in 1843 that the intellectual assault on religious belief was the foundation for all other critiques. In 1862 Darwin's French translator declared that it was impossible to reconcile scientific progress with Christian faith. Scientists and clerics alike continued to seek to reconcile scientific and theological ideas, but this required a certain flexibility and, above all, a willingness to abandon the idea that the Bible contained the direct word of God. The dilemma for the devout was that one could either accept that the Scriptures, while containing essential religious truths, could not be taken literally as the revealed word of God, or else one had to see Darwinism and biblical criticism as attacks on divine authority itself.

In Germany, Darwin's theory appealed initially to liberals and radicals who saw in science a way of continuing the ideological struggle against the old regime in the 1860s. Carl Vögt and Ludwig Büchner were amongst those professors who, having lost their university posts in the reaction after 1848, joined others, such as Ludwig Feuerbach, as the most vocal German supporters of Darwin. Darwinists sought to capitalise on Bismarck's *Kulturkampf* with the Catholic Church in the 1870s, and Darwin's great populariser, Ernst Haeckel, hoped that evolution would be taught in schools and that clerical influence would be rolled back. This went too far for Bismarck, whose struggle against the Church in any case ran out of steam. None the less, popular science was widely read in the workers' reading rooms organised by the Social Democrats. In France, republicans who established libraries in the 1860s reported that popularised science was a favourite topic among working-class readers.[6] Darwin's theory did not, however, have a free run amongst French philosophers and scientists, even anticlericals. Positivists were sceptical about a theory which they regarded as ingenious but based on thin evidence. Other anticlericals of the Third Republic, however, saw the use in Darwin's ideas. Anatole France would later write of his youth that 'the books of Darwin were our Bible'.[7] In Spain after 1900, Darwin's theory found fertile ground in the anticlerical Modern Schools established in Catalonia by the League of

Free Thinkers, which produced cheap, popular versions of Darwin, Nietzsche and Voltaire. The schools were particularly popular with anarchists and the clergy regarded them as more dangerous to popular morality than brothels. In Valencia, an alarmed Spanish schoolteacher, Manuel Polo y Peyrolon, tried to rally the population against Darwinism, warning his compatriots that 'official Spanish science is *evolutionist*, that is, enemy of independent creation and therefore of the doctrine of Genesis'.[8]

The secular belief in science and progress was attacked by Pope Pius IX in the 'Syllabus of Errors', which was issued in 1864 and which, among other things like liberalism and socialism, condemned rationalism, including the claim that theological matters were subject to the scrutiny of philosophy and science.[9] European Catholic scientists none the less made their peace with Darwin. The Catholic *Revue des Questions Scientifiques* (published in Brussels) opposed evolutionary theories at its foundation in 1877. Yet at successive conferences Catholic scientists gradually accepted the theory of evolution through natural selection. The Third Congress, held in 1894 in Brussels, supported a motion which accepted scientists who made researches into evolution, but who did so 'under the supreme magistrature of the teaching church'. The discoveries of a Moravian friar, Gregor Mendel, inadvertently added grist to the Darwinian mill. In the 1850s Mendel experimented with successive generations of the peas which grew in the monastery garden in Brno. He laid the foundations for modern genetics, arguing that particular characteristics were inherited. Mendel's results were published from 1865 and, while the implications were not at first recognised, genetic inheritance opened up further explanations as to how natural selection operated. It was one thing, however, for clerics and scientists to find ways of reconciling religion and science, but quite another for popular opinion to do so. Exposed both to baroque forms of piety and to Darwinism in various vulgarised forms, it could not help but see the struggle between religion and science in manichean terms, in which religion was defined in opposition to Darwinism, and vice versa.

Darwin's ideas were widely disseminated, not only because of the metaphysical storm arising from them but because they seemed to explain so much in human society as well. Darwin saw his theory as a reason for humility: man, after all, was related directly to the animals, but others had different uses for his ideas. The idea that diversity in any given environment was beneficial was often missed in favour of an emphasis on the notion that the natural world was ordered by a struggle for survival. 'Social Darwinism' – a bastardised form of the scientist's ideas applied to human society – stressed the 'survival of the fittest' and became a pseudo-scientific justification for laissez-faire economics. Among the most important proponents of this was the philosopher Herbert Spencer. He argued that if natural selection was beneficial to the entire species, no social system should interfere with the competitive laws of nature. To socialists, on the other hand, Darwin's emphasis on environmental factors suggested that a restructuring of society – the human environment – would shape new human instincts and social habits. Darwin also inadvertently added grist to the satanic mill of what is now known as 'scientific racism'. His book appeared as there was debate about the origins of racial characteristics at the London Anthropological Society, between the monogenists, who argued that all humans descended from one common species, and the polygenists, who suggested that the races were in fact different human species. In an article published in the society's journal in 1864, the evolutionist Alfred Russell Wallace suggested that Darwin's theory could end the controversy once and for all. Natural selection, he argued, had already shaped the different races before the species became recognisably human. Once human beings had developed the intellect to respond to their environment without having to undergo physical change – by forging tools, stitching clothing, and so on – evolution ceased to have much direct effect on the shaping of racial characteristics. Intellectual and moral capacities rather than physical qualities, Wallace claimed, became essential in the struggle for survival. He concluded that:

> It is the same great law of '*the preservation of favoured races in the struggle for life*', which leads to the inevitable extinction of all those low and mentally undeveloped populations with which Europeans come in contact. . . . The intellectual and moral, as well as the physical qualities of the European are superior; the same power and capacities which have made him rise in a few centuries from the condition of the wandering savage with a scanty and stationary population to his present state of culture and advancement . . . enable him when in contact with the savage man, to conquer in the struggle for existence, and to increase at his expense.[10]

Social Darwinism helped to rationalise the rapid imperial expansion of the later nineteenth century. 'Natural selection', imperialists claimed, showed that races with the greater intelligence and strength ('the fittest') would have superiority over the others. In 1896, F. C. Selous declared that Africans had no other choice than that of either accepting the laws of the Europeans or dying. It was, he explained, 'the inexorable law which Darwin has aptly termed the "survival of the fittest" '.[11]

The process of reconciling religious faith with social, economic, political and cultural change became no less complicated in the twentieth century, not least because new scientific theories began to challenge the very empirical basis upon which nineteenth-century science had been based. Heralds of this uncertain future included the Austrian Sigmund Freud (1865–1939) and the German Albert Einstein, who was born in Ulm in 1879, though he studied in Switzerland, and who first published his theory of relativity in four papers in 1905. Freud trained as a doctor and from the 1880s became interested in psychology. A personal crisis in his life in the 1890s (provoked partly by the anti-Semitism which pervaded much of Viennese society at the time, for Freud was Jewish) led him to explore the nature of repressed sexuality and the subconscious. The fruit of this work was *The Interpretation of Dreams*, first published in 1900. Freud argued that subconscious impulses and emotions influenced people's behaviour. This implied that the human intellect (upon which much of nineteenth-century liberal, scientific and positivist thinking had based its beliefs) was actually weak. Such ideas divided the scientific world, not least between those who still believed that science could explain everything and those who no longer did. They also did nothing to close the apparent chasm between science and religion. As in the eighteenth century, there remained a breach between what Strauss called 'our modern world' and the more traditional beliefs which rested on faith.[12] Yet by the early twentieth century, the schism was more significant, not least because scientific ideas reached a much wider audience than before. Alongside the widespread influence of social theories such as positivism and Marxism, Darwin's theory of evolution and Freud's foundation of psychoanalysis helped to shape a more secular world-view, one in which God was a very distant figure, if He was present at all. The idea of humanity being alone in an empty universe, subject only to the brutally competitive laws of nature and aggressive human impulses, was a frightening prospect. The 'Madman' penned by the German writer Friedrich Nietzsche proclaims: 'God is dead. God remains dead. And we have killed him. How shall we, the murderers of all murderers, comfort ourselves?'[13]

Education and Literacy

The expansion of education and, more specifically, the role of the state within it, advanced secular values. In France, republicans firmly believed, with Jean Macé, that 'he who controls the school, controls the world'[14] and, under the Third Republic, the Ferry laws of the early 1880s replaced the teaching of the catechism with 'moral and civic education' in primary schools. By the law of 1886, teaching staff at primary schools for boys were to be laicised within five years, although nuns teaching at girls' schools were only to be replaced gradually, on death or retirement. In 1901 the law on associations was vigorously interpreted to ban all religious orders not authorised by the state. This led to the closure of thousands of schools, so that while in 1886–7 a third of all primary pupils were taught in Catholic schools, they accounted for only a fifth on the eve of the First World War. Secularisation did not, of course, occur without a struggle. Catholic areas such as Brittany and Flanders saw communities defending religious education by establishing private schools and so avoiding the provisions of the Ferry laws. In Germany, Bismarck's *Kulturkampf* finished with a compromise with the Catholic Church. In Italy, Catholics were angered by the 1911 law which removed control of primary education from the municipalities, for in regions which they controlled, like Venetia, they had been able to use their influence to control the curriculum and teaching appointments. In Russia, both church and Ministry of Education schools sought to promote religion, morality and obedience (an 1884 rule for the church schools described their purpose as being 'to uphold the teachings of the Orthodox faith and Christian morality among the people, and to impart useful information'.[15] The ministry's 1897 programme dedicated nine out of twenty-four hours of schooling a week to religion and church Slavonic, alongside reading, writing and arithmetic. Most *zemstva* schools, responding to the demands of parents, also provided suitably religious content in their curricula, but where they fell under liberal influence they were also more likely to add science, history and geography. It would be an exaggeration to say that the advance of education encouraged religious scepticism, but it certainly allowed secular ideas to pervade rural life. Under the Third Republic, the French village schoolteacher became the missionary of laic, republican values, in competition with the village priest for the hearts and minds of the community.

Advances towards mass literacy helped to shape this secular mind. Cultural developments in the later nineteenth century challenged old certainties and ways of life. The expansion in literacy helped to forge a mass culture based on the printed word but, in the process, undermined traditional forms of leisure where oral tradition predominated, such as the rural French *veillées*. The intellectual and political elites certainly fretted about the consequences; they feared the demoralising effects of popular literature, theatre and the cinema (the 'moving picture' was developed by the brothers Louis and Auguste Lumière in 1895). Liberals worried that cultural 'trash' prevented the forging of a national culture inspired by the great works of classical literature, art and music.

Yet the phenomenon of mass culture was partially a result of the efforts of governments and churches themselves. A concern to equip citizens with basic literacy and numeracy skills arose from the 1860s for several reasons. Economic growth, particularly with the application of new technology and the expansion of the market, required larger numbers of people who could read, write and calculate. Mass conscription demanded some literacy from recruits, particularly when the period of active service was reduced, which meant that they could no longer be taught 'on the job'. In Russia, only 21 per cent of raw recruits could read in 1874, but by 1913 that proportion had climbed to 68 per cent. In countries with universal male suffrage, such as France and Germany, the state and political parties had an interest in stressing the importance of education, because universal schooling allowed them to spread a homogeneous, 'national' message. Literacy gave opposition messages a better chance of reaching the population, but those who controlled the schools and the curriculum – the Church and the State – had a head start. Mass democracy would not have emerged in the way it did without mass literacy, but nor would the totalitarian regimes of the twentieth century.

The great expansion in education took place at primary level, where basic literacy skills and national values were instilled. Plans and ideas for universal education had been circulating, of course, since the eighteenth century, and much earlier in some European countries. Sweden had been one of the leaders, with a universal system legislated in 1842, but elsewhere governments were reluctant to commit to the cost – and frequently the conflict – until later. In France, the Guizot law of 1833 ordered all communes to establish primary schools, but these were neither compulsory nor free. None the less, in practice by the early 1860s almost every commune had a school, and fees were waived for pupils from poorer families (in the 1850s and 1860s the proportion of pupils admitted free hovered around 40 per cent). However, as schooling was not yet compulsory, some six hundred thousand children in 1863 did not attend, and illiteracy stood at 39 per cent in 1866. France had to wait for the laws sponsored by Jules Ferry under the Third Republic making primary education free (1881) and compulsory (1882). In England, the system was typically introduced gradually, with elementary schools made universal in 1870, compulsory ten years later and free in 1886, though in Scotland the primary school had long been the responsibility of each parish. In Russia, the state did not establish a universal system of education, but the *zemstva*, the Orthodox Church, the Ministry of Education and the peasants themselves vied with each other to establish local schools. At the end of the 1870s there were 22,770 primary schools in Russia and by the outbreak of the First World War there were 108,280. Owing to the political and economic importance of basic education, the state began to assume a greater role than before. In Sweden, the government took over responsibility for paying all teachers in 1875. In Russia, the Ministry of Education ran only 964 of the primary schools in 1894, but by 1914 it controlled 21,996. This occurred at the expense of the 'peasant schools' run by the village communes. In Italy, truancy and the wide regional diversity in primary education led to a 1911 law which shifted control of schools from the municipalities to a schools council, half elected and half appointed by the government.

Yet the expansion in education was not simply imposed from above by State and Church. It was also shaped by the demands of local communities whose people were moved to acquire literacy and numeracy for a whole stock of reasons. Trade unions encouraged literacy to enhance working standards and to empower their members in their dealings with employers. Technological developments placed a premium on workers who could read, write and calculate. Literacy was driven by the expansion of the market, rising standards of living and the precocious emergence of mass consumption. The expansion of the state, which published laws and regulations, the introduction of national service in the army and the development of social security all made literacy more important to people than before. Where conscription was imposed, literate recruits were often better off than the illiterates. According to the 1874 Russian army reform, recruits who had passed through primary school with a certificate would serve only four years on active duty, while others would have to survive six years. The spread of urban culture into the countryside, involving the simple pleasure of reading cheap, mass-produced novelettes and newspapers, was often reason enough to learn how to read. As a child in the 1870s, Maxim Gorky, who would become one of Russia's greatest writers, was taught to read by his mother. He was reluctant until his fellow pupils at school scoffed at his taste for Russian folk stories ('Fairy tales are rubbish! But *Robinson Crusoe* – there's a story for you!'). Gorky stole a rouble from his stepfather (the banknote was hidden inside a book by Alexandre Dumas) and bought Daniel Defoe's epic.[16] As David Vincent writes, 'a function of the historian is to remind a culture which now is excited by a means of communication only if it is attached to a plug, of the sheer thrill of first encountering the printed page'.[17]

The establishment of thousands of Russian peasant schools in the decades after 1861, paid for by the communes, reflected a genuine popular desire for education. In the 1880s an estimated 300,000–400,000 pupils attended such schools, which numbered somewhere between fifteen and twenty thousand. In France an 1864 government report claimed that in the impoverished department of the Basses-Alpes 'it is in the poorest areas that education is sought after with the most eagerness'.[18] For many parents, literacy and numeracy offered their children an escape from a barren existence. Poverty, however, could equally be a bar to schooling, even when it became free and compulsory. Poorer families could ill afford the loss of an extra pair of hands at home and at work. In 1881 an Austrian journal warned that compulsory schooling (introduced into Austria in the late 1860s) was causing resentment from the peasant who 'may not use his children for light field-work until they are fourteen' and who then had to hand them over for military service.[19] In parts of France the rhythm of schooling had to follow the cycles of the seasons – schools emptied during the summer in particular – to allow children to help their parents work the land and to engage in seasonal occupations so vital to the family economy. The idea of regular attendance with a precise leaving age sat awkwardly with rural habits.[20] For older generations, schooling was irrelevant or even a danger to the patriarchal society of the village; in Russia it was frequently the elderly who opposed the establishment of a school. Urban areas, too, had their absentees; the unskilled tended to keep their children away, while the better-paid skilled workers and artisans were more likely to value education. In 1882, therefore, the Third Republic introduced the *certificat d'études primaires* and ten years later it became compulsory for any child working in manufacturing (though not agriculture) to have such a certificate. Absenteeism declined markedly, although it still remained high in poorer areas, such as the 13th *arrondissement* in Paris, where it stood at 20 per cent in 1894. Germany and the Scandinavian countries were the most successful in imposing compulsion, but elsewhere attendance could be sparse. In Spain in 1897, 40 years after the Moyano law legislated for a universal system of primary education, an estimated 2.5 million children of school age were still not attending. In Russia, which had no compulsory system before the 1917 Revolution, about half of all children aged between eight and eleven were not at a school in 1914. In any case, educational opportunities were all too brief. An Italian law of 1904 ordered larger villages to provide six years of compulsory education, but in practice the most a rural child could expect was three years in a primary school. After 1882, French children were meant to attend school from the ages of six to thirteen, but poorer children were often removed by parents anxious to have them working. Prussia, however, had steamed ahead; as early as 1864, 90 per cent of all males aged between 14 and 64 had received eight years of schooling.

Moreover, uniform, national 'systems' of education did not really emerge. Liberals may have hoped, in principle, that universal education and literacy would act as a cultural cement which would bind together all classes and ensure social stability. Yet in practice bourgeois and nobles alike were worried by the implications: a common culture and universal literacy would undercut their claims to social and political leadership. From a government point of view, it was all very well for the masses to be able to read, write and do arithmetic, but it was important that their education did not go too far. As Robert Lowe, a British Whig, put it in 1862, 'we do not profess to give these children an education that will raise them above their station and business in life . . . but to give them an education that may fit them for that business'.[21] In many countries, therefore, primary and secondary education were kept apart as two separate systems; a pupil did not necessarily progress seamlessly from the former to the latter. Secondary schools were originally intended for the elites. In the German *Gymnasien*, the French *lycées*, the Italian *ginnasi* and *licei* and the misnamed British 'public' schools, the main curricular emphasis was on the classics. This frequently reflected the demands of middle-class and aristocratic parents, for whom a classical education was a sign of polish and social status and a preparation for entry into state service and the liberal professions. In 1866, *lycée* pupils at a prize-giving in Rouen were told that 'in a country where the political edifice rests on universal suffrage . . . power is reserved to those whom a strong classical education has raised above their fellow-men'.[22] Until the Ferry Laws of the 1880s, when schools were to inculcate explicitly secular, republican values, French primary education aimed to instil some national culture and to encourage obedience among the masses. This was why, until the 1880s, most regimes were fairly relaxed about the persistence of clerical influence in primary schools, but not in the *lycées*, from where the state drew its officials. The Prussian *Gymnasien* followed a classical curriculum, which was also reflected in their monopoly of entrance into both the universities and training for the liberal professions. In one of the British public schools in 1870, 17 out of 22 hours of teaching were devoted to the classics.

For all its elitism, the social mobility offered by the French system was broad. While the *lycées* charged fees, they were low enough that by 1848 about half of the population could afford secondary education for one of their children. While the great Parisian *lycées* were still virtually monopolised by the elites, in the 1860s half of all graduates from the provincial secondary schools were sons of peasants, shopkeepers, white- and blue-collar workers and soldiers. Scions of landowners and liberal professionals were more likely to share classes with sons of peasants and artisans in France than in schools across the Channel or the Rhine. In Germany, the social division was reflected in the fact that, in the last quarter of the nineteenth century, 50 per cent of all students in the *Gymnasien* had fathers who were professionals, civil servants or landowners. Children of industrial and commercial entrepreneurs made up a growing proportion of the rest, but the sons of artisans and workers were twice as likely to go to the more technical *Oberrealschulen* than the *Gymnasien*. In Italy, the classical curricula of the *ginnasi*, *licei* and the universities were accused of breeding a class of parasites, an oversized 'intellectual proletariat' of lawyers (of whom 1700 were graduating each year) who were unable to find jobs. Alongside them, however, technical institutes and, from 1910, the *liceo moderno*, expanded, emphasising science, mathematics and modern languages. Most Italian workers who wanted more than just a basic education were, however, obliged to nourish their hunger for knowledge by joining one of the 51 (in 1906) 'popular universities', or continuing education classes run by the universities and by workers' organisations.[23] Polish primary schools were very basic, intended for peasants and the poorer urban working class, while the secondary schools were consciously shaped for the sons of nobles and the middle class. Consequently, the nobles made up 85 per cent of the pupils in secondary schools between 1864 and 1904, while the peasants provided only 5–8 per cent. These figures, however, hide a wider schooling among the general population, as they relate only to the schools supported by the Russian Tsarist regime; there also existed a clandestine educational network.

The prevailing attitude towards women's education in the mid-nineteenth century was, at most, that women were the best teachers of children, so some basic education was certainly required. Such learning, however, was to encourage the domestic, nurturing and maternal instincts of girls; it was not intended to empower them for work or public life. While the usefulness of literacy was increasingly recognised amongst peasants and workers, it was considered much less necessary for women than for men, not least because a girl was expected to be encumbered with domestic duties from a very early age. A Russian peasant responded to one investigator in the 1860s: 'Why should I teach a girl to read and write? She won't be a soldier, she won't be a shop assistant, and a peasant woman has no time to busy herself with reading books the way the lords do.'[24]

These attitudes were reflected in the state's treatment of girls' education, which lagged behind provision for boys. In 1842 the administration of the department of the Nord in France explained that all that was required of a country girl was 'how to sew, read, write and reckon . . . a firm grasp of religious education and . . . a perfect understanding of all those manual skills which might be useful to her'.[25] Official opinion in France opposed co-education because of moral anxieties about mixing the sexes, particularly when it involved male teachers instructing girls. The Falloux law of 1850 made a separate girls' school compulsory in all but the smallest communes. As was probably intended, the teaching here was usually taken over by the Catholic religious orders, because religious education was seen as particularly apt for girls, who would nurture their children accordingly.[26] Yet the Catholicisation of French girls' education was challenged by republicans in the later 1860s. In 1867 Victor Duruy, Napoleon III's education minister, enacted a law improving conditions for lay women teachers and increasing the number of secular girls' primary schools. Under his anticlerical ministry (1863–9), the proportion of girls taught by religious orders was almost halved (from 60 per cent). Duruy and the republicans could agree that if women were meant to instil morality in their children, it would be a secular form of virtue.

There were practical reasons for educating middle-class women beyond primary level. In Russia, the government understood that women could play an important role in teaching, medicine and commerce, although it was very careful to circumscribe the educational opportunities. In 1876 a statute laying down the curriculum for women permitted female technical schools and university-level courses. In France, there were no *lycées* for women until after 1880. Until then, middle-class girls were sent to lay boarding-schools (*pensionnats*) or to educational convents. One of Duruy's proposals in 1867, to arrange *lycée* courses for girls, was met with horror by the Catholic clergy, who feared that women would be exposed to freethinkers and turned away from 'Christian and French womanhood'. The *baccalauréat*, the key to entering the liberal professions, was denied to the vast majority of women, who were not allowed to study the classics. Most had to pursue the *brevet*, the teaching qualification for primary teachers, even if they had no plans for a career in that profession. In Britain, Cambridge University allowed women to sit its exams leading to school certificates in 1863. The Endowed Schools Act of 1869 allowed funds to be diverted to establish separate grammar schools for girls and 90 such institutions had been established by the end of the century.

German middle-class prejudices against girls receiving a fuller education were broken down as it became wiser for daughters to receive some vocational training as an economic safety net. As one Prussian official rather bluntly informed his daughters, 'You are not pretty, you have no money, so marriage is out of the question', so learning for a profession was their only option. For such young women, education beyond the higher schools was not easily available until 1893–4, when courses were opened in Berlin, Karlsruhe and Leipzig to prepare women for the *Abitur*, the diploma offered by the elite *Gymnasien*. The founder of the Berlin course was Helene Lange, who had waged an arduous petitioning campaign since 1887 and who had reacted to the hostile reception by creating the *Realkurse* in late 1889, two-year courses for women which covered science, economics, mathematics, history, modern languages and Latin. This enabled German women to qualify for acceptance as medical and dental students in the United States and the Universities of Zurich and Bern. In 1899 Baden became the first German state to allow women formally to matriculate at its universities, followed by Bavaria in 1903 and Württemberg in 1904. Prussia resisted until 1909, after which the rest of the German states could scarcely hold out. By 1911–12, women still only made up 4.8 per cent of all enrolments at the German universities. In Britain, University College London had led the way in 1878 when it went co-educational, and the University of London allowed women to take degrees. The Scottish universities awarded degrees to women from the 1890s, and Trinity College Dublin from 1904. By the outbreak of the First World War, women accounted for one in five students at British universities. In France by 1914, 10 per cent of students at the University of Paris were women and they first entered the great teacher-training institution, the *École Normale Supérieure*, in 1910. In Austria–Hungary, women were allowed to register in the arts and medical faculties in 1897 and 1900 respectively, but law and technical institutes were barred to them until 1919. Russian women were allowed only to audit courses after the 1905 Revolution. Even this advance was reversed in 1908, although the special university-level courses were allowed to award degrees in 1911. In all, there were

34,000 women enrolled in higher education in Russia by 1914 compared with 93,000 men, so that women made up more than a third of students.[27]

As education expanded, so European society advanced towards mass literacy. Literacy needs careful definition: in 1886 a study of 50 million Germans demonstrated different forms of literacy, ranging from the 20 million who could handle commonly available rural almanacs and religious books, such as the Bible and hymnals, to the 10 million who could grapple with 'demanding literary subjects'. Essentially, the survey identified gradations in the range between nominal literacy (the ability to make sense of the written word) and functional literacy, the additional capacity to string sentences together in writing and to engage with ideas and problems. A reliable gauge of functional literacy is the volume of correspondence, which was first measured by the Universal Postal Union founded in 1874. The volume of items sent through the mail increased impressively up to 1913, from 3 billion letters and postcards a year to 25 billion – or 50,000 items each minute. Paradoxically, just as most European states were beginning to triumph in their wars on illiteracy, so a new form of communication was allowing long-distance transmission of the spoken voice: Alexander Graham Bell invented the telephone in 1876. Yet the spread of telecommunications (including the telegraph, which had been invented much earlier; its first commercial use was in 1842) did not endanger the dominance of letter-writing as the preferred form of contact between distant friends, relatives and associates. In 1913 there were still 100 letters for every 21 telephone calls; only in 1972 did the use of the phone outstrip the post. Use of the telephone was not to the exclusion of literacy anyway; it was first in Sweden (1899) and then in Denmark (1909) where the number of telephone calls first overtook the use of letters. These were two countries which were approaching universal literacy.[28]

In 1800, only in Scandinavia, Scotland, Geneva and parts of England, France and Germany were the populations beginning to approach mass (though far from universal) literacy. As one travelled away from these areas, high levels of literacy could be found amongst the middle class and aristocracy. The closer one journeyed towards the fringes of southern and eastern Europe, the more such skills could not be taken for granted, even among the nobility, with Russia, the Habsburg monarchy, south-eastern Europe, southern Italy, Spain and Portugal all scoring very poor marks, with literacy levels of less than 25 per cent. The first half of the century witnessed a gradual change, particularly in countries with already good standards; by the 1860s, Prussia (which was at the top of this particular class during the nineteenth century) was approaching universal literacy. Those countries which had struggled in 1800 were still doing so in 1860. Spain was facing an illiteracy rate of over 80 per cent among men and 90 per cent among women, while in Russian-ruled

Poland, 90 per cent of the population was illiterate, although the figure was better in urban centres (79 per cent in 1864). In the last three decades of the nineteenth century, illiteracy was determinedly squeezed out across much of Europe. In the west and the north by 1900, literacy levels reached more than 90 per cent, although in Belgium and Ireland 25 per cent of men could still not sign their name. In the states of south-eastern Europe, literacy ranged from 12 per cent to 39 per cent, mostly among urban workers and rural artisans rather than the peasantry – but this was an improvement on the earlier part of the century. By the time of the Revolution, literacy in Russia had reached 70 per cent in the larger cities, but it was also growing in the countryside. In 1885 an approving observer commented on one village: 'You go along the street and what do you see? Now in one cottage and then in another, a little lamp burns on the table . . . and at the table an adolescent boy or girl sits reading a book, and all the family members listen. Neighbours also come by to hear a bit.'[29]

As this evidence suggests, there was an uneven spread of literacy between generations. The relatively high levels of illiteracy recorded in Ireland and Belgium in 1900 obscure important nuances: the schooled younger generations were literate, while their grandparents were less so. Across Europe, the urban centres were more likely to have high levels of literacy than the countryside; in 1871 male literacy was near-universal in Berlin at 98.8 per cent, but in rural West Prussia it stood at 66.8 per cent. The growth of national education systems did much to break down the differences between town and country. Towards the end of the century the literacy gap between the genders was also narrowing. Whereas around 1860 in the more advanced regions male literacy had outstripped that of women by 10–25 per cent (a reflection of a wider neglect of girls' education), by 1914 there was a difference of only a few percentage points.

The expansion of education and literacy had a 'homogenising' effect on society by making a national culture more easily imposed and accepted. The press played an important role in this development. Advances in papermaking, printing (the introduction of the rotary press) and distribution (by rail) allowed publishers to produce larger, cheaper runs which made books, pamphlets and newspapers more affordable than they had been at the opening of the century. In relation to the wages of rural labourers, Parisian newspapers became cheaper: with 1910 taken as the index of 100, the real cost of newspapers declined from 821 in 1795 to 131 in 1889.[30] In Italy from the turn of the century, dailies began to carry sports pages, and newspapers such as the *Giornale d'Italia*, which carried reviews, short stories and extracts from novels, had a wide, national influence over cultural attitudes and taste. Much of the press reported not only on politics but also on sport or fashion, which may have stimulated popular aspirations to imitate bourgeois, urban culture, breaking down regional, class and urban–rural differences.[31] The provincial press was especially important in France: while total daily circulation increased from 1.5 million in 1875 to 12.5 million in 1914, the provincial dailies increased from half a million to 4 million. These papers carried stories which were first gleaned from the Parisian periodicals but which, with the development of the telegraph from the 1850s and the growth of news agencies, reported on national and international events more directly, exposing their readers to worldwide affairs. News – especially the more sensational stories – began to replace traditional forms of conversation, such as folk tales. An observer in Gascony in 1910 recorded that peasants naturally discussed the weather and crops as they always had done, but they also talked about politics.[32] With the spread of a 'national' culture, rural dialects and provincial idioms were heard less across the counters of village cafés. The French state saw schools as a key to imposing French as the universal language and to instilling a sense of national identity amongst the peasantry. Etienne Bertin, the narrator in Emile Guillaumin's 1904 story of a sharecropper's life, *The Life of a Simple Man*, swaps stories with his grandson, François, sometime in the 1880s. While the ageing Etienne tells fairy tales, the boy repeats the stories he has learned and read about at school: 'he talked of kings and queens, of Joan of Arc, Bayard, Richelieu, Robespierre, of crusades and wars and massacres'.[33] Literacy and education were not the only agencies of cultural integration. In a seminal work on France before the First World War, Eugen Weber argued that 'peasants' were turned into 'Frenchmen' by a combination of factors: roads, railways, expanding markets, military service, education and cultural change figured heavily, and his evidence suggests that the full weight of these integrating factors was not felt in some areas until the very eve of the First World War.[34] Nineteenth-century observers would have agreed with his assessment of the factors but not with his timescale. In 1864 a report on education confidently predicted that *patois*, at least, would soon die out thanks to a combination of education and the railways, which 'will be the best teachers of the French and will complete the work'.[35] Weber's work tends to look at less economically advanced areas of France, such as the Massif Central, Brittany and the Pyrenees, and so it has been criticised for drawing an overly-pessimistic picture of peasant backwardness and, above all, of country folk's lack of politicisation.[36] It is perhaps best to see, as Peter McPhee suggests, 'change . . . occurring everywhere in rural France but varying in timing, nature and intensity according to region, class and gender'.[37]

It is certainly true that the extent of cultural homogeneity should not be exaggerated. Everywhere in Europe, the rapid expansion of a more uniform culture of taste and interests did not happen simultaneously, in all regions or among all social groups. In Austria, an article published in

1909 in a peasant newspaper criticised rural women who wore city clothes. A 'peasant's daughter' sent a robust letter in reply, demanding, 'Can't we buy the things the people have in the cities?' The woman was staking her claim to share in a modern, urbanised culture. Yet the editors' response is also significant: the author of the original article, they explained, lived in a region where most people still wore traditional peasant dress, and he did not want to see this lost.[38] In Russia, the expanding reading public was bombarded with a deluge of printed works, which doubled between 1887 and 1895 and more than tripled up to 1914. More frequent exposure to a greater range of books and periodicals encouraged a wider outlook. Yet in most rural communities the 'urban' culture represented by the printed word, new fashions and the manners of young people returning from the cities lived in an uneasy and sometimes violent co-existence with the communal, rural values which some villagers (frequently the older generations) tried to defend. Even in the most industrialised regions of Germany, such as the Rhineland, working-class life was not entirely assimilated into the dominant culture promoted by the state or even by the Social Democrats. The Social Democrats stressed respectability, education and self-improvement (hence their promotion of libraries, leisure clubs and cultural associations). Yet many workers responded to the pressures of industrial life by falling back on their own subculture, often involving plenty of alcohol to 'lubricate' working-class recreation. As the workers' best defence against state repression, however, the labour movement did make inroads into working-class culture and, in the process, larger numbers of German workers absorbed the mores of 'respectability' and self-improvement stressed by the SPD.[39]

Cultural homogeneity was precisely the goal of European liberals and conservatives alike across Europe, as they saw in it a means of integrating workers and peasants into the social and political order. Yet it was hard to get workers and peasants to open the 'right' books. In the twilight of the Second Empire, the French republican historian Jules Michelet, whose works aspired to galvanise social unity by giving all French people a founding myth in the Revolution and popular democracy, despaired of ever being able to communicate with the masses.[40] This did not mean that a homogeneous culture would not emerge; it was just that it would not take the shape desired by liberals or, for that matter, conservatives.

It was one thing to be literate, but what one did with the skills was a different matter. Political or edifying themes did not always attract a high readership. In Germany, even the borrowing records of SPD reading rooms showed that working-class readers preferred fiction ranging from the German classics to mass-produced pulp, although works on history, religion and Darwinism were also popular. In France, the most popular newspaper was the *Petit Parisien*, which offered its readers news, but of the scandalous, racy or violent kind – 'human interest' stories with a diet of sex, crime and tragedy. The same could be said for the explosion of popular literature witnessed across Europe. German entrepreneurs grew rich on printing series of what in Britain were called 'penny novelettes' – cheap pamphlets of between 30 and 80 pages in length, each with a plot-driven story and an eye-catching, colour illustration on the front cover. This phenomenon of cheap popular literature was not new to Europe: French people had consumed the *Bibliothèque Bleue* in the eighteenth century, while in Germany there was a long-standing tradition of the 'folk booklet'. In Russia, the *lubki* were works of popular literature taking their name from the printed pictures which had been distributed by pedlars among the illiterate peasantry. What was new was that the publications were aimed at a larger and increasingly urban market. Stories were updated for modern tastes and they reached a wider readership, not only because of higher literacy rates but also because of the commercial prospects offered by the industrial economy. Large print runs kept costs down, while people could buy pulp fiction from railway kiosks, tobacconists, stationers and street vendors. The material was not meant to be edifying, educational or political, but escapist. Stories about the 'Wild West', adventure and crime were standard fare for the urban working class in Germany and Russia. This sort of reading material was later recalled by an embarrassed German socialist, Otto Gotsche: 'I can still see before my eyes the terrifying and bloodthirsty pictures and the screaming titles as well . . . Such trash passed through our hands by the dozens of copies. It was terrible!'[41]

Ronald Fullerton has suggested that the consumption of pulp fiction in Germany encouraged 'passivity' among the people and sapped their desire 'to shape their own popular culture'. It is certainly true that the political and social implications of a growing reading public were not necessarily revolutionary. Yet it may well have been that working-class culture also influenced elite cultural life. From the 1850s the British music hall, for example, was a form of entertainment rooted in working-class culture, but middle-class people attended the concerts. In Glasgow in the 1880s, university students were reported to attend 'surreptitiously', but towards the end of the century the gala openings of music halls were accompanied by the glitter of people of 'quality'. While not representative of audiences at normal performances, it does suggest that the relationship between working-class and bourgeois culture may at least have been ambiguous, with middle-class culture as likely to adopt working-class forms as the latter was to be imposed upon by the former.[42] Moreover, the fact that working-class people attended popular theatre or read pulp fiction did not mean that they were passive over political and social issues. Russian peasants did not always pick up the propaganda produced by the Tsarist regime, but sometimes that of the revolutionary opposition. In 1906 one Socialist Revolutionary claimed that after the excitement of the 1905 Revolution a group of peasants continued to gather to read newspapers and discuss politics.[43] That such claims could be made with any credibility at all demonstrates the plausibility of the idea that Russian peasants were being politicised with the help of the printed word. The popularised versions of Darwin read by German workers might have carried implicit or explicit social or political messages. In the 1860s, popular works in the French public libraries sponsored by the republican *Ligue de l'enseignement* included biographies, popular science, travel, practical advice on industry and agriculture, novels and history; workers did not read pulp fiction all the time. Under the Third Republic, many French readers may have purchased newspapers primarily for the sports pages, but these stories sat alongside others dealing with politics. Popular culture was not so much a sphere upon which conservative, middle-class values imposed themselves, rather an arena in which conflicting values vied for attention and acceptance.

Amongst the pulp fiction, the sport and the fashion, the wider public sphere also encouraged more people to relate their own problems to national issues and so to think in political terms. It certainly encouraged the spread of radical ideas. In France, the socialist newspaper *L'Humanité* enjoyed a circulation of 88,000 by 1914 (though this was tiny compared with the 1.4 million claimed by the *Petit Parisien*). In Russia, the St Petersburg *Gazeta Kopeika* (the first newspaper to sell at one kopek, which became a model for other Russian mass dailies) was published between 1908 and 1917. It reached its peak in 1910, with a circulation of a quarter of a million. The *Gazeta Kopeika*, which seems to have aimed at a mainly working-class and peasant readership, dissociated itself from the revolutionary left, but none the less prided itself on its 'progressive' views. It championed the cause of Mendel Beilis, a Jew who, in a *cause célèbre* in 1910, was acquitted of ritual murder. When celebrating its second anniversary, it proclaimed its purpose as acting as 'the heart of social conscience', demanding tolerance for the Empire's national and religious minorities.

Yet mass culture in Europe was not an onward march towards a more tolerant society, but a place of fierce competition between different social groups and political organisations seeking to make their ideas prevail. In 1867 the French Senate received and debated a petition from conservatives protesting against the opening of a library in the industrial town of Saint-Étienne because it would stock books penned by such dangerous writers as Voltaire, Rousseau, Proudhon and Michelet. This assault and other clerical demands like it were rejected. A panic about the alarming effects of mass literacy occurred in Germany after 1900. Conservatives, alarmed that 'trashy literature' was sapping the moral fibre of the youth, organised associations (such as the bluntly-named 'People United Against Trash in Print and Literature') to publish more wholesome reading material and to organise boycotts and demonstrations. They succeeded in persuading the local authorities in Hamburg, Leipzig and Württemberg to ban the sale of pamphlet literature. Meanwhile, trade unions and socialists expanded their own provision of Social Democratic libraries and reading rooms, shadowed by Catholic groups who did the same. In Russia, observers around 1900 were vexed by what they saw as a breakdown of traditional society and were alarmed by the moral vacuum which seemed to be emerging. The younger generation of peasants who had absorbed urban, individualistic values were thought to be undermining the solidarity of the peasant community, and responsible for what contemporaries called 'hooliganism' – crime, gambling, alcoholism and debauchery. These anxieties were held by conservatives as well as revolutionary populists, whose socialism was based on an idealised vision of the peasant commune.[44] Just as 'progressive' ideas threaded their way through the growing, amorphous body of mass culture, so too did more authoritarian, ultranationalist impulses. Popular culture provided a home for right-wing demagogues no less than it did for socialism.

Part IV

The Emergence of Mass Politics, 1879–1914

14 Towards Democracy? Feminism, Anarchism, Socialism

> The monarchy is disintegrating while still alive; it is doomed! . . . This era no longer wants us! This era wants to create independent nation-states! People no longer believe in God. The new religion is nationalism. Nations no longer go to church. They go to national associations. . . . The Emperor of Austria–Hungary must not be abandoned by God. But God *has* abandoned him![1]

The theme of decline pervades Joseph Roth's gloomy and poignant 1932 novel, *The Radetzky March*. The story follows the Slovenian Trotta family, who loyally serve Emperor Francis Joseph from one generation to the next, but, even as 1914 approaches, their world is already decaying. Flesh-and-blood contemporaries could not shake off a similar sense of decadence; the French writer Albert Robida wrote in 1888, 'nearly all centuries end badly, ours appears to follow the common law'. For Robida, the malaise stemmed from the agonies and stresses of industrial society; the age, he warned, would choke itself 'in an ingestion of iron and steel and chemical products'.[2] Robida's contemporaries across Europe looked anxiously at the destructive capacities of technology, at the emergence of mass culture, at the red and black flags flown by working-class militants, at the dark forces of ultra-nationalism and authoritarianism and at tensions in international relations and saw in them dangers not only to the political order but also to society itself. Some historians have seen the era before 1914 as one quivering on the edge of catastrophe. In his classic study of Britain between 1906 and 1914, George Dangerfield argues that a combination of interwoven political and social crises brought the British Isles to the very brink of 'such extreme disorder that nobody made much pretence any more of being able to correct it'. Domestic disaster for Britain was only averted by the outbreak of the First World War, which 'animated and united every one of her warring particles' with 'an almost incredible vigour'.[3]

Yet when people looked back at the decades before the charnel-house of the First World War, they called them, nostalgically, the *Belle Époque*: a period of stability, certainty, comfort and creativity, spiced with a touch of sensuality. In fact, contemporary fears that the old order was doomed and later nostalgia for the *Belle Époque* are two sides of the same European coin. The improvements in standards of living for many people in the later nineteenth century stimulated the emergence of mass culture and a more open civil society, with all its excitement and uncertainties. 'Democratisation' has been identified as a theme for the period from the 1870s until 1914.[4] In 1880 only a handful of states had universal male suffrage, including France, Germany, Bulgaria, Greece and Switzerland. By 1914, others, including Spain, Belgium, Russia, Finland, Romania, Norway and Italy, had joined them, but the extent of the process should not be exaggerated. Other states, such as Britain, expanded the electorate but not to all adult males, while all political systems operated to ensure that power at the centre remained with the elites. Europe was characterised less by democracy than by parliamentary government, which is not the same thing. By 1914 all European states had some form of parliamentary rule, and that included the formerly autocratic Russian Empire. Modern parliamentary government was more widespread in Europe between 1905 and 1917 than at any time in the two centuries between the French Revolution and the Revolutions of 1989–91. Women, though allowed to vote in local elections in Britain (from 1869 in some cases) and in the Habsburg monarchy, were fully enfranchised only in Finland (1906) and Norway (1907).

Feminism and Women's Emancipation

The legal position of women was enhanced in a variety of ways in the later nineteenth century. Divorce was legalised, though often with severe restrictions, in England and Wales in 1857 and in France in 1884.[5] The German law code of 1900 made divorce harder, but women were no longer legally bound to 'obedience' towards their husbands or fathers. From 1912, unmarried French mothers or their children were allowed to sue fathers for financial support. Women's property rights were also gradually enhanced. Wives were allowed to hold on to their earnings from 1870 in England and Wales, 1900 in Germany and 1907 in France. Two years later, French women were given a legal say in the disposal of family property. Women's rights were therefore inching their way towards equality with those of men, but otherwise the overall subordination of women to men in almost every conceivable way was not reversed.

Gender inequalities reflected the social attitudes of the time, particularly the doctrine of 'separate spheres' and the 'sexual double standard'. In turn, these social mores help to explain why women's political rights remained so heavily circumscribed before 1914. The ideology of 'separate spheres' was tied to the view that women were by nature domestic creatures, while men were more attuned to public life and to work. In 1892 the French republican, Jules Simon, asked, 'What is man's vocation? It is to be a good citizen. And woman's? To be a good wife and a good mother.'[6] In Russia, the attitude was summed up by the secret police: 'Can a woman be a good mother and a good housekeeper if she spends half the day in a bureau or office filled with men?'[7] Even socialists implicitly accepted the idea of separate spheres. The German socialist ideologue August Bebel envisaged that clear gender roles would exist even in a socialist society; women would still shoulder the duty of caring for 'hearth and home'.[8] The 'sexual double standard' was based on the premise that women, as nurturing, virtuous mothers and 'angels of the hearth', were meant to be sexually pure, chaste and faithful, while men had natural urges which needed to be indulged and so their sexual adventures outside marriage might be overlooked. This double standard was enshrined in law. In France, the Napoleonic Code (until 1884) condemned a husband's adultery only if he had the brass neck to have his mistress living in his marital home, while a wife could be imprisoned wherever she might have been unfaithful. If a husband found his wife 'at it' with her lover, the law forgave him if he slaughtered her in a rage (a *crime passionnel*). The idea that women had to be chaste was not always observed among the poorer parts of society. In both France and Germany, 'concubinage' (men and women living together before marrying or without marrying at all) was common practice amongst urban workers, not least because getting married could be expensive. German authorities looked darkly upon such 'illegitimate' unions; in Brunswick, the police were empowered to arrest the offending couples.[9] In peasant Russia, both men and women ideally were chaste before marriage, though a certain amount of adolescent canoodling was tolerated or even encouraged during courtship. Yet a woman who was thought to have abandoned all sexual restraint could be subjected to public rituals of shaming: her front door marked with tar, or a window broken.[10] However, if unmarried women were meant to be chaste but virile young men had unfortunate but natural urges, then the latter would need some sexual outlet before marriage. Consequently, a minority of women – prostitutes – were sacrificed in order to preserve the virtue of the majority. The British historian W. E. H. Lecky explained in 1869 that the prostitute was in fact 'the most efficient guardian of virtue. But for her the unchallenged purity of countless happy homes would be polluted.'[11] The prostitute was seen as shamefully necessary but also as a problem, a dangerous, deviant figure who led men astray and who spread disease. These attitudes shaped official policy in states as diverse as France, Germany, Italy, Russia and Britain (where the Contagious Diseases Act operated in the 1860s). Governments condoned a regulated sex trade, tolerating brothels and subjecting the women in them to regular and degrading health checks in order to control the spread of venereal disease.

It was against these prevailing attitudes that campaigns for women's political rights struggled. In 1897 Millicent Garrett Fawcett forged a

British organisation, the National Union of Women's Suffrage Societies. Although one of its petitions gathered 30,000 signatures from working-class women, it remained primarily a middle-class movement. While these 'suffragists' took a strictly legal approach, the 'suffragettes' of the Women's Social and Political Union (WSPU), established by Emmeline Pankhurst in 1903, were more militant. Emmeline's daughter, Sylvia, mobilised women workers in the East London Federation, and the WSPU engaged in civil disobedience and then attacks on property, with the more violent acts peaking in 1912–14. The tactics of the British suffragettes appalled most French feminists, such as Maria Deraismes and Léon Richer. They were closely associated with the republican opposition to Napoleon III and so the overriding priority of their Association for the Rights of Women (1871) and the French League for the Rights of Women (1882) was the defence of the Republic itself. The socialist Hubertine Auclert grew impatient with this prevarication and in 1883 formed her own organisation, Women's Suffrage, which urged women to go on a tax strike. In 1909 the French Union for Women's Suffrage was established to forge links between all suffrage organisations and by 1914 it had 65 affiliated groups and 12,000 members. In Germany, the suffrage movement was united from the 1890s in the Union of German Women's Organisations (BDF), which campaigned not only for suffrage but also against regulated prostitution. The Italian women's emancipation movement had roots in both Catholicism and the radical left. Feminists associated with the latter formed For Women in 1898. This was followed five years later by a more moderate National Council of Italian Women and then by the Catholic Union of Women. All three organisations supported women's suffrage. In the 1905 Revolution in Russia, women became involved in political meetings and organised strikes. The liberals among them established the Union for Women's Equality, calling for legislation protecting women workers, women's health insurance and an equal share in land reform.

Prevailing attitudes conspired against giving women the right to vote in almost every country in Europe before 1914. These attitudes seem to have been shared by many European women themselves. French Catholic organisations opposed to women's suffrage dwarfed those of their feminist opponents. The Joan of Arc Federation boasted 350,000 members in the early twentieth century, and the Patriotic League of Frenchwomen had 320,000. Both aimed at 'rechristianising' France rather than pressing for the vote. On 5 July 1914 a suffrage demonstration led by Marguerite Durand rallied a mere 6000 people compared with the massive, quarter-million-strong suffragette march in London in 1908. A British anti-suffrage movement arose among women who were not always surrendered wives. In 1889 the popular writer Mrs Humphrey Ward welcomed the expansion of women's opportunities in work and education. She saw the role of women on education and poor law boards as a natural expression of their nature, but, she argued, 'the emancipating process has now reached the limits fixed by the physical constitution of women' and by the natural differences between the sexes.[12]

While facing hostility or indifference, the feminist movements were often divided over their priorities. French republican feminists accepted the argument that a premature extension of the suffrage to women would be political suicide, since women were more religious than men and so were more likely to be influenced by the Catholic Church. 'If they voted today,' Léon Richer explained in 1888, 'the Republic would not last six months.'[13] Socialists often put the class struggle before the battle for women's emancipation. In Germany, the SPD's Erfurt programme of 1891 demanded the abolition of all gender inequalities and suffrage for all citizens 'regardless of sex', yet co-operation with 'bourgeois' suffragists was sometimes rocky; August Bebel described the latter as 'enemy sisters'. Social Democrat women were to avoid contact with middle-class feminists.[14] After 1905, Russian socialists criticised the bourgeois nature of Russian feminism. Alexandra Kollontai claimed that the Union for Women's Equality was simply a capitalist tool to reform the predicament of women, allowing the existing political and social system to survive. Women workers and peasants, she urged, should join the class struggle rather than the battle for gender equality.

Social rather than political issues often seemed more pressing than the vote. In 1909 the National Council of French Women was established and grew to 100,000 members in 123 local societies. Its priorities were women's legal rights, education, working conditions, public health, temperance and prostitution. In Germany, Louise Otto-Peters founded the All German Women's Union in 1865, with an emphasis on education and work.[15] In Russia, a Women's Progressive Party was established in 1906, demanding equality in financial and work-related matters, and a more liberal divorce law. Above all, women's organisations targeted the regulated system of prostitution, as it infringed women's civil rights and entrenched the sexual double-standard. Josephine Butler led a successful charge (in 1866) against the Contagious Diseases Acts. Other European feminists tried to follow suit – a campaign in Hamburg was led by Lida Heymann in the early 1900s,[16] while trafficking in women was the subject of a special congress in St Petersburg in 1910. Feminists were, therefore, not united in their priorities or methods. Yet if suffrage campaigns were unsuccessful in most countries before 1914, the mobilisation of women around other issues, such as property, marriage, education, work and prostitution, drew hundreds of thousands of middle-class and, increasingly, working-class women into political activity, often for the first time.

Anarchism

In the half-century before the First World War, social protest evolved as food riots and machine-breaking became rarer and new methods of mobilising workers and peasants, such as trade unions, strikes and political parties, emerged. In the process, a working-class consciousness was more widely articulated. Ideologues of the left hoped that by organising the working class and the peasantry, they could forge a more egalitarian society, but they were divided over how to rally the starvelings and toilers of Europe. Some argued that revolution was the only way to destroy the old order, while others sought to work within parliamentary systems until parties representing the masses captured power by legal means. The left was also ideologically split, the most important division being between socialists and anarchists. Most anarchist movements hoped to forge some form of highly decentralised, egalitarian society. Some aimed to bring about the collapse of the established order by dramatic deeds which inspired the masses to rise and some emphasised a more classic form of revolution, while others still envisaged the bourgeois state caving in under the weight of a general strike.

This last aim was the ultimate goal of the anarcho-syndicalist movement in France, where anarchist outrages involving bomb attacks in Paris in 1893 and the assassination of President Carnot in Lyon in 1894 were the acts of only a minority of alienated intellectuals and workers. These acts provoked repressive legislation in the *lois scélérates*, but they also stirred widespread alarm and revulsion and, in the 1890s, the revolution seemed a long way off. Instead, Parisian workers fearing the erosion of their skills, mechanisation and the growth of the factory system frequently turned to another form of anarchistic thinking, which drew on the revolutionary socialism of Auguste Blanqui (who died in 1881) and the ideas of Jean Allemane. By stressing the importance of strikes, Allemanism helped to inspire the anarcho-syndicalism which gripped the labour movement from the 1890s. Anarcho-syndicalists dreamed of a general strike organised by a nationwide network of local *syndicats* (trade unions), each formed of workers in the same trade. In 1895 the *Confédération générale du travail* (CGT) was founded to encourage the affiliation of these diverse unions to one great union, and the movement gained momentum after 1900 as a result of mounting disillusion over the limits of the Third Republic's social reforms. In 1902, when its Socialist rivals were in turmoil, the CGT scored a coup when it absorbed the *Fédération des bourses*, the trade unions based since 1887 in the government-sponsored labour exchanges (*bourses du travail*). In the first years of the new century there was an annual average of 1000 work stoppages, culminating in 1906 when a general strike was planned for 1 May. The alarm generated by the industrial unrest was enough to dampen republican willingness to exert government influence on behalf of the workers. Whereas in 1900–2 Waldeck-Rousseau's Radical ministry had intervened in industrial disputes, forcing employers to make concessions, within a few years the authorities were more likely to throw their weight behind the management. The Radical prime minister, Georges Clemenceau, responded to the general strike threat in May 1906 by massing 35,000 troops in Paris and arresting the CGT's leaders. Now that the state was crushing strikes, rather than acting as mediator, the success of anarcho-syndicalism in winning concessions diminished. Consequently, working-class enthusiasm for the anarcho-syndicalist unions cooled; growth in their membership had run at a rapid 9 per cent a year between 1884 and 1907, but the rate halved thereafter. From 1910 the new leadership of the CGT accepted a need both to work within the existing social system and to co-operate with the Socialists.[17]

Syndicalism did not, however, fail only because of government repression. French union membership in general was weak; in 1906, of some seven or eight million non-agricultural workers, only 10 per cent belonged to trade unions, of whom a quarter (or around two hundred thousand) were in the CGT. Much of the labour force consisted of independent, self-employed artisans, who were unlikely to strike against themselves. Workers in smaller workshops tended to join the 'moderate' (meaning non-revolutionary) unions, which supported reformist socialism rather than anarcho-syndicalism. Moderate unions boasted the largest organisations – those of the printers, miners and railway workers. Unskilled workers were frequently uprooted peasants who protested with spontaneous, violent strikes rather than through union organisation. Where their small unions were poorly funded, French workers also adopted forms of protest other than strikes, such as go-slows and sabotage. Although women constituted a third of the workforce, they were involved in only 10 per cent of strikes; as they undercut male wages, they were frequently excluded from unions. Finally, in practice most workers – anarcho-syndicalist, socialist or otherwise – would rally to the defence of the 'bourgeois' Republic when it was threatened, as it was in 1914. The Republic was the bearer of the democratic inheritance from the French Revolution, which cut across class identity.

The small scale of Italian manufacturing at first attracted urban workers to anarchism rather than to socialism. The Italian section of the Workers' International, founded in 1869, was anarchist. Claiming 4000 members, mostly artisans who felt threatened by large-scale capital, it drew inspiration from the Paris Commune, aspiring to small-scale self-government rather than to socialist state control. Anarchism was particularly strong in the urban areas of northern and central Italy, but made little impact in the predominantly rural south. An attempt to seize Bologna in 1874 and an insurrection in the Matese in southern Italy in 1877 failed against the strength of the police, the army and the indifference of the peasantry. Individual acts of violence, including (in 1878) the attempted assassination of King Umberto (he was saved, ironically enough, by a former republican – the Prime Minister Benedetto Cairoli) and the killing of two people with a bomb in Florence, caused public outrage. Despite Cairoli's heroics, the government fell and its successor enforced strong police action against anarchists over the next year. Although anarchism survived as an idea – particularly in the form of syndicalism – reformist socialism began to look like a more promising route by which workers might have their grievances addressed. Anarchism in Italy resorted to desperate, terrorist methods, exploding bombs in Rome and finally hitting their target when they assassinated Umberto in 1900.

In Spain, conversely, anarchism remained a viable political force, competing with the socialists wherever the republicans failed to attract support. In the 1880s and 1890s the republican opponents of the Restoration had no social programme (beyond offering cheap credit to farmers) which would allow them to break out of their urban strongholds and to gather a mass following. Instead, anarchism would become the great peasant movement. It took the form of terrorist brutality in the 1890s: more than twenty people were killed in a theatre-bombing and ten at a religious procession, and Canovás himself was assassinated. Yet the mainstream movement tapped into latent peasant traditions, particularly in Andalusia, where social antagonism between an impoverished peasantry and the great landowners was reinforced by long-standing dreams of the *reparto* (division of the great estates). Despite rigorous government repression, outbursts of peasant violence and anarchist-led strikes recurred in the 1880s and 1890s, and the movement gathered momentum. Anarchism was also becoming an urban phenomenon, particularly in Barcelona, where, as in France, small-scale workshops, combined with the intransigent hostility of the state and employers, underscored the appeal of anarcho-syndicalism. Anarchist ideas were also brought in by the migration of poor southern labourers, who swelled the ranks of Barcelona workers.

Fuel was injected into the anarchist movement – and into the left in general – by the United States' crushing defeat of Spain in 1898. When the first rumours of the defeat arrived, riots and strikes broke out across the country, and the government declared a state of emergency in May. Intellectuals, politicians, journalists, demagogues and ecclesiastics of all political stripes spoke of the urgent need for 'regeneration'. The government's own efforts at reform were too little to save liberal Spain from intense political assaults from both the left and the right. In 1908 the conservative prime minister, Antonio Maura, proposed to deal with anarchism with a law empowering the government to deport anarchists, close down newspapers and disperse political meetings. In 1909 a call-up of reservists for a campaign in Spanish Morocco provoked demonstrations across the country and in Barcelona on 26 July a preplanned anarchist general strike brought the city to a standstill. The military governor declared martial law, opening Barcelona's 'Tragic Week', in which the workers, strongly influenced by anarchist propaganda, burned 50 churches, monasteries and Catholic schools. On 29 July, troops from outside Catalonia were brought in to crush the insurrection. Working-class districts held out for two days, battered by artillery. By 2 August, when the last flickers of the revolt were snuffed out, over one hundred people had been killed. There were 2000 arrests, 1700 courts martial, 600 guilty verdicts and 17 death sentences, of which four were carried out. A fifth victim was Francisco Ferrer Guardia, 'the Spanish Dreyfus', a republican who had not been involved in the insurrection, but who was executed nevertheless.[18]

Alfonso XIII dismissed Maura and appointed a Liberal government, which from 1910 until his assassination in June 1912 was led by José Canalejas. Canalejas sought to calm tempers with a series of reforms, but he was beset by labour unrest. In 1911 the anarchists established the *Confederación Nacional del Trabajo* (CNT) to prepare a general strike. While Canalejas respected stoppages aimed at ameliorating working conditions and wages, his government came down hard on politically-motivated strikes, declaring martial law against 12,000 striking railway workers in 1912. While for conservatives, therefore, Canalejas was too soft on the left, for socialists, anarchists and republicans he was a monarchist stooge – 'the last cartridge of Liberalism'.[19] His assassination, however, probably deprived the Restoration of a statesman who offered the best chance of combining liberal reforms with political order.[20] Spain remained neutral during the First World War, but in the aftermath the monarchy would not survive its shock waves.

Socialism

The British labour movement predated the spread of socialist ideas, which shaped its generally moderate, reformist character. In the 1870s British trade unions were organisations of skilled craftworkers and of large-scale industries, such as railways, mining and shipbuilding. In many of these trades, workers had undertaken apprenticeships and were fully aware of the differences (not least the wage differentials) which distinguished them from unskilled workers. The commitment of the Trades Union Congress to legal methods was rewarded with two laws in 1871 and 1875 allowing peaceful strikes and protecting the funds of trade unions. The emphasis of the 'old' unionism was respectability and conciliation with employers,[21] which may have reflected both the 'elite' consciousness of skilled workers and unionism's weakness as a result of its low membership. This does not mean, however, that there were no tensions between craftsmen and employers. After 1870 the emergence of strong international competition put the latter under pressure to cut costs (namely wages), and introduce new machinery and new ways of organising production, all of which threatened to deskill the workers. There were strikes in the 1860s and 1870s, usually over wage levels, but also over the working day and control over the production process.

From the late 1880s a 'new' unionism emerged which was more explicitly socialist in colour. A grave slump in 1879 brought several years of high unemployment and, with workers in a poor bargaining position, wages fell. By the end of the decade, therefore, the TUC's moderation seemed inadequate to defend workers' interests. The economy recovered in the late 1880s and a more radical movement emerged, drawing on traditional sources of unionism, such as miners, but also unskilled workers such as gas workers and dockers. The first sensational success of 'new' unionism came in 1887 when the women workers ('match girls') of the Bryant and May match factory, organised by the socialist Annie Besant, won a strike for better conditions. 'New' unions, such as the Miners' Federation (founded in 1888), were willing to use violence in strikes, to which all their funds were to be dedicated. A renewed economic downturn after 1890 gave employers their chance to grapple back the concessions made during the strike wave of the late 1880s. This counter-offensive, combined with the spread of militant mass unions, caused mutual antagonism which was sometimes violently expressed during industrial disputes. None the less, the transient nature of their first victories led the new unions to seek more lasting achievements and they began to emphasise collective bargaining and even mutual benefits, making them more akin to the 'old' unions.

Many of the 'new' unions were first organised by socialists and, though the TUC leadership remained in the hands of 'old' union moderates, by 1890 a quarter of the delegates were socialists. The vigorous response of employers (which included lock-outs, the use of 'blackleg' labour to break strikes and the formation of employers' associations), supported by some legal judgements which went against strikers, helped to erode the barriers between the 'old' and the 'new' unions and to politicise the labour movement.[22] In 1899 the appeal court narrowly defined 'peaceful' picketing. A strike in the Taff Vale Railway Company in South Wales led to a court judgement, finally upheld by the House of Lords in 1901, which made unions liable for damages. Political action appeared to be the only means of protecting the legal rights of unions against the arm of the law.

Violence was one possibility. The Social Democratic Federation, founded by H. M. Hyndman in 1884 to spread socialist propaganda, had sponsored demonstrations by unemployed Londoners in 1886–7 which erupted into violence. Yet this proved to be counter-productive, as it tarnished socialism in general. The SDF haemorrhaged some of its best blood, such as H. H. Champion, for whom a more practical political solution for workers was to secure independent labour representation in parliament.[23] An alternative tendency existed among middle-class Victorian radicals in the Fabian Society, established in 1884, which sought to persuade the existing powers of the wisdom of socialism and reform. It initially opposed separate parliamentary representation of labour, as an explicitly class-based party was counter-productive to the Fabian aim of 'permeating' the social and political elites.

This was not attractive to working-class radicals, whose loyalty to the Liberals was being sorely tested. Many Liberal MPs, who were often employers themselves, opposed such union demands as the eight-hour day and they refused to support the 1884 miners' strike. Local Liberal Associations invariably rejected working-class candidates, including the Scottish socialists Keir Hardie (1888) and Ramsay MacDonald (1894). These figures deserted the Liberals, and Hardie and two others won three parliamentary seats for independent labour in 1892. The following year in Bradford, Hardie steered a congress of socialist and trade-union delegates towards the creation of the Independent Labour Party. The ILP was socialist in its aims 'to secure the collective ownership of the means of production, distribution and exchange',[24] but the Fabians and the SDF, though at the Bradford congress, held aloof. Even the term 'socialist' was avoided because the ILP wanted to create a broad party appealing to moderate unionists who, 'when it came to revolution', as Ben Tillett put it, 'sneaked under the nearest bed'.[25] The ILP won elections to municipal councils and school boards. Its propaganda permeated wider society: Robert Blatchford's popular socialist tract, *Merrie England* (1894), sold 750,000 copies.[26] Though the ILP had a successful social and campaigning organisation, the Clarion Movement, it failed to win any seats in the 1895 elections (which were, in any case, a disaster for the Liberals too).

The party received its most important boost from the conversion of the trade-union movement. The employer offensive of the 1890s and judicial hostility towards unionism encouraged the spread of more militant ideas and made even the moderate unions more receptive to separate worker representation, if not to socialism. In 1899 the TUC voted to support the election of Labour MPs. The following year, a congress of different socialist organisations (including the ILP, the SDF and the Fabians) established the Labour Representation Committee, whose purpose was to find Labour parliamentary candidates. The affiliated unions were initially small in number, representing no more than 200,000 workers (10 per cent of all union membership in 1900), but the Taff Vale decision in 1901 prodded more unions to link up with the LRC. By 1903 the number of workers represented by affiliated unions soared over the million mark, assuring Labour of a deep well of funding and of votes. The Liberals, with an eye on the next elections, would ignore Labour at their peril. An electoral pact secretly forged in 1903 committed Labour MPs to support a Liberal government, while the Liberals would give the LRC a free hand to fight the Conservatives in 30 seats. In the event, the Liberals came to power in 1906 with a landslide. They scarcely needed the support of the 29 victorious Labour MPs, who now styled themselves 'the Labour Party'.

The Liberal government reversed the Taff Vale judgement in 1906, but their other great reforms danced very much to a Liberal tune rather than a Labour one. It rejected Ramsay MacDonald's 'Right to Work' bill, which would have obliged local authorities to find work for the unemployed. Disastrously for Labour in 1909, the (Tory-dominated) House of Lords passed down the Osborne judgement, which made it illegal for a trade union to fund any political party. Moreover, while at its pre-war peak Labour secured 45 MPs (1910), they were rarely successful when they were opposed by a Liberal candidate. Labour's apparent anaemia provoked a militant reaction among some unions and other socialist organisations. Renegade local branches of the ILP drew closer to the SDF, forming the predecessor of the British Communist Party, the British Socialist Party, in 1911. The more radical trade unions drew inspiration from French syndicalism, welding together great federations of workers. In 1914 a 'Triple Alliance' was sealed between the miners', transport and railway unions to co-ordinate strike action. This militancy was responsible for a period of labour unrest in 1911–14, but it was a minority movement. Trade-unionism expanded dramatically in this period – from 1,661,000 in 1911 to 2,682,000 in 1913 – but this may have been as much to do with the unions' role in administering the National Insurance scheme introduced by the Liberals in 1911 as with militancy. Despite the weakness of the Labour Party in forcing the pace of reform before 1914, the number of unions affiliating to it continued to rise, representing 1,572,391 workers – or well over half of organised labour – by 1914. This growth at the grassroots would make Labour a formidable political force in the future.[27]

Irish socialism conflated the workers' struggle with that of the political fight against the British state. The Irish Trades Union Congress was established in 1894, but 'new' unionism was slow to develop and the ITUC could only boast 60,000 skilled workers as members by 1900. This was partly because Dublin had few large-scale industries, while its unskilled workers were impoverished casual labourers. At the same time, Irish nationalism, particularly when supported by the Catholic Church, was hostile to state intervention, and the fact that social reformers were often Protestant did not help. Yet just before the First World War, socialist militancy did make headway, and was inspired by British 'new' unionism. It was, however, strongest in the north; in Belfast, Ireland's most dynamic industrial centre, socialist unity broke across the Protestant–Catholic divide.

In France, a separate working-class political movement was weak in the decade after the Commune. Hoping to divert the workers away from socialism, Gambetta sponsored the creation of moderate workers' organisations (*chambres syndicales*), but they attracted only the most skilled artisans, amounting to some twenty thousand workers in Paris by 1876. Over the next three years a breach between middle-class republicans and working-class socialists began to crack open. In 1876 the first-ever national labour congress, representing skilled workers, resolved that, with the triumph of the Republic, it was now time for the working class to 'affirm its own interests and to seek the means by which it could transform its economic condition'.[28] This commitment was hedged in by a statement of obedience to the law and was an affirmation of the co-operative socialism of Proudhon. The congress envisaged a syndicalist association in each trade, which, by accumulating income from membership dues, would slowly absorb private enterprises. The *syndicats* would thus free the workers from the wage system and eliminate poverty.

The republicans, on the other hand, had shelved their social reforms in order to consolidate the support of the peasantry and small businesses, which threatened to discredit the gradualist methods preferred by the 1876 Congress. The influence of Marxists, led by Jules Guesde, made inroads and, at the 1879 Congress in Marseille, persuaded the workers' delegates to found the first French socialist party. None the less, the divisions between the moderates (called the 'possibilists' because they adhered to the Proudhonist programme of co-operation with the republicans) and the Marxists were too deep to sustain unity for long. The long-term economic depression and strikes involving violent confrontations with troops (Anzin in 1884, Decazeville in 1886 and Fourmies in 1891) rallied working-class voters to the socialist cause, but the moderates benefited no less than the Marxists. The possibilist Paul Brousse declared that 'Fourmies achieved more than all the pamphlets of Lafargue,[29] the doctrines of Karl Marx and the speeches of Guesde.'[30] Guesde's Marxist *Parti ouvrier* had only limited success in attracting mass support. It made inroads only where it was not competing with pre-existing labour organisations, as in large-scale textile, coal and metallurgical factories. The possibilists were more successful because the idea of workers' co-operatives reflected French artisans' and craftworkers' personal experience of working in smaller-scale workshops. Moreover, these socialists made a material difference when they won power on local councils. By 1887 they had won some nine seats on the Paris municipality, having campaigned on local issues such as public transport and housing. By 1890 French socialism was, therefore, a divided movement, though it did have some political success. In 1881 the first socialist was elected to the National Assembly, which had a 12-strong 'labour group' by 1889.

The return of economic prosperity in the 1890s encouraged moderate tendencies: it was clear that revolution was not imminent, so it was better to settle down to work through legal means. The integration of the socialist movement into the Third Republic was helped by some common ground with the republican Radicals. Radicals and socialists disagreed over their ultimate goals – the former advocated a small property-owning democracy, while the latter espoused collective ownership – but they agreed on details such as secularisation, constitutional reform, income tax and some nationalisation. They often worked together in the same newspapers and their voters transferred their electoral support from one to the other for tactical reasons. Even Guesde, while insisting that he still awaited the revolution, thought it best to work within the parliamentary system so that, when the revolution came, there would be a rump of socialist deputies who could assume its leadership. Reformism was given a boost in 1896, with Alexandre Millerand's Saint-Mandé programme, emphasising the ballot-box as the means by which socialism would be achieved. None the less, Millerand went too far for most of the socialist leadership when in 1899 he tried to demonstrate that socialists could make great gains by joining bourgeois parties in government when he accepted a position in the Radical cabinet. He was discredited when his proposals for social reform (including pensions) floundered on three rocks: a wave of strikes in 1900–2, the refusal of employers to make concessions to organised labour, and the Senate, which voted down the pension bill. This failure split the socialists between the reformists under Jaurès, who formed the *Parti socialiste français*, and the revolutionaries under Guesde and the Blanquist, Edouard Vaillant, who created the *Parti socialiste de France*. While Jaurès's party might vote with Radicals, it could not yet stomach its leaders joining a bourgeois government, and Millerand was expelled from the PSF in 1904. Pressure from the Socialist International brought the two factions to forge a single party, the *Section française de l'internationale ouvrière*, in 1905.

The SFIO became, by 1914, the second largest in the Chamber of Deputies, but its relationship with the working class was ambiguous. Its electoral success came in part because of its anti-militarism: the SFIO, along with the rest of the French left, opposed the 1913 law which raised the period of military service from two to three years. Guesdist factory workers contributed to its 1.4 million votes (and 103 seats), but so did a lower middle class of peasants, low-ranking civil servants, teachers and retailers, attracted by the SFIO's promises of protection for small producers and its defence of the republican values of democracy and secularism. Their shift of loyalty away from the Radicals was conditional on the socialists following a reformist tack. In turn, however, many workers turned their back on the SFIO, though this would become more apparent in the aftermath of the First World War.

When the European crisis unfolded in the summer of 1914, Jaurès tried to form an alliance with the anarcho-syndicalist CGT in the hope of co-ordinating general strikes in both France and Germany to stop the war. The mood changed rapidly once the German attack in the west came; the CGT leader, Léon Jouhaux, declared on 3 August that the Austrians and the Germans were to blame for the conflict. Though the French labour and socialist movements did not accept the existing social and economic order, they rallied around the Republic against foreign aggression, particularly when their German counterparts offered little sign of reciprocating French expressions of international class solidarity, rallying instead around the Kaiser.

This betrayal of which French socialists accused their German comrades seemed all the more surprising because all too often the Social Democrats had felt the crushing, authoritarian weight of the German state. Bismarck's anti-socialist law in 1878 left hundreds of newspapers outlawed, societies closed down and socialists arrested. 'Minor states of siege' were declared in SPD strongholds such as Berlin, Frankfurt and Leipzig, allowing the authorities to exile activists. Yet the SPD's subculture ensured its survival, with Social Democratic sports and leisure societies, associations for women and for youth, reading clubs, social insurance and funeral policies. It even had its own postal system, allowing activists to distribute its underground newspaper, the *Sozialdemokrat*. This made the Social Democrats a wider cultural and social force, appealing primarily to the skilled workers. Yet, despite the persecution between 1878 and 1890 (when the laws were allowed to lapse), the socialists never, in practice, became a revolutionary party. In 1880 the SPD reacted to the repression by formally adopting 'all means necessary' to achieve a socialist, democratic state, and it certainly became more avowedly Marxist, culminating in the Erfurt programme in 1891. None the less, the SPD's very popularity gave renewed credibility to the legalist (or 'revisionist') approach. Its vote rose from 312,000 in 1881 to 4.25 million in 1912. By 1914 the party would boast a membership which rose comfortably over a million. By sheer force of numbers, it seemed, the SPD could force change through legal means.

The growth of unions was also impressive from 1895; by 1914 a quarter of the workforce was unionised (only Britain and Austria had a greater proportion of workers in unions). The half-million strong Metalworkers' Union was the largest in the world, though not all German unions were socialist. Catholic unions had 343,000 members and the liberal Hirsch-Duncker unions 122,000 in 1913. Yet the 'Free Unions' affiliated to the SPD accounted for by far the greatest proportion of membership, boasting more than two and a half million members that year. Most, however, resisted socialist calls for political strikes, preferring to use stoppages for improving wages and conditions, and there was a dramatic upsurge in strike action for such economic purposes after 1900.

Yet workers' apparent adaptation to the conservative order should be taken with some caution. The relentless growth in the SPD reflects not only the expansion of the German working class, but also a reaction against the harassment and petty regulations of the authoritarian state. Even after the lapse of the anti-socialist laws, socialists were still watched by police and excluded from public employment. Workers were subjected to different forms of police interference and regulation. Large firms and cartels blacklisted unionised or striking workers. Strikes meant confrontation with the police and even the army, so while they may have been initiated by industrial tensions, they often demanded deep commitment from the workers. Political strikes did occur. In January 1906 Hamburg city council increased the annual income required to qualify for the vote, in order to forestall socialist gains in the municipal elections. The SPD and the unions responded by calling a general strike, which was followed by riots. So while in practice for most of the time the SPD worked within the existing political and social order because it suited them to do so, the gradualist approach itself was not formally adopted by the party leadership before 1914, nor (probably) by most of the SPD's vast membership. The growing vote for the SPD reflected the workers' alienation from the political and social order – and for non-unionised workers, voting socialist was often their only safe form of protest.[31]

Working-class and socialist loyalties were doubtful even in 1914. The SPD had taken a battering at the polls in 1907 when Chancellor Bülow rallied conservatives and nationalists against the Catholic Centre and the socialists, who opposed his colonial policies. While the socialists lost about half their seats (dropping from 81 to 43), their share of the vote did not, in fact, decline by much and remained the largest in the Reich. The electoral system hid how far working-class voters were resistant to patriotic appeals to support the conservative order. In 1913 the SPD appeared to abandon its anti-militarism when it supported Germany's most extravagant military budget yet. This did not mean, however, that they had been seduced by the brand of patriotism advertised by the nationalists. They had accepted the bill because it was financed by a property tax for which they had long campaigned. Moreover, if war was imminent, the socialists saw it in terms of a conflict against the repressive Tsarist regime, which was why they also voted for war credits in 1914. The behaviour of the SPD's deputies in the *Reichstag* did not necessarily reflect the feelings of the rank and file towards the existing order, which was beset by a crescendo of strikes as the war approached. There was, as Countess Marie Radziwill warned, a 'latent antagonism between two very different Germanies'.[32]

By comparison with Germany, socialism was weak in Spain and Italy. The Spanish Socialist Workers' Party (PSOE) was established in 1879 but, though it attracted the articulate support of the Madrid print-workers, its trade-union organisation, the *Unión General de*

Trabajadores (UGT) which was founded in 1882, failed to plant deep roots in Barcelona, where it competed with both radical republicans and anarchists. After 1900 the bedrock of its support would be in Madrid and in the industrialising Basque regions, particularly amongst miners. The Spanish socialists had no clear agrarian programme to appeal to the peasantry, so the anarchists were more successful in winning rural converts.

In Italy, mutual aid societies, credit banks and co-operatives were sponsored by the employers, the Catholic Church or the authorities, while artisans' co-operative societies were conservative. Anarchists and socialists alike sought to politicise popular protests, but they were usually spontaneous, sparked by traditional grievances such as taxation and high food prices, as in Milan in 1898. Strikes first appeared in the 1870s, but socialist trade unions were rarely behind them. As in France and Spain, socialists also competed with both the anarchists and the radical republicans for popular support.

Yet they made inroads as workers and peasants absorbed the impact of economic change, particularly during the Great Depression and the tariff war with France, which began in 1887. In 1882 the former anarchist Andrea Costa became Italy's first socialist deputy, sitting for Ravenna. Agricultural regions such as Emilia and Lombardy were to become bedrocks of rural socialism as landowners tried to cut costs by reducing wages and turning sharecroppers into landless labourers.[33] Italy's first united socialist party was formed at a congress in Genoa in 1892, calling itself the Italian Socialist Party (PSI) from 1895. It survived a period of repression under Francesco Crispi in 1894 to emerge as the first Italian party to embrace the possibilities of mass politics, with local branches, party congresses, membership cards, internal elections, and its own newspaper, *Avanti!* (inspired by the German *Vorwärts*), and by 1897 it had a membership of 27,000. In 1900 (before universal male suffrage was introduced) the PSI secured 216,000 votes and 32 parliamentary seats.

Workers, meanwhile, found that strikes could be organised through the government-sponsored labour exchanges, the Chambers of Labour, or, better still, they could mediate industrial disputes. By 1902 a quarter of a million workers were organised in socialist unions, although they were mostly skilled, northern men. Inroads were made among the peasantry of the Po valley. In 1901 one of the earliest Italian agricultural unions, the *Federterra*, was founded for agricultural labourers and by 1913 accounted for nearly half the membership of the umbrella trade-union organisation, the General Confederation of Labour (formed in 1906). Emilia-Romagna witnessed the growth of socialist rural collectives, which by 1910 boasted 218,000 members across Italy, farming 37,000 hectares.

Yet not all socialist activity was peaceful. In 1893 endemic protest against a prolonged agrarian crisis in Sicily exploded into open revolt. Socialist *Fasci* (meaning 'bundles' – groups of people who sought political power) led strikes, ran for the municipal councils and appealed to the peasantry by demanding the redistribution of the great estates, the latifundia. Violence and arson mounted. An anarchist insurrection in Tuscany in 1894 seemed to show that the revolt had spread to the mainland. Crispi, the prime minister, declared martial law in Sicily and, on the mainland, the new Socialist Party was banned and was forced to meet clandestinely in 1895. The repression resumed in 1897–9 against a further wave of violent protests up and down the country in a reaction to high food prices in 1898; at least eighty people were killed and hundreds more wounded in Milan.

Both the liberal regime and the socialist movement, therefore, were confronted with a dilemma: for the former, the problem was whether to repress or to integrate the socialists; for the latter, it was whether to seek change through legal means or by revolutionary violence. These issues were never entirely resolved, but in practice the socialist movement was domesticated within the liberal order. This was the result, first, of a convergence between the PSI's middle-class leadership and the Radicals, and, secondly, of reforming initiatives from liberal governments after 1900. As early as 1895, the PSI and the Radicals found a common cause in their opposition to Crispi, and they allied in fighting local elections. Italian socialists therefore began to act like their French comrades, working within the parliamentary system, pressing for greater democratisation and social reform, collaborating with middle-class radicals and, when necessary, defending the freedoms of the liberal state from authoritarian impulses. At the same time, the liberal regime worked to integrate the socialists within the political system. Giovanni Giolitti, interior minister from 1901 and prime minister from 1903, created arbitration bodies to mediate labour disputes and a Supreme Labour Council to advise the government on industrial relations and labour welfare, all with workers' representatives. The government invested heavily in public works and secured PSI support for a package of welfare reforms.

Yet Giolitti had (in Martin Clark's graphic metaphor) 'swallowed the head, but not the backbone'[34] of Italian socialism. The PSI rank and file were less convinced that co-operation with the liberal regime was the best way forward. Unions, spurred by the economic growth up to 1910, became more militant as they saw the opportunity to press their demands. The relationship between workers, peasants and the liberal state was always ambiguous. As in Germany, a working-class subculture was nurtured by independent organisations, with workers engaging in self-improvement and political education, publishing their own newspapers, organising educational associations, campaigning against alcoholism and domestic abuse, and in favour of monogamy. They also ran their own co-operative shops and housing associations. They challenged the moral authority of Catholicism, engaging in a localised cultural struggle for hearts and minds, with socialist processions, funerals and other rituals to rival those of the Church. Moreover, though legal, strikes were still violent as confrontations between pickets, blacklegs and police led to over two hundred deaths or injuries between 1900 and 1904. The killing of a miner in 1904 led to a general strike which was particularly widespread across the north. While the strike itself eventually collapsed, its success in mobilising the workers lent weight to the revolutionary, syndicalist argument within the PSI. The revolutionaries held the majority at the 1904 party congress. Though the reformists regained control in 1908, they lost it to the revolutionaries again in 1912, when Giolitti took Italy into a war for the conquest of Libya. The reformists, Giolitti's parliamentary allies, cautiously supported the government, but the rank and file held fast to their anti-imperialism, which led the PSI as a whole to be tarred with the same unpatriotic brush. Isolated in parliament and derided outside for organising anti-war demonstrations, the socialists split between the discredited reformists and the revolutionaries. The latter secured a majority at the party congress, and among the intransigent leadership was Benito Mussolini, who took over the editorship of *Avanti!* Ironically, it would be under this rather cryptic and theatrical character that the seeds of authoritarian, populist nationalism would bear their bitter fruit in the aftermath of the First World War.

The Austrian labour movement had a bad start in the 1870s: first, despite the constitutional guarantees of free association, working-class political activity was proscribed and some leaders were arrested. Austrian trade-unionism in the 1880s alarmed the authorities enough for the government to pass an anarchist law in 1886, which denied trial by jury to those accused of 'anarchist' or 'subversive' tendencies. It was the Marxist Viktor Adler, however, who managed to forge the Social Democratic Party from the wreckage, on a socialist programme adopted at its first conference at Hainfeld in December 1888–January 1889. It drew most of its support from Czech and German workers, and so, with its stress on the unity of the international working class, in theory stood astride the most bitter of the national divisions within Austrian politics. By 1897, however, it had to make allowances for the different nationalities within the party, and it created a federal structure with a branch for each nationality of Cisleithania, albeit united by common acceptance of the Hainfeld programme and a biannual all-Austrian congress. None the less, many of the German members – like Adler himself – had assumed that they would lead the new socialist state. The German leadership gave the game away at the first all-Austrian congress at Brno in 1899. Their draft resolution stated that, though a socialist Austria would be a democratic federation of peoples, as a 'practical necessity', German should be kept as the common language 'as there [was] no other choice'. This brought opposition from the Czech delegates, and in 1911 the Czechs split off to form their own separate party and trade unions. In the end, national aspirations ran as deeply as social issues.

The restricted franchise in Hungarian politics meant that, unlike in Austria, parties stressing social rather than nationality issues did not make much headway. Labour organisations were permitted, but under tight restrictions. Their ineffectiveness in wringing concessions from the state and from employers led, in 1890, to the foundation of the Hungarian Social Democratic Party, which adopted the Austrian Hainfeld programme. The brutality with which the government put down strikes drove workers into the labour movement. In the later 1890s 51 workers were killed and 114 wounded in battles with the police. The army was used against the first national railway strike in 1904 and a strike by 30,000 Budapest metalworkers in the summer of 1905 (which was supported by 25,000 rural labourers). The ranks of the Social Democratic trade unions swelled to 32,000 by 1912, but the membership of the party itself had only grown to 4000; without universal male suffrage there was little point in joining a party when one could not vote for it. The Hungarian Social Democrats were, moreover, unsure about the role of the peasantry. Their failure to support a strike of rural labourers in 1897 split the socialist movement, with an Independent Socialist Party emerging to demand the nationalisation of all larger farms and their redistribution among the poorer peasantry. In the repression which followed in 1898, all socialist parties were repressed and strikers were dispersed by the gendarmerie. To soothe social tensions, Kálmán Széll's government (1899–1903) legalised trade unions, but farm labourers were subjected to the 'whipping-bench law', which gave them some workers' rights, but also allowed the landlords to inflict corporal punishment. In 1903, while still not appealing to the peasantry, the Social Democrats drafted a new programme recognising the equality of the national minorities and their rights to self-determination. Yet they could not decide whether the party itself should pursue the goal of autonomy for Hungary's nationalities and whether or not Hungary itself should be independent of Austria. Thus the Hungarian socialists neither rallied the peasantry to their cause nor forged a wide transnational party. They did, however, press for universal suffrage, which, if it had been secured, might have led them in those directions. In 1905–6 it supported the suffrage reform threatened by Francis Joseph against the Magyar opposition, organising a 200,000-strong demonstration in 1907 in its favour. It honed its internationalist credentials by opposing the annexation of Bosnia-Herzegovina in 1908, and in 1912 engaged in violent demonstrations against the new military bill and for democratic reform.

Russia: Socialism, Liberalism and Revolution

Russian socialism was in disarray after the assassination of Tsar Alexander II in 1881. Revolutionary activity was suppressed as leaders were executed or in exile. Populism put its faith in the latent egalitarianism of the Russian peasantry and had hoped to avoid the social agonies of industrialisation. Yet it was confronted with the uncomfortable reality that Russia was undergoing that very process. 'Neo-Populists' therefore argued that the growing industrial working class and the peasantry were united by their poverty in the struggle against the Tsarist regime. Seeking to propagandise among the workers and the peasants, the Neo-Populists formed their own party in exile in 1901: the Socialist Revolutionaries, under Victor Chernov. The Socialist Revolutionaries were willing to accept a bourgeois parliamentary regime and believed in civil liberties, but they were still determined that 'propaganda by deed' would spark the revolution. They opened a bitter terrorist campaign, shooting and blowing apart over a hundred government officials by 1904.

Meanwhile, another form of socialism was beginning to make an impact: Marxism. Initially, Marxist influence was faint, as few revolutionaries considered the conditions for a proletarian revolution to exist in Russia. Indeed in 1872 the Tsarist censor allowed Marx's *Das Kapital* to be translated on the grounds that no one would bother to read it, let alone understand it. Yet industrialisation created a small but expanding working class from the 1880s, while Populist failures of the 1870s suggested that faith in the peasants' revolutionary potential was misplaced. Populists such as Georgii Plekhanov ('the founder of Russian Marxism') were attracted by the 'scientific' nature of Marx's ideas, with their close analysis of economic and social developments. In 1895 Vladimir Ulyanov (Lenin) and Yuli Martov formed the short-lived Union of Struggle for the Emancipation of the Working Class, which, before its leaders were arrested, helped to organise a strike of 30,000 textile workers in St Petersburg in 1896. Two years later, Lenin and Martov were among the founders of the Russian Social Democratic Workers' Party, to which the Bund, a separate Marxist party formed by Jewish workers in Vilna and the northern 'Pale' in 1897, affiliated. The ideological problem for the Marxists was that Russia had no sizeable liberal bourgeoisie who would challenge the 'feudal' Tsarist order in the historical stage before the revolution of the proletariat. In 1903 this issue (as well as some blistering personal friction) led to the split in the party. The Mensheviks, including Plekhanov and Martov, argued for co-operation with liberals and support for a bourgeois parliamentary democracy first, while waiting for the economic and social preconditions for the workers' revolution to evolve. The Bolsheviks, led by the iron-willed Lenin, disagreed. In his 1902 pamphlet, *What is to be Done?*, Lenin argued that Russia could leap directly to the proletarian revolution through a small, tightly-disciplined party of professional revolutionaries. They would educate workers in class-consciousness, galvanising them into revolution. Allied with the mass of the peasantry, the workers would topple the Tsarist regime, whereupon the war against the bourgeoisie – and the property-owning peasantry – would begin immediately under a dictatorship of the proletariat.

Neo-Populism and Marxism would exploit the opportunities which arose from 1905, when the autocracy collapsed, but the liberals, not the socialists, were the initial beneficiaries. The Russian Revolution of 1905 had its roots in the great famine of 1892, which ravaged the area of southern Russia from the Black Sea to the Urals and which was followed by a cholera epidemic. The government tried to cope with the crisis, but the most impressive efforts came from Russian society. The *zemstva* organised a relief campaign, distributing food and medicine; professional associations and liberal nobles formed committees to raise money and assistance, and medical students volunteered to work in cholera hospitals. This public mobilisation has led some historians to date the emergence of Russian civil society (*obshchestvennost*) to 1892.[35] A sense reawakened amongst intellectuals, professionals and liberal nobles – especially the 'Third Element', the 70,000 experts employed by the *zemstva* – that they should have a greater voice in the running of the Empire. They hoped that the Tsar could be persuaded to reform peacefully but, after his accession in 1894, Nicholas II warned them not to entertain 'senseless dreams'.

Their efforts to organise politically in the late 1890s were met with police harassment, so it was in Switzerland in 1902 that representatives of the *zemstva* and the intelligentsia met and formed Russia's first liberal party, the Union of Liberation, aimed at forging a democratic, constitutional monarchy. In 1904, with the outbreak of the Russo-Japanese War, it began to emerge from the underground, distributing its newspaper, *Liberation*, and holding reform banquets. The socialist parties had to contend with this liberal organisation and, at a meeting in Paris, they all agreed to co-operate in the common goal of toppling the autocracy and convoking a democratic legislative assembly.

The prospects for an upheaval were strong as the twentieth century opened. A poor harvest in 1902 sparked endemic rural unrest, especially in the impoverished Black Earth region, where peasants enviously eyed the rich pickings of the gentry estates. Almost a third of all incidents of peasant violence and protest in 1905–7 took place in this central area of Russia.[36] In the industrial regions, the growth of a working class to some fifteen million by 1913 – over three million of them in factories and mines – provided fertile soil for the dissemination of revolutionary ideas. Many were peasants who sent money back to their villages, travelling back when they could and maintaining plots of land there. Class-consciousness and politicisation was less developed among these peasant-workers than among the 'hereditary' working class – those born and raised in the urban, industrialised environment. Yet the worker-peasants were frequently the conduits by which political ideas flowed into the countryside. They were also among the leaders of the peasant insurrections of 1905. In the cities they added a traditional but violent and anarchic (*buntarstvo*) edge to labour protest, including machine-breaking, looting and rioting. None the less, political leadership fell to the skilled, literate and urbanised workers, who were the most politicised and who could organise, articulate demands and maintain the discipline needed for strikes.

The government made some concessions, such as an eleven-and-a-half-hour day in 1896, but by 1904 the autocracy was facing a unique situation in which large sections of society – peasants, workers, the liberal 'Third Element' and the non-Russian nationalities (to be discussed in the next chapter) – were demanding reform. The Tsar hoped that the war against Japan that year would be short and victorious and would strengthen the regime, enabling it to defeat the revolutionary threat at home. Instead, it was a military disaster fatal to the autocracy. A strike involving 120,000 St Petersburg workers in January 1905 culminated in a march led by Father Georgii Gapon to the Winter Palace. Their petition asked, in the most supplicating of terms, for an end to the war, a constituent assembly and civil liberties. Troops opened fire, slaughtering some two hundred people and wounding hundreds more. 'Bloody Sunday' was a great turning-point: it tore away the mystique of a paternalistic, holy Tsar and provoked a wave of spontaneous strikes. Liberals now became strident in their demands for constitutional concessions. In June a mutiny in the Black Sea fleet (including the *Potemkin*) and among troops returning from the war in the east compounded the crisis. In rural violence which lasted into 1907, 3000 noble houses went up in smoke as peasants tried to drive the gentry off the land. The peasants were also beginning to mobilise politically: a Peasant Union was formed in Moscow province in May.

In October 1905, delegates of striking workers, mostly organised by the Mensheviks, joined representatives of the main socialist parties in a 50-strong council (soviet), initially to organise the general strike which gathered pace that month, but rapidly assuming responsibility for the militia, food supply and a newspaper, *Izvestiia*. It became an alternative government for the workers. The Tsar, in desperation, recalled Sergei Witte (whom he had dismissed in 1903) and his new prime minister advised making concessions to the liberals, which might split them from the socialists. This Nicholas did in the Manifesto of 17 October, which created a parliament (Duma) elected by universal male suffrage.

The October Manifesto opened the gates to mass politics. Politicians and activists, from ultra-conservatives to socialists, had to mobilise the population in a manner to which it was wholly unaccustomed. Initially, those who drew the most advantage from this were the liberals, despite a permanent division in October. The more conservative 'Octobrists' – *zemstva* nobles worried by the peasant violence and industrialists dependent upon government contracts – stood by the October Manifesto, opposing further reforms and advocating martial law to restore order. The more radical liberals formed the Constitutional–Democratic ('Kadet') Party in October 1905, led by the historian Pavel Miliukov. The Kadets rejected the October Manifesto as wholly inadequate. They demanded direct suffrage, the expropriation (with compensation) of noble land to calm the countryside, an eight-hour day for workers, progressive income tax, universal and compulsory primary education, and self-determination for the nationalities – a programme more radical than that of any other liberal party in Europe. The 100,000-strong party, consisting of radical *zemstva* nobles, professionals and intelligentsia, was well-placed for the elections to the duma. By the time elections were held in February 1906, it had 200 branches across Russia and made efforts to reach the peasantry, distributing its manifesto and campaigning for social justice. Meanwhile, the Peasant Union itself grew to 200,000 members, with up to five thousand branches across twelve provinces, although this merely scratched the surface of rural Russia. When the duma met in April, 179 of 478 seats were held by Kadets and 230 by independent peasant deputies. There were only a handful of socialists, as the left-wing parties had boycotted the elections.

After the Fundamental Laws of 1906, which fell far short of liberal political demands (for one, Nicholas refused to relinquish his claims to autocracy), the Kadets followed a policy of uncompromising opposition to the Tsar. Yet the Kadets could not forge a lasting alliance with the peasant deputies, from among whom the Trudovik socialist group was formed. They wanted to expropriate all private land without compensation, which went too far for the liberals. When the Tsar dismissed the first duma in July, Kadet appeals for a campaign of civil disobedience received only a muted response. Fear of government reprisals was undoubtedly a factor, but it was also an alarming sign that the Kadets' primarily political programme did not reach across the great chasm in Russian society. Despite their claims to the contrary, they did not speak for the popular masses. Instead, the socialist parties stepped into the breach.

The reactionary years of 1907–11 narrowed the scope for legal political activities and discredited the Menshevik dream of a 'Europeanised' (that is, legal, open and democratic) labour movement. At the same time, however, the revolutionary potential of the socialist parties was 'pulverised' by determined political repression, a counter-offensive by employers against labour and their own internal divisions. Yet there was a revival of unrest in the two years before the war. This was partly due to a resurgence in economic growth, which made the workers more confident in challenging their employers. Yet trade unions, though legalised for the first time in 1905, were still broken up by the government, and skilled workers became disillusioned with Menshevik gradualism.

The Bolsheviks were therefore able to challenge the influence of the moderate socialists (including a group of Right Socialist Revolutionaries, who would only use legal methods). The readership of the Bolshevik newspaper, *Pravda*, reached 40,000 – the largest circulation of any socialist journal in Russia – and they won six of the nine workers' curiae in the 1912 elections. The persistent Mensheviks, however, had a hand in organising new unions and a wave of strikes erupted through Russian industry after 500 striking gold miners on the Lena River were shot dead in April 1912. The number of strikes swelled from 2032 in 1912 to 3534 in 1914 (almost 8000 in all in 1912–14) and involved more than three million workers.[37] The Bolsheviks steadily gained ground within the legal trade unions, winning control of at least eleven out of fifteen in St Petersburg. Yet the role of the Bolsheviks in the labour unrest of these years should not be overestimated. The unions themselves were weak, accounting for only 28,000 of all workers in St Petersburg, yet at the same time 61 per cent of all strikes and 83 per cent of strikers were politically motivated in 1912–14. The Bolsheviks were, therefore, an influence, but only one in a range of socialist alternatives, including the Mensheviks and the Left Socialist Revolutionaries. The inchoate nature of the revolutionary opposition to the Tsarist regime is illustrated by the 'general strike' of July 1914 (in fact it was joined by 28 per cent of the workforce in St Petersburg and 2–3 per cent in Moscow). On the very eve of the war, St Petersburg workers demonstrated against the brutal suppression of a strike in the Baku oilfields. Although preceded by Bolshevik agitation, most strikers came out spontaneously at the news that, once again, police had fired into the crowd of demonstrators. As the strikers clashed with police and toppled streetcars to use as barricades, the strike turned into an insurrection which the Bolsheviks feared, rightly, would not spread beyond the capital and would be suppressed. They pleaded with the workers 'to refrain from extreme measures'.[38] Yet the workers ignored the Bolsheviks, as well as the Menshevik and Socialist Revolutionary alternatives, and the strike continued before being defeated by lock-outs and police action in mid-July. For all the drama, therefore, Russia was not quite on the brink of a new revolution. The general strike embraced a relatively small section of the workers (particularly when compared with February 1917), while the Tsarist regime was, unlike in 1917, still able to use force to crush the demonstrations. Meanwhile, the socialist parties, including the

Bolsheviks, were unable to impose their leadership, while (and here again 1917 would be different) liberal opinion amongst the Kadets and in the duma held itself aloof from the unrest.[39] It would take the extreme social pressures of two and a half years of war to produce the February Revolution of 1917.

15 The Nationalist Challenge

From the 1870s until the outbreak of the First World War, nationalism generally worked against the forces of the left, undermining the internationalist appeals of socialism and anarchism. Some socialist parties sought to combine the social struggle with nationalist aims – Józef Piłsudski's Polish Socialist Party attempted to do just that. In the end, however, all socialist movements had to choose between the class war, with its internationalist implications (since the proletariat existed in every European country) and the national struggle, which implied an appeal based on ethnic lines, reaching over internal social and economic differences. The Polish socialists eventually split over precisely this issue, with Piłsudski giving priority to independence rather than to social revolution. In contrast, the Serbian Social Democrats rejected all manifestations of South Slav nationalism – whether that took the form of 'Greater Serbia' or Yugoslavia – but then the Serbian socialists remained a tiny party.[1] Even in countries where national independence was not at stake, such as France and Germany, socialists were faced, in the international crisis immediately before and during 1914, with an awkward choice between their internationalist dedication to the working class and their loyalty to their own nation. With a few bold exceptions, European socialists did not find it too difficult to choose the latter. Otherwise, it was rare for nationalism and socialism to inhabit the same political movement; where they did, the strange union gave birth to a populist, authoritarian ideology. Governments made nationalist appeals to win over public support against the challenge of the left or to domesticate socialist and labour movements. Yet in the multinational empires of Austria–Hungary and Russia, nationalism amongst the subject peoples was potentially a grave, centrifugal danger. Among the stateless peoples of central and eastern Europe, where boundaries, governments and regimes had changed frequently, language, culture and national symbols took on an extreme importance. Where ethnic groups did not feel that they had a full stake in the political order, so the survival and development of their language and culture provided the thread, giving them a sense of their own heritage and identity. This helps to explain why even the smallest slights by the dominant nationality frequently provoked furious reactions. It also explains why governments also worked so hard at 'Germanisation', 'Magyarisation' or 'Russification' in order to undermine the national identities of their subject peoples. Such efforts were met with an opposite reaction, but just how real the danger of disintegration was to these multinational empires is the source of some debate.

Western-European states did not escape similar pressures from national or ethnic groups. The most dramatic development occurred in Scandinavia. In 1905, Norway separated from Sweden, breaking a union which had existed formally since 1815, but it was a crisis which was resolved peacefully because of the willingness of both sides to negotiate and to make concessions.[2] In Spain, Catalan and Basque nationalism arose from a sense that their special interests had been neglected by the state. The ultra-Catholic Basque Nationalist Party (PNV) was founded in 1894, demanding full independence and unity with the Basque lands in France. It envisaged a racial community, where marriage to non-Basques would be discouraged. Catalanism originally sought to promote the Catalan language and to protect Catalonia's manufacturing with tariffs. It also drew support from peasant Carlists who resented the centralising tendencies of the liberal state. Finally, it became a political movement seeking regional autonomy: the 'Bases de Manresa', penned by Prat de la Riba in 1892, demanded a Catalan state within a federal Spain. In 1893, Prat's 'Catalan Union' became a political party, later called the *Lliga Regionalista*. In Belgium, a conflict arose between Flemish cultural nationalists, 'flamingants', who sought to promote their language and the Catholic faith against the godless influence of the French and the Walloons (French-speaking Belgians).[3]

The most violent separatist movement in the west was in Ireland. In the late 1870s tenants' resistance to their landlords stirred under the sting of poor harvests. Led by Charles Stewart Parnell, the Land League encouraged rent strikes and 'boycotts' (the word originated in Ireland), which meant ostracising landlords, while Fenians tried to channel peasant anger into violence. In May 1882 the Chief Secretary for Ireland and his under-secretary were murdered. Gladstone himself was now convinced that reform was necessary in Ireland.[4] In 1881 a Land Act was passed, which gave the Irish tenants their 'Three Fs' – fair rents, fixity of tenure and freedom to sell their leases. The Irish electorate, enlarged in 1884 to include a large stratum of Catholic tenants and labourers, now came into play. After the General Election of December 1885, Parnell's Irish Parliamentary Party held the exact balance at Westminster. Yet Gladstone's conversion to Home Rule for Ireland was not merely a cynical ploy to secure nationalist support. He seems to have been sincerely convinced that it was now the only means by which Ireland could be governed by consent. Further land reform would produce a class of Irish property-owners who would be a force for stability.[5] Gladstone's 1886 Home Rule bill fell, however, not only before the ranks of the Conservative opposition, but against Liberals who split off from Gladstone's party – Whigs and 'Liberal Unionists' led by Joseph Chamberlain. They were not necessarily knee-jerk reactionaries – most professed to want some reform – but sectarian fear of Catholic dominance in Ireland certainly lurked among them. This issue focused minds on the question of the Protestant north; a Unionist MP for Belfast (where riots exploded on the streets) shrilly warned that Home Rule 'would be resisted by the people of Ulster at the point of the bayonet'.[6] The ideological alignment between Protestantism and Unionism was cemented by the co-operation of Orange Lodges and Conservative politicians during the crisis, which polarised Irish politics along religious lines. The episode also affected Scotland. Aggrieved nationalists grumbled that while troublesome, violent Ireland was offered reform and even Home Rule, the reinstatement of the position of Scottish Secretary in 1885 was a pallid recognition for Scottish loyalty and legality. The Scottish Liberal peer Lord Rosebery could well growl ironically, 'I leave for Scotland next week with the view of blowing up a prison or shooting a policeman.'[7]

After the failure of another Irish Home Rule Bill introduced by Gladstone in 1893, Irish nationalism received a boost from a cultural flourish. This was the early age of W. B. Yeats and James Joyce, but in its more militant form Irish cultural nationalism could frequently be atavistic (equating modernity with Englishness), ethnic (aligning Irishness with the Celts) and sectarian (equating Irishness with Catholicism). Sinn Fein ('Ourselves') was established in 1905 under Arthur Griffith to promote Gaelic culture, but in 1908 it stood its first parliamentary candidate. Home Rule returned close to the top of the legislative agenda when the Liberal government became dependent upon Labour and the IPP for support after the elections of January 1910. The IPP leader, John Redmond, used this as leverage to coerce the government to introduce a new bill in April 1912. This brought Ireland to the brink of civil war. Unionist organisations, co-ordinated by the Ulster Unionist Council and encouraged by British Conservatives, demanded partition – the separation of the Protestant northern counties from an Ireland with Home Rule. In September 1912 a 'Solemn League and Covenant', signed by 250,000 people, pledged to use 'all means which may be found necessary to defeat the present conspiracy to set up a Home Rule Parliament'.[8] In January 1913 the Ulster Volunteer Force was created and armed by illegal imports of some twenty-five thousand weapons and ammunition. The Unionist Council also drafted plans for a provisional government in a separatist Ulster and, by the summer of 1914, plans were in place for a coup d'état, which the UVF, now with 23,000 men, could undoubtedly have carried off against the province's 1000 British soldiers. Nationalists responded by forming a force of their own, ostensibly to uphold the rule of law, which was led by a Provisional Council. These Irish Volunteers openly imported 1500 crusty old rifles in the summer of 1914 to provoke a confrontation with their Unionist opponents. The Home Rule Bill passed the House of

Commons in May 1914, but the Lords amended the bill to exclude nine counties permanently from Home Rule – the legislative roots of the partition of 1921. That – and the Irish civil war which erupted with it – was delayed by the First World War.

The war would also at first postpone, but then forcibly resolve, the nationality problems of central and eastern Europe. The Polish population in eastern Germany was considered to be a danger to the integrity of the Reich. During Bismarck's *Kulturkampf* against the Catholic Church, measures targeted Polish cultural life in West Prussia, Posen and Silesia. In 1872 German became the language of instruction in all state schools, except in religious education, while Polish could not be taught even as a foreign language. All law-courts and all state-run offices, down to the railway and postal services, were to use German exclusively. In 1885, Prussian police arrested and expelled from the Reich 30,000 Poles and Polish Jews whose residency papers were not in order. The following year, Bismarck established an organisation called, with startling bluntness, the Colonisation Commission, which tried to encourage German settlement in the Polish areas. With interethnic tensions stretched, German ultra-nationalists in Posen organised the Society for the Eastern Borders (*Deutscher Ostmarkenverein*) in 1894 to defend the German language and German interests against the Slavic hordes. Street names and public signposts were changed from Polish to German. The Poles resisted the Colonisation Commission by establishing, in 1897, a Land Purchase Bank and agricultural co-operatives which encouraged Polish occupancy of vacant farmland. In 1901 a school strike followed attempts to teach even religious education in German, while the example of the academic strike in Russian-ruled Poland around the 1905 Revolution was copied in Prussian Poland in 1906–7. Corrosive as their relations with the Germans were, the Poles did not seriously threaten to secede. Polish nationalists dreamed someday of restoring an independent, united Poland, but for now the stark alternative appeared to be the iron Russian grip of Tsarism. In 1914 the Polish deputies in the *Reichstag* feared a Russian invasion enough to support the Kaiser when war broke out.[9]

How seriously one judges the threat of nationalism to have been to the integrity of the Russian Empire depends very much upon how one looks at the evidence. David Saunders argues that the centrifugal and centripetal forces were roughly equal in strength, though at certain moments – such as during the fragmentation of 1917–20 – that equilibrium was 'punctuated'.[10] Norman Davies points out that, for all the charges one can level at the Tsarist regime, it at least treated all its non-Russian subjects with equal brutality and it treated its Russian people the worst.[11] None the less, the Tsar's peoples each felt his lash differently. 'Russification' was not consistently pursued as a policy and it meant variously the imposition of Russian administration, language, culture and religious values on some minorities, and their voluntary adoption by others.[12] Where they were imposed, the intensity varied from one ethnic group to the next.

Poland and the Ukraine suffered heavily after the 1863 insurrection, while the German-speaking nobles of the Baltic provinces, who remained loyal to the Tsar, were spared for another two decades. After the initial reaction from 1864, the Polish 'Congress Kingdom' was dissolved in 1874. Between 1883 and 1894, the Polish language was banned from all law-courts and at all levels of administration, including (impossibly) the village communes. Polish officials were purged from senior and middle ranks, being allowed only to work as postal and railway clerks. Even legal organisations, such as the Catholic Church, had to use Russian in their internal correspondence, while railway signs, street signs and place names in Polish were replaced with Cyrillic. The teeth of Russification also sank deeper into the primary school system. From 1885 all subjects had to be taught in Russian, except for religion and Polish grammar, while the political allegiance of teachers was scrutinised. In secondary education, Russian teachers with Polish sympathies were sacked. Although Catholicism was never expurgated, Orthodox chapels and choirs were established. Meanwhile, students' movements and activities were closely monitored by informers and by new residence requirements. If, on paper, Russification in Poland was thorough, in practice the Tsar's officials had a sublime ability to contradict each other, while the underpaid police and low-ranking functionaries were eminently corruptible.[13]

Ukrainian books on most topics were banned after the uprising of 1863–4 and, from 1876, they could no longer be imported and nor could the language be used in the theatre. This law, though relaxed briefly in 1881–5, became progressively stricter in subsequent years and was not repealed until the 1905 Revolution. An important consideration for the Tsarist regime may have been demographic. The Ukrainians were an immense bulk of the empire's population, consisting of 18 per cent of the Tsar's subjects in 1897. During the drafting of the 1876 law, a senior official commented that it was all right for the Tsar to tolerate the emergence of literature in Latvian, because, with a population of about a million, the Latvians would scarcely threaten the integrity of the Empire. On the other hand, to encourage the separatism of 'Little Russians' (as the Ukrainians were called) would be catastrophic, particularly with the activities of Ukrainian nationalists based in Austrian Galicia, regarded as the Ukraine's 'Piedmont'. The authorities were alarmed less by the outpourings of Ukrainian 'high literature' (as Mikhail Katkov caustically remarked, 'no one reads them and even those that do don't understand them'), than by 'low-brow' works intended for the peasant masses. The Kiev section of the Imperial Geographical Society was closed down for producing such material. As one of its leading lights, Mykhailo

Drahomanov, fled into exile, he lamented that the 1876 law had stopped the distribution of thousands of affordable pamphlets which he and others had disseminated amongst Ukrainian peasants in 1874–5. Despite Tsarist efforts, however, only a small proportion of the Ukrainian population – about 1.4 million out of 25 million – seem to have 'Russified' in the last four decades of the nineteenth century.[14]

The potential for the punitive measures imposed on Poland, Belarus and the Ukraine to expand into a broader Russification policy was always present. A law of July 1864 made Russian, with some exceptions, the only teaching language in primary schools across the Empire and was explicitly aimed at restricting linguistic diversity.[15] Under Tsar Alexander III, Russification was inflicted even on loyal nationalities. The reason was partly ideological: turning his back on his father's 'Great Reforms', the new Tsar wrapped himself in Nicholas I's banner of 'Orthodoxy, Autocracy, and Nationality'. Together 'Orthodoxy' and 'Nationality' implied either the dominance of the Russian people or the assimilation of the non-Orthodox and non-Russians into their faith and culture. Alexander III was therefore more inclined to listen to conservative nationalists such as Mikhail Katkov and Iurii Samarin, who argued that the empire could only become a unitary national state if all its peoples accepted the Russian language and religion as their own. There were also practical reasons. The unification of Germany and Russia's economic development thrust forward new strategic concerns. The Baltic provinces guarded the approaches to St Petersburg from Germany, but they also stood astride the Western Dvina River, an important outlet for Russian exports, a point emphasised from 1870 by the construction of a railway line along the same route. Estonia, Latvia and Lithuania, were, along with Poland, among the most economically advanced and urbanised regions of the Empire. Lutheran pastors in Estonia and Latvia had developed the national languages amongst the peasantry by developing systems of near-universal education.[16] The government's main concern, however, was the loyalty of the elites. From Alexander III's point of view, the unification of Germany made the devotion of the German-speaking nobles questionable. On his accession in 1881 he refused to recognise their privileges, Russian courts were subsequently introduced, and the Russian language was made compulsory in administration, law and all but elementary schools. In 1893 the German-language university at Dorpat (Tartu) was closed and reformed as a Russian institution.[17]

Since its annexation in 1809, quiescent Finland could claim a parliament, although only on paper for most of the time. A special committee for Finnish affairs (which Alexander II restored in 1857) and a Finnish secretary of state gave implicit recognition to its distinctiveness. With the Polish insurrection of 1863, the government sought to lure the nobles from seeking Swedish protection and reconvened the Finnish diet (which had not met since 1809). It was eventually allowed to meet every three years. Two years later, the Bank of Finland was permitted to issue its own currency, marks, which, when placed on the gold standard in 1878, gave Finland monetary independence from Russia. That same year, the Tsar permitted the Finns to raise their own armed forces, which would serve only in Finland and would be deployed for the protection of 'the throne and the fatherland'.[18] The elites and the intelligentsia divided between the 'Fennomans', who wanted to promote the use of Finnish as a means of building up a sense of nationhood, and the 'Svecomans', who preferred to keep Swedish as the language of government, law and higher education. The Tsarist regime gave cautious encouragement to 'Fennomania', seeking to develop the Finnish language as a means of outflanking Swedish-speaking liberals. Yet this velvet-gloved handling made the emergence of the mailed fist of repression in the 1890s all the more shocking to Finns. There were several reasons for the reversal of policy. The Finnish diet sat uneasily with Tsar Nicholas II's autocratic urges. Pressure from Russian nationalists, alarmed at the prospect of Finnish 'separation', was also mounting. The decisive factor, however, was probably the emergence of new international alignments. As neighbouring Sweden seemed to favour Germany, a semi-autonomous Finland, with its own army and parliament, now appeared to be much more of a liability.[19] Between 1899 and 1902 the Tsar stripped the diet of its legislative authority (which was met by a protest which gathered half a million signatures), the Russian language was made compulsory in higher administration and in secondary schools, the separate army was abolished and conscription into the imperial army introduced (which provoked passive resistance: only half of all Finnish conscripts reported for duty in 1902).

Russification in the later nineteenth century also meant the imposition of Orthodoxy, which entailed persecution, especially for the Jews. In the wake of Alexander II's assassination, the authorities connived in pogroms – violent attacks on Jewish communities – in Moscow, St Petersburg and Warsaw. Alexander III himself was notoriously anti-Semitic and the ultra-nationalist Slavophiles shared his prejudices. In 1882, Jews were banned from buying rural property, forbidden to enter the legal, military and medical professions, and quotas were imposed on their entry into secondary schools and universities. They were denied the vote in *zemstva* and municipal elections and in 1891 all Jews in Moscow residing without permits were expelled. Further pogroms were to occur in the early twentieth century, the first in Bessarabia in 1903 (in which 47 Jews were killed and 400 wounded), but worse was to come in 1905–6, when over three thousand Jews died. Jews were the greatest victims of the savagery of popular Russian chauvinism and official Russification, but other non-Orthodox peoples felt its blows. Alexander II had permitted some thirty-five thousand Latvians and Estonians to reconvert from Orthodoxy to Lutheranism, but under his successor 37,000 were forced to convert back to Orthodoxy. 60,000 Muslims and other 'heathens' (according to one triumphant report in 1894) were converted to Orthodox Christianity in Central Asia and the Far East.

Russification naturally provoked opposition amongst the nationalities, although it was rarely united. Poles withdrew from public life and even from socialising with Russians. Polish language, literature and history were kept alive by a clandestine education network which provided teachers and published and distributed books in Polish. In 1900 the Russian authorities themselves estimated that these secret schools were teaching a third of the population.[20] A 'flying' university, meeting at different locations to avoid suppression, operated for 20 years from 1882. Politically, the Polish opposition was divided. The 'conciliators' sought to avoid confrontation with the regime, believing violence to be counter-productive. They hoped that cultural, economic and social progress would offset the minimal political concessions which could ever be expected from the Tsar. From this camp sprang Roman Dmowski, who in 1897 founded the National Democratic Movement (known as the NDs or *Endecja*). Another, 'loyalist' tendency consisted of conservatives who sought to find common ground with the Tsar in opposing socialism and revolution. When Alexander III signed a Concordat with Pope Leo XIII in 1883, the Catholic Church formally supported the loyalist position. Yet both loyalists and conciliators lost credibility with the renewed Russification of the 1880s. Initiative therefore fell to the revolutionary opposition, embodied by Dmowski's lifelong opponent, Józef Piłsudski of the Polish Socialist Party (PPS) founded in 1892. PPS commitment to complete independence by violent means brought it into conflict with the *Endecja*. Both parties tapped into an emerging seam of Polish nationalism, based no longer on the *szlachta*, but on mass politics. The Tsarist regime saw the PPS as the most dangerous of all the Polish opposition groups (which also included the Jewish Bund and Feliks Dzierżyński's Social Democracy of the Kingdom of Poland and Lithuania, which opposed Piłsudski's nationalism).[21]

The Ukrainian opposition was also split: the socialist Revolutionary Ukrainian Party, which had been founded clandestinely in Kiev and Kharkov in the late 1890s, supported a united Ukraine, but under the protective shell of a liberalised Russian Empire. In 1899 a moderate Ukrainian National Democratic Party, modelled on the *Endecja*, emerged in Austrian Galicia, while the more explicitly separatist National Ukrainian Party was formed within the Russian Empire in 1902 with the slogan 'Ukraine for the Ukrainians'. None of these organisations, however, managed to secure a mass following before the 1905 Revolution.[22] Belarussian populists established the Social–Revolutionary Group, with a clandestine magazine called *Homon* (Clamour) in 1884, though it was closed down after two issues.[23] The Finnish opposition disagreed over methods. The 'Old Finns' advocated working within the Tsarist administration, while the 'Young Finns' argued for more active resistance. The Finnish Social Democratic Party, established in 1898, supported the Young Finns, drawing in worker and peasant support. After the Russian governor-general, Nikolai Bobrikov, arrested and exiled the leadership of the opposition, he was assassinated in June 1904.

During the 1905 Revolution, the most violent opposition to the Tsar came from the nationalities of the Empire. In Poland, protests first stirred when the Russo-Japanese war broke out in 1904. Piłsudski's PPS prepared for a violent insurrection by forming *bojówki* (battle squads) in May. The war caused a social crisis because it shut Polish goods out of Asian markets. Unemployment, social distress, strikes and demonstrations gathered pace and, in November, protesters were gunned down in Warsaw. With news of the 'Bloody Sunday' massacre in St Petersburg in January 1905, a general strike was joined by 400,000 workers, and over the next two years there were almost seven thousand strikes involving 1.3 million workers and farm labourers. Middle-class support came in the form of a school and university strike, lasting until 1907. Meanwhile, Piłsudski's squads waged a terrorist campaign with assassinations and bombings in a bitter insurgency lasting into 1908. Some concessions were briefly wrung from the wounded regime. In the spring of 1905 the Uniate Church was granted toleration, the Polish school board recognised (though Polish was still only permitted as the language of instruction in private schools) and Poles were to be allowed to buy land. When the Polish socialist parties boycotted the 1906 elections to the duma and the loyalists were hammered at the polls, Dmowski's *Endecja* took most of the Polish seats. Though it sought to press for Polish autonomy, it refused to work with the Ukrainians, Belarussians and Lithuanians, whose claims might contradict those of the Poles.[24] Tsarist manipulation of the curia system, in any case, ensured that Polish representation overall would be severely reduced by the third duma in 1907. In desperation, the *Endecja* revealed its seamier side: anti-Semitism, which appealed to its largely lower middle-class following. As Dmowski's rhetoric against Jews became increasingly virulent, socialist and Jewish voters combined to deny him his Warsaw seat in the elections to the fourth duma in 1912. The National Democrat movement, which combined ultra-nationalist rhetoric with a moderate programme, had been blunted.

Yet the direct action favoured by the Polish left was also beaten down, though with difficulty. Even as the Tsarist regime appeared to relent on paper, it began to strike back on the ground. In the winter of 1906–7, workers were locked out of factories, forcing them to face starvation or to accept the owners' terms. Thousands of strikers were arrested and sent back to their villages. Piłsudski's terrorist raids became more desperate, not least because a third of all workers joined the National Democratic organisation, the National Workers' League, which aimed primarily at breaking the socialist grip on the working-class movement, even copying the PPS's battle squads. In the internecine struggle, some forty or fifty Poles were being killed each week. The PPS split under the pressure, between the *Lewica* (Left), which sought to pursue the class struggle, and Piłsudski's *Rewolucja*, which continued the fight for independence. PPS-*Lewica* eventually joined the Social Democracy of the Kingdom of Poland and Lithuania (SDKPiL), which would evolve into the Polish Communist Party. With the Polish revolution in disarray, the Tsarist regime managed to reassert its authority, but it never regained the grudging quiescence which most Poles had offered before 1904.[25]

In Finland, workers in Helsinki joined a general strike which helped bring the autocracy to its knees in 1905. In 1906 the opposition summoned a new diet, which would be the most democratic parliament in Europe, elected by universal male and female suffrage. The politicisation of the working class gathered speed: in the summer, a 'Red' insurrection in Helsinki was suppressed by the conservative 'Whites', but the Social Democrats emerged as the largest single party in the 1907 elections to the Finnish parliament. From 1908 the Tsar regained his grip on Finnish affairs and, by the outbreak of war, Finland was once more being administered by Russian officials. Across the Baltic provinces, peasants went on rent strike and refused to co-operate with officials and judges. Passive resistance developed into violent assaults on landlords' property and, depending upon the region, between 19 per cent and 38 per cent of all manor houses were set aflame. After the Tsarist regime had restored order, the bloodshed on both sides left a bitter legacy. The government itself sought a reconciliation with the German elites as a guarantee of social order, but the German landowners were no longer so certain that the Tsar was the best protector against the Estonian and Latvian peasants. They began to seek safety in ethnic solidarity, forming educational and social associations which sought to bring all Baltic Germans together, regardless of social status.

Belarus saw the publication of two newspapers in Belarussian, one of them produced by the Belarussian Socialist Union, *Hramada*. Although it was at first suppressed by the authorities in 1906, the journal re-emerged as *Naša Niva* ('Our Cornfield') and continued to publish until 1915. It none the less only enjoyed a circulation of 4500.[26] In the Ukraine, the Russian socialist parties exploited the issue of peasant land-ownership to win support, but there was a Ukrainian cultural resurgence. Newspapers and journals appeared and the language was briefly permitted in primary and secondary schools. The Revolutionary Ukrainian Party reformed itself as the Ukrainian Social Democratic Worker's

Party, advocating (for now) autonomy within the Russian Empire, with a parliament in Kiev. Ukrainian liberals co-operated with the Russian Kadets, while the Marxists would join up with their Russian equivalents in 1908. All Ukrainian political tendencies, therefore, envisaged some form of relationship with Russia in their short-term future.[27]

The Russian Empire cracked open during the upheavals around 1905. Yet few of the national movements demanded full independence; the Polish socialists were among the few within Russia's European Empire who did so. That the Tsarist regime managed to reassert its authority within a few years suggests that, even where there was mass opposition, the Empire would only fragment when the regime was weakened at its heart. Repeatedly, in 1905, 1917 and 1991, this occurred because of Russia's international predicament and a domestic revolution. 1905 and 1917 (but perhaps not 1991?) were, to paraphrase David Saunders, 'bouts of punctuated equilibrium'.[28]

In Austria–Hungary, the national issue dominated politics for the entire period from the Compromise of 1867 to the First World War. For many Austrian Germans, the concessions to the Hungarians went too far, while for radical Magyars, they did not go far enough. The other nationalities resented the predominance the *Ausgleich* gave to the Germans and the Hungarians. For the majority of the population – workers, artisans, peasants – socio-economic problems were undoubtedly the main issue, but, as local society in many parts of the monarchy was structured along national lines, these grievances were often expressed in ethnic terms.

Despite the tensions between Austria and Hungary over the common policies of the monarchy, there was enough support at the centre of Hungarian politics to make the Compromise work. Yet there were troublesome opponents, including radical supporters of Lajos Kossuth who wanted to restore the 1848 Constitution and who formed a separate 'Independence and '48 Party' in 1884. They struck a chord with the small country nobles, wealthier peasants, provincial lawyers and middle-class urban intellectuals who resented interference by imperial officials, who were usually Germans and Czechs. The Independence Party eventually won an absolute majority in the 1906 elections.[29]

Yet until the late 1880s the Hungarian political landscape was calm, partly because of the Liberal dominance under Kálmán Tisza, prime minister from 1875 to 1890. His government ensured parliamentary support by manipulation of the restricted suffrage: officials pressurised voters through tax assessment, but they were also known to falsify electoral registers, quarantine defiant villages and even close 'unsafe' bridges on the way to the polls. Under Tisza, about a hundred and sixty constituencies were in Liberal pockets, and formed a phalanx of deputies dubbed Tisza's 'mameluke guard'.[30] Although the Liberals supported the Compromise, they were also sensitive to imperial encroachments on Hungarian autonomy. The precise relationship between Hungary, the Crown and the other nationalities of the empire – called the 'issue of public law' – dominated Hungarian politics up to the war. The main sources of conflict were the combined imperial army and the economic terms of the Compromise, both of which were subject to renewal every ten years.

With regard to the imperial army, disputes arose over the respective contributions to be made by Austria and Hungary and over the language of command. The latter issue brought the period of relative stability in Austro-Hungarian relations to a stormy end. In 1888 Tisza's government had secured some reductions in the German-language regulations in the imperial army. This did not go far enough for the radicals, who condemned the combined force as 'alien, dynastic and absolutist'. In 1889, when the bill was presented to parliament, the opposition mobilised demonstrations in Budapest and the provinces, which had to be put down by troops. Tisza managed to steer through a revised bill, but, hounded and exhausted, he resigned in March 1890. When the next revision came belatedly in 1902, the Independence Party responded to a proposal for an increase in recruitment by demanding further reductions in the use of German and for Hungary's separate army, the *Honvéd*, to have artillery. This last demand alarmed Francis Joseph, who, still mindful of 1848, was adamantly against giving the Hungarians such firepower. The radicals were again supported by riots and the Emperor dismissed his Liberal prime minister, Kálmán Széll, in June 1903. In September he declared the unity of the imperial army, provoking further storms of protests. Another Hungarian cabinet was swept from power and the imperial government prepared plans for the military occupation of the country. In a final effort to reach a peaceful solution, the Emperor appointed István Tisza (Kálmán's son) as prime minister. The younger Tisza brokered another compromise, which he tried to strongarm through parliament in November 1904. The opposition parties formed a 'Coalition' which, with the refusal of the bureaucracy to support the usual vote-rigging processes, defeated the Liberals – who had ruled for 30 years – in the 1905 elections. Against a chaotic backdrop of strikes inspired by the Russian Revolution of 1905, the Coalition declared 'national resistance', calling on the Hungarian counties not to co-operate with tax collection and recruitment. Francis Joseph's interior minister, József Kristóffy, suggested breaking the deadlock by introducing universal male suffrage which, it was thought, would rally the peasantry, the workers and, in particular, the non-Magyar population behind the monarchy. The strategy worked, in a way. When the Coalition balked at this reform, there were popular demonstrations in support of it. The government finally sent in the army to clear parliament in February 1906. These measures (and the lack of support from the urban workers) brought the Coalition to heel: secretly, it agreed to the army bill in return for the withdrawal of universal male suffrage. In 1912 István Tisza pushed the next renewal through, surviving an attempt on his life while protesting crowds were dispersed with troops. To gain the necessary votes, however, the government had to concede artillery to the *Honvéd*.

A dispute over the economic compromise coincided with the turn-of-the-century army crisis. The 1887 economic compromise had been passed in the stable days of Kálmán Tisza, but in 1896, with renewal looming, the Austrian parliament was in crisis and unable to approve it for Cisleithania. The imperial government therefore secured an agreement with the Hungarian ministry, then led by Dezső Bánffy, that the 1887 agreement could simply be extended until 1907, unless either the Austrian *Reichsrat* or the Hungarian diet repudiated it. The latter did, in a charge led by the Independence Party which claimed that this agreement was an infringement of Hungary's constitutional rights. Bánffy was forced to resign in 1899 and it was Széll who successfully brokered a solution, extending the 1887 agreement in return for tariffs to satisfy the Magyar gentry. To the chagrin of nationalists in 1907, the economic compromise was again renewed, for the last time, with an increased share in the Hungarian financial contribution to the common expenses of the monarchy. Even so, Hungary's burden of these costs remained proportionately lower than that of Austria. Austria, with 46.7 per cent of the population in 1910, paid 63.6 per cent of the common expenses, as compared with the 36.4 per cent paid by Hungary, which accounted for 51.3 per cent of the population.[31] This apparently unequal distribution actually took into account Austria's more advanced economy, but it fuelled anti-Magyar feeling among Austrians. In 1895 Karl Lueger told the *Reichsrat* that 'Dualism' was 'the greatest misfortune which my fatherland has ever had to suffer, a greater misfortune even than the wars we lost'.[32]

Yet the Compromise survived until 1918. For all the violence of their pre-war opposition, the Hungarians would fight loyally during the First World War. Even the radicals of the Independence Party, while wanting to destroy the *Ausgleich*, did not seek separation from the monarchy itself. Most Magyars recognised that outright independence would leave their country prey to assaults by Russia which might, moreover, stir up the Slav population within Hungary. The Compromise did little to soothe Austro-Hungarian relations, but the Magyar reaction was not fatal to the Empire.

While Austrians and Hungarians both disliked the *Ausgleich*, the other nationalities detested it. On paper, the ethnic distribution of the franchise in Hungary was not shockingly biased towards the Magyars. Of the restricted electorate (7 per cent of the population could vote in 1905), Magyars, with around 54 per cent of the population, had around 60 per cent of the votes. None the less, the suffrage operated in such a way that a Magyar candidate would require fewer votes to win in a peripheral (and usually non-Magyar) constituency, than in one located in the Magyar-populated centre. Magyars therefore controlled 90 per cent of the parliamentary seats.[33] Some liberals, such as Deák and Kossuth (who died in 1894), counselled care in dealing with the nationalities, but in general the Magyar elites clung to the notion that 'Magyarisation' could force the minorities to imbibe Magyar culture until a strong, unitary nation-state emerged, which would dominate the Habsburg monarchy.[34] Magyar was made a compulsory subject in primary schools in 1879. In 1898 all towns and villages were meant to be known by their Magyar names (or they would be invented where no such equivalent existed). In 1907 a law ordered that 13 out of 30 hours of every secondary school week should be devoted to lessons on the Magyar language. Yet while some 90 per cent of employees in state service spoke Magyar by 1914, the success of Magyarisation was restricted to certain ethnic groups in urban parts of central Hungary, where people were more likely to have brushes with the state. The country's 700,000 Jews eagerly seized the opportunity to assimilate. In the rural regions of the periphery, children and parents saw little need to speak Magyar and they did not retain what they did learn because the language was not spoken at home.

Magyarisation also sparked resistance. The Germans ('Saxons') of Transylvania sought refuge in cultural associations, their own schools and their churches. Their Romanian neighbours were among the most intransigent. Insisting on political autonomy, they refused to send deputies to the diet in Budapest. The government responded by banning the United Romanian Party, which had been formed in 1881. Ten years later, the Romanian Cultural League took up the torch in exile, although it stressed its loyalty to the Habsburg monarchy. In 1892 when it submitted a petition outlining Romanian grievances to Francis Joseph, he warned them that this was an illegal gesture (since constitutionally his Romanian subjects had to seek redress from the Hungarian diet). The petition was published abroad in several languages, for which several of its authors were imprisoned. Transylvania was then subjected to more intense Magyarisation. Slovaks, who in the mid-1870s saw their high schools closed down and their cultural association, the *Matiča Slovenška*, banned, found a leader in a priest named Andrej Hlinka. In 1906 he was sentenced to two years in prison for 'agitation against a nationality' (which meant, of course, against the Magyars). On his release, Hlinka's efforts to consecrate a Slovak church in defiance of the authorities led to clashes with police, in which 15 people were killed.

A strong reaction arose among the South Slavs of Hungary, particularly among the Croatians, who sought to defend the *Nagodba* against Magyarisation. The problem with Croatian nationalism, however, was that it was split at least three ways up to 1914. Traditionalists emphasised 'state right', or historic claims to Croatian unity and independence.

Supporters of the Illyrian (or, as it was becoming more commonly known, 'Yugoslav') ideal wanted a united state of all the South Slavs. A third tendency – the majority – supported the one goal or the other, but within a reformed Habsburg empire. The problem with all these visions was that the Croats had to come to some accommodation with the Serbs, who, with the absorption of the Military Frontier into Civil Croatia in 1881, constituted a quarter of the population. Depending upon their aspirations, Croatian nationalists regarded Serbs as long-lost Croats, fellow South Slavs or a different people altogether. Croatian nationalists also claimed Bosnia as part of Croatia, while 'Greater Serb' nationalists envisaged it within an enlarged Serbian kingdom.[35] The Hungarian government could undercut Croatian demands by supporting the Serbian minority in Croatia, as the Hungarians tried to Magyarise the country, while Croats worked for a revision of the *Nagodba*. In 1883 Zagreb rioted over the addition of Magyar inscriptions on public buildings. The Ban appointed by the Hungarian government, Károly Khuen-Héderváry, responded by placing Serbs in government and promoting their economic and social interests. He manipulated the electorate (which represented only 2 per cent of the population) to secure pro-Magyar majorities in the *Sabor*. The *Nagodba* clauses sticking in Croatian throats were those giving Budapest a large share of Croatian revenue for common expenses. In 1903 a Hungarian refusal to amend these rules led to further riots, and a coalition of Croatian opposition parties won the 1906 elections. The Hungarians punished this defiance by decreeing that all employees on the State Railways, including those on lines in Croatia, should speak Hungarian. Public meetings in Croatia called for separation from Hungary. The Ban tried to silence the opposition by dissolving the *Sabor*. Further repression followed after the annexation of Bosnia-Herzegovina in 1908, because of Magyar anxieties about this new addition to the Slav population. In 1909 a number of Croatian leaders were put on trial and in 1912, after several assassination attempts on the Ban, the constitution was suspended. None the less, for all the violence, most of the Croatian opposition was working for change within the empire, not to secede from it.

In Cisleithania, the nationality question revolved around *Besitzstand*: the presumed right of the Austrian Germans to political office and to social and economic predominance. *Besitzstand* was justified on the grounds of demographics, economics and custom. In 1910 the Germans were the largest single group in Austria, with 36 per cent of the population. They accounted for 52 per cent of manufacturing and commercial activity and they had traditionally provided the monarchy with state officials, army officers and clergy. Statutes periodically enforced German as the language of government, while Germans had 45 per cent of the seats in the *Reichsrat*. Austrian Germans were deeply conscious of their special relationship with the state: they were the *Staatsvolk*, their language the *Staatssprache*.[36] The other nationalities reacted strongly against these pretensions, although in this period there was no consistent effort at 'Germanisation'. Interethnic struggles were waged at many different levels – on the streets and in cultural organisations, as well as in local councils, the *Landtage* and the *Reichsrat*.

The 750,000 Italians of the Trentino (in the south Tyrol) and along the Adriatic coast nursed, potentially, the deepest separatist impulses. For Italian nationalists, the Trentino was *Italia irredenta* (rightly belonging to Italy). Although there were incidents (such as riots in Trieste in 1882), not all Italians of the Tyrol wanted to separate from Austria. The Catholic Church supported the Empire, the nobles were divided and the local political party, the *Partito Populare*, counted pro-Austrians amongst it members. Italians, Slovenians and Croats sat together on the fault line between Latin and Slav Europe. The Slavs were hostile to Italian claims to Gorizia and Istria, while, as Catholics, the Slovenians also nursed suspicions of the Orthodox Serbs, so most preferred the security which the Empire offered against both Italian and Greater Serbian nationalism.

In return for their loyalty to the Habsburg monarchy, the Poles of Galicia, with 46 per cent of the population, were allowed to dominate the mostly peasant Ukrainians (or 'Ruthenians'), who accounted for 42 per cent, both politically and socially. A socialist deputy to the local diet (*Sejm*), described the province as 'an estate leased to the Polish *szlachta*'.[37] The defence of their position in Galicia led most Poles to oppose the introduction of universal male suffrage in 1907. A more serious, long-term threat to the monarchy came from the Ukrainians, who began to show a developing national consciousness. Despite efforts by the Polish nobility to obstruct the introduction of compulsory education from the 1860s, it made an impact. While literacy remained low (by 1900 two-thirds of the Ruthenian peasantry were still illiterate), there was enough of a readership in the villages to support a growing popular press, with an average of one new publication appearing each year from the mid-1880s. In 1868 the 'national populists' established *Prosvita* ('Enlightenment'), which argued that the Ruthenians were part of a greater Ukrainian nation. *Prosvita* fostered village reading clubs (usually led by well-to-do peasants, priests or teachers), printed pamphlets and published a monthly, popular newspaper, the *Batkivshchyna* (Fatherland) between 1879 and 1896. By 1914 *Prosvita* had 36,500 members, but the reading clubs could boast a substantial 197,000.[38] Originally confined to intellectuals and clergy, a Ukrainian national consciousness had awakened amongst the Galician peasantry. Around 1900, middle-class Ukrainian and Polish students violently clashed in Lviv (Lwow), and the Polish governor of the province was assassinated. Despite these stirrings of nationalism, however, most Ukrainians in Galicia generally remained loyal to the Habsburgs, whom they still saw as their best protector against their Polish landlords. This was shown by the electoral success of the Ukrainian National Democratic Party (founded in 1899), which campaigned for reform within the Habsburg monarchy. In 1914 the government pressured the Poles into accepting a reform which increased Ukrainian representation in the *Sejm*, and promised schools and a university for the Ukrainians.

The greatest headache in Cisleithania came from the fraught relations between the Czechs and the Germans. This was partly because the Czechs were numerically and economically important, second only to the Germans. They constituted 23 per cent of the population in 1910, and almost half of them were engaged in manufacturing and commerce. The Czechs had the second-largest group in the *Reichsrat*. They also enjoyed a strong historical sense of nationhood, based on memories of their 'ancient liberties' guaranteed back in 1526, and the unity of the Czech crownlands: Bohemia, Moravia and Silesia. This national identity was reinforced by a strong educational system, by high standards of literacy among the workers and lower middle class of artisans, shopkeepers and petty officials, and by organisations such as the gymnastic organisation, the *Sokol*. Meanwhile, they sought to assert their dominance over the German population within the Czech lands themselves. The struggle between the Czechs and the Germans was the most maddening of all the frustrations in pre-war Austrian politics.

Count Eduard Taafe, minister-president from 1879 until 1893, claimed that he governed Austria by 'keeping all nations in a state of well-tempered discontent'.[39] In fact, he was kept in power by his 'iron ring' of conservative Poles, Slovenes and Austrians in the *Reichsrat*, while showing flexibility towards the Czechs, who were boycotting parliament. In 1879 he extended the use of Czech in local administration, added more representation for the Czechs in the first electoral *curia*, created a Czech section of the University of Prague and widened the franchise. The Czechs ended their boycott of the *Reichsrat* and in 1883 the broader suffrage enabled them to overturn the German majority in the Bohemian diet. The problem was that no government could make concessions to the Czechs without infuriating the Germans, and vice versa. In the furious storm of German protest, three of Taafe's six ministers resigned. The most important consequence of the episode was that the (mostly German-speaking) Austrian liberals, who had claimed to be an anational party representing all the peoples of Cisleithania, now withdrew to protect German interests.

Yet there was a darker side to German defensiveness, expressed most virulently by the emergence on the extreme right of a new nationalist movement. As elsewhere in Europe, it combined a commitment to social reform with chauvinism and anti-Semitism. The German National Association was founded in 1882 by Georg von Schönerer, whom Adolf Hitler would regard as one of his antecedents. Schönerer sought to 'raise ethnic consciousness' in Austria by organising mass meetings, distributing propaganda, gathering petitions and supporting radical nationalists during elections.[40] Schönerer combined social reform and the defence of German interests with authoritarianism and anti-Semitism. His solution to the ethnic question was 'pan-German', aiming ultimately at the unity of the entire German people. He proposed to rid the German parts of the empire of the Slavs by giving them autonomy – except for the Czechs, among whom lived a substantial German population. Slavs within the German territories would then assimilate or lose their rights as citizens and, eventually, Austria would unite with the German Reich. Schönerer's anti-Semitism appealed to the core of the movement, chauvinistic Austrian students and workers who identified capitalism with the Jews. While the association itself was small – by 1885 it had fewer than a hundred members in Vienna – it had branch offices across Austria and it tended to work through sympathetic organisations and publishers. One of the great weaknesses of the pan-German movement, however, was its fragmentation: scores of less influential groups with similar aims emerged from the 1880s, although there was an attempt to form a confederation of about a hundred and sixty organisations in 1900. While the People's Party (founded in 1881 with aims similar to those of Schönerer, who had seceded from it) had a presence in the *Reichsrat*, Schönerer's association itself never influenced more than four deputies. There was, after all, a contradiction between the association's German separatism and loyalty to the multinational Habsburg monarchy. Moreover, Schönerer's pan-Germanism led him to embrace Lutheranism, associated with Prussia. Around 1900 he persuaded some fifty thousand Austrian Catholics to convert to Protestantism, but he also alienated much of the lower middle class and the peasantry.

Another expression of the German reaction was the founding of a populist Christian Social Party by Karl Lueger in 1891. Its supporters were peasants and lower middle-class groups who felt beleaguered by both large-scale capitalism and socialism. Lueger offered an alternative which, unlike Schönerer's, was Catholic and loyal to the monarchy. He proposed social reforms, the extension of the suffrage and the protection of the 'small man' against both liberal capitalism and socialism, but he articulated these aspirations in anti-Semitic terms; in 1890 Lueger appealed for the 'unity of all anti-Semites'.[41] His work among the artisans and shopkeepers in Vienna won him leadership of the city council in 1895 and 1897. Francis Joseph at first refused to accept his election, but his popularity in the city was so overwhelming that the Emperor was forced to yield. Lueger was mayor until his death in 1910 and Vienna was controlled by the Christian Social Party until 1918.

By 1890 the shrill pitch of German opposition had alarmed Francis Joseph, but Taafe's brokering of a compromise between the Czech and German parliamentary leaders could not prevent the drift towards extremes. The compromise was repudiated by the radical 'Young Czechs', who went on to trounce the moderate 'Old Czechs' in the 1891 elections. On the German side, the liberals lost seats to the German nationalists, including Lueger's Christian Social Party. In the new *Reichsrat*, the Czechs blocked Taafe's efforts to cool German passions with concessions, while riots in Bohemia brought a state of emergency and the arrest of members of a subversive Czech organisation, the *Omladina*. Taafe fell in 1893, when his 'iron ring' snapped apart over an extension of the suffrage, which the minister-president saw as the only escape from the political mire. As one of his ministers argued, the 'lower, politically uncorrupted classes . . . would make social, not national politics' and were 'dynastically minded, reliable, appreciative and easy to rule'.[42]

Taafe's successors could find no way out of the deadlock between the Czechs and the Germans, which claimed a startling succession of political scalps. Count Casimir Badeni, who received the minister-president's poisoned chalice in 1895, lifted the state of emergency in Bohemia and in 1897 introduced a fifth electoral *curia* based on universal male suffrage. Yet, as an attempt to realign politics away from national to social issues, it failed. Filibustering (*Obstruktion*) by both Germans and Czechs merely intensified, making parliament unworkable. Badeni's successors had to rule by emergency decree. Between 1900 and 1904, the national groups fell out over the pickings of a public works programme meant to bring stability. In 1907 universal and equal male suffrage, based as far as possible on constituencies cutting across nationalities, was pushed through in an effort to realign politics along social, rather than ethnic, lines. A brief period of parliamentary stability allowed the minister-president, Max von Beck, to renew the economic compromise with Hungary that same year. Yet his minor concessions to the Hungarians earned him the enmity of the heir presumptive, the anti-Magyar Franz Ferdinand, who connived with the Christian Socials to engineer Beck's downfall in 1908.

The annexation of Bosnia-Herzegovina, adding more Slavs to the Empire, was a large lump of fat dropped on to the flames. Party politics began to split along ethnic lines again. The Bohemian Germans disrupted the diet in Prague in 1908, while in the *Reichsrat* the Czechs (after trying a short-lived coalition with the South Slavs) resumed obstruction tactics. One minister-president in this period expressed the sense of haplessness when he said of one set of negotiations, 'Primarily I am interested in the talks not breaking down. Whether they achieve anything is less important.'[43] By 1913 two years of German obstruction in Prague had brought Bohemia to the verge of bankruptcy. When the minister-president, Karl Stürgkh, appointed an emergency commission to raise the funds needed, the Czechs in the *Reichsrat* denounced it as unconstitutional. Stürgkh closed down parliament on 14 March 1914;

Austria was being governed by decree on the very eve of the First World War.

The monarchy failed to heal national divisions by orientating politics around social problems, in large part because, in many regions, the social structure had evolved along ethnic lines, so national and social issues coincided. The extension of the franchise merely complicated the political landscape: to the older liberal and conservative parties were added ultra-nationalist, socialist and agrarian groups, so that by 1914 there were more than twenty-five parties in the *Reichsrat*. These parties did not represent large, transnational social groups, but rather the interests of social classes *within* their own particular ethnic group. If anything, the task of building a secure parliamentary majority had become more Herculean.[44] Austrian politics, therefore, never managed to squirm out of the sinkhole of interethnic strife, which paralysed the development of a workable parliamentary system.

Yet the Austro-Hungarian monarchy itself was not breaking apart under internal pressures. There was widespread discontent with the 1867 Compromise, but there was no groundswell amongst any nationality for complete separation from the Habsburg monarchy. Ethnic strife did stunt the growth of parliamentary politics in both Austria and Hungary. It promoted domestic political instability and even violence. However, the real danger from nationalism came from outside, from Italian, Romanian and Slav (particularly Serb) irredentists who tried to agitate among their co-nationals within the monarchy. It was this confluence of external nationalism with internal interethnic strife which made the issue potentially so dangerous towards 1914.

Nowhere was this more apparent than across the Empire's south-eastern frontier. After the disastrous war of 1877–8, Serbian nationalists continued to nourish dreams either of acting as a 'Piedmont' for the South Slavs, or of expanding into 'Greater Serbia'. Prince Milan Obrenović, however, recognised his state's military and economic limitations, while, at the Berlin Congress in 1878, Russia had accepted that Serbia would fall into Austria–Hungary's sphere of influence. Serbia sealed a commercial and political agreement with the Habsburg monarchy in 1881, in return for which it was awarded the status of a kingdom in 1882; for now, South Slav nationalism was an irritant rather than a threat. Romanian irredentism, which might have claimed Transylvania from Hungary, was also contained. In 1883 Austria–Hungary sealed an alliance with Romania, where public opinion was hostile to Russia (the Tsar had bitten off territory from the new kingdom and had supported a hostile 'Greater Bulgaria'). The dual monarchy was also one of Romania's most important trading partners.

None the less, three forces, at different times pulling in a myriad of directions, conspired to ensure that the relatively stable situation in south-east Europe would not last. The first of these was the internal weakness of the Ottoman Empire. The reforms of the *Tanzimat* were opposed by the Sultan's privileged Muslim subjects. The Muslim elites in Albania went so far as to demand autonomy and repeatedly rebelled, as in 1881 and 1897. The second, more serious danger was irredentism among the emerging states of south-east Europe. The remaining swathe of Ottoman territory there, including Albania, Epirus, Thrace and Macedonia, rested uneasily between the emerging states of Greece, Serbia and Bulgaria. Nationalists in these countries anticipated having to fight over the spoils when, as expected, the Turks would be unceremoniously ejected from the entire region. Yet the third problem was that the great European powers, particularly Austria–Hungary and Russia, had their own strategic reasons for exploiting the disputes among these smaller nations. For these reasons, the region was emerging as one of the great fault-lines in European politics.

This great-power interference aggravated nationalism. Just as Serbia was drawn into the Habsburg orbit, so the principality of Bulgaria (nominally under Turkish suzerainty) was a Russian satellite. Its constitution was vetted by the Tsar, who, in an ironic twist, permitted universal male suffrage because the peasantry was allegedly Russophile. The Tsar supplied the upper ranks of the Bulgarian army and exerted direct influence through the Russian consul in Sofia, even to the point of interfering in elections. Bulgarian nationalists, meanwhile, hungrily eyed the Bulgarian province of Eastern Rumelia (also under Ottoman suzerainty), demanding its annexation. Tsar Alexander III supported such a union, but wanted to secure it on his terms so that Russia's strategic position would expand with Bulgaria. He – so fiercely reactionary in Russia – actually sponsored subversive activity within the southern province. The nationalists, however, resented Russian interference and wanted to shake the Tsar off Bulgaria's back. A Revolutionary Central Committee fomented a military coup in the province's capital, Plovdiv, in September 1885 and proclaimed the union of Eastern Rumelia with Bulgaria. The revolutionaries threatened Bulgaria's prince, Alexander of Battenberg, with nothing less than 'annihilation' if he did not accept the annexation on their terms. The unfortunate prince understandably agreed, but in the process infuriated not only the Tsar (who recalled his army officers), but also Serbia and Greece, who jealously feared Bulgarian unification as a threat to Macedonia. In October King Milan launched a preventive war to forestall Bulgarian expansionism, but his poorly motivated forces were shattered in a three-day battle at Slivnitsa in November 1885, after which the Bulgarians poured into Serbia itself. Austria–Hungary, alarmed at the conquest of its satellite, threatened war if the Bulgarians did not withdraw back across the frontier. This brief conflict showed that the great powers could be drawn into regional conflicts by the ambitions of their own client-states. Nationalists learned that their territorial ambitions could only be fulfilled if they had strong armed forces recruited from a motivated, patriotic peasantry and either the acquiescence or the active support of a great power. For now, however, the great powers resisted the temptation to press forward their own strategic interests by manipulating regional rivalries.

Greece had wanted to join in the mêlée in 1885, but had been prevented from doing so by Britain, one of the guarantors of Greek independence. Another opportunity to pursue the 'Great Idea' arose in 1896, with an insurrection against Ottoman rule in Crete. A Greek expeditionary force arrived in support in 1897, igniting a full-scale Graeco-Turkish war in which the Greeks were only saved from annihilation by the great powers. The Greeks had to withdraw from the island, which was occupied by an international force until 1909. Yet the great prize for Greece, Serbia and Bulgaria alike remained Macedonia, the great ache in the western flank of the Ottoman Empire. Perhaps half of the Macedonian population was Muslim, but there was also a mingling of ethnicities, including Bulgarians, Greeks and Serbs. The three rivals waxed lyrical about an independent Macedonia, while each aimed to devour the territory whole. They based their claims on dubious historic claims and on conflicting (and inevitably 'fudged') population statistics which – naturally – always showed that one's own ethnic group predominated.[45] None of the contenders had the military strength to expel the Turks on its own, but nor could they swallow their mutual suspicions to co-operate. It was not long, therefore, before the Macedonian question erupted into violence. In 1893, IMRO (the Internal Macedonian Revolutionary Organization) emerged with the slogan 'Macedonia for the Macedonians'. The Bulgarians, Greeks and Serbs responded by sponsoring their own Macedonian revolutionary movements, which fought each other as well as the Turks. In ugly terrorist campaigns, they bombed trains, ships and banks and sabotaged public amenities such as water and electricity. In cosmopolitan Salonika, they hurled bombs in bars, hotels and theatres in the quarter frequented by subjects of the great powers. In 1903 IMRO sparked an insurrection in the province of Monastir and succeeded in driving out the Turkish garrison at Kruševo before being crushed. In the repression, 119 villages were burned to the ground and 30,000 refugees fled across the frontiers. In October, Austria and Russia, working together for one of the last times, forced the Sultan to accept international monitoring of the region.

Such co-operation was all too brief and the next crisis was sparked by a revolution in Turkey. Radical Turkish students and army officers, frustrated by the Ottoman decay, demanded the restoration of the Constitution of 1876. The most important of their various underground organisations was the Committee for Union and Progress (CUP, or the 'Young Turks') founded in 1899 by Enver Bey and Mustafa Kemal (later Atatürk), who were stationed in Salonika. Their own Third Army Corps had been bloodied in the bitter fighting against the Macedonian insurgents and was infected with mutiny. Moreover, they resented great-power interference in Turkish affairs, and news of a meeting between Tsar Nicholas II and King Edward VII to discuss the Macedonian question in 1908 sparked the Young Turk revolution. Sniffing a great-power conspiracy to wrest the region from the Ottoman Empire, the revolutionaries assassinated the Sultan's most trusted commander in Macedonia and proclaimed the Constitution of 1876. As one garrison after the next joined the coup, Abdülhamid II conceded. In the ensuing disorder, the Young Turks deposed him (1909) and resorted to authoritarian rule. They had aspired to strengthen the Empire, but their revolution merely encouraged Serbian, Bulgarian and Greek nationalists, who saw the 1908 Revolution as a sign of terminal Turkish illness. Bulgaria declared full independence, while Greece, in the wake of a nationalist coup which eventually brought Eleutherios Venizelos to power, once more declared its annexation of Crete, although it came to nothing. For Austria–Hungary, the revolution spelled danger over the future of Bosnia-Herzegovina, which was still legally a Turkish domain, but which had been under Austro-Hungarian occupation since 1878.

Habsburg anxiety was fuelled by distrust of Serbia, with which relations had rapidly deteriorated. In 1903, Serb army officers slaughtered the unpopular, pro-Austrian King Alexander Obrenović, his queen, her two brothers and three of his generals. They replaced him with the scion of the rival Serb dynasty, Peter Karadjordjević, who reintroduced parliamentary government but was frequently reminded by the army of his debt to them. Serbia began to assert its independence from its erstwhile Habsburg patron. In 1905 it signed a commercial treaty with Bulgaria, sparking the commercial 'Pig War' (after Serbia's important export) with Austria–Hungary between 1906 and 1911. Politically, the Serbian government now looked to Russia as its protector. This assertiveness, and the real possibility of a Turkish collapse in 1908, persuaded Vienna to annex Bosnia-Herzegovina that year. The Serbs regarded Bosnia-Herzegovina as part of 'Greater Serbia', or 'Yugoslavia', and there were massive demonstrations in Belgrade, where parliament voted emergency funds to prepare for war. Montenegro, which also had its eye on territory in the region, mobilised its forces. The Russians were already politically involved because, although the Austrians had consulted them before the annexation, the Austrian foreign minister, Alois von Aehrenthal, succeeded in outraging Russian public opinion by publicly (and falsely) declaring that the Russian government had consented unconditionally. Russia now promised to support Serbia diplomatically, but made it clear that it would not go to war over the provinces. With German backing, Aehrenthal replied with an ultimatum in February 1909, warning that unless Russia and Serbia recognised the annexation, Austria–Hungary would invade Serbia. Russia yielded, avoiding great-power conflict, but the humiliation was hard to bear.[46] The defeat also unleashed a strong Serb nationalist reaction. The 'National Defence', a cultural organisation which emphasised military training, was established, and Austrian intelligence reports suggested that it was drilling bands of guerrillas. Even more sinister was the secret society, 'Union or Death', which its enemies called the 'Black Hand', dedicated to Serb nationalist goals through terrorism.

Nationalist aspirations and international rivalries were given a new outlet with another sign that Turkish power was crumbling. The Italian attack on Libya in 1911–12 entangled Turkish forces in North Africa, giving Greece, Bulgaria, Serbia and Montenegro the inducement to overcome their differences. They held a series of painstaking negotiations for an alliance intended to drive Turkey out of Europe and to divide up the spoils. Russian encouragement of this 'Balkan League' was primarily aimed against Austria–Hungary; smarting from the Bosnian crisis, Russia wanted to forge a reliable alliance with the smaller states against the penetration of the region by Austro-Hungarian and, increasingly, German interests.[47]

The alliance bore its first bitter fruit in the First Balkan War, which opened in October 1912. Montenegro, followed by the other allies, attacked Turkey in a conflict which stretched from the Adriatic to the fortress of Adrianople. In six weeks the Turks were driven almost entirely out of Europe. In November Turkey requested international intervention, and in December two conferences were held concurrently in London: the peace negotiations between the belligerents and the London Ambassadors' Conference, which aimed to broker a new settlement of the 'Eastern question', replacing that of 1878. Macedonia was the bone sticking in all throats, but the boundaries of an independent Albania were also a source of contention. These fiery debates were interrupted when the war resumed in 1913 after another Young Turk coup. They were afraid that the Liberal government would surrender Adrianople (colourfully described by the Turkish ambassador as a 'window into our harem') to Bulgaria. The Treaty of London finally brought the war to an end in May 1913, but it brought no resolution to the Macedonian question and there were border skirmishes amongst the erstwhile allies. In June, Bulgarian troops finally launched a surprise attack on the Greeks and the Serbs in Macedonia. In this Second Balkan War, the Turks and Romanians joined the Serbs, Greeks and Montenegrins in a joint mauling of Bulgaria, which was overrun within a month. The Treaty of Bucharest in August 1913 stripped Bulgaria of much of what it had gained in the First Balkan War. While the Bulgarians clung on to some of their Macedonian conquests, most of the region was carved up between Greece and Serbia.

During the wars of 1912–13, south-eastern Europe was visited by the horrors which would shortly ravage the rest of the continent. For the first time, a military aircraft (Romanian) was seen flying over a large civilian centre (Sofia), albeit on reconnaissance. All sides, in both wars, committed appalling atrocities against civilians. Military casualties were also horrendous: of all the troops mobilised by Bulgaria (a staggering 600,000 out of a male population of just over 1.9 million), 21 per cent were killed or wounded, or died from disease. In all, combat casualties outweighed deaths from disease, owing perhaps to the artillery barrages and full-frontal attacks by infantry against well-prepared positions. It was, a British observer reported, 'the most futile and wasteful thing, he had ever seen in his life'. His words grimly foreshadowed the experience of the next great European war.[48]

16 Authoritarian and Conservative Responses

In the later nineteenth century, new forms of right-wing ideology evolved from older tendencies, creating movements which, while authoritarian, did not necessarily revolve around traditional conservative poles such as the Church, the monarchy, and the traditional elites, a form of conservatism which none the less persisted. The new authoritarianism put greater emphasis on the people as a source of power and sovereignty. For this reason, it gathered ideological momentum from sources which were hitherto usually associated with the left. It frequently rejected the hierarchical, paternalist conservatism of monarchists, while emphasising nationalism and social reform. It was also hostile to the allegedly corrupt, degenerating effects of parliamentary politics, which it sought to restrict or to destroy outright. It did not like capitalism, either, mainly for the effects which competition from big business had on small producers – peasant farmers, shopkeepers, artisans – who were frequently its core supporters. The interests of 'the people' would be pursued by strong government – a dictatorship or a powerful monarchy in alliance with its people – which would rise above the corruption of liberal parliamentarianism to improve social conditions for the masses and invigorate the nation as a whole. That nation was often defined as racially exclusive, denying, in particular, that Jews could ever be part of the national community. They rejected socialism because it emphasised class conflict over national strength and unity. The frequently ambiguous mix of ideas at work is best summed up in the term 'national socialism', which was coined not in twentieth-century Germany, but in nineteenth-century France, by the neo-royalist Maurice Barrès.[1]

France had already experienced populist, authoritarian government in the shape of the Second Empire, but the democratic, 'Jacobin' origins of the 'new right' in France can be seen in the *Ligue des patriotes*, established in 1882 with the aim of encouraging patriotism through propaganda and education. Radical republicans could applaud such goals, but its leader, Paul Déroulède, soon injected the toxins of xenophobia, anti-Semitism, social Darwinism and authoritarianism into its veins, opposing the parliamentary system and seeking to prepare the French 'race' for a war of revenge against Germany. The *Ligue des patriotes* struck a chord among some of the urban lower middle classes, who felt threatened by both large-scale capitalism and working-class militancy. It mushroomed to 100,000 members – 30 per cent of them in Paris. Although French Jews made up a tiny quarter per cent of the population, they were popularly associated not only with big business and finance, but also with support for the Revolution and the Republic, which the ultra-nationalists despised. Edouard Drumont exploited this seam of racial hatred, and his book, *La France juive* (1886), went through no fewer than 200 editions in 15 years. The extremes of the Catholic Church made their own noise: the newspaper, *La Croix*, which had a circulation of 170,000, condemned liberal Catholics and republicans alike in the wake of the secularising legislation of the 1880s. Its anti-Semitism, originally based on traditional religious arguments, also took on the racial elements adopted by the *Ligue*. Economic, religious and racial anti-Semitism were, ultimately, inter-related and provided the common ground between the different currents of anti-republicanism.

In the late 1880s the 'new right' found a figurehead. In some ways, General Georges Boulanger was an unlikely candidate: he saw himself as a Jacobin and his first real taste of political power came when he was appointed war minister in a Radical government in 1885. He loathed Drumont and refused to use anti-Semitism to promote his cause. Yet a nationalist cult developed around Boulanger because he introduced reforms in the army and struck a tough anti-German pose. In 1887 he went eyeball-to-eyeball with Bismarck to secure the release of a French officer accused of espionage. The politicians, alarmed at the dangers of a new form of 'Bonapartism', engineered the fall of the entire government in May. An unholy alliance coalesced behind Boulanger: the *Ligue* (which would provide the thugs for street-fighting); monarchists, such as the exuberant Legitimist, the duchesse d'Uzès (who secretly financed Boulanger) and the Orleanist comte de Paris; ex-Bonapartists; disaffected Radicals, such as Henri Rochefort; and revolutionary socialists, workers from the industrial suburbs who followed the doctrines of Auguste Blanqui. 'Boulangism', therefore, had no real sense of direction; it was bound together only by a common hatred of the Third Republic. The plan (such as it was) was for Boulanger to stand repeatedly in by-elections, which would be hailed as mini-plebiscites, forcing elections to a new assembly which would reshape France, though precisely in what image no one knew for sure. A series of electoral victories by Boulanger in 1888, a duel with the Radical prime minister, strikes and Boulangist demonstrations kept the situation on the boil until January 1889. That month, Boulanger triumphed in a Paris by-election, which his excited supporters interpreted as a sign of swelling popular support ahead of the general elections that year. Yet the Boulangists met their match in the dark and determined figure of Ernest Constans,[2] the interior minister who confined troops to barracks, massed police in the centre of Paris, banned all demonstrations and public gatherings, and recruited a 100-strong 'political brigade' – a police force which would keep watch on Boulangist leaders. The *Ligue des patriotes* was banned in March and its leaders subjected to house searches, which allowed Constans to put about the false rumour that evidence had been uncovered of Boulanger's treason. The General fled and committed suicide over his mistress's grave in Brussels in 1891.

In the General Elections of October 1889, government money, violence between republicans and Boulangists, and electoral 'manipulation' ensured that the republicans won an outright majority. The regime had survived its gravest danger since 1871, although to do so it had had to resort to authoritarian measures. None the less, in subsequent elections the very existence of the Third Republic would no longer be challenged. The Boulanger affair, however, crystallised the authoritarian tendencies on the extreme right. It was also an awe-inspiring exercise in mass politics. In 1889 the Boulangists distributed no fewer than five million posters in Paris alone and millions more in the provinces, along with 100,000 photographs of the General and a million pamphlets. Pictures of the whiskered General pasted on farmhouse walls may have been, as one republican official grumbled, merely a pastiche of the 'evil Napoleonic legend', but the republicans had to redouble their efforts to win over the peasantry. 'Boulangism', Michael Burns suggests, 'went a long way in preparing the rural politics of the twentieth century'.[3]

The defeated Boulangists seized the opportunity for revenge opened up by the Dreyfus Affair. In 1894 Alfred Dreyfus, a Jewish artillery captain assigned to the general staff, was court-martialled and sentenced to life imprisonment on Devil's Island for allegedly passing secrets to the Germans. Initially, few people doubted Dreyfus's guilt, but his relatives worked doggedly to clear his name. The army stubbornly refused to reopen the case, even after it was revealed that some of the evidence used to convict the captain was forged. The real spy, a dissipated officer named Marie Charles Esterhazy, was acquitted in January 1898. Yet to increasing numbers of republican intellectuals and politicians, the case against Dreyfus appeared to be founded on anti-Semitic prejudice. The novelist Émile Zola responded to Esterhazy's acquittal with a thunderous article, '*J'Accuse*!', in Clemenceau's paper, *L'Aurore*, accusing the army and the War Ministry of misleading the public and of perverting justice. This opened the affair proper, which was a struggle between two broad sweeps of opinion.

On the one hand there were those who believed that Dreyfus was guilty, pure and simple, or who, like many moderate republicans ('Opportunists'), may have had doubts but did not want to alienate the army. France, they feared, would be weakened if the honour of the army were to be questioned. The most venomous poison came from those who tried to mobilise anti-Semitic feeling against the Republic as a whole, namely the *Ligue des patriotes*, the ultra-Catholic Assumptionist Order, the newspaper *La Croix*, Drumont's journal *La Libre Parole*, and royalist army officers. Collectively, the various anti-Dreyfusard attitudes probably represented most of French opinion; 80 per cent of the French press condemned Dreyfus, and the affair sparked anti-Semitic riots in some sixty towns over an 80-month period. Many committed republicans, however, rallied to the Dreyfusard cause, seeing the struggle in terms of justice and human rights against clerical reaction. Young middle-class men had been made liable to conscription in 1889 and the liberals among them channelled their resentment against 'militarism'. The Dreyfusards virtually forgot the issue of Dreyfus's innocence and saw their cause as a defence of the Republic, its institutions and its values against its opponents among the Catholic clergy, royalists and ultranationalists. Radicals, socialists, Opportunists and a significant minority of moderate Catholics alike combined in a front for 'republican defence'.

When President Félix Faure died in February 1899 (he was in an amorous clinch with his mistress), his successor, Emile Loubet, supported a retrial. The reaction of the *Ligue des patriotes* and the especially nasty *Ligue antisemitique française*, which had fomented most of the anti-Dreyfus riots, was to plot a coup which was forestalled by Déroulède's arrest for treason. Though he was acquitted, he was rearrested in June after another nationalist demonstration which was met with an overwhelming Radical and Socialist counter-protest mustering 100,000 people. That same month, the divided Opportunist government fell from power and was succeeded by a Radical-orientated ministry of 'republican defence' under René Waldeck-Rousseau, which banned the *Ligues* and the Assumptionists. Dreyfus was at last retried in Rennes and, though the court martial stubbornly found the captain guilty, it added that it had been 'with extenuating circumstances', whereupon Dreyfus was pardoned. The government, however, put the army under close surveillance and made promotion dependent upon political reliability. While these measures no doubt helped to curb royalist impulses within the officer corps, they poisoned civil–military relations up to the eve of the First World War.

The political consequences of the affair were profound. It tore open the long-standing division between republicans and devout Catholics. Sore feelings had already been aggravated, particularly under Jules Ferry's ministry of 1882–5, which expelled the Jesuits, legalised divorce and excluded the clergy from the education system. Yet from 1890 a Catholic movement – the *ralliement* – had arisen for reconciliation with the Republic. Led by Cardinal Charles Lavigerie and encouraged by Pope Leo XIII, who issued an encyclical in February 1892, many French Catholics (including half of their bishops) now tried to work within the Republic in order to defend their Church. They were met halfway by Opportunists, eager to heal the rift in French society and to forge a broad, conservative coalition against the radicals and socialists. Yet the *ralliement* was ruptured by the Dreyfus affair. In 1901 a law on associations legalised all organisations except religious orders, which still had to seek authorisation. The Radicals won the elections in 1902, with the anticlerical Emile Combes forming the new government. Combes rigorously enforced the new law, dissolving all religious orders. In 1904 the regular clergy were banned from teaching in any kind of school, which led to the closure of Catholic schools. Diplomatic relations with the Vatican were broken and, in December 1905, Church and State were formally separated, which meant that all state support for the clergy (guaranteed since the Concordat of 1802) was withdrawn. Catholics protested against separation and there was violent resistance in some twenty departments. In practice, however, separation was not the death-knell of Catholic influence: local authorities and congregations came to informal agreements over religious activities; public collections paid priests' salaries; a youth movement developed alongside Catholic sports clubs and, though some one thousand, eight hundred Catholic schools had been closed by 1911, most of their pupils went to new, private schools run by Catholic lay teachers. None the less, the *rallié* attempt to forge a conservative Catholic–republican alignment had failed.

For the extreme right, the Dreyfusard victory had merely offered further 'proof' that the Republic was being manipulated by Jewish interests. It also reinforced the tendencies which had emerged during the Boulanger affair: the ability of right-wing groups to work together and their capacity for marshalling popular support with appeals to nationalism and anti-Semitism. In 1899 Charles Maurras founded *Action française*, a group prone to street violence, which combined ultra-Catholic royalism with anti-Semitism. Its newspaper of the same name, established in 1908, attracted (rather alarmingly!) a student readership. Amongst the French middle classes, the Dreyfus Affair also produced the ultra-nationalist *Ligue de la patrie française* in 1899, which, in 1901, helped to form the 'Yellow Unions' which, at their peak, attracted some hundred thousand workers. They emphasised co-operation with employers in resolving disputes but they were swept away in the upsurge of left-wing strike action from 1908.[4] The use of the popular press, street demonstrations, violence and the mobilisation of paramilitary groups presaged the totalitarian movements of the inter-war period.[5]

In Italy, disillusionment with the parliamentary system was far more pronounced. *Trasformismo* left a smouldering feeling that Italian politics were unresponsive to the needs of society. A banking scandal in 1893, which brought down one prime minister, left a reek of corruption hovering over the liberal regime. A generation after unification, the parliamentary monarchy had not been able to forge a strong sense of loyalty to the new state; the people of the *mezzogiorno* were still impoverished and devout Catholics continued to boycott elections. Yet their traditional, conservative opposition to the regime evolved.

Lay confraternities, such as the *Opera dei Congressi e dei Comitati Cattolici* established in 1874, were encouraged to run Catholic libraries, newspapers and social activities to win people over to the cause of the Church against the liberal state. The Pope discouraged the creation of a clerical party akin to the Centre in Germany, for fear that it would be drawn into Italian parliamentary politics and so give them legitimacy. In 1887 Francesco Crispi met with Vatican officials to discuss a reconciliation between the State and the Church, but a storm of intransigent protests from both Catholics and liberals washed away this germinating seed. Crispi's social reforms of 1887–91 then undermined the Church's role as a charitable institution. The *Opera*'s response was to develop into an alternative agency of 'social Catholicism', promoting welfare schemes to draw workers and peasants away from socialism (in Spain, similar organisations, the Catholic Circles, also flourished). In 1891 'social Catholicism' won the support of the Pope, whose encyclical, *Rerum Novarum*, criticised capitalist society and admonished Catholics to transform it. Yet, inevitably, Catholics became more active in local politics in order to influence the way welfare was dispensed, which drew them deeper into Italian politics. Moreover, for many Italian Catholics, the parliamentary state appeared to be a bulwark against socialist and anarchist agitation. After the 1904 General Strike, the Pope relaxed the *non expedit*, allowing Italian Catholics to vote against socialist candidates in the elections. Catholic deputies appeared in the legislature, keen for reconciliation with the liberal order. At the same time, however, Pius X (1903–14) sought to stamp his authority on the lay organisations, fearing that the Church had unleashed a political force beyond Vatican control. He broke up the *Opera dei Congressi* in 1904 and 'social Catholicism' lost momentum. None the less, Catholicism was now a political force at the very heart of the liberal order; Giolitti, Italy's last great pre-war prime minister, was dependent upon Catholic support in parliament from 1912, when he lost socialist support over the Italian war in Libya.

A wider Italian malaise with *trasformismo* and parliamentary politics in general fuelled a willingness to find authoritarian solutions to Italy's problems. In 1892 Pasquale Villari graphically expressed his disgust: 'Parliament is a real cesspit of baseness and immorality, and if the head of state were to kick out the occupants of the filthy stable of Montecitorio tomorrow, the whole nation would applaud.'[6] Francesco Crispi was convinced that Italy needed a 'great man' to complete the moral unification of Italy by 'making Italians' and, until his death in 1901, he convinced himself that the 'great man' *was* Francesco Crispi.[7] Although hindsight has almost certainly distorted historical judgments of this important figure, one can understand why Crispi should later have been regarded as a forerunner of Italian Fascism.[8] Even Crispi's opponents, such as the socialist intellectual, Guglielmo Ferrero, saw

Italy's salvation in a leader who could drag Italy along a progressive course. Crispi never fulfilled the role of saviour, but during his two terms as prime minister (1887–91 and 1894–6), he strove to 'make Italians' by invigorating patriotism with an aggressive foreign policy. His attempts to expand the Italian colonies in Eritrea and Somalia brought both his ministries to an end when they were parried by Emperor Menelik of Abyssinia, first in 1891 and then in 1896. On the second occasion, Crispi fell when an Italian force of 17,000 was destroyed at Adua, with 5000 killed and 2000 taken prisoner (some of whom were castrated). It was not the first time that Africans had defeated a European army, but the blow to national pride sent shock waves through Italian society. The appeal to patriotism and military glory as a means of bridging the chasm between 'real' and 'legal' Italy had proved to be a frustrating and costly failure. The deep sense of humiliation played havoc on Italian politics into the twentieth century.

Yet the parliamentary system survived – for the time being. Against the background of social unrest and socialist and anarchist agitation in the closing years of the century, the grumbling authoritarian voices became louder. In 1899, determined filibustering by socialists, radicals and republicans prevented a government under General Luigi Pelloux from passing laws to curtail civil liberties. King Umberto himself was convinced of the stabilising merits of parliamentary government, and Italy's appeals court declared Pelloux's measures illegal when he tried to issue them by decree. When Pelloux dissolved parliament and called elections, they were won by the left. The parliamentary system had worked – and the electorate had got rid of an authoritarian government by legal means.

Yet authoritarianism took on a new face which turned unambiguously against the liberal order and took the shape of ultra-nationalism. It fed off the sense of humiliation after Adua and fretted over Italy's decadence, its industrial backwardness and its need for regeneration through war and sacrifice. The nationalist movement's intellectual leadership came from the poet Gabriele d'Annunzio, who glorified war and death, while the former radical, Alfredo Rocco, gave it its political voice, persuading the 1914 nationalist congress to reject parliamentarianism. These ideas were transmitted through a nationalist press, which had newspapers in every major Italian city. Nationalist thugs were used to break a strike in Bologna in 1906 and the movement's hostility to socialism struck a chord with landowners and the middle class, but its economic theory was not capitalist, but 'corporatist'. The state would organise the economy, determining wage levels, conciliating workers and employers and raising tariffs. Trade unions would become associations of employers and workers in each trade and industry, and would be controlled by the state. While liberalism brought class struggle and economic competition, corporatism would bring co-operation – enforced if necessary. The parliamentary regime, nationalists argued, was merely encouraging socialism and sapping the vigour of the Italian people. They demanded larger armed forces, and it was partly to silence them that Giolitti ordered the conquest of Libya in 1911. It was a divided nation which entered the First World War in 1915.

Britain, with its old, glacially evolving parliamentary system, was not immune to what Robert Gildea has called the 'bitter pill of militarism'[9] in the years immediately before the First World War. The Liberal government was anxious about labour militancy (a general strike was threatened in 1914, but was called off with the war), but their main opponents remained, as always, the Conservatives. Relations between the two main parties were so strained that the rhetoric suggests that there was a verbal civil war going on. The Tories were enraged by the effects of the Liberal reform programme and by the idea of giving Home Rule to Ireland. The Liberals, they argued, were attacking landed property and destroying the integrity of the British Empire. Ireland itself was on the brink of a civil war with real blood and bullets, even as the crisis unfolded in Europe in the summer of 1914. Militarism played a part in stoking the political crisis. In order to pay not only for the welfare reforms but also for the armaments programme (namely, building the Dreadnoughts), the government had to find new sources of revenue. For the Tories, the naval race with Germany was a cudgel with which to batter the Liberals. In 1909 the Conservatives found an ally in the *Daily Mail*, whose polemics were summed up by the call for more Dreadnoughts: 'We Want Eight and We Won't Wait!'[10] Yet raising tariffs to pay for this, as some Conservatives demanded, was out of the question, as that would have boosted food prices and burdened the poor. The irony of the Tories' predicament was that the Liberals were – partly – responding to the pressure of the very popular chauvinism which the Conservatives had harnessed. Lloyd George's 'People's Budget' of 1909 put more weight on to the shoulders of the propertied, imposing higher levels of taxation on the wealthy, especially on their land. This horrified the Conservatives, who castigated the budget as 'the beginning of the end of the rights of property' and as a 'ruinous scheme of social reconstruction'. When, on the other hand, it became clear that the Conservative majority in the House of Lords would reject the budget, the Liberals' battle cry became 'the peers versus the people'.[11] The Lords repeatedly rejected the budget and in December 1910 – three elections and a vain effort at cross-party talks later – the new King, George V, intervened. He threatened the Conservatives that he would flood the Lords with Liberal peers unless they yielded. The upper house relented and the budget passed, but this could not obscure the depth of mutual anger felt by both sides. With the 1911 Parliament Act reducing the veto powers of the House of Lords, the Liberal prime minister Herbert Asquith was heckled as a 'Traitor! Traitor!' by Conservatives. Their own leader, Arthur Balfour, was forced to step down in November because he was considered to be too conciliatory towards the Liberals. In 1912 the Tory hardliner, Austen Chamberlain, surveying the political crisis, labour and suffragette militancy and a gathering storm in Ireland, warned of impending 'economic collapse' and 'civil war'. From this perspective, Britain's entry into the First World War begins to look like a desperate attempt to unite a bitterly divided country.

Germany was no less faced with a political schism made white-hot by the demagogic rhetoric of mass politics. As the government applied authoritarian solutions, including repression and encouraging popular chauvinism, it thwarted the possibility that the German Reich would move away towards a more liberal constitutional order. After Bismarck's break with the Liberals in 1879, they declined as a political force, both in the *Reichstag* and in the Prussian civil service, which was gradually filled with reliable, conservative figures. Bismarck embarked on a brief period of imperialist expansion in 1884 in order to emasculate the opposition. The National Liberals, under Johannes Miquel, made another shift to the right when they supported colonial policy and military spending, while their more radical liberal opponents, the Radicals, were hammered at the polls in an outburst of chauvinism among voters. In 1887 the government again exploited nationalist feeling to inflict a further defeat on its liberal opponents when it clashed with them over army funding. The Septennat (the seven-year army budget) was up for renewal in 1888, but tensions with France (gripped with Boulangism) demanded early assurances of increased military spending. In November 1886 the Catholic Centre and the Radicals demanded in return that the army budget be renewable every three years. In January, Bismarck dissolved the *Reichstag* and exploited German fears of French sabre-rattling to swing voters behind him. A pro-Bismarck majority – a conservative *Kartell* which included the National Liberals – secured the renewal of the Septennat and increased tariffs on grain. Yet distribution of parliamentary seats hid the reality of a divided Germany: the opposition (including the Centre, the Radicals and the SPD) actually secured half a million more votes than the *Kartell.* Bismarck was toppled not by a groundswell of public opinion but by the new Kaiser, Wilhelm II (enthroned in June 1888). Though autocratic at heart, Wilhelm was strongly influenced by evangelical ultra-conservatives with 'Christian Social' ideas. He sought to base his authority on an alliance with the working class by offering social reform underpinned by Christian, monarchist principles. He therefore backed the National Liberals when they abandoned the *Kartell* in 1889 because Bismarck proposed making the anti-socialist legislation permanent. When the *Kartell* parties were defeated at the polls in February 1890, Bismarck's parliamentary power base was broken. With the Kaiser unwilling to keep him on as Chancellor (as he might have done, despite the *Reichstag* majority stacked against him), Bismarck resigned in March.

The new Chancellor, Leo von Caprivi, declared that his task would be to bring politics back to 'the prose of everyday life'[12] with a policy of conservative reform, addressing some of the tensions in German politics and society while conceding little of the imperial government's power. In contrast to Bismarck's combative political style, Caprivi tacked on to a 'new course', in which he sought reconciliation and a halt to the persecution of socialists. There was a new burst of social reform and, between 1891 and 1894, Caprivi tried to address worker discontent by negotiating a series of treaties with several countries, lowering German tariffs on grain, cattle and timber, while assuring German industry of markets for 12 years. The 'new course' was derailed over two persistent problems: military spending and fear of social unrest. The left defeated the 1892 military bill, which would have reduced the period of service and allowed the *Reichstag* to review the military budget every five years but would also have increased the size of the army. Caprivi dissolved parliament and, in the elections of 1893, the parties which had supported the bill – the Conservatives and National Liberals – were able, as in the past, to play the patriotic card and increase their seats. Caprivi's 'new course' could not reconcile increased army spending with conciliation of the left. Meanwhile, the greatest opposition to Caprivi's conciliatory policies came from Prussia, where National Liberals and Conservatives alike were alarmed by democratic and socialist trends in German society. The Kaiser himself resented Caprivi's reformist policies and he listened to voices at court who urged a coup to reduce the powers of the *Reichstag* and allow the government to introduce further anti-socialist legislation. Caprivi resigned, his 'new course' having failed to silence the socialists but having stimulated shrill conservative opposition in the country at large. A middle way between authoritarian and democratic solutions to Germany's problems remained elusive.

Indeed, a head of steam was building behind authoritarianism within civil society. The Agrarian League was formed by Junkers in 1893 to oppose Caprivi's lower tariffs and to press for government assistance to agriculture. Though led by the traditional elites, it was joined by farmers and peasants, so that it had over two hundred thousand members by the end of 1894. Closely allied to the Conservative Party, the Agrarian League was a vociferous voice, demanding, as the British philosopher Bertrand Russell scornfully explained, 'a minimum of constitutional government . . . and a maximum of agricultural protection . . . When agriculture is not sufficiently protected to please them, they can use language for which any Social Democrat would get years of imprisonment.'[13] In the past, Prussian Junker conservatism had not been particularly populist, but, to protect their political and social position, the elites now sought to seduce the peasantry and the lower middle class by adopting a demagogic programme – protectionist, anti-socialist, anti-Semitic and ultra-nationalist.

In so doing they encouraged forces which they could not control. In the 1890s, primarily middle-class organisations such as the Pan-German League (formed in 1891), the German Colonial Society (1892) and the Navy League (1898) emerged, adopting radical nationalist programmes which spouted the superiority of German culture and demanded a vigorous foreign policy, greater military expenditure and the acquisition of colonies. Peasantry and artisan movements, such as the Bavarian Peasants League and the Central-German Peasants Association sought more protection for the 'small man' against 'unfair competition' and opposed policies which, they claimed, favoured Jews at their expense. These sentiments gave momentum to conservatives. The Navy League, in fact, was established with the help of Admiral Alfred von Tirpitz to mobilise public support behind his naval-building programme. Yet the elites, whether heavy industrialists or Junkers, were trying to ride on the back of a dragon which could turn back to bite them. Half of the seats won by the populist, ultra-nationalist groups in the 1893 elections were at the expense of Conservatives. While useful allies against the left, the demagogues were also shrill, sometimes hysterical, critics of the conservative order when it failed to meet their radical expectations.[14]

Yet the mobilisation of right-wing populism also drew middle-class support away from the National Liberals, and liberalism in general began to slide into political oblivion. The National Liberals won around a hundred seats in the *Reichstag* for the last time in 1887. In elections from 1893 until 1912 they and the Radicals together hovered around forty to fifty seats. The decline of the liberal centre in the two decades before the First World War was an ominous sign of polarisation towards ultra-nationalists on the right and the SPD to the left. Yet in the mid-1890s the liberals still had enough fight in them to combine with other parties, such as the Centre and the socialists, to resist the authoritarian drift. The *Reichstag* voted down an 'anti-subversion' bill in 1895, an attempt to restrict the suffrage, and, in 1899, a bill to outlaw unions and strikes. Caprivi's successor, Prince Chlodwig von Hohenlohe, also resisted conservative and royal pressure to strike at the parliament and he obstructed the Kaiser's efforts to ban socialist meetings and organisations in Prussia. The Chancellor had no wish to inflame political passions any further.

Conservatives in the later 1890s sought to overcome the schism within German society by rallying all non-socialists around the Kaiser's throne. 'Social imperialism' through *Weltpolitik*, which meant asserting German nationalism on a global scale, would leave the internationalist socialists out in the cold as 'unpatriotic'. The architect of this policy was Bernhard von Bülow, who became foreign minister in 1897 (and Chancellor in 1900), asserting that 'only a successful foreign policy can help to reconcile, pacify, rally, unite'.[15] Sure enough, only the SPD and the Radicals opposed Admiral Alfred von Tirpitz's 1898 bill for the construction of 16 battleships, which was supported by a loud campaign waged by the Navy League. A further bill to build three warships a year for six years was carried in 1900. The government extended the welfare system between 1900 and 1903, but these measures did little to undercut support for the SPD, whose vote streaked upwards by a million to just over 3 million in 1903, since the navy programme was paid for by increases in agricultural tariffs in 1902. Bülow fretted about the 'incalculable consequences' of the socialist danger and, when the expected revenue increases did not yield enough to feed the accelerating naval race with Britain, Bülow was forced to introduce tax increases to parliament in 1906. The tax bill was pummelled from all sides in their attempts to avoid shouldering the burden, which ultimately fell on to the workers. This came just as the authorities were bracing themselves for the tail of the storm from the Russian Revolution of 1905. The authorities saw the 'red menace' behind SPD protests against restrictions on the franchise in Hamburg in 1906. In 1907, after his colonial policies were attacked by the Centre and the left, Bülow dissolved the *Reichstag* and, in the elections, the Chancellor campaigned once more on the nationalist ticket, deriding his opponents – with the help of ultra-nationalist groups – as unpatriotic.

These so-called 'Hottentot' elections slashed the SPD presence in the *Reichstag* to only 43 seats. Both National Liberals and Radicals had joined the conservative parties in the anti-socialist campaign. Yet this so-called 'Bülow bloc' proved to be an unworkable coalition and it fell apart in 1909, forcing the Chancellor's resignation in July. Meanwhile, the left continued to exert pressure. In 1908, Prussian workers clashed with police when the SPD, despite winning almost a quarter of the vote, were given only seven seats in the Prussian parliament. More riots followed in 1910 when the Kaiser's hasty promise of political reform was not delivered. Reform of the Prussian constitution, particularly in light of the adoption of universal male suffrage (Württemberg, Alsace-Lorraine) or direct elections (Baden, Bavaria) by other parts of the Reich, became one of the key political issues for German liberals and socialists.

Bülow's successor, Theobald von Bethmann Hollweg, was determined to stop 'the disturbing descent into parliamentarianism that was threatening to become a habit'.[16] Yet he was faced with the difficult task of holding together a crumbling political wall against the socialists. He did little to offend the conservative parties; in 1910 a bill for reform of the Prussian parliament was withdrawn and a tax on inheritances was rejected. This meant, however, that Bethmann Hollweg had to cut government expenditure – even on the navy, leading the ultra-nationalists to criticise him for lack of patriotic steel. In the 1912 elections the government was punished for its conservative policies with a swing to the left. Radicals and socialists had made electoral pacts in certain constituencies, and the SPD, with 4.25 million votes – or a third of the electorate – and 110 seats, became the largest party in the *Reichstag*. Yet no party had an absolute majority and so there was parliamentary stalemate, which merely encouraged the authoritarian tendencies at court and in the government. The Kaiser leaned more heavily towards the army, not only because of heightened international tensions but also because he wanted to shore up his defences against the 'red menace'. The surge of the left caused panic in conservative circles, who established the 'Prussian Alliance' to launch a wholesale attack on democratic trends in Germany. The authoritarian and militarist tendencies within the system were revealed after an incident in Alsace in November 1913. Some ill-advised remarks by an army officer about the locals led to demonstrations in Zabern, where the army, bypassing civilian channels, imposed a state of siege. While liberal opinion was outraged, conservatives, including the Kaiser, rallied to the defence of the army. The *Reichstag* passed a vote of no confidence in the Chancellor, but had no right to dismiss ministers; only the Kaiser could do that, and Wilhelm gloated that he could ignore the vote. In the words of William Carr, 'the Zabern affair was a lightning-flash which suddenly illuminated the horizon',[17] revealing the divisions between those who wanted to move towards wider constitutional rule and those defending militarism and the prerogatives of the Crown. It showed, moreover, that the *Reichstag* could not control the army and that neither the Chancellor nor the monarchy was responsible to parliament. On the very eve of war, Germany had still not settled on one of the essential foundations of constitutional monarchy.

Before 1905, Russia was the conservative state par excellence. After 1905 it was a constitutional monarchy, but one prone to the temptations of popular chauvinism and authoritarianism. Tsar Alexander III, who stepped over his father's mangled corpse to accede to the throne in 1881, had always been chary of the great reforms, and the assassination merely steeled his determination to restrict their liberalising effects. He promulgated an emergency statute, which remained in force up to 1905. It allowed the government to declare states of emergency and to act with varying degrees of severity towards public order. It gave provincial governors and the police wide-ranging powers to deal with unrest and threats to state security. In severe cases, the governor could impose martial law and close down the *zemstva*, municipal councils, schools and newspapers. In 1881 the statute was first imposed on ten provinces, affecting some 27.5 million of the Tsar's subjects, leading Lenin to remark that the statute was 'the real constitution of Russia'.[18] Civil liberties were reeled back. Educational opportunities were blocked: an order of 1887 admonished officials to keep the children of 'coachmen, servants, cooks, washerwomen, small shop-keepers'[19] and others out of secondary schools. In 1883 a secret police, the *Okhrana*, was established to investigate 'state crimes' to prevent strikes, and to watch suspects, public meetings, demonstrations, educational institutions and social clubs.[20] With detachments only in Moscow, St Petersburg and Warsaw in 1900, it was hopelessly undermanned to carry out this wide remit, but in practice it had an 'external service' of secret agents, informers and agents provocateurs, to whom most of its budget went. These people ran into thousands, while a 'Black Office' employed hundreds of civil servants to read the people's mail. Yet Russia, even when one adds the regular police, was less densely policed than Britain at the time, and an estimated 5000 revolutionaries were still working underground during Alexander III's reign.

The impact of peasant emancipation and the powers of the *zemstva* were hemmed in. In 1889, land captains, to be appointed from among the nobility, were empowered to overturn decisions made by peasant communes and cantons and were to enforce the will of the central government in the villages. Judicial independence was undermined with abolition of the justices of the peace, except in some urban areas. The land captains supervised the district (*volost*) courts, which since 1861 had handled justice among the peasants. Until 1904 they could order the public flogging of peasants for misdemeanours such as trespass on gentry land. The *zemstva* reform law of 1890 denied both the land-owning peasants and the Jews the right to vote for the provincial *zemstva*, whose membership and measures had to be confirmed by the provincial governor and the interior ministry. Their budgets were capped and their employees were harassed by police. Similar measures were inflicted on the municipal councils in a statute of 1892.[21]

While the regime's grip relaxed from time to time, about a quarter of the population was living under the provisions of the 1881 Emergency Statute in 1905. In the explosive events of that year, the autocracy itself collapsed. Yet the monarchy's authoritarian impulses did not. The Tsarist order resolutely clawed back some of its losses from the wreckage. It crushed the socialist revolution in the cities; in December 1905, troops arrested the St Petersburg Soviet and an insurrection, led by the Bolshevik-dominated Moscow Soviet, was crushed. That defeat unleashed the regime's counter-revolutionary campaign. From 1906 to 1909, 5000 members of the socialist parties were condemned to death and a further 38,000 exiled or imprisoned. 300,000 troops were used to stamp out the revolt in Poland, and 1200 peasants were killed in the Baltic provinces. In Russia, Cossacks and regular troops galloped through the countryside, imprisoning, flogging, hanging and shooting peasants. In all, 15,000 people were executed, thousands more were wounded and 45,000 were exiled even before the first duma met. Between August 1906 and April 1907, military tribunals hanged a further 2700 peasants. The government had also counter-attacked on the constitutional front. It created an indirect voting system, similar to that in Prussia, whereby the voters were divided up into separate *curiae* of nobles, burghers, peasants and workers, ensuring that representation in the duma would be heavily weighted in favour of the nobility. In February 1906, as the elections were under way, the Tsar created an upper house, the Council of State, half elected by the *zemstva*, the Church, the nobles and other elite, corporate bodies, and the other half nominated by the Tsar himself. Then, as the duma assembled in April, the Tsar issued the Fundamental Laws, declaring that he was still an autocrat and giving himself and the State Council a veto. When the duma was not in session, the Tsar could rule by decree. His ministers were not answerable to parliament, but the deputies could at least question ministers and propose legislation, and had immunity from arrest.

From July 1906, when the Tsar prorogued the first duma, the man given responsibility for the salvation of the monarchy was Peter Stolypin. Nicholas liked him because of his iron will in repressing the insurrection – nooses became known as 'Stolypin's neckties' – but he was a flexible conservative who also wanted to address the underlying causes of revolution. His premiership was marked by efforts at wide-ranging reform. He wanted, on the one hand, to create a responsible, loyal citizenry by guaranteeing civil rights and reforming local government, education, justice (including the abolition of the separate peasant courts) and even the government's emergency powers. He also wanted to broaden the social basis of the monarchy; while most of the nobility now rallied to the Tsar, Stolypin understood that this was too narrow a foundation. He set out, therefore, to create 'a wealthy, well-to-do peasantry, for where there is prosperity, there is also, of course, enlightenment and real freedom'.[22] A prosperous, property-owning peasantry would have been a force for stability. Stolypin's agrarian reforms, promulgated as an emergency measure in November 1906, gave the peasants the right to break away from the commune in order to form their own consolidated, private farms. It was, Stolypin would tell the duma in 1908, a 'wager . . . on the sturdy and the strong'. Peasants were sceptical; the commune offered a measure of collective welfare for the peasants, who also worried that the wealthier among them would separate with the best land. Conservative village patriarchs exerted intense and frequently violent pressure on members of the community not to do so. Of 6 million applications received by the government by 1915, a third were withdrawn because of pressure or intimidation. By 1916 only 10 per cent of peasant households in European Russia had consolidated their holdings into independent farms. They would be among the first targets of the peasant revolution in 1917.

Stolypin's reforms were also vehemently opposed by ultra-conservatives, who mobilised popular chauvinism in the streets. While some organisations were traditionally monarchist, such as the 'Russian Assembly' composed of government officials and army officers, the largest group was similar to the new authoritarian movements in western

Europe. The 'Union of the Russian People' (the 'Black Hundreds') spoke of a popular autocracy, was opposed to liberalism and socialism, and was anti-Semitic and ultra-nationalist. By the end of 1906 it had attracted 300,000 members in 1000 branches, mostly shopkeepers and artisans, low-ranking civil servants, police officers, and peasant-workers. They fought socialists and liberals in the streets and attacked Jews. In the weeks after the October Manifesto, they were behind most of the 690 pogroms which killed over three thousand Jews – 800 of them in Odessa. The Black Hundreds were supported by the Tsar, who hoped that it would develop into a popular conservative party, and their publications were financed by the ministry of the interior. Opposed by both left and extreme right, Stolypin's policies fell apart. The second duma, which opened in February 1907, reflected the political polarisation and was dissolved three months later. The government immediately changed the suffrage (with the Electoral Law of 3 June 1907) so that the most privileged 1 per cent of the country would control 300 of the duma's seats. In the third duma, therefore, the conservative Octobrists leapt to 154 seats, but the ultra-conservatives won 150 seats. The Electoral Law thus proved to be double-edged for the government. The Octobrists supported Stolypin's reforms, which would favour the peasantry, but the ultra-conservatives did not. Stolypin was also faced with mounting hostility from the Tsar himself, for whom his reforms went too far. By the time he was shot by a lone gunman – who, as it turned out, worked for the secret police – on 1 September 1911, Stolypin was already a lame political duck. The Tsarist regime's intransigence made further social and political instability almost certain, although the First World War would determine its cataclysmic nature in 1917.

17 Imperialism

In 1899, Earl's Court in London hosted the 'Greater Britain Exhibition', which celebrated the achievements of the British Empire. 'Greater Britain', the catalogue boasted, 'is the synonym of the greatest nation which has become the greatest empire the world has ever seen.'[1] Yet by that date the proud sway of British imperialism was being challenged by other European powers, particularly France, Germany and Russia, while other countries, such as Italy and Belgium, were snapping at the heels of the front runners in what had developed into a race for empire. Citizens of these states made similar claims to national greatness, a grandeur which they related to the extent of their imperial dominions, although popular enthusiasm for empire oscillated over time and varied from one European country to the next. Set in the context of the entire period from 1789, the European imperial race was a sprint rather than a marathon.

Yet there were also continuities with imperialism in earlier decades. European overseas commercial interests had led to more complicated political entanglements. 'Informal' imperialism, in which the European power was the dominant economic partner, would be in evidence in the later nineteenth century, just as it had been in the middle decades. Some earlier conquests were, like much of the feverish land-grabbing of the later phase, pre-emptive, crudely aimed at preventing another European power from seizing the same territory. Conflict sparked by local resistance to an alien culture drew European governments into asserting political control. Imperial possessions were seized by freelancing military officers acting either without orders or in flagrant breach of them, but ministers then had to be wary of relinquishing the ill-gotten gains for fear of enraging public opinion sensitive to slights against national prestige. The earlier European conquests therefore set important precedents for the 'fevered pitch'[2] of imperialism, which began in earnest in the early 1880s and continued up to 1914 – or to 1920 if one includes the carve-up of the defeated German and Ottoman Empires after the First World War.

Yet the catalysts for the great territorial scramble need to be explained. Despite earlier conquests, by 1880 there was little sign that the European powers would partition the whole African continent, for example. The Colonial Office in London had, in fact, been considering giving up all the British possessions in Africa except for the Cape for two decades, while the demoralised French had abandoned the Ivory Coast in the wake of their defeat in the Franco-Prussian War. They also considered evacuating other West African colonies 'because of the trivial scale of French interests there'.[3] Yet in the space of three decades, from 1882 until 1912, all of Africa, except for two independent states, Liberia and Abyssinia (Ethiopia), had been gorged upon by the European powers in an expansionist orgy. European (and American) feet also trampled through Asia and the Pacific, subjugating old kingdoms and prising concessions from local governments (see Map 17.1).

One of the most important differences between the piecemeal expansionism of the earlier period and the imperial burst of the late nineteenth century was the growing importance of public opinion. A fusion of popular imperialist attitudes with nationalism was a bitter cocktail which governments ignored at their peril. These attitudes were honed by increasingly tense international relations in the four decades before the First World War. In 1885 Jules Ferry had justified French imperialism by warning, 'in today's Europe, in this competition of the many rivals whose power we see growing around us . . . abstention is, very simply, the road to decadence!'[4] Social Darwinist ideas, moreover, suggested that, in the fierce competition between peoples and races, the losers would face an undignified if not nasty fate. As the scramble gathered pace, imperialists were nagged by an overwhelming sense that the world itself was, for once and never again, to be partitioned. Moreover, colonies might have some value some day, even when it was not immediately obvious. German ambitions were driven by this *Torschlusspanik* – literally, a panic that the door was being closed to Germany in the race for empire. It was best to join the dash rather than be left behind while the other powers shared out the prizes. As the *Korrespondent* newspaper put it in 1883, Germany could not watch 'other nations appropriate great tracts of territory and the very rich natural resources that go with them'.[5] In 1893 the British Foreign Secretary, Lord Rosebery, adopted the language of gold prospectors: 'We are engaged . . . in pegging out claims for the future.'[6] An explanation for the scramble for concessions in China was that the powers anticipated that it would be territorially partitioned like Africa. For King Leopold II of Belgium, the concession of the Beijing–Hankow railway line in 1898 was to be the first stage towards asserting claims to territory in China.[7]

The sense of urgency was not just coldly voiced in the corridors of power, but had a wide public resonance. Popularised versions of Darwinist, nationalist and racist ideas circulated widely before and during the great imperialist explosion. In Germany in 1881 the Hamburg lawyer Wilhelm Hübbe-Schleiden published an influential book which argued that international competition was a struggle to the death between races. Only those peoples who managed to spread their culture over wider areas of the world would survive. It was, therefore, imperative for Germany to establish overseas colonies.[8] One of the more extreme versions of British social Darwinism argued that 'feeble races

Map 17.1 European Overseas Empires, 1914

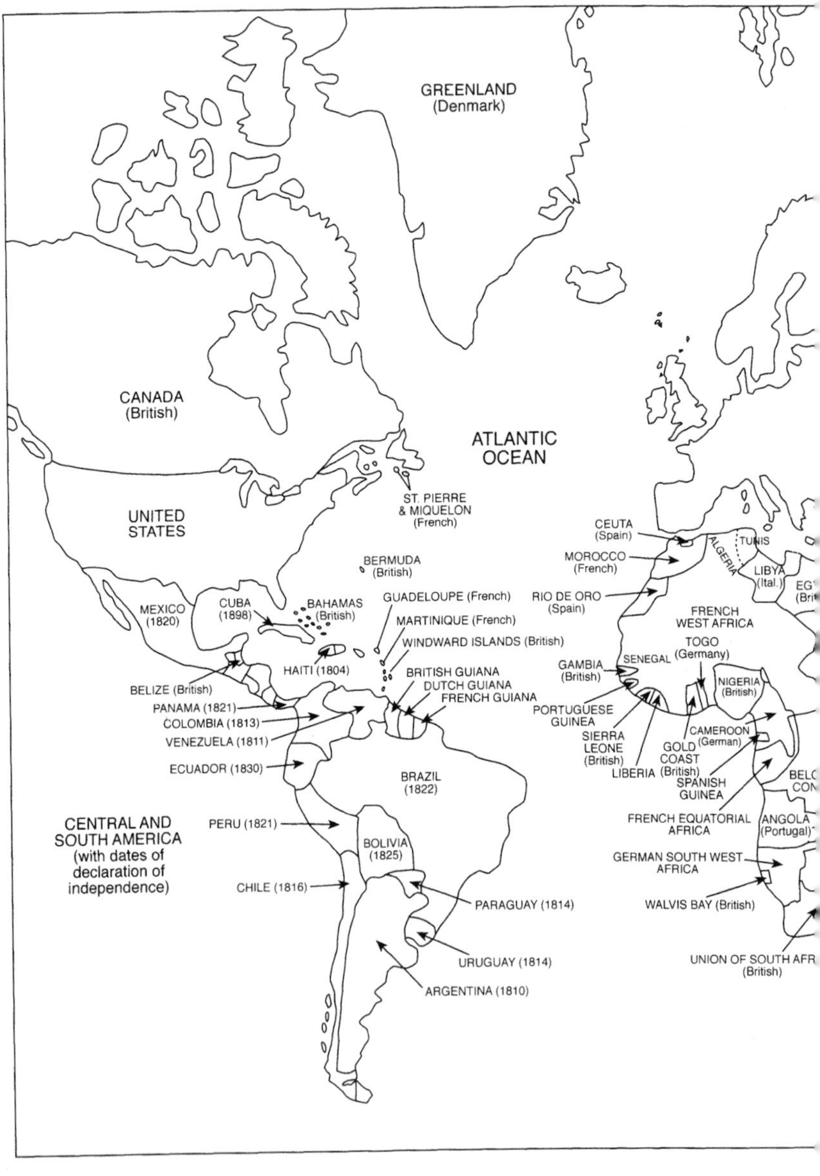

RUSSIAN EMPIRE
Russian (annexed from 1854)
St Petersburg
Moscow
Trans-Siberian Railway
Russian (annexed from 1854)
CAUCASUS
TASHKENT
CHINA
MONGOLIA
MANCHURIA
AMUR
JAPANESE EMPIRE
PACIFIC OCEAN
Port Arthur
Wei-Hai-Wei (British)
Kiaochow (German)
Hong Kong (British)
Shanghai
Ningpo
Kwangchow (French)
AFGHANISTAN
PERSIA
Russian sphere of influence
British sphere of influence
TIBET (occupied by China)
NEPAL
INDIA (British)
ERITREA (Italian)
FRENCH SOMALILAND
DIU (Port.)
GOA (Port.)
Yanaon (French)
Pondicherry (French)
Karikal (French)
ADEN (British)
BRITISH SOMALILAND
ETHIOPIA
ITALIAN SOMALILAND
UGANDA (British)
BRITISH EAST AFRICA
ZANZIBAR (British)
GERMAN EAST AFRICA
NYASALAND (British)
MADAGASCAR (French)
RÉUNION (French)
PORTUGUESE EAST AFRICA
RHODESIA (British)
BECHUANALAND (British)
(British)
CEYLON
MALAYA
INDIAN OCEAN
BURMA
SIAM
INDOCHINA
Macao (Port.)
Taiwan
Amoy
PHILIPPINES (USA)
SARAWAK (British)
MARIANAS (German)
MARSHALL ISLANDS (German)
CAROLINES (German)
EAST TIMOR (Port.)
KAISERWILHELMLAND (German)
BISMARCK ARCHIPELAGO (German)
DUTCH EAST INDIES
NEW GUINEA (British)
British spheres of influence
French sphere of influence
AUSTRALIA (British)
NEW CALEDONIA (France)
NEW ZEALAND (British)
Amoy Chinese Treaty Ports

are being wiped off the earth and the few great, incipient species arm themselves against each other. . . . Now, with the whole earth occupied and the movements of expansion continuing, [Britain] will have to fight to the death against successive rivals'.[9]

Such ideas presupposed the superiority of the European races over the others. In 1898 Benjamin Kidd informed his audience that 'the *natural* inhabitants of the tropics . . . represent the same stage in the history of the development of the race that the child does in the history of the development of the individual'.[10] Such people, it was implied, would benefit from the firm guidance of European rule. The Earl of Cromer, looking back at his days as governor of Egypt, explained to his readers that Egyptian hostility towards the British 'has been mitigated by the respect due to superior talents, and by the benefits which have accrued to the population from British interference'.[11] In 1885 Jules Ferry justified French overseas expansion by proclaiming the French *mission civilisatrice* (civilising mission): 'Can anyone deny that there is more justice, more material and moral order, more equity, more social virtue in North Africa since France carried out its conquest?'[12] Religious motives also played a role: Christian missionaries played up the 'backwardness' and the 'degradation' in which they found indigenous peoples. Indeed, while in French domestic politics republicans and Catholics waged a virtual civil war, republicans grudgingly admitted that, *overseas*, the clergy had a useful role to play as the agents of French influence.[13] Imperialist attitudes became deeply embedded in popular culture. A German showman delighted crowds with his display of 'exotic' people, including a Cameroonian dubbed 'Prince Dido', complete with top hat and tails. Songs in British working-class music halls tended to emphasise British imperialism as a liberating force, bringing help to the backward, enslaved peoples of the world, but increasingly they became more strident and xenophobic. The term 'jingoism', describing such chauvinism, stemmed from popular theatre.[14]

The apparent popularity of imperialism has led some historians to argue that governments seized on overseas adventures to divert public attention away from domestic conflicts. This was 'social imperialism', a mechanism by which Hans-Ulrich Wehler explains Bismarck's imperialism in the 1880s: 'to divert attention away from the . . . consequences of uneven economic growth, away from social tensions and away from the emancipatory task of modernizing German constitutional life and of democratizing society'.[15] Critics of Wehler's thesis, including Geoff Eley, have suggested that membership of the key groups promoting imperialism, such as the Colonial Society (founded in 1882) and the Navy League (1898), tended to attract the elites and the middle classes, rather than the workers, whom they failed to mobilise. 'Social imperialism', therefore, failed to seduce workers away from the blandishments of socialism and rally them around the conservative order. Moreover, their ultra-nationalism was as much a nuisance to the ruling elites as it was a force for stability.[16] Other critics have suggested that while Bismarck's policies were not a case of social imperialism, the later *Weltpolitik* pursued by governments from 1897 almost certainly was. Bismarck, argues Paul Kennedy, did not trumpet the success in acquiring South West Africa, Togo and the Cameroons in 1884, which one would expect from some one seeking to manipulate public opinion. Unlike Bülow, who from 1897 did follow a social imperialist policy of overseas expansion, Bismarck had no commitment to construct a great German navy, which would have been an essential component of a sustained and meaningful strategy of appealing to nationalist and imperialist impulses.[17] Bismarck casually argued in 1889 that Germany had no political interests in Samoa, but a decade later Bülow urged that 'the entire Samoan question has absolutely no material, but an ideal and patriotic interest for us'. By that stage, public attitudes had changed; in 1890 Bismarck lost power partly because he ignored the swell in imperialist attitudes. By 1897 German support for empire was widespread enough to make *Weltpolitik* a viable weapon with which to blast the socialist and radical opposition. Bülow explicitly argued that building a navy and the German bid for empire were driven by a need 'to direct the gaze from petty Party disputes and subordinate internal affairs on to the world-shaking and decisive problems of foreign policy'.[18]

Italian dreams of an empire in Africa were certainly intended for domestic consumption. Political unity alone had not forged a national consciousness, and veterans of the *Risorgimento*, such as Francesco Crispi, who had passed through the fiery crucible of war and revolution, believed that conflict was the anvil upon which patriotic Italians could be forged. Under domestic political pressure in 1894, Crispi believed that a 'baptism of blood' was needed to rally popular support behind the liberal state and to 'make Italians' in a surge of patriotism. As Italy was preparing for war against Menelik II, Emperor of Ethiopia, the newspaper *La Riforma* trumpeted, 'the new Italy has begun to be formed . . . we can now claim that not only Italy, but also Italians, have been made!'[19] Yet the evidence that public opinion took the bait is ambiguous, to say the least. When Crispi's forward policy came to grief at Adua in March 1896, there were some demonstrations in support of the war in Sicily, but riots elsewhere, though led by radicals and socialists, were no less an expression of popular anger. Public enthusiasm for Italian imperialism remained lukewarm, if not downright hostile, right up to the outbreak of the First World War, even during the Libyan conflict in 1911–12.[20]

In France, consistent public support for imperialism proved to be equally elusive. The *parti colonial* (French colonial lobby) never numbered more than 10,000 at any time before 1914. The various businesses and groups with colonial interests were not incorporated into an umbrella organisation, the *Union Coloniale Française*, until 1893. Unlike in Germany, the French ultra-nationalist movement was hostile to an empire. The French, they argued, should not dissipate their energies overseas, but should muster their strength for the recapture of Alsace and Lorraine; 'I had two sisters', Paul Déroulède roared, 'and you are offering me twenty domestic servants.' On the left, Radicals agreed that colonial entanglements sapped French strength for the next war. Meanwhile, the resources would be better deployed helping French people at home. Georges Clemenceau fumed in 1885, 'while you are lost in your colonial dreams, there are at your feet men, Frenchmen, who call for useful and beneficial efforts to develop French genius'.[21] In 1913 the colonial lobby fretted that France lacked 'that "imperial" consciousness which, in Britain, makes the humblest of subjects quiver with pride at the merest evocation of British power'.[22] Popular interest in French imperialism tended to be ignited in times of crisis, as it was after the Fashoda incident and during the two Moroccan crises of 1905 and 1911. Such reactions were not symptoms of support for colonialism itself, but rather a response to slights on national honour by other European powers. Defeat by a non-European power brought a different reaction. In 1885, when the Chinese forced the French to retreat from Langson in Indochina, the humiliation not only ended Jules Ferry's career, but the subsequent elections produced the Third Republic's most anti-imperialist parliament. Even British popular attitudes, which the French colonial lobby viewed so enviously, could be ambiguous. In the 1880s British opinion was apathetic until British soldiers were killed. Gladstone was crucified in the press when General Charles Gordon died at Khartoum, but, between such crises, public discussion was muted. The *Spectator* wryly commented, 'our people hardly watch or listen unless some favourite officer falls dead'. When Gordon was impaled by a Mahdist spear, the same journal commented on the 'chasm' between the newspaper reports and the 'true drift of British opinion . . . the former are often fierce, frothy and fickle; while the latter is slow, calm, and steady'.[23]

Public opinion, therefore, was not consistently supportive of imperialism but could sustain it at decisive moments. It was stirred less by the prospect of overseas dominion over non-Europeans than by a defensive reflex to national humiliation and defeat. Yet if colonial lobbies and organisations only fully captured public imagination intermittently, they were still able to force their policies on a reluctant (or, more usually, indifferent) public for two reasons. Domestically they had friends in high places, while overseas the agents whose activities they supported often acted on their own initiative, forcing the government to react to the consequences of their behaviour. The German colonial movement read, in the words of one historian, 'like a "Who's Who" '[24] of leading business figures, including Siemens, Krupp and David Hansemann (also a leading National Liberal). A combination of the Kaiser and figures from the imperial lobby helped to squeeze Bismarck, who had lost interest in colonies after his brief foray in 1884, out of office in 1890.[25] In France, the *parti colonial* was a small but well-organised group of businessmen, lawyers, professionals and journalists. It consistently knew what it wanted, as against an inchoate body politic and public opinion which, while indifferent to colonies, was still strongly nationalist – an emotion which could be exploited by imperialists. Neither voters nor politicians were indifferent when they believed that French honour had been slighted. At such critical junctures, therefore, governments ignored the combination of popular chauvinism and well-oiled colonial interests at their peril.

Many contemporaries explained the surge of European power as a natural consequence of the rise of industrialism and as a 'social imperialist' safety valve for the pressures of social change. Emigration creamed off the surplus population of European countries, but the people who went to independent states such as the United States or Argentina were then 'lost' to their mother country. Colonies, on the other hand, would ensure that emigrants would remain loyal citizens, while also providing a diversion from social antagonisms. In 1895 Cecil Rhodes argued, 'in order to save the 40,000,000 inhabitants of the United Kingdom from a bloody civil war, we colonial statesmen must acquire new lands to settle the surplus population'.[26] In 1910 Enrico Corradini, the ideologue of the Italian Nationalist Association, declared with self-disgust, 'We are an emigrant nation . . . a proletarian nation', but argued that an empire in Africa would allow Italians to retain their identity in Italian colonies, rather than lose their nationality in immigrant countries such as the United States. In Germany, Friedrich Fabri, who led a Protestant Missionary Society, published a book on colonisation in 1879, arguing that modern industrial society could not nurture the 'German' characteristics which belonged to a fast-disappearing age but agrarian colonies could, thus preserving the natural virtues and vigour of the German race.

Explanations for imperialism as a product of economic development focus mainly on international competition and the search for markets. Lenin defined imperialism as the 'monopoly stage of capitalism', by which he meant the inevitable growth of capitalism from its youthful, free-market phase to another level, in which great firms and cartels dominate world markets. Imperialism, he wrote in 1916, is driven by the need to find export markets for capital; 'the division of the world by the international trusts [i.e. companies] has begun . . . and the partition of all the territory of the earth by the greatest capitalist countries has been completed'.[27] Marxist views, therefore, relate imperialism to industrialisation in Europe, the expansion of world markets, a need for food supplies and raw materials, and increasing competition among the industrialising powers for a share in these global markets and resources. The economic stimulus to imperialism cannot easily be refuted, though it was not consistently the main factor.

The rise of international competition, which became especially fierce in the late nineteenth century, challenged British predominance of world markets, which meant that the policy of 'a fair field and no favour' no longer seemed so attractive, neither to the British nor to the latecomers. These rivals included not just European powers such as Germany but also the United States, Japan and, in textiles, India, which between 1885 and 1913 was challenging its British masters in some markets. In the words of one economic historian, 'economic growth was now also economic struggle' and, combined with political rivalries, it was expressed 'in that final surge of land hunger and that chase for spheres of influence that have been called the New Imperialism'.[28] British trade in 'visible' (agricultural and manufactured) products had been running at a balance of trade deficit since 1800, a deficit which increased every decade. In other words, Britain was importing more visible products than it was exporting, not least because the population was dependent upon food imports to feed itself. Until 1890 this deficit was covered by an impressive growth in 'invisible' exports, such as banking, insurance and other financial services, while a third source of income, investments overseas, also brought in a significant return. After 1890, with the rise of foreign competition, invisible exports were no longer enough to cover the annual deficit in visible trade, so overseas investments became correspondingly more important. While some British critics argued that the best remedy was to invest in British manufacturing to boost industrial exports, for others the remedy was for the government to act, first, to maintain and widen overseas markets, and, secondly, to expand openings for overseas investment. In the last decade of the nineteenth century, 92 per cent of new British investments overseas went to countries outside Europe, half to Africa, Asia and Australasia, while a third of all British exports went to the British Empire. These markets were, however, rapidly being cornered by other European powers, which were then raising colonial tariff barriers against their rivals. While the British stubbornly adhered to free trade, the government was drawn into taking action to ensure that British commerce was not unduly disadvantaged by European powers who gave special privileges and protection to their own subjects. The protection of colonies and markets became an important element in British imperialism in the later nineteenth century. Sometimes that meant annexing territory which, while strategically important, may have had little commercial worth.[29]

In 1885, as Germany joined the 'scramble for Africa', Bismarck – a renowned sceptic about colonialism – explained, 'Our colonizing efforts are measures designed . . . to help German exports', being 'nothing more than an additional means of promoting the development . . . of German economic life.'[30] The Great Depression, which was in an acute phase in the mid-1880s, had put Bismarck under immense pressure to help boost the German economy through an export drive. As other industrialising countries were also seeking similar markets and, like Germany since 1879, were turning to protectionism, free trade no longer seemed enough to meet the needs of German industry. German colonies in Africa provided lucrative contracts for railway investment, while, in return, German firms profited from imports of rubber, ivory, peanuts, palm oil and cotton. Portuguese imperialism was even more driven by economics. The slump in agricultural prices in the 1870s and the simultaneous rise of international competition against its nascent industries were disastrous for the Portuguese economy and state, which was facing bankruptcy by the early 1890s. High tariffs were imposed in 1892 to protect Portuguese trade with the empire, so that by 1914 the proportion of exports, particularly wine and cotton fabrics, being shipped from Portugal to its colonies increased from 3 per cent to 15 per cent.[31] By 1914 the French empire accounted for 9.4 per cent of French imports and 13 per cent of its exports, but the colonies were vital for *specific* French industries, such as bleached cotton, beer, shoes, and iron and steel building materials and rails. Meanwhile France drew the vast majority of its rice, cane sugar, table wine, olive oil, phosphate and groundnuts (used for soap and as an industrial lubricant) from its empire.[32]

A prime example of imperialism as a jealous urge to ensnare overseas markets was the forcible opening of trade leases by European powers in China between 1898 and 1902. This 'unhinged' the 'open door' policy, which had been forced on the Ch'ing dynasty in the middle decades of the century by the British, whereby Chinese 'treaty ports' would be open to all for free trade. When Japan heavily defeated China in the war of 1894–5, Chinese power collapsed, as the Japanese seized Taiwan and Korea and imposed a heavy indemnity. When the Emperor went begging to the Western powers for loans, Britain's commercial rivals saw their chance. They offered funds in return for their individual, exclusive use of Chinese ports and trading privileges in China, particularly in railways, mining and shipping. The British saw off the challenge to their commercial preponderance for three years, but the cracks appeared when Germany forced China to cede Kiaochow at the end of 1897, followed by the Russian acquisition of Port Arthur and the French lease of Kwangchow Bay in 1898. This unleashed the 'scramble for concessions', as European powers raced for exclusive use of Chinese ports, and from there hoped to establish spheres of influence and even direct control within the hinterland. Trying to stop the scramble was, as *The Times* put it, like 'trying to keep out the ocean with a mop'[33] so the British joined in the mêlée. They seized the port of Wei-hai-wei in the north, leased more of the Kowloon peninsula opposite Hong Kong and secured the rich commercial route of the Yangtse River. Britain at least hoped to preserve Chinese territorial integrity and did so with a series of agreements with Germany, France and Russia in 1899–1900. This shielded China from Africa's fate, while Britain's 1902 alliance with Japan restored some regional stability, but the free-trading 'open door' policy was over, as each imperial power jealously guarded its ports, its concessions and its 'spheres of influence' from the other. The consequences were dramatic: the Boxer rebellion of 1900 was a reaction not just against Christian, European and American influence, but also against the Emperor K'ang Yu-wei's attempts to strengthen the central government by introducing administrative centralisation and other 'Westernising' policies. The rebellion, encouraged by the Dowager Empress, who declared war on the European powers, was crushed with an international effort. China was further saddled with an indemnity and European garrisons. The Empress had to yield control of Chinese customs and duties to the Europeans. The crumbling power of the Ch'ing dynasty hastened its overthrow in the Revolution of 1911, after which President Sun Yat-sen sought to forge a democratic, nationalist regime.

When the dust began to settle after the global stampede, the colonies, protectorates and concessions did not emerge as the great markets and sources of raw materials anticipated by some imperialists. The Portuguese found that, important as the colonial markets were for cotton and wine, they did not absorb all the surplus production accumulating in the metropolis. While the French economy was certainly entangled with colonial markets, only certain sectors were deeply involved. Local interests, such as the ports of Marseille and Bordeaux and the silk-weaving city of Lyon, were islands of enthusiasm for economic imperialism within a rather placid sea of indifference.[34] For French investors, Europe was a more attractive prospect than the empire. By 1914 half of the 45 billion francs invested abroad remained in Europe, of which an impressive 11.3 billion were sunk into Russia. Only 4 billion went to the colonies.[35] The relatively poor return from colonial markets certainly helps to explain the short-lived eagerness (if he was ever truly eager at all) with which Bismarck approached Germany's overseas acquisitions. In 1886 he admitted that he was 'unenthusiastic about overseas colonial policy'.[36] Up to 1914, colonial trade accounted for only 1 per cent of German imports and exports. Most of the 2 million marks invested in Africa by 1914 was sunk into regions other than the German colonies. Germany was increasingly dependent upon non-European imports for food and raw materials (rising from 25 per cent to 45 per cent between 1890 and 1914), but most of these came from Australia and the Americas.[37]

The relative unimportance of colonial trade for most European countries should not obscure the fact that important economic interests *believed* – however fleetingly – in the commercial and financial benefits of empire. Bismarck's hunch that German economic interests would be better served by informal, commercial exploitation rather than by imperial control proved in the long run to be correct. None the less, as before, the European seizure of territory sometimes took place when older economic arrangements broke down in the face of bankruptcy or local resistance. The British occupation of Egypt in 1882, which unleashed the European scramble for African territory, occurred after the ruler, Khedive Ismail, went bankrupt in 1875. Over the next seven years, political and financial control by Europeans grew by stealth as they sought to protect their investments. Egyptian nationalists and Muslim leaders, resentful of this foreign influence, responded by toppling the Khedive in 1879. The growing cohesion of the Egyptian national movement confronted the French and the British with a choice: either to cut all their losses and abandon Egypt or to assume direct rule. In 1882 the British opted for the latter course of action.[38]

Yet there were capitalist critics for whom neither free trade nor capitalism was intrinsically imperialistic; to Cobden's voice in the mid-nineteenth century one could add J. A. Hobson's study, *Imperialism*, first published in 1902. Hobson believed that capitalism would ultimately benefit everyone. Imperialism was actually a perversion of capitalism by a selfish minority of businessmen who exerted a disproportionate influence over both government and public opinion. It is certainly true that some economic exploitation was based on methods more reminiscent of seventeenth-century mercantilism than free-market capitalism. In 1892, to bolster government revenue, the Portuguese government effectively restored seigneurialism on the *prazos*, the plantations of Mozambique. Tenants on state-owned plantations were to perform labour services as a means of commuting their tax obligations, while African workers were not allowed to leave the estate without permission.[39] In the Dutch East Indies, Indonesians were forced to perform labour services for the colonial government and to dedicate a fifth of their land to the production of cash crops such as coffee, tea, sugar and indigo, to be surrendered to the government in lieu of taxation and in return for which the farmers received wages. Dutch liberals, adhering to free-trade principles, roundly criticised this 'cultivation system' and, in 1870, they passed an agrarian law aimed at encouraging European settlement and developing the Indonesian economy based on free labour and private property. The reforms failed and the fiscally lucrative cultivation system persisted until 1915.[40] Attempts to exploit indigenous workers in German East Africa (present-day Tanzania) led to a long revolt, the Maji-Maji rebellion of 1904–6. It was so called because the insurgents believed that a sprinkling of holy water (*maji*) made them impenetrable to German bullets. It proved not to be so, but the colonists were forced to introduce a regime based on incentives rather than forced labour.

If European imperialism was driven partially by international competition, then strategic concerns, such as the defence and cornering of markets and the protection and consolidation of trade routes, would also have been important. Such concerns bound imperialism up with political rivalries. The great age of imperialism, while not afflicted by a major European war, was an epoch of sharpening international antagonisms. Imperialism, therefore, may have been the bitter fruit of such rivalries. The French were allowed to occupy Tunisia in 1881–2 because Bismarck wanted to channel French energies away from European affairs. In 1890, Germany recognised British dominance in the Nile Valley and a British protectorate over Zanzibar in return for a reward much closer to home: the British withdrawal from the North Sea island of Heligoland, a potentially threatening naval base. Imperial possessions, in other words, could be used as leverage in European politics. Conversely, disputes over imperial spoils could rebound on European affairs.

A potential source of conflict was the vast Congo Basin. In 1884 the British had forced the Portuguese to relinquish their dreams of forging a great African empire linking Angola with Mozambique. The ensuing British–Portuguese agreement, however, conflicted with the dreams of other European powers. King Leopold of the Belgians feared that his possessions in the Congo would be cut off from the Atlantic by the Portuguese, the British and the French (who had their own Congolese colonies on the coast). When the Germans had declared a protectorate over South West Africa (along with the Cameroons and Togo) in 1884, they had also refused to recognise the British–Portuguese treaty. European governments, therefore, grew increasingly apprehensive about the impact which these disputes were having on international relations. Bismarck summoned an international conference in Berlin, which was held from November 1884 to March 1885. The conference accepted Leopold's claims, giving him a vast territory, named the Congo Free State, south of the River Congo. This became Leopold's personal fiefdom until his brutal mismanagement led the Belgian government to take it over in 1908. French claims to the right bank of the Congo, the Gabon and the vast hinterlands were recognised, as was Germany's seizure of the Cameroons and South West Africa (Namibia). The Portuguese grip on Angola was confirmed.

The Berlin Conference may have eased tensions, but it did not satisfy European hunger for more expansion and so it did not resolve the underlying diplomatic conflicts. The British–Portuguese dispute was reignited later in the decade. Cecil Rhodes's dreams of linking the Cape to Cairo with a red carpet of British territory dissected Portuguese ambitions to link Mozambique with Angola. Rhodes's forces clashed with the Portuguese, forcing Scottish missionaries (who were opposed to colonialism) in Nyasaland (Malawi) to call reluctantly for protection. A

British ultimatum in 1890 forced the Portuguese to back down, a 'humiliation' which had serious domestic consequences in Portugal. German–British tensions would be inflamed over this region when, during the British war against the South African Boers (1899–1902), the Germans twice proposed a 'continental league' which would force the British to end the war.

Further north, in 1898, the British and the French nearly went to war over the Sudan. The origins of the clash lay in the British occupation of Egypt in 1882, which left the French, who had economic interests in the country, simmering in near-impotent rage. The British position in Egypt was challenged, however, when supporters of the Sudanese Islamic sheikh, the Mahdi, disrupted Egyptian rule (and therefore British influence) in the Sudan, culminating in the death of Gordon at Khartoum in 1885. This left the Sudan open to other European powers, and the French greedily eyed the Upper Nile Valley. They hoped to link their colonies in Western and Equatorial Africa to the Red Sea and also to dislodge the British from Egypt. Over a decade later, a French expedition finally struck out from the French Congo. At Fashoda in 1898 it confronted a British force, fresh from defeating the Mahdists at Omdurman. The French government backed down and, though the humiliation had serious domestic consequences, war was avoided.

Colonial rivalries certainly inflamed tensions among the European powers, and governments were not above exploiting imperial frictions for diplomatic leverage. Germany's behaviour over Morocco in 1905 and 1911 would provide further examples of this. Imperialism provided a wider field upon which European states challenged each other. Yet European ministers were often reluctant imperialists. They were frequently driven into imperialist adventures less for 'rational' political and economic reasons than because they were responding to popular impulses which they either shared or which they sought to contain or exploit. Indeed, cooler political calculations might have militated *against* trying to satisfy imperialist urges. Under Italian nationalist pressure to seize Libya from Turkey in 1911, Giolitti wondered whether it really was in Italy's interests to provoke the break-up of the Ottoman Empire, a 'cornerstone' upon which was 'founded the equilibrium and peace of Europe'.[41] Yet such careful calculations were frequently too subtle for those who had invested too much energy and emotion in the glories of overseas expansion, and Giolitti succumbed to nationalist pressure and approved the assault on Libya. To ascribe to governments a consistent strategic and diplomatic rationale for overseas expansion gives them credit for a control over events which they never really had.

This is especially true of the behaviour of zealous imperialists on the ground. Their actions, supported by the colonial lobbies at home, could suck governments into the imperialist whirlpool. The very distances which separated the metropolis from adventurers such as the Briton

Cecil Rhodes, the French explorer Pierre de Brazza and the German Carl Peters made them almost uncontrollable. These people often forced the pace of imperialism when they exceeded whatever authority they may have had and ran into trouble with local people. Meanwhile, the domestic lobby, or public opinion in general, appealing to national prestige, demanded government action to salvage the situation. A ministry willing to ignore public pressure, force the imperialist hero to back down and then bear the storm of nationalist indignation would be a government with a political death wish. The French explorer, Pierre de Brazza, undertook a series of expeditions into the Congo and Gabon between 1875 and 1885. The government authorised the exploration, but not Brazza's 1882 treaty with the Batéké, who ceded what became 'Moyen-Congo' (Middle Congo) to France. Yet parliament ratified the annexation, not because public opinion was interested in France acquiring the Congo but because it was inflamed by the British occupation of Egypt that same year. The colonialists exploited this feeling, organising a 'committee for the defence of French interests threatened by Britain'. Brazza became a national hero and the government had no choice but to defend his conquests at the Berlin conference in 1884. Lieutenant-Colonel Borgnis-Desbordes ignored explicit orders when he undertook a series of expeditions from Senegal, occupying Bamako on the Niger River and then thrusting into the Soudan (present-day Mali). 'Once in the Soudan I can thumb my nose at everybody, and it will take a brave man to stop me from doing whatever I think best', he cheerfully wrote home.[42] Berlin found German agents equally difficult to keep on a leash. In the mid-1880s Carl Peters, founder of the *Gesellschaft für Deutsche Kolonisation*, and sponsor of the German East Africa Company, made several expeditions into Africa, negotiating with local rulers until he had accumulated some sixty thousand square miles of territory. He presented these acquisitions to a flabbergasted Bismarck, who reluctantly placed the territory under German protection, securing international recognition at the Berlin conference. The incorrigible Peters then explored Uganda and Tanzania between 1888 and 1890, alarming the British, for whom Peters was getting too close to the Nile for comfort. When the British protested, the Germans were only too happy to relinquish any claims to the Nile in return for the British withdrawal from Heligoland. Peters's behaviour profoundly irritated the German government, whose primary concerns were diplomatic, and he was tried in 1897 for official misconduct while serving as government commissioner in German East Africa. Governments may have exploited imperialist attitudes when it suited them, but in doing so they were unleashing a force which they could not always control.

18 The Origins of the First World War

On 28 June 1914 a car carrying the heir to the Austro-Hungarian throne, Archduke Franz Ferdinand, made its way along the quay on the Miljacka River in Sarajevo, the capital of Austria–Hungary's provinces of Bosnia-Herzegovina. In a twist of fate, the chauffeur had missed his turning and so was forced to reverse back along the quayside, giving a nervous young assassin, Gavrilo Princip, his chance. He fired two shots. The first struck the Archduke and the second went astray as an onlooker tried to knock the gun from Princip's hand. It hit the Archduke's wife, Sophie, the Duchess of Hohenberg. She was already dead when the mortally wounded Archduke begged her to live for their children. He died trying to reassure those around him by whispering, 'It is nothing . . . it is nothing.'

Events were to prove that he was tragically wrong. Princip was a member of the Young Bosnians, recruited from tough young peasants, who dreamed of an independent Yugoslav state. They had sought the support of the Black Hand, an ultra-nationalist Serbian organisation bitterly hostile to Austria–Hungary. Its leader, Colonel Dragutin Dimitrijević ('Apis'), had allowed the Young Bosnians to be supplied with bombs and pistols. The Habsburg monarchy was far from blameless in the ensuing crisis. Voices in the imperial government alleged that the Serbian government itself sponsored the terrorists and the assassination became the excuse needed by Austria–Hungary to settle accounts with its prickly southern neighbour. Why this regional crisis escalated into the first general European war since 1815 needs to be explained. Princip himself, who would die in prison in Terezín in 1917, spent the rest of his days ridden with guilt (and tuberculosis), but his only consolation was a suspicion that sooner or later the war would have broken out anyway. He was probably right.[1]

In the immediate aftermath of the conflict, the most convenient explanation for the victors was German responsibility (the notorious 'war guilt' clause in the Treaty of Versailles in 1919). Some politicians, however, argued that the international system itself had broken down. In David Lloyd George's graphic image, 'the nations in 1914 slithered over the brink into the boiling cauldron of war'. Others blamed the proliferation of arms in the years before 1914; the British foreign minister in 1914, Sir Edward Grey, suggested that 'the enormous growth of armaments in

Europe, the sense of insecurity and fear caused by them – it was these that made war inevitable'. Historians have also focused on the role of different powers, namely the rivalry between Austria–Hungary and Russia over south-eastern Europe, and French and British relations with Germany. In fact, these factors were bound up with two major geo-political issues: the 'German question' (the place of the new, dynamic German state within the European and, indeed, world order) and the persistent 'Eastern question'.

In the 1870s these two issues were causes for co-operation, although the usual mistrust between the great powers never lurked far beneath the surface. After German unification, Bismarck sought to secure the new German state from a resurgent, vengeful France by cultivating conservative, monarchical solidarity between Germany, Austria–Hungary and Russia. This was the purpose of the *Dreikaiserbund*, which broke up on the reef of the 'Eastern crisis' of 1875–8. Yet the Congress of Berlin in 1878 enabled Bismarck to act as 'honest broker' between the powers, presenting Germany as a force for peace. However, Bismarck also saw the integrity of the Habsburg empire as a keystone to the stability of the new European order, so he tended to back Austria against Russia. In 1879, therefore, he persuaded the reluctant Kaiser to seal an alliance with his old enemy, Austria. The purpose was defensive: Austria–Hungary and Germany would support each other if Russia attacked either. For the battered Habsburgs, this alliance was a welcome guarantee of security. For Bismarck, the alliance would enable Germany to restrain Austrian behaviour in south-eastern Europe and, by creating a front ostensibly aimed at Russia, would persuade the Tsar to remain on good terms with Germany. Bismarck also persisted in trying to keep France isolated by drawing Italy into the agreement, forging the Triple Alliance in 1882. For a few years after 1878, therefore, it looked as if careful brinkmanship and diplomacy had secured Germany's position in Europe (Bismarck sought to reassure the powers by announcing that Germany was 'satiated'). Bismarck's alliances worked to contain the rivalries between Germany, Austria–Hungary and Russia. In 1887 Bismarck revealed the precise terms of the Austro-German alliance to the Russian ambassador in order to convince him to sign a 'Reassurance Treaty' with Germany. France was kept isolated and, therefore, resolutely pacific within Europe. Britain, still the pre-eminent, though no longer unchallenged, global power, sought to avoid the commitment of alliances altogether. These balancing acts were upset by developments from the 1890s. The French broke out of their diplomatic isolation, Germany made a push for global power, and irredentism in south-eastern Europe intensified. As Paul Schroeder suggests, after 1890 Germany 'lost control of the system' which Bismarck had constructed.[2]

The Dual Alliance between France and Russia, sealed in 1893 (and ratified by France in January 1894), was, in many ways, the inadvertent product of German actions. While in France the desire for revenge (*revanche*) and the recuperation of Alsace and Lorraine fluctuated, no one could honestly expect France and Germany to be on warm terms after the experience of 1870–1. French *revanchisme* and German Francophobia were rekindled in the 1870s and 1880s by periodic war scares and border incidents. Military discussions between France and Russia had begun in the 1870s as a means of meeting the challenge of the German industrial–military powerhouse. Moreover, Bismarck inadvertently strengthened Russia's financial ties with France. In 1887 his ban on the sale of Russian government bonds on the Berlin Stock Exchange (to coerce Russia into a more co-operative mood) merely drove Russia to look for other sources of capital for its industrialisation programme. Tsarist bonds proved popular with French small investors, giving closer political ties to St Petersburg a popular basis. The Franco-Russian alliance was explicitly defensive against the Triple Alliance ('having no other object than to meet the necessities of a defensive war, provoked by an attack of the forces of the Triple Alliance') and against German aggression in particular.[3] From Russia's perspective, the alliance would safeguard its western frontiers as it turned eastwards, developing its Siberian hinterland and pressing into Manchuria and China. It would also preserve the balance of power in Europe, which for Russia seemed most endangered by the military and industrial might of Germany.[4]

Although both the Triple and Dual Alliances were defensive, the secrecy of European diplomacy (for example, the public was not aware of the Franco-Russian agreement until 1897 and most French ministers were kept in the dark about its precise terms until war broke out) did little to ease mutual suspicions. Even when the signatories publicly acknowledged their alliance, other powers could not be certain that it was secretly not more than defensive. Moreover, balance-of-power politics had assumed that when one state threatened the others with hegemony, the others, or some of them, would coalesce to cut that state back down to size. The functioning of this system required flexibility in international relations, since different states endangered the balance of power at different times. Alliances, however, are concrete agreements which, if they are to survive, require consistent engagement and demonstrations of mutual support. Russia's commitment to the balance of power was henceforth expressed in terms of the defence of France against Germany, while Germany was bound to prevent the disintegration of Austria–Hungary in the face of Russian pressure. The existence of the two alliances, therefore, narrowed the room for manoeuvre in European relations, encouraged the great powers to make assumptions about the hostile intentions of the other camp and fostered a need to support allies in times of crisis.

In the 1890s, however, an actual war between the two alignments still seemed remote. Austria–Hungary was facing a domestic political crisis. Russia was industrialising and concerned with eastward expansion. *Revanchisme* in France began to cool off from around 1895 as the Franco-Prussian War began to pass into memory and as it sought to continue its overseas expansion, which proved more likely to bring it into conflict with Britain than with Germany. In 1899, after the Fashoda incident, the French and Russians renegotiated their alliance to include a defensive clause against Britain. None the less, German reluctance to support French claims to Morocco after 1900 and to reach an agreement with Britain over imperial expansion in Asia led, in 1901, to the two Western powers opening discussions to bury the hatchet over certain imperial issues.

Britain, moreover, had another good reason to reach an accommodation with her French and Russian competitors. From 1897 Germany embarked earnestly on a drive for world power (*Weltpolitik*), which ensured that the relative stability among the great powers would not survive into the twentieth century. It was not as if Germany could be accused of being the only state indulging in overseas expansion. The problem was that Germany's drive for world power posed a direct challenge to Britain, whose empire was the most obvious obstacle to Germany's assumption of its global position. British opinion was, above all, unsettled by the German programme of naval construction. The German government did not envisage an offensive naval war against Britain. Admiral Tirpitz, in line with contemporary strategic thinking, believed that if Germany had two battleships for every three floated by Britain, then the German navy stood a chance of victory if it was on the defensive. He calculated that, given Britain's widespread colonial commitments, the 2:3 ratio would eventually – by 1920 – give Germany a balance with Britain in the North Sea but not dominance. The German navy was to be capable of inflicting such serious damage on the British fleet that the British would not contemplate fighting. Tirpitz hoped that a fleet of some sixty battleships lurking so close to British shores would persuade the British to yield concessions to Germany overseas.[5]

Weltpolitik and the naval programme had two consequences: the British responded with shipbuilding of their own and Britain's foreign relations were realigned as it resolved its imperial disputes with France and Russia. British naval thinking was driven by the 'two-power standard', whereby the Royal Navy was to be stronger than the combined fleets of the next two maritime powers. Although Britain was fully aware of the danger from the burgeoning German navy (the diplomat Sir Francis Bertie put it colourfully: 'the Germans' aim is to push us into the water and steal our clothes'[6]), the response became more vigorous after 1904 when Sir John Fisher became First Sea Lord. In 1906 the navy built the *Dreadnought*, the most advanced warship of the day, rendering Tirpitz's ships obsolete. The next phase of the naval race was, therefore, more costly and was turning into a marathon which the Germans could not win. The pressure was piled on with the British emergence from self-imposed diplomatic isolation. In fact, the drawn-out Boer War of 1899–1902 had already exposed the difficulty faced by Britain in sustaining its position against its competitors. The British, therefore, signed an alliance with Japan in 1902 in order to contain Russian and German influence in China and Manchuria. In 1904 Britain and France reached an agreement primarily over their colonial rivalries. The Entente Cordiale allowed Britain to consolidate its hold on Egypt, while France would be allowed to create a protectorate over Morocco. Moreover, Siam would be left as an independent buffer between British possessions in Burma and French Indochina. While neither an alliance nor an agreement necessarily aimed at Germany, it was a headache for German policy-makers, who had long assumed that the Franco-British rivalry was insurmountable and that sooner or later Britain would have to confer with Germany over global issues. Germany, therefore, tried to break the Entente in 1905 when the Kaiser landed at Tangier in Morocco, declaring his support for Moroccan independence and demanding equality for German commerce there. French politicians talked about the potential for conflict with Germany, while the British feared German plans for a naval base on the Atlantic coast. The Algeciras conference in January 1906 recognised French influence in Morocco (which none the less remained an independent state). This first Moroccan crisis also gave the British and the French occasion to consider the military possibilities of the Entente. Concurrently with the conference, French and British staff officers discussed co-operation in the event of war with Germany. As the crisis unfolded, the Russian navy was destroyed in the war with Japan, severely blunting another danger to the British Empire. The Russian government, meanwhile, was now keen to improve relations with Britain, so it could consolidate its hold on its eastern possessions without fear of interference. In 1907, Britain and Russia reached an entente, with both powers settling their differences over Persia, Afghanistan and Tibet.

By 1907, therefore, the rivalry between Britain and Germany had brought the former out of isolation and into agreements – though not formal military alliances – with France and Russia. The role of imperialism as a root cause of the First World War should not, however, be exaggerated; right up to 1914, Britain and Germany were able to negotiate over their imperial differences on a case-by-case basis. An agreement over British and German involvement in extending the Baghdad railway to Basra on the Persian Gulf – to which Britain's Entente partners were opposed – was signed less than two months before the war broke out. Yet for Germany the danger of diplomatic isolation arose at the Algeciras conference, where Austria–Hungary was the only power to support its position. Italy proved to be an unreliable ally: in 1902 the

Italian government had promised to support French claims to Morocco in return for a free hand in Libya, and the two sides agreed to remain neutral if either was attacked by another power.

With only Austria–Hungary as a reliable but apparently dependent ally, there was talk in Germany of 'encirclement' by the Entente powers. Once the Franco-Russian alliance became known in 1897, German plans had been drafted for a two-front war. In 1905 the Chief of the General Staff, Alfred von Schlieffen, drew up his plan for a lightning-strike against France, after which Germany would turn eastwards and fight a longer war against Russia. This does not mean that Germany was planning to go to war, although there were some people in the military, including Schlieffen himself, who advocated a pre-emptive strike against Britain and France. It does show, however, that military planning and expectations were being shaped by emerging diplomatic alignments. German fears of 'encirclement' – and an aggressive response to it – were forcefully vented during the crisis which followed the Austro-Hungarian annexation of Bosnia-Herzegovina in 1908. German backing helped to force the Russians to yield, but war was also avoided because Russia, recovering from the 1905 Revolution, could not afford international conflict.

Yet peace came at a price in 1908–9. The Bosnian crisis, coming hard on the heels of Russia's humiliation at Japanese hands, left a deep residue of bitterness in its relations with Austria–Hungary and Germany. In 1914, when Austria again threatened Serbia, Russia was determined neither to abandon its Slav ally nor to bow to German bullying a second time.[7] Meanwhile, although Austria–Hungary and Serbia would sign a trade agreement which would bring the 'Pig War' to an end in 1911, relations between the two states would progressively deteriorate. In 1908–9, Francis Joseph and his foreign minister, Aehrenthal, were reluctant to take any steps against Serbia which would portray Austria–Hungary as the aggressor. Yet others within the government, like the Chief of General Staff, Conrad von Hötzendorf, fretted over the dangers posed by Serb or Yugoslav nationalism to the integrity and security of the Austro-Hungarian monarchy. In the spring of 1909 Hötzendorf urged war. He was overruled, but in subsequent years – and especially in the summer of 1914 – he would lament what he saw as a lost opportunity to deal with the Serb threat before it developed.[8] The Bosnian crisis thrust the unpalatable 'Eastern question' back on to the international table in a way not seen since 1878.

A series of imperial disputes stretched international tensions further. The second Moroccan crisis in 1911 stemmed from the French attempt to establish a protectorate. In the spring of that year, riots against the Sultan in Fez gave France the pretext to send troops into the town to protect the French population. This put central Morocco under direct French control and, even when order had been restored, the soldiers remained, which breached the accords reached at Algeciras and a later agreement in 1909 giving some rights to Germany, who now seized on this opportunity to demand compensation. In July the German gunboat, *Panther*, anchored off the Moroccan port of Agadir. Talks opened, with the Germans demanding – and the French refusing – all of the French Congo. Anti-German elements in the French government, particularly the colonial lobby, considered the possibility of war, but those who favoured conciliation were strengthened by a warning from Joseph Joffre, the French Chief of the General Staff, that the French military was not prepared. Voices in the British government, alarmed at the prospect of a strong German presence in Morocco, made it clear that Britain would be prepared to support France by going to war against Germany. Austria–Hungary, meanwhile, repaid staunch German support over Bosnia by failing to back Germany, because Vienna had no vital interests at stake. In November 1911, therefore, the French and German governments came to an agreement whereby Morocco would become a French protectorate in return for economic concessions to German interests there and a helping of Congolese territory.

The consequences of the second Moroccan crisis were profound. It inflamed French public opinion, rekindling *revanchisme*, which had been muted for a few years. The French government had at least begun to recognise that the population of Alsace and Lorraine was less and less interested in reunion with France. In Germany, nationalist opinion was aroused not just against France but against Britain, whom it blamed for blunting Germany's African initiative. None the less, both the British and German governments still nursed the hope that they could resolve their own imperial differences. The danger of military conflict over Morocco shocked both governments, and negotiations over the naval race, unsuccessful in 1909–10, were reopened in February 1912. These, however, floundered in April when the Kaiser and Tirpitz stubbornly resisted Chancellor Bethmann Hollweg's urgings to accommodate the British by reducing naval expenditure. The Chancellor also failed to secure his primary goal – a promise of British neutrality in the event of war in Europe. Britain was now sufficiently worried about German intentions to make a naval agreement with France. The Royal Navy would guard the English Channel and the North Sea, while the French would concentrate on the Mediterranean. The Entente Cordiale was now looking more like a military alliance. Britain still made efforts to calm down the naval race in 1913 and Tirpitz reduced his programme, but, as Earl Grey put it, this was not out of 'love for our beautiful eyes, but the extra 50 millions required for increasing the German Army',[9] a reaction to the two Balkan Wars of 1912–13.

Neither of those conflicts – crises more serious than the assassination at Sarajevo in 1914 – sparked a wider European war. The First Balkan War might very well have done. When Serb forces reached the Adriatic through Albania in November 1912, Austria–Hungary threatened war unless they withdrew immediately. As such an intervention would have provoked a Russian response, the great powers stepped in. Suspicion lurked beneath this international co-operation. The Austrians wanted a strong, independent Albanian state to hem Russia's Serbian allies in, while Russia wanted a smaller Albania in order to ensure gains for Serbia and Montenegro. The Second Balkan War saw the Russian-sponsored Balkan League shatter and, with it, its hopes of securing the balance of power in south-eastern Europe with a broad alliance against the Habsburgs. The most serious consequence of the Balkan Wars, however, was that an enlarged Serbia became the predominant Slav power in the region, stoking Austro-Hungarian anxieties that it might, more than ever, become a competing source of loyalty for the Empire's South Slavs. From the Russian perspective, Serbia was now (apart from Montenegro) Russia's only ally in the region, since Bulgaria felt betrayed after its defeat in 1913.

The wider international consequence of the Balkan Wars was the proliferation in arms; to cite David Stevenson, 1912–14 were the years of 'the great acceleration' in the arms race.[10] Italy raised its levy of recruits in June 1913, while Germany and France passed army laws in July and August 1913, the latter responding to the former. Austria–Hungary followed suit in March 1914. On the eve of war, Russia embarked on its 'Great Programme' of war preparations. For all sides, this did not just include increasing the size of the armed forces, but also investing in strategic infrastructures, such as railways and fortifications. France urged Russia to press ahead with railway construction and Germany responded by developing further track towards its eastern frontiers. The arms race did not cause the war, but it did show that the European powers were preparing for a major conflagration.

No other power was anticipating conflict more than Germany. Fritz Fischer has argued that the Junker elites sought a war in order to resolve the crisis in German domestic politics. Moreover, Germany had aspired not only to an overseas empire but also to expansion within Europe (*Mitteleuropa*).[11] The war which 'the German politicians started in July 1914' was 'an attempt to defeat the enemy powers before they became too strong, and to realize Germany's political ambitions which may be summed up as German hegemony over Europe'.[12] Most of all, Germany feared Russia, whose economic development was gathering pace. By the end of 1912 the Kaiser himself had come to the conclusion that Germany's differences with France and Russia could no longer be resolved by diplomatic means. On 8 December 1912 the Kaiser summoned Moltke, Tirpitz and two senior admiralty officials to a 'War Council' in response to a British warning that if Austria–Hungary invaded Serbia (as it was threatening to do during the First Balkan War), Britain could not remain 'a quiet bystander'. The Kaiser told this small group of officials that if Russia was ready to defend Serbia against Austria, then Germany would consider war unavoidable – a prospect which Wilhelm II was willing to face. Moltke supported the Kaiser: 'I believe a war to be unavoidable and: the sooner the better.' The longer Germany waited, the stronger its enemies would become. Tirpitz, however, warned that the fleet would require another 18 months of preparation if it were to take on Britain in 'the great fight'. The record of the meeting bluntly summarised the deadlock: 'The result was pretty well zero.'[13]

Fischer's controversial views have not, of course, gone unchallenged. Gerhard Ritter argued that German imperialism must be seen in the context of the imperialism of other colonial powers. He denied that the German leadership wanted a world war, claiming that it was rather overwhelmed by events in July 1914.[14] More recently, Holger Herwig has denied that Germany went to war in order to 'drive for world power', arguing rather that Germany was seeking to secure and enhance the borders of 1871. There was no plan for war before the Sarajevo crisis: 'the decision for war was made in July 1914 and not . . . at a nebulous 'war council' on 8 December 1912'. The German government had no prior 'shopping list' of war aims, but rather they were hastily drafted in September 1914 when German forces were already fighting in France.[15] Certainly Fischer himself appears to admit that, for the 'war council' of 8 December 1912 at least, the German staff had given no consideration as to what might be favourable conditions in which to start a war. This is not, unfortunately, the place to wade into the intricate details of the highly charged debate over Germany's aims in the years before 1914. Germany's plans for expansion were neither new nor, at the time, unique. Throughout the nineteenth century, all European states had expansionist aspirations, whether in Europe or overseas, whether in terms of political and economic influence or formal political control. The question which needs to be answered, therefore, is why these conflicting aspirations should have catastrophically shattered the general European peace which had lasted since 1815. As Paul Schroeder puts it, 'the answer to "Who started the war?" does not constitute an answer to "What caused the war?" '[16]

There is no doubt that one of the answers *is* the long-term effects of Germany's drive for world power, which, as we have seen, caused such distrust and hostility among the European powers. Yet the European powers had worked together in the past to restrain the ambitions of one power or another. The answer, therefore, lies in the breakdown of the international system, caused by the realignment of European politics around alliances and ententes; the renewal of bitter international competition through the imperial scramble, whether overseas or in south-eastern Europe ('the feast of vultures', as one Austrian diplomat put it), and the arms race. The resulting climate of mutual suspicion and hostility could scarcely be dented by negotiations on individual issues.

This culminated in July 1914 when Germany, Austria–Hungary and Russia abandoned restraint and pushed the new Bosnian crisis towards a European war. The German government certainly welcomed the diplomatic opportunities offered by the crisis. Bethmann Hollweg seems to have hoped that it would remain a regional conflict; supporting Austria–Hungary unconditionally against Serbia (the so-called 'blank cheque' of 5 July 1914) would allow Germany to bolster what it saw as its endangered diplomatic position in the east.[17] That means, however, that, even if Germany had no desire to go to war in 1914, it had no intention of restraining Austria–Hungary as an ally and so bears responsibility for the escalation which followed the assassinations in Sarajevo.

Both Austria–Hungary and Russia threw off restraint in July 1914. This was because the regional balance of power had been significantly altered by the Balkan Wars. Austria–Hungary's South Slav population, while restive, was not separatist, but the enlarged Serbian state, whose nationalists laid claim to Bosnia, now looked like a real danger to the integrity of the monarchy. The Austrians hoped to defeat nationalism by confronting South Slav agitation and reducing – if not destroying altogether – the South Slav appeal of Serbia. Austria–Hungary naturally hoped that the conflict would remain regional, but, unlike in 1908–9, Russia could not force Serbia to accept the Austrian ultimatum of 23 July 1914. The Russian government feared that, if it did so, the pro-Russian Karadjordjević dynasty would be toppled. The Tsar therefore ordered the partial mobilisation of Russian forces in support of Serbia, which may have stiffened Serb resolve. The Austrian declaration of war which followed on 28 July threatened Serbia with destruction. This was the great difference between the Bosnian crisis of 1908–9 and that of 1914: in the former, the very existence of Serbia did not appear to be at stake; now, the fate of Russia's only friend in the Balkans seemed to be dangerously precarious.

Moreover, the strength of the Tsarist regime within Russia depended to a large extent on its ability to preserve the Empire and its international prestige: weakness would invite revolution, as it did in 1905. The Russian monarchy could not afford another diplomatic reversal such as that sustained in 1909. Russia therefore stood by Serbia and found itself at war, not only against Austria–Hungary (against which Russia mobilised on 30 July), but also against Germany, which declared war on 1 August. France, hesitating while awaiting a promise of British support, none the less went to war against Germany that same day in support of its Russian ally. Germany, anticipating the French move, had already set in motion the Schlieffen Plan and, on 2 August, issued an ultimatum to Belgium, demanding the right to send troops through that country against France. King Albert and the Belgian parliament unanimously rejected this breach of their neutrality and, on 4 August, Germany invaded. This was the final proof for a divided British government that

Germany posed a direct threat not only to the European balance of power but also to Britain's vital interests. It declared war when its ultimatum demanding a German withdrawal expired at midnight.

It was said that patriotic euphoria, even among opponents of the existing regime, greeted the outbreak of the conflict. When they made their decisions for war, one of the calculations made by European governments, so many of which were beset by political polarisation and social unrest, may have been that the nation would at last unite behind the established order. Yet political truces such as the *Burgfrieden* in Germany and the *Union sacrée* in France were fragile. Most German socialists supported the war, but primarily because the Russian mobilisation convinced them that they were defending their fatherland against the reactionary Tsarist regime. In France, once the invasion of Belgium made the danger of German aggression abundantly clear, the left went to war to defend its own vision of the Republic, anticipating that, with the defeat of the old regime in Germany, conditions would be riper for international socialism or revolution. In Russia, the French ambassador meditated with some prescience as he watched columns of troops march through St Petersburg: 'As I looked at them I reflected that a large number of them were already marked out for death. But what will be the feelings of those who return? What notions, reflections and clamours, what new spirit or new soul will they bring back with them to their own firesides?'[18]

It did not take long for the underlying political and social divisions in the belligerent states to break open again under the agonising strains of the conflict. In 1905 Jaurès had warned:

> From a European war a revolution may spring up and the ruling classes would do well to think of this. But it may also result, over a long period, in crises of counter-revolution, of furious reaction, of exasperated nationalism, of stifling dictatorships, of monstrous militarism, a long chain of retrograde violence.[19]

Jaurès would not live to see whether or not his predictions would be fulfilled. On 31 July 1914, though he was coming around to the idea that France was fighting a legitimate war of defence, he was shot dead by a nationalist fanatic. The patriotic unity with which European societies greeted the arrival of the conflict was a thin crust. It buckled and cracked under the deeper political and social forces which had been gathering in the decades before 1914. The industrialised furnace of the First World War brought the social antagonisms and political extremes boiling violently back up to the surface, ensuring that, for the next three decades at least, twentieth-century Europe would be a dangerous place.

Notes

Preface

1. Quoted in J. Alvarez-Junco, *The Emergence of Mass Politics in Spain: Populist Demagoguery and Republican Culture, 1890–1910* (Brighton, 2002), vii. I have tried in vain to find the direct source of this quotation, and I thank my medievalist colleagues for their heroic assistance in the quest.

1 Europe in 1789

1. *Memoirs and Correspondence of Sir R. M. Keith* (1849), extract in A. Lentin (ed.), *Enlightened Absolutism (1760–1790): A Documentary Sourcebook* (Newcastle-upon-Tyne, 1985), 154–5.
2. For the background on agricultural change, see P. Bairoch, 'Agriculture and the Industrial Revolution 1700–1914', in C. M. Cipolla (ed.), *The Fontana Economic History of Europe*, III, *The Industrial Revolution* (Glasgow, 1973), especially 455–71; W. Doyle, *The Old European Order 1660–1800* (Oxford, 1978), 21–7. For the persistence of old techniques in France, see R. Price, *An Economic History of Modern France 1730–1914* (Basingstoke, 1981), 62–7.
3. See, for example, the economy of the Aquitaine in A. Forrest, *The Revolution in Provincial France: Aquitaine 1789–1799* (Oxford, 1996), 4–5.
4. See, for example, the case of the medical profession in France in C. Jones, 'The Great Chain of Buying: Medical Advertisement, the Bourgeois Public Sphere and the Origins of the French Revolution', *AHR*, CI (1996), 13–40.
5. T. C. W. Blanning, *The Origins of the French Revolutionary Wars* (London, 1986), 37; P. Anderson, *Lineages of the Absolutist State* (London, 1974), 58.
6. For peasant agitation in the wake of Joseph's decree, see É. H. Balázs (trans. T. Wilkinson), *Hungary and the Habsburgs 1765–1800: An Experiment in Enlightened Absolutism* (Budapest, 1997), 216–28.
7. For discussions of communications, literacy and the 'public sphere', see especially T. C. W. Blanning, *The Culture of Power and the Power of Culture: Old Regime Europe 1660–1789* (Oxford, 2002), especially 103–82; T. Munck, *The Enlightenment: A Comparative Social History 1721–1794* (London, 2000), especially 46–72.

2 The French Revolution, 1789–1804

1. As subtly argued in such 'Marxist' classics as G. Lefebvre (trans. R. R. Palmer), *The Coming of the French Revolution* (Princeton, NJ, 1947).

2. The revisionist assault opened with Alfred Cobban, *The Social Interpretation of the French Revolution* (Cambridge, 1968). A now classic discussion of the great debate is W. Doyle, *Origins of the French Revolution* (Oxford, 1980).
3. See especially G. Chaussinand-Nogaret (trans. W. Doyle), *The French Nobility in the Eighteenth Century* (Cambridge, 1984) and C. Lucas, 'Nobles, Bourgeois and the Origins of the French Revolution', *P&P*, 60 (August 1973), 84–126; D. M. G. Sutherland, *The French Revolution and Empire: The Quest for a Civic Order* (Oxford, 2003), 347; Doyle, *Origins*, 211–12.
4. See, for example, P. McPhee, *A Social History of France 1789–1914*, 2nd edn (Basingstoke, 2004), 24.
5. The ground-breaking works which interpreted the Revolution in terms of the transformation of political culture are F. Furet (trans. E. Forster), *Interpreting the French Revolution* (Cambridge, 1981) and L. Hunt, *Politics, Culture, and Class in the French Revolution* (Berkeley, CA, 1984). See also the articles by K. M. Baker, *Inventing the French Revolution: Essays on French Political Culture in the Eighteenth Century* (Cambridge, 1990).
6. P. M. Jones, *Reform and Revolution in France: The Politics of Transition, 1774–1791* (Cambridge, 1995), 78.
7. Some historians doubt whether this was anything new in the period immediately before 1789: see W. Doyle, 'Was there an Aristocratic Reaction in Pre-Revolutionary France?', in *Officers, Nobles and Revolutionaries: Essays on Eighteenth-Century France* (London, 1995), 49–74, which originally appeared as an article in *P&P*, 57 (1972), 97–122. Others emphasise its intensity in the pre-revolutionary years: see P. M. Jones, *The Peasantry in the French Revolution* (Cambridge, 1988), 42–59; D. Andress, *French Society in Revolution 1789–1799* (Manchester, 1999), 23–4; McPhee, *Social History of France 1789–1914*, 16–17.
8. The classic work on the 'Great Fear' is G. Lefebvre (trans. J. White), *The Great Fear of 1789: Rural Panic in Revolutionary France* (London, 1973).
9. A. Soboul (trans. G. Lewis), *The Parisian Sans-Culottes and the French Revolution 1793–4* (Oxford, 1964), 50. But see also the different views of R. M. Andrews, 'Social Structures, Political Elites, and Ideology in Revolutionary Paris, 1792–4' *JSH*, XIX (1985–6), 71–112; M. Sonenscher, 'Artisans, Sans-Culottes and the French Revolution', in A. Forrest and P. Jones (eds), *Reshaping France: Town, Country and Region in the French Revolution* (Manchester, 1991), 105–21.
10. C. Jones, *The Great Nation: France from Louis XV to Napoleon* (London, 2002), 470.
11. The debate is expertly summarised in H. Gough, *The Terror in the French Revolution* (Basingstoke, 1998).
12. See Furet, *Interpreting the French Revolution* and Hunt, *Politics, Culture and Class*.
13. S. Schama, *Citizens: A Chronicle of the French Revolution* (New York, 1989), 447.
14. A point suggested by K. M. Baker, 'Introduction: Conceptualizing the Terror', in *The French Revolution and the Creation of Modern Political Culture*, IV, *The Terror* (Oxford, 1994), xvi.
15. Gough, *The Terror*, 52–4.

16. R. Magraw, *France 1815–1914: The Bourgeois Century* (London, 1983), 25; Sutherland, *French Revolution*, 347; P. McPhee, *The French Revolution 1789–1799* (Oxford, 2002), 184.
17. Andress, *French Society*, 165.
18. W. Doyle, *The Oxford History of the French Revolution* (Oxford, 1989), 97.
19. M. Crook, *Elections in the French Revolution: An Apprenticeship in Democracy, 1789–1799* (Cambridge, 1996).
20. McPhee, *French Revolution 1789–1799*, 125.
21. Sutherland, *French Revolution*, 180.
22. Andress, *French Society*, 65.
23. D. Godineau (trans. K. Streip), *The Women of Paris and their French Revolution* (Berkeley, CA, 1998), 270.
24. R. Phillips, 'Women and Family Breakdown in Eighteenth-Century France: Rouen 1780–1800', *SH*, II (1976), 197–218.

3 The European Impact, 1789–1815

1. Quoted in B. Simms, *The Struggle for Mastery in Germany, 1779–1850* (Basingstoke, 1998), 55.
2. Quoted in Blanning, *Origins*, 134.
3. E. V. Macleod, *A War of Ideas: British Attitudes to the Wars Against Revolutionary France, 1792–1802* (Aldershot, 1998), 184; Blanning, *Origins*, 161.
4. Quoted in J. J. Sheehan, *German History 1770–1866* (Oxford, 1989), 242.
5. Simms, *Struggle for Mastery*, 63–4; Sheehan, *German History*, 243–6.
6. For other Russian motives for entering the War of the Third Coalition, see D. Saunders, *Russia in the Age of Reaction and Reform 1801–1881* (London, 1992), 38.
7. N. Hampson, 'The Idea of the Nation in Revolutionary France', in Forrest and Jones, *Reshaping France*, 25.
8. J. A. Lynn, *The Bayonets of the Republic: Motivation and Tactics in the Army of Revolutionary France, 1791–94* (Oxford, 1996), especially 119–62.
9. H. Strachan, 'The Nation in Arms', in G. Best (ed.), *The Permanent Revolution: The French Revolution and its Legacy 1789–1989* (London, 1988), 54; T. C. W. Blanning, *The French Revolutionary Wars 1787–1802* (London, 1996), 118.
10. Doyle, *Oxford History*, 358.
11. Quoted in Blanning, *Origins*, 178.
12. M. Broers, *Europe under Napoleon 1799–1815* (London, 1996), 113.
13. M. Lyons, *Napoleon Bonaparte and the Legacy of the French Revolution* (Basingstoke, 1994), 235.
14. J. A. Davis, 'The Napoleonic Era in Southern Italy: An Ambiguous Legacy?' *PBA*, LXXX (1991), 133–48.
15. G. Ellis, *The Napoleonic Empire* (Basingstoke, 1991), 82–93.
16. See J. A. Davis, 'The 'Santafede' and the Crisis of the 'Ancien Regime' in Southern Italy', in J. A. Davis and P. Ginsborg (eds), *Society and Politics in the Age of Risorgimento: Essays in Honour of Denis Mack Smith* (Cambridge, 1991), 1–25.

17. A. Grab, 'From the French Revolution to Napoleon', in J. A. Davis (ed.), *Italy in the Nineteenth Century* (Oxford, 2000), 28–9.
18. Broers, *Europe under Napoleon*, 269–70; T. C. W. Blanning, *The French Revolution in Germany: Occupation and Resistance in the Rhineland 1792–1802* (Oxford, 1983), 323–8.
19. See, for example, the problems highlighted by Charles Esdaile in 'Popular Mobilisation in Spain, 1808–1810: A Reassessment', in M. Rowe (ed.), *Collaboration and Resistance in Napoleonic Europe: State-formation in an Age of Upheaval, c. 1800–1815* (Basingstoke, 2003), 90–106.

4 The Conservative Order

1. A useful summary of views on the 'Restoration' can be found in M. Broers, *Europe after Napoleon: Revolution, Reaction and Romanticism, 1814–1848* (Manchester, 1996), 1–8 and in D. Laven & L. Riall, *Napoleon's Legacy: Problems of Government in Restoration Europe* (Oxford, 2000), 1–26.
2. The settlement's more recent critics have included G. Best, *War and Society in Revolutionary Europe, 1770–1870* (Oxford, 1982), 192; C. Church, *Europe in 1830: Revolution and Political Change* (London, 1983), 15–16; H. Hearder, *Italy in the Age of the Risorgimento 1790–1870* (London, 1983), 172–6. Its defenders have included H. Nicolson, *The Congress of Vienna: A Study in Allied Unity: 1812–1822* (London, 1948) and, more recently, P. W. Schroeder, *The Transformation of European Politics 1763–1848* (Oxford, 1994), especially 575–82, 797–804; see also P. W. Schroeder, 'International Politics, Peace, and War, 1815–1914', in T. C. W. Blanning (ed.), *The Nineteenth Century* (Oxford, 2000), 158–65. For the view, with which Schroeder disagrees, that the Congress of Vienna restored a 'balance of power' arrangement, see the essays in A. Sked (ed.), *Europe's Balance of Power* (London, 1979).
3. Quoted in R. Albrecht-Carrié (ed.), *The Concert of Europe* (London, 1968), 32.
4. Text in Albrecht-Carrié, *Concert of Europe*, 33–4.
5. For the policing of the Habsburg monarchy, see especially D. E. Emerson, *Metternich and the Political Police: Security and Subversion in the Hapsburg Monarchy (1815–1830)* (The Hague, 1969); A. Sked, *The Decline and Fall of the Habsburg Empire 1815–1918* (London, 1989), 44–51.
6. D. Laven, 'Law and Order in Habsburg Venetia 1814–1835', *HJ*, 39 (1996), 383–403.
7. G. de Bertier de Sauvigny (trans. L. M. Case), *The Bourbon Restoration* (Philadelphia, PA, 1966), 165.
8. For British politics in this period, see J. C. D. Clark, *English Society 1688–1832: Ideology, Social Structure and Political Practice during the Ancien Régime* (Cambridge, 1985), 349–420; J. Cannon, *Parliamentary Reform 1640–1832* (London, 1972), 165–203; F. O'Gorman, *The Long Eighteenth Century: British Political and Social History 1688–1832* (London, 1997), 351–76; L. Colley, *Britons: Forging the Nation 1707–1837* (New Haven, CT, 1992), 321–63. For Scotland, see W. Ferguson, *Scotland 1689 to the Present* (Edinburgh, 1968), 266–90; B. P. Lenman, *Integration*

and Enlightenment: Scotland 1746–1832 (Edinburgh, 1981), 129–67. On Ireland, see K. T. Hoppen, *Ireland since 1800: Conflict and Conformity* (London, 1999), 11–24.

9. C. Esdaile, 'Enlightened Absolutism versus Theocracy in Spain 1814–50', in Laven and Riall, *Napoleon's Legacy*, 73.
10. W. M. Reddy, 'Condottieri of the Pen: Journalists and the Public Sphere in Postrevolutionary France (1815–1850)', *AHR*, XCIX (1994), 1546n; P. Pilbeam, *The 1830 Revolution in France* (Basingstoke, 1991), 30–1.
11. D. Blackbourn, *The Fontana History of Germany 1780–1918: The Long Nineteenth Century* (London, 1997), 128.
12. N. Davies, *God's Playground: A History of Poland*, 2 vols (New York, 1982), II, 21, 38–9.
13. M. Beaven, 'Readership in Early Nineteenth-Century Russia: Recent Soviet Research', *SR*, XLIII (1984), 276–80.
14. R. Tempest, 'Madman or Criminal: Government Attitudes to Petr Chaadaev in 1836', *SR*, XLIII (1984), 281–7.
15. Reddy, 'Condottieri of the Pen', 1548–9.
16. N. Pushkareva (trans. E. Levin), *Women in Russian History from the Tenth to the Twentieth Century* (Stroud, 1999), 197.
17. C. J. Esdaile, *Spain in the Liberal Age: From Constitution to Civil War, 1808–1939* (Oxford, 2000), 54.
18. For details on the Portuguese revolution of the 1820s, see S. G. Payne, *A History of Spain and Portugal*, 2 vols. (Madison, WI, 1973), II, 513–21.
19. For details on the revolutions of 1820–1 and their consequences in Italy, see Hearder, *Risorgimento*, 54–5, 136–41; S. J. Woolf, *A History of Italy 1700–1860: The Social Constraints of Political Change* (London, 1979), 255–65; D. Mack Smith, *A History of Sicily: Modern Sicily after 1713* (London, 1968), 352–61.
20. Cannon, *Parliamentary Reform*, 169.
21. Quoted in Cannon, *Parliamentary Reform*, 167.
22. These issues are discussed fully in M. Levinger, *Enlightened Nationalism. The Transformation of Prussian Political Culture, 1806–1848* (Oxford, 2000), 113–25. On the *Burschenschaften*, see, for example, K. H. Wegert, 'The Genesis of Youthful Radicalism: Hesse-Nassau, 1806–19', *CEH*, X (1977).
23. Levinger, *Enlightened Nationalism*, 138–9.
24. G. A. Kertesz (ed.), *Documents in the Political History of the European Continent 1815–1839* (Oxford, 1968), 67–9.
25. For Hungarian politics in this era, see B. K. Király, 'The Young Ferenc Deák and the Problem of the Serfs 1824–1836', *S–F*, XXIX (1970), 91–8; R. J. W. Evans, 'The Habsburgs and the Hungarian Problem, 1790–1848', *TRHS*, 5th Series, XXXVIII (1989), 41–62; I. Deak, *The Lawful Revolution: Louis Kossuth and the Hungarians 1848–1849* (New York, 1979), 13–17.
26. J. Gooding, *Rulers and Subjects: Government and People in Russia 1801–1991* (London, 1993), 28.
27. For details on the Decembrists, see A. G. Mazour, *The First Russian Revolution, 1825. The Decembrist Movement: Its Origins, Development, and Significance* (Stanford, CA, 1964); Saunders, *Russia*, 87–115; W. B. Lincoln, 'A Re-examination of Some Historical Stereotypes: An Analysis of the Career Patterns and Backgrounds of the Decembrists', *JGO*, XXIV (1976), 357–68.

28. For Nicholas I's secret police and censorship, see P. S. Squire, *The Third Department: The Establishment and Practices of the Political Police in the Russia of Nicholas I* (Cambridge, 1978); C. A. Ruud and S. A. Stepanov, *Fontanka 16: The Tsar's Secret Police* (Quebec, 1999), 17–25. For a stimulating discussion of the alienation of the intelligentsia, see N. V. Riasanovsky, *A Parting of Ways: Government and the Educated Public in Russia 1801–1855* (Oxford, 1976).
29. Text in M. Walker (ed.), *Metternich's Europe* (London, 1968), 128–30.
30. Text in Walker, *Metternich's Europe*, 132–6.
31. E. J. Hobsbawm, *The Age of Revolution 1789–1848* (London, 1962), 132–3.

5 Social Crises and Responses, 1815–1848

1. Quoted in H. J. Habakkuk, *Population Growth and Economic Development since 1750* (Leicester, 1971), 65.
2. Quoted in W. Köllmann, 'The Population of Germany in the Age of Industrialism', H. Moller (ed.), *Population Movements in Modern European History* (New York, 1964), 101.
3. W. W. Rostow, *The Stages of Economic Growth: A Non-Communist Manifesto*, 2nd edn (Cambridge, 1971), 7–8.
4. P. McPhee, *A Social History of France 1780–1880* (London, 1992), 152–73; Price, *Economic History of Modern France*, 192–200.
5. See the table in T. Nipperdey (trans. D. Nolan), *Germany from Napoleon to Bismarck, 1800–1866* (Dublin, 1996), 88.
6. Nipperdey, *Germany*, 149.
7. H. Böhme, *An Introduction to the Social and Economic History of Germany: Politics and Economic Change in the Nineteenth and Twentieth Centuries* (Oxford, 1978), 22.
8. A. Lyttelton, 'Landlords, Peasants and the Limits of Liberalism', in J. A. Davis (ed.), *Gramsci and Italy's Passive Revolution* (London, 1979), 115–16.
9. S. L. Hoch, *Serfdom and Social Control in Russia: Petrovskoe, a Village in Tambov* (Chicago, 1986), 15–37, 45–51.
10. Banking and credit is examined in detail in P. Mathias, *The First Industrial Nation: The Economic History of Britain 1700–1914*, 2nd edn. (London, 1983), 148–59.
11. A. Gerschenkron, *Economic Backwardness in Historical Perspective: A Book of Essays* (Cambridge, MA, 1966), 17.
12. E. Melton, 'Proto-Industrialization, Serf Agriculture and Agrarian Social Structure: Two Estates in Nineteenth-Century Russia', *P&P*, 115 (1987), 69–106; M. E. Falkus, *The Industrialisation of Russia 1700–1914* (Basingstoke, 1972), 29, 36–7, 39.
13. C. H. Johnson, 'Patterns of Proletarianization', in L. R. Berlanstein (ed.), *The Industrial Revolution and Work in Nineteenth-Century Europe* (London, 1992), 83–5.
14. W. Cooke Taylor, *Notes of a Tour in the Manufacturing Districts of Lancashire* (1842), extract in B. I. Coleman (ed.), *The Idea of the City in Nineteenth-Century Britain* (London, nd), 81–6.
15. Quoted in L. Chevalier (trans. F. Jellinek), *Labouring Classes and Dangerous Classes in Paris during the First Half of the Nineteenth Century* (New York, 1973), 205–6.

16. Quoted in W. H. Sewell, *Work and Revolution in France: The Language of Labor from the Old Regime to 1848* (Cambridge, 1980), 224.
17. For the gruesome details, see R. J. Evans, *Death in Hamburg: Society and Politics in the Cholera Years 1830–1910* (Oxford, 1987), 226–56.
18. Quoted in Evans, *Death in Hamburg*, 119.
19. D. G. Boyce, *Nineteenth-Century Ireland: The Search for Stability* (Dublin, 1990), 69.
20. For the French system, see R. Price, 'Poor Relief and Social Crisis in Mid-Nineteenth-Century France', *ESR*, XIII (1983), 423–54 and D. H. Pinkney, 'Les Ateliers de secours à Paris (1830–1831): précurseurs des ateliers nationaux de 1848', *RHMC* XII (1965), 65–70.
21. On the Prussian system, see H. Beck, 'The Social Policies of Prussian Officials: the Bureaucracy in a New Light', *JMH* LXIV (1992), 263–98.
22. Quoted in P. Pilbeam, *Republicanism in Nineteenth-Century France 1814–1871* (Basingstoke, 1995), 181.
23. Quoted in Pilbeam, *Republicanism*, 169.
24. On socialism, see Broers, *Europe after Napoleon*, 80–90; Pilbeam, *Republicanism*, 155–84.
25. Quoted in E. Hobsbawm, *Industry and Empire* (Harmondsworth, 1969), 94.
26. J. M. Merriman, 'The *Demoiselles* of the Ariège, 1829–1831', in *1830 in France* (New York, 1975), 87–118.
27. M. Gailus, 'Food Riots in Germany in the late 1840s', *P&P*, 145 (1994), 173.
28. J. L. Snell, *The Democratic Movement in Germany, 1789–1914* (Chapel Hill, NC, 1976), 59.
29. For details of the Galician peasant uprising of 1846, see S. Kieniewicz, *The Emancipation of the Polish Peasantry* (Chicago, 1969), 113–26.
30. R. Bohac, 'Everyday forms of Resistance: Serf Opposition to Gentry Exactions, 1800–1861', in E. Kingston-Mann and T. Mixter (eds), *Peasant Economy, Culture and Politics of European Russia, 1800–1921* (Princeton, NJ, 1991), 237, 241–3.
31. R. Price, *A Social History of Nineteenth-Century France* (London, 1987), 238.
32. Quoted in Sheehan, *German History*, 649.
33. Quoted in Sheehan, *German History*, 650.
34. Quoted in R. J. Rath, *The Viennese Revolution of 1848* (New York, 1969), 15n.
35. Quoted in Sewell, *Work and Revolution in France*, 212–13.

6 Europe Overseas

1. See, for example, T. C. W. Blanning, 'Introduction: The End of the Old Regime', *Nineteenth Century*, 2.
2. Quoted in R. Aldrich, *Greater France: A History of French Overseas Expansion* (Basingstoke, 1996), 94.
3. Quoted in C. M. Andrew and A. S. Kanya-Forstner, 'Centre and Periphery in the Making of the Second French Colonial Empire, 1815–1920', *JICH*, XVI (1988), 10, 9–34.
4. Quoted in Andrew and Kanya-Forstner, 'Centre and Periphery', 14.

5. Quoted in Andrew and Kanya-Forstner, 'Centre and Periphery', 11.
6. Quoted in O. MacDonagh, 'The Anti-Imperialism of Free Trade', in A. G. L. Shaw (ed.), *Great Britain and the Colonies 1815–65* (London, 1970), 164–83.
7. Quoted in B. Porter, *The Lion's Share: A Short History of British Imperialism 1850–1983*, 2nd edn (London, 1984), 11.
8. Quoted in Porter, *Lion's Share*, 3.
9. Quoted in Porter, *Lion's Share*, 6.
10. A. G. Hopkins, 'Overseas Expansion, Imperialism, and Empire, 1815–1914', in Blanning, *Nineteenth Century*, 222–3.
11. Quoted in Porter, *Lion's Share*, 6.
12. For a sceptical view of this point, however, see D. C. M. Platt, 'Further Objections to an "Imperialism of Free Trade", 1830–60', *EHR*, XXVI (1973), 77–91.
13. Quoted in Hopkin, 'Overseas Expansion', 221.
14. J. Gallagher and R. Robinson, 'The Imperialism of Free Trade', *EHR* VI (1953), 1–15.

7 Europe between Revolutions, 1830–1848

1. For a discussion of the economic crisis, see Pilbeam, *1830 Revolution*, 37–59.
2. A. B. Spitzer, 'The Bureaucrat as Proconsul: The Restoration Prefect and the *Police Générale*', *Comparative Studies in Society and History* VIII (1964–1965), 374–5; R. S. Alexander, 'Restoration Republicanism Reconsidered', *FH*, VIII (1994), 458.
3. U. Frevert, *Women in German History: From Bourgeois Emancipation to Sexual Liberation* (Oxford, 1989), 69.
4. Quoted in Nipperdey, *Germany*, 328.
5. Quoted in R. Carr, *Spain 1808–1975*, 2nd edn (Oxford, 1982), 184.
6. K. Marx and F. Engels, *Manifesto of the Communist Party* (Moscow, 1977), 36.
7. F. M. L. Thompson, *The Rise of Respectable Society: A Social History of Victorian Britain, 1830–1900* (London, 1988), 105.
8. Quoted in L. O'Boyle, 'The Problem of an Excess of Educated Men in Western Europe, 1800–1850', *JMH*, XLII (1970), 488.
9. P. Pilbeam, *The Middle Classes in Europe 1789–1914: France, Germany, Italy and Russia* (Basingstoke, 1990), 17.
10. R. D. Anderson, *Education in France 1848–1870* (Oxford, 1978), 11.
11. J. J. Sheehan, *German Liberalism in the Nineteenth Century* (London, 1982), 26–7.
12. Quoted in J. Kocka, 'The European Pattern and the German Case', in J. Kocka and A. Mitchell (eds), *Bourgeois Society in Nineteenth-Century Europe* (Oxford, 1993), 10.
13. R. Tombs, *France 1814–1914* (London, 1996), 357.
14. Details of the September Laws in H. A. C. Collingham, *The July Monarchy: A Political History of France 1830–1848* (London, 1988), 165–6.
15. Pilbeam, *Republicanism*, 129–40.
16. Quoted in D. Moon, *Russian Peasants and Tsarist Legislation: Interaction between Peasants and Officialdom, 1825–1855* (Basingstoke, 1992), 67.

17. Quoted in Saunders, *Russia*, 153.
18. G. Hosking, *Russia: People and Empire 1552–1917* (London, 1998), 271–5.
19. Simms, *Struggle for Mastery*, 157–68.

8 The European Revolution, 1848–1850

1. For the economic crisis, see, for example, T. J. Markovitch, 'La Crise de 1847–1848 dans les industries parisiennes', *RHES*, XLIII (1965), 256–60 and Gailus, 'Food Riots in Germany'.
2. P. Ginsborg, *Daniele Manin and the Venetian Revolution of 1848–49* (Cambridge, 1979), 88.
3. R. Price, *The French Second Republic: A Social History* (London, 1972), 109.
4. *Le National*, in R. Price, *Documents on the French Revolution of 1848* (Basingstoke, 1995), 102.
5. J. Sperber, *Rhineland Radicals: The Democratic Movement and the Revolution of 1848–1849* (Princeton, NJ, 1991), 228.
6. Quoted in Rath, *Viennese Revolution*, 178.
7. Quoted in Rath, *Viennese Revolution*, 296.
8. W. J. Orr, jun., 'East Prussia and the Revolution of 1848', *CEH*, XIII (1980), 316.
9. F. Lewald (trans. H. Ballin), *A Year of Revolutions: Fanny Lewald's Recollections of 1848* (Oxford, 1997), 121, 129, 133.
10. Quoted in full in Rath, *Viennese Revolution*, 196.
11. The full translated text of his letter is in *SEER*, XXVI (1947–48), 303–8.
12. Rath, *Viennese Revolution*, 263.
13. I. Deak, 'István Széchenyi, Miklós Wesselényi, Lajos Kossuth and the Problem of Romanian Nationalism', *AHY* XII–XIII (1976–77), 75; Deak, *Lawful Revolution*, 122.
14. Carpathinus (pseud.), '1848 and Roumanian Unification', *SEER*, XXVI (1947–48), 399–401.
15. Deak, *Lawful Revolution*, *passim*, but see especially 174.
16. T. W. Margadant, *French Peasants in Revolt: The Insurrection of 1851* (Princeton, NJ, 1979), 3–39.
17. S. Z. Pech, *The Czech Revolution of 1848* (Chapel Hill, NC, 1969), 67–8.
18. Quoted in Sperber, *Rhineland Radicals*, 252.
19. Quoted in S. Zucker, 'German Women and the Revolution of 1848: Kathinka Zitz-Halein and the Humania Association', *CEH*, XIII (1980), 240.
20. Quoted in Zucker, 'German Women', 244. For women's role in the 1848 Revolutions in France, see D. Barry, *Women and Political Insurgency: France in the Mid-Nineteenth Century* (Basingstoke, 1996).
21. D. Saunders, 'A Pyrrhic Victory: The Russian Empire in 1848', in R. J. Evans and H. Pogge von Strandmann, *The Revolutions in Europe, 1848–49: From Reform to Reaction* (Oxford, 2000), 135–55.

9 A New Era?

1. The term is from Eric Dorn Brose, in *German History 1789–1871: From the Holy Roman Empire to the Bismarckian Reich* (Oxford, 1997), 264–85.

2. J. F. McMillan, *Napoleon III* (London, 1991), 54.
3. Quoted variously: see Tombs, *France*, 398; McMillan, *Napoleon III*, 55.
4. For the *bienio* of 1854–6, see V. G. Kiernan, *The Revolution of 1854 in Spanish History* (Oxford, 1966).
5. For Spain under O'Donnell, see Carr, *Spain*, 257–64; Kiernan, *Revolution of 1854*, 239–52.
6. Quoted in E. J. Evans, *The Forging of the Modern State: Early Industrial Britain 1783–1870* (London, 1983), 326.
7. Quoted in D. Mack Smith, *Victor Emanuel, Cavour and the Risorgimento* (London, 1971), 42.
8. Quoted in Sked, *Decline and Fall*, 147.
9. Manteuffel and Ranke quoted in Sheehan, *German History*, 710, 727.
10. Quoted in L. Gall, *Bismarck: The White Revolutionary*, 2 vols, I, *1815–1871* (London, 1986), 99.
11. J. P. LeDonne, *The Russian Empire and the World 1700–1917: The Geopolitics of Expansion and Containment* (New York, 1997), 117–26.
12. Quoted in B. Jelavich, *Russia's Balkan Entanglements, 1806–1914* (Cambridge, 1991), 114.
13. Quoted in W. Baumgart, *The Crimean War 1853–1856* (London, 1999), 136.
14. Her story can be read in her autobiography, *The Wonderful Adventures of Mrs Seacole in Many Lands* (1857), (London, 1999).
15. Quoted in W. E. Mosse, *The Rise and Fall of the Crimean System 1855–71: The Story of a Peace Settlement* (London, 1963), 33.

10 Unifications and State-Building

1. Extract in D. Mack Smith (ed.), *The Making of Italy 1796–1870* (London, 1968), 237.
2. Cavour to Victor Emanuel, quoted in M. Walker (ed.), *Plombières: Secret Diplomacy and the Rebirth of Italy* (New York, 1968), 34.
3. D. Mack Smith, *Mazzini* (New Haven, CT, 1994), 130.
4. Details on the Sicilian peasant insurrection in Mack Smith, *Victor Emanuel, Cavour*, 190–224.
5. Quoted in Gall, *Bismarck*, I, 143.
6. Figures from D. Düding, 'The Nineteenth-Century German Nationalist Movement as a Movement of Societies', in H. Schulze (ed.), *Nation-Building in Central Europe* (Leamington Spa, 1987), 47 and Sheehan, *German Liberalism*, 98.
7. Quoted in Gall, *Bismarck*, I, 163.
8. Extracts from Bismarck's 'Blood and Iron' speech in D. G. Williamson, *Bismarck and Germany 1862–1890* (London, 1998), 97.
9. Quoted in O. Pflanze, *Bismarck and the Development of Germany*, 3 vols (Princeton, NJ, 1963), I, 212.
10. Quoted in A. J. P. Taylor, *Bismarck: The Man and the Statesman* (London, 1965), 47.
11. On this episode, see E. E. Kraehe, 'Austria and the Problem of Reform in the German Confederation, 1851–1863', *AHR*, LVI (1951), 276–94.
12. Quoted in Sheehan, *German Liberalism*, 113.
13. A. J. P. Taylor, *The Course of German History: A Survey of the Development of German History since 1815* (London, 1993), ch. 6.

14. The problem of absorbing Prussia's conquests is discussed in detail in H. A. Schmitt, 'From Sovereign States to Prussian Provinces: Hanover and Hesse-Nassau, 1866–1871', *JMH*, LXXV (1985), 24–56.
15. Quoted in Pflanze, *Bismarck*, I, 322.
16. Quoted in W. Carr, *A History of Germany 1815–1990* (London, 1991), 105.
17. For a defence of the liberals, see G. R. Mork, 'Bismarck and the "Capitulation" of German Liberalism', *JMH*, XLIII (1971), 59–75. For an unambiguous statement to the contrary, see Alexander Schwan, 'German Liberalism and the National Question in the Nineteenth Century', in Schulze, *Nation-Building*, 65–80.
18. O. von Bismarck, *Otto von Bismarck: The Man and the Statesman, being the Reflections and Reminiscences of Otto Prince von Bismarck*, 2 vols (London, 1898), II, 100.
19. Quoted in Pflanze, *Bismarck*, I, 480.
20. Quoted in D. Beales and E. F. Biagini, *The Risorgimento and the Unification of Italy*, 2nd edn (London, 2002), 157.
21. A. M. Birke, 'German Catholics and the Quest for National Unity', in Schulze, *Nation-Building*, 59.
22. M. Clark, *Modern Italy 1871–1995*, 2nd edn (London, 1996), 83.
23. Bismarck, *Reflections and Reminiscences*, II, 138–9.
24. For a contemporary discussion of the problem, see, for example, the extract in S. J. Woolf (ed.), *The Italian Risorgimento* (London, 1969), 75.
25. Cited in C. Duggan, 'Politics in the Era of Depretis and Crispi, 1870–96', in Davis, *Italy in the Nineteenth Century*, 164–5.

11 Containing the Tempest: Reform and Consolidation

1. Address to the Moscow nobility, 31 August 1858, in G. Vernadsky (ed.), *A Source Book for Russian History from Early Times to 1917*, 3 vols (New Haven, CT, 1972), III, 591.
2. Quoted in F. Venturi, *Roots of Revolution: A History of the Populist and Socialist Movements in Nineteenth-Century Russia* (Chicago, 1960), 173.
3. See, for example, the quotation in A. B. Ulam, *In the Name of the People:Prophets and Conspirators in Prerevolutionary Russia* (New York, 1977), 102.
4. Quoted in Ulam, *Name of the People*, 82.
5. R. F. Leslie, *Reform and Insurrection in Russian Poland, 1856–1865* (London, 1963), 83.
6. Quoted in P. S. Wandycz, *The Lands of Partitioned Poland, 1795–1918* (Seattle, WA, 1975), 175.
7. J. Zaprudnik, *Belarus: At a Crossroads in History* (Boulder, 1993), 61–2.
8. For Ukrainian nationalism in this period, see J. Remy, 'The Ukrainophile Intelligentsia and its Relation to the Russian Empire in the beginning of the reign of Alexander II (1856–1863)', in C. J. Chulos and J. Remy (eds), *Imperial and National Identities in Pre-Revolutionary, Soviet and Post-Soviet Russia* (Helsinki, 2002), 177–98.
9. Quoted in Hosking, *Russia: People and Empire*, 379.
10. 'Catechism of a Revolutionist', in Vernadsky, *Source Book for Russian History*, III, 649–50.

11. Ulam, *Name of the People*, 225–6.
12. A. J. P. Taylor, *The Habsburg Monarchy 1809–1918* (London, 1990), 117.
13. R. A. Kann, *The Multinational Empire: Nationalism and National Reform in the Habsburg Monarchy 1848–1918*, 2 vols (New York, 1950), II, 128.
14. Quoted in Taylor, *Habsburg Monarchy*, 142.
15. Quoted in Taylor, *Habsburg Monarchy*, 160.
16. E. H. Kossmann, *The Low Countries 1780–1940* (Oxford, 1978), 287–8.
17. Quoted in Evans, *Forging of the Modern State*, 346.
18. Extract in D. G. Wright, *Democracy and Reform: 1815–1885* (Harlow, 1970), 131–2.
19. Quoted in G. Best, *Mid-Victorian Britain, 1851–75* (London, 1979), 289.
20. McMillan, *Napoleon III*, 65–6.
21. Quoted in Tombs, *France*, 417.
22. Pilbeam, *Republicanism*, 252–3.
23. Quoted in S. H. Elwitt, *The Making of the Third Republic: Class and Politics in France, 1868–1884* (Baton Rouge, LA, 1975), 43. See also S. H. Elwitt, 'Politics and Social Classes in the Loire: The Triumph of Republican Order, 1869–1873', *FHS*, VI (1969), 93–112.
24. Quoted in Tombs, *France*, 421.
25. Quoted in Elwitt, *Making of the Third Republic*, 50.
26. For a discussion of *caciquismo*, see Carr, *Spain*, 366–79.

12 The Sinews of Power and the Means of Existence

1. The chapter title is partially borrowed from J. Brewer, *The Sinews of Power: War, Money and the English State, 1688–1783* (London, 1989).
2. For introductions to this debate, see especially C. Heywood, *The Development of the French Economy, 1750–1914* (Basingstoke, 1992); R. Magraw, ' "Not Backward but Different"? The debate on French "Economic Retardation" ', in M. S. Alexander (ed.), *French History since Napoleon* (London, 1999), 336–63.
3. Quoted in T. H. von Laue, *Sergei Witte and the Industrialization of Russia* (1963) (New York, 1974), 1.
4. P. R. Gregory, *Russian National Income, 1885–1913* (Cambridge, 1982).
5. P. Gatrell, *The Tsarist Economy 1850–1917* (London, 1986), 139.
6. On sharecropping in Italy, see Lyttelton, 'Landlords, Peasants and the Limits of Liberalism', 104–35, and F. M. Snowden, 'From Sharecropper to Proletarian: The Background to Fascism in Rural Tuscany, 1880–1920', in Davis, *Gramsci and Italy's Passive Revolution*, 136–71.
7. S. B. Saul, *The Myth of the Great Depression*, 2nd edn (Basingstoke, 1985).
8. See B. Dicks, 'Choice and Constraint: Further Perspectives on Socio-Residential Segregation in Nineteenth-Century Glasgow with particular reference to its West End', in G. Gordon (ed.), *Perspectives of the Scottish City* (Aberdeen, 1985), 91–124.
9. Quoted in R. L. Glickmann, *Russian Factory Women: Workplace and Society, 1880–1914* (Berkeley, CA, 1984), 13.
10. Quoted in Frevert, *Women in German History*, 90.
11. For a discussion of this issue, among others see T. McBride, 'Women's Work and Industrialization', in Berlanstein, *The Industrial Revolution and Work*, 63–80.

12. Quoted in J. McDermid and A. Hillyar, *Women and Work in Russia: A Study in Continuity through Change 1880–1930* (London, 1998), 79.
13. M. R. Reinhard and A. Armengaud, *Histoire générale de la population mondiale* (Paris, 1961), 307–16.
14. M. R. Manus, 'Social Drinking in the *Belle Époque*', *JSH*, VII (1974), 115–41.
15. M. Grüttner, 'Working-Class Crime and the Labour Movement: Pilfering in the Hamburg Docks 1888–1923', in R. J. Evans, *The German Working Class 1888–1933* (London, 1982), 56–7.
16. For the welfare reforms, see, for example, J. R. Hay, *The Origins of the Liberal Welfare Reforms 1906–1914* (Basingstoke, 1983); G. C. Peden, *British Economic and Social Policy: Lloyd George to Margaret Thatcher*, 2nd edn (London, 1991), which has a helpful chapter on the 'People's Budget'; G. R. Searle, *The Quest for National Efficiency: A Study of British Politics and Political Thought, 1899–1914* (London, 1990); J. H. Weiss, 'Origins of the French Welfare State: Poor Relief in the Third Republic, 1871–1914', *FHS*, XIII (1983), 47–77; P. Nord, 'The Welfare State in France, 1870–1914', *FHS*, XVIII (1994), 821–38.

13 The Cultural Clash and the Growth of the Public

1. Quoted in D. G. Charlton, *Secular Religions in France 1815–1870* (London, 1963), 43.
2. W. M. Simon, *European Positivism in the Nineteenth Century: An Essay in Intellectual History* (Ithaca, NY, 1963), 85n.
3. Quoted in Simon, *European Positivism*, 80.
4. J. C. Greene, *The Death of Adam: Evolution and its Impact on Western Thought* (Ames, 1996), 79.
5. C. W. Goodwin, 'On the Mosaic Cosmology', *Essays and Reviews* (1860), text in T. Cosslett, *Science and Religion in the Nineteenth Century* (Cambridge, 1984).
6. Anderson, *Education in France*, 149.
7. Quoted in Charlton, *Secular Religions*, 195.
8. Quoted in J. H. Brooke, *Science and Religion: Some Historical Perspectives* (Cambridge, 1991), 296.
9. A translated text of the 'Syllabus of Errors' may be found in Kertesz, *Documents*, 233–41.
10. Quoted in Greene, *Death of Adam*, 318.
11. Quoted in Brooke, *Science and Religion*, 295.
12. Brooke, *Science and Religion*, 275–6.
13. Quoted in J. J. Sheehan, 'Culture', in Blanning, *Nineteenth Century*, 133.
14. Quoted in Price, *Social History*, 317.
15. Quoted in J. Brooks, *When Russia Learned to Read: Literacy and Popular Literature, 1861–1917* (Princeton, NJ, 1985), 47.
16. M. Gorky (trans. R. Wilks), *My Childhood* (Harmondsworth, 1966), 213–14.
17. D. Vincent, *The Rise of Mass Literacy: Reading and Writing in Modern Europe* (Cambridge, 2000), 22.
18. Quoted in Anderson, *Education in France*, 159.

19. Quoted in G. Lewis, 'The Peasantry, Rural Change and Conservative Agrarianism: Lower Austria and the Turn of the Century', *P&P*, 81 (1978), 137.
20. Anderson, *Education in France*, 163–5.
21. Quoted in F. Bédarida, *A Social History of England 1851–1990* (London, 1991), 157.
22. Quoted in Anderson, *Education in France*, 150.
23. Clark, *Modern Italy*, 170–1.
24. Quoted in Brooks, *When Russia Learned to Read*, 13.
25. Quoted in Price, *Social History*, 319.
26. Quoted in Price, *Social History*, 319.
27. See J. C. Albisetti, *Schooling German Girls and Women: Secondary and Higher Education in the Nineteenth Century* (Princeton, NJ, 1988), 292–305, for statistics and comparative discussion of women's access to secondary and higher education.
28. D. Vincent, *The Rise of Mass Literacy: Reading and Writing in Modern Europe* (Cambridge, 2000), 1–4.
29. Quoted in Brooks, *When Russia Learned to Read*, 30.
30. Price, *Social History*, 354.
31. R. A. Fullerton, 'Toward a Commercial Popular Culture in Germany: The Development of Pamphlet Fiction, 1871–1914', *JSH*, XII (1978–79), 503; Price, *Social History*, 355.
32. E. Weber, *Peasants into Frenchmen: The Modernization of Rural France, 1870–1914* (Stanford, CA, 1976), 469.
33. E. Guillaumin, *The Life of a Simple Man* (London, 1982), 176.
34. Weber, *Peasants into Frenchmen*, *passim*, but especially 195–374.
35. Quoted in Anderson, *Education in France*, 169.
36. See, for example, the interesting remarks by Magraw, *France 1815–1914*, 318–23. Weber answers some of his critics in 'Comment la politique vint aux paysans: a second look at peasant politicization', *AHR*, LXXXVII (1982), 357–89.
37. McPhee, *A Social History of France 1789–1914*, 210.
38. Quoted in Lewis, 'Peasantry, Rural Change', 141.
39. See L. Abrams, *Workers' Culture in Imperial Germany: Leisure and Recreation in the Rhineland and Westphalia* (London, 1992), 3–11.
40. Anderson, *Education in France*, 144–52.
41. Quoted in Fullerton, 'Toward a Commercial Popular Culture', 497.
42. P. Maloney, *Scotland and the Music Hall 1850–1914* (Manchester, 2003), 186–7.
43. Brooks, *When Russia Learned to Read*, 28–9.
44. S. P. Frank, 'Confronting the Domestic Other: Rural Popular Culture and its Enemies in Fin-de-Siècle Russia', in S. P. Frank and M. D. Steinberg (eds), *Cultures in Flux: Lower-Class Values, Practices, and Resistance in Late Imperial Russia* (Princeton, NJ, 1994), 75.

14 Towards Democracy? Feminism, Anarchism, Socialism

1. J. Roth (trans. J. Neugroschel), *The Radetzky March* (1932) (London, 1995), 161–2.

2. Quoted in E. Weber, *France: Fin de Siècle* (Cambridge, MA, 1986), 67.
3. G. Dangerfield, *The Strange Death of Liberal England* (London, 1966), 328, 340.
4. E. Hobsbawm, *The Age of Empire 1875–1914* (London, 1994), 84.
5. T. McBride, 'Public Authority and Private Lives: Divorce after the French Revolution', *FHS*, XVII (1992), 759–60.
6. Quoted in J. F. McMillan, *Housewife or Harlot: The Place of Women in French Society 1870–1940* (Brighton, 1981), 12.
7. Quoted in Pushkareva, *Women in Russian History*, 237.
8. Quoted in Frevert, *Women in German History*, 141.
9. See S. Bajohr, 'Illegitimacy and the Working Class: Illegitimate Mothers in Brunswick, 1900–1933', in Evans, *German Working Class*, 142–73.
10. O. Semyonova Tian-Shanskaia (ed. D. L. Ransel), *Village Life in Late Tsarist Russia* (Bloomington, IN, 1993), 4–5.
11. Quoted in Bédarida, *Social History of England*, 161.
12. Quoted in B. G. Smith, *Changing Lives: Women in European History since 1700* (Lexington, MA, 1989), 358.
13. Quoted in McMillan, *Housewife or Harlot*, 84.
14. Frevert, *Women in German History*, 141, 146.
15. Smith, *Changing Lives*, 254.
16. R. J. Evans, 'Prostitution, State and Society in Imperial Germany', *P&P*, 70 (1970), 122–3.
17. G. C. Friedman, 'Revolutionary Unions and French Labor: The Rebels behind the Cause; or, Why Did Revolutionary Syndicalism Fail?' *FHS*, XX (1997), 155–81.
18. Alvarez-Junco, *Mass Politics in Spain*, 147.
19. Quoted in Carr, *Spain*, 495.
20. Payne, *History of Spain and Portugal*, II, 591.
21. See, for example, the declaration of a coalminers' union in the west of Scotland, cited in W. W. Knox, *Industrial Nation: Work, Culture and Society in Scotland, 1800–Present* (Edinburgh, 1999), 118.
22. P. Adelman, *The Rise of the Labour Party 1880–1945*, 2nd edn (London, 1986), 25.
23. H. Pelling, *Origins of the Labour Party*, 2nd edn (Oxford, 1965), 42–4.
24. Quoted in Pelling, *Origins*, 118.
25. Quoted in Pelling, *Origins*, 118.
26. See the extract in Adelman, *Rise of the Labour Party*, 108–9.
27. J. J. Smyth, *Labour in Glasgow, 1896–1936: Socialism, Suffrage, Sectarianism* (East Linton, 2000), 10–27.
28. Quoted in B. Moss, *The Origins of the French Labor Movement, 1830–1914: The Socialism of Skilled Workers* (Berkeley, CA, 1976), 66.
29. Paul Lafargue, Marx's son-in-law, who helped Guesde spread the Marxist message.
30. Quoted in R. D. Anderson, *France 1870–1914: Politics and Society* (London, 1977), 125.
31. These issues are discussed by R. J. Evans, 'Introduction: The Sociological Interpretation of German Labour History', and by D. Geary, 'Identifying Militancy: The Assessment of Working-Class Attitudes towards State and Society', in Evans, *German Working Class*, 15–53, 220–46.
32. Quoted in V. R. Berghahn, *Imperial Germany 1871–1914: Economy, Society, Culture and Politics* (Oxford, 1994), 275.
33. Lyttelton, 'Landlords, Peasants and the Limits of Liberalism', 117.

34. Clark, *Modern Italy*, 141.
35. See, for example, O. Figes, *A People's Tragedy: The Russian Revolution 1891–1924* (London, 1996), 162–3.
36. M. Perrie, 'The Russian Peasant Movement of 1905–7: Its Social Composition and Revolutionary Significance', in B. Eklof and S. P. Frank (eds), *The World of the Russian Peasant: Post-Emancipation Culture and Society* (Boston, 1990), 197.
37. L. Haimson, 'The Problem of Social Stability in Urban Russia, 1905–1917' (Part One), *SR*, XXIII (1964), 627, 631.
38. Quoted in R. B. McKean, *St Petersburg between the Revolutions: Workers and Revolutionaries June 1907–February 1917* (New Haven, CT, 1990), 310.
39. There is considerable debate over the nature of the 'general strike' of July 1914. For contrasting views, see Haimson, 'The Problem of Social Stability', which stresses the importance of the Bolsheviks and the revolutionary potential of the strikes and McKean, *St Petersburg*, 297–317, 491–3, which plays down both.

15 The Nationalist Challenge

1. I. Banac, *The National Question in Yugoslavia: Origins, History, Politics* (Ithaca, NY, 1984), 110.
2. Details of the Swedish–Norwegian drama may be found in T. K. Derry, *A History of Scandinavia: Norway, Sweden, Denmark, Finland and Iceland* (Minneapolis, 1979), 268–74.
3. See M. Van Ginderachter, 'Belgium and the Flemish Movement: From Centralised Francophone State to Multilingual Federation (1830–2000)', in G. Hálfdanarson and A. K. Isaacs (eds), *Nations and Nationalities in Historical Perspective* (Pisa, 2001), 67–77; K. Deprez and L. Vos (eds), *Nationalism in Belgium: Shifting Identities, 1780–1995* (Basingstoke, 1998).
4. D. G. Boyce, 'Gladstone and Ireland', in P. J. Jagger (ed.), *Gladstone* (London, 1998), 111.
5. A. O'Day, *Irish Home Rule 1867–1921* (Manchester, 1998), 111.
6. Quoted in O'Day, *Irish Home Rule*, 114.
7. Quoted in R. J. Finlay, *A Partnership for Good? Scottish Politics and the Union since 1880* (Edinburgh, 1997), 41.
8. Quoted in R. F. Foster, *Modern Ireland 1600–1972* (London, 1988), 466–7n.
9. Davies, *God's Playground*, II, 126–37.
10. D. Saunders, 'Regional Diversity in the Later Russian Empire', *TRHS*, 6th Series, X (2000), 163.
11. Davies, *God's Playground*, II, 108.
12. M. H. Thaden, M. H. Haltzel, C. L. Lundin, A. Plakans, T. U. Raun and E. C. Thaden, *Russification in the Baltic Provinces and Finland, 1855–1914* (Princeton, NJ, 1981), 8; P. Waldron, *The End of Imperial Russia, 1855–1917* (Basingstoke, 1997), 109–21; Hosking, *Russia: People and Empire*, 376–97.
13. R. E. Blobaum, *Rewolucja: Russian Poland, 1904–1907* (Ithaca, NY, 1995), 2–10.

14. D. Saunders, 'Russia's Ukrainian Policy (1847–1905): A Demographic Approach', *EHQ* XXV (1995), 181–208.
15. Saunders, 'Regional Diversity', 159.
16. Thaden et al., *Russification*, 4–5
17. Hosking, *Russia: People and Empire*, 382–3.
18. Quoted in Derry, *History of Scandinavia*, 276. Details on Russo-Finnish relations in Thaden et al., *Russification*, 29–32.
19. Derry, *History of Scandinavia*, 277.
20. See J. Miąso, 'Education and Social Structure in the Kingdom of Poland in the Second Half of the Nineteenth Century', *HE*, X (1981), 101–9.
21. Davies, *God's Playground*, II, 43–54; Blobaum, *Rewolucja*, 28–39.
22. Wandycz, *Lands of Partitioned Poland*, 306–7.
23. Zaprudnik, *Belarus*, 59, 61–2.
24. R. E. Blobaum, *Rewolucja: Russian Poland 1904–1907* (Ithaca, NY, 1995), 230.
25. Davies, *God's Playground*, II, 369–77.
26. Zaprudnik, *Belarus*, 63–5.
27. Wandycz, *Lands of Partitioned Poland*, 315–16.
28. Saunders, 'Regional Diversity', 163.
29. T. Zsuppán, 'The Hungarian Political Scene 1908–1918', in M. Cornwall (ed.), *The Last Years of Austria–Hungary* (Exeter, 1990), 65.
30. A. C. János, *The Politics of Backwardness in Hungary 1825–1945* (Princeton, NJ, 1982), 96–7.
31. Based on figures in Sked, *Decline and Fall*, 278–9. The remaining 2 per cent of the population of the empire is accounted for by Bosnia-Herzegovina, annexed in 1908.
32. Quoted in Sked, *Decline and Fall*, 189.
33. C. A. Macartney, *The House of Austria: The Later Phase 1790–1918* (Edinburgh, 1978), 207; Sked, *Decline and Fall*, 209.
34. J. K. Hoensch (trans. K. Traynor), *A History of Modern Hungary 1867–1986* (London, 1988), 29.
35. These different tendencies are discussed by Banac, *National Question in Yugoslavia*, 89–103.
36. A. G. Whiteside, 'The Germans as an Integrative Force in Imperial Austria: The Dilemma of Dominance', *AHY*, III (1967), 1, 157–200.
37. Quoted in Wandycz, *Lands of Partitioned Poland*, 278.
38. For details on the politicisation of the Ukrainian peasantry of Galicia, see J.-P. Himka, *Galician Villagers and the Ukrainian National Movement in the Nineteenth Century* (Basingstoke, 1988), especially 59–104, 143–215.
39. Quoted in A. G. Kogan, 'The Social Democrats and the Conflict of Nationalities in the Habsburg Monarchy', *JMH*, XXI (1949), 205.
40. A. G. Whiteside, *The Socialism of Fools: Georg Ritter von Schönerer and Austrian Pan-Germanism* (Berkeley, CA, 1975), 90.
41. Quoted in Whiteside, *Socialism of Fools*, 147.
42. Quoted in Macartney, *House of Austria*, 181–2.
43. Quoted in L. Höbelt, 'Austrian Pre-War Domestic Politics', in Cornwall, *Last Years of Austria–Hungary*, 57.
44. For an interesting and sophisticated explanation for the failure of parliamentary politics in Austria, see J. W. Boyer, 'The End of an Old Regime: Visions of Political Reform in Late Imperial Austria', *JMH*, LVIII (1986), 159–93. See also S. G. Konirsh, 'Constitutional Aspects of the Struggle

between Germans and Czechs in the Austro-Hungarian Monarchy', *JMH*, XXVII (1955), 231–61.

45. See the figures in J. Macarthy, *The Ottoman Peoples and the End of Empire* (London, 2001), 58–9.
46. D. Stevenson, *Armaments and the Coming of War: Europe 1904–1914* (Oxford, 1996), 128.
47. Jelavich, *Russia's Balkan Entanglements*, 227–8.
48. Details on both Balkan Wars can be found in R. C. Hall, *The Balkan Wars 1912–1913: Prelude to the First World War* (London, 2000).

16 Authoritarian and Conservative Responses

1. Tombs, *France*, 453.
2. See B. Fulton, 'The Boulanger Affair Revisited: The Preservation of the Third Republic, 1889', *FHS*, XVII (1991).
3. M. Burns, *Rural Society and French Politics: Boulangism and the Dreyfus Affair 1886–1900* (Princeton, NJ, 1984), 117.
4. G. L. Mosse, 'The French Right and the Working Classes: *Les Jaunes*', *JCH*, VII (1972), 185–208.
5. V. Caron, 'The "Jewish Question" from Dreyfus to Vichy', in Alexander, *French History since Napoleon*, 176–80. For the impact of the Dreyfus affair on rural politics (about which there is some debate over the extent), see Burns, *Rural Society*, and N. Fitch, 'Mass Culture, Mass Parliamentary Politics, and Modern Anti-Semitism: The Dreyfus Affair in Rural France', *AHR*, XCIII (1992), 55–95.
6. Quoted in C. Duggan, *Francesco Crispi: From Nation to Nationalism* (Oxford, 2002), 679.
7. C. Duggan, 'Nation-building in 19th-Century Italy: The Case of Francesco Crispi', *History Today*, LII, 2 (February 2002), 15.
8. Duggan, *Francesco Crispi*, 7.
9. R. Gildea, *Barricades and Borders: Europe 1800–1914* (Oxford, 1987), 418–21.
10. Quoted in Z. S. Steiner, *Britain and the Origins of the First World War* (Basingstoke, 1977), 133.
11. Quoted in Steiner, *Britain and the Origins*, 135.
12. Quoted in Carr, *History of Germany*, 163.
13. Quoted in F. L. Carsten, *A History of the Prussian Junkers* (Aldershot, 1989), 137–8.
14. For discussions of the radical nationalist and populist organisations, see D. Blackbourn, 'The Politics of Demagogy in Imperial Germany', *P&P*, 113 (November 1986), 152–84; D. Blackbourn, 'Peasants and Politics in Germany, 1871–1914', *EHQ*, XIV (1984), 47–75; D. Blackbourn, 'The Wilhelmine Right: How it Changed' and I. Farr, 'Populism in the Countryside: The Peasant Leagues in Bavaria in the 1890s', in R. J. Evans (ed.), *Society and Politics in Wilhelmine Germany* (London, 1978), 112–35 and 136–59; G. Eley, 'Defining Social Imperialism: Use and Abuse of an idea', *SH*, III (1976), 265–90.
15. Quoted in K. A. Lerman, 'Bismarck's Heir: Chancellor Bernhard von Bülow and the National Idea 1890–1918', in J. Breuilly (ed.), *The State of Germany: The National Idea in the Making, Unmaking and Remaking of a Modern Nation–State* (London, 1992), 109.

16. Quoted in W. J. Mommsen (trans. R. Deveson), *Imperial Germany 1867–1918: Politics, Culture, and Society in an Authoritarian State* (London, 1995), 153.
17. Carr, *History of Germany*, 185.
18. P. Waldon, 'States of Emergency: Autocracy and Extraordinary Legislation, 1881–1917', *RR*, VIII (1995), 1–25.
19. Quoted in Gooding, *Rulers and Subjects*, p. 79.
20. P. A. Zaionchkovsky (trans. D. R. Jones), *The Russian Autocracy under Alexander III* (Gulf Breeze, FL, 1976), 93.
21. For an (overly) optimistic assessment of these statutes, see W. B. Lincoln, *The Great Reforms. Autocracy, Bureaucracy, and the Politics of Change in Imperial Russia* (De Kalb, IL, 1990), 175–91.
22. Quoted in Waldron, *End of Imperial Russia*, 35.

17 Imperialism

1. Quoted in R. F. Betts, *The False Dawn: European Imperialism in the Nineteenth Century* (Minneapolis, 1976), 30.
2. Aldrich, *Greater France*, 87.
3. Quoted in R. E. Robinson and J. Gallagher, 'The Partition of Africa', in *New Cambridge Modern History*, XI, *Material Progress and World-Wide Problems: 1870–1898* (Cambridge, 1962), 603.
4. Quoted in Aldrich, *Greater France*, 99.
5. Quoted in H.-U. Wehler, 'Bismarck's Imperialism 1862–1890', *P&P*, 48 (August 1970), 134.
6. Quoted in Porter, *Lion's Share*, 133.
7. J. Stengers, 'King Leopold's imperialism', R. Owen and B. Sutcliffe (eds), *Studies in the Theory of Imperialism* (London, 1972), 257.
8. W. D. Smith, 'The Ideology of German Colonialism, 1840–1906', *JMH* XLVI (1974), 650–1.
9. Quoted in Porter, *Lion's Share*, 126.
10. Quoted in Betts, *False Dawn*, 155.
11. Earl of Cromer, *Modern Egypt*, 2 vols (London, 1908), I, 5–6.
12. Quoted in Aldrich, *Greater France*, 98–9.
13. Aldrich, *Greater France*, 129.
14. P. Summerfield, 'Patriotism and Empire: Music Hall Entertainment 1870–1914', in J. M. Mackenzie (ed.), *Imperialism and Popular Culture* (Manchester, 1986), 17–48; P. Maloney, *Scotland and the Music Hall*, 167.
15. Wehler, 'Bismarck's Imperialism', 143.
16. Eley, 'Defining Social Imperialism', 265–90.
17. P. Kennedy, 'German Colonial Expansion. Has the "Manipulated Social Imperialism" been Ante-Dated?', *P&P*, 54 (February 1972), 134–41.
18. Bismarck and Bülow quoted in Kennedy, 'German Colonial Expansion', 137–8.
19. Quoted in Duggan, *Francesco Crispi*, 692.
20. R. J. B. Bosworth, *Italy, the Least of the Great Powers: Italian Foreign Policy before the First World War* (Cambridge, 1979), 189.
21. Quoted in Aldrich, *Greater France*, 113.
22. Quoted in C. M. Andrew, 'The French Colonialist Movement during the Third Republic: The Unofficial Mind of Imperialism', *TRHS*, 5th Series, XXVI (1976), 144–5.

23. Quoted in Porter, *Lion's Share*, 115.
24. Blackbourn, *Fontana History of Germany*, 333.
25. H. Pogge von Strandmann, 'Domestic Origins of Germany's Colonial Expansion under Bismarck', *P&P*, 42 (February 1969), 157–9.
26. Quoted in Porter, *Lion's Share*, 132.
27. *Imperialism: the Highest Stage of Capitalism*, quoted in T. Kemp, 'The Marxist Theory of Imperialism', in R. Owen and B. Sutcliffe, *Studies in the Theory of Imperialism* (London, 1972), 22.
28. D. S. Landes, *The Unbound Prometheus: Technological Change and Industrial Development in Western Europe from 1750 to the Present* (Cambridge, 1970), 240–1.
29. Porter, *Lion's Share*, 139–47.
30. Quoted in Wehler, 'Bismarck's Imperialism', 136.
31. G. Clarence-Smith, *The Third Portuguese Empire 1825–1975: A Study in Economic Imperialism* (Manchester, 1985), 81–112.
32. Aldrich, *Greater France*, 196.
33. Quoted in Porter, *Lion's Share*, 157.
34. A. Porter, *European Imperialism, 1860–1914* (Basingstoke, 1994), 47.
35. Porter, *European Imperialism*, 40.
36. Quoted in Wehler, 'Bismarck's Imperialism', 127.
37. Blackbourn, *Fontana History of Germany*, 333–5.
38. For more detail, see R. Owen, 'Egypt and Europe: From French Expedition to British Occupation', in Owen and Sutcliffe, *Studies*, 205–7.
39. Clarence-Smith, *Third Portuguese Empire*, 100–1.
40. H. L. Wesseling, 'The Giant that was a Dwarf, or the Strange History of Dutch Imperialism', *JICH*, XVI (1988), 61–2.
41. Quoted in Bosworth, *Italy*, 145.
42. Quoted in Andrew and Kanya-Forstner, 'Centre and Periphery', 20.

18 The Origins of the First World War

1. Details on Princip and the assassination in A. J. May, *The Passing of the Hapsburg Monarchy 1914–1918*, 2 vols (Philadelphia, PA, 1966), I, 29–39. See also M. Glenny, *The Balkans 1804–1999: Nationalism, War and the Great Powers* (London, 1999), 250–1, 304–5 and J. Remak, *Sarajevo* (New York, 1959).
2. P. W. Schroeder, 'World War I as Galloping Gertie: A Reply to Joachim Remak', in H. W. Koch (ed.), *The Origins of the First World War: Great Power Rivalry and German War Aims*, 2nd edn (Basingstoke, 1984), 106.
3. J. F. V. Keiger, *France and the Origins of the First World War* (Basingstoke, 1983), 13.
4. D. C. B. Lieven, *Russia and the Origins of the First World War* (Basingstoke, 1983), 26–7.
5. Details in V. R. Berghahn, *Germany and the Approach of War in 1914* (New York, 1973), 23–42.
6. Quoted in Berghahn, *Germany and the Approach of War*, 48.
7. Lieven, *Russia*, 37. Compare Lieven's account, based on Russian sources, with that of Samuel R. Williamson, *Austria–Hungary and the Origins of the First World War* (Basingstoke, 1991), 67–72.
8. See S. Wank, 'Some Reflections on Conrad von Hötzendorf and his Memoirs Based on Old and New Sources', *AHY*, I (1965), 74–89.

9. Quoted in Steiner, *Britain and the Origins*, 98.
10. Stevenson, *Armaments and the Coming of War*, 231–328.
11. See F. Fischer, *Germany's Aims in the First World War* (London, 1967), especially 3–49, and F. Fischer, *War of Illusions: German Policies from 1911 to 1914* (London, 1975).
12. Fischer, *War of Illusions*, 470.
13. Fischer, *War of Illusions*, 160–2.
14. See the two essays in Koch, *The Origins of the First World War* by J. Joll, 'The 1914 Debate Continues: Fritz Fischer and his Critics', 30–45, and K.-H. Janssen 'Gerhard Ritter: A Patriotic Historian's Justification', 292–318.
15. H. Herwig, *The First World War: Germany and Austria–Hungary 1914–1918* (London, 1997), 19.
16. Schroeder, 'International Politics', 206.
17. Mommsen, *Imperial Germany*, 162.
18. M. Paléologue, *An Ambassador's Memoirs 1914–1917* (London, 1973), 65.
19. Quoted in J. Joll, *Europe since 1870: An International History*, 3rd edn (Harmondsworth, 1983), 195.

Bibliographic Essay

This can only be a small selection of the vast array of excellent writings available on this period; on average 2000 items are published annually on the French Revolution alone. Works absent from the list below are more likely to have been omitted owing either to constraints of space or to my own ignorance, rather than to any judgement on their quality. Space restrictions also mean that most articles used in the preparation of this book have been omitted: for these, readers may refer to the notes. In this bibliography I have generally cited those articles which have not been referenced there. While documentary collections are not generally included (though some are cited in the notes), those textbooks which include documents are asterisked. This bibliographic essay opens with two sections on general surveys, followed by a section dealing with economic, social and cultural themes. The rest of the essay discusses works relating to political developments, broken down into sections corresponding roughly with the chronological breakdown of this book.

General European Surveys

The 'long nineteenth century' is well-served by broad introductory surveys, notably R. Gildea, *Barricades and Borders: Europe 1800–1914*, 2nd edn (Oxford, 1996) which is elegantly written. T. C. W. Blanning (ed.), *The Nineteenth Century* (Oxford, 2000) is a collection of lively, digestible essays. Despite the apparently narrow focus implied by the title, the articles in I. Woloch (ed.), *Revolution and the Meanings of Freedom in the Nineteenth Century* (Stanford, CA, 1996) are actually broad introductions to political history. The entire period is also covered by a number of series. From a Marxist perspective, with engaging detail, see E. Hobsbawm, *The Age of Revolution 1789–1848* (London, 1962), *The Age of Capital* (London, 1975) and *The Age of Empire, 1875–1914* (London, 1987). The Fontana series covering the same era comes from an eclectic mix of viewpoints, including G. Rudé, *Revolutionary Europe, 1783–1815* (Glasgow, 1964) which is still useful, and J. Droz, *Europe between Revolutions 1815–1848* (London, 1967) which is rather dated. More recent and helpful are J. A. S. Grenville, *Europe Reshaped, 1848–1878* (London, 1980) and N. Stone, *Europe Transformed, 1878–1919* (London, 1985). Together, F. Ford, *Europe 1780–1830* (London, 1970); H. Hearder, *Europe in the Nineteenth Century, 1830–1880* (London, 1966) and J. M. Roberts, *Europe 1880–1945* (London, 1967) offer a wealth of detail. Up-to-date surveys of the first half of the period also include J. Sperber, *Revolutionary Europe, 1780–1848* (London, 2000) and the briefer C. Breunig and M. Levinger, *The Revolutionary Era 1789–1850*, 3rd edn (London, 2002). The later part of the era is discussed in detail in J. Joll, *Europe since 1870: An International History* (Harmondsworth, 1976), but especially enjoyable is M. Larkin, *Gathering Pace: Continental Europe 1870–1945* (London, 1969) – it opens with an imaginary balloonist's eye-view of Europe in 1870. International affairs are discussed in P. W. Schroeder, *The Transformation of European Politics 1763–1848* (Oxford, 1994), which argues that the shock of the French Revolutionary and Napoleonic Wars caused international politics to shift from a precarious balance of power system to one based on a consensus to avoid conflict. A. J. P. Taylor, *The Struggle for Mastery in Europe 1848–1918* (Oxford, 1954) is now a classic.

Specific Countries and Regions

Books covering individual regions and countries are very numerous. For France, R. Tombs, *France 1814–1914* (London, 1996) has some wonderful detail and is a great read; it is probably the best introduction for students. R. Magraw, *France 1815–1914: The Bourgeois Century* (London, 1983), written from a Marxist perspective, is a mine of information, particularly on social and economic developments. The collection of essays in M. S. Alexander (ed.), *French History since Napoleon* (London, 1999) provides some up-to-date surveys on a broad range of topics, as does M. Crook (ed.), *Revolutionary France 1788–1880* (Oxford, 2002). S. Gemie, *French Revolutions, 1815–1914: An Introduction* (Edinburgh, 1999)*, is attuned to current trends by discussing political culture. For Italy, the best general textbook for the period up to unification is S. Woolf, *A History of Italy 1700–1860: The Social Constraints of Political Change* (London, 1979), though students coming to the topic for the first time might be swamped by all the detail. H. Hearder, *Italy in the Age of the Risorgimento 1780–1870* (London, 1983) covers all the separate states prior to 1860, as well as the process of unification itself. D. Beales and E. F. Biagini, *The Risorgimento and the Unification of Italy*, 2nd edn (London 2002)* is a good introduction and includes a chapter on the role of women. Martin Clark, *Modern Italy 1871–1995*, 2nd edn (London, 1996) is especially informative, while J. A. Davis (ed.), *Italy in the Nineteenth Century* (Oxford, 2000) is a stimulating collection of essays, as is J. A. Davis and P. Ginsborg (eds), *Society and Politics in the Age of Risorgimento: Essays in Honour of Denis Mack Smith* (Cambridge, 1991). Spain is covered comprehensively by R. Carr, *Spain 1808–1975*, 2nd edn (Oxford, 1982), but a quality, up-to-date perspective is offered by C. J. Esdaile, *Spain in the Liberal Age: From Constitution to Civil War, 1808–1939* (Oxford, 2000). The second volume of S. G. Payne, *A History of Spain and Portugal*, 2 vols (Madison, 1973) is less detailed, but is helpful not least because it is one of the rare works in English which covers Portugal. On Britain, E. J. Evans, *The Forging of the Modern State: Early Industrial Britain 1783–1870* (London, 1983) offers a wealth of information. The essays in H. C. G. Matthew (ed.), *The Nineteenth Century: The British Isles, 1815–1901* (Oxford, 2000) are up-to-date surveys. For the Scottish dimension, see the pithy J. F. McCaffrey, *Scotland in the Nineteenth Century* (Basingstoke, 1998). For Ireland, D. G. Boyce, *Nineteenth-Century Ireland: The Search for Stability* (Dublin, 1990) is primarily a political history, but it skilfully weaves social developments into the narrative. See also K. T. Hoppen, *Ireland since 1800: Conflict and Conformity* (London, 1999). The standard 'revisionist' work (in the sense that it challenges nationalist versions of Irish history) is R. F. Foster, *Modern Ireland 1600–1972* (London, 1988). Northern Europe is well-served by T. K. Derry, *A History of Scandinavia: Norway, Sweden, Denmark, Finland and Iceland* (Minneapolis, 1979). The equivalent book for Belgium and the Netherlands is E. H. Kossmann,

The Low Countries 1780–1940 (Oxford, 1978). The sometimes turbulent history of the Swiss in this period is chronicled by E. Bonjour, H. S. Offler and G. R. Potter, *A Short History of Switzerland* (Oxford, 1952).

On Germany, D. Blackbourn, *The Fontana History of Germany 1780–1918: The Long Nineteenth Century* (London, 1997) is readable and informative. W. Carr, *A History of Germany 1815–1990* (London, 1991) is also very useful. T. Nipperdey (trans. D. Nolan), *Germany from Napoleon to Bismarck, 1800–1866* (Dublin, 1996) is a detailed book, a theme of which is a search for the roots of Germany's authoritarian tendencies. E. D. Brose, *German History 1789–1871: From the Holy Roman Empire to the Bismarckian Reich* (Oxford, 1997) has less detail, but is readable. Together, J. J. Sheehan, *German History 1770–1866* (Oxford, 1989) and G. A. Craig, *Germany 1866–1945* (Oxford, 1981) are excellent. B. Simms, *The Struggle for Mastery in Germany, 1779–1850* (Basingstoke, 1998) stresses the importance of foreign policy in the emerging political shape of Germany. The essays in J. Breuilly (ed.), *The State of Germany: The National Idea in the Making, Unmaking and Remaking of a Modern Nation-State* (London, 1992) cover much of this period. A more comprehensive collection of essays is J. Breuilly (ed.), *19th Century Germany: Politics, Culture and Society 1780–1918* (London, 2001). On the Habsburg empire, a readable classic, focusing on political developments, is A. J. P. Taylor, *The Habsburg Monarchy 1809–1918* (Harmondsworth, 1964). C. A. Macartney, *The Habsburg Empire 1790–1918* (London, 1968) is the most detailed general work and has been helpfully abridged as *The House of Austria: The Later Phase 1790–1918* (Edinburgh, 1978). A. Sked, *Decline and Fall of the Habsburg Empire 1815–1918* (London, 1989) includes an extensive discussion of historiography. A. C. János, *The Politics of Backwardness in Hungary 1825–1945* (Princeton, NJ, 1982) is not an easy read, but it offers some important insights. J. K. Hoensch (trans. K. Traynor), *A History of Modern Hungary 1867–1986* (London, 1988) is a good introduction to political developments from the Compromise. For the Russian Empire, J. N. Westwood, *Endurance and Endeavour: Russian History 1812–1992*, 4th edn (Oxford, 1993) is becoming a classic, while J. Gooding, *Rulers and Subjects: Government and People in Russia 1801–1991* (London, 1993) is written in a refreshingly direct style. G. Hosking, *Russia: People and Empire 1552–1917* (London, 1998) argues that the historic association of Russia with its empire stored up future problems for Russian national identity. D. Saunders, *Russia in the Age of Reaction and Reform 1801–1881* (London, 1992) is superb, and is followed up well by H. Rogger, *Russia in the Age of Modernisation and Revolution, 1881–1917* (London, 1983). P. Waldron, *The End of Imperial Russia, 1855–1917* (Basingstoke, 1997) is an excellent introduction to the problems facing the later Tsarist regime. On Poland, the authority in the English language is N. Davies, *God's Playground: A History of Poland*, 2 vols (New York, 1982), especially the second volume. His briefer *Heart of Europe: A Short History of Poland* (Oxford, 1984) is also useful. P. S. Wandycz, *The Lands of Partitioned Poland, 1795–1918* (Seattle, WA, 1975) is extremely thorough, covering those areas of Lithuania and the Ukraine lost for Poland in the partitions. For an often overlooked part of the Russian Empire, see J. Zaprudnik, *Belarus: At a Crossroads in History* (Boulder, 1993). South-eastern Europe is described in often gruesome detail in the readable M. Glenny, *The Balkans 1804–1999: Nationalism, War and the Great Powers* (London, 1999). S. K. Pavlowitch, *A History of the Balkans, 1804–1945* (London, 1999) is comprehensive for the nineteenth century. See also J. Macarthy, *The Ottoman Peoples and the End of Empire*

(London, 2001) and B. Jelavich, *Russia's Balkan Entanglements, 1806–1914* (Cambridge, 1991). C. and B. Jelavich, *The Establishment of the Balkan National States, 1804–1920* (Seattle, WA, 1977) is an excellent introduction, carefully explaining all the terms and complexities of the region's history. For Romania before unification, see K. Hitchins, *The Romanians 1774–1866* (Oxford, 1996) and, for afterwards, see, by the same author, *Rumania, 1866–1947* (Oxford, 1994).

Economic, Social and Cultural Life

The causes and effects of the demographic pressure from 1750 are discussed in H. J. Habakkuk, *Population Growth and Economic Development since 1750* (Leicester, 1971). H. Moller (ed.), *Population Movements in Modern European History* (New York, 1964) is an interesting collection of older essays, but the most useful book of all on this topic is W. R. Lee (ed.), *European Demography and Economic Growth* (London, 1979). M. R. Reinhard and A. Armengaud, *Histoire générale de la population mondiale* (Paris, 1961) has some useful statistics. General economic histories include C. M. Cipolla (ed.), *The Fontana Economic History of Europe*, Part III, *The Industrial Revolution* (London, 1973) and Part IV, 2 vols, *The Emergence of Industrial Societies* (London, 1973), though some of the articles now appear rather dated. See also T. Kemp, *Industrialization in Nineteenth-Century Europe* (London, 1969) and, especially, D. S. Landes, *The Unbound Prometheus: Technological Change and Industrial Development in Western Europe from 1750 to the Present* (Cambridge, 1969) and S. Pollard, *Peaceful Conquest: The Industrialization of Europe 1760–1970* (Oxford, 1981). For the development of wider markets, see S. Pollard, *European Economic Integration 1815–1870* (London, 1974). The most helpful works on industrialisation are A. Milward and S. B. Saul, *Economic History of Continental Europe* (London, 1973) and *The Development of the Economies of Continental Europe 1850–1914* (London, 1977) and M. M. Postan and H. J. Habbakuk (eds), *The Cambridge Economic History of Europe*, VI, Parts 1 and 2, *The Industrial Revolutions and After*, 2 vols (Cambridge, 1966). W. W. Rostow, *The Stages of Economic Growth: A Non-Communist Manifesto*, 2nd edn (Cambridge, 1971) posits the notion of industrial 'take-off'. For the leading European industrial nations, see P. Mathias, *The First Industrial Nation: The Economic History of Britain 1700–1914*, 2nd ed. (London, 1983) and H. Böhme, *An Introduction to the Social and Economic History of Germany: Politics and Economic Change in the Nineteenth and Twentieth Centuries* (Oxford, 1978). M. Kitchen, *The Political Economy of Germany 1815–1914* (London, 1978) relates political to economic developments. S. B. Saul, *The Myth of the Great Depression*, 2nd edn (Basingstoke, 1985) is, as the title suggests, sceptical about the impact of falling prices on the British economy after 1873. None the less, in European countries which were still primarily agricultural, the effects seemed to have been real enough. A. Gerschenkron, *Economic Backwardness in Historical Perspective: A Book of Essays* (Cambridge, MA, 1966) offers his thesis that the precise obstacles to economic growth in any country will determine the way in which that country's economy develops. Gerschenkron's theory has been challenged in the cases of several countries, including Russia. M. E. Falkus, *The Industrialisation of Russia 1700–1914* (Basingstoke, 1972) accepts some of Gerschenkron's ideas, but not all. Recent work has been more critical: see, for example, P. Gatrell, *The Tsarist Economy 1850–1917* (London, 1986) and P. R. Gregory, *Russian National Income, 1885–1913* (Cambridge, 1982). These works also challenge the classic image of the backwardness of agriculture in late imperial Russia, embodied, for example, in the work of G. T. Robinson, *Rural Russia under the Old Regime: A History of the Landlord–Peasant World and a Prologue to the Peasant Revolution of 1917* (Berkeley, CA, 1932). W. E. Mosse, *Perestroika under the Tsars* (London, 1992) examines the role of the Russian government. Particularly readable on that subject is T. H. von Laue, *Sergei Witte and the Industrialization of Russia* (New York, 1974). The 'backwardness' of French economic development is also the subject of debate, discussed in C. Heywood, *The Development of the French Economy, 1750–1914* (Basingstoke, 1992). See also F. Crouzet, 'French Economic Growth in the Nineteenth Century Reconsidered', *History*, LIX (1974), 167–79, which finishes on an optimistic note. R. Price, *An Economic History of Modern France 1730–1914* (Basingstoke, 1981) offers plenty of facts and figures. D. F. Good, *The Economic Rise of the Habsburg Empire 1750–1914* (Berkeley, CA, 1984) debunks some of the more pessimistic assessments of 'backwardness'. For a dense discussion of the economy of south-eastern Europe, see J. R. Lampe and M. R. Jackson, *Balkan Economic History 1550–1950: From Imperial Borderlands to Developing Nations* (Bloomington, IN, 1982).

There are many good social histories of specific countries. Life in Victorian Britain is discussed in engaging detail by G. Best, *Mid-Victorian Britain, 1851–75* (London, 1979) and A. N. Wilson, *The Victorians* (London, 2002). E. Hobsbawm, *Industry and Empire* (Harmondsworth, 1969) is a powerful account of the impact of economic change on British society. F. Bédarida, *A Social History of England 1851–1990* (London, 1991) is a good warts-and-all description. See also F. M. L. Thompson, *The Rise of Respectable Society: A Social History of Victorian Britain, 1830–1900* (London, 1988). French society is discussed in two excellent books, P. McPhee, *A Social History of France 1789–1914*, 2nd edn (Basingstoke, 2004) and R. Price, *A Social History of Nineteenth-Century France* (London, 1987). Social problems in Italy are explored by the essays in J. A. Davis (ed.), *Gramsci and Italy's Passive Revolution* (London, 1979). For Russian society after 1861, see the essays in C. E. Black, *The Transformation of Russian Society: Aspects of Social Change since 1861* (Cambridge, MA, 1960). The impact of industrialisation on working and living conditions for men and women are the subject of the essays in L. R. Berlanstein (ed.), *The Industrial Revolution and Work in Nineteenth-Century Europe* (London, 1992). An interesting Russian case study is C. Wynn, *Workers, Strikes, and Pogroms: The Donbass–Dnepr Bend in Late Imperial Russia, 1870–1905* (Princeton, NJ, 1992). For Scotland, see W. W. Knox, *Industrial Nation: Work, Culture and Society in Scotland, 1800–Present* (Edinburgh, 1999). For Germany, R. J. Evans (ed.), *The German Working Class 1888–1933* (London, 1982) is thought-provoking. French cases can be compared in M. P. Hanagan, *The Logic of Solidarity: Artisans and Industrial Workers in Three French Towns 1871–1914* (Chicago, 1980). The emergence of a middle class has absorbed social historians, whose findings are synthesised in P. Pilbeam, *The Middle Classes in Europe 1789–1914: France, Germany, Italy and Russia* (Basingstoke, 1990). J. Kocka and A. Mitchell (eds), *Bourgeois Society in Nineteenth-Century Europe* (Oxford, 1993) is a provocative series of comparative essays. F. L. Carsten, *A History of the Prussian Junkers* (Aldershot, 1989) charts the political responses of the Prussian elites to the challenges of the age.

Urbanisation, city life and culture can be explored by reading the essays in

M. F. Hamm (ed.), *The City in Late Imperial Russia* (Bloomington, IN, 1988) and R. J. Evans, *Death in Hamburg: Society and Politics in the Cholera Years 1830–1910* (Oxford, 1987). Those who wish to read about the ghastlier conditions endured by many nineteenth-century Europeans can find plenty of material in M. Durey, *The Return of the Plague: British Society and the Cholera 1831–2* (Dublin, 1979), as well as Evans, just cited. On German cities, see W. Köllmann, 'The Process of Urbanization in Germany at the height of the industrialization period', *JCH*, IV (1969), 59–76, and for life in an industrialised region, see D. F. Crew, *Town in the Ruhr: A Social History of Bochum, 1860–1914* (New York, 1979) which has some vivid detail. P. Hanák, *The Garden and the Workshop: Essays on the Cultural History of Vienna and Budapest* (Princeton, NJ, 1998) is an eclectic and interesting bag of articles. L. Chevalier (trans. F. Jellinek), *Labouring Classes and Dangerous Classes in Paris during the First Half of the Nineteenth Century* (New York, 1973) investigates the effects of mid-century urban poverty from different perspectives. A British classic is A. Briggs, *Victorian Cities* (Harmondsworth, 1968). For the Scottish experience, see G. Gordon (ed.), *Perspectives of the Scottish City* (Aberdeen, 1985). Rural life can be investigated by reading A. Moulin (trans M. C. and M. F. Cleary), *Peasantry and Society in France since 1789* (Cambridge, 1991). The ground-breaking work on France was E. Weber, *Peasants into Frenchmen: The Modernization of Rural France, 1870–1914* (Stanford, CA, 1976) and it continues to spark debate about peasant politicisation. S. L. Hoch, *Serfdom and Social Control in Russia: Petrovskoe, a Village in Tambov* (Chicago, 1986) is a fascinating case study of Russian serfdom. The limits of reform before 1861 are discussed in D. Moon, *Russian Peasants and Tsarist Legislation: Interaction between Peasants and Officialdom, 1825–1855* (Basingstoke, 1992). More general themes are explored in E. Kingston-Mann and T. Mixter (eds), *Peasant Economy, Culture and Politics of European Russia, 1800–1921* (Princeton, NJ, 1991). There are also some excellent essays in B. Eklof and S. P. Frank (eds), *The World of the Russian Peasant: Post-Emancipation Culture and Society* (Boston, MA, 1990). Older but still informative articles are collected in W. S. Vucinich (ed.), *The Peasant in 19th Century Russia* (Stanford, CA, 1968). The fluctuating fortunes of the Polish peasantry are charted in S. Kieniewicz, *The Emancipation of the Polish Peasantry* (Chicago, 1969).

For state intervention in the social question in the last decades of the period, see J. R. Hay, *The Origins of the Liberal Welfare Reforms 1906–1914* (Basingstoke, 1983) and G. R. Searle, *The Quest for National Efficiency: A Study of British Politics and Political Thought, 1899–1914* (London, 1990). Recent work on French social reforms include B. Taithe, *Defeated Flesh: Welfare, Warfare and the Making of Modern France* (Manchester, 1999); A. R. Aisenberg, *Contagion: Disease, Government, and the 'Social Question' in Nineteenth Century France* (Stanford, CA, 1999); J. R. Horne, *A Social Laboratory for Modern France: The Musée Social and the Rise of the Welfare State* (Durham, NC, 2002) and T. B. Smith, *Creating the Welfare State in France, 1880–1940* (Montreal, 2003), which focuses on the case of Lyon: for the pre-1914 period, see ch. 2.

The role of women in society and politics has been the subject of a wealth of research in recent decades. B. G. Smith, *Changing Lives: Women in European History Since 1700* (Lexington, MA, 1989)* is a good general history. U. Frevert, *Women in German History: From Bourgeois Emancipation to Sexual Liberation* (Oxford, 1989) covers women of all social classes and of different political perspectives, while J. F. McMillan, *France and Women 1789–1914:*

Gender, Society and Politics (London, 2000) does the same service for France. See also his *Housewife or Harlot: The Place of Women in French Society 1870–1940* (Brighton, 1981). N. Pushkareva (trans. E. Levin), *Women in Russian History from the Tenth to the Twentieth Century* (Stroud, 1999) is a readable introduction to the topic. J. McDermid and A. Hillyar, *Women and Work in Russia: A Study in Continuity through Change 1880–1930* (London, 1998) is peppered with interesting detail and covers rural and urban work, as well as women from the elites and the revolutionary parties. See also R. L. Glickmann, *Russian Factory Women: Workplace and Society, 1880–1914* (Berkeley, CA, 1984). B. A. Engel, *Between the Fields and the City: Women, Work, and Family in Russia, 1861–1914* (Cambridge, 1994) is excellent. D. Barry, *Women and Political Insurgency: France in the Mid-Nineteenth Century* (Basingstoke, 1996) deals with the period from 1815 to 1871. Women's education is discussed in J. C. Albisetti, *Schooling German Girls and Women: Secondary and Higher Education in the Nineteenth Century* (Princeton, NJ, 1988). For single mothers, see R. G. Fuchs and L. P. Moch, 'Pregnant, Single, and Far from Home: Migrant Women in Nineteenth-Century Paris', *AHR*, XLV (1990), 1007–31. Prostitution and its regulation was a central issue for feminists in many nineteenth-century countries. R. J. Evans, 'Prostitution, State and Society in Imperial Germany', *P&P*, 70 (1970), 106–29, is a key article, but see also the books by A. Corbin, *Women for Hire: Prostitution and Sexuality in France after 1850* (Cambridge, MA, 1996), the content of which is less salacious than the title might suggest. See also J. Harsin, *Policing Prostitution in Nineteenth-Century Paris* (Princeton, NJ, 1985) and L. Bernstein, *Sonia's Daughters: Prostitutes and their Regulation in Imperial Russia* (Berkeley, CA, 1995).

The most accessible introduction to the question of literacy is the readable D. Vincent, *The Rise of Mass Literacy: Reading and Writing in Modern Europe* (Cambridge, 2000). For the thorny struggle over French education, see R. D. Anderson, *Education in France, 1848–1870* (Oxford, 1975) and R. Gildea, *Education in Provincial France 1800–1914: A Study of Three Departments* (Oxford, 1983). The essays in S. P. Frank and M. D. Steinberg (eds), *Cultures in Flux: Lower-Class Values, Practices, and Resistance in Late Imperial Russia* (Princeton, NJ, 1994) offer engaging detail on popular culture. J. Brooks, *When Russia Learned to Read: Literacy and Popular Literature, 1861–1917* (Princeton, NJ, 1985), is an entertaining examination of the *lubki*. For popular culture in Germany, see L. Abrams, *Workers' Culture in Imperial Germany: Leisure and Recreation in the Rhineland and Westphalia* (London, 1992), while an interesting study from the British Isles is P. Maloney, *Scotland and the Music Hall 1850–1914* (Manchester, 2003). E. Weber, *France: Fin de Siècle* (Cambridge, MA, 1986) is bedside reading. At a more highbrow level, the challenge of secular ideas to religion can be traced by reading D. G. Charlton, *Secular Religions in France 1815–1870* (London, 1963) and W. M. Simon, *European Positivism in the Nineteenth Century: An Essay in Intellectual History* (Ithaca, NY, 1963). The best introduction to the challenge of science to revealed religion is J. H. Brooke, *Science and Religion: Some Historical Perspectives* (Cambridge, 1991), which includes a discussion of the impact of nineteenth-century biblical scholarship. J. C. Greene, *The Death of Adam: Evolution and its Impact on Western Thought* (Ames, 1996), is also accessible, since it approaches its subject through mini-biographies of the scientists. T. Cosslett (ed.), *Science and Religion in the Nineteenth Century* (Cambridge, 1984)* offers useful glosses on the texts presented.

The French Revolution, Napoleon and the European Impact, 1789–1815

The French Revolution has been derided and defended in almost equal measure since the event itself. Classic accounts include G. Lefebvre, *The French Revolution*, 2 vols (New York, 1962–4); A. Soboul, *The French Revolution 1787–1799*, 2 vols (London, 1974) and N. Hampson, *A Social History of the French Revolution* (London, 1963). Of the most recent works, W. Doyle, *The Oxford History of the French Revolution* (Oxford, 1989) is probably the most balanced. D. Andress, *French Society in Revolution 1789–1799* (Manchester, 1999)* is critical of the Revolution's failures, but offers a lively and spirited defence of its achievements. P. McPhee, *The French Revolution 1789–1799* (Oxford, 2002) is in a similar vein. Highly critical of the Revolution is S. Schama's controversial, but readable, *Citizens: A Chronicle of the French Revolution* (New York, 1989). Other recent general histories include G. Lewis, *The French Revolution: Rethinking the Debate* (London, 1993) which is a rejoinder to revisionist views, and D. M. G. Sutherland, *The French Revolution and Empire: The Quest for a Civic Order* (Oxford, 2003). Helpful collections of essays include G. Best (ed.), *The Permanent Revolution: The French Revolution and its Legacy 1789–1989* (London, 1988); A. Forrest and P. Jones (eds), *Reshaping France: Town, Country and Region in the French Revolution* (Manchester, 1991); G. Lewis and C. Lucas (eds), *Beyond the Terror: Essays in French Regional and Social History, 1794–1815* (Cambridge, 1983) and C. Lucas (ed.), *Rewriting the French Revolution: The Andrew Browning Lectures* (Oxford, 1991). Recent contributions to the various debates and historiographical trends can be traced through some excellent readers, which include G. Kates (ed.), *The French Revolution: Recent Debates and New Controversies* (London, 1998); P. Jones (ed.), *The French Revolution in Social and Political Perspective* (London, 1996) and R. Schechter (ed.), *The French Revolution: The Essential Readings* (Malden, MA, 2001).

Students seeking to grasp the old debate over whether or not the French Revolution was bourgeois and/or capitalist in origin can find no better source of help than W. Doyle, *Origins of the French Revolution* (Oxford, 1980, with editions since). The classic 'Marxist' case is put by G. Lefebvre (trans. R. R. Palmer), *The Coming of the French Revolution* (Princeton, NJ, 1947), while the opening salvo of the 'revisionist' assault is Alfred Cobban, *The Social Interpretation of the French Revolution* (Cambridge, 1968). Further contributions to the 'revisionist' case include G. Chaussinand-Nogaret (trans. W. Doyle), *The French Nobility in the Eighteenth Century* (Cambridge, 1984) and C. Lucas, 'Nobles, Bourgeois and the Origins of the French Revolution', *P&P*, 60 (August 1973), 84–126. More recent work has been informed by the 'linguistic turn', which interprets the Revolution as an ideological and cultural transformation. This view took off with F. Furet (trans. E. Forster), *Interpreting the French Revolution* (Cambridge, 1981) and L. Hunt, *Politics, Culture, and Class in the French Revolution* (Berkeley, CA, 1984). See also the articles by K. M. Baker, *Inventing the French Revolution: Essays on French Political Culture in the Eighteenth Century* (Cambridge, 1990). The emphasis on revolutionary ideology or 'discourse' has led some historians to suggest that the Terror was inherent in the Revolution from the start. An excellent introduction to the debate sparked by this view is H. Gough, *The Terror in the French Revolution* (Basingstoke, 1998). The later phases of the Revolution are well covered by M.

Lyons, *France under the Directory* (Cambridge, 1975) and, by the same author, *Napoleon Bonaparte and the Legacy of the French Revolution* (Basingstoke, 1994)*.

Work in English on the Revolution in the provinces took off from the 1970s. Among the wealth of excellent writing, a taste can be had by reading C. Lucas, *The Structure of the Terror: The Example of Javogues and the Loire* (Oxford, 1973) and, more recently, A. Forrest, *The Revolution in Provincial France: Aquitaine 1789–1799* (Oxford, 1996). An important aspect of political practices in the Revolution is discussed in M. Crook, *Elections in the French Revolution: An Apprenticeship in Democracy, 1789–1799* (Cambridge, 1996). For the impact of the Revolution on French society, see Andress, already cited, as well as works on specific groups. Books on the peasantry include P. M. Jones, *The Peasantry in the French Revolution* (Cambridge, 1988) and G. Lefebvre (trans. J. White), *The Great Fear of 1789: Rural Panic in Revolutionary France* (London, 1973). The effects of the Revolution on women's place in society – and their political role – are discussed in O. Hufton, *Women and the Limits of Citizenship in the French Revolution* (Toronto, 1992) and D. Godineau (trans. K. Streip), *The Women of Paris and their French Revolution* (Berkeley, CA, 1998). See also the essays in S. E. Melzer and L. W. Rabine (eds), *Rebel Daughters: Women and the French Revolution* (Oxford, 1992). The role of the urban militants is described by A. Soboul (trans. G. Lewis), *The Parisian Sans-Culottes and the French Revolution 1793–4* (Oxford, 1964); G. Rudé, *The Crowd in the French Revolution* (Oxford, 1959) and R. Cobb, *The Police and the People: French Popular Protest 1789–1820* (Oxford, 1970). The devastating effects on the Church and its subsequent recovery are thoroughly discussed in N. Aston, *Religion and Revolution in France 1780–1804* (Basingstoke, 2000), which also looks at Jews and Protestants.

The final two chapters of W. Doyle, *The Old European Order 1660–1800* (Oxford, 1978) provide a brief introduction to the impact of the French Revolution on the rest of Europe. It is ironic that, just as an important trend in writing on the French Revolution should now emphasise ideology rather than circumstances to explain the Terror, one of the circumstances emphasised by the traditional historiography – the war – should be the subject of renewed interest. T. C. W. Blanning, *The Origins of the French Revolutionary Wars* (London, 1986) is an excellent and thorough discussion as to how the conflict began. The same author's *The French Revolutionary Wars 1787–1802* (London, 1996) is written with characteristic wit. Its sequel is D. Gates, *The Napoleonic Wars 1803–1815* (London, 1997). While Blanning stresses power politics as the underlying factor in the war, E. V. Macleod, *A War of Ideas: British Attitudes to the Wars Against Revolutionary France, 1792–1802* (Aldershot, 1998) shows how ideology helped to shape responses in Britain. A brief but convenient overview of the French Revolutionary and Napoleonic Wars is provided by C. J. Esdaile, *The French Wars, 1792–1815* (London, 2001). The 'revolutionary' nature of French tactics and motivation is researched in J. A. Lynn, *The Bayonets of the Republic: Motivation and Tactics in the Army of Revolutionary France, 1791–94* (Oxford, 1996) and, for a wider discussion of revolutionary warfare, see G. Best, *War and Society in Revolutionary Europe 1770–1870* (Oxford, 1982).

The impact of the French Revolution and of Napoleon on Europe is the subject of a number of excellent works. J. Godechot, *La Grande Nation: l'expansion révolutionnaire de la France dans le monde de 1789 à 1799*, 2nd edn

(Paris, 1983) is a gold mine, but awaits its translator. The same author's *France and the Atlantic Revolution of the Eighteenth Century, 1770–1799* (London, 1965) has some helpful detail. Godechot and R. R. Palmer were proponents of the 'Atlantic' thesis, arguing that the French Revolution was part of a wider, broadly 'democratic' movement which affected the western hemisphere in the later eighteenth century. Palmer's case is put in *The Age of the Democratic Revolution*, 2 vols (Princeton, NJ, 1959–64). The theory has since been exploded, but Palmer's work is still a good source for essential detail. Critics of the Palmer–Godechot thesis have included those working on the impact of the French Revolution and Napoleon in specific countries, emphasising the importance of local conditions. The most accessible studies of this kind include T. C. W. Blanning, *The French Revolution in Germany: Occupation and Resistance in the Rhineland 1792–1802* (Oxford, 1983); S. Schama, *Patriots and Liberators: Revolution in the Netherlands 1780–1813* (London, 1992); M. Broers, *Napoleonic Imperialism and the Savoyard Monarchy: State-Building in Piedmont, 1773–1821* (Lewiston, 1997); M. Elliott, *Partners in Revolution: The United Irishmen and France* (New Haven, CT, 1982); H. T. Dickinson (ed.), *Britain and the French Revolution 1789–1815* (Basingstoke, 1989) and H. T. Dickinson, *British Radicalism and the French Revolution 1789–1815* (Oxford, 1985). The Polish insurrection and its aftermath can be investigated by reading J. Lukowski, *The Partitions of Poland, 1772, 1793, 1795* (London, 1999) and A. Zamoyski, *The Last King of Poland* (London, 1992). The Russian response to the French Revolution may be gauged from J. T. Alexander, *Catherine the Great: Life and Legend* (Oxford, 1989) and I. de Madariaga, *Russia in the Age of Catherine the Great* (London, 1981). The early reform efforts under Alexander I can be explored with M. Raeff, *Michael Speransky: Statesman of Imperial Russia 1772–1839* (The Hague, 1957) which should be compared with J. Gooding, 'The Liberalism of Michael Speransky', *SEER*, LXIV (1986), 401–24. For broad European overviews, see M. Broers, *Europe under Napoleon 1799–1815* (London, 1996); A. Grab, *Napoleon and the Transformation of Europe* (Basingstoke, 2003); G. Ellis, *The Napoleonic Empire* (Basingstoke, 1991); M. Rowe (ed.), *Collaboration and Resistance in Napoleonic Europe: State-Formation in an Age of Upheaval, c. 1800–1815* (Basingstoke, 2003) and P. G. Dwyer (ed.), *Napoleon and Europe* (Harlow, 2001).

1815–1848

Political ideology and practice in the post-Napoleonic order are discussed in M. Broers, *Europe after Napoleon: Revolution, Reaction and Romanticism, 1814–1848* (Manchester, 1996)*. The essays in D. Laven and L. Riall (eds), *Napoleon's Legacy: Problems of Government in Restoration Europe* (Oxford, 2000), are thought-provoking. A lively narrative is offered by P. Johnson, *The Birth of the Modern: World Society 1815–1830* (New York, 1991). A classic work on the peace settlement at Vienna is H. Nicolson, *The Congress of Vienna: A Study in Allied Unity: 1812–1822* (London, 1948), while the diplomatic consequences are explored by Schroeder, already cited, and by the essays in A. Sked (ed.), *Europe's Balance of Power* (London, 1979).

For Germany in general during this period, Simms and Nipperdey, already cited, are especially useful, while a classic is T. S. Hamerow, *Restoration, Revolution, Reaction: Economics and Politics in Germany, 1815–1871*

(Princeton, NJ, 1958). The politics of conservatism against reformism in Prussia can be explored by reading the stimulating work by M. Levinger, *Enlightened Nationalism. The Transformation of Prussian Political Culture, 1806–1848* (Oxford, 2000) which has a much broader focus than the title might suggest. For discussions of the oppressive nature (or not) of the Habsburg monarchy, see Sked, *Decline*, already cited; D. E. Emerson, *Metternich and the Political Police: Security and Subversion in the Hapsburg Monarchy (1815–1830)* (The Hague, 1969) and D. Laven, *Venice and Venetia under the Habsburgs 1815–1835* (Oxford, 2002). An accessible biography of the architect of the conservative system is A. Palmer, *Metternich: Councillor of Europe* (London, 1972). G. de Bertier de Sauvigny (trans. L. M. Case), *The Bourbon Restoration* (Philadelphia, PA, 1966), while making no secret of its Bourbon sympathies, is a readable and often remarkably balanced account of the period in France. The standard book on the White Terror of 1815 is D. P. Resnick, *The White Terror and the Political Reaction after Waterloo* (Cambridge, MA, 1966). The liberal regime which followed the Bourbon restoration is comprehensively dealt with in H. A. C. Collingham, *The July Monarchy: A Political History of France 1830–1848* (London, 1988). The role of the army in Spanish politics is detailed in E. Christiansen, *The Origins of Military Power in Spain 1800–1854* (London, 1967), though it assumes some knowledge and is best read in conjunction with one of the more general textbooks on Spanish history. One of the few books in English on the Carlist War is J. F. Coverdale, *The Basque Phase of Spain's First Carlist War* (Princeton, NJ, 1984). British politics in this period are covered by J. Cannon, *Parliamentary Reform 1640–1832* (London, 1972) and F. O'Gorman, *The Long Eighteenth Century: British Political and Social History 1688–1832* (London, 1997). An interesting, if ultra-conservative, perspective is offered by J. C. D. Clark, *English Society 1688–1832: Ideology, Social Structure and Political Practice during the Ancien Régime* (Cambridge, 1985) which virtually laments the demise (or, as Clark would have it, surrender) of the hierarchical, confessional state.

For the liberal and radical opposition to the conservative order in France, see P. Pilbeam, *Republicanism in Nineteenth-Century France 1814–1871* (Basingstoke, 1995). On the labour movement, see W. H. Sewell, *Work and Revolution in France: The Language of Labor from the Old Regime to 1848* (Cambridge, 1980). A still useful collection of essays on the British working-class movement is A. Briggs (ed.), *Chartist Studies* (London, 1959). For Russia, A. G. Mazour, *The First Russian Revolution, 1825. The Decembrist Movement: Its Origins, Development, and Significance* (Stanford, CA, 1964)* is getting rather dated. More recent is P. O'Meara, *The Decembrist Pavel Pestel: Russia's First Republican* (Basingstoke, 2003). The consequences of the Decembrist uprising are explored in P. S. Squire, *The Third Department: The Establishment and Practices of the Political Police in the Russia of Nicholas I* (Cambridge, 1978)* and C. A. Ruud and S. A. Stepanov, *Fontanka 16: The Tsar's Secret Police* (Quebec, 1999). See also N. V. Riasanovsky, *A Parting of Ways: Government and the Educated Public in Russia 1801–1855* (Oxford, 1976). For Germany, besides Levinger, already cited, see J. L. Snell, *The Democratic Movement in Germany, 1789–1914* (Chapel Hill, NC, 1976), though J. J. Sheehan, *German Liberalism in the Nineteenth Century* (London, 1982), is rooted more firmly in social developments. The Greek War of Independence is the subject of a readable narrative history by D. Dakin, *The Greek Struggle for Independence 1821–1833* (London, 1973). For analysis, see the essays by Richard Clogg (ed.), *The Struggle for Greek Independence* (Basingstoke, 1973).

See also J. S. Koliopoulos, 'Brigandage and Irredentism in Nineteenth-Century Greece', *EHQ*, XIX (1989), 193–228. The revolutions of the early 1830s have not been as widely written about as those of 1848. Notable works, however, include C. Church, *Europe in 1830: Revolution and Political Change* (London, 1983), P. Pilbeam, *The 1830 Revolution in France* (Basingstoke, 1991) and J. M. Merriman (ed.), *1830 in France* (New York, 1975). A venerable account of the Polish insurrection is R. F. Leslie, *Polish Politics and the Revolution of November 1830* (London, 1956).

The European Revolutions, 1848–50

There are some excellent general studies of the mid-century revolutions. The best scholarly work is J. Sperber, *The European Revolutions, 1848–1851* (Cambridge, 1994): as much as two-fifths of the book is devoted to a dense discussion of the social and political background. A briefer introduction is provided by R. Price, *The Revolutions of 1848* (Atlantic Highlands, 1989). An entertaining narrative is P. Robertson, *Revolutions of 1848: A Social History* (New York, 1952). A series of older articles dedicated to the Revolutions were published for the centenary in *SEER*, XXVI (1947–8). The essays by R. J. Evans and H. Pogge von Strandmann (eds), *The Revolutions in Europe, 1848–49: From Reform to Reaction* (Oxford, 2000) explore the European dimension as well as the revolutions in individual countries. For the revolution in France, the best book is R. Price, *The French Second Republic: A Social History* (London, 1972), but see also the lively narrative by G. Duveau (trans. A. Carter), *1848: The Making of a Revolution* (London, 1967), which deals with the collapse of the July Monarchy. P. H. Amman, *Revolution and Mass Democracy: The Paris Club Movement in 1848* (Princeton, NJ, 1975), begins where Duveau leaves off, examining the revolution through the eyes of the radical political societies. From a different perspective, F. A. de Luna, *The French Republic under Cavaignac, 1848* (Princeton, NJ, 1969), looks at a nemesis of the working-class movement. The violent peasant reaction to Louis Napoleon's coup is examined in T. W. Margadant, *French Peasants in Revolt: The Insurrection of 1851* (Princeton, NJ, 1979). For Germany, J. Sperber, *Rhineland Radicals: The Democratic Movement and the Revolution of 1848–1849* (Princeton, NJ, 1991), is a rich discussion of the radical revolutionary movement in the west. For Austria, R. J. Rath, *The Viennese Revolution of 1848* (New York, 1969), is a readable narrative, based on extensive quotations from primary sources. For the Hungarian perspective, see I. Deak, *The Lawful Revolution: Louis Kossuth and the Hungarians 1848–1849* (New York, 1979), which is also a good read. S. Z. Pech, *The Czech Revolution of 1848* (Chapel Hill, NC, 1969) is solid. For Croatia, see G. E. Rothenberg, 'Jelačić, the Croatian Military Border, and the Intervention against Hungary in 1848', *AHY*, I (1965), 45–68. For Italy, P. Ginsborg, *Daniele Manin and the Venetian Revolution of 1848–49* (Cambridge, 1979), is excellent. Equally good, but providing a different perspective, is A. Sked, *The Survival of the Habsburg Empire: Radetzky, the Imperial Army and the Class War, 1848* (London, 1979). G. M. Trevelyan, *Garibaldi's Defence of the Roman Republic 1848–9* (London, 1920) is worth a read.

1850–1879

The breakdown of the Vienna system in the carnage of the Crimean War is discussed in both its military and diplomatic dimensions by W. Baumgart, *The Crimean War 1853–1856* (London, 1999). The international consequences of the war are considered in W. E. Mosse, *The Rise and Fall of the Crimean System 1855–71: The Story of a Peace Settlement* (London, 1963). The most accessible introduction to the Second Empire in France is J. F. McMillan, *Napoleon III* (London, 1991). The initial agony of the Third Republic in France is explored by B. Taithe, *Citizenship and Wars: France in Turmoil 1870–1871* (London, 2001). The Paris Commune in particular has been the subject of an enormous amount of work. R. Tombs, *The Paris Commune 1871* (London, 1999) is a good place to start, but see also E. Schulkind, *The Paris Commune of 1871* (London, 1971), a handy introductory pamphlet. The social foundations of the Third Republic are discussed in S. H. Elwitt, *The Making of the Third Republic: Class and Politics in France, 1868–1884* (Baton Rouge, LA, 1975). For Spanish politics around mid-century, see V. G. Kiernan, *The Revolution of 1854 in Spanish History* (Oxford, 1966). On Italian unification, L. Riall, *The Italian Risorgimento: State, Society and National Unification* (London, 1994) is especially impressive, providing an excellent synthesis of historiography. For a straightforward introductory narrative, try J. Gooch, *The Unification of Italy* (London, 1986). Anything by D. Mack Smith is good, but see especially *Victor Emanuel, Cavour and the Risorgimento* (London, 1971), a series of essays broader than the title implies. His biography of *Mazzini* (New Haven, CT, 1994) is also outstanding. G. M. Trevelyan, *Garibaldi and the Thousand* (London, 1909) is a good read and is partly based on interviews with survivors. F. J. Coppa, *The Origins of the Italian Wars of Independence* (London, 1992) provides the diplomatic background to the *Risorgimento*. The problems of integrating the new Italian state are explored in J. Schneider (ed.), *Italy's 'Southern Question': Orientalism in One Country* (Oxford, 1998). An interesting case study can be gleaned from D. Mack Smith, *A History of Sicily: Modern Sicily after 1713* (London, 1968) and, more up to date, L. Riall, *Sicily and the Unification of Italy: Liberal Policy and Local Power, 1859–1866* (Oxford, 1998). An accessible introduction to German unification is J. Breuilly, *The Formation of the First German Nation–State, 1800–1871* (Basingstoke, 1996). For Bismarck's role in German unification, see L. Gall, *Bismarck: The White Revolutionary*, 2 vols (London, 1986); O. Pflanze, *Bismarck and the Development of Germany*, 3 vols (Princeton, NJ, 1963); A. J. P. Taylor, *Bismarck: The Man and the Statesman* (London, 1965) and D. G. Williamson, *Bismarck and Germany 1862–1890* (London, 1998)*. The small but vocal liberal nationalist organisation is described in L. O'Boyle, 'The German *Nationalverein*', *JCEA*, XVI (1957), 333–52. R. J. Bazillion, 'Economic Integration and Political Sovereignty: Saxony and the *Zollverein*, 1834–1877' *CJH*, XXV (1990), 189–213 is an interesting case study of the political role played by the customs union. Discussions of other themes like religion and the role of civic organisations are gathered in H. Schulze (ed.), *Nation-Building in Central Europe* (Leamington Spa, 1987).

W. B. Lincoln, *The Great Reforms. Autocracy, Bureaucracy, and the Politics of Change in Imperial Russia* (De Kalb, IL, 1990) is a detailed discussion of the process by which the Great Reforms in Russia were implemented. See also the articles in B. Eklof, J. Bushnell and L. Zakharova (eds), *Russia's Great Reforms,*

1855–1881 (Bloomington, IN, 1994). A. J. Rieber, 'Alexander II: A Revisionist View', *JMH*, XLIII (1971), 42–58 argues that the reforms were driven primarily by military considerations. The revolutionary opposition in Russia is discussed in detail in F. Venturi, *Roots of Revolution: A History of the Populist and Socialist Movements in Nineteenth-Century Russia* (Chicago, 1960), which gives plenty of space to ideological developments. A. Gleason, *Young Russia: The Genesis of Russian Radicalism in the 1860s* (Chicago, 1983) and A. B. Ulam, *In the Name of the People: Prophets and Conspirators in Prerevolutionary Russia* (New York, 1977) are especially readable. The study of the Polish uprising of 1863 is R. F. Leslie, *Reform and Insurrection in Russian Poland, 1856–1865* (London, 1963), but see also S. Kieniewicz, 'Polish Society and the Insurrection of 1863', *P&P*, 37 (July 1967), 130–48. A useful work on the projects for dealing with the nationalities of the Habsburg empire and the attitudes which underpinned them is R. A. Kann, *The Multinational Empire: Nationalism and National Reform in the Habsburg Monarchy 1848–1918*, 2 vols (New York, 1950).

1880–1914

For students of social and political conflict, the decades before the First World War are a fertile field. A good general history of France during this era is R. D. Anderson, *France 1870–1914: Politics and Society* (London, 1977). R. Gildea, *France 1870–1914*, 2nd edn (London, 1996)* is a useful short introduction. A central figure in British politics in this period is the subject of the essays in P. J. Jagger (ed.), *Gladstone* (London, 1998). G. Dangerfield, *The Strange Death of Liberal England* (London, 1966) is a classic, written in a florid style, and argues that British society on the eve of the First World War was on the verge of a meltdown. There are many excellent books on the German Reich. V. R. Berghahn, *Imperial Germany 1871–1914: Economy, Society, Culture and Politics* (Oxford, 1994) is comprehensive in its coverage of an exhaustive range of themes, but it lacks narrative drive. R. J. Evans (ed.), *Society and Politics in Wilhelmine Germany* (London, 1978) has some penetrating essays. W. J. Mommsen (trans. R. Deveson), *Imperial Germany 1867–1918: Politics, Culture, and Society in an Authoritarian State* (London, 1995) is a translated collection of articles by a leading German historian. The essays in M. Cornwall (ed.), *The Last Years of Austria–Hungary* (Exeter, 1990) are easy to digest. For Russia, O. Figes, *A People's Tragedy: The Russian Revolution 1891–1924* (London, 1996) is the most readable book.

For the left-wing challenge in France, see B. Moss, *The Origins of the French Labor Movement, 1830–1914: The Socialism of Skilled Workers* (Berkeley, CA, 1976), which comes from a Marxist perspective. J. Alvarez-Junco, *The Emergence of Mass Politics in Spain: Populist Demagoguery and Republican Culture, 1890–1910* (Brighton, 2002) is a biography of an important Spanish republican, Lerroux. The standard work on the British socialist movement is H. Pelling, *Origins of the Labour Party*, 2nd edn (Oxford, 1965), but P. Adelman, *The Rise of the Labour Party 1880–1945*, 2nd edn (London, 1986)* is a good introduction to the subject. For a Scottish perspective, see J. J. Smyth, *Labour in Glasgow, 1896–1936: Socialism, Suffrage, Sectarianism* (East Linton, 2000). For the revolutionary threat in Russia, see L. Haimson, 'The Problem of Social Stability in Urban Russia, 1905–1917' (Part One), *SR*, XXIII

(1964), 619–42 and (Part Two), XXIV (1965), 1–22. Haimson's views have been challenged by R. B. McKean, *St Petersburg between the Revolutions: Workers and Revolutionaries June 1907–February 1917* (New Haven, CT, 1990) which is essential reading. See also V. E. Bonnell, *Roots of Rebellion: Workers' Politics and Organizations in St Petersburg and Moscow, 1900–1914* (Berkeley, CA, 1983).

For the reaction on the right in France, see R. Rémond, *The Right Wing in France: From 1815 to de Gaulle* (Philadelphia, PA, 1966), which is still the best introduction to the subject. The saga of Boulangism is described in F. H. Seager, *The Boulanger Affair: Political Crossroad of France, 1886–1889* (Ithaca, NY, 1969). The excellent D. Johnson, *France and the Dreyfus Affair* (London, 1966) reads like a novel and is the best place to start on that polarising conflict. M. Burns, *Rural Society and French Politics: Boulangism and the Dreyfus Affair 1886–1900* (Princeton, NJ, 1984) gauges the impact on the countryside. For the consequences, see M. Larkin, *Church and State after the Dreyfus Affair: The Separation Issue in France* (London, 1974). For Germany, K. A. Lerman, *The Chancellor as Courtier: Bernhard von Bülow and the Governance of Germany 1900–1909* (Cambridge, 1990) examines a figure who saw himself as heir to the Bismarckian tradition. C. Duggan, *Francesco Crispi: From Nation to Nationalism* (Oxford, 2002) is a biography of a character traditionally taken as a Fascist predecessor. For the reaction in Russia under Alexander III, see P. A. Zaionchkovsky (trans. D. R. Jones), *The Russian Autocracy under Alexander III* (Gulf Breeze, FL, 1976). For repression in the last years of imperial Russia, see I. Lauchlan, *Russian Hide-and-Seek: The Tsarist Secret Police in St Petersburg, 1906–1914* (Helsinki, 2002).

On nationalist movements, see the collection of brief essays in G. Hálfdanarson and A. K. Isaacs (eds), *Nations and Nationalities in Historical Perspective* (Pisa, 2001)*. For the evolution of nationalist ideas in the south-east, see I. Banac, *The National Question in Yugoslavia: Origins, History, Politics* (Ithaca, NY, 1984). Belgium nationalism is explored by the essays in K. Deprez and L. Vos (eds), *Nationalism in Belgium: Shifting Identities, 1780–1995* (Basingstoke, 1998). An accessible introduction to the 'Irish question' is A. O'Day, *Irish Home Rule 1867–1921* (Manchester, 1998)*. The place of Scotland in the United Kingdom is discussed in R. J. Finlay, *A Partnership for Good? Scottish Politics and the Union since 1880* (Edinburgh, 1997). An important recent study of nationalism in the Habsburg empire is C. E. Nolte, *The Sokol in the Czech Lands to 1914: Training for the Nation* (Basingstoke, 2002). See also the essays in P. Brock and H. G. Skilling (eds), *The Czech Renascence of the Nineteenth Century* (Toronto, 1970). The political evolution of a populist, anti-semitic form of nationalism in Austria is discussed by A. G. Whiteside, *The Socialism of Fools: Georg Ritter von Schönerer and Austrian Pan-Germanism* (Berkeley, CA, 1975). Nationalism in the 'Ukrainian Piedmont' is investigated in J.-P. Himka, *Galician Villagers and the Ukrainian National Movement in the Nineteenth Century* (Basingstoke, 1988). The national opposition in Poland is explored in R. E. Blobaum, *Rewolucja: Russian Poland, 1904–1907* (Ithaca, NY, 1995), which has broad introductory chapters. The turn of important tendencies within Polish nationalism towards anti-semitism is charted by B. A. Porter, *When Nationalism Began to Hate: Imagining Modern Politics in Nineteenth-Century Poland* (Oxford, 2000). The nationalities in the north-west of the Russian empire are dealt with comprehensively in M. H. Thaden, M. H. Haltzel, C. L. Lundin, A. Plakans, T. U. Raun and E. C. Thaden, *Russification in the Baltic Provinces and Finland, 1855–1914* (Princeton, NJ, 1981). The bitter fruit of nationalism in south-east Europe is described by R. C. Hall, *The Balkan Wars 1912–1913: Prelude to the First World War* (London, 2000), which is based on sources in many languages.

European Imperialism

A narrative history of European imperialism in the nineteenth century is R. F. Betts, *The False Dawn: European Imperialism in the Nineteenth Century* (Minneapolis, MN, 1976). Some of the older theories of imperialism are explored by the essays in R. Owen & B. Sutcliffe, *Studies in the Theory of Imperialism* (London, 1972). A. Porter, *European Imperialism, 1860–1914* (Basingstoke, 1994), however, is probably the best introduction to both old and recent interpretations. R. Aldrich, *Greater France: A History of French Overseas Expansion* (Basingstoke, 1996) is useful for details on the French empire. The most accessible general history of British imperialism is B. Porter, *The Lion's Share: A Short History of British Imperialism 1850–1983*, 2nd edn (London, 1984), which is enlivened by bursts of irreverence. Themes in British imperialism are explored in A. G. L. Shaw (ed.), *Great Britain and the Colonies 1815–65* (London, 1970). Russian expansionism and the efforts of other European powers to restrict it are considered in J. P. LeDonne, *The Russian Empire and the World 1700–1917: The Geopolitics of Expansion and Containment* (New York, 1997). The reasons for the Italian drive for empire are discussed in R. J. B. Bosworth, *Italy, the Least of the Great Powers: Italian Foreign Policy before the First World War* (Cambridge, 1979). G. Clarence-Smith, *The Third Portuguese Empire 1825–1975: A Study in Economic Imperialism* (Manchester, 1985) reasserts the importance of economic motives in one case of European overseas expansion. Much recent work, however, has explored the culture of imperialism and the impact of empire on European culture. For examples of such approaches, see J. M. Mackenzie (ed.), *Imperialism and Popular Culture* (Manchester, 1986).

The Origins of the First World War

Books and articles are legion, but good introductions include J. Joll, *The Origins of the First World War* (London, 1984), which is probably the best of the general works available. L. C. F. Turner, *Origins of the First World War* (London, 1970) provides a useful narrative, while R. Henig, *The Origins of the First World War*, 2nd edn (London, 1993) is a pithy introduction to both the events and conflicting interpretations. The 'Fischer controversy' may be followed by reading, first, the books which fired the whole debate in the first place, namely F. Fischer, *Germany's Aims in the First World War* (London, 1967) and the same author's *War of Illusions: German Policies from 1911 to 1914* (London, 1975). Secondly, the essays in H. W. Koch (ed.), *The Origins of the First World War: Great Power Rivalry and German War Aims*, 2nd edn (Basingstoke, 1984) include conflicting responses to Fischer. The debate continues in the papers of a symposium published in *CEH*, XXI, 3 (1988). D. Stevenson, *Armaments and the Coming of War: Europe 1904–1914* (Oxford, 1996) explores a central issue in pre-war international politics. For the role of individual countries, V. R.

Berghahn, *Germany and the Approach of War in 1914* (New York, 1993) is an excellent refuge for readers seeking to make sense of the debate on German responsibility. Z. S. Steiner, *Britain and the Origins of the First World War* (Basingstoke, 1977); J. F. V. Keiger, *France and the Origins of the First World War* (Basingstoke, 1983); R. J. B. Bosworth, *Italy and the Approach of the First World War* (Basingstoke, 1983); D. C. B. Lieven, *Russia and the Origins of the First World War* (Basingstoke, 1983) and S. R. Williamson, *Austria–Hungary and the Origins of the First World War* (Basingstoke, 1991) are all pretty comprehensive.

Index

Note: For names of individual cities, see 'cities'. For monarchs, see under individual countries.